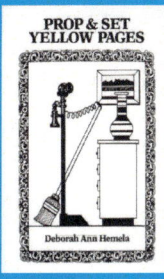
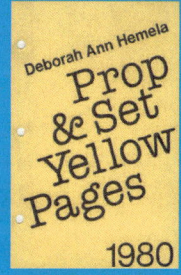

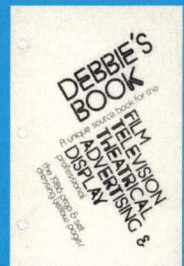

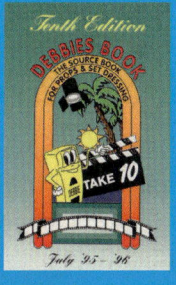
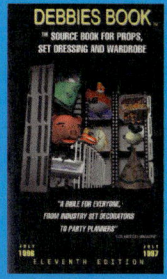

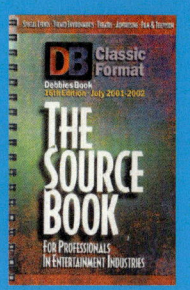

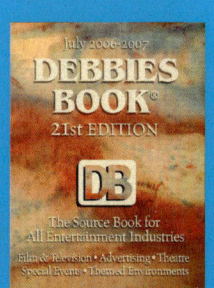
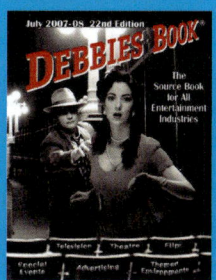

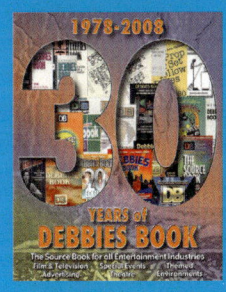

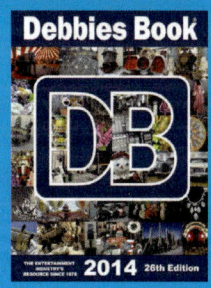
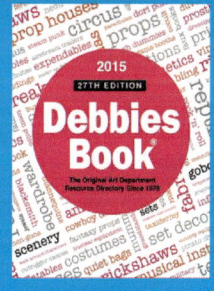

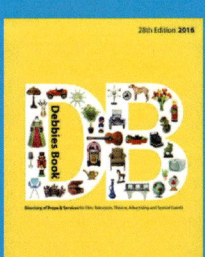

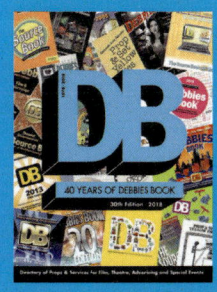

DB Debbies Book®

CELEBRATING 40 YEARS

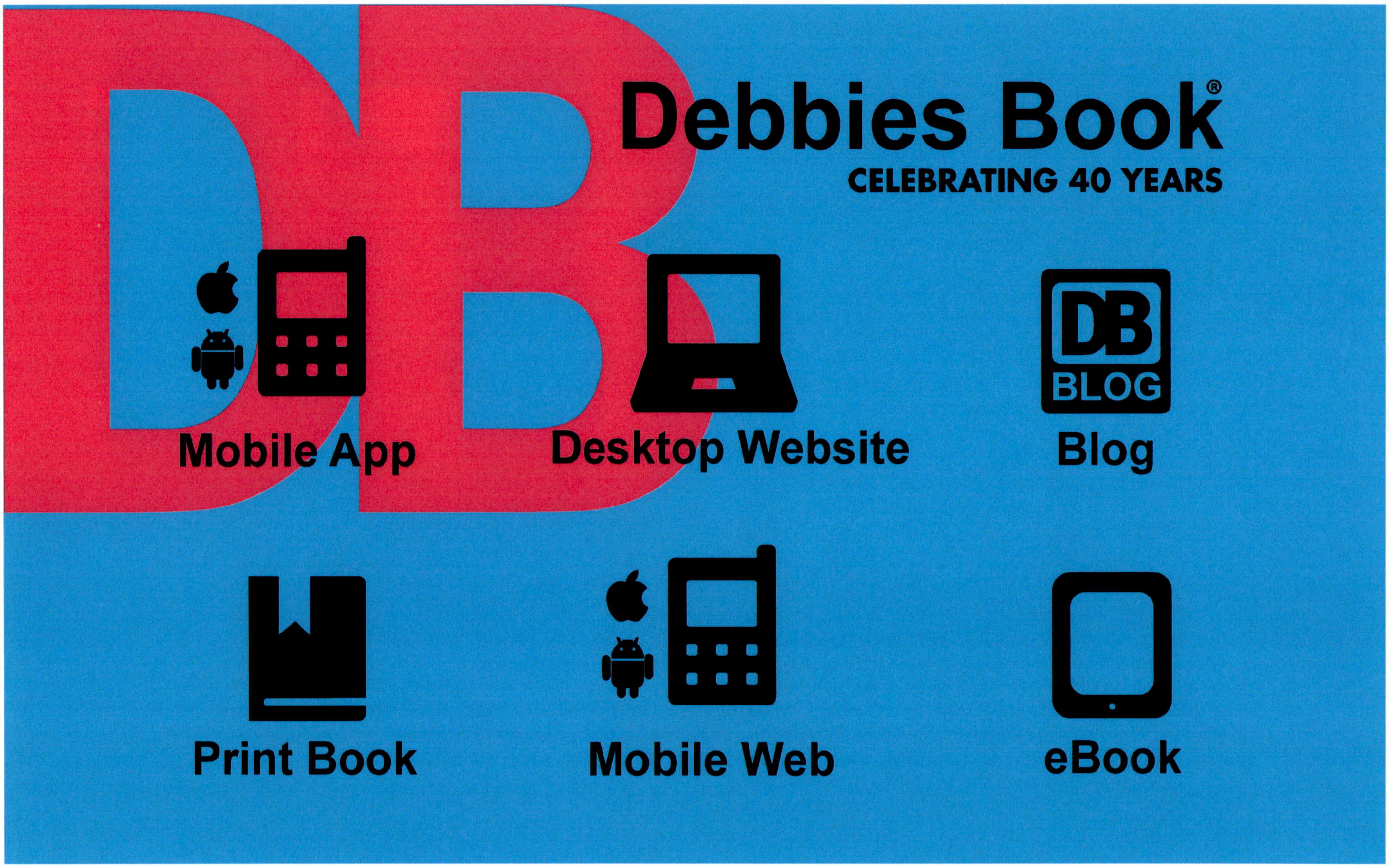

DB Debbies Book®

CELEBRATING 40 YEARS

Mobile App

Desktop Website

Blog

Print Book

Mobile Web

eBook

A REMINDER: In print book, **Prop House & Costume Rental House**

All listings are shortened to 1-2 lines to save space. Full contact information/addresses located within their respective categories.

Thank you Bryce Nicholson, Kyle Casey, Leah Tadena, and of course, Ruby & Lulu.
And, as always, Earl Carlson, Jim Newton and Don Roberts.

Debbies Book®, Inc.
P.O. Box 6378
Altadena, CA 91003-6378

Phone (626) 797-7699
www.debbiesbook.com
email: info@debbiesbook.com

Accessories

See: Decorative Accessories* Leather (Clothing, Accessories, Materials)* Wardrobe, Accessories

Acrylics

See: Plastics, Materials & Fabrication

Adding Machines

See: Business Machines

Adhesives, Glues & Tapes

See Also: Expendables

Harris Industries, Inc. (800) 222-6866
5181 Argosy Ave, Huntington Beach, CA, 92649
Tapes; safety, caution, anti-skid, barricade, flagging, custom
www.harrisind.com

R. S. Hughes (818) 686-9111
10639 Glenoaks Blvd Ste 1, Pacoima, CA, 91331
Adhesives, sealants, fillers & glues
www.rshughes.com

Adirondack Chairs

See: Furniture, Outdoor/Patio

Adult Toys & Novelties

See: Goth/Punk/Bondage/Fetish/Erotica Etc.

Advisors

See: Art, Artists For Hire* Research, Advisors, Consulting & Clearances* Search Tools, Directories, Libraries

Aerobic Equipment

See: Exercise & Fitness Equipment

Aerospace

See Also: Aircraft, Charters & Aerial Services* Locations, Airport Dressing & Hangars* Space Shuttle/Space Hardware* Space Suits

LCW Props (818) 243-0707
Jet Parts, Exterior Lighting of Planes, Wind Tunnel, Test Planes, Titanium & Inconel Parts, Turbines, Exhaust, Cones

6439 San Fernando Rd. Glendale, CA 91201
Phone: 818-243-0707 - www.lcwprops.com

N.S. Aerospace Props (818) 765-1087
7429 Laurel Canyon Blvd, N Hollywood, CA, 91605
Rocket Engines, Rocket Components, Hardware, Fittings and Industrial parts for various time periods, consultations too.
nortonsalesm@aol.com * www.nortonsalesinc.com

Afghans

See: Linens, Household

African Themed Parties

See: Costume Rental Houses* Events, Decorations, Supplies & Services* Events, Design/Planning/Production* Prop Houses* Themed Environment Construction* Travel (City/Country) Themed Events

African/Oceanic Decorative Items

See Also: Furniture, Moroccan

Badia Design, Inc. (818) 762-0130
5420 Vineland Ave, N Hollywood, CA, 91601
Moroccan handmade furniture, home decor, tribal rugs, brass chandeliers, mosaic tables, tiles, themed event rentals
info@badiadesign.com * www.badiadesign.com

The Hand Prop Room LP. (323) 931-1534

History For Hire, Inc. (818) 765-7767
masks, tools, weapons

Hollywood Studio Gallery (323) 462-1116
masks & shields

Oceanic Arts (562) 698-6960
thatching & hut roofing, bamboo, shields, masks, dugout canoe

Omega/Cinema Props (323) 466-8201
African/oceanic items of various types from masks and religious items to artwork and vases.

Prop Services West (818) 503-2790

Universal Studios Property & Hardware Dept (818) 777-2784
African masks, African spears, African sculptures, African busts, African wood carvings and much more.

Warner Bros. Studios Property Department (818) 954-2181
Masks, spears, shells, driftwood, coastal accessories and decorative items

ZG04 DECOR (818) 853-8040

Air Cannons

See: Special Effects, Equipment & Supplies

Air Cargo & Freight

See: Transportation, Trucking and/or Storage* Aircraft, Charters & Aerial Services

Air Conditioning & Heating, Production/Event

See Also: Plumbing Fixtures, Heating/Cooling Appliances

Aggreko Event Services (818) 767-7288
13230 Cambridge St, Santa Fe Springs, CA 90670
big, quiet power, heating & HVAC systems, over 130 locations globally for filming, tours, events
www.aggreko.com

Castex Rentals (323) 462-1468
1044 N Cole Ave, Hollywood, CA, 90038
portable air conditioning units, misters, floor fans, propane heaters, electric heaters
service@castexrentals.com * www.castexrentals.com

Studio Air Conditioning, Inc. (818) 222-4143
5171 N Douglas Fir Rd Unit 6, Calabasas, CA, 91302
Studio air conditioners, mount-less AC's, convenient air conditioning, studio AC
www.studioair.com

Air Conditioning Vents

See: Plumbing Fixtures, Heating/Cooling Appliances

Air Hockey Game

See: Game Tables & Equipment

Air Tools

See: Tools

Air Tubulars

See: Balloons & Balloon Sculptures

Aircraft, Charters & Aerial Services

See Also: Locations, Airport Dressing & Hangars
Aerial Focus (805) 455-3142
Call for Appt
extreme sports cinematography, base jumping, wing walking, skydiving, hang gliding
www.aerialfocus.com

Aerial Stunt Service (310) 543-2222
3128 Via La Selva, Palos Verdes, CA, 90274
aerial cinematography & coordination, skydivers/stunts, extreme sports & stock footage
www.skydive.tv

Aero Jet Services (800) 582-3641
8014 E McClain Dr. Suite 200, Scottsdale AZ, 85260
Jet charters, maintenance, management & purchasing
www.aerojetservices.com

AirCharter World (925) 602-5330
395 Taylor Blvd, Ste 100, Pleasant Hill, CA, 94523
Air & charter worldwide, Biz Jets & transport aircraft available
larry@acworld.com * www.acworld.com

AirNet II LLC (877) 293-8463
3041 George Page Jr., Columbus, OH, 43217
Jet services, charter, express, bank, medical, government, private, cargo, sales
www.airnet.com

Airpower Aviation Resources (805) 499-0307
702 Paseo Vista, Thousand Oaks, CA, 91320
Aircraft-airplanes & helicopters: civilian, military,commercial, vintage & antique. Full aerial coordination services.
airpowerinc@earthlink.net * www.airpower-aviation.com

Camera Copters (888) 463-7953
copters & planes, camera mounts & systems, SAG pilots, aerial coord. for stunts, location scouting & pre-prod.
www.cameracopters.com

Celebrity Helicopters (877) 999-2099
961 W. Alondra Blvd, Compton, CA, 90220
wide variety of helicopters, with camera mounts, FAA approved "Movie Manual" for special camera positions
www.celebheli.com

Goodyear Blimp (310) 327-6565
19200 S. Main St, Gardena, CA, 90248
"Spirit of America" follows a line of Goodyear blimps that have appeared in dozens of movies.
www.goodyearblimp.com

Jet Productions (818) 781-4742
13351 Riverside Dr Suite 530, Sherman Oaks CA, 91423
jet charters including private & production transportation, & photo shoot
www.jetproductions.net

Orbic Helicopters, Inc. (805) 389-1070
777 Aviation Dr, Camarillo, CA, 93010
helicopter tours/charters, aerial filming
www.orbichelicopters.com

Rock-It Air Charter (310) 702-6770
Web Based Business
executive jet charters, 24X7, 95 offices worldwide
www.rockitair.com

Stunt Wings/Adventure Sports Productions (818) 367-2430
12623 Gridley St, Sylmar, CA, 91342
hang gliding, paragliding, ultralight talent & equipment, cinematography, stunts
www.stuntwings.com

Airplane & Aircraft Mockups

See Also: Locations, Airport Dressing & Hangars Locations, Insert Stages & Theatres*
Aero Mock-Ups (888) 662-5877
Aviation prop house. Complete airplane interiors & airport dressing, service area gallery model airplanes. No hangars.

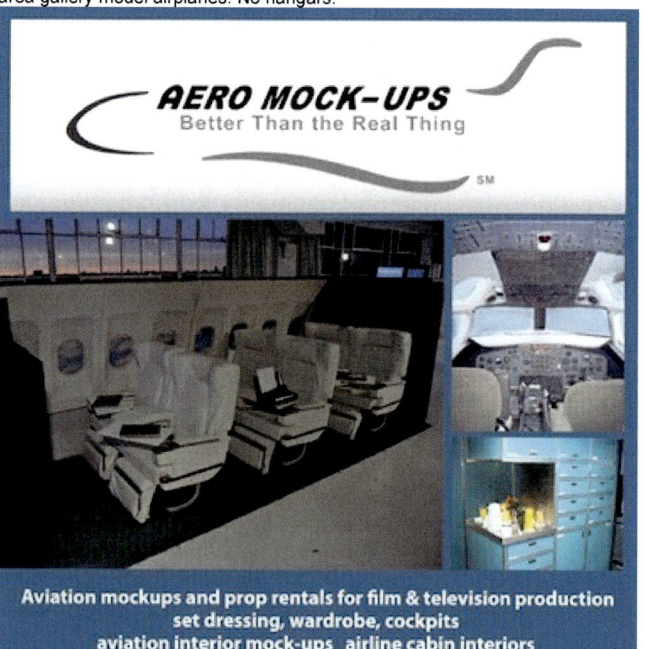

Aviation mockups and prop rentals for film & television production
set dressing, wardrobe, cockpits
aviation interior mock-ups   airline cabin interiors

Air Hollywood - Prop House & Standing Sets (818) 890-0444
13240 Weidner St, Los Angeles, CA, 91331
airplane sets for rent
info@airhollywood.com * www.airhollywood.com

Airpower Aviation Resources (805) 499-0307
702 Paseo Vista, Thousand Oaks, CA, 91320
Aircraft-airplanes & helicopters: civilian, military,commercial, vintage & antique. Full aerial coordination services.
airpowerinc@earthlink.net * www.airpower-aviation.com

RJR Props (404) 349-7600
Large commercial airline interior; navy helicopter

Airstream Trailers

See: RV Vehicles & Travel Trailers, Equip & Parts

Aladdin Lamps

See Also: Arabian Decorations
Badia Design, Inc. (818) 762-0130
5420 Vineland Ave, N Hollywood, CA, 91601
info@badiadesign.com * www.badiadesign.com

The Hand Prop Room LP. (323) 931-1534
Brass lamps, Aladdin lamps, oil lamps, eastern lamps

History For Hire, Inc. (818) 765-7767
good selection

Alarms

See Also: Security Devices or Services Security Walk-Through & Baggage Alarms*
Alley Cats Studio Rentals (818) 982-9178
burglar, fire, modern, period

E.C. Prop Rentals (818) 764-2008
burglar, fire, modern to period, multiples

LCW Props (818) 243-0707
Bells, Fire Alarms, Fire Pulls, Electronic, Emergency Lights

Mike Green Fire Equipment Co. (818) 989-3322
11916 Valerio St, N Hollywood, CA, 91605
Fire Alarms, Fire Alarm Strobes, Fire Alarm Bells, Fire Bells. Vintage to New.
info@mgfire.com * www.Mgfire.com

Modern Props (323) 934-3000
contemporary alarms, futuristic alarms, electronic alarms, radio alarm clocks, oversized alarms, contemporary and vintage alarm clocks, security alarms

RJR Props (404) 349-7600
Security alarms, alarm panels, fire alarm pulls and more for rent.

Aliens

See Also: Futuristic Furniture, Props, Decorations

Dapper Cadaver   **(818) 771-0818**
Alien bodies & monsters. Alien skulls & enlongated human skulls. Autopsy tables & instruments. Oddities & specimen jars.

LCW Props   **(818) 243-0707**
Alien Body Parts, Alien Corpses, Men In Black Dressing

Modern Props   **(323) 934-3000**
Prints, sculptures, skulls, monster mounted heads, pinball machine, futuristic weapons and futuristic equipment.

Alley Dressing

AIR Designs   **(818) 768-6639**
Trash cans, barrels, pallets, signage, dumpsters, crates & boxes, lighting & more.

Alley Cats Studio Rentals   **(818) 982-9178**
clean metal rolling dumpsters, pallets, crates, fence. New York Street Dressing. street lamps, platform construction

C. P. Two   **(323) 466-8201**
Fire hydrants and other pieces of alley dressing.

E.C. Prop Rentals   **(818) 764-2008**
Clean Dumpsters, Pallets, Crates, Trash Cans, Clutter, Shopping Carts, Clean Bags of Trash

The Hand Prop Room LP.   **(323) 931-1534**
barricades, drums, crates, trash cans

History For Hire, Inc.   **(818) 765-7767**

LCW Props   **(818) 243-0707**
Our Specialty, We Own Our Own Recycling Center Next Door, Quantity And Quality Cannot Be Beat

6439 San Fernando Rd. Glendale, CA 91201
Phone: 818-243-0707 - www.lcwprops.com

Sony Pictures Studios-Prop House (Off Lot)   **(310) 244-5999**
dumpsters, trash cans & bins, fire escape, exterior stairs, exterior stair lights

Universal Studios Property & Hardware Dept   **(818) 777-2784**
Alley dressing; trash dumpsters, trash bins, trash cans, traffic barricades, recycling bins more

Ambulance/Paramedic

See Also: Hospital Equipment* Medical Equip/Furniture, Graphics/Supplies* Stretchers* Vehicles/Picture Vehicles

A-1 Medical Integration   **(818) 753-0319**
Medical devices for Set Decoration & Property, from minor procedures to detailed hospital units.

Alpha Companies - Spellman Desk Co.   **(818) 504-9090**
complete interior ambulance dressing from the #1 source for medical in the industry.

The Hand Prop Room LP.   **(323) 931-1534**

History For Hire, Inc.   **(818) 765-7767**
period & contemporary

LCW Props   **(818) 243-0707**
Heart Defibrillators, Medical Bags, Gurneys, Crash Unit, First Aid

American Folk Art

See: Antiques & Antique Decorations* Carved Figures* Furniture, Early American/Colonial* Paintings/Prints

American Indian

See: Native American* Rugs

Americana

See: Antiques & Antique Decorations* Furniture, Early American/Colonial* Furniture, Rustic* Paintings/Prints

Ammunition & Blanks

See: Guns & Firearms

Amusement Park

See: Animal Costumes & Walk Around Characters* Arcade Equipment, Games & Rides* Carnival Dressing/Supplies* Flags/Banners* Kiosks* Ticket Booths

Anatomical Charts & Models

See: Body Parts* Bones, Skulls & Skeletons

Anchors

See: Nautical Dressing & Props

Anesthesia Equipment

A-1 Medical Integration　　　　　　　　(818) 753-0319
Anesthesia Machines, Ventilators, Vitals Monitors, IV Pumps, Endotracheal Tubes, Oxygen Masks & Tubing, Anesthetic Drugs.
LCW Props　　　　　　　　　　　　　　(818) 243-0707
Full Hospital Setup, Hospital Equipment, Syringes, Sharps Containers

Angels & Cherubs

See: Christmas

Animal Cages

E.C. Prop Rentals　　　　　　　　　　(818) 764-2008
Large castered stainless & heavy metal, small animal type
LCW Props　　　　　　　　　　　　　　(818) 243-0707
Large Selection Of Different Sizes, Single Cages or Banks, Rolling
Universal Studios Property & Hardware Dept　(818) 777-2784
Lots of birdcages, hamster cages, large animal cages and more.

Animal Costumes & Walk Around Characters

See Also: Costumes Prop Design & Manufacturing*
The Costume House　　　　　　　　　　(818) 508-9933
rabbit walk around, bunny walk around, eagle walk around, chicken walk around, roach walk around
Geppetto Studios　　　　　　　　　　(718) 398-9792
839 Broad St, Utica NY, 13501
full body puppet costumes, puppet displays, walkarounds
www.geppettostudios.com
Heritage Costumes　　　　　　　　　　(310) 320-6392
mascots, body, oversized heads
Marylen Costume Design　　　　　　　(800) 628-6417
5 Corning Court, Medford, OR, 97504
over 2,500 animal, character & mascot costumes
online@marylen.com * www.marylen.com
Sony Pictures Studios-Wardrobe　　　(310) 244-5995
alterations, call (310) 244-7260
Stagecraft Inc.　　　　　　　　　　　(513) 541-7150
3950 Spring Grove Ave, Cincinatti, OH, 45223
walkaround cartoons, animals, & illusion walkarounds
www.stagecraftinc.com
Tech Works FX Studios　　　　　　　　(504) 722-1504
13405 Seymour Meyers Blvd #5, Covington, LA, 70433
Specializes in Costume Design, Creature Suits, Make Up FX, Monsters and Custom Characters.
info@techworksstudios.com * www.techworksstudios.com
Ursula's Costumes, Inc.　　　　　　　(310) 582-8230
2516 Wilshire Blvd, Santa Monica, CA, 90403
www.ursulascostumes.com

Animal Glue

See: Expendables

Animal Hides & Mounted Heads

See: Costume/Wardrobe/Sewing Supplies Prop Houses* Rugs* Taxidermy, Hides/Heads/Skeletons*

Animal Mock-ups

See: Fiberglass Products/Fabrication Puppets, Marionettes, Automata, Animatronics* Taxidermy, Hides/Heads/Skeletons*

Animal Skulls & Skeletons

See: Bones, Skulls & Skeletons Jungle Dressing* Taxidermy, Hides/Heads/Skeletons*

Animals (Live), Services, Trainers & Wranglers

See Also: Aquariums & Tropical Fish Horses, Horse Equipment, Livestock*
All Creatures Great & Small　　　　　(914) 232-3623
3 Little Lane, White Plains, NY, 10605
professional trainers & handlers, all animal talent incl. cats & dogs, farm, exotic, birds, reptiles, insects
www.animalagent.com
All Star Animals　　　　　　　　　　(516) 569-5014
Call for Appt
dogs & cats, farm animals, exotics, also animal locator, live promotional events in NY area
allstaranimals@gmail.com * www.allstaranimals.com
American Humane Association　　　　(818) 501-0123
12711 Ventura Blvd, Studio City, CA 91604
National HQ in Denver, CO - guidelines for production; protects all animals in film & media
filmunit@americanhumane.org * www.humanehollywood.org
Animal Actors of Hollywood, Inc.　　(805) 495-2122
860 W. Carlisle Rd, Thousand Oaks, CA, 91361
hoofstock, domestic animals, reptiles, small exotics
www.animalactors.net
Bee & Insect People Unltd.　　　　　(800) 924-3097
P.O. Box 343, Claremont, CA, 91711
bees, insects, spiders & wasps, stunt people
honeycott@verizon.net
Benay's Bird & Animal Source　　　(818) 881-0053
By Appointment Only
Birds, dogs & cats, farm animals, forest animals, primates, exotics, hoofstock, insects, rodents, reptiles, sea lions
benaysanimals@gmail.com * www.benaysanimals.com
Birds & Animals Unlimited　　　　　(877) 542-1355
animal & trainer talent, offices in S. Cal., Florida, NY, & London
www.birdsandanimals.com
Bob Dunn's Animal Services　　　　(818) 896-0394
16001 Yarnell St, Sylmar, CA, 91342
birds, dogs, cats, apes, exotics, insects, hoofstock, monkeys, reptiles, rodents
www.animalservices.com
Boone's Animals for Hollywood　　(661) 257-0630
32727 Merritt Rd, Acton, CA 93510
dogs, cats, birds, rodents
info@boonesanimals.com * www.boonesanimals.com
Bow Wow Productions　　　　　　　(760) 948-9430
Northern & Southern California
domestic & exotic animals & wranglers for film/TV, special events
bowwowprod@aol.com * www.bowwowproductions.com
Critters of the Cinema　　　　　　　(661) 724-1929
PO Box 378, Lake Hughes, CA, 93532
dogs & cats, big cats, aquatic mammals, birds, primates, hoofed small/large mammals, insects, kangaroos, reptiles
Rob@crittersofthecinema.com * www.crittersofthecinema.com
Exotic Life Fish & Reptiles　　　　　(818) 341-1007
9919 Topanga Canyon Blvd, Chatsworth, CA, 91311
fresh/salt water fish, wide variety reptiles, tortoises, tanks, equip., service
www.exoticlifefishandreptilesla.com
Gentle Jungle　　　　　　　　　　　(661) 248-6195
801 Lebec Rd., P.O. Box 832, Lebec, CA, 93243
animals/trainers, domestic dogs/cats, small animals, livestock/horses, big cats, wolves & exotics
www.gentlejungle.com
Hollywood Animals　　　　　　　　　(661) 299-9000
PO Box 2088, Santa Clarita, CA 91386
Lions, working pride, tigers, bears, elephants, leopards, panthers & animal stunts for film, TV & print ads
hollywoodanimals@me.com * www.hollywoodanimals.com

Jules Sylvester's Reptile Rentals Inc.   **(818) 621-4101**
Thousand Oaks, CA
Reptiles, Snakes, Spiders, Scorpions, Frogs, Turtles, Tortoises, Alligators, bugs and more!
reptilerentals@gmail.com * www.reptilerentals.com

Jungle Exotics   **(909) 887-3500**
P.O. Box 90538, San Bernardino, CA 92427
cats & dogs, lions, wolves, wide variety of birds & reptiles
info@junglexotics.com * www.junglexotics.com

Living Art Aquatic Design, Inc.   **(310) 822-7484**
2301 South Sepulveda Blvd, Los Angeles, CA, 90064
30 yrs exp. fish wrangler, custom aquarium setups, saltwater/freshwater
ron@aquatic2000.com * www.aquatic2000.com

Paws For Effect   **(877) 729-7439**
PO Box 650, Lake Hughes, CA, 93532
dogs & cats, birds, exotics (lions, tigers) reptiles, insects, offices in CA, NY, CT, MI, IL
www.pawsforeffect.net

Phil's Animal Rentals   **(805) 521-1100**
PO Box 309, Piru, CA, 93040
Domestic/exotic. Horses, dogs, birds, cows, yak, water buffalo, flamingos, huge variety wagons & carriages, vintage prop
www.philsanimalrentals.com

Randy Miller's Predators in Action   **(909) 499-9064**
PO Box 1691, Big Bear City, CA, 92314
exotic large cats, wolves, black & grizzly bears, controlled wrestling & attacks, snarls & roars on cue
www.predatorsinaction.com

Silver Screen Animals   **(661) 269-0231**
34540 Brock Lane, Acton, CA, 93510
dogs & cats, farm animals, forest animals, some insects, birds, exotic animals, barnyard animals, rodents.
www.silverscreenanimals.com

Studio Animal Services   **(661) 257-4798**
28230 San Martinez Grande Canyon Rd, Castaic, CA, 91384
small/med/large dogs, cats, hoofstock, birds, & exotics (bears, wolves, monkeys, etc.)
www.studioanimals.com

Talented Animals   **(310) 858-8722**
1033 N Carol Dr Ste 401, W Hollywood, CA, 90069
birds, cats & dogs, exotics, hoofstock, primates, reptiles, rodents, wild animals incl. wolves
www.talentedanimals.com

Working Wildlife   **(661) 245-2406**
Call for Appt.
Animal rental; exotic cats & dogs, chimps, primates, bears, wolves, foxes, raccoons, birds, reptiles, reindeer, and more
info@workingwildlife.com * www.workingwildlife.com

Worldwide Movie Animals, LLC   **(661) 252-2000**
P.O. Box 802474 Santa Clarita CA, 91380
dogs/cats, birds, primates, reptiles, insects, camels, kangaroos, porcupines, beavers
www.worldwidemovieanimals.com

Animation Control Systems

See: Puppets, Marionettes, Automata, Animatronics* Special Effects, Electronic

Animatronics

See: Prop Design & Manufacturing* Puppets, Marionettes, Automata, Animatronics* Special Effects, Electronic* Special Effects, Make-up/Prosthetics

Antenna

E.C. Prop Rentals   **(818) 764-2008**
rooftop TV, satellite, antenna towers
LCW Props   **(818) 243-0707**
Large Selection, TV, Satellite, Radio, High Frequency, Wifi, Dual Band, Large & Small

Antiques & Antique Decorations

See Also: Asian Antiques, Furniture, Art & Artifacts* Linens, Household* Salvage, Architectural

Angelus Medical & Optical Co., Inc.   **(310) 769-6060**
13007 S Western Ave, Gardena, CA, 90249
Antique Medical Furniture & Antique Medical Equipment
www.angelusmedical.com

Castle Antiques & Design   **(818) 765-5000**
11924 Vose St, N Hollywood, CA, 91605
We offer a wide variety of types and styles of Antique Furniture and Decor for rental and purchase
info@castleantiques.net * www.castleprophouse.com

CASTLE ANTIQUES
&DESIGN

The largest selection of authentic Antique and Mid-Century Modern pieces to choose from!
20,000 Square Feet

We are open to decorators and the general public
Monday - Friday
from 9am to 5pm

11924 Vose Street
North Hollywood, CA 91605

(818) 765-5000

info@castleantiques.net

www.CastleAntiques.net

Clifford Antiques   **(747) 283-1272**
3429 Magnolia Blvd, Burbank, CA, 91505
British Antiques shipped from Scotland 18th Century to Mid Century a family run business with over 40 years experience
wfcliffordantiques@yahoo.com * www.cliffordantiques.com

Design Mix Furniture   **(323) 939-7500**
442 S La Brea Ave, Los Angeles, CA, 90036
Global imports of Indian, Indonesian, Chinese, African, Moroccan art, acc., antiques, reprod. & Industrial Furniture
alyssashah@earthlink.net * www.mixfurniture.com

Galerie Sommerlath - French 50s 60s   **(310) 838-0102**
9608 Venice Blvd, Culver City, CA, 90232
Over 10,000 sq ft of Mid-Century, 70's & 80's furniture, lighting, accessories, home decor, art, sculptures, paintings.
info@galeriesommerlath.com * www.galeriesommerlath.com

The Hand Prop Room LP.   **(323) 931-1534**
History For Hire, Inc.   **(818) 765-7767**

LISTINGS FOR THIS CATEGORY CONTINUE ON THE
FOLLOWING PAGE

International Printing Museum   **(714) 529-1832**
315 Torrance Blvd, Carson, CA, 90745
antique printing/office equipment 1450-1980. old presses, machines, related furniture, period artwork
mail@printmuseum.org * www.printmuseum.org

Jan's & Co. European Antiques, Inc.   **(323) 735-6455**
1904 W Adams Blvd, Los Angeles, CA, 90018
European furnishings and antiques
info@jansantiques.com * www.jansantiques.com

Jas. Townsend & Son, Inc.   **(574) 594-5852**
133 N 1st St, P.O. Box 415, Pierceton, IN, 46562
catalog sales; American Colonial period inspired reprod. of wardrobe & household items, books/patterns of Colonial perio
www.jas-townsend.com

King Richards Antique & Vintage Center   **(562) 698-5974**
12301 Whittier Blvd, Whittier, CA, 90602
Largest antiques & vintage store in CA. Over 1 acre of furniture, jewelry, collectibles, props. Great filming location.
martha@kingrichardsantiques.com * www.kingrichardsantiques.com

Ob-jects   **(818) 351-4200**
Antique chairs, Antique furniture, antique upholstery, folk furniture, antique objects

Old N Country Prop Shop, LLC   **(818) 423-2599**
A wide variety of mainly "East Coast" Antiques and Accessories, and Americana.

Omega/Cinema Props   **(323) 466-8201**
Antique furniture, items and tools.

Pasadena Antique Center and Annex   **(626) 449-7706**
480 South Fair Oaks Ave, Pasadena, CA, 91105
A wide array of decorative antiques and functional antique pieces from across the globe.
pasadenaantiqecenterandannex@gmail.com * bit.ly/PasadenaAntiqueCenter

Pasadena Antiques & Design   **(626) 389-3938**
330 S Fair Oaks Avenue, Pasadena, CA, 91105
Antiques of all ages and descriptions. 17th. through 20th. century
roy@antiquesofpasadena.com * www.antiquesofpasadena.com

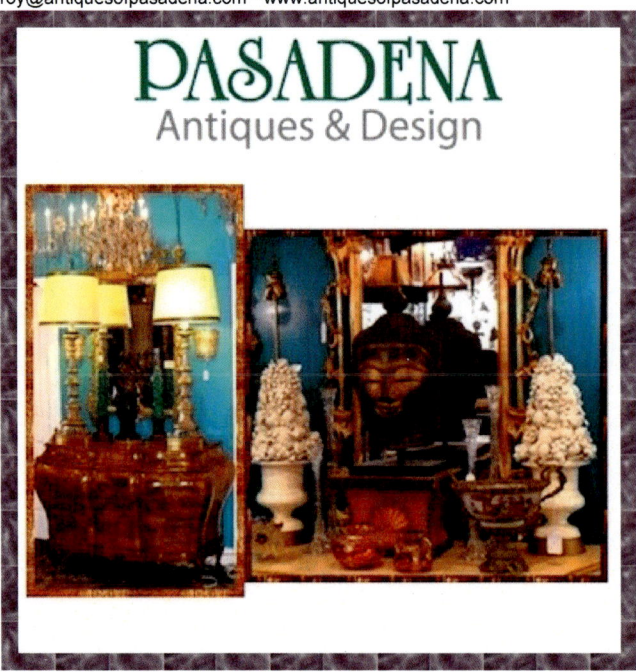

The Rational Past   **(310) 476-6277**
By Appointment, West Los Angeles, CA
Authentic science, industrial, technical antiques & collectibles. Many professions & eras represented. See web site.
info@therationalpast.com * www.therationalpast.com

The Seraph   **(740) 369-1817**
5606 State Route 37 E, Delaware, OH, 43015
Mfg. authentic reprod. 17th/18th C. furnishings & case goods, etc. 1000s of items, hrs Th-Sun, 10-5 Eastern, call for ca
www.theseraph.com

Sony Pictures Studios-Prop House (Off Lot)   **(310) 244-5999**

Susanne Hollis, Inc.   **(626) 441-0346**
230 Pasadena Ave, South Pasadena, CA, 91030
20th - 17th century Antiques, Accessories, and Fine Art from around the world in our 19,000sqft. warehouse and showrooms
sales@susannehollis.com * www.susannehollis.com

Universal Studios Property & Hardware Dept   **(818) 777-2784**
Antiques from antique lamps, antique fixtures and antique decorations of all kinds.

Used Church Items, Religious Rentals   **(412) 220-2272**
115 East Barr Street, Mcdonald, PA, 15057
1000's of Vintage Antique Religious items for large cathedrals, churches, and home chapels.
www.religiousrentals.com

Warner Bros. Studios Property Department   **(818) 954-2181**
Large collection period and antique furniture, hand props, fixtures and accessories

Apothecary

See: Drugstore/Apothecary Lab Equipment*

Apple Boxes

See: Expendables

Appliances

See Also: Refrigerators Stoves* Vacuum Cleaners* Washing Machines/Dryers*

C. P. Two   **(323) 466-8201**

The Hand Prop Room LP.   **(323) 931-1534**
sm. household

Kimos Appliance LLC   **(818) 787-8995**
15430 Cabrito Road #1, Van Nuys, CA, 91406
We rent and/or sell all major home appliances. Most makes, models, styles, sizes, and colors available. Call today!!
kimosappliances@yahoo.com * www.kimosappliances.com

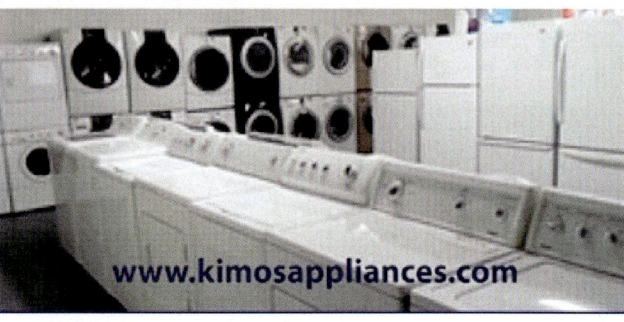

LCW Props (818) 243-0707
Commercial, Disabled For Debris, Non-Working, Old, Rusty
Modern Props (323) 934-3000
contemporary, household, backs cut out, vintage, refrigerators, stoves, freezers, countertop appliances, toy appliances.
NEST Studio Rentals, Inc. (818) 942-0339
small household
Omega/Cinema Props (323) 466-8201
Residential appliances and commercial appliances from period to contemporary.
RC Vintage, Inc. (818) 765-7107
40s, 50s, 60s & 70s selection Fridges, Toasters, Blenders, Large selection of Vintage Stoves, Refrigerators, and more
Sony Pictures Studios-Prop House (Off Lot) (310) 244-5999
Air conditioner, coffee maker, compacter, dishwasher, dryer, fountains, freezers, furnaces, hair dryers, ironing boards and more.
Studio Plumbing Rentals (323) 829-9339
7373 Atoll Ave, N Hollywood, CA, 91605
studioplumbingrentals@gmail.com * www.studioair.com
Universal Studios Property & Hardware Dept (818) 777-2784
Appliances from coffee makers and refrigerators to stoves and toasters, commercial appliances and residential appliances.
Warner Bros. Studios Property Department (818) 954-2181
Refrigerators, stoves, washing machines, dryers, microwaves, household appliances
ZG04 DECOR (818) 853-8040
Kitchen appliances

Aprons

See: Protective Apparel Uniforms, Trades/Professional/Sports* Wardrobe*

Aquariums & Tropical Fish

See Also: Plastics, Materials & Fabrication
Living Art Aquatic Design, Inc. (310) 822-7484
2301 South Sepulveda Blvd, Los Angeles, CA, 90064
30 yrs exp. fish wrangler, custom aquarium setups, saltwater/freshwater
ron@aquatic2000.com * www.aquatic2000.com

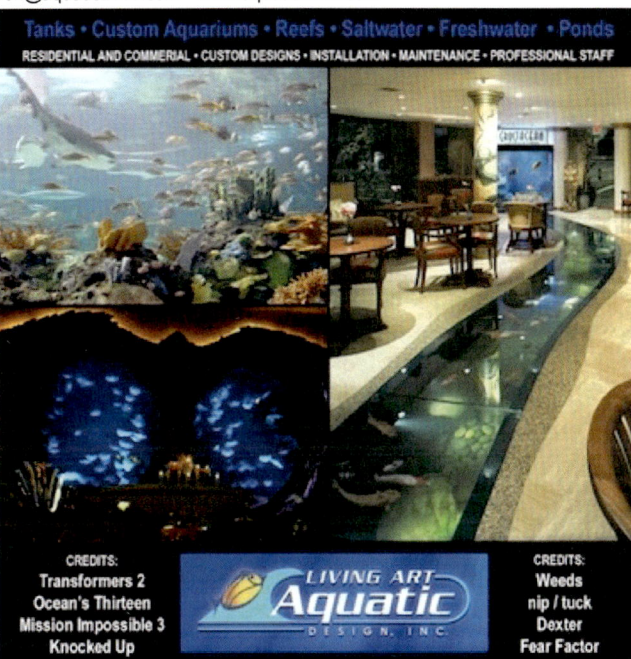

Tanks • Custom Aquariums • Reefs • Saltwater • Freshwater • Ponds
RESIDENTIAL AND COMMERIAL • CUSTOM DESIGNS • INSTALLATION • MAINTENANCE • PROFESSIONAL STAFF

CREDITS:
Transformers 2
Ocean's Thirteen
Mission Impossible 3
Knocked Up

CREDITS:
Weeds
nip / tuck
Dexter
Fear Factor

RC Vintage, Inc. (818) 765-7107
Full Selection of Shapes and sizes Saltwater and Freshwater Available, Aquarium with matching stand, tropical fish!

Arabian Decorations

Badia Design, Inc. (818) 762-0130
5420 Vineland Ave, N Hollywood, CA, 91601
brass arabian decorations, hanging lanterns, metal moroccan furniture, moroccan pillow
info@badiadesign.com * www.badiadesign.com
History For Hire, Inc. (818) 765-7767
brass, fabrics

Arcade Equipment, Games & Rides

See Also: Pinball Machines Scales* Vendor Carts & Concession Counters* Video Games*
AIR Designs (818) 768-6639
Video, skill, claw, pinball, rides, dart, pool & more.
Arcade Amusements (866) 576-8878
802 West Washington Ave Ste E, Escondido, CA, 92025-1644
Planning a Party? How about having some games there? How about 10? How about 20? How about... Well, you get the idea.
phil@arcadeamusements.com * www.arcadeamusements.com

ARCADE AMUSEMENTS
CLASSIC VIDEO & ARCADE GAMES
INTERACTIVE GAMES
TABLE GAMES
WWW.ARCADEAMUSEMENTS.COM

L. A. Party Works (888) 527-2789
9712 Alpaca St, S El Monte, CA, 91733
in Vancouver tel. 604-589-4101 photo booth, kiddie rides, carnival games, dunk tank, Mocap Boxing Arcade
partyworks@aol.com * www.partyworksinteractive.com
LCW Props (818) 243-0707
Arcade Games, Gaming Systems, Joysticks, Coin Operated, Money Changers
Lennie Marvin Enterprises, Inc. (Prop Heaven) (818) 841-5882
pinball, video games, kiddie rides & more
RC Vintage, Inc. (818) 765-7107
30s-90s free standing games/rides, mutoscope, fortune tellers, Pinballs and Video Games. Funhouse Mirrors. Clown Heads!

Archery Equipment, Training

See Also: Sporting Goods & Services Weaponry, Historical* Weaponry, Medieval*
The Hand Prop Room LP. (323) 931-1534
real, mfg., stunts, crossbows, sport, medieval, Native American
History For Hire, Inc. (818) 765-7767
ethnic & period bows & arrows
Sony Pictures Studios-Prop House (Off Lot) (310) 244-5999
Sword & Stone (818) 562-6548
longbows, crossbows, arrows, bolts, quivers
Universal Studios Property & Hardware Dept (818) 777-2784
Archery equipment such as bows and arrows, arrow quivers, archery trophy and more.

Architectural Lighting

See: Searchlights/Skytrackers, Architectural Lights

Architectural Pieces & Artifacts

See Also: Columns* Doors* Fiberglass Products/Fabrication* Pedestals* Salvage, Rubble, Clutter & Trash (Prop)* Scenery/Set Construction* Scenery/Set Rentals* Staff Shops

Charisma Design Studio, Inc.   **(818) 252-6611**
8414 San Fernando Blvd, Sun Valley, CA, 91352
high-end 1-off large scale metal/glass/wood art
info@charismadesign.com * www.charismadesign.com

Eric's Architectural Salvage   **(213) 413-6800**
1540 W 6th St, Los Angeles, CA, 90017
Erics Architectural Salvage has been salvaging items hands for over 18 years and now we are finally open to the public.
ericstiques@aol.com * www.ericsarchitecturalsalvage.com

Freeway Building Materials & Supply   **(323) 261-8904**
1124 S. Boyle Ave, Los Angeles, CA, 90023
bricks, steel windows
www.freewaybuildingmaterials.us

The Hand Prop Room LP.   **(323) 931-1534**
Monument Sign Mfg. LLC   **(800) 711-3626**
805 N Warren St, Orwigsburg, PA, 17961
catalog sales; custom made foam, wide variety arch. applications
www.monumentmfg.com

Olde Good Things, Inc.   **(213) 746-8600**
1800 S Grand Ave, Los Angeles, CA, 90015
Interior/exterior doors, antique paneling, hardware, windows, salvaged antiques, anchor leg tables, pine tables
www.oldegoodthings.com

Pasadena Architectural Salvage   **(626) 535-9655**
2600 E Foothill Blvd, Pasadena, CA, 91107-3408
circa 1880s-1930s entry doors, s/g windows, iron gates, columns, mantels, footed tubs, spec. Arts & Crafts period
pasarcsalvage@aol.com * www.pasadenaarchitecturalsalvage.com

Sword & Stone   **(818) 562-6548**
gargoyles, stone work, custom design-wrought iron & sheet metal

Universal Studios Property & Hardware Dept   **(818) 777-2784**
Architectural pieces and architectural artifacts.

Warner Bros. Studios Hardware Rentals   **(818) 954-1335**
4000 Warner Blvd Bldg 30, Burbank, CA, 91522
Door Knobs & Door Plates, Door Hinges, Window Fixtures, Elevator Panels, Train Accessories & Boat Accessories
wbsfproperty@warnerbros.com * www.wbpropertydept.com

Warner Bros. Studios Staff Shop   **(818) 954-2269**
Manufacturer of exterior & interior details used for the creation of sets in all architectural styles & eras.

Architectural Research

See: Research, Advisors, Consulting & Clearances

Archiving Media/Records Management

Bonded Services   **(818) 848-9766**
3205 Burton Ave, Burbank, CA, 91504
media storage archives/vaults, climate control, physical distribution, studio services
www.bonded.com

Iron Mountain   **(800) 899-IRON**
1 Federal St, Boston, MA 02110
locs. in Hollywood, NY, PA, & International; climate controlled vaults, media storage, records mgmt, film preservation
www.ironmountain.com

Keep It Self Storage   **(818) 769-5477**
4444 Vineland Ave, Toluca Lake, CA, 91602
All media, film-tape, self-storage, climate control, 24 hr access, electronic security; + more loc. in S. Cal.
www.keepitselfstorage.com

Pacific Title Archives   **(818) 760-4223**
10717 Vanowen St, N Hollywood, CA, 91605
film & video storage, high security, p/u & delivery, database mgmnt, film/video inspection/preservation
www.pacifictitlearchives.com

Producers Film Center   **(323) 851-1122**
948 N Sycamore Ave, Hollywood, CA, 90038
film/videotape storage, climate control, 24 hr guards, computerized inventory, immediate access
www.filmstorage.net

Repro-Graphic Supply   **(818) 771-9066**
9838 Glenoaks Blvd, Sun Valley, CA, 91352
Digital archiving & archiving services. All media; paper / art to Flash Drives, portable hard drives, CDs, and emails.
info@reprographicsupply.com * www.reprographicsupply.com

Arenas

See: Locations, Stages/Studios, Film/TV/Events

Armoires

See: Antiques & Antique Decorations

Armor, Chainmail, Suits of Armor

See Also: Weaponry, Historical* Weaponry, Medieval

Costume Armour Inc.   **(845) 534-9120**
2 Mill Street, Building 1 Suite 101, Cornwall, NY 12518
theatrical armor
info@costumearmour.com * www.costumearmour.com

The Costume House   **(818) 508-9933**
bathing suits, vintage beach wear, mens bathing suit, women bathing suit, children bathing suits

Omega/Cinema Props   **(323) 466-8201**
Suits of armor, coat of arms, shields, samurai armor, and armor display stands.

Sony Pictures Studios-Wardrobe   **(310) 244-5995**
alterations, call (310) 244-7260

Sword & Stone   **(818) 562-6548**
aluminum, bronze, chainmail, mesh, human-horse, shields, historic & future

Universal Studios Property & Hardware Dept   **(818) 777-2784**
Suit of armor; helmets, shields, breastplates and more from different time periods and countries.

Warner Bros. Studios Costume Dept   **(818) 954-1297**
Gothic, Medieval, European, English, Japanese, Hoods, Suits, Hats, Boots

Army-Navy Equipment

See: Military Props & Equipment* Military Surplus/Combat Clothes, Field Gear* Walkie-Talkies* Weapons

40 YEARS OF DEBBIES BOOK

Richard Pryor was playing at the Pantages Theatre. **Cheech & Chong's "Up In Smoke"** was down the street at the movie theatre. California voters approved Proposition 13. **President Carter** raised the mandatory retirement age to 70, **Pope John Paul** became the first non-Italian pope in 465 years, and the first public edition of Debbies Book hit the streets. Norman Lear and Mary Tyler Moore were in full swing, Metro Media (then Channel 11) had 4 stages and 6 rehearsal halls spinning out sitcoms. (Now it's a high school) **"Annie Hall", "Deer Hunter", "Grease"** and **"Animal House"** were the top grossing movies that year while **"Rockford Files"** and **"All in the Family"** were in top form. **"Dallas", "Mork & Mindy", "Taxi", "WKRP in Cincinnati"** were getting ready to debut and independent prop houses were booming.

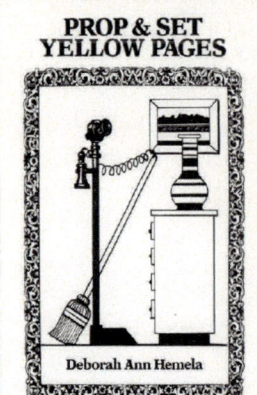

PROP & SET
YELLOW PAGES

Deborah Ann Hemela

Shoppers for shows during this period used the yellow pages and a handful of prop houses, plus the major studios. In Hollywood, Santa Monica Blvd. was the locale of most independent sources like Cinema Props, Cinema Mercantile, Omega, Roschu and P.S.W. Billy Wolf, First St. Furniture, House of Props, Ellis Mercantile and Earl Hays Press were all tucked away on the side streets. Walter Allen Plant Rentals was across from Paramount Stuidos, Jackson Shrub Supply was out on Sepulveda. ("The Valley" in those days seemed so far away.) The two major hand prop houses were Ellis Mercantile on La Brea and The Hand Prop Room on the west side of town. I.S.S. had just opened, started by a couple of prop masters who hand found a niche. Who would have thought that it would outlive Ellis Mercantile and grow so much larger years down the road. Yep...small, independent sources were poppin' up all over town. It was crazy. It was fun.

Art & Picture Framing Services

See Also: Easels

Clearedart.com/El Studio Granados   **(818) 240-4421**
958 Verdugo Circle Dr, Glendale, CA, 91206
Complete one-stop custom-framing services, over 4000 mouldings, plexi
boxes, museum mounting.
fineart@elstudiogranados.com * www.clearedart.com

Dina Art Co.   **(323) 469-4073**
6433 W Sunset Blvd, Los Angeles, CA, 90028
Cleared art, art posters, custom framing, hand colored prints & more. Over
3,000 images in 22 categories available.
dina@dinaart.com * www.dinaart.com

The Hand Prop Room LP.   **(323) 931-1534**
Hollywood Cinema Arts   **(818) 504-7333**
Certified museum grade framers that can make any artwork look like a
masterpiece.

Hollywood Studio Gallery   **(323) 462-1116**
classical to posters, fast turnaround-mounting services

Omega/Cinema Props   **(323) 466-8201**
Photography frames, art frames, old picture frames, contemporary picture
frames, wood frames, antique frames, ornate frames.

U-Frame It Gallery   **(818) 781-4500**
6203 Lankershim Blvd, N Hollywood, CA, 91606
Over 1,000 frames in stock, 1-hr. turnaround. We also do frame repairs.
uframit@aol.com * www.uframeitgallery.com

Custom Framing For Film & Television
1-hour framing service available • Pick-up and delivery
Thousands of styles available • Access to cleared artwork
New Location!
www.uframeitgallery.com

Art Deco Carpet & Rugs

Modern Props   **(323) 934-3000**
Art deco rugs, modern rugs, contemporary rugs, many patterns, many colors,
wool rugs, silk rugs, and more.

RC Vintage, Inc.   **(818) 765-7107**
large patterned rugs, multiple designs, hand woven looks, water colored, house
hold rugs, shag rugs, vintage carpet

Universal Studios Property & Hardware Dept   **(818) 777-2784**
Art deco carpets and art deco rugs

Art Deco Dressing/Accessories

History For Hire, Inc.   **(818) 765-7767**
smalls

Old N Country Prop Shop, LLC   **(818) 423-2599**
We have lots of art deco dressing / accessories: pottery, purses, tables, dishes,
decor, and lots more.

Universal Studios Property & Hardware Dept   **(818) 777-2784**
Art deco dressing; art deco trays, art deco sconces, art deco chairs, art deco
vases, art deco plateware and more.

Art Deco Furniture & Rugs

See: Art Deco Carpet & Rugs* Art Deco Dressing/Accessories*
Furniture, Art Deco

Art For Rent (Cleared Art)

See Also: Art, Artists For Hire* Carved Figures* Glass & Mirrors,
Art/Finishing/Etching/Etc.* Paintings/Prints* Photographs* Posters,
Art/Movie/Travel/Wanted Etc.* Sculpture

Alpha Companies - Spellman Desk Co.   **(818) 504-9090**
cleared art, abstract, landscapes, oil paintings, photographs

Art By Kidz   **(818) 625-1477**
Call for Appt, Glendale, CA, 91207
100s of ORIGINAL CHILDRENS 2D & 3D ARTWORKS for rent at low flat rates
based on size. Cleared copyright, located in Glendale.
artbykidz@gmail.com * www.artbykidz.com

Art Dimensions Inc.   **(310) 433-8934**
Web Based Business
Cleared contemporary art for lease including paintings, prints, sculptures and
photography by more than 80 artists.
info@artdimensionsonline.com * www.artdimensionsonline.com

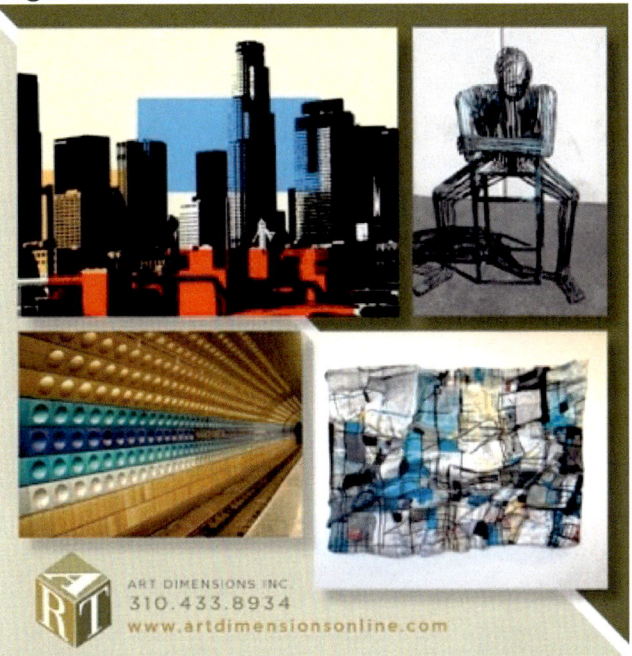

ART DIMENSIONS INC.
310.433.8934
www.artdimensionsonline.com

ART PIC   **(818) 503-5999**
6826 Troost Ave, N Hollywood, CA, 91605
Contemporary Art Rental and Sales. All mediums ALL ART CLEARED. Open
M-F 9-5. We ship worldwide.
artpicla@mac.com * www.artpic2000.com

ART•PIC
818 - 503 5999
all cleared art
M-F 9-5

LISTINGS FOR THIS CATEGORY CONTINUE ON THE
FOLLOWING PAGE

ARTagogo.net   (310) 753-9991
2041 Glencoe Ave, Venice, CA, 90291
Cleared art & photography; custom art & graphics, delivery available. Call Cynthia Hill for unlisted items not on web.
cynthiahill@mac.com * www.artagogo.net

Artery Props   (877) 732-7733
7684 Clybourn Ave 2nd Floor Unit C, Sun Valley, CA, 91352
100% cleared artwork & owned artwork: posters, stickers, flyers, gold records, signs, CDs, DVDs, albums, mic flags, more
info@arteryprops.com * www.arteryprops.com

Artspace Warehouse   (323) 936-7020
7358 Beverly Blvd, Los Angeles, CA, 90036
Huge selection of cleared original art in stock for same day rent or sale at affordable prices.
info@artspacewarehouse.com * www.artspacewarehouse.com

Breen/Graham   (323) 663-3426
Call for appointment.
Unusual art made from recycled materials
www.claregraham.com

Bridge Furniture & Props Los Angeles   (818) 433-7100
We carry modern & traditional furniture, lighting, accessories, cleared art, & rugs. Items are online for easy shopping.

Chris's Art Resource (C.A.R.)   (323) 480-2942
1035 N Myra Ave, Los Angeles, CA, 90029
Hundreds of CLEARED paintings, All Sizes and Styles-Sleek to Cozy, All Art on Premises
w99lulu@yahoo.com * www.chrisartresource.com

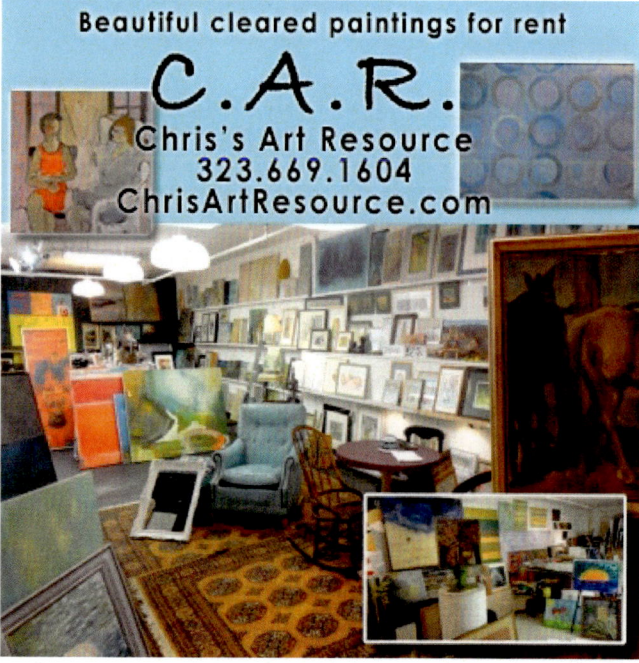

Clearedart.com/El Studio Granados　　　(818) 240-4421
958 Verdugo Circle Dr, Glendale, CA, 91206
Galleries full of eclectic fine art in a variety of mediums and techniques for gallery installations, & corporate decor.
fineart@elstudiogranados.com * www.clearedart.com

ClearedINK　　　(310) 505-2433
Web Based Business
ClearedINK is an online platform, providing direct access to contemporary cleared artwork around the clock.
art@clearedink.com * www.clearedink.com

CLEAREDINK

Cope Studios: The Haven　　　(818) 913-7187
926 Western Ave Ste A & B, Glendale, CA, 91201
Various items are available for rent ranging from sculptures, paintings, tools, easels, and more.
figurativesculptor@hotmail.com * www.copestudios.com

Dina Art Co.　　　(323) 469-4073
6433 W Sunset Blvd, Los Angeles, CA, 90028
Cleared art, art posters, custom framing, hand colored prints & more. Over 3,000 images in 22 categories available.
dina@dinaart.com * www.dinaart.com

Enchanted Studio Props, LLC　　　(818) 561-4550
3000 W Empire Ave, Burbank, CA, 91504
Hundreds of copyright cleared artworks available on site, ready for immediate pick-up.
espart4film@gmail.com * www.espart4film.com

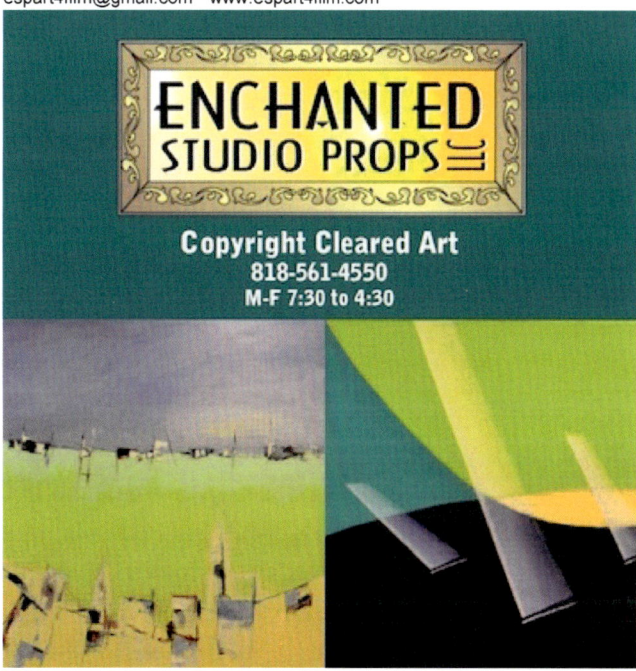

LISTINGS FOR THIS CATEGORY CONTINUE ON THE FOLLOWING PAGE

Faux Library Studio Props, Inc.   **(818) 765-0096**
Cleared Art, cleared photographs, book artwork and more including presidential portraits!

FILM ART LA   **(323) 461-4900**
Culver City Warehouse at Jefferson & Hauser. Call for address.
Period-Contemporary Art. Cleared art rentals available for immediate pick up. 13000 high rez images, print to all sizes.
filmartla@gmail.com * www.filmartla.com

Western Tanager by Astrid Preston

888-858-7107

FILMARTOLA

Hollywood Cinema Arts   **(818) 504-7333**
Artwork for every type of set. Paintings, Prints, Sculptures and Photography.

Hollywood Cinema Arts
Largest Motion Picture Art Gallery In The World!

Custom Framing • Cleared Art • Jewelry & Small Props

FormDecor, Inc.   **(310) 558-2582**
America's largest event rental supplier of 20th Century furniture and accessories for Modern and Mid-Century styles.

Galerie Sommerlath - French 50s 60s   **(310) 838-0102**
9608 Venice Blvd, Culver City, CA, 90232
Over 10,000 sq ft of Mid-Century, 70's & 80's furniture, lighting, accessories, home decor, art, sculptures, paintings.
info@galeriesommerlath.com * www.galeriesommerlath.com

Ghettogloss Cleared Art   **(323) 871-8100**
Web Based Business
Cutting edge contemporary paintings & photography 100% Cleared. Street Art, Graffiti, Outsider Art, Low Brow & Pop.
www.ghettogloss.com

The Hand Prop Room LP.   **(323) 931-1534**
lrg sel. cleared pieces

Hollywood Studio Gallery   **(323) 462-1116**
60,000 items on display in our art rental gallery. Cleared art rentals and sales

RENTALS • SALES • CUSTOM FRAMING • PHOTO SERVICES

HOLLYWOOD STUDIO GALLERY
ART & FRAMING
FOR THE IMMEDIATE WORLD

1000'S OF CLEARED
OR CLEARABLE WORKS

THE INDUSTRY'S MOST
EXTENSIVE COLLECTION

SINCE 1979

LCW Props (818) 243-0707
Cleared Artwork; Paintings, Sketches, Photos, Custom Graphics, Art Supplies, Kiln, Pottery Wheel

Little Bohemia Rentals (818) 853-7506
11940 Sherman Rd, N Hollywood, CA, 91605
cleared modern photography, cleared original artworks, wall hangings, tapestries, fiber art, framed and unframed
sales@wearelittlebohemia.com * www.wearelittlebohemia.com

Modern Props (323) 934-3000
modern art for rent, contemporary prints, originals, wall art, sculptures & more cleared art

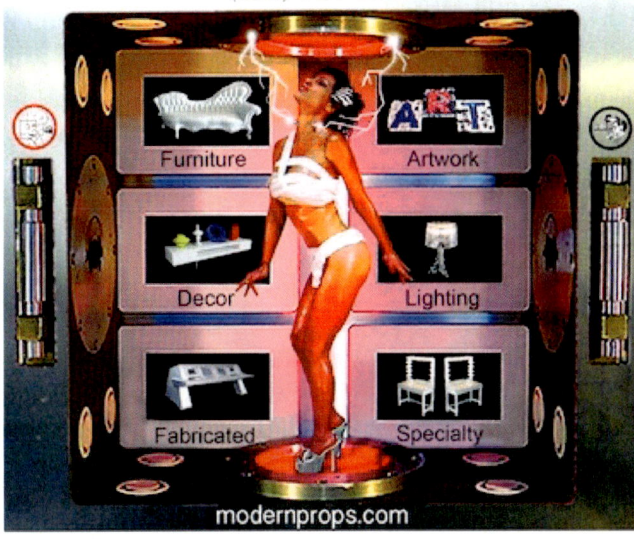

Modernica Props (323) 664-2322
Cleared artwork - MidCentury Artwork & Retro Artwork

NEST Studio Rentals, Inc. (818) 942-0339
Cleared artwork including cleared paintings, prints, photographs, family photos, kid's artwork in stock

Ob-jects (818) 351-4200
Cleared art and art rentals of various kinds

Old N Country Prop Shop, LLC (818) 423-2599
Cleared artwork and custom artwork, in a variety of styles and sizes.

Omega/Cinema Props (323) 466-8201
Paintings, sculptures, photographs, prints, tribal artifacts, portraits, needlepoint, presidential artwork and prints

Prop Services West (818) 503-2790
Art for rent/cleared art of all kinds including Masters Artwork.

RC Vintage, Inc. (818) 765-7107
Cleared Art, many framed pictures, framed paintings, paintings of ships, flowers, vases, people, instruments, you name it!

Schmidli Backdrops LA (323) 938-2098
5830 W Adams Blvd, Culver City, CA, 90232
Providing hand painted Textured and Scenic backdrops to the commercial, film, and fashion industry for over 20 years.
backdrops@schmidli.com * www.schmidli.com

Sculpture by Bruce Gray (323) 223-4059
688 South Avenue 21, Los Angeles, CA, 90031
modern sculptures, abstract paintings, mobiles, unique furniture, giant objects, kinetic art, custom metal work, metal a
bruce@brucegray.com * www.brucegray.com

Sony Pictures Studios-Prop House (Off Lot) (310) 244-5999
acrylic artwork, glass artwork, metal artwork, wood artwork, cleared artwork

Susanne Hollis, Inc. (626) 441-0346
230 Pasadena Ave, South Pasadena, CA, 91030
20th - 17th century Antiques, Accessories, and Fine Art from around the world in our 19,000sqft. warehouse and showrooms
sales@susannehollis.com * www.susannehollis.com

U-Frame It Gallery (818) 781-4500
6203 Lankershim Blvd, N Hollywood, CA, 91606
Cleared photographs, wide variety, custom framing
uframit@aol.com * www.uframeitgallery.com

Wallspace (323) 930-0471
607 N La Brea, Los Angeles, CA, 90036
Contemporary abstract art gallery and photography. Available for rent and sale with permission to use on tv film & print
art@wallspacela.com * www.wallspacela.com

ZEdonk ART (818) 693-1082
5330 Derry Ave Ste P, Agoura Hills, CA, 91301
ZEdonk ART has a spectacular collection of over 5000 pieces of handcrafted Children's Artwork cleared & ready to rent!
kelly@zedonkart.com * www.ZEdonkART.com

ZG04 DECOR (818) 853-8040
Cleared Art, Paintings, Drawings, Photography

Art Glass, Hand Blown/Leaded Etc.

See: Glass & Mirrors, Art/Finishing/Etching/Etc.

Art, Artists For Hire

Charisma Design Studio, Inc. (818) 252-6611
8414 San Fernando Road, Sun Valley, CA, 91352
custom metal/glass/wood/stone mixed media functional art
info@charismadesign.com * www.charismadesign.com

Clearedart.com/El Studio Granados (818) 240-4421
958 Verdugo Circle Dr, Glendale, CA, 91206
Commissions considered for original paintings, drawings, sculptures,
installations, murals, maps, masks, and miniatures.
fineart@elstudiogranados.com * www.clearedart.com

Cope Studios: The Haven (818) 913-7187
926 Western Ave Ste A & B, Glendale, CA, 91201
Our studio has 45 artists ranging in all styles, techniques, and mediums.
figurativesculptor@hotmail.com * www.copestudios.com

Enchanted Studio Props, LLC (818) 561-4550
3000 W Empire Ave, Burbank, CA, 91504
Along w/ hundreds of copyright cleared artworks available on site, commissions
of all kinds available.
espart4film@gmail.com * www.espart4film.com

Famous Frames (310) 642-2721
5839 Green Valley Circle, Ste 104, Culver City, CA, 90230
In NY call (212) 980-7979: Artist reps for storyboards, comps, illustrations &
animatics
www.famousframes.com

Fauve Associates (818) 481-2019
6553 Randi Ave, Woodland Hills, CA, 91303
Art direction, concept & graphic design; fine art, all styles & media; sculpture;
mega-murals & backings
info@fauveassociates.com * fauveassociates.com

FILM ART LA (323) 461-4900
Culver City Warehouse at Jefferson & Hauser. Call for address.
Painted & Digital Commissions Art, Murals, Portraits. Cleared art rentals We
clear and print famous artists and artwork.
filmartla@gmail.com * www.filmartla.com

Ghettogloss Cleared Art (323) 871-8100
Web Based Business
We have artists available for art commissions of all kinds. There is no job that is
too big or small for us. Just ask.
www.ghettogloss.com

HPR Graphics (323) 556-2694
5674 Venice Blvd, Los Angeles, CA, 90019
Graphic design, photo retouching, photo compositing, custom graphics, and
more.
hprcan@earthlink.net * www.hprgraphics.net

Kathleen Swaydan (626) 798-7637
Call for Appt.
Fine reproductions & art historical research specializing in Italian Renaissance.
Call for appt.
www.artid.com/members/kdswaydan

KIHL STUDIOS (818) 812-9594
9701 Owensmouth Ave Unit 1, Chatsworth, CA, 91311
Original dimensional artwork and decor created by sculptor and designer
Brandon Kihl.
design@kihlstudios.com * www.kihlstudios.com

PropArt (323) 461-5842
Hollywood, CA, 91605
Script specific art, props & set dressing. Commissioned fine art paintings &
sculpture, also student & character driven
wright-douglas@sbcglobal.net * www.specialtysetprops.com

Wallspace (323) 930-0471
607 N La Brea, Los Angeles, CA, 90036
Contemporary abstract art gallery and photography. Available for rent and sale
with permission to use on tv film & print
art@wallspacela.com * www.wallspacela.com

ZEdonk ART (818) 693-1082
5330 Derry Ave Ste P, Agoura Hills, CA, 91301
ZEdonk ART has a talented team of Artists with paint brushes drawn & ready!
kelly@zedonkart.com * www.ZEdonkART.com

Art, On The Floor

See: Carpet & Flooring

Art, Supplies & Stationery

See Also: Certificates Desk Dressing* Easels* Hobby & Craft
Supplies* Pens, Fountain* Art & Picture Framing Services*

Blick Art Materials (323) 933-9284
7301 W Beverly Blvd, Los Angeles, CA, 90036
www.dickblick.com

Carter Sexton Fine Art Materials (818) 763-5050
5308 Laurel Canyon Blvd, N. Hollywood, CA, 91607
wide selection of artist supplies
www.cartersexton.com

Cheap Joe's (800) 227-2788
374 Industrial Park Dr, Boone, NC, 28607
Catalog: extensive selection of artist supplies
www.cheapjoes.com

Continental Art Supplies (818) 345-1044
7041 Reseda Blvd, Reseda, CA, 91335
artist supplies & drafting materials
www.continentalart.com

Francis-Orr Fine Stationery (310) 271-6106
320 N. Camden Dr, Beverly Hills, CA, 90210
huge sel. of fine papers: in-stock & custom, unique desk access. & gifts,
calligraphy services, no art supplies
www.francisorrbeverlyhills.com

Jerry's NY Central (646) 678-5474
111 4th Ave, New York, NY, 10003
primed/unprimed linen canvas, fine art supplies, handmade paper 100 years in
business
www.jerrysretailstores.com

LCW Props (818) 243-0707
Easels, School Art & Science Projects, Paperwork

Michael's (Burbank) (818) 260-0527
1551 N Victory Pl, Burbank, CA, 91502
www.michaels.com

Michael's (Pasadena) (626) 431-2850
1155 E Colorado Blvd, Pasadena, CA, 91106
www.michaels.com

Mittel's Art Center (310) 399-9500
2499 Lincoln Boulevard, Venice, CA, 90291
www.mittelsartcenter.com

Repro-Graphic Supply (818) 771-9066
9838 Glenoaks Blvd, Sun Valley, CA, 91352
Art supplies and hobby supplies for sale.
info@reprographicsupply.com * www.reprographicsupply.com

Sony Pictures Studios-Prop House (Off Lot) (310) 244-5999
Art & Craft supplies, artist paint box, artist drawing box, art set, canvas, clay,
paints, tracing light box, acorn, animal art

Sticker Planet (Original Farmers Market) (323) 939-6933
6333 W 3rd Street, Los Angeles, CA, 90036
Creative, artistic stickers for decorating, crafting & collecting. Thousands of
stickers in many themes and sizes.
www.stickerplanetLA.com

Swain's (818) 243-3129
537 N Glendale Ave, Glendale, CA, 91206
www.swainsart.com

Art, Tribal & Folk

See Also: Asian Antiques, Furniture, Art & Artifacts Baskets*
Mexican Decorations*

Badia Design, Inc. (818) 762-0130
5420 Vineland Ave, N Hollywood, CA, 91601
Moroccan Decorations, Moroccan Art, traditional African art, Moroccan
ornaments
info@badiadesign.com * www.badiadesign.com

Clearedart.com/El Studio Granados (818) 240-4421
958 Verdugo Circle Dr, Glendale, CA, 91206
Cleared multi-media fine art; paintings, folk art carvings and sculptures, masks,
miniatures, and hero items.
fineart@elstudiogranados.com * www.clearedart.com

The Hand Prop Room LP. (323) 931-1534
masks, totems, figures, Native American

History For Hire, Inc. (818) 765-7767

Prop Services West (818) 503-2790

Sony Pictures Studios-Prop House (Off Lot) (310) 244-5999
masks & drums

Artificial Food

See: Food, Artificial Food

Artificial Plants & Trees

See: Flowers, Silk, Plastic & Dried Greens*

Arts & Crafts Furniture

See: Furniture, Arts & Crafts

Asian Antiques, Furniture, Art & Artifacts

See Also: Pottery Shoji Screens*
Bali & Beyond   (818) 837-9485
11856 Balboa Blvd Ste 318, Granada Hills, CA, 91344
Traditional & Contemporary Wayang Kulit Shadow Puppets, Gamelan
Instruments & Music, Art & Artifacts from Bali & Beyond.
maria@balibeyond.com * http://balibeyond.com/commissionsrentals.html

Bali & Beyond • Rentals
818/837-9485
balibeyond.com/commissionsrentals.html

• Wayang Kulit Shadow Puppets
• Western Shadow Figures
• Gamelan Instruments
• Balinese Set Decorations

For More Information
Call MaRia Bodmann
a Culture Bearer and
Translator of Traditional
Balinese Arts and Ritual

Serving Southern California since 1990

Castle Antiques & Design   (818) 765-5000
11924 Vose St, N Hollywood, CA, 91605
Asian decorative antiques and Asian furniture for rent and purchase.
info@castleantiques.net * www.castleprophouse.com

Design Mix Furniture   (323) 939-7500
442 S La Brea Ave, Los Angeles, CA, 90036
Global imports of Indian, Indonesian, Chinese, African, Moroccan art, acc.,
antiques, reprod. & Industrial Furniture
alyssashah@earthlink.net * www.mixfurniture.com

MIX

MIXFURNITURE.COM 323-852-3078

F. Suie One Company   (626) 795-1335
1335 E Colorado Blvd, Pasadena, CA, 91106
Open 11-5 Wed-Sat or by Appt. Our specialty
fsuieone@earthlink.net

F. Suie One co.

Established 1888. Specializing in fine Asian
antiques and furniture for over 100 years.

**LISTINGS FOR THIS CATEGORY CONTINUE ON THE
FOLLOWING PAGE**

1980
40 YEARS OF DEBBIES BOOK

Ronald Reagan was elected president, John Lennon was shot and **CNN & MTV** were born. Quite a year! **"The Empire Strikes Back"** and "Nine to Five" were in theatres, "Kramer vs. Kramer" won the Oscar that year. Mount St. Helens erupted in 1981. Prince Charles and Lady Diana Spencer were married. Everyone was in love with **"Magnum PI"**. We left the 70's behind with Watergate, pet rocks and bell-bottoms, humming along with The Eagles and Fleetwood Mac.

Deborah Ann Hemela
Prop & Set Yellow Pages
1980

In 1980, the second edition of Debbies Book was published, still hand-typed on an electric typewriter. Not many changes occurred during the early years to the format or the frequency of the book, publishing it every other year up until 1992 with the 7th Edition. But then the book content changed so often that I started doing Debbies Book full time every year with a new edition hitting the streets ready for the new TV season each July. Common categories listed in the book were 'Manuscript Typing Services', 'Stop Watches', 'Magnetic Signs' and 'Morticians Wax'. Liquor and smoking was still very much in, so 'Cigar, Cigarettes & Tobacco' were acceptable. 'Condom Machines' were added to the long list of vending machine types.

Faux Library Studio Props, Inc.　　　　　　(818) 765-0096
Asian antiques and more for rent.

The Hand Prop Room LP.　　　　　　(323) 931-1534
History For Hire, Inc.　　　　　　(818) 765-7767
smalls, lots of Japanese items
Hollywood Studio Gallery　　　　　　(323) 462-1116
panels, prints, paintings
J.F. Chen Antiques　　　　　　(323) 463-4603
1000 N. Highland Ave, Los Angeles, CA 90038
antique & reproduction Continental, Asian and vintage furniture & accessories
www.jfchen.com
Modern Props　　　　　　(323) 934-3000
Asian ceramics including contemporary asian antiques, futuristic asian art,
asian sculptures to asian prints
Ob-jects　　　　　　(818) 351-4200
Asian styled furniture, wall pieces, museum mounted
Omega/Cinema Props　　　　　　(323) 466-8201
Samurai armor, asian portraits, persian rugs, asian themed furniture, asian
trunks, and more.
Pasadena Antique Center and Annex　　　　　　(626) 449-7706
480 South Fair Oaks Ave, Pasadena, CA, 91105
A large assortment of art, artifacts, and collectibles from all across Asia and
from all eras and styles.
pasadenaaantiqecenterandannex@gmail.com * bit.ly/PasadenaAntiqueCenter
Sony Pictures Studios-Prop House (Off Lot)　　　　　　(310) 244-5999
Universal Studios Property & Hardware Dept　　　　　　(818) 777-2784
Antique asian carts, antique asian jars, antique asian trays and more.

Asian Themed Parties

See: Costume Rental Houses* Events, Decorations, Supplies &
Services* Events, Design/Planning/Production* Travel (City/Country)
Themed Events

Associations

See: Guilds, Unions, Societies, Associations

Astrological

The Hand Prop Room LP.　　　　　　(323) 931-1534
crystal balls, charts
History For Hire, Inc.　　　　　　(818) 765-7767
Modern Props　　　　　　(323) 934-3000
Astrological props; crystal balls, globe statues, desk globes with maps spinning
and solid mount, oversized ribbed globes

Athletic Equipment

See: Boxing, Wrestling, Mixed Martial Arts (MMA)* Exercise &
Fitness Equipment* Sporting Goods & Services* Sportswear* Track &
Field Equipment* Uniforms, Trades/Professional/Sports

Athletic Themed Parties

See: Events, Decorations, Supplies & Services* Events,
Design/Planning/Production* Events, Entertainment* Sports &
Games Themed Events

Atmospheric Effects

See: Expendables* Fog Machines* Snow, Artificial & Real* Special
Effects, Equipment & Supplies

ATMs (Automated Teller Machines)

See: Bank Dressing

Audience Cutouts & Inflatables

Gonzo Brothers　　　　　　(310) 828-4989
2834 Colorado Ave #34, Santa Monica CA, 90404
Audience cutouts
www.gonzobrothers.com
Universal Studios Graphic Design & Sign Shop　　　　　　(818) 777-2350
Standees

Audience Response Systems

See: Game Show Electronics & Equipment

Audience Seating

See Also: Bleachers & Grandstand Seating* Folding Chairs/Tables*
Stages, Portable & Steel Deck* Theater Seating
Bill Ferrell Co.　　　　　　(818) 767-1900
10556 Keswick St, Sun Valley, CA, 91352
Stages, risers, steps, handrails, casters and ramps for audience seating and
handicap lifts. Set construction.
www.billferrell.com
C. P. Two　　　　　　(323) 466-8201
Theatre seating and other various seating options; theater seating, stadium
seating, auditorium seating
Mike Brown Grandstands　　　　　　(800) 266-2659
2300 Pomona Blvd, Pomona, CA, 91768
chair to grandstand risers, audience seating
www.mbgs.com
RC Vintage, Inc.　　　　　　(818) 765-7107
stadium seats Baseball and Football and Soccer!
Spec Seats　　　　　　(800) 535-2048
19516 S Susana Rd, Rancho Dominguez, CA, 90221
Multi-purpose folding chairs, custom logo chairs, stools, storage carts and
accessories.
http://specseats.com
Steeldeck, Inc.　　　　　　(323) 290-2100
3339 Exposition Place, Los Angeles, CA, 90018
rentals@steeldeck.com * www.steeldeck.com
Universal Studios Property & Hardware Dept　　　　　　(818) 777-2784
Various audience seating
Upstage Rentals Inc.　　　　　　(818) 247-1149
8238 Lankershim Blvd, N Hollywood, CA, 91605
www.upstagerentals.com

Audio Equipment

See Also: Control Boards* Editing Equipment & Services* Lighting &
Sound, Concert/Theatrical/DJ/VJ* Microphones* Phonographs*
Radio/TV Station* Recording Studio (Prop)* Stereo Equipment* Tape
Recorders* Victrolas/Gramophones
Ametron Audio & Video　　　　　　(323) 464-1144
1546 N. Argyle Ave, Hollywood, CA, 90028
Parking available in the back
www.ametron.com
Astro Audio Video Lighting, Inc.　　　　　　(818) 549-9915
6615 San Fernando Rd, Glendale, CA, 91201
PA system small/large concert, DJ system, soundboards, mics
www.astroavl.com
Coast Recording Audio Props　　　　　　(818) 755-4692
10715 Magnolia Blvd, N Hollywood, CA, 91601
Professional Audio Equipment, Radio Station, Recording Studio, DJ Setup.
1950s - Present. Audio equipment props, practical audio parts
props@coastrecording.com * www.coastrecordingprops.com
E.C. Prop Rentals　　　　　　(818) 764-2008
speakers; lg/sm, indoor/outdoor, wall/pole mounts

EFX- Event Special Effects   (626) 888-2239
125 Railroad Ave, Monrovia, CA, 91016
PA- Stage- Concert- Sound
info@efxla.com * www.efxla.com

The Hand Prop Room LP.   (323) 931-1534

History For Hire, Inc.   (818) 765-7767
microphones, mixers, etc., very complete

LCW Props   (818) 243-0707
DJ, Mixing Boards, Headphones, Stage Lighting, On Air, Recording Studio, Microphones, Reel To Reel

Modern Props   (323) 934-3000
contemporary audio equipment, futuristic audio equipment, home audio equipment & commercial audio equipment

RJR Props   (404) 349-7600
Audio mixers, microphones, and more audio props for rent.

Sony Pictures Studios-Prop House (Off Lot)   (310) 244-5999
radios, mics, microphone, mic stand, speakers, tape recorder player, walkie talkie, walkman, turntables

Warner Bros. Studios Production Sound & Video   (818) 954-2511
4000 Warner Blvd Bldg 43, Burbank, CA, 91522
A/V Equipment Rental, Design, Presentations, Install & Support; Visual Display Creation; Communication.
wbsfproductionsound@warnerbros.com * www.wbsoundandvideo.com

Woody's Electrical Props   (818) 503-1940
period to futuristic consoles, panels & electrical equipment

Audio/Visual Film Equipment

See Also: Audio Equipment* Motion Picture Projectors* Themed Environment Construction* Video Camera Equipment & Services

Astro Audio Video Lighting, Inc.   (818) 549-9915
6615 San Fernando Rd, Glendale, CA, 91201
We can design & install integrated, intelligent AVL systems
www.astroavl.com

Edwards Technologies, Inc.   (310) 536-7070
139 Maryland St, El Segundo, CA, 90245
designs multisensory media & technology systems, for themed environments
www.edwardstechnologies.com

Electrosonic, Inc   (818) 333-3600
3320 N. San Fernando Blvd, Burbank, CA, 91504
Design, mfg & install specialized systems; projection, audio, interactives, show control & event scheduling
www.electrosonic.com

Harkness Hall   (540) 370-1590
10 Harkness Blvd, Fredericksburg, VA, 22401
Design & mfg. custom front & rear projection screen systems, for indoor/outdoor themed environments
www.harkness-screens.com

LCW Props   (818) 243-0707
Plasma, LCD, Monitors, Stage Lighting, AV Server Racks, Media Centers, Consoles, Presentation, Projectors & Screens

Mad Systems, Inc.   (714) 259-9000
733 N Main St, Orange, CA, 92868
Specialize in innovative multimedia solutions, interactives, & exhibits, systems design & integration
www.madsystems.com

Old N Country Prop Shop, LLC   (818) 423-2599
Lots of vintage cameras and projectors of many types (8mm, slides, etc.), screens on stands, more.

RJR Props   (404) 349-7600
Video mixers, studio monitors and more audio/visual equipment for rent.

TechnoMedia Solutions   (407) 351-0909
4545 36th St, Orlando, FL, 32811
media-based concept, production & development, NY office: (212) 452-1100
www.gotechnomedia.com

Thorburn Associates, Inc.   (818) 569-0234
1317 N San Fernando Blvd #212, Burbank, CA, 91504
Acoustics, audio visual, themed entertainment, presentation lighting, & technology systems design
www.ta-inc.com

Automata

See: Robots

Automobiles

See: Police Car, Police Motorcycle* RV Vehicles & Travel Trailers, Equip & Parts* Vehicle Preparation Services* Vehicles/Picture Vehicles

Automotive/Garage Equip. & Parts

See Also: Chain Hoists* Emissions Analyzers* Gas Pumps/Islands, Gas Station* License Plates* Ramps, Automobile* RV Vehicles & Travel Trailers, Equip & Parts* Tires* Tools

AIR Designs   (818) 768-6639
Nascar, gas station, junk & wrecking yard, chop shop, diagnostic, mechanic, home, racing, period & modern.

Alley Cats Studio Rentals   (818) 982-9178
gas station/garage/mechanic dressing, motorcycle parts

E.C. Prop Rentals   (818) 764-2008
commercial & residential, diagnostic equip., tool boxes/chests

E.C. PROP RENTALS
11846 SHERMAN WAY NORTH HOLLYWOOD CA 91605
818-764-2008

The Hand Prop Room LP.   (323) 931-1534

History For Hire, Inc.   (818) 765-7767
period

LCW Props   (818) 243-0707
Tools, Shelving, Hoses, Presses, Cleared Paint Cans

Old N Country Prop Shop, LLC   (818) 423-2599
Lots of vintage garage tools to stage that garage.

Sony Pictures Studios-Prop House (Off Lot)   (310) 244-5999
car battery charger, car alarm control, automotive parts, bike parts, buckets, pales, car club, air compressors, more

Autopsy Equipment

See: Morgue

Awards

See: Calligraphy* Certificates* Engraving* Prop Houses* Trophies/Trophy Cases

Awnings

See Also: Canopies, Tents, Gazebos, Cabanas* Canvas* Sewing
Services, Industrial* Window Treatments

American Awning (323) 222-7500
1901 N San Fernando Rd, Los Angeles, CA 90065
info@americanawningabc.com * www.americanawning1.com

Canvas Specialty (323) 722-1156
PO Box 22268, Los Angeles, CA, 90022-0268
www.can-spec.com

LCW Props (818) 243-0707
store awnings

Sarris Interiors & Marine (562) 531-8612
8225 Alondra Blvd, Paramount, CA, 90723
mfg. & fabrication, will ship anywhere, for semi trailers, dressing room trailers,
household
www.sarrisinteriors.com

Warner Bros. Drapery, Upholstery & Flooring (818) 954-1831
4000 Warner Blvd Bldg 30, Burbank, CA, 91522
Soft pipe awnings with & without wings: custom manufacturing; many colors &
fabrics
wbsfdrapery@warnerbros.com * www.wbdrapery.com

Baby Doubles, Realistic Babies

See: Puppets, Marionettes, Automata, Animatronics

Baby Items

See: Children's & Baby Clothing* Children/Baby Accessories &
Bedroom

Back Packs

See: Camping Equipment* Prop Houses* Sporting Goods & Services

Backdrops

See: Backings* Scenery/Set Construction

Backings

See Also: Events, Backings & Scenery* Printing, Graphics, Digital &
Large Format* Scenery/Set Rentals

Apollo Design Technology (260) 497-9191
4130 Fourier Dr, Ft Wayne, IN, 46818
Gobos, largest mfg. of custom glass & steel patterns; plus accessories,
adhesives, filters & motion effects
www.apollodesign.net

Fauve Associates (818) 481-2019
6553 Randi Ave, Woodland Hills, CA, 91303
No image too complex, any size and style of backings. Known for our
large-format pictorial work
info@fauveassociates.com * fauveassociates.com

Grosh Scenic Rentals, Inc. (323) 662-1134
4114 Sunset Blvd, Hollywood, CA, 90029
theater, dance, themed event
www.grosh.com

iWeiss Theatrical Solutions (888) 325-7192
815 Fairview Ave #10, Fairview, NJ 07022
digitally printed day & night drops
info@iweiss.com * www.iweiss.com

J. C. Backings (310) 841-0123
5905 Smiley Dr, Culver City CA, 90232
Painted backings, photo backings and digital print backings
info@jcbackings.com * http://www.jcbackings.com

Modern Props (323) 934-3000
carnival backings, amusement drops, many colored block-glass divider walls,
wood dividers

Schmidli Backdrops LA (323) 938-2098
5830 W Adams Blvd, Culver City, CA, 90232
Providing hand painted Textured and Scenic backdrops to the commercial, film,
and fashion industry for over 20 years.
backdrops@schmidli.com * www.schmidli.com

SCHMIDLI BACKDROPS
LOS ANGELES. NEW YORK. LONDON. HAMBURG. SHANGHAI. SYDNEY

RANKIN.

DAVID ROEMER.

CARLOS SERRAO.

EASTON SCHIRRA.

Schmidli Backdrops NY (800) 724-0171
601 West 26th St, 10th floor, New York, NY, 10001
High end texture & scenic backdrops for Film/TV & photography. Full
installation service & custom paintings.
backdrops@schmidli.com * www.schmidli.com

Studio Dynamics (800) 595-4273
7245 Alondra Blvd, Paramount CA, 90723
canvas & muslin, textures, chromakey, scenic, custom motorized lifts
customerservice@studiodynamics.com * www.studiodynamics.com

UV/FX Scenic Productions (310) 821-2657
171 Pier Ave Suite 355, Santa Monica, CA, 90405
leader in day to night, dual image, completely invisible, & 3D scenic effects &
scenery
www.uvfx.com

Warner Bros. Studios Scenic Art & Sign Shop (818) 954-1815
4000 Warner Blvd Bldg 44, Burbank, CA, 91522
hand-painted art to grand-format digital printing for backings, billboards, murals
and portraits
wbsigns@warnerbros.com * www.wbsignandscenic.com

Badges, Patches & Buttons

See Also: Engraving* Memorabilia & Novelties* Name Plates*
Promotional Items & Materials

G-Man Emblem (727) 862-7419
11832 Aranda Ct, Hudson, FL 34667
Embroidered patches, lapel pins, challenge coins, direct garment embroidery &
silk screening for law enforcement, milita
www.gmanemblem.com

The Hand Prop Room LP. (323) 931-1534
U.S., custom, foreign, federal, police, fire, name pins

History For Hire, Inc. (818) 765-7767
Police, paramedic, security guard, props

Hollywood Studio Gallery (323) 462-1116
framed patches only

RHS Enterprises (714) 840-4388
PO Box 5779, Garden Grove, CA, 92846-0779
Police & Federal law enforcement badges, patches, credentials, history,
consulting, books. We answer Federal questions
rhsenterprises@earthlink.net * www.raymondsherrard.com

Sony Pictures Studios-Prop House (Off Lot) (310) 244-5999
Federal Badges, Fire Department Badges, Security Badges, Sheriff Badges,
Marshall Badges, dog tags, employee IDs and more

Sony Pictures Studios-Wardrobe (310) 244-5995
alterations, call (310) 244-7260

Sword & Stone (818) 562-6548
Patches, badges and buttons along with other costume accessories.

Universal Studios Property & Hardware Dept (818) 777-2784
Various badges, patches and buttons.

Western Costume Co. (818) 760-0900

Bag Lady Carts

E.C. Prop Rentals	**(818) 764-2008**
shopping carts only	
The Hand Prop Room LP.	**(323) 931-1534**
fully outfitted	
LCW Props	**(818) 243-0707**
Carts, Recyclables, Dressed, Large Quantity	
Universal Studios Property & Hardware Dept	**(818) 777-2784**
Shopping carts, commercial shopping carts, and grocery shopping carts.	

Bags & Sacks

See: Boxes* Expendables* Packing/Packaging Supplies, Services* Promotional Items & Materials* Shopping Bags (Silent)

Bakery

See Also: Delicatessen Equipment* Display Cases, Racks & Fixtures (Store)* Food, Artificial Food

AIR Designs	**(818) 768-6639**
Glass cases, racks, ovens, pie cases, trays, counters, signage, display items, faux food & more.	
The Hand Prop Room LP.	**(323) 931-1534**
fake cakes, breads, rolls, rolling pins	
LCW Props	**(818) 243-0707**
Racks, Misc. Equipment, Display Cabinets	
Lennie Marvin Enterprises, Inc. (Prop Heaven)	**(818) 841-5882**
rolling racks, glass cases, fake cakes/bread, pastry	
Machinery & Equipment Co., Inc.	**(909) 599-3916**
115 N Cataract Ave, San Dimas, CA, 91773	
Used commercial bakery equipment including mixers, screens, fillers, conveyors stainless steel racks, sinks and more.	
sherri@machineryandequipment.com * www.machineryandequipment.com	
Modern Props	**(323) 934-3000**
Bakery dressing including stainless steel racks, display shelves and display cases,	

Balance Beam

See: Gymnasium & Gymnastic Equipment

Ball Park Concessions

See: Carnival Dressing/Supplies

Ballet Barres & Dance Mirrors

See Also: Dance Floors

C. P. Two	**(323) 466-8201**
Ballet barres, metal ballet bars, wooden ballet barres, adjustable ballet bars, wall mounted ballet bars, and more.	
Dance Equipment International	**(800) 626-9258**
2103 Lincoln Ave, Ste C, San Jose, CA, 95125	
glassless mirrors, adjustable portable/wallmount barres	
www.danceequipment.com	
E.C. Prop Rentals	**(818) 764-2008**
free standing dance castered mirrors	
Warner Bros. Studios Property Department	**(818) 954-2181**
Castered dance mirrors, can have ballet barres attached.	

Balloon (Hot Air) Gondolas

See Also: Aircraft, Charters & Aerial Services

History For Hire, Inc.	**(818) 765-7767**
wicker	

Balloons & Balloon Sculptures

See Also: Inflatables, Custom

Aah-Inspiring Balloons	**(562) 494-7605**

Call for an Appointment.
After 14 years in the TV and Film Industry, Aah-Inspiring Balloon Decor has been seen in over 200 TV shows and Films.
aahinspiring1@aol.com * www.aahinspiringballoons.com

Amazing Balloons By Gee	**(310) 676-1524**

4516 W Broadway Ave, Hawthorne, CA, 90250
Since 1994, Arches, bouquets, columns, drops and theme decor for the "right look".
claudiagee@socal.rr.com * www.amazingballoonsbygee.com

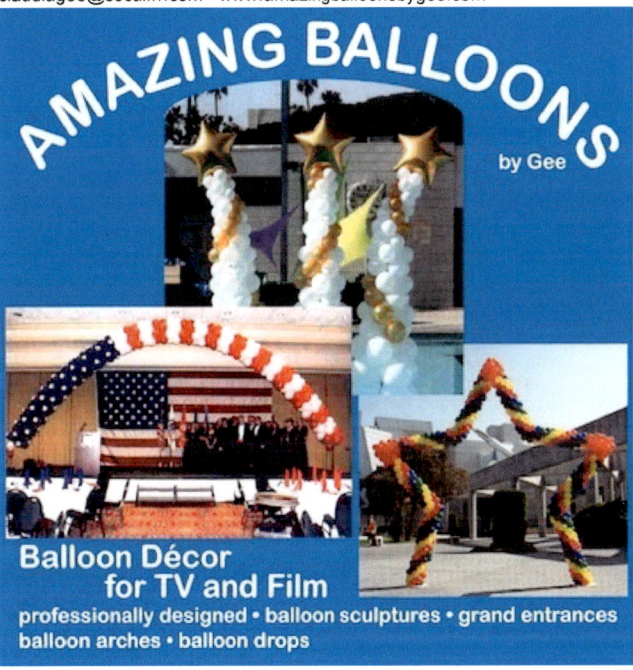

LISTINGS FOR THIS CATEGORY CONTINUE ON THE FOLLOWING PAGE

Balloon Haven   (888) 591-8449
Call for appointment.
26 year balloon pros, diverse, timely & professional. Rush service, on location.
Helium rentals.
www.balloonhaven.com

Bill Ferrell Co.   (818) 767-1900
10556 Keswick St, Sun Valley, CA, 91352
Balloon drops for conventions and special events.
www.billferrell.com
L. A. Party Works   (888) 527-2789
9712 Alpaca St, S El Monte, CA, 91733
in Vancouver tel. 604-589-4101
partyworks@aol.com * www.partyworksinteractive.com

Bamboo

See: Greens* Tikis & Tropical Dressing

Bank Dressing

See Also: Metal Detectors* Money (Prop)* Security Walk-Through &
Baggage Alarms* Surveillance Equipment
Advanced Liquidators Office Furniture   (818) 763-3470
Bank dressing including bank teller stations, bank deposit stations, and
lighting.
AIR Designs   (818) 768-6639
Exterior ATM Machines, Signage, Stanchions
Alley Cats Studio Rentals   (818) 982-9178
ATM machines
ATM Cash Connect/Financial Product, Inc.   (818) 848-1025
624 S San Fernando Blvd, Burbank, CA, 91502
ATMs: all models, full function, custom paint/enclosures/screens manipulate
cash dispensing, other bank machines
www.financialproductinc.com

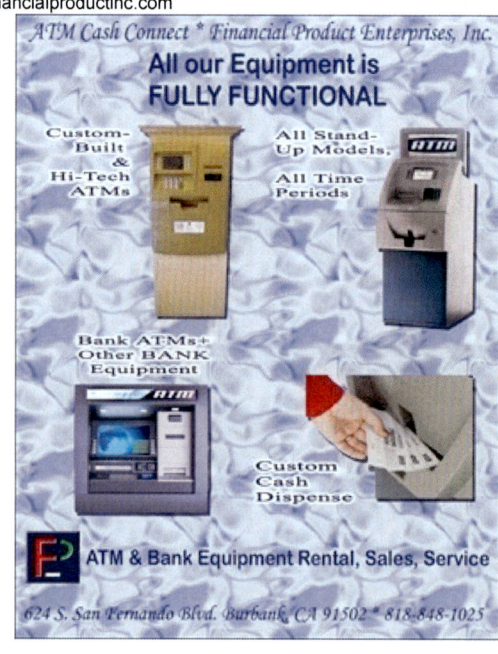

C. P. Two   (323) 466-8201
Bank teller counters, bank dressing, bank counters, bank name plates,
mortgage rate chart, floor displays and more.
History For Hire, Inc.   (818) 765-7767
safe deposit boxes, bank tables, moneybags etc.
Hollywood Studio Gallery   (323) 462-1116
signage only

LCW Props (818) 243-0707
ATM's, Bank Printer, Card Sliders, Money Counters, Check Encoders, Fake Money / Coins

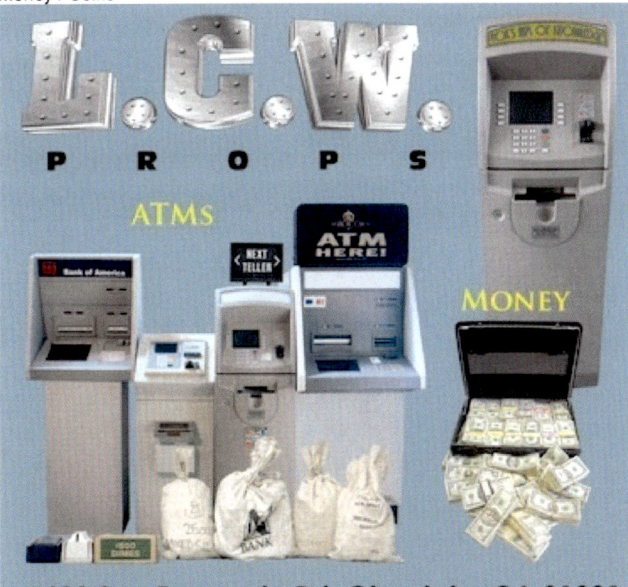

6439 San Fernando Rd. Glendale, CA 91201
Phone: 818-243-0707 - www.lcwprops.com

Modern Props (323) 934-3000
Bank dressing including ATMs, bank counters, bank stanchions, bank kiosks
RJR Props (404) 349-7600
Bank dressing/bank props including teller terminals, money counters, cash drawers, check scanners and more for rent.
Universal Studios Property & Hardware Dept (818) 777-2784
Bank dressing from banker's lamps, banker signs, bundled money and more.

Banners

See: Flags/Banners* Sign Painters* Signs

Banquets/Booths (Seating)

AIR Designs (818) 768-6639
Restaurant, Diner, Bar, Cafeteria, Fast Food, Booths & Modular Seating
C. P. Two (323) 466-8201
Various restaurant booths, restaurant settees, cafe tables, porcelain coffee cups, table tops, formica tables & more.
FormDecor, Inc. (310) 558-2582
America's largest event rental supplier of 20th Century furniture and accessories for Modern and Mid-Century styles.
Lux Lounge EFR (888) 247-4411
106 1/2 Judge John Aiso St #318, Los Angeles, CA, 90012
Banquet Seating: Curved Banquettes, High Back Banquette, Straight Banquette
info@luxloungeefr.com * www.luxloungeefr.com
RC Vintage, Inc. (818) 765-7107
Diner restaurant dressing; restaurant booths, restaurant tables, restaurant chairs, diner counters, etc
Universal Studios Property & Hardware Dept (818) 777-2784
Banquettes and restaurant booths.

Bar Stools

See: Bars, Nightclubs, Barware & Dressing* Chairs* Stools

Barbecues

Alley Cats Studio Rentals (818) 982-9178
large & small, gas grills vintage to contemporary, grill smokers
C. P. Two (323) 466-8201
Charcoal barbecues, gas barbecues, personal barbecues, barrel barbecues, barbecue accessories, portable barbecues
The Hand Prop Room LP. (323) 931-1534
Weber, large, charcoal, gas, stainless steel, open pit, barbecue utensils
History For Hire, Inc. (818) 765-7767
Weber, 55-gallon drum style
RC Vintage, Inc. (818) 765-7107
BBQ's, barbecue carts, bbq pig sign
Sony Pictures Studios-Prop House (Off Lot) (310) 244-5999
BBQs, barbeques, barbeque tools, barbecue tools
Universal Studios Property & Hardware Dept (818) 777-2784
Barbecue tools, hibachi barbecues and barbecues including a 55-gallon one.

Barbells

See: Exercise & Fitness Equipment* Weightlifting Equipment

Barber Shop

See Also: Beauty Salon* Make-up & Hair, Supplies & Services* Salon & Spa Equipment* Shaving, Old Fashion, Non-Electric
The Hand Prop Room LP. (323) 931-1534
barber shop dressing
History For Hire, Inc. (818) 765-7767
chairs, signs, products, accessories
Lennie Marvin Enterprises, Inc. (Prop Heaven) (818) 841-5882
chairs,poles,coat racks,towels,steamers,signage,period-modern
RC Vintage, Inc. (818) 765-7107
40s-60s, poles-chairs, general supplies/products; full barber shop, barber shop waiting room, barber set, chairs & sofas
Sony Pictures Studios-Prop House (Off Lot) (310) 244-5999
barber cloth, salon brush, salon comb, salon clippers, salon comb jar, salon equipment holder, finer soaker, manicure set
Universal Studios Property & Hardware Dept (818) 777-2784
Barber shop dressing; barber shop chairs, barber shop aprons, barber shop accessories, barber shop poles & more.

Barns

See: Western Americana

Barrels & Drums, Wood/Metal/Plastic

See Also: Crates/ Vaults* Oil Cans & Drums* Wine Kegs
AIR Designs (818) 768-6639
5-55 Gallon Drums, Wine Barrels & Racks, Plastic Drums
Alley Cats Studio Rentals (818) 982-9178
many sizes and styles & drums, also cardboard
C. P. Two (323) 466-8201
Hollywood's largest selection! All shapes, all sizes, all types.
E.C. Prop Rentals (818) 764-2008
multiples of sizes & styles

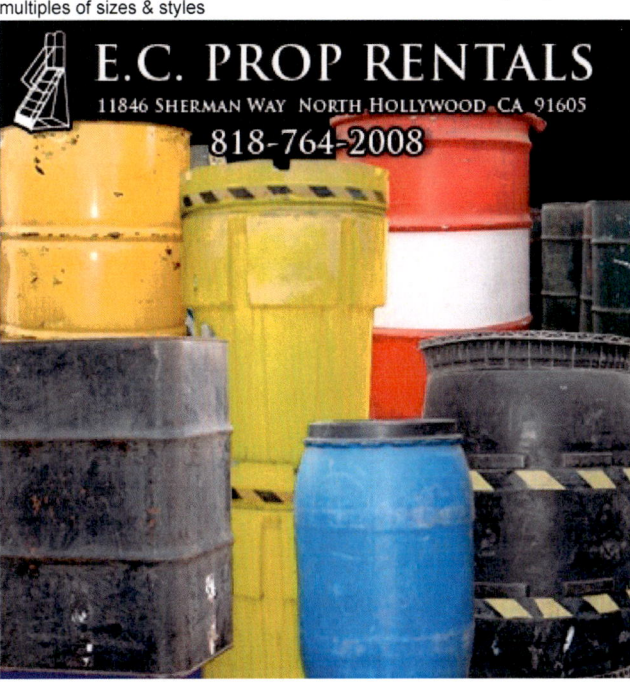

E. C. PROP RENTALS
11846 SHERMAN WAY NORTH HOLLYWOOD CA 91605
818-764-2008

Evans Family Barrels (818) 523-8174
7918 Fairchild Ave, Canoga Park, CA, 91306
59 gal oak wine barrels and 53 gal oak whiskey barrels, whole and half sizes, and products made from barrels
evansbarrels@gmail.com * www.EvansFamilyBarrels.com
The Hand Prop Room LP. (323) 931-1534
wood, metal
History For Hire, Inc. (818) 765-7767
LCW Props (818) 243-0707
Wood, Metal, Plastic, Colored. Large Quantities
Sony Pictures Studios-Prop House (Off Lot) (310) 244-5999
Universal Studios Property & Hardware Dept (818) 777-2784
All kinds of barrels; whiskey barrels, wine barrels, wooden barrels, metal barrels, cask barrels and more.

Barricades

See Also: Crowd Control: Barricades, Turnstiles Etc.* Fences*
Stanchions & Rope* Traffic/Road Signs, Lights, Safety Items

AIR Designs (818) 768-6639
Police barricades, Construction, Cones, Bollards, Parking Blocks, Cafe Railing,
Pedestrian

Alley Cats Studio Rentals (818) 982-9178
wood, plastic w/flashing lights, guard gate arm, short metal stand up barricade
units, Stand up chain link fences.

E.C. Prop Rentals (818) 764-2008
K-rails, freeway guardrails, construction, crowd control, police, traffic, military
checkpoint

E.C. PROP RENTALS
11846 SHERMAN WAY NORTH HOLLYWOOD CA 91605
818-764-2008

The Hand Prop Room LP. (323) 931-1534
police, parade, road cones, construction, working signs

History For Hire, Inc. (818) 765-7767
old style wood

LCW Props (818) 243-0707
Police, Crowd Control, Concert

Statewide Traffic Safety & Sign (714) 468-1919
13261 Garden Grove Blvd, Garden Grove, CA, 92840
signage, barricades, equipment, traffic control personnel many credits
www.statewidesafety.com

Sterndahl Enterprises, Inc. (818) 834-8199
11861 Branford St, Sun Valley, CA, 91352
traffic control equipment, signage, barricades, striping, trucks & bobcats
www.sterndahl.com

STERNDAHL ENTERPRISES, INC.

Traffic Control Equipment / K-rail / Signals
(Trucks/Cones / Arrow boards / Signs & more)
Certified Traffic Control Tech.
Striping / Marking & Removals / Bobcats
(Thermoplastic / Paint / Temporary Tape)

Universal Studios Property & Hardware Dept (818) 777-2784
many barricades; traffic barricades, road barricades, street barricades, &
orange cones of various styles and sizes.

ZG04 DECOR (818) 853-8040

Bars, Nightclubs, Barware & Dressing

See Also: Banquets/Booths (Seating)* Beer Equipment, Taps & Coolers* Chairs* Dance Floors* Darts & Dartboards* Irish, All Things Irish* Liquor Bottles* Pool/Billiard Tables & Accessories* Pub Signs* Sports Bar Dressing* Tables

AIR Designs (818) 768-6639
Neon, Bar Smalls, Bottles, Taps, Bars (Front & Back), Tables, Chairs, Stools, Glassware, Complete Set Ups

Astro Audio Video Lighting, Inc. (818) 549-9915
6615 San Fernando Rd, Glendale, CA, 91201
Nightclub lighting, nightclub sound systems, and nightclub video for rent or purchase.
www.astroavl.com

C. P. Two (323) 466-8201
Bar dressing, portable bars, commercial bars, modular bar setup, bar stools, bar chairs, saloon to contemporary

The Hand Prop Room LP. (323) 931-1534
signs, bottles, glasses, labels

History For Hire, Inc. (818) 765-7767
bottles, glasses, pitchers, cash registers

LCW Props (818) 243-0707
Seating, Bars, Glassware, Taps, Neons, Sporting Memorabilia, Display Cases

Lennie Marvin Enterprises, Inc. (Prop Heaven) (818) 841-5882
Full bar, nightclub dressing. Barware, liquor bottles, bar signs and more.

LM Treasures (626) 252-7354
Car inspired Sofas, Clocks, shelves, & Bars all allow for more uniqueness & personality in any type of restaurant.

Lux Lounge EFR (888) 247-4411
106 1/2 Judge John Aiso St #318, Los Angeles, CA, 90012
Event Bar Rentals: Tufted Bars, Illuminated Bars, Circle Bar
info@luxloungeefr.com * www.luxloungeefr.com

Modern Props (323) 934-3000
contemporary bar dressing, futuristic bar dressing, bar glassware, bar lighting, bar seating

Old N Country Prop Shop, LLC (818) 423-2599
A variety of stools, glasses, trays, mugs, bars, and more.

RC Vintage, Inc. (818) 765-7107
40s, 50s & 60s large selection, high tables Stools and Many Bar Counter tops....Many Bar Lamps

Sony Pictures Studios-Prop House (Off Lot) (310) 244-5999
bar organizer, beer taps, bottle openers, bottle trays, liquor caddy, bar tables, equipment, glassware, dishes and more

Universal Studios Property & Hardware Dept (818) 777-2784
Bar dressing including; bar stools, bar lighting, bar glasses, and more.

ZG04 DECOR (818) 853-8040

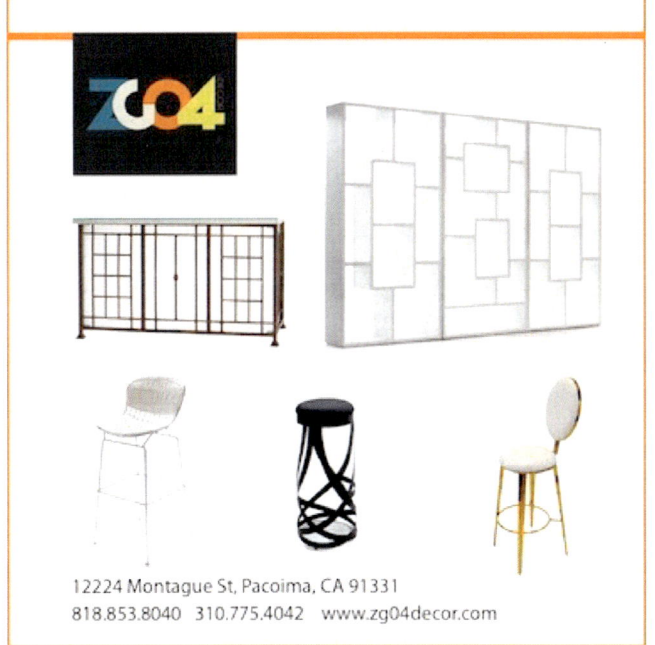

12224 Montague St, Pacoima, CA 91331
818.853.8040   310.775.4042   www.zg04decor.com

Baseball Equipment

See: Baseball Pitching Machine* Scoreboards & Scoring Systems* Sporting Goods & Services* Sports/Athletic Field Lining/Graphics

Baseball Pitching Machine

The Hand Prop Room LP. (323) 931-1534
baseballs, pitching machine, vintage pitching machine, softballs

L. A. Party Works (888) 527-2789
9712 Alpaca St, S El Monte, CA, 91733
Variety of different baseball pitching machines available, direct source.
partyworks@aol.com * www.partyworksinteractive.com

1983

40 YEARS OF DEBBIES BOOK

Debbies Book went high tech. For the first time, the book layout was done on a computer and then sent to a printer. Personal computers were just beginning. Little did we all realize how computers and the internet would be a force to come in the near future. Cell phones made their first appearance in the States, remember those big, clunky first models? We were treated to Wendy's ads of **"Where's the Beef?"** and there were protests over the new Coca-Cola formula. We said good-bye to **"Mash"** and hello to **"Cheers"** and **"Hill St. Blues"**. Canada got its independence from the U.K., and the first woman walked in space. **"Flashdance"** and **"Star Wars: Episode 5 Return of the Jedi"** hit the big screen and **"Gandhi"** took Oscar's Best Picture.

Prop Houses were beginning to move north of Hollywood. Earl Hays Press relocated and Independent Studio Services, Lennie Marvin, Woody's Electronic Props on San Fernando Rd. marked the beginning of the move to Sun Valley. Back in Hollywood, the movement of independent prop houses gobbling up smaller ones began. Omega Props was the first, it purchased Modern Furniture Rentals that was up on Hollywood Blvd. and then continued acquiring: First St. Furniture, Cinema Props, the list goes on... 25 years ago props were a lot more simple. The typical categories listed in the book were 'License Plates', 'Record Players', 'Phonographs' and 'Turntables' (both for records and Scenery Construction). Xeroxing of scripts was a pain, one has to remember that we didn't have Kinkos, you had to go to small companies who had Xerox services. (Ah, and now years later... that name is gone, changed to FedEx.)

Basketball Court & Backboards

See Also: Carpet & Flooring* Sporting Goods & Services
Alley Cats Studio Rentals (818) 982-9178
outdoor rim, chain & cloth net, metal backboard, fixed park basketbal rims and stand up home basketball hoops
The Hand Prop Room LP. (323) 931-1534
wall-mounted, portable
L. A. Party Works (888) 527-2789
9712 Alpaca St, S El Monte, CA, 91733
Portable basketball courts/basketball flooring and basketball baskets. Panel system flooring
partyworks@aol.com * www.partyworksinteractive.com

888-527-2789

FULL & HALF COURT FLOORING / BRANDING / PRO GOALS / SHOT CLOCKS / BALL RACKS

PARTYWORKS
I N T E R A C T I V E

Universal Studios Property & Hardware Dept (818) 777-2784
Basketball backboards; garage mounted basketball backboards, portable basketball backboards and freestanding basketball backboards

Baskets

The Hand Prop Room LP. (323) 931-1534
History For Hire, Inc. (818) 765-7767
many types
Old N Country Prop Shop, LLC (818) 423-2599
Picnic baskets, wicker baskets, Longaberger baskets, laundry baskets and more, in a variety of sizes, shapes and colors.
Omega/Cinema Props (323) 466-8201
Baskets: American Indian baskets, fishing baskets and much more.
Prop Services West (818) 503-2790
Sony Pictures Studios-Prop House (Off Lot) (310) 244-5999
large selection
Universal Studios Property & Hardware Dept (818) 777-2784
All kinds of baskets; woven baskets, decorative baskets, picnic baskets, bread baskets, laundry baskets and more.

Bath Tubs

See: Bathroom Fixtures* Plumbing Fixtures, Heating/Cooling Appliances* Prop Houses

Bathing Suits, Swim & Beach Wear

The Costume House (818) 508-9933
20s to 60s, M/W/children
Sony Pictures Studios-Wardrobe (310) 244-5995
alterations, call (310) 244-7260
TYR Sport, Inc. (714) 897-0799
15391 Springdale St, Huntington Beach, CA, 92649
product placement: M/W/ children's swimwear, multi-sport / triathlon apparel, contact PR Dept.
www.tyr.com
Universal Studios Costume Dept (818) 777-2722
Rental, mfg., & alterations
Warner Bros. Studios Costume Dept (818) 954-1297
One-Piece, Two-Piece, Bikini, Mallet, Tankini, Halter, Bandeau, Caftans, Cover-Ups, Shorts, Hats

Bathroom Decorations

History For Hire, Inc. (818) 765-7767
everything but the plumbing
Modern Props (323) 934-3000
contemporary bathroom decorations, futuristic bathroom decorations, hardware & accessories, bathroom sinks, bathtubs
NEST Studio Rentals, Inc. (818) 942-0339
small furnishings, decorative accessories, linen
Ob-jects (818) 351-4200
furniture
Prop Services West (818) 503-2790
Universal Studios Property & Hardware Dept (818) 777-2784
Bathroom dressing, bathroom fixtures, bathroom toiletries, bathroom vanity, bathroom scales and more.

Bathroom Fixtures

See Also: Plumbing Fixtures, Heating/Cooling Appliances* Prop Houses* Sinks
E.C. Prop Rentals (818) 764-2008
Hand dryers, soap & towel dispensers, wash fountains, stainless steel mirrors, signage
LCW Props (818) 243-0707
Stalls, Sinks, Toilets, Lighting
RC Vintage, Inc. (818) 765-7107
40s, 50s & 60s, sconces, outlet lights, sink units and more
Sony Pictures Studios-Fixtures (310) 244-5996
5933 W Slauson Ave, Culver City, CA, 90230
period to present day, fixtures, hardware, cloth towel dispenser, condom dispenser, commercial hand dryer
www.sonypicturesstudios.com
Studio Plumbing Rentals (323) 829-9339
7373 Atoll Ave, N Hollywood, CA, 91605
studioplumbingrentals@gmail.com * www.studioair.com

Batteries & Battery Chargers

See: Automotive/Garage Equip. & Parts* Electrical/Electronic Supplies & Services* Expendables

Beach Props

See Also: Sporting Goods & Services* Surfboard, Wakeboard* Volleyball Setup
E.C. Prop Rentals (818) 764-2008
set of volleyball poles, signage, trash cans, bike racks
The Hand Prop Room LP. (323) 931-1534
beach, nautical props, cruiser bikes, kayaks
History For Hire, Inc. (818) 765-7767
umbrellas, cabanas, folding chairs etc.
LCW Props (818) 243-0707
Chairs, Umbrellas, Surf Boards, BBQ's, Kayaks, Towables
Lennie Marvin Enterprises, Inc. (Prop Heaven) (818) 841-5882
Lifeguard chairs, lifeguard shacks, beach signs, beach umbrellas, beach chairs
Sony Pictures Studios-Prop House (Off Lot) (310) 244-5999
Universal Studios Property & Hardware Dept (818) 777-2784
Beach props, beach chairs, beach umbrellas, beach towels, beach lounge chairs, Polynesian torches and more.

Beach Theme Events

See: Events, Backings & Scenery* Events, Decorations, Supplies & Services* Events, Design/Planning/Production* Events, Entertainment

Beaded Curtains

See: Events, Backings & Scenery* Theatrical Draperies, Hardware & Rigging

Beads & Beading

See: Costume/Wardrobe/Sewing Supplies* Embroidery, Screen Printing, Etc.* Jewelry, Costume* Jewelry, Fine/Reproduction

Bean Bag Chairs

See: Bedroom Furniture & Decorations* Futons & Bean Bag Chairs

Beatles Musical Instruments

See: Musical Instruments

Beauty & Grooming Supplies

See: Make-up & Hair, Supplies & Services* Shaving, Old Fashion, Non-Electric

Beauty Salon

See Also: Barber Shop* Make-up & Hair, Supplies & Services* Salon & Spa Equipment

Galaxy Enterprises, Inc.   **(323) 728-3980**
5411 Sheila St, Los Angeles, CA, 90040
Mfg. of complete line of beauty & barber salon equipment. stylish, modern, wide variety, antique items too!
sales@galaxymfg.com * www.galaxymfg.com

History For Hire, Inc.   **(818) 765-7767**
beauty parlor items, hair dryers, etc. period products too.

RC Vintage, Inc.   **(818) 765-7107**
period hair dryers and chairs, 40s-60s supplies/products, more

Sony Pictures Studios-Prop House (Off Lot)   **(310) 244-5999**
furniture, dressing, supplies

Universal Studios Property & Hardware Dept   **(818) 777-2784**
Beauty shop chairs, hair cutting accessories, blow driers, curling irons, cosmetics, and more.

Bedding

See: Linens, Household

Bedroom Furniture & Decorations

See Also: Children/Baby Accessories & Bedroom* Prop Houses

Blueprint Furniture   **(310) 657-4315**
8600 Pico Blvd. Los Angeles, CA, 90035
Modern furniture lighting accessories early classic bauhaus mid-century contemporary design. Good studio rental history.
www.blueprintfurniture.com

Bridge Furniture & Props Los Angeles   **(818) 433-7100**
We carry modern & traditional furniture, lighting, accessories, bedroom art, & rugs. Items are online for easy shopping.

Castle Antiques & Design   **(818) 765-5000**
11924 Vose St, N Hollywood, CA, 91605
We have beds, bed frames, head boards, bookcases, mirrors, side tables, end tables, chests, dressers, vanities and more!
info@castleantiques.net * www.castleprophouse.com

LCW Props   **(818) 243-0707**
Armoires, Head Boards, Dressers, Tables, Chairs, Lighting

Little Bohemia Rentals   **(818) 853-7506**
11940 Sherman Rd, N Hollywood, CA, 91605
headboards, dressers, nightstands, vanities, benches, shelving
sales@wearelittlebohemia.com * www.wearelittlebohemia.com

Lori Wall Beds   **Not Listed**
Web Based Business
DIY kits for Murphy Beds/Wall Beds
www.loriwallbeds.com

Martin Iron Design   **(818) 760-3636**
10750 Cumpston St, N Hollywood, CA, 91601
All wrought iron beds are made to order in Queen, California King and Eastern King sizes. Custom finishes are available.
martinirondesign@yahoo.com * www.martinirondesign.com

Modern Props   **(323) 934-3000**
contemporary bedroom, futuristic bedroom furniture, bedroom accessories & beds, end tables, many head boards

NEST Studio Rentals, Inc.   **(818) 942-0339**
contemporary, queen sets, juvenile

Ob-jects   **(818) 351-4200**
Biedermeier, vanity mirrors, chaises, daybeds, chest of drawers, bedroom cabinets

Old N Country Prop Shop, LLC   **(818) 423-2599**
Bedframes, bedroom dressers, end tables and more.

Omega/Cinema Props   **(323) 466-8201**
Bedroom dressers, bedroom mirrors, cheval mirrors, furniture & accessories, contemporary to period.

P. J.s Sleep Company Inc.   **(800) 628-8288**
4707 E 49th St, Vernon CA, 90058
mattresses, bedroom furniture, a unique bedroom store for less
www.pjssleep.com

Prop Services West   **(818) 503-2790**

A Royal Suite Home Furinishings   **(661) 259-7000**
26536 Carl Boyer Dr, Santa Clarita, CA, 91350
A Royal Suite, family-owned since 1978, Features AMERICAN-MADE Furniture, and the Finest Furniture at the Greatest Value
norb@ars-email.com * www.aroyalsuite.com

Sony Pictures Studios-Prop House (Off Lot)   **(310) 244-5999**
clothes brush, coat hangars, headrest, jewelry holder, shoe dryer, tie rack, bed warmers

Universal Studios Property & Hardware Dept   **(818) 777-2784**
Bedroom furniture; dressers, nightstands, wardrobe cabinets, chest of drawers, bedroom lamps & more.

ZG04 DECOR   **(818) 853-8040**
Beds, Dressers, Bed frames, Headboards, Highboys, Nightstands, Upholstered Headboards, Vanitys, Mattresses

Beds

See: Bedroom Furniture & Decorations* Children/Baby Accessories & Bedroom

Beer Equipment, Taps & Coolers

See Also: Bars, Nightclubs, Barware & Dressing

AIR Designs   **(818) 768-6639**
Beer Taps, Towers, Coolers, Kegs, CO2 Canisters, Glassware & More

C. P. Two   **(323) 466-8201**
Beer glasses, taps, coolers, pitchers, cleared beer taps, beer kegs, corked kegs, wooden kegs, metal beer kegs and more.

California Beverage   **(818) 997-3831**
PO Box 44366, Panorama City, CA, 91412-0366
beer - soda, practical - prop; I make it work for you, since 1971
bruhozer@yahoo.com * www.californiabev.com

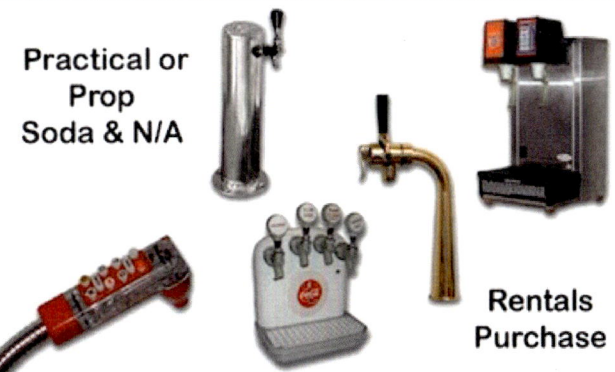

The Hand Prop Room LP.   **(323) 931-1534**
kegs, coolers, beer taps, beer much, beer signs, beer neon signs

History For Hire, Inc.   **(818) 765-7767**
huge supply of vintage cans

LCW Props   **(818) 243-0707**
Kegs, Taps, Vendor Signs, Jockey Boxes

Machinery & Equipment Co., Inc.   **(909) 599-3916**
115 N Cataract Ave, San Dimas, CA, 91773
Used commercial brewery equipment including kettles, tanks, filters, pumps, canning & bottling equipment and more.
sherri@machineryandequipment.com * www.machineryandequipment.com

RC Vintage, Inc.   **(818) 765-7107**
period, 40s, 50s & 60s European Vintage Bar Taps, and American Stainless Modern

Sony Pictures Studios-Prop House (Off Lot)   **(310) 244-5999**
taps & coolers, beer kegs, beer bottles, liquor bottles

Universal Studios Property & Hardware Dept   **(818) 777-2784**
Beer coolers, beer taps, beer glassware

Bees & Beekeeping

See: Animals (Live), Services, Trainers & Wranglers

Bells

See: Chimes & Bells

Belt Massagers

See: Exercise & Fitness Equipment

Belts

See: Military Surplus/Combat Clothes, Field Gear* Uniforms, Military* Uniforms, Trades/Professional/Sports* Wardrobe, Accessories

Benches

See Also: Audience Seating* Courtroom Furniture & Dressing* Theater Seating

AIR Designs (818) 768-6639
Bus Benches, Park Benches, Airport Seating, Interior & Exterior Restaurant & Bar

Alley Cats Studio Rentals (818) 982-9178
wood, metal work benches, fiberglass park tables w/benches, bleachers

C. P. Two (323) 466-8201
Various benches of various styles

E.C. Prop Rentals (818) 764-2008
Exterior park/bus stop/fiberglass/aluminum/aluminum w/back, and interior locker room/jail with handcuff bars

E.C. PROP RENTALS
11846 SHERMAN WAY NORTH HOLLYWOOD CA 91605
818-764-2008

FormDecor, Inc. (310) 558-2582
America's largest event rental supplier of 20th Century furniture and accessories for Modern and Mid-Century styles.

The Hand Prop Room LP. (323) 931-1534
park benches, bus stop benches, playground benches, antique benches, vintage benches, wooden benches, sports, signage

History For Hire, Inc. (818) 765-7767
sports, bus, park

Jackson Shrub Supply, Inc. (818) 982-0100
park benches, bus benches, garden benches in lightweight reinforced foam/fiberglass

LCW Props (818) 243-0707
Locker Room, Court Room, Bus, Prison, Library, Park

Lennie Marvin Enterprises, Inc. (Prop Heaven) (818) 841-5882
all styles, shapes, sizes of bus, park,comp,metal,wood

Modern Props (323) 934-3000
outdoor benches, modern benches, metal benches, aluminum benches

Old N Country Prop Shop, LLC (818) 423-2599
Farm benches, handmade benches, cobbler benches, workman benches

Omega/Cinema Props (323) 466-8201
Various benches of various styles

Prop Services West (818) 503-2790

RC Vintage, Inc. (818) 765-7107
business, parks and court.

Sony Pictures Studios-Prop House (Off Lot) (310) 244-5999
general, park benches, bus benches; wood benches & metal benches

Universal Studios Property & Hardware Dept (818) 777-2784
Period to modern benches; courtroom benches, park benches, bus benches, church benches, workout benches and more.

Warner Bros. Studios Property Department (818) 954-2181
Park, picnic, church, weight, outdoor, bus, children's, wicker, rattan, rustic, piano/organ

Beverages

See: Beer Equipment, Taps & Coolers* Food, Artificial Food

Bibles

See: Books, Real/Hollow & Faux Books* Religious Articles

Bicycles & Bicycling Supplies

See Also: Prop Houses* Sporting Goods & Services

Alley Cats Studio Rentals (818) 982-9178
bicycles & racks

Beverly Hills Bike Shop (310) 275-2453
10546 W Pico Blvd, Los Angeles, CA, 90064
any contemporary bicycle need
www.bhbikeshop.com

The Bicycle Kitchen (323) 662-2776
4429 Fountain Ave, Los Angeles, CA, 90029
bicycle repairs, Sat-Sun 12-6, M 12-5, T-TH 6:30-9:30PM
www.bicyclekitchen.com

C. P. Two (323) 466-8201
Kids bikes, mountain bikes, street bikes, highwheeler bikes, tricycles, bike racks, and more.

E.C. Prop Rentals (818) 764-2008
Bike racks and distressed bicycle frames

The Hand Prop Room LP. (323) 931-1534
period-present, mountain, amazing restored collection

History For Hire, Inc. (818) 765-7767
contemp & period, men, women, children

I. Martin Imports (323) 653-6900
8330 Beverly Blvd, Los Angeles, CA, 90048
www.imartin.com

Lennie Marvin Enterprises, Inc. (Prop Heaven) (818) 841-5882
mens bikes, ladies bikes, childrens bikes, tandem bikes, from high wheeler to contemp.

Little Bohemia Rentals (818) 853-7506
11940 Sherman Rd, N Hollywood, CA, 91605
Dutch, Holland, China, Flying Pigeon, European, Fixies, City, Step-Through; Bicycles & bicycle accessories.
sales@wearelittlebohemia.com * www.wearelittlebohemia.com

Palms Cycle Shop (310) 838-9644
3770 Motor Ave, Los Angeles, CA, 90034
Rentals & sales of new, used and classic bikes & accessories
palmscycle@yahoo.com * www.palmscycle.com

PALMS CYCLE
STUDIO RENTALS
Custom Bikes • Rentals
Road Bicycles • Cruisers
Fixed Gear Bikes
Mountain Bikes • BMX
Specializing in
Schwinn Classic Bicycles

Prop Services West (818) 503-2790
contemp & period, children's

Sony Pictures Studios-Prop House (Off Lot) (310) 244-5999
period & contemp., adult & child

Universal Studios Property & Hardware Dept (818) 777-2784
men & women, period to present

Billboards & Billboard Lights

See Also: Street Dressing, Exterior Signs

Alley Cats Studio Rentals   (818) 982-9178
lights-working, on goosenecks/poles

E.C. Prop Rentals   (818) 764-2008
high multiples in many styles, w/goosenecks & straight pipe

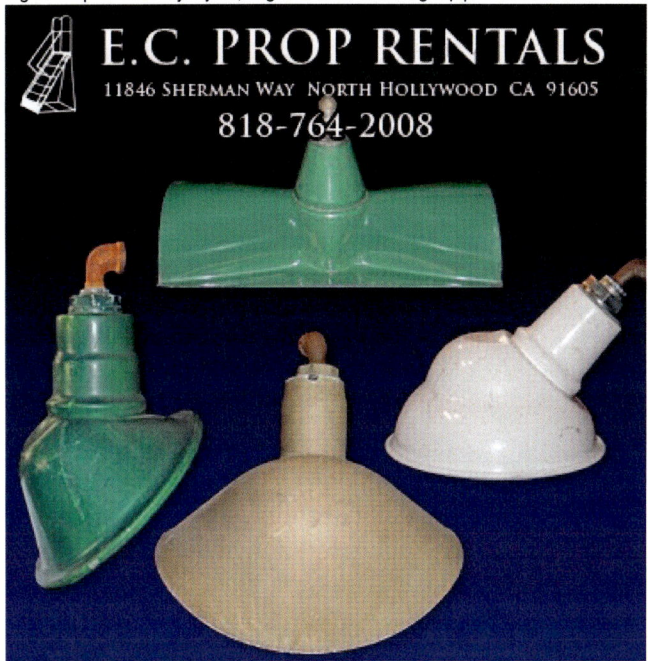

E.C. PROP RENTALS
11846 SHERMAN WAY NORTH HOLLYWOOD CA 91605
818-764-2008

LCW Props   (818) 243-0707
Neon Signs, Custom Graphics

Billiards

See: Bowling Equipment Game Tables & Equipment* Pool/Billiard Tables & Accessories*

Bingo

See: Gambling Equipment

Binoculars, Scopes & Telescopes

Alley Cats Studio Rentals   (818) 982-9178
pier binoculars

The Hand Prop Room LP.   (323) 931-1534
personal/military binoculars, night vision scopes, telescopes

History For Hire, Inc.   (818) 765-7767
large selection

Jadis   (310) 396-3477
2701 Main St, Santa Monica, CA, 90405
Antique & replica binoculars & telescopes. Period microscopes.
jadis1@gmail.com * www.jadisprops.com

LCW Props   (818) 243-0707
Star Gazing, Bird Watching, Hunting, Rifle Scopes, Period - Present

Omega/Cinema Props   (323) 466-8201
New binoculars and vintage binoculars with carrying cases.

Orion Telescopes & Binoculars   (800) 447-1001
89 Hangar Way, Watsonville CA, 95076
catalog sales; telescopes, binoculars, spotting scopes night vision equipment
www.telescope.com

The Rational Past   (310) 476-6277
By Appointment, West Los Angeles, CA
Authentic science, industrial, technical antiques & collectibles. Many
professions & eras represented. See web site.
info@therationalpast.com * www.therationalpast.com

Sony Pictures Studios-Prop House (Off Lot)   (310) 244-5999

Bird Baths

See: Fountains, Decorative & Garden Garden/Patio*

Bird Cages/Houses

Badia Design, Inc.   (818) 762-0130
5420 Vineland Ave, N Hollywood, CA, 91601
info@badiadesign.com * www.badiadesign.com

Dapper Cadaver   (818) 771-0818
Decorative birdcages and ornate birdcages.

The Hand Prop Room LP.   (323) 931-1534

History For Hire, Inc.   (818) 765-7767
cages

LCW Props   (818) 243-0707
large & small

Omega/Cinema Props   (323) 466-8201
Decorative bird cages; vintage bird cages, antique bird cages, wooden bird
cages, classic bird cages, steel bird cages

Prop Services West   (818) 503-2790

RC Vintage, Inc.   (818) 765-7107
bird cages Brass Vintage, swivel bird cages, hanging bird cages, cages on
stands

Sony Pictures Studios-Prop House (Off Lot)   (310) 244-5999
bird cages, cricket cages

Universal Studios Property & Hardware Dept   (818) 777-2784
Many bird cages/birdcages and bird houses/birdhouses

Birds

See: Animal Cages Animals (Live), Services, Trainers & Wranglers*
Bird Cages/Houses* Feathers*

Birthing Room

See Also: Hospital Equipment Medical Equip/Furniture,
Graphics/Supplies* Intensive Care Unit / NICU (Natal Intensive Care
Unit)*

A-1 Medical Integration   (818) 753-0319
Medical devices for Set Decoration & Property, from minor procedures to
detailed hospital units.

Alpha Companies - Spellman Desk Co.   (818) 504-9090
The #1 source for medical equipment in the Industry.

Blackboards

See: Chalk Boards Office Equipment & Dressing* School Supplies,
Desks & Dressing*

Blacklights

See: Lighting & Sound, Concert/Theatrical/DJ/VJ

Blacks

See: Theatrical Draperies, Hardware & Rigging

Blacksmith Shop/Foundry

The Hand Prop Room LP.   (323) 931-1534
hammers, anvil, bellows, tongs

Harry Patton Horseshoeing Supplies   (626) 359-8018
223 W. Maple Ave, Monrovia, CA, 91016
blacksmith shop avail. as location; horseshoeing supplies, can locate farriers
harrypattonhorseshoes@gmail.com * www.harrypatton.com

History For Hire, Inc.   (818) 765-7767
anvils, blacksmith items, etc.

LCW Props   (818) 243-0707
Tools, molds, Equipment

Sword & Stone   (818) 562-6548
Full blacksmith shop including anvil, bellows, tongs, hammers. Medieval
available

Blankets

See: Linens, Household Native American*

Blanks

See: Guns & Firearms

Bleachers & Grandstand Seating

See Also: Audience Cutouts & Inflatables* Audience Seating* Crowd Control: Barricades, Turnstiles Etc.* Rigging, Equipment or Services* Stages, Portable & Steel Deck

Alley Cats Studio Rentals　　　　　　(818) 982-9178
9' four row bleacher and 4' three row bleacher available for rent.

Alley Cats Props

www.alleycatsprops.com

Brown-United Grandstands & Staging　　　　(800) 442-7696
PO Box 1700, Monrovia, CA, 91017
Service/Sales/Rentals, grandstands; massive.
info@brownunited.com * www.brownunited.com

E.C. Prop Rentals　　　　　　　　　　(818) 764-2008
15' long & 9' long 4-tier aluminum bleachers, castered

E.C. PROP RENTALS
11846 SHERMAN WAY NORTH HOLLYWOOD CA 91605
818-764-2008

J.E.M F/X Inc　　　　　　　　　　　　(818) 398-1578
By Appointment Only
Finish units 6'11"H by 24'W made of four units that roll. Can be painted school colors, custom Vinyl wraps can be added.

Merrill Carson Entertainment　　　　　(818) 780-1735
Call for Appt.
bleachers, staging, benches, chair & choir risers
carsonentertainment@gmail.com * www.merrillcarson.com

Blinds

See: Window Treatments

Bling

10 Karat Rentals　　　　　　　　　　(818) 635-4124
7100 Tujunga (At RC Vintage), N Hollywood, CA, 91605
10karatrentals@gmail.com

AIR Designs　　　　　　　　　　　　(818) 768-6639
20"/22"/24"/26" Chrome Wheels for Pimped Out Rides

The Hand Prop Room LP.　　　　　　　(323) 931-1534
rapper jewerly in stock & will mfg

LCW Props　　　　　　　　　　　　　(818) 243-0707
Jewelry, Gold, Silver, Gaudy, Rings, Watches, Over The Top

Rhinestone Guy　　　　　　　　　　　(888) 594-7999
We Ship To You.
rhinestones & other jewelry making supplies
rhinestoneguy@yahoo.com * www.rhinestoneguy.com

ShopWildThings　　　　　　　　　　　(928) 855-6075
2880 Sweetwater Ave, Lake Havasu City, AZ, 86406
Event Decor, Beaded Curtains, Chain Curtains, String Curtains & Columns, Crystal Columns. Reliable service & delivery.
help@shopwildthings.com * www.shopwildthings.com

Block And Tackle Sets

See: Automotive/Garage Equip. & Parts* Chain Hoists* Construction Site Equipment* Factory/Industrial* Nautical Dressing & Props* Rigging, Equipment or Services

Blood

See Also: Special Effects, Make-up/Prosthetics

A-1 Medical Integration　　　　　　　(818) 753-0319
Medical devices for Set Decoration & Property, from minor procedures to detailed hospital units.

Dapper Cadaver　　　　　　　　　　　(818) 771-0818
Resin blood pools. Blood paint. Mouth blood. FX blood gel, powder and paste.

The Hand Prop Room LP.　　　　　　　(323) 931-1534
fake blood, prop blood, lab test tubes, capsules

Blu-Ray Rentals/Sales Store

See: Video Store Dressing* Video Rental/Sales Store

Blue Screens

See: Green Screens, Blue Screens

Blueprint Equipment & Supplies

LCW Props (818) 243-0707
Tons Of Blueprints, Buildings, Offices, Residential

Repro-Graphic Supply (818) 771-9066
9838 Glenoaks Blvd, Sun Valley, CA, 91352
drafting & engineering supplies, equipment & service, all Ind.'s. large format xerographics printing
info@reprographicsupply.com * www.reprographicsupply.com

Steven Enterprises (800) 491-8785
17952 Skypark Circle Unit E, Irvine, CA, 92614
Wide Format Printers. Rent/Buy. Authorized Dealer: HP, KIP, Canon, Oce, Epson. We service & supply everything we install
sales@plotters.com * www.plotters.com

Board Games

See: Sporting Goods & Services

Boats & Water Sport Vehicles

See Also: Nautical Dressing & Props Nautical/Marine Services & Charters* Sporting Goods & Services*

Alley Cats Studio Rentals (818) 982-9178
8' dinghies, 8' lap strakes, 12 ' rowboat with oars

Gondola Adventures, Inc. (949) 646-2067
3101 West Coast Highway Ste 110, Newport Beach, CA, 92663 **x801**
Authentic Venetian gondolas, both in and out of water, piloted by professional gondoliers. Expert staff. Since 1993
cruises@gondola.com * www.gondola.com

The Hand Prop Room LP. (323) 931-1534
antique canoes, rowboats/kayaks, past-present

LCW Props (818) 243-0707
Kayak, Boat Parts, Outboard Engines, Dock Buoys, Large Outdoor Kitchen BBQ

Sony Pictures Studios-Prop House (Off Lot) (310) 244-5999
shipwrecked row boats, canoes, dinghy

Tally Ho Marine Salvage & Decor (310) 548-5273
406 22nd St, San Pedro, CA, 90731
If we don't have it & can't find it, we can build it. rowboats

Universal Studios Property & Hardware Dept (818) 777-2784
Inflatable boats, rowboats, kayaks, canoes

West Marine (800) 262-8464
4750 Admiralty Way, Marina Del Rey, CA 90292
catalog sales; 400+ stores, compl. line boating access., inflatable boats, dinghies, kayaks, motor/sail boats & clothing
www.westmarine.com

Bobbinettes

See: Theatrical Draperies, Hardware & Rigging

Bobble Heads

See: Nodders

Bobcats

See: Construction Site Equipment

Body & Face Painting

See: Tattoos (Temporary) Body/Face Painting

Body Parts

See Also: Anatomical Charts & Models Bones, Skulls & Skeletons* Mannequins* Special Effects, Equipment & Supplies*

Dapper Cadaver (818) 771-0818
Lifelike fake body parts, bodies & dummies. Severed heads, fake arms & legs, hearts & organs. Wound, burn & custom FX.

Gorygirl Halloween Event Staging and Prop Rental (818) 912-6902
Prop rubber body parts. Items in Bulk only available with 2-4 week lead time and subject to availability.

The Hand Prop Room LP. (323) 931-1534

History For Hire, Inc. (818) 765-7767

LCW Props (818) 243-0707
Misc. Limbs, Skeletons, Anatomical Models

Body Piercing

See: Goth/Punk/Bondage/Fetish/Erotica Etc. Tattoo & Body Piercing Equipment & Supplies*

Boiler Room

See: Plumbing Fixtures, Heating/Cooling Appliances

Bondage

See: Goth/Punk/Bondage/Fetish/Erotica Etc. Leather (Clothing, Accessories, Materials)*

Bones, Skulls & Skeletons

See Also: Dinosaurs* Fossils* Taxidermy, Hides/Heads/Skeletons
Dapper Cadaver (818) 771-0818
Human skeletons; medical, crime & Halloween. Lifecast, forensic skull & bone
replicas. Animal & dinosaur. T-rex skeleton.
Gorygirl Halloween Event Staging and Prop (818) 912-6902
Rental
Plastic Skeletons, plastic skulls; animal skeletons and Skeleton style props and
set dressing
The Hand Prop Room LP. (323) 931-1534
human, animal, sealife, human bones, loose bones, skeletons, skulls, animal
skulls, steer head, taxidermy animals
History For Hire, Inc. (818) 765-7767
complete skeletons,parts,human & animal
KIHL STUDIOS (818) 812-9594
9701 Owensmouth Ave Unit 1, Chatsworth, CA, 91311
Human skull & bone reproductions, animal bone reproductions, skeleton art,
sci-fi/fantasy skeletons.
design@kihlstudios.com * www.kihlstudios.com
LCW Props (818) 243-0707
Skeletons, Heart, Lungs, Reproductive Models, Brain, Prosthetics
Sony Pictures Studios-Prop House (Off Lot) (310) 244-5999
Sword & Stone (818) 562-6548
Human skeletons
Universal Studios Property & Hardware Dept (818) 777-2784
Various bones from human bones to animal bones

Boneyard (Junk)

See: Architectural Pieces & Artifacts Salvage, Rubble, Clutter &
Trash (Prop)*

Bonnets

See: Headwear - Hats, Bonnets, Caps, Helmets Etc.

Book Covers & Bookbinding

Faux Library Studio Props, Inc. (818) 765-0096
Book coverings, book art, faux book covers, book casing, experts at creating a
real looking fake library
Gibbs Bookbinding (213) 223-6921
6646 Hollywood Blvd Ste 206, Hollywood, CA, 90028
Custom books and boxes of all sizes. Leather, cloth, and paper, in current or
historic/aged styles. Fast turnaround.
stephaniegibbs@gmail.com * www.GibbsBookbinding.com
H & H Book Services (818) 242-2665
236 N. Glendale Ave, Glendale, CA, 91206
repair & restorations, fine bindings, book bindery, book binding
www.hhbookservices.com
Kater-Crafts Bookbinders (562) 692-0665
4860 Gregg Rd, Pico Rivera, CA, 90660
Custom work, any size. Fine hand binding. Industry credits. Museum quality
restoration.
sales@katercrafts.com * www.katercrafts.com

Books, Real/Hollow & Faux Books

See Also: Paperwork, Documents & Letters, Office* Scrapbooks
Alpha Companies - Spellman Desk Co. (818) 504-9090
hollow books, law books, school books, medical books, novels, journals
Book Decor (858) 336-8370
Web Based Business
Real antique leather bound books in Danish for set decor. Various sizes and
colors, pristine condition to worn and aged.
sales@bookdecor.com * www.bookdecor.com

Books For Libraries, Inc. (800) 321-5596
28064 Ave Standford Unit L, Santa Clarita, CA, 91355
Books for Libraries offers complete real book academic libraries up to 50,000,
by type, subject or mixed
JStitz@pacbell.net * www.booksforlibraries.com
Booth & Williams (844) 429-2665
3000 Shawnee Industrial Way, Ste 114, Suwanee, GA, 30024
Over 1,000,000 vintage & modern book prop rentals. Any age, color, subject,
style or condition.
props@boothandwilliams.com * www.boothandwilliams.com

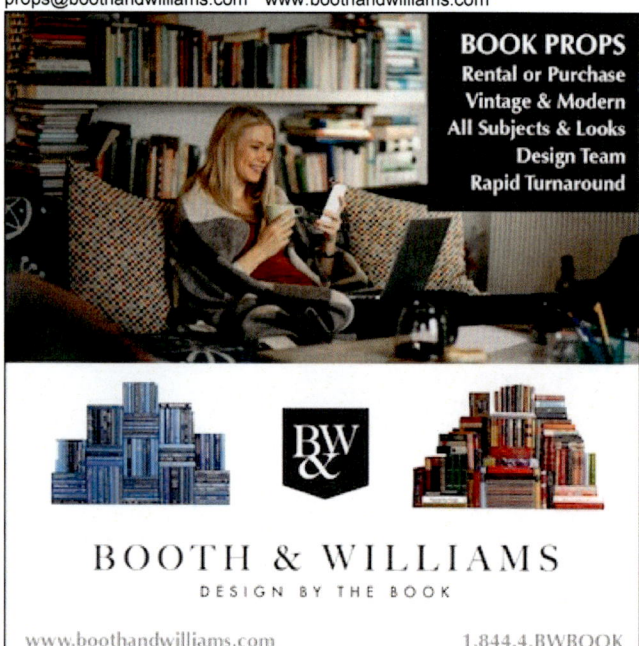

Book Decor   (858) 336-8370
Web Based Business
Real antique leather bound books in Danish for set decor. Various sizes and
colors, pristine condition to worn and aged.
sales@bookdecor.com * www.bookdecor.com

Collins Visual Media   (818) 686-6581
10518 Johanna Ave, Shadow Hills, CA, 91040
We create and distress fabric and leather hard-cover books, any size, plus we
design and print dust jackets.
www.collinsvisualmedia.com

E.C. Prop Rentals   (818) 764-2008
manuals, binders, printouts

Faux Library Studio Props, Inc.   (818) 765-0096
1000s of feet of hollow books, medical to classics, library shelving, real books,
hollow books, faux books.

Prop Books • Libraries • Furniture
huge collection • 60,000 sq ft • furniture • accessories • modern • antiques
Faux Library Studio Props

Gibbs Bookbinding   (213) 223-6921
6646 Hollywood Blvd Ste 206, Hollywood, CA, 90028
Custom books and boxes of all sizes. Leather, cloth, and paper, in current or
historic/aged styles. Fast turnaround.
stephaniegibbs@gmail.com * www.GibbsBookbinding.com

The Hand Prop Room LP.   (323) 931-1534
period-present wide sel.

History For Hire, Inc.   (818) 765-7767
specialty book mfg

LCW Props   (818) 243-0707
Large Selection, Legal, Fiction, Non-Fiction, Reference, Leather Bound

Ob-jects   (818) 351-4200
leather sets, coffee table, cook, garden

Omega/Cinema Props   (323) 466-8201
Cookbooks, recipe books, leather bound books, king james replica bible, faux
books and more.

Picture Start Props   (818) 255-5472
Many different styles and colors from antique to contemporary coffee table
books.

Prop Services West   (818) 503-2790
law books, paper backs, children, novels

Sony Pictures Studios-Prop House (Off Lot)   (310) 244-5999
paperbacks to law, autographed books, binders, bookends, bookmaker, comic
books, composition books, cookbooks, diary, dictionary

Universal Studios Property & Hardware Dept   (818) 777-2784
All manner of books available.

Warner Bros. Studios Property Department   (818) 954-2181
Faux, hardcover, soft cover, research, cookbooks, antique, travel, law, faux

ZG04 DECOR   (818) 853-8040
Cleared Books, Magazines, Comics

Bookstores

See Also: Search Tools, Directories, Libraries

Psychic Eye Book Shops, Inc.   (818) 906-8263
13435 Ventura Blvd, Sherman Oaks, CA, 91423
new age, metaphysical, self help, occult, astrology, also several other stores in
LA area
www.pebooks.com

Alexandria II New Age Bookstore   (626) 792-7885
170 S. Lake Ave, Pasadena, Ca 91101
Metaphysical books, DVDs, music, incense, gifts, Tarot cards, altar items, yoga
supplies & more
www.alexandria2.com

Book Soup   (310) 659-3110
8818 Sunset Blvd, W.Hollywood, CA, 90069
open 7 days, 9AM to 9PM
www.booksoup.com

Cook Books by Janet Jarvits   (626) 344-9275
1353 N Hill, Pasadena, CA, 91104
over 15,000 used & rare cookbooks
www.cookbookjj.com

Distant Lands   (800) 310-3220
20 S. Raymond Ave, Pasadena, CA, 91105
traveler's bookstore & outfitter, international maps
www.distantlands.com

Drama Book Shop   (212) 944-0595
250 W. 40th St, New York, NY, 10018
www.dramabookshop.com

Faux Library Studio Props, Inc.   (818) 765-0096
Complete bookstore dressing, books & bookcases, book shelving, book
shelves.

Hennessey & Ingalls, Inc.   (213) 437-2130
300 S. Santa Fe Ave., Suite M, Los Angeles, CA 90013
books on the visual arts, and architecture.
www.hennesseyingalls.com

Larry Edmunds Bookshop   (323) 463-3273
6644 Hollywood Blvd, Hollywood, CA, 90028
Also we carry posters, memorabilia, photos & novelties
www.larryedmunds.com

Samuel French, Inc.   (866) 598-8449
7623 Sunset Blvd, Hollywood, CA, 90046
www.samuelfrench.com

Strand Bookstore, Inc.   (212) 473-1452
828 Broadway (at 12th St), New York, NY, 10003-4805
world's largest used book store, see Jenny McKibben X150
www.strandbooks.com

U.S. Government Bookstore   (866) 512-1800
710 N Capitol St NW, Washington, DC, 20401
Online sales for all government publications
http://bookstore.gpo.gov

Vroman's Bookstore   (626) 449-5320
695 E Colorado Blvd, Pasadena, CA, 91101
www.vromansbookstore.com

Boom Lifts

See: Construction Site Equipment

Booths

See: Banquets/Booths (Seating) Carnival Dressing/Supplies* Game
Booths* Telephone Booths & Pay Telephones* Ticket Booths*

Boots

See: Shoes, Boots & Footwear Western Wear*

Bottles

See Also: Bars, Nightclubs, Barware & Dressing* Glassware/Dishes*
Liquor Bottles* Milk Bottles & Cans

AIR Designs   **(818) 768-6639**
Liquor, Wine, Beer, Display Bottles, Crates, Boxes, Multiples & Generic
E.C. Prop Rentals   **(818) 764-2008**
5 Gallon Water Coolers, Glass Bottles, Plastic Bottles
The Hand Prop Room LP.   **(323) 931-1534**
period-present personal, medical, liquor, household, soda, beer
History For Hire, Inc.   **(818) 765-7767**
soda, liquor, other
LCW Props   **(818) 243-0707**
Jars, Lab Glassware, We Own The Recycling Center Next Door
Modern Props   **(323) 934-3000**
contemporary bottles, futuristic bottles, household bottles & commercial bottles
Old N Country Prop Shop, LLC   **(818) 423-2599**
Wide variety of Vintage and Antique, MARKED glass bottles for whiskey,
cleaning, medicine and soft drinks.
Omega/Cinema Props   **(323) 466-8201**
All kinds of bottles: Classic and period bottles, clay bottles, tonic bottles, glass
bottles, apothecary bottles & more.
Prop Services West   **(818) 503-2790**
Sony Pictures Studios-Prop House (Off Lot)   **(310) 244-5999**
champagne bottles, liquor bottles, decorative bottles, milk bottles, oil bottles,
vinegar bottles, spice bottles, sports bottles
Universal Studios Property & Hardware Dept   **(818) 777-2784**
All manner of bottles.

Bounce Houses

See: Inflatables, Custom

Bouquets

See: Balloons & Balloon Sculptures* Florists/Floral Design

Bourns & Pouffes

See: Hotel, Motel, Inn, Lodge

Bowling Equipment

See Also: Sporting Goods & Services
The Hand Prop Room LP.   **(323) 931-1534**
bowling shoes, bowling bags, vintage bowling, bowling pins, bowling trophies,
rubber bowling pins, bowling balls
History For Hire, Inc.   **(818) 765-7767**
pins, bags & shoes, trophies
Universal Studios Property & Hardware Dept   **(818) 777-2784**
Bowling balls, bowling ball bags, bowling gloves, bowling pins
US Bowling Corporation Murrey International   **(909) 548-0644**
5480 Schaefer Ave, Chino, CA, 91710
Ball returns, seating, tables, ball racks, lanes, custom graphics
sales@usbowling.com * www.usbowling.com

Bows & Arrows

See: Archery Equipment, Training* Native American* Sporting Goods
& Services* Weapons

Boxes

See Also: Crates/ Vaults* Gift Wrapping* Packing/Packaging
Supplies, Services

Acme Display Fixture & Packaging   **(888) 411-1870**
3829 S Broadway St, Los Angeles, CA, 90037
Complete store setups: garment racks, displays/display cases, counters,
packaging, shelving, hangers, mannequins
sales@acmedisplay.com * www.acmedisplay.com
Basaw Manufacturing, Inc.   **(818) 765-6650**
7300 Varna, N Hollywood, CA, 91605
Basaw builds crates to order, large inventory in stock. wooden, corrugated,
specialized packs
fredy@basaw.com * www.basaw.com
E.C. Prop Rentals   **(818) 764-2008**
wood, metal, fiberglass, cardboard
History For Hire, Inc.   **(818) 765-7767**
wood, hat, shoe
Kater-Crafts Bookbinders   **(562) 692-0665**
4860 Gregg Rd, Pico Rivera, CA, 90660
Custom work. Clamshell boxes, slipcases, portfolio/photo boxes. Museum
quality.
sales@katercrafts.com * www.katercrafts.com
LCW Props   **(818) 243-0707**
Wood Crates, Molded Plastic, Cardboard, Large & Small, New & Old
Sony Pictures Studios-Prop House (Off Lot)   **(310) 244-5999**
apothecary boxes, candy boxes, cheese box, cigar boxes, cigarette boxes,
decorative boxes, display boxes, wrapped gift

Boxing, Wrestling, Mixed Martial Arts (MMA)

See Also: Exercise & Fitness Equipment* Gymnasium & Gymnastic
Equipment
Boxing Ring Rental   **(323) 460-4644**
1060 Vine Street, Hollywood, CA, 90038
Boxing ring rentals and boxing ring space for rent.
info@BoxingRingRental.com * www.BoxingRingRental.com

Modern Boxing Rings
Classic Boxing Rings
Aged Boxing Ring
Pro Fight Boxing Rings
Boxing Accessories

1060 Vine Street, Hollywood, CA, 90038 (323) 460-4644

BoxingRing.com   **(855) 776-5278**
11555 Whittier Blvd, Whittier, CA, 90601
We sell all kinds of equipment including uniforms, weapons, and rings for
boxing, wrestling, Mixed Martial Arts & more.
info@BoxingRing.com * www.BoxingRing.com

(855) 776-5278
BOXINGRING.COM
RINGS, CAGES AND
ACCESSORIES

History For Hire, Inc.   (818) 765-7767
boxing gloves, bells

L. A. Party Works   (888) 527-2789
9712 Alpaca St, S El Monte, CA, 91733
Boxing rings available. Our print shop can customize the graphics and branding too!
partyworks@aol.com * www.partyworksinteractive.com

REGULATION PRO RING / CUSTOM COLORS & BRANDING / BOXING MACHINES

888-527-2789
partyworksusa.com

PARTYWORKS
I N T E R A C T I V E

Lennie Marvin Enterprises, Inc. (Prop Heaven)   (818) 841-5882
Boxing and martial arts equipment

MMA Cage Rental   (323) 305-7311
1058 Vine Street, Hollywood, CA, 90038
MMA cage rentals and MMA cage fighting space.
info@MMACageRental.com * www.MMACageRental.com

MMA cage rentals • MMA cage fighting space

Gear
Punching Bags
Mats
Protective Gear
Pads

MMA CAGE RENTAL

1058 Vine Street, Hollywood, CA, 90038 (323)305-7311
WWW.MMACAGERENTAL.COM

Pro Boxing Supplies   (818) 760-9500
4405 Laurel Canyon Blvd, Studio City, CA, 91607
Boxing rings, Wrestling rings, MMA cages, punching bags, boxing gloves, heavy bags, weapons, dummies, and much more...
proboxingsupplies@yahoo.com * www.proboxingsupplies.com

PBS PRO

Pro Boxing Supplies
"Where the Pros shop"

Boxing Rings
Fight Cages
Punching Bags
Boxing Equipment
Protective Gear
Punch Mitts
& Shields

Awards, Belts
& Novelties

Fitness Apparel,
Shoes & Accessories

Martial Arts
Equipment

Pro Fight Shop   (323) 460-4600
1062 Vine Street, Hollywood, CA, 90038
Boxing rings, Wrestling rings, Punching bags, Boxing gloves, Heavy bag stands, MMA cages, MMA Rings, Fight Rings, Mats
profightshop@yahoo.com * www.profightshop.com

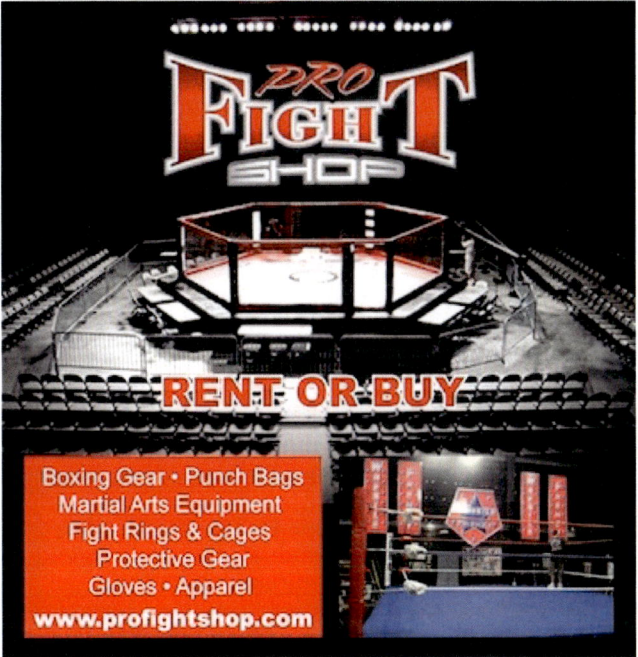

PRO FIGHT SHOP

RENT OR BUY

Boxing Gear • Punch Bags
Martial Arts Equipment
Fight Rings & Cages
Protective Gear
Gloves • Apparel
www.profightshop.com

Sony Pictures Studios-Prop House (Off Lot)   (310) 244-5999
boxing equipment, punching balls, speed bags

Brass Accessories

See: Decorative Accessories Prop Houses*

Brass Lamps

See: Light Fixtures

Break Room

AIR Designs (818) 768-6639
Vending Machines; Soda & Snack, Coffee Machines, Counters, Seating, Refrigerators

E.C. Prop Rentals (818) 764-2008
employee break room dressing

Breakaways (Glass, Props, Scenery)

See Also: Expendables* Special Effects, Equipment & Supplies

Alfonso's Breakaway Glass, Inc. (818) 768-7402
8070 San Fernando Rd, Sun Valley, CA, 91352
largest mfg; 1000 breakaway glass,props & scenery, windshield to test tube, & custom
info@alfonsosbreakawayglass.com * www.alfonsosbreakawayglass.com

Collins Visual Media (818) 686-6581
10518 Johanna Ave, Shadow Hills, CA, 91040
We have the best tech for creating breakaways. From circus horses to football players we give the best breaks.
www.collinsvisualmedia.com

General Veneer Manufacturing Co. (323) 564-2661
8652 Otis St, South Gate, CA, 90280
Breakaway balsa wood sheets & boards
balsasales@generalveneer.com * www.generalveneer.com

The Hand Prop Room LP. (323) 931-1534
designed to your needs, glasses, vases, plates, etc.

HPR Custom (323) 931-1534
5700 Venice Blvd, Los Angeles, CA, 90019
Breakaway chairs, breakaway tables, breakaway guitars, breakaway branches, breakaway clubs, breakaway pool cues and more
www.hprcustom.com

J & M Special Effects, Inc. (718) 875-0140
524 Sackett St, Brooklyn, NY, 11217
Formerly Jauchem & Meeh. bottles, glasses,breakaway bottles,breakaway vases, breakaway wine bottles
info@jmfx.net * www.jmfx.net

New Rule FX (818) 387-6450
7751 Densmore Ave, Van Nuys, CA, 91406
Breakaway props-all types & categories. Balsa furniture, Fake food. Foam Weapons. Tools, custom props, molding & casting
ryan@newrulefx.com * www.NewRuleFX.com

Breakaway Props • Custom Props • Expendables
Breakaway Glass • Breakaway Bricks & Masonry
Fake Food • Foam & Rubber Weapons and Tools

Peter Geyer Action Props, Inc (818) 768-0070
8235 Lankershim Blvd Ste G, N Hollywood, CA, 91605
balsa furniture
www.actionprops.com

Rohan Glass Company, Inc (818) 984-1000
12442 Oxnard St, N Hollywood, CA, 91606
breakaway sheet glass, 2-way mirrors, regular glass windows etc
rohanglass@yahoo.com * www.rohanglasscompany.com

Universal Studios Property & Hardware Dept (818) 777-2784
Breakaways and breakaway fabrication

Breaker Boxes

See Also: Control Boards* Control Panels/Boxes* Electrical/Electronic Supplies & Services* Electronic Equipment (Dressing)* Gas & Electric Meters

AIR Designs (818) 768-6639
Home Breaker Boxes & Industrial Breaker Boxes

Alley Cats Studio Rentals (818) 982-9178
period, modern

E.C. Prop Rentals (818) 764-2008
extensive sel., period-contemp.

LCW Props (818) 243-0707
Tons of Different Styles & Sizes, Rigged, With Conduit, Can Make Custom

Brick

See: Concrete Block, Brick, Gravel, Sand, Rocks, Etc.

Bridal Dress

See: Wedding Attire

Briefcases

See Also: Luggage

The Hand Prop Room LP. (323) 931-1534
period-present, great selection, rigged, custom design

History For Hire, Inc. (818) 765-7767
huge sel, all periods

LCW Props (818) 243-0707
Haliburton, Rigged With Electronics, Spy Kits, Surveillance Style, Bomb Detonators

Modern Props (323) 934-3000
contemporary briefcases, futuristic briefcases, espionage briefcases

Sony Pictures Studios-Prop House (Off Lot) (310) 244-5999

Universal Studios Property & Hardware Dept (818) 777-2784
Leather briefcases, lockable briefcases, aluminum briefcases, worn briefcases, computer briefcases, and more.

Broadcast Studio

See: Radio/TV Station* Video Camera Equipment & Services

Bronzes

See: Sculpture

Brush Hauling

See: Transportation, Trucking and/or Storage

Bubble Gum Machines

See: Vending Machines

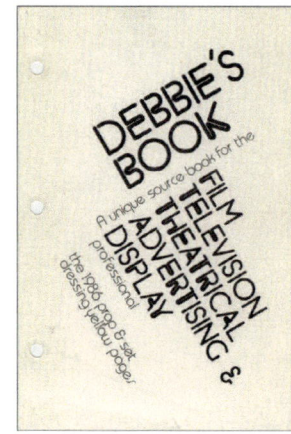

Bubble Machines

Astro Audio Video Lighting, Inc. (818) 549-9915
6615 San Fernando Rd, Glendale, CA, 91201
Bubble machines and bubble machine fluid available.
www.astroavl.com
EFX- Event Special Effects (626) 888-2239
125 Railroad Ave, Monrovia, CA, 91016
Bubble Machies- Bubble Master- Fluid
info@efxla.com * www.efxla.com
L. A. Party Works (888) 527-2789
9712 Alpaca St, S El Monte, CA, 91733
Bubble machines for rent
partyworks@aol.com * www.partyworksinteractive.com
LCW Props (818) 243-0707
Working Machines
Universal Studios Special Effects Equip. (818) 777-3333

Bubble Wrap

See: Expendables Packing/Packaging Supplies, Services*

Buckboard

See: Carriages, Horse Drawn

Buckets

See Also: Barrels & Drums, Wood/Metal/Plastic Western Dressing*
E.C. Prop Rentals (818) 764-2008
new/used, metal/plastic
The Hand Prop Room LP. (323) 931-1534
wood, metal
History For Hire, Inc. (818) 765-7767
metal, wood, tin, enamel
LCW Props (818) 243-0707
Large & Small, Stainless Steel, Plastic, Metal, Ice
Old N Country Prop Shop, LLC (818) 423-2599
A variety of different size and styled buckets and pails.
Sony Pictures Studios-Prop House (Off Lot) (310) 244-5999
Universal Studios Property & Hardware Dept (818) 777-2784
Many kinds of buckets from mop to coal, many periods.

Buggies

See: Carriages, Horse Drawn

Bugs

See: Animals (Live), Services, Trainers & Wranglers Insects, Artificial*

Building Supply, Lumber, Hardware, Etc.

See Also: Architectural Pieces & Artifacts Concrete Block, Brick, Gravel, Sand, Rocks, Etc.* Glass & Mirrors* Hardware, Decorative* Paneling, Veneers & Laminates* Tile, Marble, Granite, Etc.*
A & A Building Materials (626) 447-3595
310 N Santa Anita Ave, Arcadia, CA, 91006
drywall, lath, plaster; limited lumber, plywood, sand
www.aamaterials.com
A & G Lumber (310) 838-6222
5942 W Washington Blvd, Culver City, CA, 90232
www.aglumber.com
Anawalt Lumber (323) 464-1600
1001 N. Highland, Hollywood, CA, 90038
multiple locations in north L.A.
info@anawaltlumber.com * www.anawaltlumber.com
Anderson International Trading (714) 666-8183
1171 N. Tustin Ave, Anaheim, CA, 92807
1/64" to 1" plywood & veneers, curves & cylinders, musical drums, bendable substrates
www.aitwood.com

Anderson Plywood Sales (310) 397-8229
4020 Sepulveda Blvd, Culver City, CA, 90230
info@andersonplywood.com * www.andersonplywood.com
Arrow Fence & Lumber (818) 686-3553
10865 Sutter Ave, Pacoima, CA, 91331
lumber/plywood, beams, peeler poles
www.arrowfenceandlumber.com
Arroyo Building Materials (818) 365-6170
890 Arroyo St, San Fernando, CA, 91340
stone, steel products, lumber, drywall, doors/windows etc.
www.arroyobuildingmaterials.net
Austin Hardwoods & Hardware (714) 953-4000
610 N Santiago St, Santa Ana, CA, 92701
Exotic/domestic hardwoods, sheet goods, hardware, woodworking tools
www.austinhardwoodsonline.com
B & B Hardware (310) 390-9413
12450 W. Washington Blvd, Los Angeles, CA, 90066
Bear Forest Products, Inc (951) 727-1767
4685 Brookhollow Circle, Riverside, CA, 92509
Wood construction materials, Plywood- Softwood and Hardwood. MDF, PB, etc. Lumber 1x3, 1x4, 2x4, etc.
matto@bearfp.com * www.bearfp.com
BMC (818) 982-6046
7151 Lankershim Blvd, N Hollywood, CA, 91605
multiple locations in L.A.
www.buildwithbmc.com
Bourget Bros. Building Materials (310) 450-6556
1636 11th St, Santa Monica, CA, 90404
www.bourgetbros.com
C & E Lumber Co. (909) 626-3591
2692 N. Towne Ave, Pomona, CA, 91767
lumber/plywood, peeler poles, rail fencing
www.celumber.com
California Do-It Center (818) 845-8301
3221 W. Magnolia Blvd, Burbank, CA, 91505
multiple loc. in L.A.
www.doitcenter.com
Dykes Lumber (212) 582-1930
124 East 124th St, New York, NY, 10035
8 loc. in NYC area, lumber, mouldings, const. products
www.dykeslumber.com
E.C. Prop Rentals (818) 764-2008
construction dressing, shelving, fencing, power & hand tools
Far West Plywood (818) 885-1511
18450 Parthenia Pl, Northridge, CA, 91325
www.farwestplywood.com
Feldman Lumber (718) 786-7777
1281 Metropolitan Ave., Brooklyn, NY 11237
www.feldmanlumber.com
Forest Plywood (714) 523-1721
14711 Artesia Blvd, La Mirada, CA 90638
lumber, plywood, melamine, etc.
www.forestplywood.com
Goldenwest Plywood & Lumber (562) 867-3386
17326 Woodruff Ave, Bellflower, CA, 90706
lumber/plywood
www.goldenwestplywood.com
Home Depot (323) 461-3303
5600 W. Sunset Blvd, Hollywood, CA, 90028
mult. loc. in LA/NYC: website has store locator function
www.homedepot.com
Jansen Ornamental Supply Co., Inc. (800) 423-4494
10926 Schmidt Rd, El Monte, CA, 91733
architectural ornamental hardware, stair railings, wholesale only
www.jansensupply.com
Jones Lumber (323) 564-6656
10711 S. Alameda St, Lynwood, CA, 90262
extensive
www.joneslumber.com
Lenoble Lumber (718) 784-5230
38-20 Review Ave, Long Island City, NY, 11101
no hardware
www.lenoblelumber.com

LISTINGS FOR THIS CATEGORY CONTINUE ON THE FOLLOWING PAGE

Neiman Reed Lumber Co.   (818) 781-3466
7875 Willis Ave, Panorama City, CA, 91402
lumber/plywood, wholesaler
http://neimanreed.com

North Hollywood Hardware, Inc.   (818) 980-2453
11847 Ventura Blvd, Studio City, CA, 91604
Full service hardware store with hard to find items.
nohohardware@gmail.com * www.ehardware2go.com

Northridge Lumber   (818) 349-6701
18537 Parthenia St, Northridge, CA, 91324
www.northridgelumberco.com

Orchard Supply Hardware   (818) 779-7292
5960 Sepulveda Blvd, Van Nuys, CA, 91411
multiple loc. in L.A., call (888) 746-7674 for store nearest you
www.osh.com

Pasadena Lumber   (626) 797-2220
1464 Lincoln Ave, Pasadena, CA, 91103

Quixote   (504) 266-2297
10289 Airline Hwy, St Rose, LA, 70087
Set Building Supplies, Set Construction, Power Tools, lumber, glues, delivery
nola@quixote.com * www.quixote.com

The ReUse People   (818) 244-5635
3015 Dolores St, Los Angeles, CA, 90065
Thousands of board feet of reused lumber and used building materials. All
denailed and ready for use.
JeffCockerell@TheReUsePeople.org * www.TheReUsePeople.org

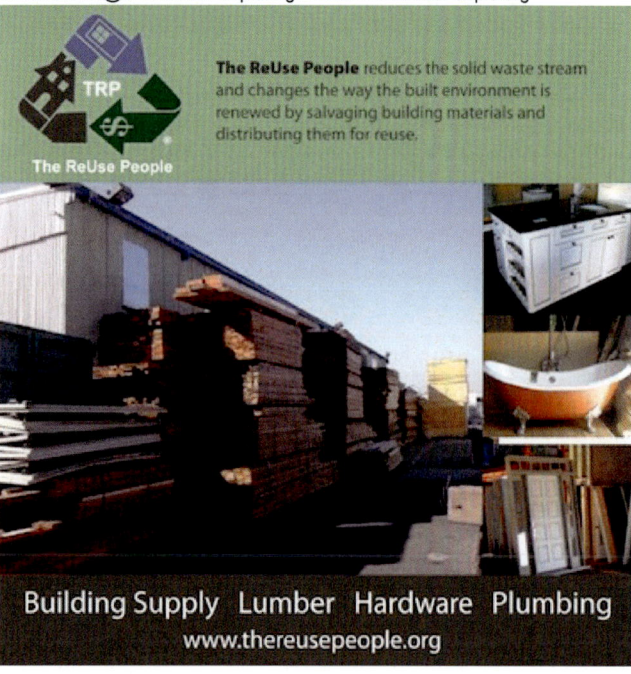

Roadside Lumber   (818) 991-1880
29112 Roadside Dr, Agoura Hills, CA, 91301
www.roadsidelumber.com

Rosenzweig Lumber & Plywood Corp.   (718) 585-8050
801 East 135th St, Bronx, NY, 10454
building supplies but no hardware
www.rosenzweiglumber.com

Royal Plywood   (562) 404-2989
14171 E Park Place, Cerritos, CA, 90703
lumber/plywood & veneers, wholesaler
www.royalplywood.com

Virgil's Hardware   (818) 242-1104
520 N Glendale Ave, Glendale, CA, 91207

Warner Bros. Studios Paint Department   (818) 954-1817
4000 Warner Blvd Bldg 47, Burbank, CA, 91522
Production expendables & supplies to the entertainment community at great
prices
www.wbpaintdept.com

Bulkhead Lights

See Also: Caged Vapor Proof Lights* Nautical Dressing & Props

E.C. Prop Rentals   (818) 764-2008
multiple sizes & styles

LCW Props   (818) 243-0707
Ship, Submarine, Train, Dock Lights

Bull Horns

See: Megaphones

Bullet Proof Vests

See: Military Props & Equipment* Police Equipment

Bulletin Boards

E.C. Prop Rentals   (818) 764-2008
many sizes & styles, wood & metal, int. wall-mount, ext. free standing

The Hand Prop Room LP.   (323) 931-1534
wall, floor, office, academic, wooden, metal

History For Hire, Inc.   (818) 765-7767
wall-mount

Hollywood Studio Gallery   (323) 462-1116
pre-dressed

LCW Props   (818) 243-0707
Large & Small, Behind Glass, Many Styles

Linoleum City, Inc.   (323) 469-0063
4849 Santa Monica Blvd, Hollywood, CA, 90029
Bulletin board cork, decorative wall cork, insulation cork, underlayment cork,
cork floors, floating cork floors.
sales@linocity.com * www.linoleumcity.com

Omega/Cinema Props   (323) 466-8201
Wooden framed bulletin boards, aluminum framed bulletin boards, cork bulletin
boards and others in many sizes available.

On Set Graphics   (661) 233-6786
Web Based Business
100% Cleared Printable Flyers, Bulletin Board Dressing, Posters, Office Notes,
Signage, and so much more.
info@onsetgraphics.com * www.onsetgraphics.com

Sony Pictures Studios-Prop House (Off Lot)   (310) 244-5999
all sizes, wall & free-standing

Universal Studios Property & Hardware Dept   (818) 777-2784
Bulletin boards including; rolling bulletin boards, hanging bulletin boards, two
sided bulletin boards and more.

Buoys

See: Nautical Dressing & Props

Bus Benches

See: Benches

Bus Depot Lockers

See: Lockers

Bus Rentals

See: Vehicles/Picture Vehicles

Bus Shelter

See Also: Benches* Street Dressing
AIR Designs (818) 768-6639
Shelters & Enclosures, Benches, Trash Cans, Signage, Poster Displays
Alley Cats Studio Rentals (818) 982-9178
complete shelters
E.C. Prop Rentals (818) 764-2008
contemp. & bus stop ad benches, multiples

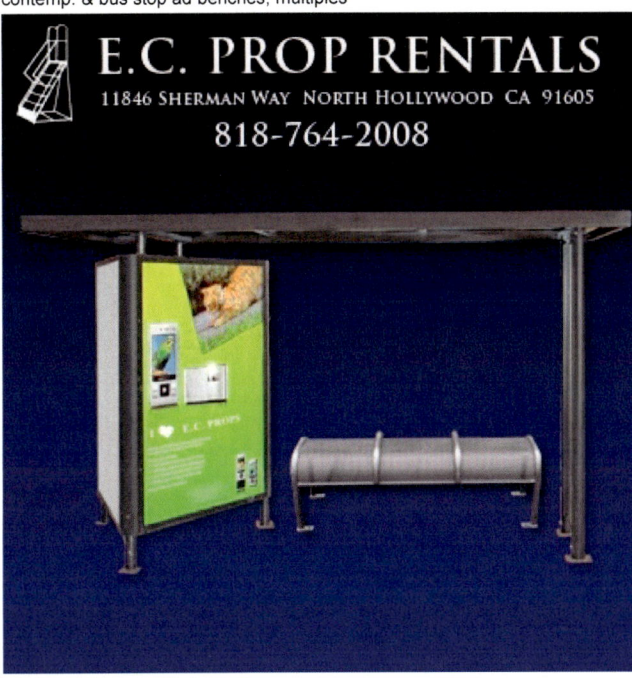

E.C. PROP RENTALS
11846 SHERMAN WAY NORTH HOLLYWOOD CA 91605
818-764-2008

Lennie Marvin Enterprises, Inc. (Prop Heaven) (818) 841-5882
various styles, quantity avail.

Business Machines

See Also: Bank Dressing* Cash Registers* Computers* Copy Machines* Office Equipment & Dressing* Typewriters
Advanced Liquidators Office Furniture (818) 763-3470
used adding machines, typewriters, vintage typewriters, vintage tape dispensers, shredders, and more
History For Hire, Inc. (818) 765-7767
period typewriters, adding machines, etc.
LCW Props (818) 243-0707
Copiers, Faxes, Printers, Large Selection Of New & Old
Modern Props (323) 934-3000
contemporary business machines, futuristic business machines, electronic business machines
Omega/Cinema Props (323) 466-8201
Period to modern business machines of various kinds.
Universal Studios Property & Hardware Dept (818) 777-2784
Prop business machines for all of your office dressing rentals.

Busts

See: Sculpture

Buttons

See: Badges, Patches & Buttons* Costume/Wardrobe/Sewing Supplies* Memorabilia & Novelties

Cabinets

See: Kitchen Counters & Cabinets* Staff Shops

Cable Covers

See: Electrical/Electronic Supplies & Services* Events, Decorations, Supplies & Services* Floor, Ground & Surface Protection

Cactus, Live & Artificial

See Also: Greens
California Cactus Center (626) 795-2788
216 S. Rosemead Blvd, Pasadena, CA, 91107
www.cactuscenter.com
California Nursery "Cactus Ranch" (818) 894-5694
19420 Saticoy St, Reseda, CA, 91335
Over 100,000 cacti & succulent plants - by appt only
www.california-cactus-succulents.com
Green Set, Inc. (818) 764-1231
Cactus, succulents and other desert plants, both live and artificial, many many types and styles of cacti
Jackson Shrub Supply, Inc. (818) 982-0100
Saguaro 5' to 18', beaver tail, succulents, live cactus, artificial cactus, fire retardant brush, plus more

Cafe Tables/Chairs/Umbrellas

See Also: Coffee House* Delicatessen Equipment* Restaurant Furniture & Dressing
AIR Designs (818) 768-6639
Round and Square, Period/Modern Diner, Cafe, Coffee Shop, Bistro, Umbrellas
C. P. Two (323) 466-8201
Cafe tables, cafe chairs, cafe lamps and more.
FormDecor, Inc. (310) 558-2582
America's largest event rental supplier of 20th Century furniture and accessories for Modern and Mid-Century styles.
LCW Props (818) 243-0707
Tables, Chairs, Patio Dressing
Lennie Marvin Enterprises, Inc. (Prop Heaven) (818) 841-5882
wrought iron, marble, tile top, bistro
Modern Props (323) 934-3000
contemporary cafe furniture, futuristic cafe furniture, various heights, cafe furniture multiples
Sony Pictures Studios-Prop House (Off Lot) (310) 244-5999

Universal Studios Property & Hardware Dept (818) 777-2784
Prop cafe tables, cafe chairs, cafe umbrellas and more for rent.

Cafeteria Counter/Line

See Also: Counters* Vendor Carts & Concession Counters
AIR Designs (818) 768-6639
Complete Cafeteria Setups, Food Prep, Heat Lamps, Trays, Dishwasher, Tables, Modular Seating, Trash Cans

Caged Vapor Proof Lights

See Also: Bulkhead Lights* Lanterns* Light Fixtures* Nautical
Dressing & Props
Alley Cats Studio Rentals   (818) 982-9178
working, w/cages
E.C. Prop Rentals   (818) 764-2008
high multiples & mounting styles, w/all globe colors

E.C. PROP RENTALS
11846 SHERMAN WAY NORTH HOLLYWOOD CA 91605
818-764-2008

Modern Props   (323) 934-3000
caged vapor proof lights/vapor lights
RC Vintage, Inc.   (818) 765-7107
Large Selection
Sony Pictures Studios-Fixtures   (310) 244-5996
5933 W Slauson Ave, Culver City, CA, 90230
period to present day
www.sonypicturesstudios.com
Universal Studios Property & Hardware Dept   (818) 777-2784
Caged vapor proof lights/vapor lights for rent.

Cages

See: Animal Cages* Bird Cages/Houses

Cakes

See: Food, Artificial Food* Food, Food Stylists

Calculators

See: Business Machines* Computers* Science Equipment

Calendars

See: Art, Supplies & Stationery* Office Equipment & Dressing

Calligraphy

Anne Robin Calligraphy   (917) 863-0899
Call for Appointment - Los Angeles & New York
Lettering and calligraphy for props, credits, titles, logos and for events
(invitations, place cards, envelopes, etc.)
anne@annerobin.com * www.annerobin.com
Collins Visual Media   (818) 686-6581
10518 Johanna Ave, Shadow Hills, CA, 91040
We change symbols and matter into spirit with our calligraphy designs and
layout at any size.
www.collinsvisualmedia.com
Designing Letters   (310) 702-4042
4032 Marcasel Ave, West Los Angeles, CA, 90066
custom lettering props, ancient/modern, manuscript & letters, logo lettering,
titles
www.deannsingh.com

Calliopes

Enchanted Melodies Music Machine Co.   (818) 894-5694
Call for Appt.
Circus Organ/Carousel Band Organ/Calliope on wheels Must see & hear to
believe! Create a festive atmosphere!

Camera Equipment

See Also: Motion Picture Camera Equipment* Motion Picture
Production Equip., Period* Motion Picture Projectors* Press
Equipment* Surveillance Equipment* Video Camera Equipment &
Services
Castex Rentals   (323) 462-1468
1044 N Cole Ave, Hollywood, CA, 90038
Profoto, lighting, soft boxes, tripods, tripod heads.
service@castexrentals.com * www.castexrentals.com

CASTEX
Hollywood *California*

*Serving the Motion Picture &
Photography Industries Since 1955*

**Production, Grip, Lighting
Expendables & More...**

1044 Cole Avenue, Hollywood, CA 90038
Tel: 323.462.1468 • Fax: 323.462.3719

www.castexrentals.com

The Hand Prop Room LP.   (323) 931-1534
Cameras and Camera Equipment
History For Hire, Inc.   (818) 765-7767
period,motion picture,still; full line period dollies, darkroom
LCW Props   (818) 243-0707
Point & Shoot, Digital SLR, Tripods, Period - Present, News, ID & Passport,
35mm
Motion Picture Marine   (310) 951-1110
578 Washington Blvd Ste 866, Marina Del Rey, CA, 90292
marine production company, camera & boats, camera stabilization mounts
including the Perfect Horizon
davidgrober1@gmail.com * www.perfect-horizon.com
Old N Country Prop Shop, LLC   (818) 423-2599
Many vintage cameras, from 8mm, Polaroid, SLR, Brownie, etc. Magic Lantern
in antique wood box. Movie projectors, etc.
Omega/Cinema Props   (323) 466-8201
Polaroid cameras, kodak cameras, instamatic cameras, and much more from
period to modern.
RJR Props   (404) 349-7600
Security cameras, movie cameras, personal cameras, news cameras and more
for rent.
Samy's Cameras   (323) 938-2420
431 S Fairfax Ave, Los Angeles, CA, 90036
everything photographic
www.samys.com
Sony Pictures Studios-Prop House (Off Lot)   (310) 244-5999
Albums, camera bags, film cans, film reels, projector screens, slide viewers,
photographic supplies, tripods, more
Universal Studios Property & Hardware Dept   (818) 777-2784
All kinds of camera equipment rentals available.

Camouflage Nets

See Also: Cargo Nets* Military Props & Equipment

Alley Cats Studio Rentals	(818) 982-9178
different sizes, shapes	
E.C. Prop Rentals	(818) 764-2008
assorted desert color	
Green Set, Inc.	(818) 764-1231
Nets & Skins, Camouflage nets including: camo brown nets, camo green nets, even erosion cloths	
The Hand Prop Room LP.	(323) 931-1534
different sizes & shapes, military nets, large camouflage nets, army nets, fishing nets, large nets	
History For Hire, Inc.	(818) 765-7767
lots	
Jackson Shrub Supply, Inc.	(818) 982-0100
erosion cloth, dirt skins, camouflage netting, camo nets	
LCW Props	(818) 243-0707
Different Sizes & Shapes, Brown, Green	
Picture Start Props	(818) 255-5472
Both brown camouflage nets and green camouflage nets	
RDD U.S.A. Inc.	(213) 742-0666
4638 E Washington Blvd, Commerce, CA, 90040	
various sizes & styles, woodland & desert	
www.rddusa.com	
Supply Sergeant	(323) 849-3744
503 N Victory Blvd, Burbank, CA, 91502	
military nets, army nets, navy nets, camping nets, camp nets	
david@jacksgt.com * www.supplysergeantshop.com	
Universal Studios Property & Hardware Dept	(818) 777-2784
Camouflage nets of various sizes for rent.	

Campers

See: RV Vehicles & Travel Trailers, Equip & Parts

Camping Equipment

See Also: Binoculars, Scopes & Telescopes* Camouflage Nets*
Canopies, Tents, Gazebos, Cabanas* Fishing Equipment & Tackle*
Lanterns* Sporting Goods & Services* Walkie-Talkies

The Hand Prop Room LP.	(323) 931-1534
stoves, ice chest, lanterns, sleeping bags, adult	
History For Hire, Inc.	(818) 765-7767
period, contemporary, great coolers	
LCW Props	(818) 243-0707
Tents, Cots, Outdoor Kitchen BBQ, Pots & pans, Backpacks, Military Surplus	
Sony Pictures Studios-Prop House (Off Lot)	(310) 244-5999
hiking backpacks, backpacking backpacks, bedrolls, sleeping bags, canteens, fanny packs, canes, walking sticks, more	
Universal Studios Property & Hardware Dept	(818) 777-2784
Prop camping equipment for rent.	

Candelabras

See Also: Lanterns

Castle Antiques & Design	(818) 765-5000
11924 Vose St, N Hollywood, CA, 91605	
All styles of brass and silver Candelabras and Candle Holders and more	
info@castleantiques.net * www.castleprophouse.com	
Dapper Cadaver	(818) 771-0818
Wrought iron candelabras. Tabletop candelabras and floor candelabras.	
The Hand Prop Room LP.	(323) 931-1534
period-present	
History For Hire, Inc.	(818) 765-7767
table top, Gothic, iron, brass	
LCW Props	(818) 243-0707
Brass, Religious, Silver Plated, Many	
Modern Props	(323) 934-3000
contemporary candlebras, futuristic candelabras	
Prop Services West	(818) 503-2790

ShopWildThings	(928) 855-6075
2880 Sweetwater Ave, Lake Havasu City, AZ, 86406	
Event Decor, Beaded Curtains, Chain Curtains, String Curtains & Columns, Crystal Columns. Reliable service & delivery.	
help@shopwildthings.com * www.shopwildthings.com	
Sony Pictures Studios-Fixtures	(310) 244-5996
5933 W Slauson Ave, Culver City, CA, 90230	
period to present day, large sel	
www.sonypicturesstudios.com	
Universal Studios Property & Hardware Dept	(818) 777-2784
Candelabras of all kinds; period to present; fancy to plain; electric to candle all for rent.	
Used Church Items, Religious Rentals	(412) 220-2272
115 East Barr Street, Mcdonald, PA, 15057	
Candelabras - 3-lite, 7-lite, floor, tabletop, wrought iron, large, small, catholic, votive stands, sanctuary.	
www.religiousrentals.com	
Warner Bros. Studios Property Department	(818) 954-2181
Period, hanging, silver, ornate, metal, floor standing, candelabra shades, brass, decorative	

Candles

See Also: Candelabras* Hobby & Craft Supplies

Antonino Ajello & Bros. House of Candles	(310) 204-4724
10315 Washington Blvd, Culver City, CA, 90232	
Double Wick Candles and Triple Wick Candles all sizes/dimensions. Cater to industry schedules. Events/home design.	
www.houseofcandlesculvercity.com	
General Wax & Candle Company	(818) 765-6357
6863 Beck Ave, N. Hollywood, CA, 91605	
Open Tues-Sat	
www.genwax.com	
ShopWildThings	(928) 855-6075
2880 Sweetwater Ave, Lake Havasu City, AZ, 86406	
Event Decor, Beaded Curtains, Chain Curtains, String Curtains & Columns, Crystal Columns. Reliable service & delivery.	
help@shopwildthings.com * www.shopwildthings.com	
Sony Pictures Studios-Prop House (Off Lot)	(310) 244-5999
battery operated candles, bar candles, candelabras, tapers, glass candels, candle holders, candle lamps, candle lanterns	
Universal Studios Property & Hardware Dept	(818) 777-2784
Scented candles, religious candles, prayer candles, tea candles and more.	
Used Church Items, Religious Rentals	(412) 220-2272
115 East Barr Street, Mcdonald, PA, 15057	
Beeswax Candles, Candle Holders, Candlesticks, Processional Candles, Votive Candles, Altar Candles	
www.religiousrentals.com	

Candy Counters

See: Candy Jars* Candy Racks* Display Cases, Racks & Fixtures (Store)

Candy Jars

See Also: Candy Racks

C. P. Two	(323) 466-8201
Glass candy jars, ceramic candy jars, apothecary candy jars, plastic candy jars.	
The Hand Prop Room LP.	(323) 931-1534
period-present	
History For Hire, Inc.	(818) 765-7767
large inventory, filled	
RC Vintage, Inc.	(818) 765-7107
40s, 50s & 60s Glass, jars to entire display cases & racks for candy specifically, incl. faux candy and gumball machines	
Universal Studios Property & Hardware Dept	(818) 777-2784
Glass jars and plastic jars for candy or with candy all for rent.	
Warner Bros. Studios Property Department	(818) 954-2181
Candy jars of all kinds, shapes and sizes.	

Candy Racks

See Also: Candy Jars

AIR Designs   **(818) 768-6639**
Displays, Convenience Store, Countertop & Free Standing

The Hand Prop Room LP.   **(323) 931-1534**
vintage candy racks, antique candy rack, metal candy rack, steel candy rack, 3 level candy rack

History For Hire, Inc.   **(818) 765-7767**
filled

Sony Pictures Studios-Prop House (Off Lot)   **(310) 244-5999**

Canes

The Costume House   **(818) 508-9933**

DutchGuard   **(800) 821-5157**
412 W. 10th Street, Kansas City, MO, 64105
customer service (816) 221-3581. canes, staffs, sword canes & walking sticks, a novel selection
www.dutchguard.com

The Hand Prop Room LP.   **(323) 931-1534**
period-present

History For Hire, Inc.   **(818) 765-7767**
plain & fancy

LCW Props   **(818) 243-0707**
Plain & Fancy

Omega/Cinema Props   **(323) 466-8201**
Walking canes & walking sticks; wooden canes, metal canes, bamboo canes

Prop Services West   **(818) 503-2790**

Universal Studios Property & Hardware Dept   **(818) 777-2784**
Walking sticks and canes of many time periods and taste all for rent.

Canoes

See: Boats & Water Sport Vehicles

Canopies, Tents, Gazebos, Cabanas

See Also: Audience Seating* Carnival Dressing/Supplies* Military Props & Equipment* Sewing Services, Industrial

2 Feathers Tipi   **(530) 816-0635**
P.O. Box 586, Westwood, CA, 96137
We specialize in tipis, including delivery and setup/strike
http://2featherstipi.com

AA Surplus Sales Co., Inc.   **(323) 526-3622**
2940 E Olympic Blvd, Los Angeles, CA, 90023
U.S. Military tents, GP Tents, Pup Tents, Hexagon Tents, Command Post Tents & more.
surplusking@hotmail.com * www.aasurplus.com

American Awning   **(323) 222-7500**
1901 N San Fernando Rd, Los Angeles, CA 90065
canopies
info@americanawningabc.com * www.americanawning1.com

Badia Design, Inc.   **(818) 762-0130**
5420 Vineland Ave, N Hollywood, CA, 91601
Badia Design Inc. has tents for your Moroccan themed party, wedding or special event.
info@badiadesign.com * www.badiadesign.com

Castex Rentals   **(323) 462-1468**
1044 N Cole Ave, Hollywood, CA, 90038
Caravan and EZ up dealer (all sizes), sales and rentals, custom canopies and canopy parts
service@castexrentals.com * www.castexrentals.com

Chattanooga Tent Co.   **(800) 843-8514**
1110 Oak St, Chattanooga, TN, 37403
event & production tents & awnings
www.chattanoogatent.com

Fall Creek Corporation   **(765) 482-1861**
PO Box 92, Whitestown, IN, 46075
Civil War era, military & civilian. historical to custom tents
ajfulks@fcsutler.com * www.fcsutler.com

History For Hire, Inc.   **(818) 765-7767**
pup tents, also cabanas

L. A. Circus   **(323) 751-3486**
Call for Appt, Los Angeles, CA, 90047
circus tents, vintage circus tents, largest circus trailers, ticket booths, circus trailers, circus linens
circusinc@aol.com * www.lacircus.com

L. A. Party Works   **(888) 527-2789**
9712 Alpaca St, S El Monte, CA, 91733
Canopies and cabanas, EZ UPs and tents for rent.
partyworks@aol.com * www.partyworksinteractive.com

LCW Props (818) 243-0707
Tents, Inflatable Domes, EZ-Ups

Panther Primitives Inc (800) 487-2684
P.O. Box 32 State Route 33, Normantown, WV, 25267
Native American Tipis, American Civil Ware Tents, French & Indian War Tents, Medieval Tents & more.
www.pantherprimitives.com

Raj Tents (310) 320-6600
1170 W. Mahalo Pl, Rancho Dominguez CA, 90220
We are best known for offering our Moroccan, Indian, and Beach Chic themes as well as a variety of others.
http://www.rajtents.com

RDD U.S.A. Inc. (213) 742-0666
4638 E Washington Blvd, Commerce, CA, 90040
largest supplier of many styles of tents & tarps
www.rddusa.com

Supply Sergeant (323) 849-3744
503 N Victory Blvd, Burbank, CA, 91502
military tents, camping tents, army tents, heavy duty tents, weather tents, military tarps, army tarps
david@jacksgt.com * www.supplysergeantshop.com

Sword & Stone (818) 562-6548
Wrought iron carnival tent

Yurts of America (317) 377-9878
4375 Sellers St, Lawrence, IN, 46226
14'-30' yurt kits
info@yurtsofamerica.com * www.yurtsofamerica.com

Canvas

See Also: Fabrics Nautical Dressing & Props*

Damian Canvas Works (310) 822-2343
322 Culver Blvd #261, Playa Del Rey, CA 90293
Mainly for boats & props. Canvas, paintings, furniture, clothing, jewelry
www.damiancanvasworks.com

Universal Studios Property & Hardware Dept (818) 777-2784
Painting canvases, canvas tents, canvas supplies and more.

Caps

See: Headwear - Hats, Bonnets, Caps, Helmets Etc.

Car Hoists

See: Automotive/Garage Equip. & Parts

Car Parts

See: Automotive/Garage Equip. & Parts

Car Seat, Child

See: Children/Baby Accessories & Bedroom

Cargo Nets

See Also: Chain & Rope Nautical Dressing & Props* Warehouse Dressing*

LCW Props (818) 243-0707
Fishing nets, fishing webb net, crate of nets, and more nautical equipment

Pacific Fibre & Rope Co. (800) 825-7673
903 Flint Ave, Wilmington, CA, 90748
moreinfo@pacificfibre.com * www.pacificfibre.com

Carhop Trays

AIR Designs (818) 768-6639
Door & Steering Wheel Mount

The Hand Prop Room LP. (323) 931-1534
vintage carhop trays, aluminum carhop trays, metal carhop trays, plastic carhop trays

History For Hire, Inc. (818) 765-7767
and the stuff that goes on them

RC Vintage, Inc. (818) 765-7107
40s, 50s & 60s, large and small trays

Sony Pictures Studios-Prop House (Off Lot) (310) 244-5999

Caribbean Dressing

See: Jungle Dressing Tikis & Tropical Dressing*

Caricature Drawings

See: Art For Rent (Cleared Art)

Carnival Dressing/Supplies

See Also: Balloons & Balloon Sculptures Calliopes* Carnival Games & Rides* Carousel Horses* Circus Equipment/Dressing/Costumes* Clowns* Fun House Mirrors* Memorabilia & Novelties* Ticket Booths* Vendor Carts & Concession Counters*

Amusement Svcs/Candyland Amusements (818) 266-4056
18653 Ventura Blvd Ste 235, Tarzana, CA, 91356
Games, rides, food stands, ticket booths. We are the owner, no middleman. Straight from the Carnival itself
raymond@candylandamusements.com * www.candylandamusements.com

Artistic Carnival & Circus Design (323) 751-3486
Call for Appointment.
Circus & carnival dressing, costumes, consulting services

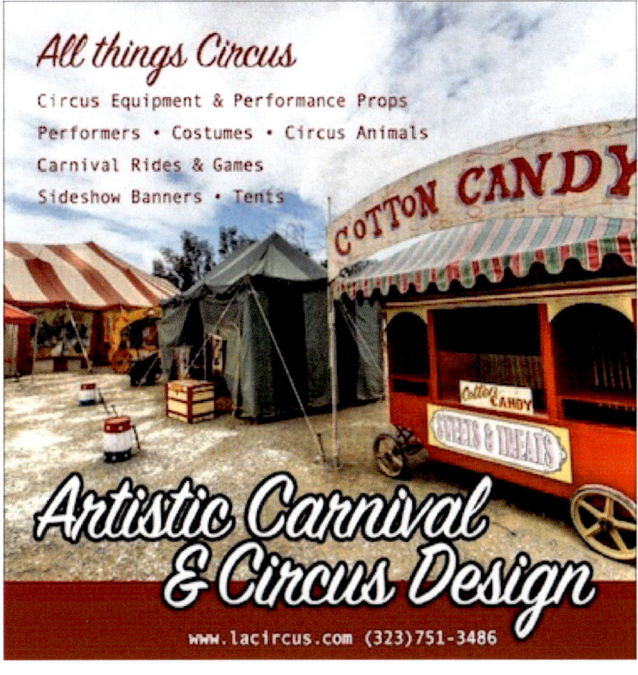

Collins Visual Media (818) 686-6581
10518 Johanna Ave, Shadow Hills, CA, 91040
We have vast knowledge and experience in creating authentic carnival and circus signage with hand-lettering and aging.
www.collinsvisualmedia.com

Dapper Cadaver (818) 771-0818
Sideshow props and poster art. Freakshow oddities and skeletons.

E.C. Prop Rentals (818) 764-2008
string lights & barricades

History For Hire, Inc. (818) 765-7767
Mardi Gras heads, trunks, bed of nails

LISTINGS FOR THIS CATEGORY CONTINUE ON THE
FOLLOWING PAGE

L. A. Circus   (323) 751-3486
Call for Appt, Los Angeles, CA, 90047
tentage, silent flags, circus posters, steam train, costumes, side show banner, circus dressing room, horses
circusinc@aol.com * www.lacircus.com

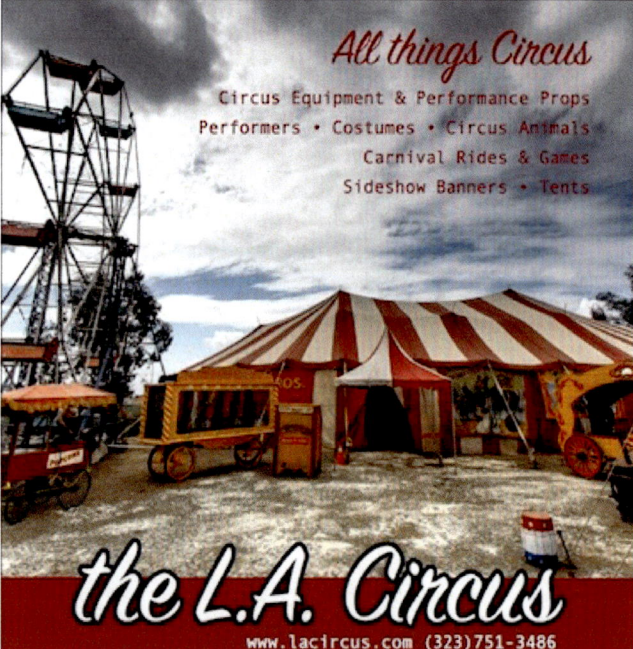

L. A. Party Works   (888) 527-2789
9712 Alpaca St, S El Monte, CA, 91733
in Vancouver tel. 604-589-4101. booths, games, vendor carts & much more
partyworks@aol.com * www.partyworksinteractive.com
Lennie Marvin Enterprises, Inc. (Prop Heaven)   (818) 841-5882
side show banners, games, machines, mechanical figures, cut-outs, Carnival/Mardi Gras pieces
RC Vintage, Inc.   (818) 765-7107
Bumper cars, Clown Head Trash Cans, Funhouse Mirrors, Carnival Games, String Lights, Trash Cans w/ Clown Head Lids

1988

40 YEARS OF DEBBIES BOOK

CD's outsell vinyl records for the first time. NASA first warns congress of the greenhouse effect and dangers of global warming. South Africa frees Nelson Mandela after 27 years.

We saw the end of the Cold War, the Persian Gulf War, and East & West Germany united. **"The Simpsons"** debuts on Fox and **"Seinfeld"** debuts on NBC. **"Murphy Brown", "Wanted", "The Wonder Years"** and **"America's Most Wanted"** were on T.V. **"Rain Man", 'Who Framed Roger Rabbit"** and **"Big"** were on the big screen and **"The Last Emperor"** was the year's big winner.

Dwight took the easy way out and just added the "#5" to the cover and we were off and running for another year. The book's category index got a little more sophisticated than it had been. This was the first year I started taking display ads in the book. Only 3 of those 8 advertisers (Dozer Office Furnishings, Omega/Cinema Props, and R.C. Vintage) are still around today. Long gone are Roschu, Hollywood Central Props, Advance Wall Covering, Cal State Store Fixtures, and Al's Studio Rentals.

5TH DEBBIE'S BOOK
A unique source book for the
FILM TELEVISION THEATRICAL ADVERTISING & DISPLAY
professional
5th edition prop & set dressing yellow pages

Carnival Games & Rides

See Also: Carnival Dressing/Supplies Carousel Horses* Circus Equipment/Dressing/Costumes* Game Booths*

Amusement Svcs/Candyland Amusements   (818) 266-4056
18653 Ventura Blvd Ste 235, Tarzana, CA, 91356
Carnival games, carnival rides, carnival food stands, ticket booths. We are the owner, no middleman.
raymond@candylandamusements.com * www.candylandamusements.com

L. A. Circus   (323) 751-3486
Call for Appt, Los Angeles, CA, 90047
tunnel of love swan, Barker Booths, Morland photo booths, ticket booths, small carrousel horses, mary go rounds
circusinc@aol.com * www.lacircus.com

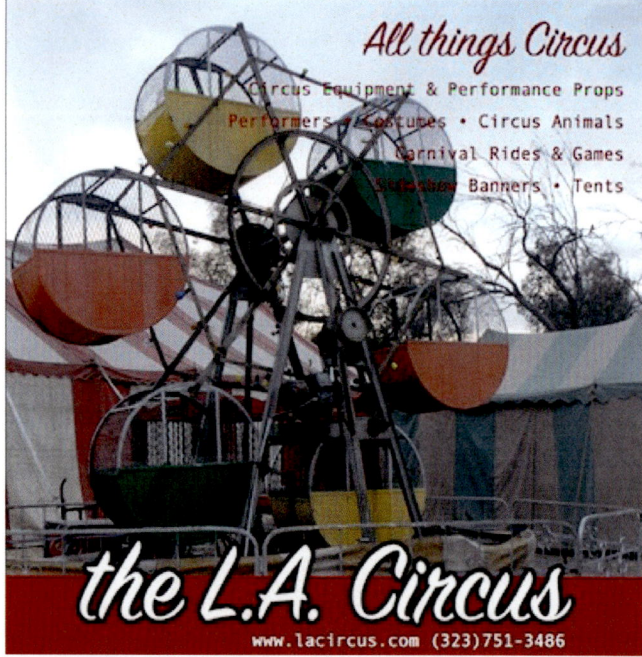

L. A. Party Works   **(888) 527-2789**
9712 Alpaca St, S El Monte, CA, 91733
in Vancouver tel. 604-589-4101. Carnival Games; dunk tanks, human bowling, crab races, zip lines & much more
partyworks@aol.com * www.partyworksinteractive.com

BOOK TODAY:
888-527-2789
partyworksusa.com

DUNK TANKS / RIDES / ZIP LINE / GAME BOOTHS / HIGH STRYKER / MORE

PARTYWORKS
INTERACTIVE

Carousel Horses

Amusement Svcs/Candyland Amusements   **(818) 266-4056**
18653 Ventura Blvd Ste 235, Tarzana, CA, 91356
carousel horses, carousel jets, carousel dragons, carousel cups, other rotating rides, tidal wave, ferris wheel, kite flyer, sizzler rock-o-plane
raymond@candylandamusements.com * www.candylandamusements.com
Universal Studios Property & Hardware Dept   **(818) 777-2784**
Prop carousel horses of many shapes, types and sizes for rent.

Carpet & Flooring

See Also: Tile, Marble, Granite, Etc. Studio Tile Flooring* Sono Tubes* Rugs* Red Carpeting, Events/Premiers* Dirt Skins* Art Deco Carpet & Rugs*

Collins Visual Media   **(818) 686-6581**
10518 Johanna Ave, Shadow Hills, CA, 91040
We print art and logos on seamless carpeting up to 16' x 60' plus we provide removable and permanent floor graphics.
www.collinsvisualmedia.com
FormDecor, Inc.   **(310) 558-2582**
America's largest event rental supplier of 20th Century furniture and accessories for Modern and Mid-Century styles.
Home Court Advantage   **(702) 400-2253**
241 W Charleston Blvd Ste 111, Las Vegas, NV, 89102
Basketball flooring/basketball paneling
www.homecourtrentals.com

Linoleum City, Inc.   **(323) 469-0063**
4849 Santa Monica Blvd, Hollywood, CA, 90029
Vinyl, Carpet, Linoleum, Hardwood, Laminate, Cork, Tile, Sisal, Seagrass, Bamboo, Area Rugs, Wall Cork, Dance Floors.
sales@linocity.com * www.linoleumcity.com

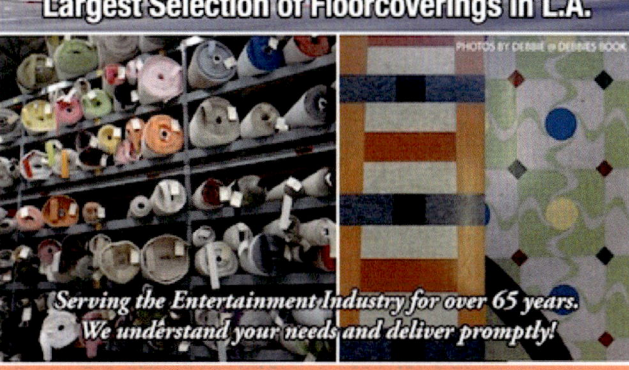

LINOLEUM CITY
Largest Selection of Floorcoverings in L.A.
PHOTOS BY DEBBIE @ DEBBIES BOOK
Serving the Entertainment Industry for over 65 years.
We understand your needs and deliver promptly!
Carpet • Vinyl • Cork • Carpet Runners • Hardwood Floors
Linoleum • Tiles • Laminate Floors • Ceramic Tiles
Window Treatments • Wall Coverings

Monarch Carpet   **(213) 388-0148**
3021 West Temple St, Los Angeles, CA, 90026
Carpet sales, carpet installation, custom rug fabricators, wood flooring, sisal, seagrass, ceramic tile, vinyl & more.
monarchcar@aol.com * www.monarchcarpet.com
Pacific Floor Company   **(818) 775-0438**
9300 Oso Ave, Chatsworth, CA, 91311
Design to Build Performance Floor Contractor; Gym Flooring, Fitness Flooring, Dance Flooring, Designer Flooring, & more.
sales@pacificfloor.com * www.pacificfloor.com

PACIFIC FLOOR   818.775.0438
PREMIUM PORTABLE MAPLE FLOORS

Services Include:
Portable Maple Basketball Court, Full Court or Half Court Rental, Portable Spalding G5 Hoops, Graphic Design Artwork for Rental, Athletic Wood Floors, and Dance Floors
www.PortableMapleBasketballFloors.com

Prop Services West   **(818) 503-2790**
Warner Bros. Drapery, Upholstery & Flooring   **(818) 954-1831**
4000 Warner Blvd Bldg 30, Burbank, CA, 91522
All grades of residential & commercial carpet; Indoor/Outdoor; Linoleum; VCT Tile; installation
wbsfdrapery@warnerbros.com * www.wbdrapery.com
ZG04 DECOR   **(818) 853-8040**

Carport Canopies

See: Awnings* Canopies, Tents, Gazebos, Cabanas

Carriages, Horse Drawn

Barton's Horse Drawn Carriages & Sleighs   **(626) 447-6693**
518 Fairview Ave, Arcadia CA, 91007
Antique carriages/sleighs, transport to site, drivers provided, realistic brown prop horse on wheels, saddles, harnesses, 1800s-1900s

Gorygirl Halloween Event Staging and Prop Rental   **(818) 912-6902**
Large Halloween style Horse Drawn Carriage Hearse Foam and wood and metal gold casket

Harris Stage Lines   **(805) 237-1860**
5995 N River Rd, Paso Robles, CA, 93446
horse drawn vehicles for hire: stagecoach, carriages, chariots.
www.harrisstagelines.com

Universal Studios Property & Hardware Dept   **(818) 777-2784**
Horse drawn carriages, horse drawn chariots, and more for rent.

Warner Bros. Studios Property Department   **(818) 954-2181**
Western carriages, Buggies, Covered Farm Wagons, Stagecoach wagons

Cars

See: Vehicle Preparation Services* Vehicles/Picture Vehicles

Carts

See: Locations, Airport Dressing & Hangars* Vendor Carts & Concession Counters

Carved Figures

History For Hire, Inc.   **(818) 765-7767**
ship's figureheads

Modern Props   **(323) 934-3000**
contemporary figurines, futuristic figurines, carved figurines/carved figures

Ob-jects   **(818) 351-4200**
carved figures/carved figurines for rent

Omega/Cinema Props   **(323) 466-8201**
Carved figurines from ancient to modern of various animals, sports and religions.

Sony Pictures Studios-Prop House (Off Lot)   **(310) 244-5999**

Sword & Stone   **(818) 562-6548**
Pirate figurines, armor figurines, skulls and more

Universal Studios Property & Hardware Dept   **(818) 777-2784**
Carved figures of different backgrounds, ethnicities, and mediums for rent.

Used Church Items, Religious Rentals   **(412) 220-2272**
115 East Barr Street, Mcdonald, PA, 15057
Patron Saints, Angels, Jesus, Joseph, Mary, Wood & Plaster, Pietas, Stations of the Cross, Scenes. All sizes.
www.religiousrentals.com

ZG04 DECOR   **(818) 853-8040**
Animal, Figurative, Relief, Tribal, African, Busts, Dogs, Horses, Male, Female

Cases

See Also: Briefcases* Crates/ Vaults* Display Cases, Racks & Fixtures (Store)* Futuristic Furniture, Props, Decorations* Luggage* Musical Instrument Cases* Trophies/Trophy Cases

Astro Audio Video Lighting, Inc.   **(818) 549-9915**
6615 San Fernando Rd, Glendale, CA, 91201
Road cases, lighting bags, Pro X Cases, Stand Cases, Turntable Cases, Keyboard Bags and more for your traveling needs.
www.astroavl.com

E.C. Prop Rentals   **(818) 764-2008**
Road boxes, specialty equipment cases, metal briefcases

The Hand Prop Room LP.   **(323) 931-1534**

LCW Props   **(818) 243-0707**
Huge selection, Molded Cases, Anvil Cases, Pelican Cases, Road Cases, Wood Cases, Any Kind.

Cash Registers

A. D. Business Solutions   **(818) 765-5353**
11412 Vanowen St, N. Hollywood, CA 91605
Cash registers, point of sale equipment, touch screens, credit card devices, time card devices & more.
info@cashandcredit.com * www.cashandcredit.com

AIR Designs   **(818) 768-6639**
Period to Modern, Practical

American Cash Registers   **(323) 664-4586**
507 N Hoover St, Los Angeles, CA, 90004
sell, rent, lease & repair; cash registers & point of sale machines from 1900 to present
erwin@american-pos.com * www.american-pos.com

FormDecor, Inc.   **(310) 558-2582**
Brass antique cash registers for rent.

The Hand Prop Room LP.   **(323) 931-1534**
period-modern

History For Hire, Inc.   **(818) 765-7767**

LCW Props   **(818) 243-0707**
Digital & Analog, Period - Present

RC Vintage, Inc.   **(818) 765-7107**
modern to early 1900s Brass and Contemporary

Sony Pictures Studios-Prop House (Off Lot)   **(310) 244-5999**

Universal Studios Property & Hardware Dept   **(818) 777-2784**
Vintage cash registers, modern cash registers, manual cash registers, electric cash registers all for rent.

Casino Gaming Equipment

See: Gambling Equipment

Caskets

See Also: Cemetery Dressing* Mortuary* Religious Articles

ABC Caskets Factory   **(323) 268-1783**
1705 N Indiana St, Los Angeles, CA, 90063
Manufacture fine wood & metal caskets and funeral dressing; biers, carts, skirts, church trucks, lowering devices & more
factorydirect@abettercasket.com * www.abettercasket.com

California Casket Co.   **(310) 963-3905**
12421 Venice Blvd Ste 1, Los Angeles, CA, 90066
Caskets, grave markers, flower arrangements, urns, also hearse rentals, funeral supplies. Can rent
calcasket@aol.com * www.losangelesfuneralservice.com

Dapper Cadaver   **(818) 771-0818**
Modern wood & metal caskets, toe-pinchers and vintage coffins. Casket stands.

Gorygirl Halloween Event Staging and Prop Rental   **(818) 912-6902**
Toe pincher distressed pallet Caskets, Half ground breaker caskets. Bulk pallet coffins need 2-4 week lead time.

The Hand Prop Room LP.   **(323) 931-1534**

History For Hire, Inc.   **(818) 765-7767**
old, new, Dracula

LCW Props   **(818) 243-0707**
Wood, Metal, Military, Rigged

Sony Pictures Studios-Prop House (Off Lot)   **(310) 244-5999**

Universal Studios Property & Hardware Dept   **(818) 777-2784**
Metal caskets & wood caskets for rent.

Cat Scratching Post, Climbers, Condos & Beds

See: Pet Furniture, Houses, Clothing

Catering

See Also: Beer Equipment, Taps & Coolers* Events, Decorations, Supplies & Services* Food, Artificial Food* Food, Food Stylists

Along Came Mary Events   **(323) 931-9082**
247 Lorriane Blvd, Los Angeles, CA 90004
www.alongcamemary.com

Big Screen Cuisine Catering   **(818) 345-0009**
6924 Canby Ave Ste 109, Reseda, CA, 91335
Catering for film/TV since 1989, quick turnaround
www.bscevents.com

Bobby Weisman Caterers   **(818) 843-9999**
736 S. Glenwood Pl, Burbank, CA, 91506
Serving the Entertainment Industry since 1984. Our mobile kitchens travel nationwide.
bobbyweisman@sbcglobal.net * www.bobbyweisman.com

Command Performance Catering   **(800) 817-3232**
5273 N. Commerce Ave, Unit # 6, Moorpark, CA, 93021
www.cpcatering.com

Java The Truck   **(310) 717-6967**
Call for Service, Los Angeles, CA
Mobile coffee shop offering the widest selection around, 24/7. Self contained, 2 barristas, no setup time, blended drink
www.javathetruck.com

Rise & Shine Catering   **(310) 649-0906**
6511 1/4 South Sepulveda Blvd, Los Angeles, CA, 90045
Breakfast & lunch catering. Film locations, office meetings, private events.
info@riseandshinecatering.com * riseandshinecatering.com

Someone's In The Kitchen   **(818) 343-5151**
5973 Reseda Blvd, Tarzana, CA, 91356
www.sitk.com

Too Tasty Catering   **(818) 355-5431**
Call For Arrangements Glendale, CA, 91201
Highest quality bistro gourmet food at affordable prices. All items hand-crafted from scratch.
www.tootasty-catering.com

Universal Studios Special Events   **(818) 777-9466**
100 Universal City Plaza, Universal City, CA, 91608
universal.specialevents@nbcuni.com * universalstudioslot.com/special-events

Wolfgang Puck Catering   **(323) 491-1250**
6801 Hollywood Blvd Ste 513, Hollywood, CA, 90028
www.wolfgangpuckcatering.com

Cats

See: Animals (Live), Services, Trainers & Wranglers

Catwalks

See: Grating, Grated Flooring, Catwalks

Cauldrons

See: Occult/Spiritual/Metaphysical

Cellular Phones

See: Telephones, Cellular

Cemetery Dressing

See Also: Caskets* Florists/Floral Design* Morgue* Mortuary

Dapper Cadaver (818) 771-0818
Tombstones, monuments, obelisks & crypts. Angels, crosses & military. Cemetery combos.

Green Set, Inc. (818) 764-1231
high quality tombstones, urns decorative and plain, many grave markers, cemetery walls

The Hand Prop Room LP. (323) 931-1534
caskets, prop headstones, fake bats

History For Hire, Inc. (818) 765-7767
headstones

Jackson Shrub Supply, Inc. (818) 982-0100
over 200 units in top quality fiberglass, grave markers, headstones, funeral dressing

LCW Props (818) 243-0707
Tombstones Real & Fake, Caskets, Coffins

Sony Pictures Studios-Prop House (Off Lot) (310) 244-5999

Universal Studios Graphic Design & Sign Shop (818) 777-2350
custom tombstones

Universal Studios Property & Hardware Dept (818) 777-2784
Prop tombstones and other cemetery dressing for rent.

Centrifuges

LCW Props (818) 243-0707
Large & Small, Working, Rigged

Machinery & Equipment Co., Inc. (909) 599-3916
115 N Cataract Ave, San Dimas, CA, 91773
Used industrial and lab centrifuges including disc stack, basket, decanter, nozzle, separators, clarifiers and more.
sherri@machineryandequipment.com * www.machineryandequipment.com

Universal Studios Property & Hardware Dept (818) 777-2784
Prop centrifuges for rent.

Ceramic Casting & Manufacturing

See: Prop Design & Manufacturing* Prop Reproduction & Fabrication* Staff Shops

Ceramics

See: Decorative Accessories* Pottery* Urns

Certificates

See Also: Art, Supplies & Stationery* Office Equipment & Dressing

The Hand Prop Room LP. (323) 931-1534
printed graphics, office dressing

History For Hire, Inc. (818) 765-7767
custom mfg.

Hollywood Cinema Arts (818) 504-7333
Thousands of Certificates in ornate custom frames to standard black frames.

Hollywood Studio Gallery (323) 462-1116
100s to choose from,custom-medical-miltary,school,etc

LCW Props (818) 243-0707
Custom Graphics, Legal, Sports, Diplomas, Dentistry, Medical, Professional

Omega/Cinema Props (323) 466-8201
Medical certificates, diplomas, dental certificates, achievement certificates and much more!

On Set Graphics (661) 233-6786
Web Based Business
100% cleared office certificates for everything from medical certificates and dental certificates to participation awards.
info@onsetgraphics.com * www.onsetgraphics.com

Prop Services West (818) 503-2790

Sony Pictures Studios-Prop House (Off Lot) (310) 244-5999
large selection

Universal Studios Graphic Design & Sign Shop (818) 777-2350
custom

Universal Studios Property & Hardware Dept (818) 777-2784
Prop certificates for rent; graduation diplomas, medical certification and more.

Chain & Rope

See Also: Camouflage Nets* Cargo Nets

Alley Cats Studio Rentals (818) 982-9178
all widths,lengths,styles rope; fake & real chain

E.C. Prop Rentals (818) 764-2008
wide assortment

The Hand Prop Room LP. (323) 931-1534
period-modern

History For Hire, Inc. (818) 765-7767
rope & chain

LCW Props (818) 243-0707
Large Selection Of Assorted Sizes & Styles. Boating, Industrial, Sporting

Memphis Net & Twine Co., Inc. (901) 458-2656
2481 Matthews Ave, Memphis, TN, 38108
Fish Nets, Seine Nets, Gill Nets, Trammel Nets, Cast Nets, Fish Netting, Trawls, Rope & Twine
sportsinfo@memphisnet.net * www.memphisnet.net

Pacific Fibre & Rope Co. (800) 825-7673
903 Flint Ave, Wilmington, CA, 90748
rope manufacturing, all kinds, as much as you need, hwr fittings, tools, nets, but no chains, rope
moreinfo@pacificfibre.com * www.pacificfibre.com

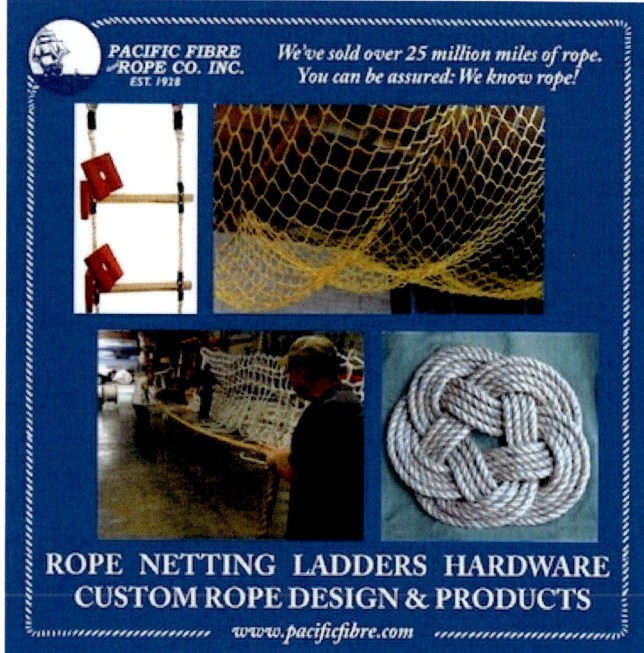

Chain Hoists

See Also: Automotive/Garage Equip. & Parts* Construction Site
Equipment* Rigging, Equipment or Services
AIR Designs (818) 768-6639
Block & Tackle Engine Hoists
Astro Audio Video Lighting, Inc. (818) 549-9915
6615 San Fernando Rd, Glendale, CA, 91201
Chain hoists and rope hoists for rigging.
www.astroavl.com
E.C. Prop Rentals (818) 764-2008
large & small, also A frames

Chain Link Fence

See: Fences

Chainmail

See: Armor, Chainmail, Suits of Armor

Chair Covers

See: Events, Decorations, Supplies & Services* Slipcovers*
Upholstery Materials/Services

Chair Risers

See: Audience Seating* Stages, Portable & Steel Deck

Chairs

See Also: Benches* Chairs, Senate Chamber (Sets)* Director's
Chairs, Bags, Pouches* Folding Chairs/Tables* Furniture,
Outdoor/Patio* Futons & Bean Bag Chairs* Opera Chairs*
Slipcovers* Stools
Advanced Liquidators Office Furniture (818) 763-3470
new & used, all quality levels, huge variety of models, designers, upholstery,
costs, purpose, and types.
AIR Designs (818) 768-6639
Restaurant/Bar, Coffee Shop, Fast Food, Bistro, Cafeteria, Interior & Exterior
Bridge Furniture & Props Los Angeles (818) 433-7100
We carry modern & traditional furniture, lighting, accessories, art, & rugs. Items
are online for easy shopping.

BRIDGE LA
FURNITURE & PROPS
3210 Vanowen St.
Burbank, CA 91505
BridgeProps.com
Tel: 818.433.7100

C. P. Two (323) 466-8201
All kinds of chairs from patio and restaurant to folding and beach.
Castle Antiques & Design (818) 765-5000
11924 Vose St, N Hollywood, CA, 91605
Chairs of all sizes and styles including benches, ottomans, armchairs, sofas,
settees, chaise lounges, and dining chairs
info@castleantiques.net * www.castleprophouse.com

Dozar Office Furnishings (310) 559-9292
9937 Jefferson Blvd, Culver City, CA, 90232
Rentals X22. Office chairs, arm chairs, reception chairs, executive chairs,
waiting room chairs, wheel chairs
dozarrents@aol.com * www.dozarrents.com
E.C. Prop Rentals (818) 764-2008
High multiples, industrial, metal/castered/stools/etc.
Faux Library Studio Props, Inc. (818) 765-0096
luxury chairs, high end chairs, classical chairs, desk chairs, posh chairs,
elegant chairs, residential office chairs
FormDecor, Inc. (310) 558-2582
America's largest event rental supplier of 20th Century furniture and
accessories for Modern and Mid-Century styles.
LCW Props (818) 243-0707
Stacking, Upholstered, Futuristic, Office, Rocket Chairs
Lennie Marvin Enterprises, Inc. (Prop Heaven) (818) 841-5882
cafe seating, restaurant chairs, contemporary chairs, high qty.
Little Bohemia Rentals (818) 853-7506
11940 Sherman Rd, N Hollywood, CA, 91605
Vintage to contemporary lounge, club, cigar, reclining, bergere, Danish modern,
leather, slipper, high back, chair & ottoman
sales@wearelittlebohemia.com * www.wearelittlebohemia.com
Lux Lounge EFR (888) 247-4411
106 1/2 Judge John Aiso St #318, Los Angeles, CA, 90012
Many Chairs: Classic Chairs, Contemporary Chairs, Armless Chairs, Lounge
Chairs, Ghost Chairs
info@luxloungeefr.com * www.luxloungeefr.com
Modern Props (323) 934-3000
contemporary chairs, futuristic chairs, multiples chairs
Modernica Props (323) 664-2322
classic, modern, contemporary, multiples
NEST Studio Rentals, Inc. (818) 942-0339
contemporary, upholstered, dining, office
Ob-jects (818) 351-4200
decorative, contemporary, traditional, upholstery, dining chairs, ottomans,
loveseats, sofas, settees, sectionals
Old N Country Prop Shop, LLC (818) 423-2599
A large selection of modern chairs, traditional chairs, and antique chairs.
Omega/Cinema Props (323) 466-8201
All kinds of chairs from patio and restaurant to folding and beach.
Picture Start Props (818) 255-5472
All kinds of chairs. Dining, arm chairs, patio chairs
Prop Services West (818) 503-2790
A Royal Suite Home Furinishings (661) 259-7000
26536 Carl Boyer Dr, Santa Clarita, CA, 91350
A Royal Suite, family-owned since 1978, Features AMERICAN-MADE
Furniture, and the Finest Furniture at the Greatest Value
norb@ars-email.com * www.aroyalsuite.com
Sony Pictures Studios-Prop House (Off Lot) (310) 244-5999
large selection/multiples, adirondack chairs, armchairs, chair backs, folding
bamboo chairs, benches, beach chairs, more
Universal Studios Property & Hardware Dept (818) 777-2784
All kinds of chairs of different styles and time periods for rent.
Warner Bros. Studios Property Department (818) 954-2181
Dining, Wingback, Patio, Upholstered, folding, stacking, side, bentwood, Bank
of England, Barcelona, executive
ZG04 DECOR (818) 853-8040
Seating, Benches, Club Chairs, Side, Client, Dining, Desk, Swivel, Vanity,
Folding Chairs, Event Seating, Multiples

Chairs, Senate Chamber (Sets)

Chalk Boards

See Also: Office Equipment & Dressing* School Supplies, Desks &
Dressing
E.C. Prop Rentals (818) 764-2008
castered & wall-mount
The Hand Prop Room LP. (323) 931-1534
wall mounted chalkboards, rolling chalkboards, dry erase boards, chalk, chalk
erasers
History For Hire, Inc. (818) 765-7767
rolling & wall-mount
LCW Props (818) 243-0707
Many Sizes, Green, Black, White Boards, Freestanding
Prop Services West (818) 503-2790
RC Vintage, Inc. (818) 765-7107
including stand up menu chalk boards,
Sony Pictures Studios-Prop House (Off Lot) (310) 244-5999
all sizes
Universal Studios Property & Hardware Dept (818) 777-2784
Chalkboards for rent; from standing blackboards to wall mounted chalkboards
& grease boards/grease pen boards.

Chandeliers

Castle Antiques & Design (818) 765-5000
11924 Vose St, N Hollywood, CA, 91605
All styles and sizes of brass, crystal, glass, or metal chandeliers.
info@castleantiques.net * www.castleprophouse.com

Lux Lounge EFR (888) 247-4411
106 1/2 Judge John Aiso St #318, Los Angeles, CA, 90012
Chandeliers: Custom made Chandeliers, Classic Chandeliers, Crystal
Chandeliers, Luxury Chandeliers, Pendant Chandeliers
info@luxloungeefr.com * www.luxloungeefr.com

Omega/Cinema Props (323) 466-8201
Period to contemporary chandeliers.

Pasadena Antique Center and Annex (626) 449-7706
480 South Fair Oaks Ave, Pasadena, CA, 91105
Antique Chandeliers & Vintage Candle and Electric Chandeliers of all eras and
styles.
pasadenaantiqecenterandannex@gmail.com * bit.ly/PasadenaAntiqueCenter

Pasadena Antiques & Design (626) 389-3938
330 S Fair Oaks Avenue, Pasadena, CA, 91105
Antique & Mid-Century Chandeliers of all descriptions.
roy@antiquesofpasadena.com * www.antiquesofpasadena.com

Prop Services West (818) 503-2790

ShopWildThings (928) 855-6075
2880 Sweetwater Ave, Lake Havasu City, AZ, 86406
Event Decor, Beaded Curtains, Chain Curtains, String Curtains & Columns,
Crystal Columns. Reliable service & delivery.
help@shopwildthings.com * www.shopwildthings.com

Sony Pictures Studios-Fixtures (310) 244-5996
5933 W Slauson Ave, Culver City, CA, 90230
period to present day, large sel,art deco, brass, candle, chinese, crystal,
contemporary, court room, crystal, empire style, french, georgian, mission,
morrocan, novelty, period, spanish, traditional, victorian, western
www.sonypicturesstudios.com

Sony Pictures Studios-Prop House (Off Lot) (310) 244-5999
period chandeliers to modern chandeliers, chandelier shipping boxes

Universal Studios Property & Hardware Dept (818) 777-2784
Chandeliers of different sizes and time periods. Gold chandeliers, plain
chandeliers, crystal chandeliers & more.

Used Church Items, Religious Rentals (412) 220-2272
115 East Barr Street, Mcdonald, PA, 15057
Large Gothic Chandeliers, Wall Scones, Hanging, Wall Mount, Sanctuary
Lights, Votive Stands and Votive Lights.
www.religiousrentals.com

Warner Bros. Studios Property Department (818) 954-2181
Hanging, ballroom, crystal, antique, Entryway chandeliers, floor standing,
period, hallway, ornate

ZG04 DECOR (818) 853-8040
Classic Chandeliers, Crystal Chandeliers, Contemporary Chandeliers,
Traditional Chandeliers

Change Machines

See: Vending Machines

Chapel

See: Church, Chapel, Synagogue, Mosque

Charities & Donations

Amusement Svcs/Candyland Amusements (818) 266-4056
18653 Ventura Blvd Ste 235, Tarzana, CA, 91356
Games, rides, food stands, ticket booths. We are the owner, no middleman.
raymond@candylandamusements.com * www.candylandamusements.com

Habitat for Humanity of Greater Los Angeles (424) 246-3637
8739 E Artesia Blvd, Bellflower, CA, 90706
Habitat's ReStores are home-improvement thrift stores, helping to fund our
mission. Free pick-up, tax-deductible.
www.ShopHabitat.org

Hollywood Cinema Production Resources (310) 258-0123
any props/set material, will pick up, charity donation

The ReUse People (818) 244-5635
3015 Dolores St, Los Angeles, CA, 90065
We accept almost all types of building supplies and offer tax-deductible
donation receipts.
JeffCockerell@TheReUsePeople.org * www.TheReUsePeople.org

Charters

See: Aircraft, Charters & Aerial Services Nautical/Marine Services &
Charters* Trains*

Chase Lights

Astro Audio Video Lighting, Inc. (818) 549-9915
6615 San Fernando Rd, Glendale, CA, 91201
Various chase lights for purchase or rent including DJ effects and more.
www.astroavl.com

Universal Studios Property & Hardware Dept (818) 777-2784
Various chase light strings for different occasions.

Chastity Belts

See: Goth/Punk/Bondage/Fetish/Erotica Etc. Wardrobe,
Antique/Historical*

Check-out Stands

See: Grocery Check-out Stands (Complete)

Chemical Lab

See: Lab Equipment

Chestnut Carts/Machines

See: Vendor Carts & Concession Counters

Chicago Themed Parties

See: Events, Decorations, Supplies & Services Events,
Design/Planning/Production* Travel (City/Country) Themed Events*

Chicken Feeders

See: Farm Equipment & Dressing

Children's & Baby Clothing

See Also: Children/Baby Accessories & Bedroom
CBS Costume Rental (323) 575-2666
doubles & triples, infants & toddlers
The Costume House (818) 508-9933
christening gowns, school clothes
Sony Pictures Studios-Wardrobe (310) 244-5995
alterations, call (310) 244-7260
Universal Studios Costume Dept (818) 777-2722
Rental, mfg., & alterations
Western Costume Co. (818) 760-0900

Children/Baby Accessories & Bedroom

See Also: School Supplies, Desks & Dressing Toys & Games*
Art By Kidz (818) 625-1477
Call for Appt, Glendale, CA, 91207
100s of ORIGINAL CHILDRENS 2D & 3D ARTWORKS for rent at low flat rates
based on size. Cleared copyright, located in Glendale.
artbykidz@gmail.com * www.artbykidz.com
The Hand Prop Room LP. (323) 931-1534
Kids furniture/baby furniture, baby toys, baby accessories and baby doubles
History For Hire, Inc. (818) 765-7767
period carriages, strollers, cradles, toys, accessories
Hollywood Studio Gallery (323) 462-1116
prints-mounted unicorn head
Modern Props (323) 934-3000
contemporary and futuristic, furniture to accessories, small collection
NEST Studio Rentals, Inc. (818) 942-0339
furniture, toys, accessories; many cleared items
Prop Services West (818) 503-2790
Children accessories and baby accessories - kids bedroom dressing
Sony Pictures Studios-Prop House (Off Lot) (310) 244-5999
crib, bed, stroller, car seat, plus accessories, baby bath, baby bottle warmer,
baby care items, baby monitor, bassinet
Universal Studios Property & Hardware Dept (818) 777-2784
Children and baby accessories for the bedroom.
ZEdonk ART (818) 693-1082
5330 Derry Ave Ste P, Agoura Hills, CA, 91301
ZEdonk ART has everything a decorator needs to embellish a child's room!
kelly@zedonkart.com * www.ZEdonkART.com

Chimes & Bells

The Hand Prop Room LP. (323) 931-1534
LCW Props (818) 243-0707
Many Sizes & Styles
Lennie Marvin Enterprises, Inc. (Prop Heaven) (818) 841-5882
Ornate bells, Liberty bell, nautical bells, Tibetan bells, cow bells, wall mounted
bells and more
Omega/Cinema Props (323) 466-8201
Decorative bells, functional bells, cow bells, brass desk bells, school bells,
copper bells, wind chimes and more.
Universal Studios Property & Hardware Dept (818) 777-2784
Wind chimes, servants bells and much more for rent.

Chimney Parts & Tops

See: Rooftop Dressing

China Hat Lights

See Also: Caged Vapor Proof Lights Lamp Posts & Street Lights*
Lamp Shades* Lamps* Lanterns* Light Fixtures* Light Fixtures,
Period* Lighting, Industrial* Warehouse Dressing*
AIR Designs (818) 768-6639
Post-Mount, Hanging, Wall-Mounted, Assorted Styles
Alley Cats Studio Rentals (818) 982-9178
Gooseneck china hat lights & hanging china hat lights.
E.C. Prop Rentals (818) 764-2008
High multiples, many styles/sizes, practical, with optional piping for all

The Hand Prop Room LP. (323) 931-1534
Modern Props (323) 934-3000
contemporary china hat lights
Sony Pictures Studios-Fixtures (310) 244-5996
5933 W Slauson Ave, Culver City, CA, 90230
period to present day
www.sonypicturesstudios.com
Universal Studios Property & Hardware Dept (818) 777-2784
Various china hat lights and china hat lamps for rent.

Chinese Art & Artifacts

See: Asian Antiques, Furniture, Art & Artifacts

Chinese Fly Streamers

See: Asian Antiques, Furniture, Art & Artifacts Flags/Banners*

Chinese Pots

See: Pottery

Choir Risers

See: Audience Seating Stages, Portable & Steel Deck*

Christmas

See Also: Candles* Costume Rental Houses* Costumes* Events,
Decorations, Supplies & Services* Events,
Design/Planning/Production* Holiday Theme Events* Sleds* Sleighs*
Snow, Artificial & Real* Soldier Toys & Drums* Thrones* Toys &
Games* Wrapped Prop Gift Packages

Almost Christmas Prop Shoppe   (818) 285-9627
5348 Vineland Ave, Building C, N Hollywood, CA, 91601
Christmas decorations and supplies.
christmasprops@gmail.com * www.christmasprops.com

Flower Art   (323) 935-6800
5859 West 3rd Street, Los Angeles, CA, 90036
If you need a little Xmas (even in July), let us transform your sets into a Xmas
wonderland w/trees, garlands wreaths!
info@flowerartla.com * www.flowerartla.com

FROST   (310) 704-8812
Call for Appointment - 21405 Madrona Ave, Torrance, CA, 90503
Holiday decor, specializing in large scale trees, Santa sets, ornaments.
Professional installations.
mdisplay@yahoo.com * www.frostchristmasprops.com

Green Set, Inc.   (818) 764-1231
Christmas trees live/artif., lights, decor, sleighs, snowman, soldiers, smalls,
outdoor and indoor dressing

The Hand Prop Room LP.   (323) 931-1534
Sleighs, decorations, lights, toys

History For Hire, Inc.   (818) 765-7767
thrones, presents, multiples of toys; Santa's workshop dressing

Jackson Shrub Supply, Inc.   (818) 982-0100
Xmas trees, snowmen, toy soldiers, reindeer, Santa throne, Santa sleigh,
Christmas decorations, string lights

LCW Props   (818) 243-0707
Decorations Big & Small, Inflatables, Lighting, Reindeer, Penguins

LM Treasures   (626) 252-7354
Santa, statues, Drummer Boy statues, Nut Cracker statues, Reindeer statues,
Thrones, and so much more.

Modern Props   (323) 934-3000
contemporary christmas dressing & period christmas dressing

Moskatels   (213) 689-4590
733 S San Julian St, Los Angeles, CA, 90014

Omega/Cinema Props   (323) 466-8201
Christmas swag, christmas trees, nutcrackers, tree toppers, christmas
stockings, christmas ornaments and much more.

ShopWildThings   (928) 855-6075
2880 Sweetwater Ave, Lake Havasu City, AZ, 86406
Event Decor, Beaded Curtains, Chain Curtains, String Curtains & Columns,
Crystal Columns. Reliable service & delivery.
help@shopwildthings.com * www.shopwildthings.com

Stats Floral Supply   (626) 795-9308
120 S Raymond Ave, Pasadena, CA, 91105
www.statsfloral.com

Universal Studios Property & Hardware Dept   (818) 777-2784
lights, decorations, props, Santa throne

Church, Chapel, Synagogue, Mosque

See Also: Clerical, Judicial, Academic Gowns/Apparel* Religious
Articles

Cardinal Church Furniture   (626) 334-5252
401 S Irwindale Ave, Azusa, CA, 91702
Church furniture & carpeting
info@cardinalchurchfurniture.com * www.cardinalchurchfurniture.com

LCW Props   (818) 243-0707
Bibles, Hymn Books, Crosses, Pews, Sound Equipment, Lighting

Omega/Cinema Props   (323) 466-8201
Church organs, church pews, church lecterns, church benches, church artwork,
bimahs, and much more.

Universal Studios Property & Hardware Dept   (818) 777-2784
Church props, synagogue props and mosque props of all time periods for rent.

Used Church Items, Religious Rentals   (412) 220-2272
115 East Barr Street, Mcdonald, PA, 15057
Catholic Statues, Crucifixes, Censors, Vestments, Votive Stands, Candelabras,
Podiums, Hanging Lights, Baptismals.
www.religiousrentals.com

Warner Bros. Studios Property Department   (818) 954-2181
Religious smalls, candle holders, religious panels, pictures, statues, crosses

Cigar Store Indian

See Also: Smoking Products

The Hand Prop Room LP.   (323) 931-1534

LM Treasures   (626) 252-7354
Life size Cigar Store Indians plus many other variety of life size Indian Statues
and cowboys.

Omega/Cinema Props   (323) 466-8201
Tobacco Indian figures, cigar store Indian statue, tobacco Indian statues

RC Vintage, Inc.   (818) 765-7107
Large 7 feet, a couple models, 2 small cigar store indians

Universal Studios Property & Hardware Dept   (818) 777-2784
Cigar store Indian statue

Cigar/Tobacco Products

See: Smoking Products

Cigarette Machines

See: Vending Machines

Cinder Block

See: Concrete Block, Brick, Gravel, Sand, Rocks, Etc.

Circus Equipment/Dressing/Costumes

See Also: Animal Cages* Animals (Live), Services, Trainers & Wranglers* Balloons & Balloon Sculptures* Calliopes* Carnival Dressing/Supplies* Carnival Games & Rides* Carriages, Horse Drawn* Clowns* Vendor Carts & Concession Counters* Wagons

Artistic Carnival & Circus Design   (323) 751-3486
Call for Appointment.
Circus & carnival dressing, costumes, consulting services

Circus Hall of Fame   (765) 472-7553
3076 E Circus Lane, Peru, IN, 46970
Big tent, vintage wagons, 10 acre historic circus site
circushalloffame@peru.com * www.circushof.com

Dapper Cadaver   (818) 771-0818
Sideshow gaffs & oddities: feejee mermaids, etc. Fortune teller decor. Scary clown & dark ride props.

History For Hire, Inc.   (818) 765-7767
trunks, animal stands, etc.

L. A. Circus   (323) 751-3486
Call for Appt, Los Angeles, CA, 90047
classic/traditional to contemporary to avant garde, incl the Roschu circus props, side show wagons, tokens
circusinc@aol.com * www.lacircus.com

L. A. Party Works   (888) 527-2789
9712 Alpaca St, S El Monte, CA, 91733
in Vancouver tel. 604-589-4101. trapeze to tightropes, snake lady, magicians and clowns
partyworks@aol.com * www.partyworksinteractive.com

Modern Props   (323) 934-3000
side show backdrops, circus banners, circus dressing pieces

RC Vintage, Inc.   (818) 765-7107
side show posters & accessories only

Cities Themed Parties

See: Events, Decorations, Supplies & Services* Events, Design/Planning/Production* Themed Environment Construction* Travel (City/Country) Themed Events

Civil War Era

See Also: Guns & Firearms* Military Props & Equipment* Prop Reproduction & Fabrication* Wardrobe, Antique/Historical* Weaponry, Historical

Caravan West Productions   (661) 268-8300
35660 Jayhawker Rd, Aqua Dulce, CA, 91390
weapons, saddlery, costumes, props, rolling stock & buckaroos
caravanwest@earthlink.net * www.caravanwest.com

Fall Creek Corporation   (765) 482-1861
PO Box 92, Whitestown, IN, 46075
Civil War era, military & civilian. high quality uniforms, equip., weapons, rifles; muskets, tentage, misc.
ajfulks@fcsutler.com * www.fcsutler.com

The Hand Prop Room LP.   (323) 931-1534
Confederate weaponry and union weaponry, all kinds of costuming dressing for soldiers of the time.

History For Hire, Inc.   (818) 765-7767
Lots! Can outfit 100s of soldiers

Sword & Stone   (818) 562-6548
Civil war era guns and civil war era swords

Clapboards

See: Slates/Clapboards

Classroom

See: Chalk Boards* School Supplies, Desks & Dressing

Cleaners & Cleaning Services

See Also: Vacuum Cleaners

Crime Scene Clean Up   (844) 255-2461
We come to you - biohazard disposal, Los Angeles, CA, 90630
Trauma scene management, licensed, bonded, insured O.S.H.A./Haz-Mat certified, Dept. of Health #TSW-003
info@crimescenecleanup.com * www.crimescenecleanup.com

Milt & Edie's   (818) 846-4734
4021 W Alameda at Pass, Burbank, CA, 91505
2-Hour cleaning & shirt laundry available 24/7/365 at no extra charge. Tailoring & Alterations available 24/7/365.
info@miltandedies.com * www.miltandedies.com

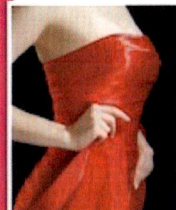

Sunset Laundraclean   (323) 653-2360
8201 Melrose Ave, Los Angeles, CA, 90046
Dry cleaning & laundry, 24 hr service, pickup/del for studios only

Cleaning Supplies

See: Expendables

Clear Vinyl

See: Floor, Ground & Surface Protection* Wall Coverings

Clearances

See: Art For Rent (Cleared Art)* Art, Artists For Hire* Private Investigations* Research, Advisors, Consulting & Clearances

Cleared Art

See: Art For Rent (Cleared Art)* Art, Artists For Hire* Paintings/Prints* Photographs* Research, Advisors, Consulting & Clearances* Sculpture

Clerical, Judicial, Academic Gowns/Apparel

Alpha Robes
1310 Hialeah Pl, Florissant, MO, 63033
Robes: children's choir, judicial, baptismal, paraments, vestments, stoles, accessories
sales@alpharobes.com * www.alpharobesales.com

C. M. Almy & Son, Inc. (800) 225-2569
228 Sound Beach Ave, Old Greenwich, CT, 06870
Mfg.-all denominations, stock & custom. vestments, clothing for clergy & choir
www.almy.com

The Costume House (818) 508-9933
priest robes, judges robes

Cotter Church Supplies (213) 385-3366
1701 James M. Wood Blvd, Los Angeles, CA, 90015
www.cotters.com

Sony Pictures Studios-Wardrobe (310) 244-5995
alterations, call (310) 244-7260

Universal Studios Costume Dept (818) 777-2722
Rental, mfg., & alterations

Western Costume Co. (818) 760-0900

Climate Control

See: Air Conditioning & Heating, Production/Event* Heaters, Indoor* Heaters, Outdoor* Plumbing Fixtures, Heating/Cooling Appliances

Clocks, Analog & Residential

See Also: Clocks, Digital & Commercial* Watches & Pocket Watches

AIR Designs (818) 768-6639
Kitchen, Restaurant, Diner, Auto

E.C. Prop Rentals (818) 764-2008
industrial, school, dual-face, multiples + time clocks

Feldmar Watch & Clock Center (310) 274-8016
9000 W. Pico Blvd, Los Angeles, CA, 90035
Repairs
www.feldmarwatch.com

The Hand Prop Room LP. (323) 931-1534
period-present, novelty

History For Hire, Inc. (818) 765-7767
desk, wall, time clocks

LCW Props (818) 243-0707
Digital, Analog, Period - Present, Large & Small, Programmable, Rigged

Modern Props (323) 934-3000
Household clocks, commercial clocks

NEST Studio Rentals, Inc. (818) 942-0339
wall, mantel, desk, novelty, kitchen

Ob-jects (818) 351-4200
decorative clocks

Old N Country Prop Shop, LLC (818) 423-2599
Vintage and antique clocks of various sizes. Huge selection of early clocks to modern day.

Omega/Cinema Props (323) 466-8201
Period clocks to contemporary clocks; wall clocks, grandfather clocks, modern clocks, mid-century modern clocks and more.

Picture Start Props (818) 255-5472
From vintage clocks to modern clocks including many wall clocks for different periods.

Prop Services West (818) 503-2790
Residential clocks in many styles

RC Vintage, Inc. (818) 765-7107
40s, 50s & 60s & time clocks Herman Miller

Sony Pictures Studios-Prop House (Off Lot) (310) 244-5999
large selection, chess timers, contessa clock, desk clocks, hourglass clocks, mantle clocks, oversized clocks, radio clocks

Universal Studios Property & Hardware Dept (818) 777-2784
All kinds of clock prop rentals

Clocks, Digital & Commercial

See Also: Lighting, LED, Fiber Optic & Specialty* Clocks, Analog & Residential

E.C. Prop Rentals (818) 764-2008
Industrial clocks, digital clocks, and more.

LCW Props (818) 243-0707
Digital clocks, racing clocks, and more

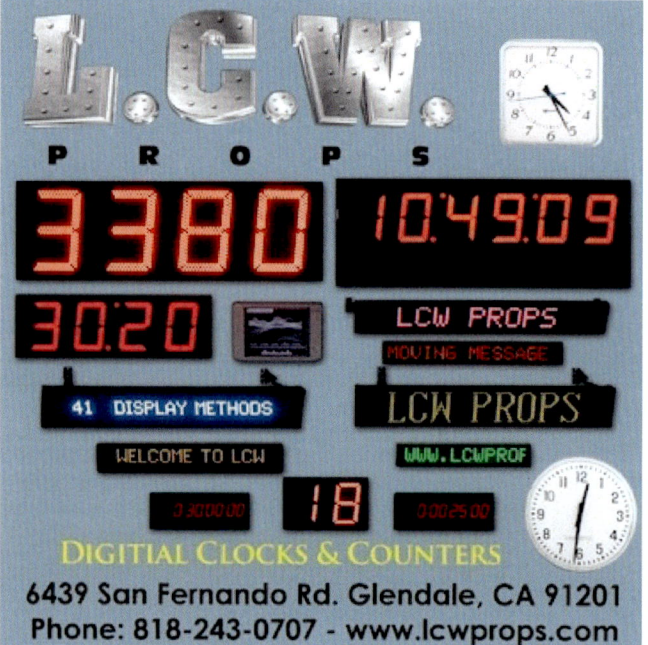

Mandex LED Displays (805) 497-8006
3248 Jessica St, Newbury Park, CA, 91320
Rental of large LED counters/LED digital Clocks/LED Timers & large digital count up down timers, w PC or remote control.
info@ledsignage.com * www.ledsignage.com

Modern Props (323) 934-3000
Futuristic clocks, digital clocks

Clowns

See Also: Carnival Dressing/Supplies* Circus Equipment/Dressing/Costumes* Make-up & Hair, Supplies & Services

Bubba's Clown Supplies (478) 733-8347
P.O. Box 65039, Orange Park, FL, 32065
face paint, noses, horns, wigs, circus music, apparel
www.bubbasclownsupplies.com

Clown Supplies Inc. (603) 435-8812
Website only.
catalog sales; clown make-up, noses, wigs, hats, buttons, props, sound makers, books, magic tricks, gag books
www.clownsupplies.com

Dapper Cadaver (818) 771-0818
Lifesize scary clown character props.

Gorygirl Halloween Event Staging and Prop Rental (818) 912-6902
Clown midget props, Large clown props, circus decor, 3D black Light wall paper

LM Treasures (626) 252-7354
Clowns can either be spooky or friendly. We provide both spooky clown statues and friendly life size clown statues.

Pricilla Mooseburger Originals (800) 973-6277
116 Division St West, Maple Lake, MN, 55358
custom tailored clown costumes, make-up supplies
www.mooseburgeronline.com

Spear's Specialty Shoe Co. (413) 739-5693
12 Orlando St, Springfield, MA, 01108
custom made clown shoes & street shoes, also slap gloves & Santa boots & belts
www.spearshoes.com

CNC Router & Laser Etching Services

See Also: Prop Design & Manufacturing Water Jet CNC Services*

Beyond Image Graphics (818) 547-0899
1853 Dana St, Glendale, CA, 91201
Over 10 years servicing the film industry, and businesses with top quality prints and signs. CNC Routing.
rafi@beyondimagegraphics.com * www.beyondimagegraphics.com

Bill Ferrell Co. (818) 767-1900
10556 Keswick St, Sun Valley, CA, 91352
CNC routing; CAD drawing; Fabrication
www.billferrell.com

Centerline Scenery (818) 252-7467
8238 Lankershim Blvd, N Hollywood, CA, 91605
meredyth@centerlinescenery.com

Charisma Design Studio, Inc. (818) 252-6611
8414 San Fernando Road, Sun Valley, CA, 91352
Bring sketches to life! Glass Etching and waterjet, experienced cutting services
info@charismadesign.com * www.charismadesign.com

SIXTH DEBBIES BOOK
THE SOURCE BOOK FOR PROP & SET DRESSING

'Grunge' movement and **Operation Desert Storm**. 'Debbies Book' title first used without an apostrophe. More advertisers found the growing Book. Prop Houses and bookstores started selling the Book, and it started evolving beyond just props and set dressing.

1990

40 YEARS OF DEBBIES BOOK

Collins Visual Media (818) 686-6581
10518 Johanna Ave, Shadow Hills, CA, 91040
We provide custom and finished CNC and laser products at any size using a wide variety of substrates.
www.collinsvisualmedia.com

D'ziner Sign Co. (323) 467-4467
801 Seward Street, Los Angeles, CA, 90038
Props, 3D carving
sales@dzinersign.com * www.dzinersign.com

depict (323) 222-1001
1460 Naud St, Los Angeles, CA, 90012
info@depict33.com * www.depict33.com

EFX- Event Special Effects (626) 888-2239
125 Railroad Ave, Monrovia, CA, 91016
Custom Fabrication- CNC- Plasma Table- Pipe & Ring Benders- 3D Renderings
info@efxla.com * www.efxla.com

Flix FX Inc. (818) 765-3549
7327 Lankershim Blvd #4, N Hollywood, CA, 91605
CNC machining, CNC wood & plastic routing, CNC tube & profile bending
info@flixfx.com * www.flixfx.com

The Hand Prop Room LP. (323) 931-1534
CNC Machine, CAD Drawing, 3D Rapid Prototyping, Laser engraving

HPR Custom (323) 931-1534
5700 Venice Blvd, Los Angeles, CA, 90019
Design, CAD drawings, fabrication, laser cutting and laser etching.
www.hprcustom.com

New Rule FX (818) 387-6450
7751 Densmore Ave, Van Nuys, CA, 91406
ryan@newrulefx.com * www.NewRuleFX.com

Scenic Highlights (818) 252-7760
10830 Cantara St, Sun Valley, CA, 91352
scenichighlights.com

Set Masters (818) 982-1506
24853 Avenue Rockefeller, Valencia, CA, 91355
CNC routing; CNC lathe; CAD drawing; Laser Engraving; CNC Plasma; 3D Renderings; Custom Fabrication and Design
info@setmasters.com * www.setmasters.com

Warner Bros. Studios Scenic Art & Sign Shop (818) 954-1815
4000 Warner Blvd Bldg 44, Burbank, CA, 91522
graphic design and production studio for signs & scenic art; digital printing to hand-painted
wbsigns@warnerbros.com * www.wbsignandscenic.com

Worlds of Wow (817) 380-4215
1800 Shady Oaks Drive, Denton, TX, 76205
Advanced CNC routing services
www.worldsofwow.com

Coal

See: Concrete Block, Brick, Gravel, Sand, Rocks, Etc.

Coca Cola Memorabilia

AIR Designs (818) 768-6639
Neon, Signage, Vending Machines, Clocks, Soda Dispensers
The Hand Prop Room LP. (323) 931-1534
signs, bottles
History For Hire, Inc. (818) 765-7767
coolers, bottles, other brands
LCW Props (818) 243-0707
Period Pieces, Large Quantity Of Soda Bottles & Glasses, Lighting
RC Vintage, Inc. (818) 765-7107
signs & machines 40s, 50s & 60s, coca cola machines

Cockpits

See: Locations, Airport Dressing & Hangars* Space Shuttle/Space Hardware

Cocktails

See: Food, Artificial Food

Coffee House

See Also: Cafe Tables/Chairs/Umbrellas* Delicatessen Equipment
AIR Designs (818) 768-6639
Cappuccino Machines/Equipment, Signs, Neon Displays, Counters, Tables & Chairs
The Hand Prop Room LP. (323) 931-1534
cappucino machines, display, dressing, coffee grinders
History For Hire, Inc. (818) 765-7767
Lennie Marvin Enterprises, Inc. (Prop Heaven) (818) 841-5882
cappuccino machines, espresso machines, signs, counter/back bar/cases/tables/stools
Modern Props (323) 934-3000
contemporary/household & commercial cappuccino machines for coffee house dressing
New Frontier Coffee (310) 839-3423
5890 Blackwelder St, Culver City, CA, 90232
We have a tremendous amount of coffee related equipment. New and vintage, prop and functional.
newfrontiercoffee@gmail.com * www.nfcoffee.com
RC Vintage, Inc. (818) 765-7107
Cappuccino machines, Coffee Machines Espresso, contemporary, Grinders. Carts. Bean bags Faux. Displays
Universal Studios Property & Hardware Dept (818) 777-2784
Coffee house dressing including signage, furniture & appliances.

Coffee Mugs

See: Promotional Items & Materials

Coffins, Wooden & Period

See: Caskets* Cemetery Dressing* Prop Houses* Religious Articles

Coin Op Rides, Machines & Cranes

See: Arcade Equipment, Games & Rides* Vending Machines

Coin-op Photo Booths

See: Photo Booths

Coins & Currency

See: Money (Prop)

Collars & Cuffs

See: Wardrobe, Accessories

Collectibles

See Also: Coca Cola Memorabilia* Comic Books & Comic Book Racks* Memorabilia & Novelties* Pepsi Memorabilia* Prop Houses* Sports Fan Items, Memorabilia, Photographs
AIR Designs (818) 768-6639
Toys, Signs, Auto, Pedal Cars, smalls
Clifford Antiques (747) 283-1272
3429 Magnolia Blvd, Burbank, CA, 91505
British Antiques shipped from Scotland we're a family run business with over 40 years experience
wfcliffordantiques@yahoo.com * www.cliffordantiques.com
The Hand Prop Room LP. (323) 931-1534
period-present, radios, clocks, sports, electronics
History For Hire, Inc. (818) 765-7767

LCW Props (818) 243-0707
Coins, Stamps, Bronzes, Metals, Rocks, Call Us First
Modern Props (323) 934-3000
contemporary/futuristic/electronic collectibles
Off The Wall (310) 652-1185
737 N. La Cienega, Los Angeles, CA 90069
unusual antiques of early 20th C., Art Deco to mid-century
www.offthewallantiques.com
Old N Country Prop Shop, LLC (818) 423-2599
Pottery, Pyrex, Depression Glass, Hall China, Midcentury linens, china, housewares, fabric, sewing notions, etc.
Pasadena Antique Center and Annex (626) 449-7706
480 South Fair Oaks Ave, Pasadena, CA, 91105
Antique and Vintage collectibles from all eras & styles representing all areas of the globe.
pasadenaantiqecenterandannex@gmail.com * bit.ly/PasadenaAntiqueCenter
Sony Pictures Studios-Prop House (Off Lot) (310) 244-5999
coin collection, gems, minerals, insect collections, spoon collections
Used Church Items, Religious Rentals (412) 220-2272
115 East Barr Street, Mcdonald, PA, 15057
Vintage Religious Catholic and Christian Antiques and Collectibles from Rosary Beads to Cathedral Stained Glass Windows
www.religiousrentals.com

Color Keyed Backgrounds

See: Green Screens, Blue Screens* Fabrics* Paint & Painting Supplies

Columns

See Also: Architectural Pieces & Artifacts* Scenery/Set Rentals* Statuary
American Wood Column Corp. (718) 782-3163
913 Grand St, Brooklyn, NY, 11211-2785
catalog sales; large sel. of millwork, architectural/decorative small finials to tall columns, plain to ornate, custom t
www.americanwoodcolumncorp.com
C. P. Two (323) 466-8201
Antique columns to vintage columns; English Victorian columns, oak columns, pine columns, and more.
Green Set, Inc. (818) 764-1231
Columns, Pedestals & Balustrades, Banister sectionals, specialized capitals, Ionic, Corinthian, Doric, and statue
Jackson Shrub Supply, Inc. (818) 982-0100
Corinthian columns, Ionic columns, modern columns, many others 8'-12' tall, fiberglass columns, and more.
LCW Props (818) 243-0707
Roman, Futuristic, Faux
Modern Props (323) 934-3000
Roman-present, fiberglass columns
MODRoto (888) 724-1228
16404 Knott Ave, La Mirada, CA, 90638
plastic, also pedestals, lightbases, colonnades, arches for wedding & events
www.modroto.com
Omega/Cinema Props (323) 466-8201
Antique columns to vintage columns; English Victorian columns, oak columns, pine columns, and more.
ZG04 DECOR (818) 853-8040
Event columns/decorative columns and Roman columns. Multiples of all

Comic Books & Comic Book Racks

See Also: Collectibles* Magazines & Magazine/Newspaper Racks
AIR Designs (818) 768-6639
Display Stands, Racks, Old & New Comic Books
The Hand Prop Room LP. (323) 931-1534
in stock & will fabricate, Vintage comic books, vintage DC Comics
Hi De Ho Comics & Books with Pictures (310) 394-2820
1431 Lincoln Blvd, Santa Monica, CA, 90401
Southern California's first & best. comic books
www.hideho.com
History For Hire, Inc. (818) 765-7767
custom mfg.
Meltdown (323) 851-7223
7522 W Sunset Blvd, Los Angeles, CA, 90046
comic books
www.meltcomics.com
P Dot's Comics & Collectibles (626) 798-1455
1505 N Lake Ave, Pasadena, CA, 91104
Comic books, comic artwork, comic exclusives and more
pdotcomics@hotmail.com *
http://stores.ebay.com/P-Dots-Comics-and-Collectibles
RC Vintage, Inc. (818) 765-7107
40s, 50s & 60s comic books, wall & standing racks, full set of matching racks
Sony Pictures Studios-Prop House (Off Lot) (310) 244-5999
Universal Studios Property & Hardware Dept (818) 777-2784
Comic book racks and comic book store dressing.

Computer Software & Services

See Also: Computers
Di-No Computers-Service Dept (626) 795-6674
2817 E Foothill, Pasadena, CA 91107
sales & repair; Pasadena's premier Apple specialist
www.di-no.com
Hi-Tech Computer Rental (818) 841-0677
172 W Verdugo Ave, Burbank, CA, 91502
Mac, PC, peripherals
www.htcr.net
LCW Props (818) 243-0707
Product Boxes For Software, Custom Graphics, Playback Software, Media
Players

Computers

See Also: Control Boards
Airwaves Wireless (818) 501-8200
13400 Riverside Dr # 103 Sherman Oaks, CA, 91423
Laptops & Convertible Tablets from Dell, Acer, Asus, Samsung, Apple,
Gateway, HP, Toshiba, Panasonic, Lenovo, Microsoft.
sales@airwaveswireless.com * www.airwaveswireless.com

The Hand Prop Room LP. (323) 931-1534

LCW Props (818) 243-0707
Large Selection Of New & Old, Servers Of Any Kind, Custom, Working, Rigged,
Our Specialty Is Servers

Modern Props (323) 934-3000
computers including contemporary laptops, flat-screen LCDs
Omega/Cinema Props (323) 466-8201
Computers, computer accessories, and computer parts.
Picture Start Props (818) 255-5472
Computers, laptops, Macs (old and new) and vintage IBM types.
Repro-Graphic Supply (818) 771-9066
9838 Glenoaks Blvd, Sun Valley, CA, 91352
Computer rentals, computer repairs and computer sales.
info@reprographicsupply.com * www.reprographicsupply.com
RJR Props (404) 349-7600
Computers and computer props are our specialty. Over 5000 computers,
accessories and more for rent from new to old.
Sony Pictures Studios-Prop House (Off Lot) (310) 244-5999
Universal Studios Property & Hardware Dept (818) 777-2784
Many prop computers and computer parts for rent
Woody's Electrical Props (818) 503-1940
period to futuristic. mockups & will fabricate any design. Fantasy sets, military
sets, industrial sets, air tower

Concert Lighting

See: Lighting & Sound, Concert/Theatrical/DJ/VJ

Concert Staging

See: Audience Seating* Stages, Portable & Steel Deck

Concession Equipment

See: Carnival Dressing/Supplies* Vending Machines* Vendor Carts &
Concession Counters

Concession Stands/Carts

See: Vendor Carts & Concession Counters

Concrete Block, Brick, Gravel, Sand, Rocks, Etc.

See Also: Building Supply, Lumber, Hardware, Etc. Tile, Marble, Granite, Etc.*

Ace Brick & Patio   (818) 781-1755
6023 Sepulveda Blvd, Van Nuys, CA, 91411
also fireplaces, BBQ's & mantels
www.acebuildingmaterials.com

American Builders Supply   (818) 768-3176
8563 San Fernando Rd, Sun Valley, CA, 91352
block, brick, pavers, stone, sand, gravel, boulders
www.absupply.com

Angelus Block Co., Inc   (818) 767-8576
11374 Tuxford St, Sun Valley, CA, 91352
mfg., every kind of cinder block, paving block, 7 plants in L.A.
www.angelusblock.com

Arroyo Building Materials   (818) 365-6170
890 Arroyo St, San Fernando, CA, 91340
new/used brick, block, stone, sand, gravel, boulders
www.arroyobuildingmaterials.net

Balboa Brick & Supply Co.   (818) 785-7492
16755 Roscoe Blvd, North Hills, CA, 91343
concrete, masonry, brick, stone, sand, stucco
www.balboabrickandsupply.com

California Quarry Products   (661) 942-3992
42057 3rd St. East, Lancaster, CA, 93535
we deliver. gravel, rocks, sand, landscape supplies
www.californiaquarryproducts.com

Central Valley Builders Supply   (818) 343-3838
7030 Reseda Blvd, Reseda, CA, 91335
also loc in Van Nuys & North Hills comprehensive: sand, gravel, rock, cinderblock, brick, etc.
www.cvbs.com

Green Set, Inc.   (818) 764-1231
gravel, sand, rocks; also prop rocks

Hanson Aggregates   (626) 856-6710
13550 E Live Oak Ave, Irwindale, CA, 91706
aggregates in large quantity, rocks to fine sand
www.lehighhanson.com

Hub Construction Specialties   (818) 547-3364
5310 San Fernando Rd, Glendale, CA, 91203
concrete specialists
www.hubhasit.com

Jackson Shrub Supply, Inc.   (818) 982-0100
desert, mountain peaks, outcroppings, river rock, pebbles, walls, coal

La Canada Rustic Stone Co.   (626) 798-7876
1385 Lincoln Ave, Pasadena, CA, 91103
wall/volcanic rock, sand, cement, brick/block, great flagstone
www.rusticstone.com

Prime Building Materials   (818) 765-6767
6900 Lankershim Blvd, N Hollywood, CA, 91605
brick, block, stone, sand, gravel, Mexican pavers
www.prime3.com

Sepulveda Building Materials   (310) 436-1400
359 E Gardena Blvd, Gardena, CA, 90248
block, brick, sand, gravel, cement, slate, boulders
www.sepulveda.com

Condom Machines

See: Vending Machines

Condoms

See: Goth/Punk/Bondage/Fetish/Erotica Etc.

Conduit

See: Electrical/Electronic Supplies & Services

Cones, Traffic

See: Traffic/Road Signs, Lights, Safety Items

Confetti

See Also: Events, Decorations, Supplies & Services

Astro Audio Video Lighting, Inc.   (818) 549-9915
6615 San Fernando Rd, Glendale, CA, 91201
Confetti canons/confetti machines available/confetti launchers
www.astroavl.com

Bill Ferrell Co.   (818) 767-1900
10556 Keswick St, Sun Valley, CA, 91352
Confetti, streamers & die-cut shapes in tissue & metallic color combinations.
Cannon systems & continuous flow launchers
www.billferrell.com

CONFETTI & FOG FX Special Effects Company   (877) 576-4239
1085 W 21st Pl, Hialeah, FL, 33010
Confetti fx and streamer fx, confetti cannons and more
Info@confettiandfogfx.com * www.caffx.com

EFX- Event Special Effects   (626) 888-2239
125 Railroad Ave, Monrovia, CA, 91016
Double Barrel Cannon- Continuous Feed Unit- Confetti
info@efxla.com * www.efxla.com

J & M Special Effects, Inc.   (718) 875-0140
524 Sackett St, Brooklyn, NY, 11217
confetti, confetti cannons, confetti blasters, confetti blowers, icicles, bubbles, floating bubbles, snow dressing products
info@jmfx.net * www.jmfx.net

L. A. Party Works   (888) 527-2789
9712 Alpaca St, S El Monte, CA, 91733
Confetti canons and more. If in Vancouver tel. 604-589-4101
partyworks@aol.com * www.partyworksinteractive.com

Universal Studios Property & Hardware Dept   (818) 777-2784
Confetti including jumbo bags of confetti and plastic boxes full of confetti.

Construction Materials

See: Architectural Pieces & Artifacts Building Supply, Lumber, Hardware, Etc.* Columns* Concrete Block, Brick, Gravel, Sand, Rocks, Etc.* Electrical/Electronic Supplies & Services* Glass & Mirrors* Metal Suppliers* Metalworking, Welding & Structural* Moulding, Wood* Paint & Painting Supplies* Paneling, Veneers & Laminates* Plastics, Materials & Fabrication* Plumbing Fixtures, Heating/Cooling Appliances* Tile, Marble, Granite, Etc.*

Construction Site Equipment

See Also: Barricades Traffic/Road Signs, Lights, Safety Items*
Welding Equipment/Stations*

AIR Designs (818) 768-6639
Tools, Port-A-Potty, Manhole, Skirt, Barricades, Cones, Mesh, Construction Dressing

Alley Cats Studio Rentals (818) 982-9178
street construction props, cement mixer, Caltrans blinking arrow, porta potties

E.C. Prop Rentals (818) 764-2008
Tools & equipment, cement mixers, barricades, orange plastic fencing, signage, k-rails

The Hand Prop Room LP. (323) 931-1534
barricades, traffic, road signs, safety items

LCW Props (818) 243-0707
Hoses, Barricades, Cones, Lights, Signs, Deliniators

Consulting Services

See: Art, Artists For Hire Research, Advisors, Consulting & Clearances* Search Tools, Directories, Libraries*

Contact Paper

See: Wall Coverings Window Treatments*

Control Boards

See Also: Computers Electronic Equipment (Dressing)*

E.C. Prop Rentals (818) 764-2008
extensive sel., including stainless w/ lights/buttons/switches

History For Hire, Inc. (818) 765-7767
radio station, recording studio, TVs, big sel.

LCW Props (818) 243-0707
Working & Rigged, Many Sizes & Styles, Period - Present

Modern Props (323) 934-3000
control boards; contemporary/futuristic-radio stations to space

Woody's Electrical Props (818) 503-1940
period to futuristic. electronic panels,read-outs. Fantasy sets, military sets, industrial sets, air tower/mission contr

Control Panels/Boxes

See Also: Electronic Equipment (Dressing) Instrument Panels*

E.C. Prop Rentals (818) 764-2008
stainless & painted-wide sel.

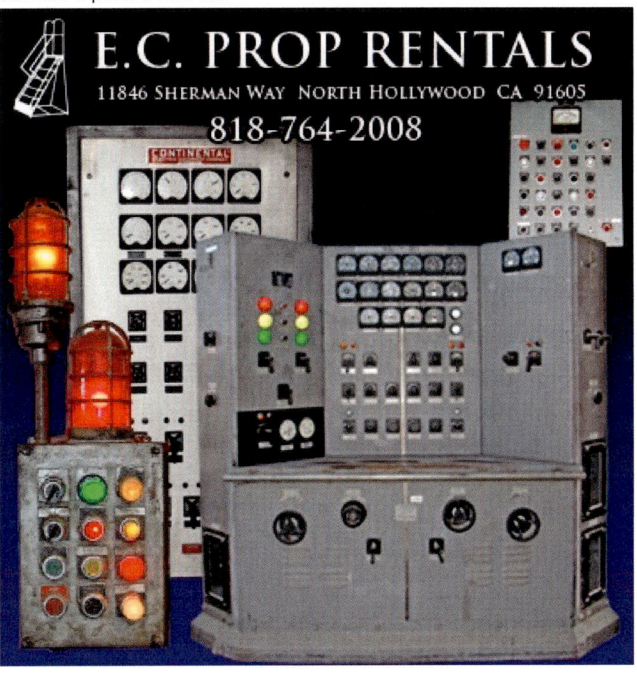

The Hand Prop Room LP. (323) 931-1534
past-future,mfg., electronic, real/dummy

Jadis (310) 396-3477
2701 Main St, Santa Monica, CA, 90405
Steampunk style large panels with vintage switches and gauges on casters. Army surplus and electronic frequency panels.
jadis1@gmail.com * www.jadisprops.com

LCW Props (818) 243-0707
Another Specialty. We Can Rig, Create, Any Of Our Very Large Selection

6439 San Fernando Rd. Glendale, CA 91201
Phone: 818-243-0707 - www.lcwprops.com

LISTINGS FOR THIS CATEGORY CONTINUE ON THE FOLLOWING PAGE

Modern Props   (323) 934-3000
control panels/control boxes; contemporary/futuristic/electronic
RJR Props   (404) 349-7600
Large control panels, industrial control panels, futuristic control panels and more for rent.
Universal Studios Property & Hardware Dept   (818) 777-2784
Many prop control panels and control boxes for rent.
Woody's Electrical Props   (818) 503-1940
period to futuristic. will design & build. Fantasy sets, military sets, industrial sets, air tower, electrical panels

Convenience Store Racks

See: Display Cases, Racks & Fixtures (Store)* Store Shelf Units & Shelving

Conventions

See: Trade Shows & Conventions

Conveyor Equipment

AIR Designs   (818) 768-6639
Straight, Curved, Grocery & Warehouse
Bill Ferrell Co.   (818) 767-1900
10556 Keswick St, Sun Valley, CA, 91352
Gravity & motorized conveyors/treadmills. Easy variable speed & reversing controllers or computer-controlled automation.
www.billferrell.com
E.C. Prop Rentals   (818) 764-2008
working electric, gravity feed, skate wheel, roller bar
LCW Props   (818) 243-0707
Conveyors, Gravity, Electronic, Rigged
Machinery & Equipment Co., Inc.   (909) 599-3916
115 N Cataract Ave, San Dimas, CA, 91773
Used conveying equipment for sale and rent. Conveyor types include belt, screw, roller, spiral, vibratory and more.
sherri@machineryandequipment.com * www.machineryandequipment.com

Cooking Equipment

AIR Designs   (818) 768-6639
Commercial Stoves, Ovens, Ranges, Fryers, Counters, Sinks, Mixers, Restaurant Kitchen Props
History For Hire, Inc.   (818) 765-7767
vintage, cooking pots, pans, skillets, iron kettles
LCW Props   (818) 243-0707
Large Outdoor BBQ's, Pots & Pans, Home & Commercial
Machinery & Equipment Co., Inc.   (909) 599-3916
115 N Cataract Ave, San Dimas, CA, 91773
Used commercial cooking equipment including kettles, mixers, ovens, braising pans, continuous cookers and more.
sherri@machineryandequipment.com * www.machineryandequipment.com
Modern Props   (323) 934-3000
contemporary/futuristic, household cooking equipment & commercial cooking equipment
Old N Country Prop Shop, LLC   (818) 423-2599
Small electrics, warmer trays, slow cookers, pressure cookers, iron skillets, aluminum, copper, stainless steel, etc.
Prop Services West   (818) 503-2790
Sony Pictures Studios-Prop House (Off Lot)   (310) 244-5999
Universal Studios Property & Hardware Dept   (818) 777-2784
All kinds of cooking equipment props for rent.
ZG04 DECOR   (818) 853-8040
Catering equipment/cooking equipment for rent.

Cool Suits

See: Environmental (Cool/Heat) Suits

Copy Machines

See Also: Office Equipment & Dressing
Cal Business Systems & Supply   (310) 470-3435
1920 Pandora Ave, Ste 7, Los Angeles, CA, 90025
short term rentals, 1 day to a year, copiers, faxes, supplies & service
LCW Props   (818) 243-0707
Large Selection Of Big & Small, Rigged, Non Working
Steven Enterprises   (800) 491-8785
17952 Skypark Circle Unit E, Irvine, CA, 92614
Wide Format Printers. Rent/Buy. Authorized Dealer: HP, KIP, Canon, Oce, Epson. We service & supply everything we install
sales@plotters.com * www.plotters.com
Universal Studios Property & Hardware Dept   (818) 777-2784
Prop photocopy machines of various sizes and types for rent.

Cork Inlay Work

See: Carpet & Flooring

Coroner

See: Morgue

Costume Jewelry

See: Jewelry, Costume

Costume Rental Houses

See Also: Costume/Wardrobe/Sewing Supplies* Costumes* Costumes, International/Ethnic* Masks* Wardrobe* Wardrobe, Accessories* Wardrobe, Antique/Historical* Wardrobe, Construction & Alterations* Wardrobe, Contemporary* Wardrobe, International/Ethnic* Wardrobe, Vintage

Action Sets and Props / WonderWorks, Inc.   (818) 992-8811
7231 Remmet Ave, Canoga Park, CA, 91303
Space shuttle & station, space suit, specialty props, miniatures, mechanical effects, cityscape, miniature buildings
www.wonderworksweb.com

Spacecraft • Spacesuits • Sets • Miniatures • SFX • Props
Photography • Museum Design • Architectural • Vehicles

WonderWorks INC
Serving Aerospace, Film, Entertainment & Education for a Third Of A Century!

Adele's of Hollywood   (323) 663-2231
5034 Hollywood Blvd, Hollywood, CA, 90027
www.adelescostumes.com
American Costume Corp.   (818) 764-2239
12980 Raymer St, N Hollywood, CA, 91605
1770s through 1970s
www.united-american.com
Bill Hargate Costumes   (323) 876-4432
1117 N Formosa Ave, West Hollywood, CA, 90046
Broadway Costumes, Inc.   (312) 829-6400
1100 W. Cermak, Chicago, IL, 60608
Chicago's oldest & largest costume house
www.broadwaycostumes.com
CBS Costume Rental   (323) 575-2666
7800 Beverly Blvd, Los Angeles, CA, 90036
Designer M/F modern, day & evening, and western 1880s
tvccostumerental@cbs.com
The Costume House   (818) 508-9933
7324 Greenbush Ave, North Hollywood, CA, 91605
http://www.thecostumehouse.com
Costume Rentals Corporation   (818) 753-3700
11149 Vanowen St, N Hollywood, CA, 91605
motion picture supplier & special order items
www.costumerentalscorp.com
The Costume Shoppe   (818) 244-1161
746 W. Doran St, Glendale, CA, 91203
Open Wed.-Sat. all periods, military, walk arounds
www.thecostumeshoppe.net
Eastern Costume   (818) 982-3611
7243 Coldwater Canyon Ave, North Hollywood, CA 91605
Full-service costume house, military, police & civilian wardrobe, 1920's to present, alterations & tailoring.
www.easterncostume.com

Helen Uffner Vintage Clothing LLC   **(718) 937-0220**
30-10 41st Avenue, 3rd Floor, Long Island City, NY, 11101
authentic 1850-1973 M/W/children apparel & accessories
uffnervintagellc@aol.com * www.uffnervintage.com

Heritage Costumes   **(310) 320-6392**
1423 Marcelina Ave, Torrance, CA, 90501
www.heritagecostumes.com

Ian Drummond Collection   **(416) 531-2591**
222 Islington Ave. #8, Toronto, Ontario, M8V 3W7
Period vintage clothing & accessories from 1900 to 1980s,
Men/Women/Children
www.iandrummondcollection.com

Make Believe, Inc.   **(310) 396-6785**
3240 Pico Blvd, Santa Monica, CA, 90405
We also sell masks, wigs, theatrical makeup & access. period, novelty &
character, accessories
www.makebelieveinccostumes.com

Motion Picture Costume Company   **(818) 557-1247**
3811 Valhalla Dr, Burbank, CA, 91505
uniforms & civilian wardrobe, 1775 to present
www.mpccwardrobe.com

Oregon Shakespeare Festival Costume Rentals   **(541) 482-2111**
408 Talent Ave, Talent, OR, 97540   **x308**
Full-service costume rental facility featuring quality garments constructed by
the Oregon Shakespeare Festival
costumerentals@osfashland.org * www.osfcostumerentals.org

Palace Costume & Prop Co.   **(323) 651-5458**
835 N Fairfax Ave, Los Angeles, CA, 90046
1850s-1980s, European, ethnic
www.palacecostume.com

Roxy Deluxe   **(818) 487-7800**
11311 Hartland St, N Hollywood, CA, 91605

Sony Pictures Studios-Wardrobe   **(310) 244-5995**
5933 W Slauson Ave, Culver City, CA, 90230
alterations, call (310) 244-7260
www.sonypicturesstudios.com

Theatrix Costume House   **(800) 977-8749**
61 Elm Grove Ave, Toronto, Ontario, M6K 2J2
Over 25,000 theatrical costumes in stock, tens of thousands of accessories,
custom tailoring & services
www.theatrixcostumehouse.com

Universal Studios Costume Dept   **(818) 777-2722**
100 Universal City Plaza, Universal City, CA, 91608
Rental, mfg., & alterations
universal.costume@nbcuni.com * http://universalstudioslot.com/costume

Warner Bros. Studios Costume Dept   **(818) 954-1297**
4000 Warner Blvd Bldg 153, Burbank, CA, 91522
Collection of period & contemporary costumes for rent categorized by era,
decade and style.
wbcostumesnewaccounts@warnerbros.com * www.wbcostumedept.com

Western Costume Co.   **(818) 760-0900**
11041 Vanowen St, N Hollywood, CA, 91605
www.westerncostume.com

Costume/Wardrobe/Sewing Supplies

See Also: Feathers Fur, Artificial & Real* Patterns* Sewing
Equipment & Workrooms* Trims, Fringe, Tassels, Beading Etc.*

Acme Display Fixture & Packaging   **(888) 411-1870**
3829 S Broadway St, Los Angeles, CA, 90037
Complete store setups: garment racks, displays/display cases, counters,
packaging, shelving, hangers, mannequins
sales@acmedisplay.com * www.acmedisplay.com

Beadcats   **(503) 625-2323**
PO Box 2840, Wilsonville, OR, 97070-2840
catalog sales; glass seed beads size 6-24, supplies, Czech pressed glass
shaped beads, books, needles, thread
www.BeadCats.com

The Button Store   **(323) 658-5473**
8344 W 3rd St, Los Angeles, CA, 90048
a large selection from Europe to Far East. huge sel, every kind of button

Eastern Costume   **(818) 982-3611**
Steamers, hangers, office supplies, tags, pins, tapes, ageing supplies, boxes,
racks, sprays, boxes, bags & accessories.

H. E. Goldberg & Co.   **(800) 722-8201**
9050 Martin Luther King Jr. Way, South Seattle, WA, 98118
catalog sales; sewing skins, pelts
www.hegoldbergfur.com

Home Sew   **(800) 344-4739**
PO Box 4099, Bethlehem, PA, 18018
catalog sales; sewing supplies, fabrics, threads, trims, notions, zippers,
patterns
www.homesew.com

Hyman Hendler & Sons, Inc   **(212) 240-8393**
142 W 38th Street, New York, NY, 10018
ribbons, lace, sequins, trims, millinery supplies + more
www.hymanhendler.com

Lacis   **(510) 843-7178**
2982 Adeline St, Berkeley, CA, 94703
trims, laces, costume supplies, reference books, website has useful links
www.lacis.com

L'Atelier   **(310) 540-4440**
1722 South Catalina Ave, Redondo Beach, CA, 90277
open 10-5 Tues-Sat; 2nd location in Redondo Beach. knitting yarn
www.latelier.com

Manhattan Wardrobe Supply   **(212) 268-9993**
245 West 29th St, 8th Floor, New York, NY, 10001
all credit cards accepted, wardrobe expendables, costume expendables
info@wardrobesupplies.com * www.wardrobesupplies.com

Renaissance Ribbons   **(530) 692-0842**
Web Based Business
catalog sales; ribbons, trims, metallic lace for trims & for costumes, notions,
upholstery & more, wholesale only
www.renaissanceribbons.com

Sculptural Arts Coating, Inc.   **(800) 743-0379**
PO Box 10546, Greensboro, NC, 27404
Mfg. of "Sculpt or Coat" nontoxic plastic cream for making props, scenery,
puppets, masks, costumes, arch. elements
www.sculpturalarts.com

Testfabrics, Inc.   **(570) 603-0432**
415 Delaware Ave, West Pittston, PA, 18643
catalog sales; synthetic & natural fabrics without additives, conservation uses:
restoration/conservation/storage
www.testfabrics.com

Wawak Corporation   **(800) 654-2235**
1059 Powers Rd, Conklin, NY, 13748
catalog sales; sewing supplies & tools, cleaning supplies & tools
www.wawak.com

Zipperstop   **(212) 226-3964**
27 Allen St, New York, NY, 10002
catalog sales; YKK zippers, ship worldwide, all major credit cards, no minimum
www.zipperstop.com

Costumes

See Also: Animal Costumes & Walk Around Characters* Holiday Costumes* Masks* Native American* Puppets, Marionettes, Automata, Animatronics* Wardrobe

Adele's of Hollywood (323) 663-2231

American Conservatory Theater (415) 439-2379
By appt only, San Francisco, CA, 94108
cfloor@act-sf.org * www.actcostumerentals.org

Artistic Carnival & Circus Design (323) 751-3486
Call for Appointment.
Circus & carnival dressing, costumes, consulting services

Broadway Costumes, Inc. (312) 829-6400
Chicago's oldest & largest costume house

Costume Co-Op (818) 752-7522
11501 Chandler Blvd, N. Hollywood, CA, 91601
Full service costume shop, alterations and made-to-order for the Film & TV industry. No inventory sales or rentals.
mail@costumeco-op.com * www.costumeco-op.com

The Costume House (818) 508-9933
theatrical, authentic 1880-1980 & Renaissance costumes

Costumes & Creatures (612) 378-2561
504 Malcom Ave. SE #200, Minneapolis, MN, 55414
full service costume/mascot design & fabrication. custom full body costumes
www.vstarentertainment.com

Eastern Costume (818) 982-3611
1920's to present, uniform & civilian wardrobe, military, alterations, hazmat, racks, ethnic costumes, NASA, and props.

Hollywood Toys & Costumes (800) 554-3444
6600 Hollywood Blvd, Hollywood, CA, 90028
Halloween, kids & adults
www.yourhollywoodcostumes.com

JFF Uniforms-Costumes (310) 320-1327
557 Van Ness Ave, Torrance, CA, 90501
Custom garments 1-10,000 pcs made from sketch or sample. Period, military, modern & more.
www.jffuniforms.com

L. A. Circus (323) 751-3486
Call for Appt, Los Angeles, CA, 90047
Circus, Vegas Showgirl, performance costumes, clown outfits, dressing tents, circus dressing rooms, circus linens
circusinc@aol.com * www.lacircus.com

Make Believe, Inc. (310) 396-6785
We also sell masks, wigs, theatrical makeup & access. character & novelty, international, accessories

Margaretrose Custom Clothing Design (323) 852-4787
1355 South Genesee Ave, Los Angeles, CA, 90019
made-to-order design, construction, pattern making, period & modern
www.margaretrosedesign.net

Norcostco (800) 220-6920
825 Rhode Island Ave S, Golden Valley, MN, 55426
multiple sales offices around the U.S. period production, classics, musicals, opera
www.norcostco.com

Oregon Shakespeare Festival Costume Rentals (541) 482-2111
Full-service costume rental facility featuring quality garments constructed **x308** by the Oregon Shakespeare Festival

Silvia's Costumes (323) 666-0680
4964 Hollywood Blvd, Los Angeles, CA, 90027
info@silviascostumes.com * http://www.silviascostumes.com

Sony Pictures Studios-Wardrobe (310) 244-5995
alterations, call (310) 244-7260

Southern Importers (713) 524-8236
4825 San Jacinto St, Houston, TX, 77004-5620
catalog sales; mask foundations & plastic animal masks
www.southern-importers.com

Sword & Stone (818) 562-6548
Roman costumes, Egyptian costumes, military costumes, viking costumes and more. Fabrication available

Tech Works FX Studios (504) 722-1504
13405 Seymour Meyers Blvd #5, Covington, LA, 70433
Specializes in Costume Design, Creature Suits, Make Up FX, Monsters and Custom Characters.
info@techworksstudios.com * www.techworksstudios.com

Universal Studios Costume Dept (818) 777-2722
Rental, mfg., & alterations

Ursula's Costumes, Inc. (310) 582-8230
2516 Wilshire Blvd, Santa Monica, CA, 90403
party costumes, wigs, masks, hats
www.ursulascostumes.com

Warner Bros. Studios Costume Dept (818) 954-1297
Collection of period & contemporary costumes for rent categorized by era, decade and style.

Western Costume Co. (818) 760-0900

1992 40 YEARS OF DEBBIES BOOK

SEVENTH
DEBBIES BOOK
THE Source Book For Prop & Set Dressing

The Cold War ended, we witnessed the **LA Riots**, CDs eclipsed cassette tapes as preferred music media, web browsers for non-geeks were being developed, and **Euro Disney** opened in France.

Television was crazy about **'Mad About You'**, **'Melrose Place'** and Jay Leno on the **'Tonight Show'**. Movies were full of sequels like **'Batman Returns'** and **'Lethal Weapon 3'**, but **'Silence of the Lambs'** took awards that year.

Life was a little scary for me, I started publishing Debbies Book full time. I added tabs and printed 3,000 copies – my biggest print run so far.

Costumes, International/Ethnic

See Also: Wardrobe, International/Ethnic
CBS Costume Rental (323) 575-2666
Middle Eastern, Asian, Caftans
The Costume House (818) 508-9933
JFF Uniforms-Costumes (310) 320-1327
557 Van Ness Ave, Torrance, CA, 90501
Custom garments 1-10,000 pcs made from sketch or sample. Period, military, modern & more.
www.jffuniforms.com
OPFOR Solutions, Inc (747) 666-7367
8100 Remmet Ave Unit #6, Canoga Park, CA, 91304
Opfor Solutions, Inc. brings you ethnic/military apparel from countries such as - Afghanistan, Iraq, Libya & more.
moe@opforsolutions.com * www.opforsolutions.com

INTERNATIONAL MILITARY COSTUMES · TRADITIONAL COSTUMES
PROPS · ATMOSPHERICS

MIDDLE EAST · SOUTH AFRICA · SOUTH AMERICA · ASIA

Sony Pictures Studios-Wardrobe (310) 244-5995
alterations, call (310) 244-7260
Universal Studios Costume Dept (818) 777-2722
Rental, mfg., & alterations
Warner Bros. Studios Costume Dept (818) 954-1297
Headpieces, Tribal, Folk, Latin, Islander, Grass Skirts, Polar, Middle Eastern
Western Costume Co. (818) 760-0900

Cotton Candy Machines

See: Vendor Carts & Concession Counters

Counters

See Also: Cafeteria Counter/Line* Display Cases, Racks & Fixtures (Store)* Kitchen Counters & Cabinets* Lunch Counters* Vendor Carts & Concession Counters
Acme Display Fixture & Packaging (888) 411-1870
3829 S Broadway St, Los Angeles, CA, 90037
Complete store setups: garment racks, displays/display cases, counters, packaging, shelving, hangers, mannequins
sales@acmedisplay.com * www.acmedisplay.com
AIR Designs (818) 768-6639
Airline, Bus Station, Auto Parts, Restaurant, Coffee Shop, Diner, Reception, Convenience Store
C. P. Two (323) 466-8201
Deli counters, restaurant counters, diner counters, meat counters, capuccino counter cart, receptionist counters and more.
FormDecor, Inc. (310) 558-2582
America's largest event rental supplier of 20th Century furniture and accessories for Modern and Mid-Century styles.
LCW Props (818) 243-0707
Desks, Airport, Digital, LED, Medical, Office
Lennie Marvin Enterprises, Inc. (Prop Heaven) (818) 841-5882
deli, coffee house, bakery, market, conv. store, diner, kitchen
Omega/Cinema Props (323) 466-8201
Deli counters, restaurant counters, diner counters, meat counters, capuccino counter cart, receptionist counters and more.
Sony Pictures Studios-Prop House (Off Lot) (310) 244-5999
display

Country Themed Parties

See: Events, Backings & Scenery* Events, Decorations, Supplies & Services* Events, Design/Planning/Production* Travel (City/Country) Themed Events

Courier Services

See: Messenger & Courier Services

Courtroom Furniture & Dressing

See Also: Scenery/Set Rentals
Alpha Companies - Spellman Desk Co. (818) 504-9090
judges benches, tables, Bank of England chairs, benches, flag posts, flags
Faux Library Studio Props, Inc. (818) 765-0096
clean quality legal book shelves, and legal office dressing including statuary, furniture, books, signs and more
The Hand Prop Room LP. (323) 931-1534
stenograph, block, hand props
History For Hire, Inc. (818) 765-7767
Omega/Cinema Props (323) 466-8201
Courtroom furniture and courtroom dressing.
RJR Props (404) 349-7600
Courtroom benches, stenographers typewriter and more for rent.
Sony Pictures Studios-Prop House (Off Lot) (310) 244-5999
Universal Studios Property & Hardware Dept (818) 777-2784
Courtroom props and dressing for rent.
Warner Bros. Studios Property Department (818) 954-2181
Courtroom benches, law books, courtroom smalls, podiums, seating

Coverlets

See: Linens, Household

Cowboy Dressing

See: Horse Saddles & Tack* Horses, Horse Equipment, Livestock* Western Wear

Cowboy Hats & Boots

See: Western Wear

Craft Supplies

See: Hobby & Craft Supplies

Cranes

See: Ladders* Scaffolding/Lighting Towers* Heavy Machinery, Equipment & Specialists

Crash Dummies

See: Dummies, Fall & Crash

Crash Pads

See: Fall Pads & Crash Pads

Crates/ Vaults

See Also: Barrels & Drums, Wood/Metal/Plastic* Boxes* Produce Crates

AIR Designs   (818) 768-6639
Fruit, Produce, Wine, Milk, Shipping Large & Small

Alley Cats Studio Rentals   (818) 982-9178
wood, metal, plastic

Basaw Manufacturing, Inc.   (818) 765-6650
7300 Varna, N Hollywood, CA, 91605
Basaw builds crates to order, large inventory in stock. all sizes & kinds, high multiples
fredy@basaw.com * www.basaw.com

C. P. Two   (323) 466-8201
Many crates of various sizes and types. Wooden crates, weathered crates, plastic crates and much more.

E.C. Prop Rentals   (818) 764-2008
wood & fiberglass, good multiples, many castered

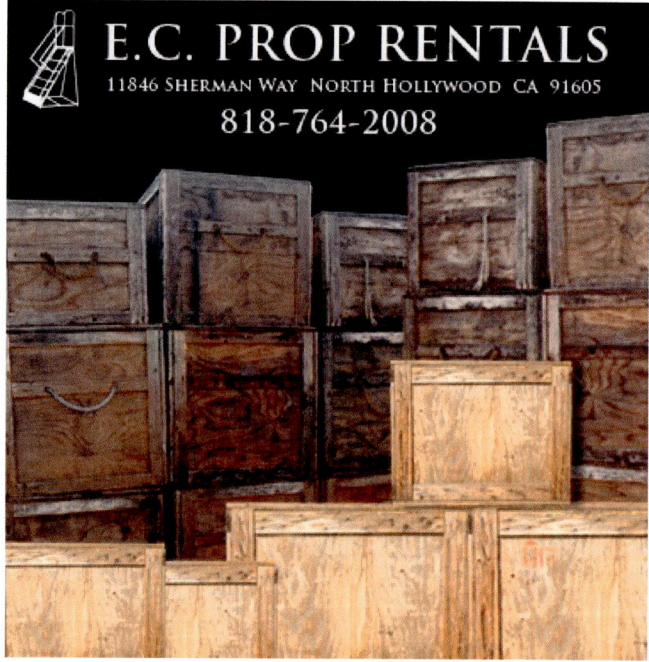

History For Hire, Inc.   (818) 765-7767
LCW Props   (818) 243-0707
Largest Selection Around. Crates Of Any Size & Shape. Wood, Plastic, Vault Storage and Marine Shipping Crates.

Sony Pictures Studios-Prop House (Off Lot)   (310) 244-5999
Universal Studios Property & Hardware Dept   (818) 777-2784
Many kinds of prop crates and vaults for rent.

Credit Card Imprint Machine

AIR Designs (818) 768-6639
Card Machines, ATM Pin Pads, Card Swipes
ATM Cash Connect/Financial Product, Inc. (818) 848-1025
624 S San Fernando Blvd, Burbank, CA, 91502
ATMs: all models, full function, custom paint/enclosures/screens manipulate cash dispensing, other bank machines
www.financialproductinc.com
Faux Library Studio Props, Inc. (818) 765-0096
Credit card imprint machines for rent or purchase.
The Hand Prop Room LP. (323) 931-1534
Digital credit card readers, vintage credit card imprint machine, card swipe machine, vintage card swipe machine
History For Hire, Inc. (818) 765-7767
LCW Props (818) 243-0707
Card Imprinters, POS, Credit Card Terminals, Credit Card Readers, Credit Card Machines
RC Vintage, Inc. (818) 765-7107
Plug in electric credit card readers/credit card machines
Universal Studios Property & Hardware Dept (818) 777-2784
Many kinds of prop credit card imprint machines and readers for rent.

Crime Scene Cleanup

See: Sanitation, Waste Disposal

Crowd Control: Barricades, Turnstiles Etc.

See Also: Barricades
E.C. Prop Rentals (818) 764-2008
Metal crowd control barricades, individual turnstiles, stanchions, high multiples

E.C. PROP RENTALS
11846 SHERMAN WAY NORTH HOLLYWOOD CA 91605
818-764-2008

History For Hire, Inc. (818) 765-7767
old style wood
Lavi Industries (888) 285-8605
27810 Hopkins Ave, Valencia, CA, 91355
mfg: retractable tape posts, stanchions & rope, railing systems rail & panels, turnstiles; hotel, restaurant, bank/theat
www.lavi.com
LCW Props (818) 243-0707
Barricades, Steel & Wood, Stanchions, Turnstile, Large Selection
Universal Studios Property & Hardware Dept (818) 777-2784
Prop barricades and turnstiles for rent.
ZG04 DECOR (818) 853-8040
Crowd control equipment and dressing; including barricades, walkie talkies, fences and more.

Crowd Stand-ups & Cutouts

See: Audience Cutouts & Inflatables

Crowns & Tiaras

See Also: Headwear - Hats, Bonnets, Caps, Helmets Etc.
The Costume House (818) 508-9933
tiaras & crowns
The Hand Prop Room LP. (323) 931-1534
Sony Pictures Studios-Prop House (Off Lot) (310) 244-5999
crowns & tiaras
Sword & Stone (818) 562-6548
in stock & custom fabricated with jewels & etching

Crucifixes & Crosses

See: Religious Articles

Cruise Ship Themed Parties

See: Events, Backings & Scenery* Events, Decorations, Supplies & Services* Events, Design/Planning/Production* Nautical Dressing & Props

Cryogenic Equipment

CONFETTI & FOG FX Special Effects Company (877) 576-4239
1085 W 21st Pl, Hialeah, FL, 33010
CO2 Effects
Info@confettiandfogfx.com * www.caffx.com
E.C. Prop Rentals (818) 764-2008
nitrogen tanks & many stainless pieces
EFX- Event Special Effects (626) 888-2239
125 Railroad Ave, Monrovia, CA, 91016
Cryo Guns- Cryo Cannons- Cyrogenics- Tanks
info@efxla.com * www.efxla.com
LCW Props (818) 243-0707
Largest Selection Around; Cryogenic Tanks/Cryogenic Tubes, Equipment, Hoses, Machines, Come Here First

Crystal Balls

See Also: Gypsy Wagon* Occult/Spiritual/Metaphysical
The Hand Prop Room LP. (323) 931-1534
Modern Props (323) 934-3000
solid glass crystal balls
Sony Pictures Studios-Prop House (Off Lot) (310) 244-5999
Universal Studios Property & Hardware Dept (818) 777-2784
Many crystal ball props for rent in different colors and sizes.

Crystal Stemware

See Also: Bars, Nightclubs, Barware & Dressing* Glassware/Dishes
The Hand Prop Room LP. (323) 931-1534
Modern Props (323) 934-3000
contemporary/futuristic, multiples of crystal stemware
Old N Country Prop Shop, LLC (818) 423-2599
Wine, champagne (hollow stem), footed champagne, after dinner drinks, etc.
Omega/Cinema Props (323) 466-8201
Wine glasses, champagne glasses and martini glasses.
Warner Bros. Studios Property Department (818) 954-2181
Crystal wine glasses, champagne flutes, champagne glasses, water glasses, assorted crystal glasses

Crystals

See: Gems, Minerals & Crystals

Cue Cards

See: Expendables* Teleprompting

Curtain/Drape Tracks & Platforms

See: Theatrical Draperies, Hardware & Rigging

Curtains

See: Drapery & Curtains* Events, Backings & Scenery* Theatrical Draperies, Hardware & Rigging* Window Treatments

Custom Props & Fabrication

See: Art For Rent (Cleared Art)* Art, Artists For Hire* Fiberglass Products/Fabrication* Furniture, Custom-made/Reproduction* Metalworking, Decorative* Metalworking, Welding & Structural* Prop Design & Manufacturing* Prop Reproduction & Fabrication* Scenery/Set Construction* Vacu-forms/Vacu-forming

Cut Outs, Audience

See: Audience Cutouts & Inflatables

Cycle Exercisers

See: Exercise & Fitness Equipment

Daggers

See: Swords & Swordplay* Weaponry, Historical* Weaponry, Medieval* Weapons

Dance Equipment

See: Ballet Barres & Dance Mirrors* Dance Floors

Dance Floors

See Also: Ballet Barres & Dance Mirrors

Astro Audio Video Lighting, Inc. (818) 549-9915
6615 San Fernando Rd, Glendale, CA, 91201
Dance floors and dance floor rentals for any event.
www.astroavl.com

Dance Equipment International (800) 626-9258
2103 Lincoln Ave, Ste C, San Jose, CA, 95125
Marley type dance floors, hardwood sprung dance floor systems
www.danceequipment.com

L. A. Party Works (888) 527-2789
9712 Alpaca St, S El Monte, CA, 91733
Portable dance floors/panel flooring including traditional and LED dance floors.
partyworks@aol.com * www.partyworksinteractive.com

888-527-2789
partyworksusa.com

ALLOWING INFINITE COMBINATIONS AND IMMERSIVE CAPABILITIES.
MULTIPLE COLORS, SHAPES AND SIZES

Linoleum City, Inc. (323) 469-0063
4849 Santa Monica Blvd, Hollywood, CA, 90029
Dance floors, stage floors, smooth floors, shiny floors, studio tiles, solid color vinyl, paint back vinyl.
sales@linocity.com * www.linoleumcity.com

ZG04 DECOR (818) 853-8040
Portable dance floors/event dance floors and permanent dance floor installation

Dance Wear

Discount Dance Supply (714) 999-0955
1501 N Raymond Ave Ste E, Anaheim, CA, 92801
catalog sales; dance wear, tights, warmups, shoes
www.discountdance.com

N2N Bodywear (213) 748-1797
1358 S Flower St, Los Angeles, CA, 90015
men's erotic wear, swimwear, underwear. contemp. men's dance & athletic wear
www.n2nbodywear.com

Sony Pictures Studios-Wardrobe (310) 244-5995
alterations, call (310) 244-7260

Danish Modern

See: Furniture, Mid-Century Modern

Darkroom

See: Camera Equipment* Photographs, Digital Processing

Darts & Dartboards

See Also: Prop Houses* Sporting Goods & Services

Billiards & Barstools (818) 897-5772
12381 Foothill Blvd, Sylmar, CA, 91342
www.billiardsandbarstools.com

The Hand Prop Room LP. (323) 931-1534

History For Hire, Inc. (818) 765-7767

Day Of The Dead

See: Mexican Decorations

Decontamination Suits

See: Protective Apparel

Decorative Accessories

See Also: Antiques & Antique Decorations* Art For Rent (Cleared Art)* Candelabras* Carved Figures* Collectibles* Linens, Household* Memorabilia & Novelties* Prop Houses* Religious Articles* Sculpture

Badia Design, Inc. (818) 762-0130
5420 Vineland Ave, N Hollywood, CA, 91601
Moroccan Home Decor and Accessories including Moroccan furniture, rugs, lamps, light fixtures and more.
info@badiadesign.com * www.badiadesign.com

Bridge Furniture & Props Los Angeles (818) 433-7100
We carry modern & traditional furniture, lighting, accessories, art, & rugs. Items are online for easy shopping.

Castle Antiques & Design (818) 765-5000
11924 Vose St, N Hollywood, CA, 91605
All styles of table top objects, vases, urns, candelabras, glass cups, crystal cups, paintings, pillows, and statues
info@castleantiques.net * www.castleprophouse.com

Clifford Antiques (747) 283-1272
3429 Magnolia Blvd, Burbank, CA, 91505
British Antiques shipped from Scotland we're a family run business with over 40 years experience
wfcliffordantiques@yahoo.com * www.cliffordantiques.com

Faux Library Studio Props, Inc. (818) 765-0096
wide selection of high-end, fresh, quality accessories to accompany book shelves, table tops and desk tops, choice ornamentation

FormDecor, Inc. (310) 558-2582
America's largest event rental supplier of 20th Century furniture and accessories for Modern and Mid-Century styles.

Galerie Sommerlath - French 50s 60s (310) 838-0102
9608 Venice Blvd, Culver City, CA, 90232
Over 10,000 sq ft of Mid-Century, 70's & 80's furniture, lighting, accessories, home decor, art, sculptures, paintings.
info@galeriesommerlath.com * www.galeriesommerlath.com

The Hand Prop Room LP. (323) 931-1534
fabulous silver collection and more

Hollywood Cinema Arts (818) 504-7333
Thousands of small props from the unusual to the ordinary.

L. A. Mart (800) 526-2784
1933 S Broadway, Los Angeles, CA, 90007
400+ showrooms in 725K sqft; giftware, merchandise, furnishings accessories to registered buyers. Call for directory.
www.lamart.com

Little Bohemia Rentals (818) 853-7506
11940 Sherman Rd, N Hollywood, CA, 91605
Antique through contemporary smalls.
sales@wearelittlebohemia.com * www.wearelittlebohemia.com

Modern Props (323) 934-3000
Hand props and decorative accessories of a wide assortment. We can fabricate too!

Modernica Props (323) 664-2322

NEST Studio Rentals, Inc. (818) 942-0339
large selection; many cleared items

N.S. Aerospace Props (818) 765-1087
7429 Laurel Canyon Blvd, N Hollywood, CA, 91605
Rocket Engines, Rocket Components, Hardware, Fittings and Industrial parts for various time periods, consultations too.
nortonsalesm@aol.com * www.nortonsalesinc.com

Ob-jects (818) 351-4200
Decorative accessories

OK the Store (323) 653-3501
8303 W 3rd St, Los Angeles, CA, 90048
unique home decor & gifts, will carry Studio accounts
www.okthestore.com

Old N Country Prop Shop, LLC (818) 423-2599
Art work, wood carvings, tins, stitchery, china, knick-knacks, salt and pepper
shakers, planters, etc.

Omega/Cinema Props (323) 466-8201
Many kinds of decorative accessories from dishes, canisters, centerpieces and
much more.

Pasadena Antiques & Design (626) 389-3938
330 S Fair Oaks Avenue, Pasadena, CA, 91105
Antique and Mid Century Accessories. A huge selection in 21,600 sq. ft.
roy@antiquesofpasadena.com * www.antiquesofpasadena.com

Prop Services West (818) 503-2790
brass, porcelain, etc.

Retro Gallery (323) 936-5261
5738 W Washington Blvd, Los Angeles, CA, 90016
20th C glass lamps, vases, objets d'art, primarily European

A Royal Suite Home Furinishings (661) 259-7000
26536 Carl Boyer Dr, Santa Clarita, CA, 91350
A Royal Suite, family-owned since 1978, Features AMERICAN-MADE
Furniture, and the Finest Furniture at the Greatest Value
norb@ars-email.com * www.aroyalsuite.com

ShopWildThings (928) 855-6075
2880 Sweetwater Ave, Lake Havasu City, AZ, 86406
Event Decor, Beaded Curtains, Chain Curtains, String Curtains & Columns,
Crystal Columns. Reliable service & delivery.
help@shopwildthings.com * www.shopwildthings.com

Sword & Stone (818) 562-6548
Tabletop statues, skulls, candelabras, gemstones and jewels

Universal Studios Property & Hardware Dept (818) 777-2784
Prop decorative accessories for rent, from smalls to large.

Used Church Items, Religious Rentals (412) 220-2272
115 East Barr Street, Mcdonald, PA, 15057
Baptismal Fonts, Votive stands, Banners, Stands, Statues, Crucifixes, Lights,
Cruets, Vestments, Altars, Angels.
www.religiousrentals.com

Warner Bros. Studios The Collection (818) 954-2181
4000 Warner Blvd Bldg 30, Burbank, CA, 91522
High end fixtures, smalls, rugs, desk accessories, linens, pillows, frames,
gadgets, kitchen dressing
wbsfproperty@warnerbros.com * www.wbpropertydept.com

ZG04 DECOR (818) 853-8040
Smalls, Ceramics, Porcelain and Ceramics, Multi Cultural, Eclectic, Tribal &
Folk, Antique

Decoys

See: Fishing Equipment & Tackle Sporting Goods & Services*

Deep Fryer

AIR Designs (818) 768-6639
Period to Modern, Baskets, Restaurant and Smaller

Omega/Cinema Props (323) 466-8201
Residential deep fryers & commercial deep fryers

Universal Studios Property & Hardware Dept (818) 777-2784
Prop commercial deep fryers, deep fryer baskets, and more for rent.

Delicatessen Equipment

See Also: Cafe Tables/Chairs/Umbrellas Coffee House* Display
Cases, Racks & Fixtures (Store)* Food, Artificial Food* Restaurant
Kitchens/Equip./Supplies* Shopping Bags (Silent)*

AIR Designs (818) 768-6639
Display Cases, Fake Food, Scales, Jars, Glass Door Coolers, Deli Slicers,
Meat Saw, Food Props

The Hand Prop Room LP. (323) 931-1534
dressing, signage, accessories, replica food

History For Hire, Inc. (818) 765-7767

LCW Props (818) 243-0707
Signs, Take A Ticket, Display Counters, Fake Meats & Cheeses

Lennie Marvin Enterprises, Inc. (Prop Heaven) (818) 841-5882
period/modern, cases, fake food, compl. deli dressing

Sony Pictures Studios-Prop House (Off Lot) (310) 244-5999

Universal Studios Property & Hardware Dept (818) 777-2784
Prop deli equipment, butcher meat carts, meat slicers, sandwich boards,
dressing and more for rent.

Dentist Equipment

See Also: Medical Equip/Furniture, Graphics/Supplies

A-1 Medical Integration (818) 753-0319
Medical devices for Set Decoration & Property, from minor procedures to
detailed hospital units.

Alpha Companies - Spellman Desk Co. (818) 504-9090
The #1 source for medical equipment in the Industry.

Dapper Cadaver (818) 771-0818
Mouth gags, tooth extruders, stainless steel instruments & instrument trays.
Open-mouth prop heads. Replica teeth.

Estrada Dental Supply (909) 989-2088
8556 Red Oak St, Rancho Cucamonga, CA, 91730
1890 to present, consulting on dentist procedures
HANKIE1@dslextreme.com * www.estradadental.com

The Hand Prop Room LP. (323) 931-1534

LCW Props (818) 243-0707
Chairs, Signs, Certificates, Tools, Lighting

Universal Studios Property & Hardware Dept (818) 777-2784
Prop dental equipment for rent

Department Store

See Also: Cash Registers Counters* Credit Card Imprint Machine*
Display Cases, Racks & Fixtures (Store)* Jewelry,
Fine/Reproduction* Prop Houses* Security Walk-Through & Baggage
Alarms* Shopping Bags (Silent)* Shopping Carts* Steel Folding
Gates & Roll-Up Doors* Store Shelf Units & Shelving* Surveillance
Equipment* Wardrobe*

Acme Display Fixture & Packaging (888) 411-1870
3829 S Broadway St, Los Angeles, CA, 90037
Complete store setups: garment racks, displays/display cases, counters,
packaging, shelving, hangers, mannequins
sales@acmedisplay.com * www.acmedisplay.com

Lennie Marvin Enterprises, Inc. (Prop Heaven) (818) 841-5882
extensive; fixtures, equipment, products, & more

Designers

See: Art, Artists For Hire Events, Design/Planning/Production*
Printing, Graphics, Digital & Large Format* Prop Design &
Manufacturing* Prop Reproduction & Fabrication* Scenery/Set
Construction* Staff Shops* Themed Environment Construction*

Desk Dressing

See Also: Globes, World Map* Maps* Office Equipment & Dressing* Office Supplies* Paperwork, Documents & Letters, Office

Advanced Liquidators Office Furniture   **(818) 763-3470**
phones, etc. desktop office equipment, desktop smalls, many desktop items for business or home desks

Alpha Companies - Spellman Desk Co.   **(818) 504-9090**
Phones, computers, staples, stack trays, desk pads

Dozar Office Furnishings   **(310) 559-9292**
9937 Jefferson Blvd, Culver City, CA, 90232
Rentals X22. Desks, book stops, desk clocks, battery clocks, speakers, desk art, artistic paper weights
dozarrents@aol.com * www.dozarrents.com

E.C. Prop Rentals   **(818) 764-2008**
lamps/file holders/letter trays/smalls

Faux Library Studio Props, Inc.   **(818) 765-0096**
1000's of desktop items, even the desks, vintage desk set, retro desk sets

huge collection • 60,000 sq ft • furniture • accessories • modern • antiques
Lightweight Books • Prop Books • Desk Dressing
Faux Library Studio Props

The Hand Prop Room LP.   **(323) 931-1534**
desk access., phones, adding machines, typewriters

History For Hire, Inc.   **(818) 765-7767**
period

LCW Props   **(818) 243-0707**
Anything You Need, Large Quantities, Everything

Modern Props   **(323) 934-3000**
contemporary/futuristic desk dressing, artificial plants, and more

Old N Country Prop Shop, LLC   **(818) 423-2599**
A variety of typewriters, desk lamps, desk accessories and assorted smalls.

Omega/Cinema Props   **(323) 466-8201**
Paperweights, ink stands, calculators, letter trays, typewriters, memo pads, pencil cups, ink wells and more.

Picture Start Props   **(818) 255-5472**
Large selection of desk dressing/desk smalls.

Prop Services West   **(818) 503-2790**

Sony Pictures Studios-Prop House (Off Lot)   **(310) 244-5999**
writing desks and dressing

Universal Studios Property & Hardware Dept   **(818) 777-2784**
Prop name plates and name plate holders along with all other kinds of desk dressing

Warner Bros. Studios Property Department   **(818) 954-2181**
Blotters & Desk Pads, Desktop Accessories, Letter Trays & Sorters, Magazine Files, Pencil Cups

ZG04 DECOR   **(818) 853-8040**
Globes, Paperwork, Binders, Books, Desk Smalls, Blotters, Desk-Sets, Desk-Frames, Note-pads, Calendars, Desk-Clocks

Desks

See: Lab Equipment* Office Furniture* School Supplies, Desks & Dressing

Dessert Carts

See: Restaurant Furniture & Dressing* Vendor Carts & Concession Counters

Detectives

See: Private Investigations

Detour Signs

See: Traffic/Road Signs, Lights, Safety Items

Diapers & Rags

See: Expendables

Digital Device Imaging, D.D.I.

See: Video 24fps / Sync System / D.D.I.

Digital Imaging

See: Art, Artists For Hire* Printing, Graphics, Digital & Large Format* Signs

Dimensional Signage

See: Printing, Graphics, Digital & Large Format* Signs

Diner Restaurant

See: Restaurant Furniture & Dressing* Restaurant Kitchens/Equip./Supplies

Dinosaurs

See Also: Bones, Skulls & Skeletons* Fossils

Dapper Cadaver   **(818) 771-0818**
Dinosaur skulls, skeletons, bones and teeth. Lifelike dinosaur statues and fossil panels. T-rex skeleton.

Kokoro Dinosaurs   **(818) 704-9094**
6800 Owensmouth Ave Suite 110, Canoga Park CA, 91303
prehistoric mammals, dinosaurs, giant insects, display exhibits, lifesize/large, animated/robotic also
www.kokorodinosaurs.com

LM Treasures   **(626) 252-7354**
We acquire a variation of extraordinary dinosaurs ranging from life size 7000 lbs. Mammoths to Baby Triceratops at 5 lbs.

Universal Studios Property & Hardware Dept   **(818) 777-2784**
Assorted prop dinosaur rentals from fossils to stuffed animals.

Director's Chairs, Bags, Pouches

See Also: Folding Chairs/Tables

C. P. Two   **(323) 466-8201**
Tall directors chairs, folding directors chairs, wooden directors chairs, metal directors chairs

Castex Rentals   **(323) 462-1468**
1044 N Cole Ave, Hollywood, CA, 90038
authorized dealer to the Industry, replacement directors chair seats & backs, Hollywood chairs, director chairs
service@castexrentals.com * www.castexrentals.com

The Hand Prop Room LP.   **(323) 931-1534**
in-house fab., logos for chair backs

History For Hire, Inc.   **(818) 765-7767**
period, current, all eras

Universal Studios Property & Hardware Dept   **(818) 777-2784**
Many types and sizes of directors chairs, including side pouches.

ZG04 DECOR   **(818) 853-8040**
Director chairs for rent

Directories

See: Search Tools, Directories, Libraries

Dirt Skins

Green Set, Inc.   **(818) 764-1231**

Jackson Shrub Supply, Inc.   **(818) 982-0100**
sheets of... dirt! Dirk skins as well as cam skins

LCW Props   **(818) 243-0707**
large quantities

Disco Balls/Mirror Balls & Drivers

AIR Designs (818) 768-6639
12" to 48"

Astro Audio Video Lighting, Inc. (818) 549-9915
6615 San Fernando Rd, Glendale, CA, 91201
12" to 40" mirror balls; all sizes with motor drives for disco dudes & divas. Fixed & variable speeds
www.astroavl.com

History For Hire, Inc. (818) 765-7767

LCW Props (818) 243-0707
Complete DJ Setup, Disco Balls, Lighting

Omega/Cinema Props (323) 466-8201

RC Vintage, Inc. (818) 765-7107
Large assortment, disco balls, laser disco ball light

ShopWildThings (928) 855-6075
2880 Sweetwater Ave, Lake Havasu City, AZ, 86406
Event Decor, Beaded Curtains, Chain Curtains, String Curtains & Columns, Crystal Columns. Reliable service & delivery.
help@shopwildthings.com * www.shopwildthings.com

Sony Pictures Studios-Fixtures (310) 244-5996
5933 W Slauson Ave, Culver City, CA, 90230
period to present day, disco ball, electronic disco ball
www.sonypicturesstudios.com

Universal Studios Property & Hardware Dept (818) 777-2784
Mirror balls and disco mirror balls for rent, in different sizes.

Disco Floors

See: Dance Floors

Dishes

See: Glassware/Dishes

Display Cases, Racks & Fixtures (Store)

See Also: Candy Racks* Comic Books & Comic Book Racks* Hat Racks* Magazines & Magazine/Newspaper Racks* Market Equipment/Fixtures* Store Shelf Units & Shelving

10 Karat Rentals (818) 635-4124
7100 Tujunga (At RC Vintage), N Hollywood, CA, 91605
10karatrentals@gmail.com

Acme Display Fixture & Packaging (888) 411-1870
3829 S Broadway St, Los Angeles, CA, 90037
Complete store setups: garment racks, displays/display cases, counters, packaging, shelving, hangers, mannequins
sales@acmedisplay.com * www.acmedisplay.com

GARMENT RACKS · STEAMERS · FORMS · MANNEQUINS · JEWELRY DISPLAYS

STORE COUNTERS · PACKAGING · GONDOLA SYSTEMS · DISPLAY CASES

AIR Designs (818) 768-6639
Mini Mart, Grocery Wire Racks/Glass Display Cases

Alley Cats Studio Rentals (818) 982-9178

Books For Libraries, Inc. (800) 321-5596
28064 Ave Standford Unit L, Santa Clarita, CA, 91355
Metal cantilever library shelving or wooden modular shelving
JStitz@pacbell.net * www.booksforlibraries.com

Custom Acrylic Fabrication Corp. (310) 844-7640
13004 S. Figueroa, Los Angeles, CA, 90061
cut to size acrylic, display cases, next day service
www.customacrylic.com

The Hand Prop Room LP. (323) 931-1534
jewelry cases, jewelry display cases, jewelry stands, wardrobe racks, antique hat stands

Henry Hanger Company (877) 436-7952
3101 S. Hill St, Los Angeles, CA, 90007
many styles of clothing hangers
www.henryhanger.com

LCW Props (818) 243-0707
Wardrobe Racks, Kiosks, Counters, Tables

Modern Props (323) 934-3000
contemporary/futuristic display cases, display racks and display fixtures

Omega/Cinema Props (323) 466-8201
Market display cases, residential display cases, commercial display cases, retail display cases, and more.

RC Vintage, Inc. (818) 765-7107
40s, 50s & 60s Department Store..

Sony Pictures Studios-Prop House (Off Lot) (310) 244-5999
retail display cases, jewelry display cases, candy display cases, wine racks, dish racks, magazine racks, postcard racks, more

Universal Studios Property & Hardware Dept (818) 777-2784
Present to period prop display cases, racks & fixtures for rent.

ZG04 DECOR (818) 853-8040
Display cases and display shelves/display shelving for rent.

Display Food

See: Food, Artificial Food* Food, Food Stylists

Diving Equipment

See: Nautical Dressing & Props* Nautical/Marine Services & Charters* Sporting Goods & Services* Wetsuits, Diving/Surfing

DJ/VJ Booths & Equipment

See: Events, Entertainment* Radio/TV Station* Lighting & Sound, Concert/Theatrical/DJ/VJ* Audio Equipment

Dock Cleats

See: Nautical Dressing & Props

Doctor's Bags

The Hand Prop Room LP. (323) 931-1534
period-present

History For Hire, Inc. (818) 765-7767

Sony Pictures Studios-Prop House (Off Lot) (310) 244-5999

Universal Studios Property & Hardware Dept (818) 777-2784
Prop doctors bags for rent.

Doctors Office

See: Dentist Equipment* Doctor's Bags* Gurneys* Hospital Equipment* Medical Equip/Furniture, Graphics/Supplies* Stretchers* X-ray Machine* X-ray Viewer* X-rays & X-ray Viewers* Waiting Room* Emergency Room* Exam Room

Documents

See: Book Covers & Bookbinding* Books, Real/Hollow & Faux Books* Printing, Graphics, Digital & Large Format* Paperwork, Documents & Letters, Office

Doghouses

See: Garden/Patio* Pet Furniture, Houses, Clothing

Dogs

See: Animals (Live), Services, Trainers & Wranglers

Dogsleds

See Also: Animals (Live), Services, Trainers & Wranglers* Christmas* Sleds

LCW Props (818) 243-0707
Period, Wood

Universal Studios Property & Hardware Dept (818) 777-2784
Prop dog sleds for rent.

Dollhouses

See Also: Dolls Toys & Games*

The Hand Prop Room LP. (323) 931-1534
design & mfg. dollhouses, antique dollhouse, vintage dollhouse, wooden dollhouse, dollhouse furniture

Merritt Productions, Inc. (818) 760-0612
10845 Vanowen St, North Hollywood, CA, 91605
specialty props, miniatures, sculpture, mech effects, set const.
www.merrittproductions.com

My Doll's House (310) 320-4828
1218 El Prado Ave Ste 136, Torrance, CA 90501
Dollhouses, Dollhouse Kits, Room Boxes, Miniatures, Collectibles, Accessories, Tools and Supplies
margiesminiatures@gmail.com * www.mydollshouse.com

Omega/Cinema Props (323) 466-8201
Various doll houses

Prop Services West (818) 503-2790

Universal Studios Property & Hardware Dept (818) 777-2784
Many kinds of prop doll houses and doll house furniture for rent.

Dollies

See: Camera Equipment Furniture Dollies, Pads & Hand Trucks*

Dolls

See Also: Children/Baby Accessories & Bedroom Dollhouses* Soldier Toys & Drums* Toys & Games*

Dolls By Sandra (818) 343-4842
7700 Rhea Ave, Reseda, CA, 91335
All dolls, modern, antique & portrait, doll repairs & doll refurbishment

The Hand Prop Room LP. (323) 931-1534

History For Hire, Inc. (818) 765-7767
vintage

Modern Props (323) 934-3000
large selection of antique chalk dolls

Monique Trading Corp. (510) 887-6200
27317 Industrial Blvd, Hayward, CA, 94545
catalog sales; parts only; doll wigs, eyes, eyelashes, stands website links to many other doll sites
sales@monique.com * www.monique.com

Ob-jects (818) 351-4200
Dolls

Old N Country Prop Shop, LLC (818) 423-2599
Vintage, Revlon doll, baby dolls, stuffed animals, porcelain head dolls, rag dolls, collectible figures, etc.

Omega/Cinema Props (323) 466-8201
Dolls of many kinds including stuffed dolls, russian stacking dolls, wooden dolls, paper dolls and more.

Prop Services West (818) 503-2790

RC Vintage, Inc. (818) 765-7107
Vintage Dolls Turn of the Century

Sony Pictures Studios-Prop House (Off Lot) (310) 244-5999
large selection, for all ages

Universal Studios Property & Hardware Dept (818) 777-2784
Prop period dolls to contemporary dolls for rent.

ZG04 DECOR (818) 853-8040
Many dolls for rent, including cleared dolls

Donations

See: Charities & Donations

Doors

See Also: Architectural Pieces & Artifacts Salvage, Architectural*

Charisma Design Studio, Inc. (818) 252-6611
8414 San Fernando Road, Sun Valley, CA, 91352
custom metal/glass/wood functional art
info@charismadesign.com * www.charismadesign.com

Coppa Woodworking, Inc. (310) 548-5332
1231 Paraiso Ave, San Pedro, CA, 90731
catalog sales; old fashioned wood screen doors
www.coppawoodworking.com

The ReUse People (818) 244-5635
3015 Dolores St, Los Angeles, CA, 90065
Hundreds of doors to choose from.
JeffCockerell@TheReUsePeople.org * www.TheReUsePeople.org

Dori Poles

See: Events, Decorations, Supplies & Services

Drafting Equipment & Supplies

See Also: Blueprint Equipment & Supplies Printing, Graphics, Digital & Large Format* Miniatures/Models* Office Equipment & Dressing* Plotters & Plotting Services*

The Hand Prop Room LP. (323) 931-1534
T-squares, micrometers, antique drafting tables, drafting tools

History For Hire, Inc. (818) 765-7767

Hopper's Office & Drafting Furniture (323) 254-7362
2901 Fletcher Dr, Los Angeles, CA, 90065
Prop rentals for art/drafting room. Over 100 Drafting tables, flat files, stools, & all drafting equipment.
www.draftingfurniture.com

Modern Props (323) 934-3000
contemporary/futuristic drafting equipment and drafting supplies

The Rational Past (310) 476-6277
By Appointment, West Los Angeles, CA
Authentic science, industrial, technical antiques & collectibles. Many professions & eras represented. See web site.
info@therationalpast.com * www.therationalpast.com

Repro-Graphic Supply (818) 771-9066
9838 Glenoaks Blvd, Sun Valley, CA, 91352
drafting & engineering supplies, equipment & service, all Ind.'s inc. architects.
See Display Ad in Blueprint Equipment
info@reprographicsupply.com * www.reprographicsupply.com

Steven Enterprises (800) 491-8785
17952 Skypark Circle Unit E, Irvine, CA, 92614
Wide Format Printers. Rent/Buy. Authorized Dealer: HP, KIP, Canon, Oce, Epson. We service & supply everything we install
sales@plotters.com * www.plotters.com

Drapery & Curtains

See Also: Flameproofing* Hampers, Theatrical* Rigging, Equipment or Services* Stanchions & Rope* Theatrical Draperies, Hardware & Rigging* Window Treatments

Astro Audio Video Lighting, Inc. (818) 549-9915
6615 San Fernando Rd, Glendale, CA, 91201
www.astroavl.com

Fox Studios Production Services (310) 369-4636
10201 W. Pico Blvd, Los Angeles, CA, 90035
www.foxstudios.com/production_services_depts

Lushes Curtains (626) 453-0337
1855 Tyler Ave Unit C, S El Monte, CA, 91733
Your Direct Velvet Curtain Manufacture! Delivering Elegant and Quality Curtains to Every Industry World Wide!
Joe@LushesCurtains.com * www.LushesCurtains.com

NEST Studio Rentals, Inc. (818) 942-0339
multiple 84" and 95" contemporary panels

Old N Country Prop Shop, LLC (818) 423-2599
Silk, gingham, linen, pom pom curtains, country check, boy prints, drapes, midcentury orange, green, etc.

Omega/Cinema Props (323) 466-8201
Drapery rentals & drapery sales, manufacturing, Local 44. Custom drapery shop.

ShopWildThings (928) 855-6075
2880 Sweetwater Ave, Lake Havasu City, AZ, 86406
Event Decor, Beaded Curtains, Chain Curtains, String Curtains & Columns, Crystal Columns. Reliable service & delivery.
help@shopwildthings.com * www.shopwildthings.com

Sony Pictures Studios-Linens, Drapes, Rugs (310) 244-5999
5933 W Slauson Ave, Culver City, CA, 90230
large selection of drapes & curtains, sheers
www.sonypicturesstudios.com

Sony Pictures Studios-Prop House (Off Lot) (310) 244-5999
Drapes, placemats, curtain sheer panels, domestic drapery, velvet theatre drapes, drapery trim, domestic drape tassels, more

Strickland's Window Coverings (910) 762-0944
5422 Oleander Dr, Wilmington, NC, 28403
Strickland's Window Coverings Set Services has been providing window coverings to the film industry for over 26 years.
beckah@stricklandsblinds.com * www.stricklandsblinds.com

TRU-ROLL (626) 599-8337
735 Los Angeles Ave, Monrovia, CA, 91016
Stage, Auditorium, Theme Park and commercial custom manufacturing of drapery and Tru Roll support track systems.
info@truroll.com * www.truroll.com

Universal Studios Drapery Dept (818) 777-2761
manufacturing

Warner Bros. Drapery, Upholstery & Flooring (818) 954-1831
4000 Warner Blvd Bldg 30, Burbank, CA, 91522
Window treatments, vintage, period, modern, deco, curtains, beaded curtains, theatrical draperies
wbsfdrapery@warnerbros.com * www.wbdrapery.com

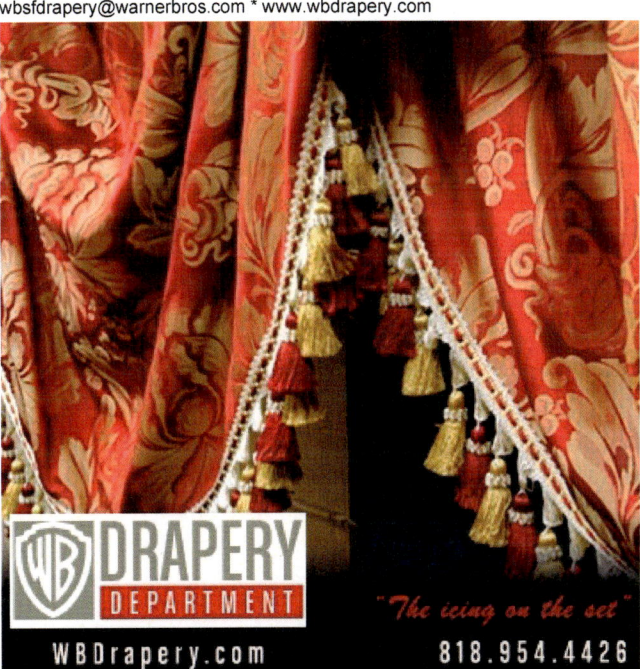

ZG04 DECOR (818) 853-8040
Custom made Drapery, Stage Curtains, Curtains, Sheers, Custom Drapery, Pillows, Table-linens, Bedding

Dress Forms

See Also: Mannequins

C. P. Two (323) 466-8201
Dress forms of many kinds.

The Hand Prop Room LP. (323) 931-1534
dress forms, rolling dress forms, antique dress forms, vintage dress forms, full size dress forms, cloth dress forms

History For Hire, Inc. (818) 765-7767
character

LCW Props (818) 243-0707
Multiple Sizes

Sony Pictures Studios-Prop House (Off Lot) (310) 244-5999

Universal Studios Property & Hardware Dept (818) 777-2784
Prop sewing dress forms, display dress forms, mens dress forms and womens dress forms for rent.

Drink & Beverage Machines/Carts

See: Beer Equipment, Taps & Coolers* Fountains, Drinking (Wall & Stand)* Soda Fountain Dressing* Vending Machines* Vendor Carts & Concession Counters

Drinking Fountains

See: Fountains, Drinking (Wall & Stand)* Soda Fountain Dressing

Drones, UAVs & UASs

AeroVironment, Inc (626) 357-9983
PO Box 5031, Monrovia, CA 91017
Committed to creating and delivering powerful new Unmanned Aircraft and Electric Vehicle solutions.
evscs@avinc.com * www.avinc.com

Drone Dudes - Aerial Cinematography Specialists (866) 856-8465
Call for Appt.
Every system we design and flight we take is driven by our love of cutting-edge cinema, music and new adventures.
bookings@dronedudes.com * www.dronedudes.com

DroneFly.com (805) 480-4033
2630 Townsgate Road Suite I, Westlake Village, CA 91361
A leader in the drone Aerospace Industry for both professional and recreational uses. We also offer full service repairs.
contact@dronefly.com * www.dronefly.com

LCW Props (818) 243-0707
Drones of various kinds

Precision Aerial Filmworks (561) 221-1450
2110 Corporate Drive, Boynton Beach, FL, 33426
FAA approved, Licensed and Insured Aerial Cinematography for Television and Cinema.
keith@pafilmworks.com * www.pafilmworks.com

Drops

See: Backings* Printing, Graphics, Digital & Large Format* Scenery/Set Construction* Theatrical Draperies, Hardware & Rigging

Drugstore/Apothecary

See Also: Candy Jars* Cash Registers* Counters* Credit Card Imprint Machine* Display Cases, Racks & Fixtures (Store)* Prop Products & Packages* Security Walk-Through & Baggage Alarms* Soda Fountain Dressing* Steel Folding Gates & Roll-Up Doors* Store Shelf Units & Shelving

Dapper Cadaver (818) 771-0818
1800s to present. Apothecary jars, specimens, glassware, labware, instruments & decor. Vintage pharmacy to modern lab.

The Hand Prop Room LP. (323) 931-1534
period-present, glasses, bottles, beakers, signage

History For Hire, Inc. (818) 765-7767

LCW Props (818) 243-0707
Huge Selection Of Apothecary Jars, Pill Bottles, Fake Drugs, Meth lab Dressing, Kilos Cocaine, Marijuana

RC Vintage, Inc. (818) 765-7107
period jars & 40s, 50s & 60s dressing of all kinds & neons

Universal Studios Property & Hardware Dept (818) 777-2784
Prop apothecary dressing and drugstore dressing for rent.

Vermont Country Store (802) 824-3184
657 Main St, Weston, VT, 05161
Catalog: hard-to-find household furnishings, clothing, food & personal care items just like old-fashioned drugstore
www.vermontcountrystore.com

Drums

See: Barrels & Drums, Wood/Metal/Plastic* Crates/ Vaults* Musical Instruments* Tanks* Wine Kegs

Dry Cleaners (Dressing)

See Also: Vacuum Cleaners
Lennie Marvin Enterprises, Inc. (Prop Heaven)   (818) 841-5882
storefront setup, steamers

Dry Cleaning Services

See: Cleaners & Cleaning Services* Laundry Carts

Dry Ice

See: Ice Sculpture

Dryers

See: Cleaners & Cleaning Services* Washing Machines/Dryers

Dulling Spray

See: Expendables

Dumbbells

See: Exercise & Fitness Equipment* Weightlifting Equipment

Dummies

See: Magicians & Props, Supplies, Dressing* Mannequins* Puppets, Marionettes, Automata, Animatronics

Dummies, Fall & Crash

Dapper Cadaver   (818) 771-0818
Poseable stunt dummies and fall dummies. Male and female. Lifelike and corpse. Wounded, burn and custom FX.
Elden Designs   (323) 550-8922
2767 W. Broadway, Eagle Rock, CA, 90041
crash test dummies, NO fall dummies
cargocollective.com/eldendesign
The Hand Prop Room LP.   (323) 931-1534
History For Hire, Inc.   (818) 765-7767
fall type
Leavittation, Inc.   (661) 252-7551
25982 Sand Canyon Rd, Santa Clarita, CA, 91387
articulated crash dummies & puppeteering,crash & stunt pads
www.stuntrev.com
Universal Studios Property & Hardware Dept   (818) 777-2784
Various prop dummies, dummy body parts, and more of different sizes, types and gender for rent.

Dumpsters

See: Alley Dressing* Construction Site Equipment

Dungeon

See: Medieval

Dunk Tanks

See: Carnival Games & Rides

Duplicating

See: Copy Machines* Photographs, Digital Processing

Dutch Shoes

See: Shoes, Boots & Footwear

Duvet

See: Linens, Household

Duvetyne

See: Expendables* Fire Extinguishers, Practical & Prop* Flameproofing

DVD Rental/Sales Store

See: Video Rental/Sales Store* Video Store Dressing

Dyeing

See: Fabric Dyeing/Tie Dyeing/Painting/Aging* Paint & Painting Supplies

Early American Furniture

See: Furniture, Early American/Colonial

Earthquake Monitoring Equipment

See: Lab Equipment

Easels

See Also: Art For Rent (Cleared Art)* Art, Artists For Hire* Art, Supplies & Stationery
Astro Audio Video Lighting, Inc.   (818) 549-9915
6615 San Fernando Rd, Glendale, CA, 91201
www.astroavl.com
The Hand Prop Room LP.   (323) 931-1534
Large and small, wall-mounted & on wheels
History For Hire, Inc.   (818) 765-7767
wood, brass
LCW Props   (818) 243-0707
Wood, Metal
Modern Props   (323) 934-3000
contemporary/futuristic, wood, aluminum, metal, walnut, acrylic, adjustable, moving, large, small, sturdy, versatile.
Sony Pictures Studios-Prop House (Off Lot)   (310) 244-5999
Universal Studios Property & Hardware Dept   (818) 777-2784
Various prop easels for rent.
ZG04 DECOR   (818) 853-8040
Easels of various sizes for rent

Editing Equipment & Services

Christy's Editorial Film & Video   (818) 845-1755
3625 W. Pacific Ave, Burbank, CA, 91505
film & digital editing supplies & equipment
www.christys.net
History For Hire, Inc.   (818) 765-7767
period, film & video
LCW Props   (818) 243-0707
Large Selection, Boards, Switchers, Custom Graphics, Audio Mixing
NBCUniversal StudioPost Editorial Facilities   (818) 777-4728
100 Universal City Plaza, Universal City, CA, 91608
170 Editorial Rooms and Suites, Exceptional 24 Hour Technical Support, Nationwide delivery and service.
universalstudioslot.com/editorial-equipment-and-facilities-rental

Egg Crate Bottom Fluorescents

See Also: Light Fixtures
E.C. Prop Rentals   (818) 764-2008
High multiples, practical, can suspended with chain or pipe

LCW Props   (818) 243-0707
large sel. of lighting
Universal Studios Property & Hardware Dept   (818) 777-2784
Prop egg crate bottom fluorescent lights for rent.

Egyptian Dressing

Dapper Cadaver	**(818) 771-0818**

Prop mummies, realistic mummified corpses and mummy characters. Egyptian statues. Obelisks and sarcophagi.

Green Set, Inc. **(818) 764-1231**
from dessert plants to Egyptian tomb dressing, many models of Egyptian statuary with some Egyptian furniture

The Hand Prop Room LP. **(323) 931-1534**
statues, mummy, masks, figures etc.

History For Hire, Inc. **(818) 765-7767**
mummy, smalls & fans

LM Treasures **(626) 252-7354**
Anything needed to help start the party such as animals, Egyptian Kings, Gods, and Sarcophaguses.

Omega/Cinema Props **(323) 466-8201**
Egyptian figurings, Egyptian busts, Egyptian books, Egyptian prints, Egyptian sculptures and much more.

Sword & Stone **(818) 562-6548**
Custom Egyptian dressing including Egyptian headdresses, Egyptian necklaces, and Egyptian crowns

Universal Studios Property & Hardware Dept **(818) 777-2784**
Prop Egyptian statues, props, weapons and more for rent.

Warner Bros. Studios Property Department **(818) 954-2181**
Egyptian Sculptures, Sarcophagus, Sphinx figures, Mummy statues, Egyptian Style Urns

Egyptian Themed Parties

See: Costume Rental Houses* Events, Decorations, Supplies & Services* Events, Design/Planning/Production* Historical Era Themed Events* Wardrobe, Antique/Historical

Electric Chairs

See Also: Prison Dressing/Jail Cell Dressing* Torture Equipment

Dapper Cadaver **(818) 771-0818**
Realistic electric chairs, interrogation chairs and restraint chairs.

History For Hire, Inc. **(818) 765-7767**
very authentic

Universal Studios Property & Hardware Dept **(818) 777-2784**
Prop electric chairs for rent

Electric Meters

See: Gas & Electric Meters

Electrical/Electronic Supplies & Services

See Also: Breaker Boxes* Computers* Control Panels/Boxes* Expendables* Insulators* Power Generation/Distribution

All Electronics Corporation **(818) 997-1806**
14928 Oxnard St, Van Nuys, CA, 91411
components retail store; new, used & industrial surplus
www.allelectronics.com

Antique Electronic Supply **(480) 820-5411**
6221 South Maple Ave, Tempe, AZ, 85283
catalog sales; electronic repair, parts & service for old radios, TVs, amps, speakers, record players, phones
www.tubesandmore.com

Apex Jr. **(818) 248-0416**
1450 West 228th St #4, Torrance, CA, 90501
new & used surplus components, wire, control panels
www.apexjr.com

Astro Audio Video Lighting, Inc. **(818) 549-9915**
6615 San Fernando Rd, Glendale, CA, 91201
Electronic equipment of all kinds. Equipment for lighting, music and more. Electronics repair also available.
www.astroavl.com

E.C. Prop Rentals **(818) 764-2008**
industrial & SS, wide sel wire & components

Electronic City **(818) 632-4494**
22287 Mulholland Highway #197, Calabasas, CA 91302
extensive inventory, esp. surveillance related
www.electroniccity.com

History For Hire, Inc. **(818) 765-7767**

LCW Props **(818) 243-0707**
Large Selection Of Electrical Panels, Boxes, Conduit, Breakers, Rigged

Old N Country Prop Shop, LLC **(818) 423-2599**
A large selection of vintage, unique, antique and rare electronic equipment and accessories, of all shapes and sizes.

Wireless for All **(818) 551-9191**
919 S Glendale Ave Ste A1, Glendale, CA, 91205
iPhone repair for iPhone 3G, iPhone 3GS, iPhone 4, iPhone 4S, and iPhone 5. Cell phone rentals.
wirelessforallsocal@gmail.com * www.instagram.com/wirelessforall

Electron Microscope

Electronic Appliances

See: Appliances* Computers* Fans-Table, Floor or Ceiling* Radios* Stereo Equipment* Telephones, Cellular* Televisions

Electronic Dart Board

See: Arcade Equipment, Games & Rides

Electronic Equipment (Dressing)

See Also: Control Boards* Game Show Electronics & Equipment* Mission Control Consoles* Read-outs

Alley Cats Studio Rentals **(818) 982-9178**
insulators, gauges, fuse boxes

Apex Electronics **(818) 767-7202**
8909 San Fernando Rd, Sun Valley, CA, 91352
Electronic & aircraft salvage parts for props & dressing, wire & cable
apexsurplus@sbcglobal.net * www.apexsurplus.com

Astro Audio Video Lighting, Inc. **(818) 549-9915**
6615 San Fernando Rd, Glendale, CA, 91201
Electronic dressing and electronic equipment dressing available for many themes including events.
www.astroavl.com

E.C. Prop Rentals **(818) 764-2008**
control boxes, consoles, electrical paneling

The Hand Prop Room LP. **(323) 931-1534**

LCW Props **(818) 243-0707**
Large Selection Of Elevator Panels, Brass, Stainless, Floor Indicators, Call Buttons

Modern Props **(323) 934-3000**
Contemporary & futuristic electronic equipment rentals, we also fabricate electronics

RJR Props **(404) 349-7600**
Hundreds of control panels, dials, gauges, indicator lights and electronic assemblies from new styles to vintage & retro.

Sony Pictures Studios-Prop House (Off Lot) **(310) 244-5999**
antenna, battery, binoculars, cable boxes, bull horn, car radio, tape player, CB Radio, CD Player, DVD Player, flash camera

Woody's Electrical Props **(818) 503-1940**
period to futuristic. digital counters & dressing. Fantasy sets, military sets, industrial sets, air tower

Elevator Dressing

See Also: Hardware, Decorative
Elevator Research & Mftg. Corp.   (213) 746-1914
1417 Elwood St, Los Angeles, CA, 90021
elevator pushbuttons, panels & related equip.
www.elevatorresearch.com
The Hand Prop Room LP.   (323) 931-1534
hdw., decorative, panels/controls w/mfg.
Hollywood Elevators/ Red Truck INC   (562) 896-6070
4707 Exposition Blvd, Los Angeles, CA, 90016
redtruck321@sbcglobal.net * hollywoodelevators.com
LCW Props   (818) 243-0707
Large Selection Of Elevator Panels, Brass, Stainless, Floor Indicators, Call
Buttons

6439 San Fernando Rd. Glendale, CA 91201
Phone: 818-243-0707 - www.lcwprops.com

Modern Props   (323) 934-3000
contemporary/futuristic elevators and elevator dressing
RJR Props   (404) 349-7600
Elevator control panels w/ working lights, exterior elevator panels; working
elevator button panels, elevator arrows.
Universal Studios Property & Hardware Dept   (818) 777-2784
Warner Bros. Studios Hardware Rentals   (818) 954-1335
4000 Warner Blvd Bldg 30, Burbank, CA, 91522
Door Knobs & Plates, Hinges, Window Fixtures, Elevator Panels, Train & Boat
Accessories
wbsfproperty@warnerbros.com * www.wbpropertydept.com

Embalming

See: Mortuary

Emblems

See: Badges, Patches & Buttons Flags/Banners*

Embroidery, Screen Printing, Etc.

See Also: Fabric Dyeing/Tie Dyeing/Painting/Aging Promotional
Items & Materials*
Big 10, Inc.   (310) 280-1610
149 S Barrington Ave Ste 812, Los Angeles, CA, 90049
embroidery, screen printing on clothing & all promotional items
www.big10promotions.com
House of Embroidery   (323) 469-4666
5273 Fountain Ave, Los Angeles, CA, 90029
By Appt. Only, custom-made embroidery for the entertainment & interior design
industries
www.houseofembroidery.net
Imprint Revolution   (310) 474-4472
10675 W Pico Blvd, Los Angeles, CA, 90064
Heat transfer, silk-screen, embroidery, custom garments, no minimums, rush
svc avail.
www.imprintrevolution.com

L. A. Party Works   (888) 527-2789
9712 Alpaca St, S El Monte, CA, 91733
in Vancouver tel. 604-589-4101. custom T-shirts
partyworks@aol.com * www.partyworksinteractive.com
Quickdraw   (310) 477-6770
2244 Federal Ave, Los Angeles, CA, 90064
custom embroidery & screen printing for clothing, bags, etc.
www.quickdraw1.com
Wizard   (323) 656-0287
13248 Victory Blvd, Valley Glen, CA, 91401
Screen printing, heat transfers, direct to garment printer, embroidery, digital
printing, sports & team apparel
debbie@thewizard.tv * www.thewizard.tv

Emergency Room

See Also: Ambulance/Paramedic Hospital Equipment* Medical
Equip/Furniture, Graphics/Supplies* Stretchers* Nurses Station*
Waiting Room* Intensive Care Unit / NICU (Natal Intensive Care
Unit)* Exam Room*
A-1 Medical Integration   (818) 753-0319
Medical devices for Set Decoration & Property, from minor procedures to
detailed hospital units.
Alpha Companies - Spellman Desk Co.   (818) 504-9090
The #1 source for medical equipment in the industry.

Emissions Analyzers

AIR Designs   (818) 768-6639
Period to Modern, Smog Machines
Alley Cats Studio Rentals   (818) 982-9178
LCW Props   (818) 243-0707
Smog Machine, Garage Tools

Engraving

See Also: Sign Painters Signs* Trophies/Trophy Cases*
D'ziner Sign Co.   (323) 467-4467
801 Seward Street, Los Angeles, CA, 90038
plastic/metal name plates, desk signs, badges
sales@dzinersign.com * www.dzinersign.com
Nights of Neon   (818) 756-4791
13815 Saticoy St, Van Nuys, CA, 91402
Computerized table router for engraving.
contact@nightsofneon.com * www.nightsofneon.com
Sword & Stone   (818) 562-6548
Same-day electrochemical metal etching & plating

Equestrian

See: Horse Saddles & Tack Horses, Horse Equipment, Livestock*
Western Dressing* Western Wear*

Erotica

See: Goth/Punk/Bondage/Fetish/Erotica Etc. Leather (Clothing,
Accessories, Materials)*

Espresso/Expresso

See: Coffee House

Etching

See: Glass & Mirrors Prop Design & Manufacturing*

Events, Backings & Scenery

See Also: Backings Scenery/Set Construction* Scenic Artists*
Centerline Scenery   (818) 252-7467
8238 Lankershim Blvd, N Hollywood, CA, 91605
meredyth@centerlinescenery.com
depict   (323) 222-1001
1460 Naud St, Los Angeles, CA, 90012
info@depict33.com * www.depict33.com
Scenic Highlights   (818) 252-7760
10830 Cantara St, Sun Valley, CA, 91352
scenichighlights.com
Schmidli Backdrops LA   (323) 938-2098
5830 W Adams Blvd, Culver City, CA, 90232
Providing hand painted Textured and Scenic backdrops to the commercial, film,
and fashion industry for over 20 years.
backdrops@schmidli.com * www.schmidli.com
ShopWildThings   (928) 855-6075
2880 Sweetwater Ave, Lake Havasu City, AZ, 86406
Event Decor, Beaded Curtains, Chain Curtains, String Curtains & Columns,
Crystal Columns. Reliable service & delivery.
help@shopwildthings.com * www.shopwildthings.com

Events, Decorations, Supplies & Services

See Also: Badges, Patches & Buttons Balloons & Balloon Sculptures* Carnival Dressing/Supplies* Catering* Columns* Confetti* Flags/Banners* Florists/Floral Design* Folding Chairs/Tables* Inflatables, Custom* Linens, Household* Disco Balls/Mirror Balls & Drivers* Neon Lights & Signs* Prop Houses* Pyrotechnics* Red Carpeting, Events/Premiers* Vendor Carts & Concession Counters* Wedding Props* Food, Food Stylists*

Aah-Inspiring Balloons (562) 494-7605
Call for an Appointment.
After 14 years in the TV and Film Industry, Aah-Inspiring Balloon Decor has been seen in over 200 TV shows and Films.
aahinspiring1@aol.com * www.aahinspiringballoons.com

AIR Designs (818) 768-6639
Diner, NASCAR, Automotive, Street Dressing, Seating

Astro Audio Video Lighting, Inc. (818) 549-9915
6615 San Fernando Rd, Glendale, CA, 91201
Event decorations and event supplies for concerts, festivals and parties.
www.astroavl.com

Bill Ferrell Co. (818) 767-1900
10556 Keswick St, Sun Valley, CA, 91352
Stages, ramps, risers, handicap lifts, turntables, winches, computer controls, custom sets, props, confetti, balloons.
www.billferrell.com

Bob Gail Special Events (310) 202-5200
1031 West Manchester Blvd Ste G, Inglewood, CA, 90301
Event decorations and event services.
eSales@BobGail.com * www.bobgail.com

Carving Ice & Big on Snow (714) 224-1455
900 S Placentia Ave Ste B, Placentia, CA, 92870
You're the best at what you do & so are we. Carving Ice & Blowing Snow for the TV & film industries for over 20 years.
info@carvingice.com * www.carvingice.com

Collins Visual Media (818) 686-6581
10518 Johanna Ave, Shadow Hills, CA, 91040
Backdrops, media walls, step & repeats, stanchions, stage displays, directional signage, installation...we have it all.
www.collinsvisualmedia.com

Dapper Cadaver (818) 771-0818
Halloween party prop central. Dinosaur props, pirate props, circus props for events & tradeshows. Rentals and customs

Fiesta Parade Floats (626) 610-0974
16016 Avenida Padilla Suite B, Irwindale, CA, 91702
parade floats, props & displays
www.fiestaparadefloats.com

Flower Art (323) 935-6800
5859 West 3rd Street, Los Angeles, CA, 90036
Award-winning, full-service floral design for movie/television sets. Located near The Grove. SDSA members since 1994
info@flowerartla.com * www.flowerartla.com

FormDecor, Inc. (310) 558-2582
America's largest event rental supplier of 20th Century furniture and accessories for Modern and Mid-Century styles.

FROST (310) 704-8812
Call for Appointment - 21405 Madrona Ave, Torrance, CA, 90503
Christmas decor prop rentals and installations for all your holiday events and productions!
mdisplay@yahoo.com * www.frostchristmasprops.com

Gorygirl Halloween Event Staging and Prop Rental (818) 912-6902
Jennifer Zuiker full service Halloween Event staging, design and decor by Appointment only.

Green Set, Inc. (818) 764-1231
theme decor. Arbors & Arches, Gazebos, Lattice, Trellis

History For Hire, Inc. (818) 765-7767
decorations, accessories

Jackson Shrub Supply, Inc. (818) 982-0100

L. A. Circus (323) 751-3486
Call for Appt, Los Angeles, CA, 90047
canvas tents, circus tents, clown mannequins, fake carnival animals: elephant, zebra, lion, horse, ferris wheel
circusinc@aol.com * www.lacircus.com

L. A. Party Works (888) 527-2789
9712 Alpaca St, S El Monte, CA, 91733
Vancouver (604) 589-4101. Event supplies; carnival, circus, competitive athletic, misting fans, virtual reality & more
partyworks@aol.com * www.partyworksinteractive.com

LISTINGS FOR THIS CATEGORY CONTINUE ON THE FOLLOWING PAGE

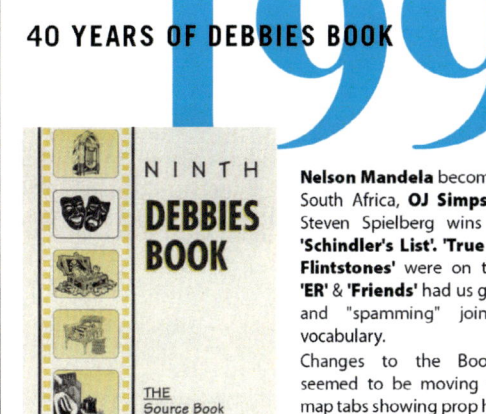

40 YEARS OF DEBBIES BOOK — 1994

NINTH

DEBBIES BOOK

THE Source Book For Prop & Set Dressing

JULY 94-95

Nelson Mandela becomes president of South Africa, **OJ Simpson** is arrested, Steven Spielberg wins 1st Oscar for **'Schindler's List'**. **'True Lies'** and **'The Flintstones'** were on the big screen, **'ER'** & **'Friends'** had us glued to the T.V., and "spamming" joined our web vocabulary.

Changes to the Book information seemed to be moving faster. I added map tabs showing prop house locations. Additional resource categories and more company data provided motivation to find ways to make the Book layout denser, a never-ending process that continues to this day.

Lennie Marvin Enterprises, Inc. (Prop Heaven) **(818) 841-5882**
props & dressing, 50s, Halloween, birthday, etc.
LM Treasures **(626) 252-7354**
Anything needed to help start the party such as animals, celebrities, or pirates will truly make it a night to remember.
Lux Lounge EFR **(888) 247-4411**
106 1/2 Judge John Aiso St #318, Los Angeles, CA, 90012
We'll add the extra touch of luxury to your event with our custom designs and event decorations.
info@luxloungeefr.com * www.luxloungeefr.com
Mandex LED Displays **(805) 497-8006**
3248 Jessica St, Newbury Park, CA, 91320
LEDIT-Flex long scrolling full color LED tickers. Entertain, create themed memorable info. at your next event.
info@ledsignage.com * www.ledsignage.com
Oceanic Arts **(562) 698-6960**
theme decor for Hawaiian, Tropical, Nautical, Polynesian, Island, Carved, Rattan, Tapa, Tiki, Luau and more
Party Pals **(858) 622-6613**
10427 Roselle St, San Diego, CA, 92121
Special events, wrap parties, TV shows, Film, set decor & more. Delivery & Set-up
www.partypals.com
Phoenix Decorating Co., Inc. **(626) 793-3174**
5400 Irwindale Ave, Irwindale CA, 91706
parade float builder
www.phxdeco.com
Sandy Rose Floral, Inc **(818) 980-4371**
6850 Vineland Ave Unit C, N Hollywood, CA, 91605
fresh & artificial florals, custom & prefab rentals, call 24 hrs.
www.sandyrose.com
Set Masters **(818) 982-1506**
24853 Avenue Rockefeller, Valencia, CA, 91355
Custom Fabrication design and Decor for all your event requirements.
info@setmasters.com * www.setmasters.com
ShopWildThings **(928) 855-6075**
2880 Sweetwater Ave, Lake Havasu City, AZ, 86406
Event Decor, Beaded Curtains, Chain Curtains, String Curtains & Columns, Crystal Columns. Reliable service & delivery.
help@shopwildthings.com * www.shopwildthings.com

Step and Repeat LA **(818) 434-7591**
10518 Johanna Ave, Shadow Hills, CA, 91040
We are passionate about our work and are here to make sure your project goes right no matter what.
Services@StepandRepeatLA.com * StepandRepeatLA.com
Universal Studios Property & Hardware Dept **(818) 777-2784**
Provides an array of event locations and services creating an exciting and unique environment for any occasion.
Universal Studios Special Events **(818) 777-9466**
100 Universal City Plaza, Universal City, CA, 91608
universal.specialevents@nbcuni.com * universalstudioslot.com/special-events
ZG04 DECOR **(818) 853-8040**

Events, Design/Planning/Production

See Also: Bleachers & Grandstand Seating* Canopies, Tents, Gazebos, Cabanas* Floor, Ground & Surface Protection* Grip Equipment* Insurance* Lighting & Sound, Concert/Theatrical/DJ/VJ* Lighting, LED, Fiber Optic & Specialty* Limousine Service* Prop Design & Manufacturing* Research, Advisors, Consulting & Clearances* Rigging, Equipment or Services* Sanitation, Waste Disposal* Searchlights/Skytrackers, Architectural Lights* Security Devices or Services* Special Effects, Equipment & Supplies* Stage Turntables* Stages, Portable & Steel Deck* Trade Shows & Conventions* Transportation, Trucking and/or Storage* Truss

Amusement Svcs/Candyland Amusements **(818) 266-4056**
18653 Ventura Blvd Ste 235, Tarzana, CA, 91356
We own our carnival equipment, games, rides and attractions; we set up. Street Fairs, commercial shoots, Carnivals, Corporate picnics
raymond@candylandamusements.com * www.candylandamusements.com
Astro Audio Video Lighting, Inc. **(818) 549-9915**
6615 San Fernando Rd, Glendale, CA, 91201
We provide event planning & event design as well as concert planning & concert design.
www.astroavl.com
EFX- Event Special Effects **(626) 888-2239**
125 Railroad Ave, Monrovia, CA, 91016
Event Design- Layouts- 3D Renderings- Management- Acitvations- Tours
info@efxla.com * www.efxla.com
Entertainment Design Corp. **(310) 641-9300**
5455 Wilshire Blvd Ste 910, Los Angeles, CA, 90036
stadium shows, corporate events, awards shows, TV & film
info@entdesign.com * www.entdesign.com
Flower Art **(323) 935-6800**
5859 West 3rd Street, Los Angeles, CA, 90036
Award-winning, full-service floral design for movie/television sets. Located near The Grove. SDSA members since 1994
info@flowerartla.com * www.flowerartla.com
L. A. Party Works **(888) 527-2789**
9712 Alpaca St, S El Monte, CA, 91733
in Vancouver tel. 604-589-4101. pre/post event PR, design to implementation
partyworks@aol.com * www.partyworksinteractive.com
Lux Lounge EFR **(888) 247-4411**
106 1/2 Judge John Aiso St #318, Los Angeles, CA, 90012
Event Design, Event Planning, Event Production: We work with you to ensure your event looks amazing!
info@luxloungeefr.com * www.luxloungeefr.com
Miziker Entertainment Group **(818) 558-1888**
4110 Riverside Dr, Burbank, CA, 91505
Concept, design, production & operations for shows, compelling places & experiences
www.miziker.com
Paradigm Shift Worldwide **(818) 831-3005**
17326 Devonshire St, Northridge, CA, 91325
all aspects of event design & production, specializing in media events & publicity stunts
www.psww.com
Premier Displays & Exhibits **(562) 598-5000**
11261 Warland Dr, Cypress, CA, 90630
Full service exhibit house providing turnkey services for trade shows, events, meetings, & permanent installations.
www.premierdisplays.com

R. W. B. Party Props, Inc. (714) 538-8629
128 S Cypress, Orange, CA, 92866
Over 50 themes, American cities to Western carts & wagons 1900s to
Futuristic, Party Props, Party Decor
lori@rwbpartyprops.com * www.rwbpartyprops.com

Route 66 Productions, Inc. (310) 823-2066
Web Based Business
full service production of corporate events: development, design, scripting &
implementation of events & media
whitneyr@artdimensionsonline.com * www.route66la.com

Rrivre Works, Inc. (323) 985-4229
2035 E Vernon Ave, Los Angeles, CA, 90058
Party and event design, planning & production
info@rrivreworks.com * www.rrivreworks.com

Tractor Vision Scenery & Rentals (323) 235-2885
340 E Jefferson Blvd, Los Angeles, CA, 90011
Specializing in entertainment, trade shows, & events, we bring your projects to
life with precision, speed & personality
sets@tractorvision.com * www.tractorvision.com

Universal Studios Special Events (818) 777-9466
100 Universal City Plaza, Universal City, CA, 91608
universal.specialevents@nbcuni.com * universalstudioslot.com/special-events

The Vox Group (310) 535-5510
1334 Parkview Ave Ste 100, Manhattan Beach, CA, 90266
Full service event marketing, production, management, and entertainment
www.voxproductions.com

ZG04 DECOR (818) 853-8040
Event design, event planning/event planners, event production and more.

Events, Entertainment

See Also: Animal Costumes & Walk Around Characters Arcade*
Equipment, Games & Rides Carnival Games & Rides* Clowns**
Events, Mobile Marketing Magicians & Props, Supplies, Dressing**
Video Games

Arcade Amusements (866) 576-8878
802 West Washington Ave Ste E, Escondido, CA, 92025-1644
Planning a Party? How about having some games there? How about 10? How
about 20? How about... Well, you get the idea.
phil@arcadeamusements.com * www.arcadeamusements.com

L. A. Circus (323) 751-3486
Call for Appt, Los Angeles, CA, 90047
canvas tents, circus tents, clown mannequins, fake carnival animals: elephant,
zebra, lion, horse, ferris wheel
circusinc@aol.com * www.lacircus.com

L. A. Party Works (888) 527-2789
9712 Alpaca St, S El Monte, CA, 91733
in Vancouver tel. 604-589-4101
partyworks@aol.com * www.partyworksinteractive.com

Quantum Rock Enterprises (310) 378-2171
PO Box 4032, Palos Verdes, CA, 90274
Rock climbing walls, mobile/indoor/outdoor up to 24', realistic, safety
staff/training/insurance, full service, easy set
www.quantumrock.com

Events, Mobile Marketing

Craftsmen Industries (800) 373-3575
3101 Elm Point Industrial Dr, Saint Charles, MO, 63301
design & build mobile trailers/vehicles, portable displays
www.craftsmenind.com

EEI Global (248) 608-7500
1400 South Livernois, Rochester Hills, MI 48307
full svc. touring & mobile marketing, vehicle construction, exhibit fabrication
www.eeiglobal.com

EFX- Event Special Effects (626) 888-2239
125 Railroad Ave, Monrovia, CA, 91016
Custom Fabrication- Marketing- Tours- Tour Management- Activations
info@efxla.com * www.efxla.com

Featherlite, Inc. (800) 800-1230
P.O. Box 320, Hwy 63 & 9, Cresco, IA, 52136
design & build custom mobile trailers for events, and for special services &
communications
www.fthr.com

L. A. Party Works (888) 527-2789
9712 Alpaca St, S El Monte, CA, 91733
in Vancouver tel. 604-589-4101. vehicles & props for marketing, promotions,
public relations
partyworks@aol.com * www.partyworksinteractive.com

MKTG (212) 366-3400
32 Avenue of the Americas, 20th Floor, New York, NY 10013
award-winning event & entertainment marketing solutions
www.mktg.com

Spevco, Inc. (336) 924-8100
8118 Reynolda Rd, Pfafftown, NC, 27040
custom vehicle design & construction
http://spevco.com

Turtle Transit (978) 365-9300
6 Fox Rd, Hudson, MA, 01749
custom built trailers & morphed vehicles
www.turtletransit.com

Exam Room

See Also: Ambulance/Paramedic Dentist Equipment* Doctor's Bags**
Hospital Equipment Medical Equip/Furniture, Graphics/Supplies**
X-ray Machine X-ray Viewer* X-rays & X-ray Viewers* Waiting*
Room Intensive Care Unit / NICU (Natal Intensive Care Unit)**
Emergency Room Radiology*

A-1 Medical Integration (818) 753-0319
Medical devices for Set Decoration & Property, from minor procedures to
detailed hospital units.

Alpha Companies - Spellman Desk Co. (818) 504-9090
The #1 source for medical equipment in the industry.

Exercise & Fitness Equipment

See Also: Physical Therapy* Weightlifting Equipment* Massage Tables* Gymnasium & Gymnastic Equipment* Fall Pads & Crash Pads* Boxing, Wrestling, Mixed Martial Arts (MMA)* Ballet Barres & Dance Mirrors

Athletic Room   (818) 764-9801
12750 Raymer St, N Hollywood, CA, 91605
Treadmills, Gym, Yoga, Boxing, ND Balls, mats, Golf, Surfboards, Tennis, Soccer, Football, Basketball, Baseball, Hockey.
athleticroom@mac.com * www.athleticroomprops.net

C. P. Two   (323) 466-8201
Weight machines, bar bells, exercise machines, medicine balls, exercise mats, gym mats, exercise balls and more.

Curtis Gym Equipment   (818) 897-2804
10275 Glenoaks Blvd Ste #7, Pacoima, CA, 91331
Prop Rentals and Servicing. Fitness Machines, Gymnastics & Weightlifting. Fake & Real Weights
curtisgymequipment@hotmail.com

Hollywood Gym Rentals   (310) 663-6161
200 West Chevy Chase Drive Unit B, Glendale, CA, 91204
Hollywood Gym Rentals specializes in short and long term rentals of fitness equipment in the Los Angeles area.
chris@hollywoodgymrentals.com * www.hollywoodgymrentals.com

I-Rep Therapy Products, Inc.   (800) 828-0852
508 Chaney St Ste B, Lake Elsinore, CA, 92530
Contact i-REP for all of your equipment and set dressing needs for physical therapy, exercise and fitness.
btwilhelm@gmail.com * www.i-reptherapyproducts.com

LCW Props   (818) 243-0707
Power Rack, Dumbbells, Fake & Real Weight Plates, Ropes, Sled, Benches, Medicine Balls, Agility Ladders

Sony Pictures Studios-Prop House (Off Lot)   (310) 244-5999
exercise benches, sports benches, boxing equipment, exercise equipment, fall pads, gym bags, jump ropes, massage tables

Exit Alarm

See: Security Walk-Through & Baggage Alarms

The Hand Prop Room LP.   (323) 931-1534
all types, prop weights

History For Hire, Inc.   (818) 765-7767
period, smalls

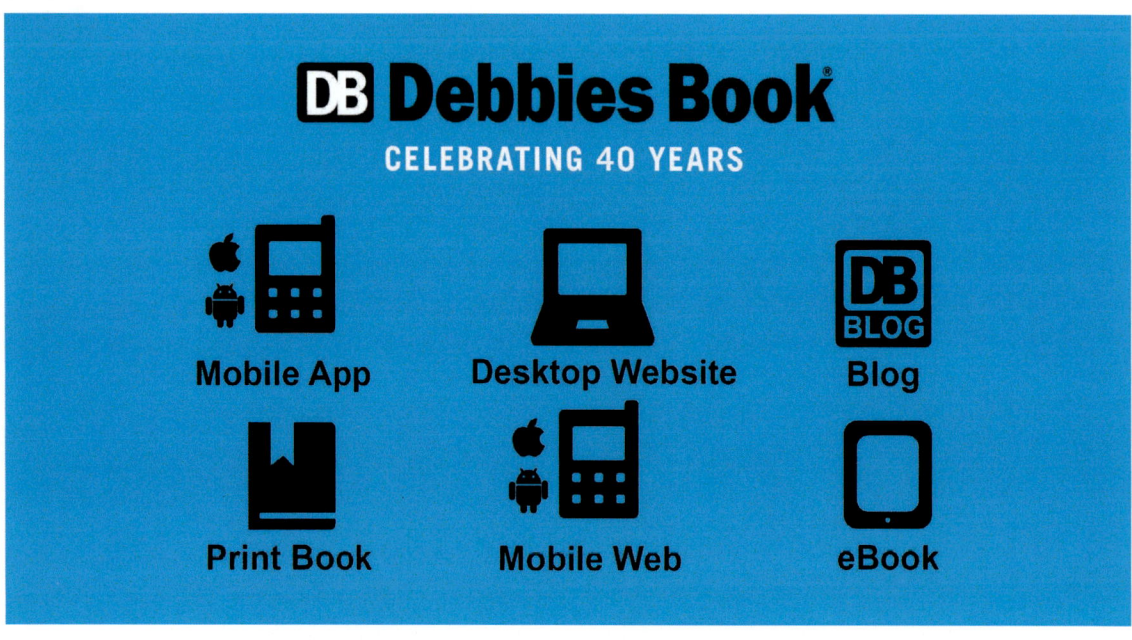

Expendables

See Also: Adhesives, Glues & Tapes* Duvetyne* Guns & Firearms* Flameproofing* Floor, Ground & Surface Protection* Grip Equipment* Janitorial Supplies* Plastics, Materials & Fabrication* Rubber Stamps

Anytime (818) 394-9675
11834 Roscoe Blvd., Sun Valley, CA 91352
expendables, digital & Chromakey tapes & paint
rentals@anytimerentals.com * www.anytimerentals.com

The Battery Hut (818) 558-6740
913 South Victory Blvd, Burbank, CA, 91502
for all your battery needs; also take old batteries for disposal
www.battery-hut.com

Bear Forest Products, Inc (951) 727-1767
4685 Brookhollow Circle, Riverside, CA, 92509
Spray adhesives for wood and paneling.
matto@bearfp.com * www.bearfp.com

Castex Rentals (323) 462-1468
1044 N Cole Ave, Hollywood, CA, 90038
tape, layout board, gels, seamless paper, gloves, knives, furniture pads etc.
service@castexrentals.com * www.castexrentals.com

Cinelease (855) 441-5500
5375 W. San Fernando Rd, Los Angeles, CA, 90039
expendables, grip/lighting equip., truck packages
cineleasesales@cinelease.com * www.cinelease.com

CONFETTI & FOG FX Special Effects Company (877) 576-4239
1085 W 21st Pl, Hialeah, FL, 33010
Expendables including confetti, special effects fluids and more
Info@confettiandfogfx.com * www.caffx.com

Expendables Plus Inc. (718) 609-6464
32 Eagle St Ste 1. Brooklyn, NY 11222
expendables only
www.expendablesplusinconline.com

Expendables Recycler (818) 901-9796
5812 Columbus Ave, Van Nuys, CA, 91411
sell & buy surplus grip/electric/camera expendables, please call before visiting us, thanks!
www.expendablesrecycler.com

The Hand Prop Room LP. (323) 931-1534
extensive

Highline Stages (212) 206-8280
440 W. 15th Street, New York City, NY, 10011
expendables, lighting, generators, grip equip.
www.highlinestages.com

MBSE Burbank (818) 303-9464
10616 Lanark St, Sun Valley, CA, 91352

Mole-Richardson Co. (323) 851-0111
12154 Montague St, Pacoima, CA 91331
Ask for Studio Depot
www.mole.com

Mutual Hardware Corp. (718) 361-2480
36-27 Vernon Blvd, Long Island City, NY, 11106
catalog sales; hardware, scenic materials, lighting, rigging
www.mutualhardware.com

New Mexico Lighting & Grip Co. (505) 506-6564
I-25 Studios 9201 Pan American Fwy NE, Albuquerque, NM, 87113
Grip & rigging equip. & services, lighting & sound. Expendable store
colin.pearman@nmlgc.com * www.newmexicolightingandgrip.com

Norcostco (800) 220-6920
825 Rhode Island Ave S, Golden Valley, MN, 55426
multiple sales offices around the U.S. full stock of theatrical expendables
www.norcostco.com

North Hollywood Hardware, Inc. (818) 980-2453
11847 Ventura Blvd, Studio City, CA, 91604
Fittings, pipes, faucets, etc. and knowledgeable staff
nohohardware@gmail.com * www.ehardware2go.com

Pacific Fibre & Rope Co. (800) 825-7673
903 Flint Ave, Wilmington, CA, 90748
rope manufacturing, all kinds, as much as you need, hwr fittings, tools, nets, but no chains, rope
moreinfo@pacificfibre.com * www.pacificfibre.com

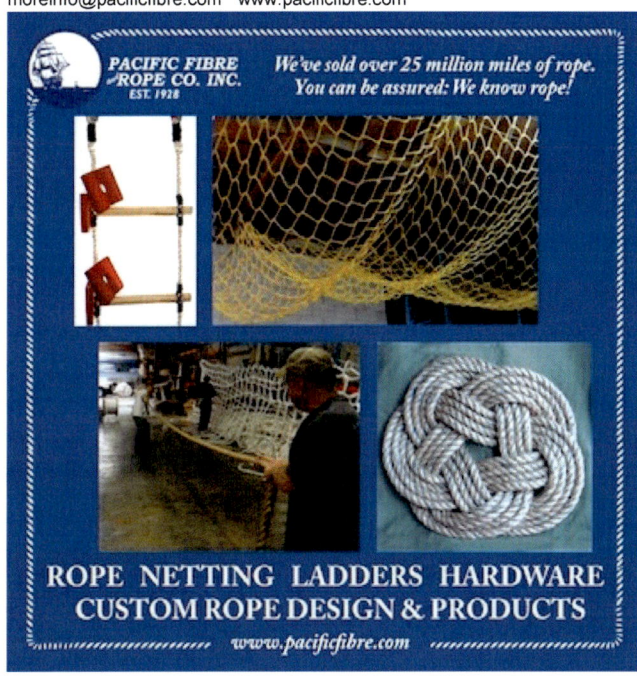

Pacific Northwest Theatre Associates (800) 622-7850
2414 SW Andover C100, Seattle, WA, 98106
catalog sales; theatrical supplies, make-up, expendables, rigging, drops, lighting, sound, effects
www.pnta.com

Panavision (Hollywood) (323) 464-3800
6735 Selma Ave, Hollywood, CA, 90028
expendables, plus camera equip., HD 900R, F23, Varicam
www.panavision.com

Quixote (504) 266-2297
10289 Airline Hwy, St Rose, LA, 70087
Grip, Electric, Camera, Art Department, Grip Tape, Gels, Foam Core, Online orders, Petty Cash Envelopes.
nola@quixote.com * www.quixote.com

Quixote Studio Store (323) 960-9191
1000 N Cahuenga, Hollywood, CA, 90038
Expendables sales & production supply rentals
store@quixote.com * www.expendables.com

Repro-Graphic Supply (818) 771-9066
9838 Glenoaks Blvd, Sun Valley, CA, 91352
Pens/Rulers/Markers/Leads Clearprint/Vellums/Diazo Film Graphic/Sketch
Paper/Title Block Cutting Supplies/Tools/Boards
info@reprographicsupply.com * www.reprographicsupply.com

Set Wear (818) 340-0540
9027 Canoga Ave Ste K, Canoga Park, CA, 91311
Work gloves (incl. Hot Hand gloves), tool pouches/belts, accessories
www.setwear.com

Sugru 011 44 20
FormFormForm Ltd, Units 1&2, 47-49 Tudor Road, London, 7998-0022
E9 7SN, United Kingdom
Self-setting rubber that can be formed by hand. Turns into a strong, flexible
silicone rubber overnight.
linda@sugru.com * www.sugru.com

TMB (818) 899-8818
527 Park Ave, San Fernando, CA, 91340
in NJ: (201) 896-8600, elect. connectors, cabling, grip/lighting components
www.tmb.com

Warner Bros. Studios Paint Department (818) 954-1817
4000 Warner Blvd Bldg 47, Burbank, CA, 91522
Production expendables & production supplies to the entertainment community
at great prices
www.wbpaintdept.com

Xeno-Lights (212) 941-9494
1 Worth Street, New York City, NY, 10013
expendables, plus grip/lighting equip.
www.xenolights.com

Experiential Marketing

See: Events, Mobile Marketing

Exterior Locations

See: Locations, Insert Stages & Theatres Locations,
Backlots/Standing Sets*

Eyewear, Glasses, Sunglasses, 3D

See Also: Wardrobe, Accessories

The Costume House (818) 508-9933
vintage

The Hand Prop Room LP. (323) 931-1534
period-futuristic

History For Hire, Inc. (818) 765-7767
period glasses, 3D glasses, lots of sunglasses

Meow (562) 438-8990
2210 E 4th St, Long Beach, CA, 90814
original "never worn" men's, women's, kids, 1950-70s frames
www.meowvintage.com

Sony Pictures Studios-Prop House (Off Lot) (310) 244-5999
large selection, glasses & sunglasses, eyepatches, eye patches, face sheild,
glasses cases, eyeglasses, goggles, monocles

Universal Studios Property & Hardware Dept (818) 777-2784
All kinds of eyewear props and accessories for rent.

EZ UP

See: Canopies, Tents, Gazebos, Cabanas

Fabric Dyeing/Tie Dyeing/Painting/Aging

See Also: Embroidery, Screen Printing, Etc.

Almore Dye House (818) 506-5444
6850 Tujunga Ave, N. Hollywood, CA, 91605

A Dyeing Art/Studio 2 (818) 246-5440
Call for Appt.
cater specifically to the Industry
www.adyeingart.com

Melissa Binder (818) 535-7085
By Appt, aging, dyeing, painting, ask for credits

Fabricators

See: Art For Rent (Cleared Art) Art, Artists For Hire* Fiberglass
Products/Fabrication* Furniture, Custom-made/Reproduction*
Metalworking, Decorative* Metalworking, Welding & Structural* Prop
Design & Manufacturing* Prop Reproduction & Fabrication*
Scenery/Set Construction* Vacu-forms/Vacu-forming*

Fabrics

See Also: Canvas Costume/Wardrobe/Sewing Supplies* Leather
(Clothing, Accessories, Materials)* Linens, Household* Linens,
Tabletop & Events* Upholstery Materials/Services*

AntiqueFabric.com (208) 921-6603
3713 Woody Dr, Boise, ID, 83703
antique fabrics in stock, mid 1800s to 1960s
fabric@antiquefabric.com * www.antiquefabric.com

Britex Fabrics (415) 392-2910
146 Geary St, San Francisco, CA, 94108
fashion & home decorating fabrics, trims, 30,000 buttons, yarn & accessories
www.britexfabrics.com

Calico Corners (818) 766-1120
12717 Ventura Blvd, Studio City, CA, 91604
upholstery, drapery, upholstering, open 7 days
www.calicocorners.com

Dazian Fabrics (877) 432-9426
10671 Lorne St, Sun Valley, CA 91352
FR theatrical fabrics, rental draperies and custom sewing services.
www.dazian.com

Dharma Trading Co. (800) 542-5227
1604 4th St, San Rafael, CA, 94901
Since 1975 the store has been serving bay area knitters, crocheters, and
weavers.
www.dharmatrading.com

Diamond Foam & Fabric Co. (323) 931-8148
611 S La Brea Ave, Los Angeles, CA, 90036
decorative fabrics & foam for upholstery, drapery & slipcovers, custom sewing
on premises
www.diamondfoamandfabric.com

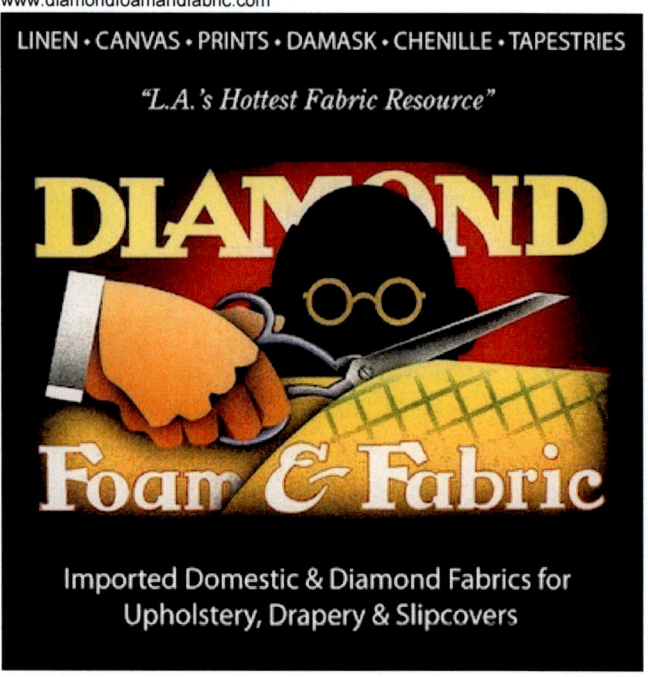

Edinburgh Imports (800) 334-6274
58406 Joshua Ln, Yucca Valley CA, 92284
1000+ plush fabrics: 1/16"-3" pile. Natural/Synthetic/felt/ultrasuede
www.edinburghimports.com

F & S Fabrics (310) 475-1637
10629 W. Pico Blvd, Los Angeles, CA, 90064
Call (310) 441-2477 for upholstery fabrics
www.fandsfabrics.com

Home Fabrics (213) 689-9600
910 S. Wall St, Los Angeles, CA, 90015
decorative drapery & upholstery at wholesale prices

International Silks & Woolens (323) 653-6453
8347 Beverly Blvd, Los Angeles, CA, 90048
notions, fabric & patterns, drapery & upholstery
www.iswfabrics.com

Leather Corral Inc (818) 764-7880
13052 Raymer St, N Hollywood, CA, 91605
Excellent source for vinyls, leathers and other fabrics.
leathercorral@yahoo.com * www.leathercorral.com

Lushes Curtains (626) 453-0337
1855 Tyler Ave Unit C, S El Monte, CA, 91733
Your Direct Velvet Curtain Manufacture! Delivering Elegant & Quality Velvet
Textiles World Wide!
Joe@LushesCurtains.com * www.LushesCurtains.com

Michael Levine, Inc. (213) 622-6259
920 S Maple Ave, Los Angeles, CA, 90015
Fabric for apparel & the home, and yarn, trims & buttons
www.lowpricefabric.com

Morgan Fabrics (323) 583-9981
4265 Exchange Ave, Los Angeles, CA, 90058
Upholstery & drapery fabrics, full rolls only
www.morganfabrics.com

National Fiber Technology, LLC (978) 686-2964
15 Union St, Lawrence, MA, 01840
catalog sales; hair & fur fabrics for wigs, headdresses, 'make-up' hair, & animal
costumes, wigs custom made.
www.nftech.com

Old N Country Prop Shop, LLC (818) 423-2599
Linens and fabrics of many colors/styles. Vintage and bolts, woolens, cottons;
prints; polyester; all colors & patterns.

Oriental Silk Co. (323) 651-2323
8377 Beverly Blvd, Los Angeles, CA, 90048
Finest imported silks, woolens, and linens from China & Orient Open Mon - Fri
9 to 5
kenwong@orientalsilk.com * www.orientalsilk.com

Outdoor Wilderness Fabrics, Inc. (800) 693-7467
123 E Simplot Blvd, Caldwell, ID, 83605
fleece, cordura, pack cloth, ripstop, waterproof/breathables, meshes, hardware
& zippers
www.owfinc.com

ShopWildThings (928) 855-6075
2880 Sweetwater Ave, Lake Havasu City, AZ, 86406
Event Decor, Beaded Curtains, Chain Curtains, String Curtains & Columns,
Crystal Columns. Reliable service & delivery.
help@shopwildthings.com * www.shopwildthings.com

Silvia's Costumes (323) 666-0680
4964 Hollywood Blvd, Los Angeles, CA, 90027
info@silviascostumes.com * http://www.silviascostumes.com

Sommer's Plastics Products (973) 777-7888
835 Bloomfield Ave, Clifton, NJ, 07012
Mfg., wide sel plastic fabrics, pleathers, fake furs, metallic, stretch, for set
decoration or costumes
Sales@Sommers.com * www.sommers.com

Testfabrics, Inc. (570) 603-0432
415 Delaware Ave, West Pittston, PA, 18643
catalog sales; synthetic & natural fabrics without additives, conservation uses:
restoration/conservation/storage
www.testfabrics.com

Warner Bros. Drapery, Upholstery & Flooring (818) 954-1831
4000 Warner Blvd Bldg 30, Burbank, CA, 91522
Sunbrella, damasks, velour, linens, cottons, sheers, lace, jacquards & prints
wbsfdrapery@warnerbros.com * www.wbdrapery.com

Facial Capture Software & Hardware

Faceware Technologies, Inc. (310) 656-6565
4515 Van Nuys Blvd Ste 301, Sherman Oaks, CA, 91403
We make Faceware - the award winning, gold-standard software and hardware
for artist-friendly facial motion capture.
sales@facewaretech.com * facewaretech.com

Factory/Industrial

See Also: Conveyor Equipment Loading Dock Dressing* Warehouse
Dressing*

AIR Designs (818) 768-6639
Drums, Lighting, Work Benches, Crates, Tools, Equipment

Alley Cats Studio Rentals (818) 982-9178
drums, gauges, pallets, pulleys

E.C. Prop Rentals (818) 764-2008
Drums, large equipment/tools, large gears metal/wood, racking, carts, knife
switches, wall dressing, and signage

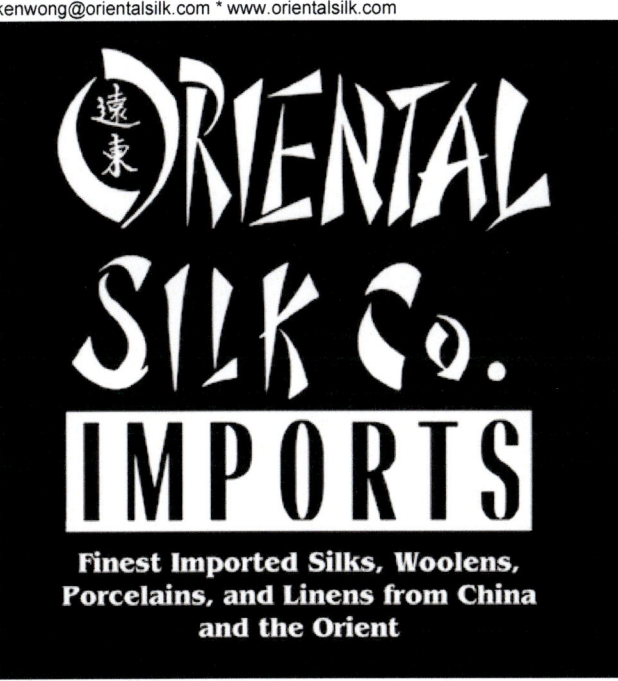

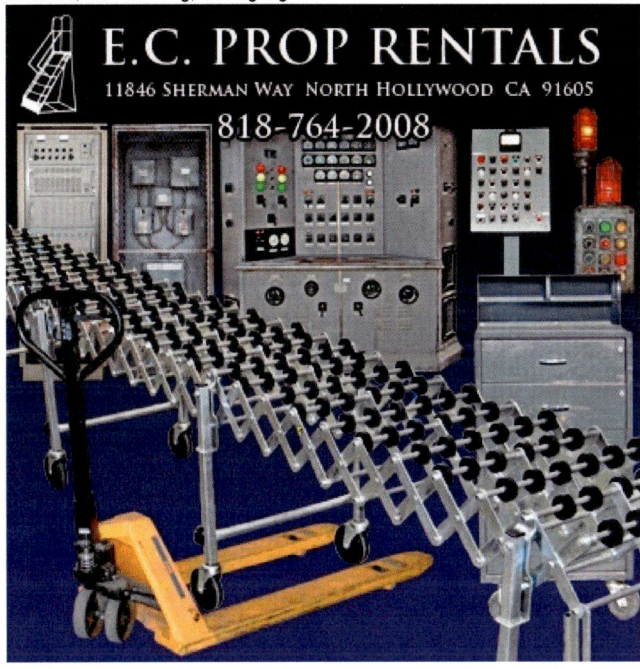

LCW Props (818) 243-0707
From Shelving To Products To Equipment

Machinery & Equipment Co., Inc. (909) 599-3916
115 N Cataract Ave, San Dimas, CA, 91773
Used industrial processing & packaging equipment. Over 5000 items available
in our inventory. Stainless steel equipment.
sherri@machineryandequipment.com * www.machineryandequipment.com

Fake Food

See: Food, Artificial Food

Fall Pads & Crash Pads

See Also: Dummies, Fall & Crash

The Hand Prop Room LP. (323) 931-1534
many sizes and types

L. A. Party Works (888) 527-2789
9712 Alpaca St, S El Monte, CA, 91733
AIR BAR Free fall air bag/fall bag for stunts and gags.
partyworks@aol.com * www.partyworksinteractive.com

Norbert's Athletic Products (800) 779-1904
431 Figueroa St, Wilmington, CA, 90744
We specialize in all sizes and styles of matting and landing pads including stunt pads, crash pads, and custom pads.
info@norberts.net * www.norberts.net

Fans, Hand

See: Wardrobe

Fans-Table, Floor or Ceiling

See Also: Air Conditioning & Heating, Production/Event* Special Effects, Equipment & Supplies

AIR Designs (818) 768-6639
Shop Fans, Fans on Stands

Alley Cats Studio Rentals (818) 982-9178
industrial, period & modern (no ceiling fans)

E.C. Prop Rentals (818) 764-2008
industrial desk/floor/ceiling/wall

The Hand Prop Room LP. (323) 931-1534
table, desk, wall period-present

History For Hire, Inc. (818) 765-7767
table & floor

LCW Props (818) 243-0707
Large Industrial, Rolling, Desk, Ceiling

Old N Country Prop Shop, LLC (818) 423-2599
A large selection of old & vintage table fans, Eskimo rotating fans, ceiling fans, all colors and sizes.

Omega/Cinema Props (323) 466-8201
Table fans, floor fans, ceiling fans, oscillating fans, box fans, portable fans and more.

Picture Start Props (818) 255-5472
Different colors and sizes from all different periods.

RC Vintage, Inc. (818) 765-7107
Vintage 40s, 50s & 60s/desk, floor, ceiling Working Condition

Sony Pictures Studios-Fixtures (310) 244-5996
5933 W Slauson Ave, Culver City, CA, 90230
period to present day, ceiling fans
www.sonypicturesstudios.com

Universal Studios Property & Hardware Dept (818) 777-2784
Period to present prop floor fans, table table, ceiling fans for rent.

Fantasy Props, Costumes, or Decorations

See Also: Aliens* Events, Backings & Scenery* Events, Decorations, Supplies & Services* Events, Design/Planning/Production* Futuristic Furniture, Props, Decorations

The Hand Prop Room LP. (323) 931-1534

Hollywood Studio Gallery (323) 462-1116
photos, drawings, prints, 3D models

LM Treasures (626) 252-7354
Everything needed to create your own fantasy story ranging from the Knight in shining Armor to the wizard and dragon.

Modern Props (323) 934-3000
fantasy props and fantasy decorations; furniture, sculpture, accessories & more

ShopWildThings (928) 855-6075
2880 Sweetwater Ave, Lake Havasu City, AZ, 86406
Event Decor, Beaded Curtains, Chain Curtains, String Curtains & Columns, Crystal Columns. Reliable service & delivery.
help@shopwildthings.com * www.shopwildthings.com

Sword & Stone (818) 562-6548
Fantasy weapons, fantasy costumes and fantasy dressing/fantasy decorations

Farm Equipment & Dressing

See Also: Animals (Live), Services, Trainers & Wranglers* Barrels & Drums, Wood/Metal/Plastic* Carriages, Horse Drawn* Horse Saddles & Tack* Horses, Horse Equipment, Livestock* Milk Bottles & Cans* Tools* Wagons* Weather Vanes

C. P. Two (323) 466-8201
Farm equipment; plows, carts, milk cans, burlap bags and burlap sacks, water pumps, farm tools, hay

The Hand Prop Room LP. (323) 931-1534

History For Hire, Inc. (818) 765-7767
farming tools, plows, butter churns, carts, chicken crates, pitchforks

Sony Pictures Studios-Prop House (Off Lot) (310) 244-5999

Farriers

See: Blacksmith Shop/Foundry

Fast Food Equipment

See: Restaurant Kitchens/Equip./Supplies* Vendor Carts & Concession Counters

Faux Books

See: Books, Real/Hollow & Faux Books

Fax Machines

See: Business Machines* Office Equipment & Dressing

Feathers

American Plume (800) 521-1132
11 Skyine Drive East, Unit 2, Clarks Summit, PA 18411
Boas/jackets/theatrical division in NYC; (800) 962-8544. feather boas, fans, gloves
apff@epix.net * www.americanplume.com

The Feather Place (213) 291-3253
719 S Los Angeles St Ste 620, Los Angeles, CA, 90014
Feather masks, boas, headdresses, wings, wigs, fans, jackets, loose feathers; peacock, pheasant, ostrich, & much more
www.featherplace.com

Gettinger Feather Corp. (212) 695-9470
45 Hoffman Ave, Hauppaug NY, 11788
catalog sales; raw & colored fancy feathers & plumes, also boas, fans & masks
info@msgfeather.com * www.msgfeather.com

Moonlight Feather (800) 468-6048
1860 Eastman Ave Suite 111, Ventura, CA, 93003
Ventura source for feathers of all kinds.
customerservice@moonlightfeather.com * http://www.moonlightfeather.com

Mother Plucker Feather Co., Inc. (213) 637-0411
2511 W 3rd St Ste 102, Los Angeles, CA, 90057
www.motherplucker.com

Fences

See Also: Barricades* Steel Folding Gates & Roll-Up Doors* Wood Shop

Alley Cats Studio Rentals (818) 982-9178
huge selection, self-standing chain link panels, chain link fences

C & C Fence Co., Inc. (818) 983-1959
12822 Sherman Way, N Hollywood, CA, 91605
chain link panel rentals, gate rentals, barbed wire and razor ribbon, install/remove/repair, fence rentals, fence props, electric iron gates
candcfence@gmail.com * www.candcfence.com

CI-Fabrics, Inc. (619) 661-7166
2325 Marconi Ct, San Diego, CA, 92154
wind screen, crowd control, sports event boundary fabric, shade cloth, sight barriers, bulk bags
www.ci-fabrics.com

E.C. Prop Rentals (818) 764-2008
Chain link/wrought iron/expanded metal all freestanding, and orange plastic construction rolls

Green Set, Inc. (818) 764-1231
Metal Fences, Wooden Fences, Bamboo Fencing

Jackson Shrub Supply, Inc. (818) 982-0100

LCW Props (818) 243-0707
Chain link, Stand Alone

Fencing Equipment

See: Sporting Goods & Services* Swords & Swordplay

Ferrellels

See: Stages, Portable & Steel Deck

Fetish

See: Goth/Punk/Bondage/Fetish/Erotica Etc.* Leather (Clothing, Accessories, Materials)

Fiberglass Products/Fabrication

See Also: Prop Reproduction & Fabrication* Scenery/Set Construction* Staff Shops* Themed Environment Construction

California Art Products   **(818) 762-4276**
11125 Vanowen St, N. Hollywood, CA, 91605
trees, rocks, animals, urns, fanciful architectural elements
www.californiaartproducts.com

Green Set, Inc.   **(818) 764-1231**
Palm trunks, Cypress swamp trunks, tree trunks, we are devoted to having it, finding it, or creating it! too!

Jackson Shrub Supply, Inc.   **(818) 982-0100**

KIHL STUDIOS   **(818) 812-9594**
9701 Owensmouth Ave Unit 1, Chatsworth, CA, 91311
Custom art fabrication and reproduction in fiberglass materials.
design@kihlstudios.com * www.kihlstudios.com

Projex International   **(661) 268-0999**
9555 Hierba Rd, Agua Dulce, CA, 91390
fiberglass & steelwork for Film & TV props, scenic, FX, many credits
www.projexinternational.com

Universal Studios Property & Hardware Dept   **(818) 777-2784**
Fiberglass props for rent, from statues and pottery to furniture and fake produce.

Warner Bros. Studios Staff Shop   **(818) 954-2269**
Manufacturer of exterior & interior details used for the creation of sets in all architectural styles & eras.

Field Striping & Lining

See: Sporting Goods & Services* Sports/Athletic Field Lining/Graphics

Fiesta Dinnerware

The Homer Laughlin China Co.   **(800) 452-4462**
672 Fiesta Dr, Newell, WV, 26050
Made in the USA since 1871
www.hlcdinnerware.com

Ob-jects   **(818) 351-4200**
Ceramic bowls, contemporary bowls,

Fifties Furniture

See: Furniture, Mid-Century Modern

Fifties Theme Parties

See: Costume Rental Houses* Costumes* Events, Backings & Scenery* Events, Decorations, Supplies & Services* Events, Design/Planning/Production* Historical Era Themed Events* Wardrobe, Vintage

Fifty-five Gal. Bar-B-Que Drum

See: Barbecues

Filing Cabinets

See Also: Office Equipment & Dressing* Police Office Dressing

Advanced Liquidators Office Furniture   **(818) 763-3470**
Large selection, various quantities, pkg deals avail.

C. P. Two   **(323) 466-8201**
All kinds of filing cabinets; steel filing cabinets, wood filing cabinets, plastic filing cabinets and more.

Dozar Office Furnishings   **(310) 559-9292**
9937 Jefferson Blvd, Culver City, CA, 90232
Rentals X22. Bookcases, mobile pedestals, vertical file cabinets, lateral file cabinets, storage cabinets
dozarrents@aol.com * www.dozarrents.com

LCW Props   **(818) 243-0707**
Large Selection, Lateral, Upright, Wood, Metal, Locking

Modern Props   **(323) 934-3000**
contemporary filing cabinets, various sizes, purposes, colors, veneered and plated. Small collection.

Omega/Cinema Props   **(323) 466-8201**
All kinds of filing cabinets; steel filing cabinets, wood filing cabinets, plastic filing cabinets and more.

Picture Start Props   **(818) 255-5472**
Modern silver/gray file cabinets and various vintage file cabinets.

Prop Services West   **(818) 503-2790**

RC Vintage, Inc.   **(818) 765-7107**
40s Wooden Filing Cabinets/Metal Filing Cabinets & Metal Filing Cabinets with locks

Sony Pictures Studios-Prop House (Off Lot)   **(310) 244-5999**

Warner Bros. Studios Property Department   **(818) 954-2181**
Lateral, Filing, Metal, Wood, Rolling, office, school, multiples, vintage, multiple drawers, period

Film Commissions

Assn. of Film Commissioners Int'l.   **(323) 461-2324**
9595 Wilshire Blvd Ste 900 Beverly Hills, CA, 90212
web site links to Film Commissions world wide.
www.afci.org

California Film Commission   **(323) 860-2960**
7080 Hollywood Blvd Ste 900, Hollywood, CA, 90028
www.film.ca.gov

Film L. A. Inc.   **(213) 977-8600**
6255 W Sunset Blvd 12th Floor, Hollywood, CA, 90028
Hollywood liaison of California Film Commission
www.filmlainc.com

Film Reels

See Also: Video Camera Equipment & Services* Video Equipment

The Hand Prop Room LP.   **(323) 931-1534**

History For Hire, Inc.   **(818) 765-7767**
Film reels for rent

Finials, Decorative

See: Lamps

Fire Extinguishers, Practical & Prop

See Also: Expendables* Fire Hoses (Prop)
AIR Designs   **(818) 768-6639**
Period to New, Handheld, 2-wheeled Carts
Alley Cats Studio Rentals   **(818) 982-9178**
modern, antique, brass
C. P. Two   **(323) 466-8201**
Fire extinguishers; period fire extinguishers, historical fire extinguishers, and modern fire extinguishers.
E.C. Prop Rentals   **(818) 764-2008**
wide sel. w/wall boxes; also alarm boxes, fire pulls, signage
The Hand Prop Room LP.   **(323) 931-1534**
rigged, prop/rubber
History For Hire, Inc.   **(818) 765-7767**
brass, most eras
LCW Props   **(818) 243-0707**
Real & Fake, Rubber, Large Selection
Mike Green Fire Equipment Co.   **(818) 989-3322**
11916 Valerio St, N Hollywood, CA, 91605
Affordable/dependable refill great pricing - large inventory, next day delivery to most areas.
info@mgfire.com * www.Mgfire.com

NEW & VINTAGE FIRE EQUIPMENT PROPS
FIRE EXTINGUISHERS • ALARMS • FIRE HOSES
SMOKE DETECTORS • FIRE SIGNAGE

MIKE GREEN
FIRE EQUIPMENT COMPANY
WWW.MGFIRE.COM

Modern Props   **(323) 934-3000**
contemporary/futuristic prop fire extinguishers, red silver, yellow, white, industrial sized nozzles,
Sony Pictures Studios-Prop House (Off Lot)   **(310) 244-5999**
bracket extinguishers, extinguisher cases, fire extinguishers
Universal Studios Property & Hardware Dept   **(818) 777-2784**
Prop fire extinguishers, vintage fire extinguishers, modern fire extinguishers and more for rent.

Fire Hoses (Prop)

E.C. Prop Rentals   **(818) 764-2008**
good multiples w/boxes & reels
The Hand Prop Room LP.   **(323) 931-1534**
History For Hire, Inc.   **(818) 765-7767**
LCW Props   **(818) 243-0707**
Large Quantities, With Or Without Nozzles, Boxes, Pulls, Extinguishers
Mike Green Fire Equipment Co.   **(818) 989-3322**
11916 Valerio St, N Hollywood, CA, 91605
Large inventory, great pricing, next day delivery to most areas.
info@mgfire.com * www.Mgfire.com
Sony Pictures Studios-Prop House (Off Lot)   **(310) 244-5999**
fire alarm boxes, fire bells, fire stand pipe, fire hydrants
Universal Studios Property & Hardware Dept   **(818) 777-2784**
Prop fire hoses, fire hose wheels, fire hose cabinets, fire hose valves and more for rent.

Fire Hydrants

See: Street Dressing

Fire Retardants

See: Fire Extinguishers, Practical & Prop* Flameproofing

Fire Sprinklers

See: Fire Extinguishers, Practical & Prop* Fire Hoses (Prop)* Flameproofing* Plumbing Fixtures, Heating/Cooling Appliances

Fire Suits

See: Costume Rental Houses* Flameproofing* Protective Apparel

Fire Trucks

See: Vehicles/Picture Vehicles

Fireman Uniforms, Hats & Equipment

See Also: Alarms* Duvetyne* Fire Extinguishers, Practical & Prop* Fire Hoses (Prop)* Flameproofing* Hoses
Allstar Fire Equipment, Inc.   **(626) 652-0900**
12328 Lower Azusa Rd, Arcadia, CA, 91006
fireman & hazmat apparel & gear
www.allstarfire.com
The Hand Prop Room LP.   **(323) 931-1534**
axes, wrenches, gear, badges, air tanks, fireman tools
LCW Props   **(818) 243-0707**
Equipment, Hoses, Nozzles, Extinguishers, Hats, Boots
Western Costume Co.   **(818) 760-0900**

Fireplaces & Mantels/Screens/Tools/Andirons

See Also: Blacksmith Shop/Foundry* Furnaces* Heaters, Indoor* Heaters, Outdoor
Encino Fireplace Shop   **(818) 881-4684**
17954 Ventura Blvd, Encino, CA, 91316
variety; free standing, glass, brass, custom made
www.encinofireplace.com
Modern Props   **(323) 934-3000**
contemporary fireplaces, small collection.
Omega/Cinema Props   **(323) 466-8201**
Fireplaces and fireplace accessories. Various fireplace screens and fireplace mantels.
Picture Start Props   **(818) 255-5472**
Some faux fireplaces and assorted tools and screens.
Prop Services West   **(818) 503-2790**
RC Vintage, Inc.   **(818) 765-7107**
vintage fireplace, vintage furnaces, stand up fireplaces, house warmers, wood burners, single room fireplaces
A Royal Suite Home Furinishings   **(661) 259-7000**
26536 Carl Boyer Dr, Santa Clarita, CA, 91350
A Royal Suite, family-owned since 1978, Features AMERICAN-MADE Furniture, and the Finest Furniture at the Greatest Value
norb@ars-email.com * www.aroyalsuite.com
Sony Pictures Studios-Prop House (Off Lot)   **(310) 244-5999**
andirons, bellows, coal braziers, coal scuttles, fireplaces, screens & tools
Sword & Stone   **(818) 562-6548**
Wrought iron tools, including fireplace andirons and fireplace tools
Universal Studios Property & Hardware Dept   **(818) 777-2784**
All things mantel and fireplace props for rent.
Universal Studios Special Effects Equip.   **(818) 777-3333**
special effects setups

Fireworks

See: Pyrotechnics

First Aid Kits

See: Ambulance/Paramedic* Medical Equip/Furniture, Graphics/Supplies

Fish

See: Aquariums & Tropical Fish

Fish Wranglers

See: Aquariums & Tropical Fish

Fish, Artificial & Rubber

See Also: Aquariums & Tropical Fish
AIR Designs (818) 768-6639
Fake Lobster, Fake Crab, Fake Fish, Etc.
The Hand Prop Room LP. (323) 931-1534
taxidermy, asst. types/sizes
Lennie Marvin Enterprises, Inc. (Prop Heaven) (818) 841-5882
taxidermy, assorted types & sizes
Sony Pictures Studios-Prop House (Off Lot) (310) 244-5999
Universal Studios Property & Hardware Dept (818) 777-2784
Prop fake fish and artificial fish for rent.
Universal Studios Special Effects Equip. (818) 777-3333
shark fins, heads

Fishing Equipment & Tackle

See Also: Fish, Artificial & Rubber* Lobster/Fish Traps
Bob Marriott's Flyfishing Store (800) 535-6633
2700 W Orangethorpe Ave, Fullerton, CA, 92833
all flyfishing, 30K+ inventory items, 325 pg catalog avail.
www.bobmarriotts.com
Fishermen's Spot (818) 785-7306
14411 Burbank Blvd, Van Nuys, CA, 91401
fly fishing & fishing tackle collectibles
www.fishermensspot.com
The Hand Prop Room LP. (323) 931-1534
full outfitting
History For Hire, Inc. (818) 765-7767
Johnny's Sports Shop (626) 797-8839
1402 Lincoln Ave, Pasadena, CA, 91103
all tackle, some camping, float tubes, live bait worms
Tally Ho Marine Salvage & Decor (310) 548-5273
406 22nd St, San Pedro, CA, 90731
If we don't have it & can't find it, we can build it. boats, nautical, block & tackle
sets, barrels, rope
Turner's Outdoorsman (626) 578-0155
835 S Arroyo Pkwy, Pasadena, CA, 91105
fishing equip. tackle, firearms; Reseda store (818) 996-5033
www.turners.com
Universal Studios Property & Hardware Dept (818) 777-2784
All things fishing props from saltwater to freshwater for rent.

Fishnets

See: Camouflage Nets* Cargo Nets* Fishing Equipment & Tackle*
Hosiery* Nautical Dressing & Props

Fitness Equipment

See: Exercise & Fitness Equipment* Massage Tables* Medical
Equip/Furniture, Graphics/Supplies

Fixtures, Display

See: Display Cases, Racks & Fixtures (Store)* Store Shelf Units &
Shelving

Fixtures, Lighting

See: Light Fixtures

Fixtures, Plumbing

See: Plumbing Fixtures, Heating/Cooling Appliances

Flagpoles

AIR Designs (818) 768-6639
8' to 35' Poles, Flags
E.C. Prop Rentals (818) 764-2008
aluminum sectional, free standing & wall-mount

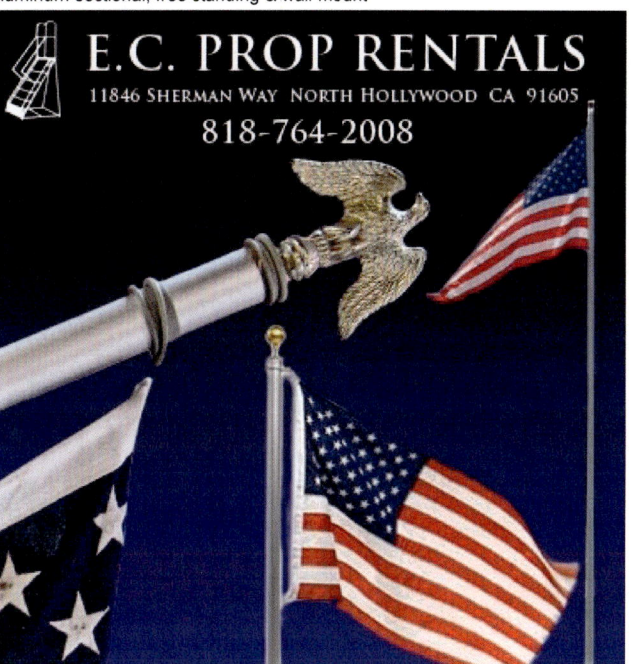

History For Hire, Inc. (818) 765-7767
inside & military style
LCW Props (818) 243-0707
Aluminum, Large & Small, Flags, Ornate
Modern Props (323) 934-3000
contemporary/futuristic, wall and free standing flagpoles, with United States flag
optional
Sony Pictures Studios-Linens, Drapes, Rugs (310) 244-5999
5933 W Slauson Ave, Culver City, CA, 90230
Large flagpoles and pennants
www.sonypicturesstudios.com
Universal Studios Property & Hardware Dept (818) 777-2784
Prop flagpoles; wall mounted flag poles, standing flag poles, and flag pole
bases all for rent.

Flags/Banners

See Also: Flagpoles* Signs* Windsocks

Beyond Image Graphics **(818) 547-0899**
1853 Dana St, Glendale, CA, 91201
Custom Banners, Back Lit Prints, Vinyl Graphics, Vinyl Lettering, Design &
Layout, Printed Banners.
rafi@beyondimagegraphics.com * www.beyondimagegraphics.com

Collins Visual Media **(818) 686-6581**
10518 Johanna Ave, Shadow Hills, CA, 91040
We fabricate custom, seamless, fabric and vinyl banner displays, both front-lit
and backlit, up to 16' x 150'.
www.collinsvisualmedia.com

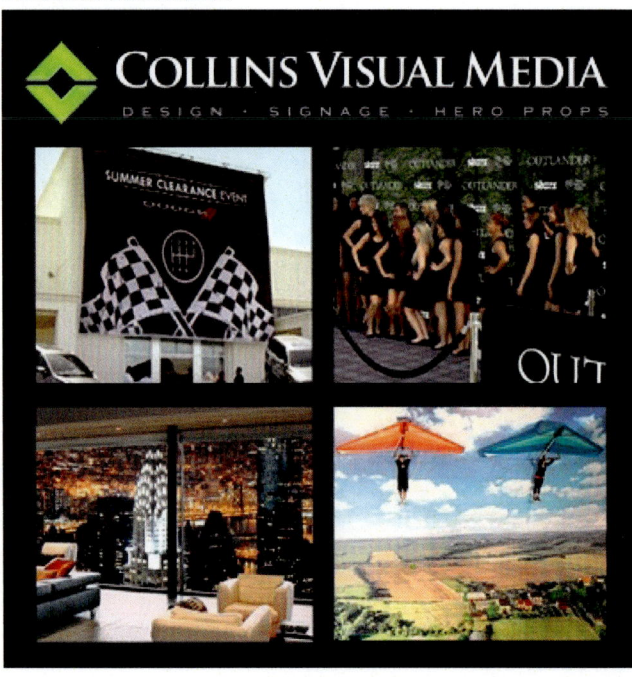

D'ziner Sign Co. **(323) 467-4467**
801 Seward Street, Los Angeles, CA, 90038
vinyl/paper, all sizes up to 20' by 200'
sales@dzinersign.com * www.dzinersign.com

depict **(323) 222-1001**
1460 Naud St, Los Angeles, CA, 90012
info@depict33.com * www.depict33.com

The Hand Prop Room LP. **(323) 931-1534**
countries, circus, graphic reprod.

History For Hire, Inc. **(818) 765-7767**
Huge selection presidential, army, etc.

L. A. Circus **(323) 751-3486**
Call for Appt, Los Angeles, CA, 90047
silent flags, antique sideshow banners, side show banners, circus banners,
circus wagons: many types
circusinc@aol.com * www.lacircus.com

LCW Props **(818) 243-0707**
Large Selection, Countries, Sports Banners, UN, Swags

Modern Props **(323) 934-3000**
United States flags framed and on stands, flag bearing figurines

Omega/Cinema Props **(323) 466-8201**
Many flags from armed forces flags to state flags and country flags.
Presidential flags & various American Flags.

Perry Flag Headquarters **(818) 526-0019**
1924 W Olive Ave, Burbank, CA, 91506
flags & flagpoles, distributors & manufacturers
flagheadquarters@att.net * www.perryflagheadquarters.com

Repro-Graphic Supply **(818) 771-9066**
9838 Glenoaks Blvd, Sun Valley, CA, 91352
Banners and flags; banner design and banner printing, flag design/flag
fabrication.
info@reprographicsupply.com * www.reprographicsupply.com

Sony Pictures Studios-Linens, Drapes, Rugs **(310) 244-5999**
5933 W Slauson Ave, Culver City, CA, 90230
all nations flags & state flags
www.sonypicturesstudios.com

Sword & Stone **(818) 562-6548**
Medieval & Renaissance

Universal Studios Graphic Design & Sign Shop **(818) 777-2350**
design, large format printing to 100" wide, & full service sign

Universal Studios Property & Hardware Dept **(818) 777-2784**
Various country, state, and religious flags in different sizes and shapes all for
rent.

Warner Bros. Drapery, Upholstery & Flooring **(818) 954-1831**
4000 Warner Blvd Bldg 30, Burbank, CA, 91522
Flags; Flag poles; Banners; Medieval Banners; Butterflies; Futuristic; Custom
manufacturing
wbsfdrapery@warnerbros.com * www.wbdrapery.com

Warner Bros. Studios Scenic Art & Sign Shop **(818) 954-1815**
4000 Warner Blvd Bldg 44, Burbank, CA, 91522
graphic design and production studio for signs & scenic art; digital printing to
hand-painted
wbsigns@warnerbros.com * www.wbsignandscenic.com

Flameproofing

See Also: Duvetyne* Fire Extinguishers, Practical & Prop* Protective
Apparel

Fabric Flameproofing Company Inc. **(323) 245-1701**
835 Milford St, Glendale, CA, 91203
fabrics, costumes, drapery, scenic backdrops, flame retardant
www.fabricflameproofingco.com

Green Set, Inc. **(818) 764-1231**
flameproofing plants, including a wide variety of cacti, dessert plants, and of
course succulents galore!

Jackson Shrub Supply, Inc. **(818) 982-0100**
Flameproofing materials, flame retardant trees, flame retardant Xmas trees, fire
retardant brush, succulents

Flash Bulbs

See: Camera Equipment

Flashlights

See: Camping Equipment* Sporting Goods & Services

Flea Markets

See: Swap Meets, Southern California

Flight Suits

See: Military Surplus/Combat Clothes, Field Gear

Floats, Nautical

See: Nautical Dressing & Props

Floats, Parade

See: Events, Decorations, Supplies & Services

Flocking

See: Fabrics* Wall Coverings

The Grateful Dead's Jerry Garcia dies, Oklahoma City's Federal Building was bombed. **Windows 95** was released and **OJ Simpson** was acquitted. 'Baywatch Nights', 'JAG', and 'Star Trek: Voyager' were on our T.V.'s. 'Toy Story', 'Batman Forever' and 'Ace Ventura' were popular, and **'Forrest Gump'** won the Oscar. We added maps, comprehensive indexing and a company index from our user's suggestions. I lost my source codes for the Book (plus a database melt-down) but **Bob Payne** rescued the data and composed the book for the first time, it has since become his permanent job.

1995

40 YEARS OF DEBBIES BOOK

Floor, Ground & Surface Protection

See Also: Flameproofing* Expendables* Duvetyne

Elasco Guard (800) 827-7887
18065 Redondo Circle, Huntington Beach CA, 92648
mfg of polyurethane products, esp. cableguards
www.elascoproducts.com

Linoleum City, Inc. (323) 469-0063
4849 Santa Monica Blvd, Hollywood, CA, 90029
Clear Vinyl, Vinyl Runners, Rubber Runner, Diamond Plate Vinyl, Embossed Flooring, Clear Carpet Runners, Entrance Mats
sales@linocity.com * www.linoleumcity.com

Largest Selection of Floorcoverings in L.A.
Serving the Entertainment Industry for over 65 years. We understand your needs and deliver promptly!
Carpet • Vinyl • Cork • Carpet Runners • Hardwood Floors
Linoleum • Tiles • Laminate Floors • Ceramic Tiles
Clear Vinyl • Window Treatments • Wall Coverings

SVE Portable Roadway Systems, Inc. (877) 384-6103
620 Compton Street, Broomfield, CO, 80020
MUD-TRAKS for protecting ground surface from tire ruts
www.sveproducts.com

Terraplas USA Inc. (903) 983-2111
1104 W State Highway 31, Kilgore, TX, 75662
turf protection from heavy crowd traffic on large or small areas
www.terraplasusa.com

Flooring

See: Carpet & Flooring* Dirt Skins* Floor, Ground & Surface Protection* Grating, Grated Flooring, Catwalks* Plastics, Materials & Fabrication* Red Carpeting, Events/Premiers* Rugs* Studio Tile Flooring* Tile, Marble, Granite, Etc.

Floral Foam

See: Foam

Florists/Floral Design

See Also: Flower Carts* Flowers, Dried* Flowers, Silk, Plastic & Dried* Greens

Floral Design by Daves Flowers   **(323) 666-4391**
4738 Hollywood Blvd, Los Angeles, CA, 90027
In business for over 40 years. We listen and create, deliver everywhere - LA, Santa Barbara, San Diego
davesflowers@aol.com * www.davesflowers.com

Unique Floral Designs EVENTS GARDEN COUTURE GIFTS

Dave's Flowers

Flower Art   **(323) 935-6800**
5859 West 3rd Street, Los Angeles, CA, 90036
Award-winning, full-service floral design for movie/television sets. Located near The Grove. SDSA members since 1994
info@flowerartla.com * www.flowerartla.com

Sandy Rose Floral, Inc   **(818) 980-4371**
6850 Vineland Ave Unit C, N Hollywood, CA, 91605
fresh & artificial florals, custom & prefab rentals, call 24 hrs. Set Florists.
www.sandyrose.com

Sandy Rose
LEGENDARY FLORALS FOR TELEVISION AND FILM

6850 Vineland Avenue C
North Hollywood, CA 91605
sandyrose.com

Flower Carts

See Also: Florists/Floral Design* Flowers, Silk, Plastic & Dried

AIR Designs   **(818) 768-6639**
Vendor Carts, Glass Cases, Stands/Display

The Hand Prop Room LP.   **(323) 931-1534**
metal flower cart, wooden flower cart, flower baskets, silk flowers, artificial flowers, outfitted flower cart

History For Hire, Inc.   **(818) 765-7767**

Jackson Shrub Supply, Inc.   **(818) 982-0100**
flower shop decor, wood flower carts, flower vendor carts, multi-tier flower carts, flower sales station props

Sandy Rose Floral, Inc   **(818) 980-4371**
6850 Vineland Ave Unit C, N Hollywood, CA, 91605
custom wood flowers carts & wood/chalkboard flower carts for rent
www.sandyrose.com

Sony Pictures Studios-Prop House (Off Lot)   **(310) 244-5999**

Flower Shop

See Also: Flower Carts* Flowers, Silk, Plastic & Dried

Jackson Shrub Supply, Inc.   **(818) 982-0100**
Flower shop decor, wood flower carts, flower vendor carts, flower sales station props.

Lennie Marvin Enterprises, Inc. (Prop Heaven)   **(818) 841-5882**

Flowers, Dried

See: Flowers, Silk, Plastic & Dried

Flowers, Silk, Plastic & Dried

Aldik Home   **(818) 988-5970**
7651 Sepulveda Blvd, Van Nuys, CA, 91405
Fake flowers, silk flowers, plastic flowers
www.aldikhome.com

Alpha Companies - Spellman Desk Co.   **(818) 504-9090**
silk florals, silk plants

Flower Art   **(323) 935-6800**
5859 West 3rd Street, Los Angeles, CA, 90036
Award-winning, full-service floral design for movie/television sets. Located near The Grove. SDSA members since 1994
info@flowerartla.com * www.flowerartla.com

Green Set, Inc.   **(818) 764-1231**
Fruit, veggies, vines, cornstalks, floral arrangements real and faux. Great for flower shop dressing & florist dressing.

Jackson Shrub Supply, Inc.   **(818) 982-0100**
suburban, classic, exotic; bushes, leaves, vintage-flowers, silk greens

Omega/Cinema Props   **(323) 466-8201**
Various plastic flowers and silk flowers, various dried flowers

Picture Start Props   **(818) 255-5472**
Large collection of various silk and plastic flowers.

Prop Services West   **(818) 503-2790**

Sandy Rose Floral, Inc   **(818) 980-4371**
6850 Vineland Ave Unit C, N Hollywood, CA, 91605
Huge collection, vintage plastics, custom & prefab silks
www.sandyrose.com

Sony Pictures Studios-Prop House (Off Lot)   **(310) 244-5999**
Plastic floral, silk floral, plastic flowers, silk flowers

Universal Studios Property & Hardware Dept   **(818) 777-2784**
Prop artificial floral arrangements, artificial plants, silk flowers, plastic flowers and more for rent.

ZG04 DECOR   **(818) 853-8040**
Realistic silk flowers & plastic flowers as well as fake greens for homes and events

Fluorescent Fixtures

See: Light Fixtures

Foam

See Also: Architectural Pieces & Artifacts* Rubber & Foam Rubber

Advanced Foam, Inc.   **(310) 515-0617**
1745 W. 134th St, Gardena, CA, 90249
www.advancedfoam.com

Astro Audio Video Lighting, Inc.   **(818) 549-9915**
6615 San Fernando Rd, Glendale, CA, 91201
Foam machines for parties and events.
www.astroavl.com

Atlas Foam Products   **(818) 837-3626**
12836 Arroyo St, Sylmar, CA, 91342
foam, sheets, small-large, cust. shape/size, floral foam
www.atlasfoam.com

Charisma Design Studio, Inc. (818) 252-6611
8414 San Fernando Road, Sun Valley, CA, 91352
cutting, sculpting & fabrication
info@charismadesign.com * www.charismadesign.com

DeRouchey Foam (888) 959-4852
13618 Vaughn Street, San Fernando, CA, 91340
We offer a full line of foam sculpting materials and services. Urethane, EPS,
HardCoat, Foam Adhesive. 24/7 Service.
info@derofoam.com * www.derofoam.com

Diamond Foam & Fabric Co. (323) 931-8148
611 S La Brea Ave, Los Angeles, CA, 90036
decorative fabrics & foam for upholstery, drapery & slipcovers, custom sewing
on premises
www.diamondfoamandfabric.com

EFX- Event Special Effects (626) 888-2239
125 Railroad Ave, Monrovia, CA, 91016
Foam Party- Foam Cannon- Foam Machines- Fluid
info@efxla.com * www.efxla.com

Foam Mart (818) 848-FOAM
628 N Victory Blvd, Burbank, CA, 91502
L-200 - L-600, closed cell foam, sculpture foams, custom foams, bead foams,
all types. Wholesale accounts welcome.
www.foammart.com

Foam Sales & Marketing (818) 558-5717
1005 W. Isabel St, Burbank, CA, 91506
rigid foam sheets, bead foam blocks, bead board
info@foamsalesandmarketing.com * www.foamsalesandmarketing.com

Williams Foam (818) 833-4343
12961 San Fernando Rd, Sylmar, CA, 91342
foam fabrication, custom work, polyethylene & polystyrene
www.williamsfoam.com

Foam Core Board

See: Expendables Paper* Styrofoam*

Fog Machines

See Also: Special Effects, Equipment & Supplies Special Effects,
Lighting & Lasers*

Astro Audio Video Lighting, Inc. (818) 549-9915
6615 San Fernando Rd, Glendale, CA, 91201
Dry ice fog machines and fluid fog machines for events and concerts including
remote controlled fog machines.
www.astroavl.com

Castex Rentals (323) 462-1468
1044 N Cole Ave, Hollywood, CA, 90038
Mole, Roscoe, D50 Hazers, fog juice, indoor fog machines & outdoor fog
machines
service@castexrentals.com * www.castexrentals.com

CONFETTI & FOG FX Special Effects Company (877) 576-4239
1085 W 21st Pl, Hialeah, FL, 33010
Fog machines including handheld fog machines and large scale fog machines
Info@confettiandfogfx.com * www.caffx.com

EFX- Event Special Effects (626) 888-2239
125 Railroad Ave, Monrovia, CA, 91016
Fog Machines- Fog- Haze- Low Lye- Dry Ice- DNG- Fluid
info@efxla.com * www.efxla.com

L. A. Party Works (888) 527-2789
9712 Alpaca St, S El Monte, CA, 91733
Fog machines fore rent
partyworks@aol.com * www.partyworksinteractive.com

Special Effects Unlimited, Inc. (323) 466-3361
1005 N Lillian Way, Hollywood, CA, 90038
many kinds
www.specialeffectsunlimited.com

Universal Studios Special Effects Equip. (818) 777-3333
bee smokers to fog guns & supplies

Folding Chairs/Tables

See Also: Chairs

Advanced Liquidators Office Furniture (818) 763-3470
many colors and models of folding chairs including padded seats and/or
padded backs. Folding tables with many high end finishes

C. P. Two (323) 466-8201
Many folding chairs, wooden folding chairs, metal folding chairs, retro folding
chairs and modern folding chairs.

Dozar Office Furnishings (310) 559-9292
9937 Jefferson Blvd, Culver City, CA, 90232
Rentals X22. Portable chairs, portable tables, folding tables, folding chairs, card
tables and more available.
dozarrents@aol.com * www.dozarrents.com

History For Hire, Inc. (818) 765-7767
chairs, card tables

LCW Props (818) 243-0707
Many, Plastic, Wood, Different Sizes, Beer Pong

Omega/Cinema Props (323) 466-8201
Many folding chairs from modern to period. Many folding tables from modern to
period.

Picture Start Props (818) 255-5472
Multiples of bamboo style folding chairs

Universal Studios Property & Hardware Dept (818) 777-2784
Many kinds of folding chairs in multiples for rent.

ZG04 DECOR (818) 853-8040
Many many kinds of folding chairs and folding tables in large quantities
multiples

Folding Screens

See: Screens, Folding

Folk Art

See: Art, Tribal & Folk

Food or Beverage Carts

See: Locations, Airport Dressing & Hangars Vendor Carts &
Concession Counters*

Food Processing Plant

See: Factory/Industrial

Food, Artificial Food

See Also: Beer Equipment, Taps & Coolers Catering* Ice Cubes,
Plastic* Soda Fountain Dressing*

Covert Cocktails (310) 714-6331
6204 Vista Del Mar, Playa Del Rey, CA, 90293
Mfg realistic faux cocktails & garnishes. Drink/drank or drunk, our cocktails
always look fresh & are 100% unspillable.
dana@covertcocktails.com * www.covertcocktails.com

Flora-Cal Products (951) 734-3672
12158 Severn Way, Riverside, CA, 92503
Artificial food/fake food
info@floracal.com * www.floracal.com

LISTINGS FOR THIS CATEGORY CONTINUE ON THE
FOLLOWING PAGE

Fosselmans Ice Cream Co. (626) 282-6533
1824 W. Main St, Alhambra, CA, 91801
best ice cream in L.A.
www.fosselmans.com

Galco's Soda Pop Stop (323) 255-7115
5702 York Blvd, Los Angeles, CA, 90042
100s of rare, regional, imported & half-forgotten soft drinks
www.sodapopstop.com

Grand Central Market (213) 624-2378
317 S. Broadway, Los Angeles, CA, 90013
fresh & preserved foods from all over the world
www.grandcentralmarket.com

Green Set, Inc. (818) 764-1231
Artificial Fruit & Artificial Vegetables, Oversized Fruits & Oversized Vegetables

The Hand Prop Room LP. (323) 931-1534
fruit to bakery goods in stock, will design & mfg.

Helena Wirth Exotic Cakes (323) 938-2286
14042 Burbank Blvd, Sherman Oaks, CA, 91401
Erotic cakes
www.helenawirthcakes.com/erotic-cakes

Hollywood Cinema Arts (818) 504-7333
Hundreds of pristine artificial food items.

Iwasaki Images of America (310) 225-2727
16927 S Main St Unit C, Gardena, CA, 90248
www.iwasaki-images.com

Jack's Wholesale Candy & Toy (213) 622-9287
777 S Central Ave, Los Angeles, CA 90021
Wholesale candy/Bulk candy, vending candy, American candy, novelty candy, pinata candy, Mexican candy
www.jackscandyandtoy.com

Jackson Shrub Supply, Inc. (818) 982-0100
fake fruit, fake vegetables, fake gourds, fake corn stalks, fake seaweed, oversized fruits, oversized vegetables

Jaqki's Cake Creations (818) 769-4967
12032 Burbank Blvd, North Hollywood, CA, 91607
Wedding cakes & custom cakes made fresh or props rental/purchase. We have 80 prop wedding cake styles to choose from.
cakesbyjaqki@yahoo.com * www.jaqkiscakes.com

LCW Props (818) 243-0707
Fake Food, Cheeses, Meats, Fruits & Vegetables

Lennie Marvin Enterprises, Inc. (Prop Heaven) (818) 841-5882
prop vegetables, fruits, meat, baked goods, cold meats, sushi, wedding cake

LM Treasures (626) 252-7354
Fruits, vegetables, ice cream, pizza, hotdogs are all pieces used to make a statement when working in the food industry.

Real Sodas In Real Bottles (310) 327-1700
2140 W 139th St, Gardena, CA, 90249
nostalgic, no longer made & hard to find sodas, will deliver
www.realsoda.com

Sony Pictures Studios-Prop House (Off Lot) (310) 244-5999
fake bread, fake cakes, fake candy, fake casserole, fake cheeses, fake chickens, fake cooked foods, fake crabs

Universal Studios Property & Hardware Dept (818) 777-2784
Prop foods/fake foods for rent.

Food, Food Stylists

See Also: Beer Equipment, Taps & Coolers* Catering* Events, Decorations, Supplies & Services* Vendor Carts & Concession Counters

Food Art L.A. (323) 791-2591
Los Angeles, CA, 90019
"Food Stylist to the Stars" TV - Film - Print - Commercial
foodartla@mac.com * www.FoodArtLA.com

Gourmet Proppers (818) 566-4140
Call for Appointment
Culinary producer & food stylist for camera ready edible food in cooking segments/demos, film, TV & commercials
bonnie@gourmetproppers.com * www.gourmetproppers.com

Helena Wirth Exotic Cakes (323) 938-2286
14042 Burbank Blvd, Sherman Oaks, CA, 91401
custom erotic cakes, sculptured & airbrushed protrait cakes, wedding cakes, real or prop
www.helenawirthcakes.com/erotic-cakes

Jaqki's Cake Creations (818) 769-4967
12032 Burbank Blvd, North Hollywood, CA, 91607
Wedding cakes & custom cakes made fresh or props rental/purchase. We have 80 prop wedding cake styles to choose from.
cakesbyjaqki@yahoo.com * www.jaqkiscakes.com

Foosball

See: Game Tables & Equipment

Foosball Game Table

See: Arcade Equipment, Games & Rides

Foot Wear

See: Shoes, Boots & Footwear

Football Equipment & Uniforms

See Also: Sporting Goods & Services* Sports & Games Themed Events

History For Hire, Inc. (818) 765-7767

L. A. Party Works (888) 527-2789
9712 Alpaca St, S El Monte, CA, 91733
Football themed games and football equipment
partyworks@aol.com * www.partyworksinteractive.com

Universal Studios Property & Hardware Dept (818) 777-2784
Football equipment

Formal Wear

See Also: Wedding Attire

CBS Costume Rental (323) 575-2666
Ladies modern evening gowns, cocktail dresses, suits

The Costume House (818) 508-9933
frock coats, morning coats, 1950s & 1970s tuxedoes

Sony Pictures Studios-Wardrobe (310) 244-5995
alterations, call (310) 244-7260

Universal Studios Costume Dept (818) 777-2722
Rental, mfg., & alterations

Western Costume Co. (818) 760-0900

Forties Furniture

See: Furniture, Mid-Century Modern

Forties Theme Parties

See: Costume Rental Houses* Costumes* Events, Backings & Scenery* Events, Decorations, Supplies & Services* Events, Design/Planning/Production* Historical Era Themed Events* Wardrobe, Vintage

Fortune-Teller & Zoltar Mahines

See Also: Carnival Dressing/Supplies* Carnival Games & Rides

L. A. Party Works (888) 527-2789
9712 Alpaca St, S El Monte, CA, 91733
Fortune-teller machine/Zoltars fortune machine
partyworks@aol.com * www.partyworksinteractive.com

Lennie Marvin Enterprises, Inc. (Prop Heaven) (818) 841-5882
Fortune teller machines, fortune teller arcade games

RC Vintage, Inc. (818) 765-7107
4 fortune-teller machines including Zoltar machines, female fortune-teller and a period fortune teller machines.

Fortuneteller

See: Fortune-Teller & Zoltar Mahines* Tarot Cards* Gypsy Wagon* Crystal Balls* Astrological

Fossils

See Also: Bones, Skulls & Skeletons* Dinosaurs

Dapper Cadaver (818) 771-0818
Standalone fossil replicas and fossil panels. Dinosaur fossils, ice age fossils and fantasy dragon fossils.

Geological Tools & Outfitter, LLC (435) 225-6421
71 N 200 W, Brigham City, UT, 84302
Fossil collecting & geology tools & equipment
www.geo-tools.com

Sword & Stone (818) 562-6548
Human skulls, bird fossils, assorted animal teeth

Wonders of the World & Beyond (310) 393-4700
1460 Lincoln Blvd, Santa Monica, CA, 90401
4-8 pm Mon-Sat, but appt preferred; real fossils, minerals lrg crystals, reprod. ancient jewelry, lrg insect specimens
www.worldsbestnaturestore.com

Foundry Dressing

See: Blacksmith Shop/Foundry

Fountain Pens

See: Pens, Fountain

Fountains, Decorative & Garden

See Also: Garden/Patio* Statuary

Badia Design, Inc. (818) 762-0130
5420 Vineland Ave, N Hollywood, CA, 91601
Moroccan Outdoor Furniture including fountains, mosaic table tops wrought
iron and more.
info@badiadesign.com * www.badiadesign.com

Green Set, Inc. (818) 764-1231
Eiffel tower, animal fountains, statue fountains, Greek fountains, Asian
fountains, multiple tier, mini and massive

Jackson Shrub Supply, Inc. (818) 982-0100
Egyptian decor, fiberglass fountains, aluminum fountains, clay fountains, and
wishing wells, bird baths

Potted (323) 665-3801
3158 Los Feliz Blvd, Los Angeles, CA, 90039
Decorative garden accessories, furniture, fountains, statues and pots
info@pottedstore.com * www.pottedstore.com

San Gabriel Nursery & Florist (626) 286-0787
632 S San Gabriel Blvd, San Gabriel, CA, 91776
large sel statuary & fountains, also plants
www.sgnursery.com

Fountains, Drinking (Wall & Stand)

See Also: Water Coolers

AIR Designs (818) 768-6639
Wall & Stand, Period & Present, Some Rigged

Alley Cats Studio Rentals (818) 982-9178
Free standing drinking fountains and wall mounted drinking fountains
available.

C. P. Two (323) 466-8201
Wall mounted drinking fountains and standing drinking fountains, period to
modern.

E.C. Prop Rentals (818) 764-2008
Porcelain/metal/stainless steel, period & contemporary

History For Hire, Inc. (818) 765-7767

LCW Props (818) 243-0707
Water Coolers, Wall Mount Fountains, Freestanding, Office, School, Prison

Modern Props (323) 934-3000
contemporary/modern, garden and public water fountains/drinking fountains.

RC Vintage, Inc. (818) 765-7107
period & modern units Prison Type, public drinking fountains, park drinking
fountains, office drinking fountains

Studio Plumbing Rentals (323) 829-9339
7373 Atoll Ave, N Hollywood, CA, 91605
studioplumbingrentals@gmail.com * www.studioair.com

Universal Studios Property & Hardware Dept (818) 777-2784
Prop standing drinking fountains & prop wall mounted drinking fountains for
rent.

Fountains, Soda

See: Soda Fountain Dressing

Frames, Eyeglass

See: Eyewear, Glasses, Sunglasses, 3D

Framing, Picture

See: Picture Frames* Art & Picture Framing Services

Freezers

See: Market Equipment/Fixtures Refrigerators* Restaurant
Kitchens/Equip./Supplies*

French Decorations

Castle Antiques & Design (818) 765-5000
11924 Vose St, N Hollywood, CA, 91605
All types of French decor and decorations for rent or purchase.
info@castleantiques.net * www.castleprophouse.com

Universal Studios Property & Hardware Dept (818) 777-2784
French decorative props for rent.

French Themed Parties

See: Events, Decorations, Supplies & Services Events,
Design/Planning/Production* Travel (City/Country) Themed Events*

Frock Coats

See: Formal Wear* Wardrobe, Antique/Historical

Fun House Mirrors

See Also: Carnival Dressing/Supplies

Get The Picture (818) 842-2968
222 South Lamer St, Burbank, CA, 91506
manufacturer, several styles & made to order

Lennie Marvin Enterprises, Inc. (Prop Heaven) (818) 841-5882
quantity available

RC Vintage, Inc. (818) 765-7107
carnival mirrors, misshaping mirrors, distortion mirrors

Funeral Dressing

See: Caskets Cemetery Dressing* Florists/Floral Design* Morgue*
Mortuary* Vehicles/Picture Vehicles*

Fur Garments

See Also: Fur, Artificial & Real Leather (Clothing, Accessories,
Materials)*

CBS Costume Rental (323) 575-2666
good quality ladies fake fur coats

Donna Salyers' Fabulous Furs (859) 291-3300
20 W 11th St, Covington, KY, 41011
catalog sales; faux fur, fabric by the yard
www.fabulousfurs.com

Madison Ave Furs LTD (212) 594-5744
118 W 27th St Ground Floor, New York, NY, 10001
Madison Avenue Furs, LTD. in NYC is a 3rd generation, family owned,
multifaceted retail & wholesale fur business.
hcfurmatcher@msn.com * www.cowitfurs.com

Roxy Deluxe (818) 487-7800
vintage women/men/child

Sword & Stone (818) 562-6548
Fur pelts, fur coats, fur lined helmets

Western Costume Co. (818) 760-0900

Fur, Artificial & Real

See Also: Leather (Clothing, Accessories, Materials)

Edinburgh Imports (800) 334-6274
58406 Joshua Ln, Yucca Valley CA, 92284
1000+ plush fabrics: 1/16"-3" pile. faux fur (synthetic plush), Schulte mohair &
alpaca, ultrasuede, felt
www.edinburghimports.com

The Indian Store (760) 639-5309
1950 Hacienda Dr, Vista, CA, 92081
beads, jewelry findings, fur, feather, leather, rawhide, pottery finished artifacts,
many books on Indian lore/tribes
www.indianstore.org

Madison Ave Furs LTD (212) 594-5744
118 W 27th St Ground Floor, New York, NY, 10001
Madison Avenue Furs, LTD. in NYC is a 3rd generation, family owned,
multifaceted retail & wholesale fur business.
hcfurmatcher@msn.com * www.cowitfurs.com

Sword & Stone (818) 562-6548
Fur pelts, fur coats, fur lined helmets

Furnaces

See Also: Heaters, Indoor Plumbing Fixtures, Heating/Cooling
Appliances*

E.C. Prop Rentals (818) 764-2008
mock coal/wood-burning & large factory-size boilers, all castered

LCW Props (818) 243-0707
Industrial, Steampunk, Brownstone, Commercial

Furniture & Art, Repair & Restoration

Adams Wood Products (423) 587-2942
5436 Jeffry Ln, Morristown, TN, 37813
catalog sales; wood furniture components & assembly kits
www.adamswoodproducts.com

Advanced Liquidators Office Furniture (818) 763-3470
repair kits, quick and no hassle - apply and let dry kits to fix almost any
upholstery, including stains and chips

Castle Antiques & Design (818) 765-5000
11924 Vose St, N Hollywood, CA, 91605
Antique and Vintage Furniture repair, restoration and upholstery available.
info@castleantiques.net * www.castleprophouse.com

Van Dyke's Restorers (800) 237-8833
PO Box 52, Louisiana, MO, 63353
catalog sales; woodworking and antique restoration supplies. antique furniture
repair parts/hardware/locks/supplies
www.vandykes.com

Warner Bros. Studios Cabinet & Furniture Shop (818) 954-1339
Antique restoration, repair, refinishing and/or replication of period to
contemporary furniture.

Furniture Dollies, Pads & Hand Trucks

Alley Cats Studio Rentals (818) 982-9178
wood, metal, period hand trucks

Castex Rentals (323) 462-1468
1044 N Cole Ave, Hollywood, CA, 90038
Super shelves, truck shelves, racks, furniture dollies, magliners, furniture pads, ratchets, rope
service@castexrentals.com * www.castexrentals.com

E.C. Prop Rentals (818) 764-2008
wide sel. & period stevedore dollies

The Hand Prop Room LP. (323) 931-1534

History For Hire, Inc. (818) 765-7767
dollies, pads, hand trucks

Universal Studios Property & Hardware Dept (818) 777-2784
Furniture dollies, furniture pads & hand trucks for rent

Furniture For Pets

See: Pet Furniture, Houses, Clothing

Furniture Oil & Polish

See: Expendables

Furniture, Antique

See: Antiques & Antique Decorations Furniture, Custom-made/Reproduction*

Furniture, Art Deco

Castle Antiques & Design (818) 765-5000
11924 Vose St, N Hollywood, CA, 91605
All types of Art Deco and Hollywood Regency style furniture for rent and purchase
info@castleantiques.net * www.castleprophouse.com

FormDecor, Inc. (310) 558-2582
America's largest event rental supplier of 20th Century furniture and accessories for Modern and Mid-Century styles.

LM Treasures (626) 252-7354
This includes a wide range of distinctively different pieces such as Lip Wall Decor, Venice Face Masks, & lady lamps.

Modern Props (323) 934-3000
furniture & accessories. Sofas, club chairs, desks, bars, tables, floor lamps, sculptures, clocks, sconces.

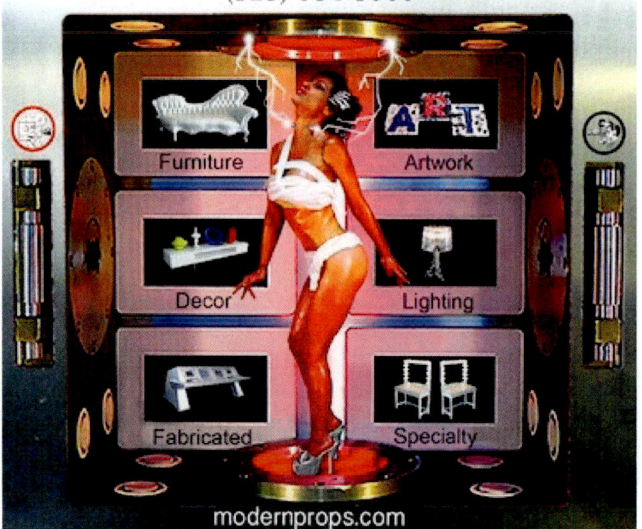

Old N Country Prop Shop, LLC (818) 423-2599
A variety of Art Deco Furniture for rent.

Omega/Cinema Props (323) 466-8201
Art deco chairs, art deco tables. art deco vanities, art deco night stands, art deco coffee tables, and more.

Pasadena Antique Center and Annex (626) 449-7706
480 South Fair Oaks Ave, Pasadena, CA, 91105
Home, office, and outdoor furnishings
pasadenaantiqecenterandannex@gmail.com * bit.ly/PasadenaAntiqueCenter

RC Vintage, Inc. (818) 765-7107
art deco chairs, fine crafted chairs, fancy tables, art deco counters, art deco sofas, comfy chairs, art deco living room sets

A Royal Suite Home Furnishings (661) 259-7000
26536 Carl Boyer Dr, Santa Clarita, CA, 91350
A Royal Suite, family-owned since 1978, Features AMERICAN-MADE Furniture, and the Finest Furniture at the Greatest Value
norb@ars-email.com * www.aroyalsuite.com

Warner Bros. Studios Property Department (818) 954-2181
High end art deco furniture

Furniture, Arts & Crafts

C. P. Two (323) 466-8201
Different types of furniture from the Craftsman style. Craftsman furniture/Craftsman bedroom furniture.

Modern Props (323) 934-3000
Craftsman furniture

Pasadena Antique Center and Annex (626) 449-7706
480 South Fair Oaks Ave, Pasadena, CA, 91105
Home, office, and outdoor furnishings
pasadenaantiqecenterandannex@gmail.com * bit.ly/PasadenaAntiqueCenter

Prop Services West (818) 503-2790

A Royal Suite Home Furinishings (661) 259-7000
26536 Carl Boyer Dr, Santa Clarita, CA, 91350
A Royal Suite, family-owned since 1978, Features AMERICAN-MADE Furniture, and the Finest Furniture at the Greatest Value
norb@ars-email.com * www.aroyalsuite.com

Sony Pictures Studios-Prop House (Off Lot) (310) 244-5999

Furniture, Asian

See: Asian Antiques, Furniture, Art & Artifacts

Furniture, Baby/Children

See Also: Children/Baby Accessories & Bedroom

Kids Cottage Furniture (818) 783-3055
14444 Ventura Blvd, Sherman Oaks, CA, 91423
Kids bedroom furniture and kids bedroom accessories
kidscottagefurniture@gmail.com * http://kidscottagefurniture.com

Old N Country Prop Shop, LLC (818) 423-2599
A large variety of children's furniture, vintage & newer.

Picture Start Props (818) 255-5472
Contemporary crib, changing table and baby furniture / toddler furniture.

Prop Services West (818) 503-2790
Childrens furniture/kids furniture

A Royal Suite Home Furinishings (661) 259-7000
26536 Carl Boyer Dr, Santa Clarita, CA, 91350
A Royal Suite, family-owned since 1978, Features AMERICAN-MADE Furniture, and the Finest Furniture at the Greatest Value
norb@ars-email.com * www.aroyalsuite.com

Furniture, Biedermeier

Omega/Cinema Props (323) 466-8201
All kinds of furniture, including bierdermeier

Prop Services West (818) 503-2790

Furniture, Contemporary

Advanced Liquidators Office Furniture (818) 763-3470
Large selection of high-end furniture, from executive quarters to secretary furniture. Innovative furniture for today

Blueprint Furniture (310) 657-4315
8600 Pico Blvd. Los Angeles, CA, 90035
Modern furniture lighting accessories early classic bauhaus mid-century contemporary design. Good studio rental history.
www.blueprintfurniture.com

Bridge Furniture & Props Los Angeles (818) 433-7100
We carry modern & traditional furniture, lighting, accessories, art, & rugs. Items are online for easy shopping.

BRIDGE LA
FURNITURE & PROPS

3210 Vanowen St.
Burbank, CA 91505

BridgeProps.com
Tel: 818.433.7100

Dozar Office Furnishings (310) 559-9292
9937 Jefferson Blvd, Culver City, CA, 90232
Rentals X22. Contemporary furniture for the office and at home.
dozarrents@aol.com * www.dozarrents.com

Faux Library Studio Props, Inc. (818) 765-0096
Modern desks; glass desks and wooden desks and Oval Office dressing

FormDecor, Inc. (310) 558-2582
America's largest event rental supplier of 20th Century furniture and accessories for Modern and Mid-Century styles.

H.D. Buttercup (310) 945-5061
3225 Helms Ave, Los Aangeles, CA, 90034
150,000 square feet. Contemporary, modern,mid-century,industrial,rustic and one of a kind pieces for your next project.
javalos@hdbuttercup.com * www.hdbuttercup.com/studio-services

Ikea (818) 842-4532
600 South Ikea Way, Burbank, CA, 91502
www.ikea.com

Little Bohemia Rentals (818) 853-7506
11940 Sherman Rd, N Hollywood, CA, 91605
sofas, chairs, coffee tables, end tables, dining sets, headboards, nightstands, desks, shelving, vanities, benches
sales@wearelittlebohemia.com * www.wearelittlebohemia.com

Lux Lounge EFR (888) 247-4411
106 1/2 Judge John Aiso St #318, Los Angeles, CA, 90012
Contemporary furniture including contemporary chairs, contemporary sofas, and contemporary tables.
info@luxloungeefr.com * www.luxloungeefr.com

Modern Props (323) 934-3000
Contemporary furniture, lamps, art, prints & accessories

Modernica Props (323) 664-2322
huge inventory of 50s-70s furniture & decor, multiples up to 500

NEST Studio Rentals, Inc. (818) 942-0339
living, dining, den, home office, bedroom

Ob-jects (818) 351-4200
upholstery, coffee tables, end tables, sofa tables

LISTINGS FOR THIS CATEGORY CONTINUE ON THE FOLLOWING PAGE

Omega/Cinema Props   **(323) 466-8201**
Contemporary furniture from Oval Office dressing to contemporary home furniture.

Pasadena Antique Center and Annex   **(626) 449-7706**
480 South Fair Oaks Ave, Pasadena, CA, 91105
Home, office, and outdoor furnishings
pasadenaantiqecenterandannex@gmail.com * bit.ly/PasadenaAntiqueCenter

Picture Start Props   **(818) 255-5472**
Assorted contemporary dressing for contemporary home or office.

Pomp Home   **(323) 592-3058**
1068 N Palm Canyon Dr, Palm Springs, CA, 92262
We are more than a furniture company, we are lovers of modern design and clean lines.
www.pomphome.com

Prop Services West   **(818) 503-2790**
Contemporary furniture rentals

Prop Services West

7040 Laurel Canyon Blvd.
No Hollywood CA 91605

www.propserviceswest.com 818-503-2790

A Royal Suite Home Furinishings   **(661) 259-7000**
26536 Carl Boyer Dr, Santa Clarita, CA, 91350
A Royal Suite, family-owned since 1978, Features AMERICAN-MADE Furniture, and the Finest Furniture at the Greatest Value
norb@ars-email.com * www.aroyalsuite.com

Sony Pictures Studios-Prop House (Off Lot)   **(310) 244-5999**
contemporary cabinets, china cabinets, computer cabinets, credenzas, entertainment centers, hutch cabinets

Universal Studios Property & Hardware Dept   **(818) 777-2784**
Contemporary furniture; contemporary chairs, contemporary tables, contemporary artwork and more for rent.

Warner Bros. Studios Property Department   **(818) 954-2181**
Contemporary bar stools, bistro tables, stacking chairs, ottomans, chaises, hanging fixtures & accessories

Warner Bros. Studios The Collection   **(818) 954-2181**
4000 Warner Blvd Bldg 30, Burbank, CA, 91522
High end Contemporary, industrial, modern, rustic & one-of-a-kind items, Oval Office Set Dressing Items
wbsfproperty@warnerbros.com * www.wbpropertydept.com

WB PROPERTY DEPARTMENT
WBPropertyDept.com

THE COLLECTION
818.954.7405

ZG04 DECOR   **(818) 853-8040**
Iconic Design, Classic-Modern, Mid-Century Furniture

12224 Montague St, Pacoima, CA 91331
818.853.8040   310.775.4042   www.zg04decor.com

Furniture, Custom-made/Reproduction

Castle Antiques & Design   **(818) 765-5000**
11924 Vose St, N Hollywood, CA, 91605
We offer custom hand-made furniture in all styles and stains including pained, distressed, and bleached finishes.
info@castleantiques.net * www.castleprophouse.com

Dan Parish LTD   **(909) 284-9227**
351 Kettering Dr., Ontario CA, 91761
Source for interior designers to create their vision without limitation. 30 years experience producing custom furniture.
dan@danparishltd.com * www.danparishltd.com

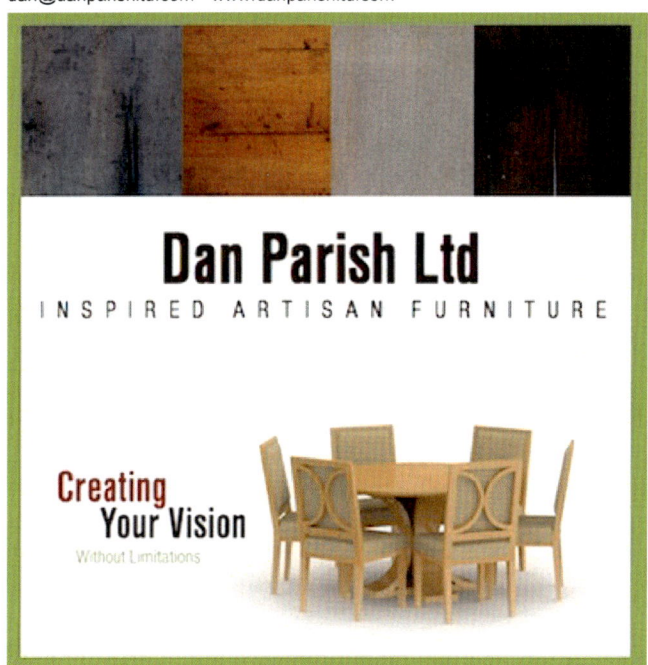

depict   **(323) 222-1001**
1460 Naud St, Los Angeles, CA, 90012
info@depict33.com * www.depict33.com

Evans Family Barrels   **(818) 523-8174**
7918 Fairchild Ave, Canoga Park, CA, 91306
Solid oak wine barrel furniture: tables, chairs, cabinets, pet furniture, home & business decor, swings, vintage barrels
evansbarrels@gmail.com * www.EvansFamilyBarrels.com

Larry St. John & Co.   **(310) 630-5828**
17021 S Broadway, Gardena, CA, 90248
Custom, heavily discounted, locally made, quality hardwood & reclaimed wood furniture, sofa sectionals and classic cars! Custom Furniture
info@larrystjohn.com * www.larrystjohn.com

LM Treasures   **(626) 252-7354**
All our items are hand painted and crafted to provide each customer with their own personally unique piece.

Lux Lounge EFR   **(888) 247-4411**
106 1/2 Judge John Aiso St #318, Los Angeles, CA, 90012
Custom furniture design & custom furniture production: Anything you can imagine, we can create.
info@luxloungeefr.com * www.luxloungeefr.com

Martin Iron Design   **(818) 760-3636**
10750 Cumpston St, N Hollywood, CA, 91601
Custom designed wrought iron furniture, anything that you can imagine.
martinirondesign@yahoo.com * www.martinirondesign.com

A Royal Suite Home Furinishings   **(661) 259-7000**
26536 Carl Boyer Dr, Santa Clarita, CA, 91350
A Royal Suite, family-owned since 1978, Features AMERICAN-MADE Furniture, and the Finest Furniture at the Greatest Value
norb@ars-email.com * www.aroyalsuite.com

Set Masters   **(818) 982-1506**
24853 Avenue Rockefeller, Valencia, CA, 91355
Source for Interior Designers; Custom Design & Manufacturing; Design Services Available
info@setmasters.com * www.setmasters.com

Stephen Kenn   **(323) 920-4210**
1250 Long Beach Ave #120, Los Angeles, CA, 90021
Stephen Kenn is available for custom design work, and The Inheritance Collection is available for purchase or rental.
contact@stephenkenn.com * www.stephenkenn.com

Warner Bros. Studios Cabinet & Furniture Shop   **(818) 954-1339**
Custom manufacturing & installation of cabinets & furniture to your specifications. Design services available.

Furniture, Early American/Colonial

Advanced Liquidators Office Furniture   **(818) 763-3470**
almost any wood style, veneered, metallic and other table top textures, colonial chairs and furniture, large variety

Castle Antiques & Design   **(818) 765-5000**
11924 Vose St, N Hollywood, CA, 91605
We have Continental and American Colonial style furniture for rent or purchase.
info@castleantiques.net * www.castleprophouse.com

Ob-jects   **(818) 351-4200**
Early American furniture/Colonial Furniture rentals

Old N Country Prop Shop, LLC   **(818) 423-2599**
Variety of Early American furniture in cherry, Ethan Allen; bed, dresser, night stands; maple, oak tables, chairs.

Omega/Cinema Props   **(323) 466-8201**

Pasadena Antique Center and Annex   **(626) 449-7706**
480 South Fair Oaks Ave, Pasadena, CA, 91105
Home, office, and outdoor furnishings
pasadenaantiqecenterandannex@gmail.com * bit.ly/PasadenaAntiqueCenter

A Royal Suite Home Furinishings   **(661) 259-7000**
26536 Carl Boyer Dr, Santa Clarita, CA, 91350
A Royal Suite, family-owned since 1978, Features AMERICAN-MADE Furniture, and the Finest Furniture at the Greatest Value
norb@ars-email.com * www.aroyalsuite.com

Universal Studios Property & Hardware Dept   **(818) 777-2784**
Colonial furniture; colonial chairs, colonial tables, colonial artwork and more for rent.

Warner Bros. Studios Property Department   **(818) 954-2181**
Chest of drawers, bedside cabinets, arm chairs, court cabinets, panels

Furniture, Eclectic

See Also: Furniture, Contemporary* Furniture, Custom-made/Reproduction

Asian Art Imports (818) 778-0852
16876 Stagg St, Van Nuys, CA, 91406
We carry an array of organic contemporary furniture with an eye for one of a kind, unique, design oriented pieces.
asianartimports@yahoo.com * www.asianartimports.com

Blackman-Cruz (323) 466-8600
836 N Highland Ave, Los Angeles, CA, 90036
unusual furniture, antique & contemp. & arch. elements
www.blackmancruz.com

Design Mix Furniture (323) 939-7500
442 S La Brea Ave, Los Angeles, CA, 90036
Global imports of Indian, Indonesian, Chinese, African, Moroccan art, acc., antiques, reprod. & Industrial Furniture
alyssashah@earthlink.net * www.mixfurniture.com

Galerie Sommerlath - French 50s 60s (310) 838-0102
9608 Venice Blvd, Culver City, CA, 90232
Over 10,000 sq ft of Mid-Century, 70's & 80's furniture, lighting, accessories, home decor, art, sculptures, paintings.
info@galeriesommerlath.com * www.galeriesommerlath.com

Martin Iron Design (818) 760-3636
10750 Cumpston St, N Hollywood, CA, 91601
Eclectic furniture; wrought iron furniture of all kinds including custom.
martinirondesign@yahoo.com * www.martinirondesign.com

Old N Country Prop Shop, LLC (818) 423-2599
A wide variety of furniture. From an Amish Bench/Table to Gossip Benches; Rope Beds; Oak Plant Pedestals; Oak Hat Stands

Picture Start Props (818) 255-5472
Large selection of eclectic furniture from mid century to now.

Prop Services West (818) 503-2790

Sony Pictures Studios-Prop House (Off Lot) (310) 244-5999
all periods, couches, chairs, bedframes, storage cabinets, liquor cabinets

Warisan (323) 938-3960
1274 Center Court Dr Ste 110, Covina, CA, 91724
www.warisan.com

Warner Bros. Studios Property Department (818) 954-2181
One of a kind eclectic furniture, hand props & light fixtures

Warner Bros. Studios The Collection (818) 954-2181
4000 Warner Blvd Bldg 30, Burbank, CA, 91522
wbsfproperty@warnerbros.com * www.wbpropertydept.com

Furniture, English/French Country

Advanced Liquidators Office Furniture (818) 763-3470

Castle Antiques & Design (818) 765-5000
11924 Vose St, N Hollywood, CA, 91605
English and French Country style furniture in stained, shabby chic, and distressed finishes.
info@castleantiques.net * www.castleprophouse.com

Clifford Antiques (747) 283-1272
3429 Magnolia Blvd, Burbank, CA, 91505
British Antiques shipped from Scotland we're a family run business with over 40 years experience
wfcliffordantiques@yahoo.com * www.cliffordantiques.com

Omega/Cinema Props (323) 466-8201

Pasadena Antique Center and Annex (626) 449-7706
480 South Fair Oaks Ave, Pasadena, CA, 91105
Home, office, and outdoor furnishings
pasadenaantiqecenterandannex@gmail.com * bit.ly/PasadenaAntiqueCenter

Prop Services West (818) 503-2790

Warner Bros. Studios Property Department (818) 954-2181
Occasional tables and chairs, Oak furniture, English cottage style furniture, pillows and floor coverings

Furniture, Forties/Fifties/Sixties

See: Furniture, Mid-Century Modern

Furniture, French Period (Louis to Empire)

Castle Antiques & Design (818) 765-5000
11924 Vose St, N Hollywood, CA, 91605
All types of French period furniture (Louis XV, Louis XVI, Louis Philippe, Empire and more) for rent or purchase
info@castleantiques.net * www.castleprophouse.com

Omega/Cinema Props (323) 466-8201

Pasadena Antique Center and Annex (626) 449-7706
480 South Fair Oaks Ave, Pasadena, CA, 91105
Home, office, and outdoor furnishings
pasadenaantiqecenterandannex@gmail.com * bit.ly/PasadenaAntiqueCenter

Universal Studios Property & Hardware Dept (818) 777-2784
French period furniture; French period chairs, French period tables, French period artwork and more for rent.

Warner Bros. Studios Property Department (818) 954-2181
Antique furniture, fixtures and floor coverings, large selection

Furniture, Functional Art

Charisma Design Studio, Inc. (818) 252-6611
8414 San Fernando Road, Sun Valley, CA, 91352
custom metal/glass/wood/stone mixed media
info@charismadesign.com * www.charismadesign.com

Gallery of Functional Art (310) 829-6990
2525 Michigan Ave E3, Santa Monica, CA, 90404
furniture & lighting & objects by artists
www.galleryoffunctionalart.com

Furniture, Futuristic

See: Futuristic Furniture, Props, Decorations

Furniture, Gothic

Omega/Cinema Props (323) 466-8201

Universal Studios Property & Hardware Dept (818) 777-2784
Gothic furniture; Gothic chairs, Gothic tables, Gothic artwork and more for rent.

Warner Bros. Studios Property Department (818) 954-2181

Furniture, Hand-Painted

See: Furniture, Eclectic* Furniture, Custom-made/Reproduction

Furniture, Home Office

See: Office Furniture

Furniture, Indian (Far East)

See: Asian Antiques, Furniture, Art & Artifacts

Furniture, Indonesian

See: Asian Antiques, Furniture, Art & Artifacts

Furniture, Industrial

See Also: Furniture, Eclectic* Furniture, Functional Art* Steampunk

Design Mix Furniture (323) 939-7500
442 S La Brea Ave, Los Angeles, CA, 90036
Global imports of Indian, Indonesian, Chinese, African, Moroccan art, acc.,
antiques, reprod. & Industrial Furniture
alyssashah@earthlink.net * www.mixfurniture.com

Modern Props (323) 934-3000
Industrial furniture for rent

Old N Country Prop Shop, LLC (818) 423-2599
Desks, filing items, staplers, commercial equipment (tile cutters), floor planes,
etc.

A Royal Suite Home Furinishings (661) 259-7000
26536 Carl Boyer Dr, Santa Clarita, CA, 91350
A Royal Suite, family-owned since 1978, Features AMERICAN-MADE
Furniture, and the Finest Furniture at the Greatest Value
norb@ars-email.com * www.aroyalsuite.com

Warner Bros. Studios The Collection (818) 954-2181
4000 Warner Blvd Bldg 30, Burbank, CA, 91522
wbsfproperty@warnerbros.com * www.wbpropertydept.com

Furniture, Iron

See: Wrought Iron Furniture & Decorations

Furniture, Japanese

See: Asian Antiques, Furniture, Art & Artifacts* Shoji Screens

Furniture, Kitchen/Dining Room

Advanced Liquidators Office Furniture (818) 763-3470

Bridge Furniture & Props Los Angeles (818) 433-7100
We carry modern & traditional furniture, lighting, accessories, kitchen art, &
rugs. Items are online for easy shopping.

Clifford Antiques (747) 283-1272
3429 Magnolia Blvd, Burbank, CA, 91505
British Antiques shipped from Scotland we're a family run business with over 40
years experience
wfcliffordantiques@yahoo.com * www.cliffordantiques.com

Little Bohemia Rentals (818) 853-7506
11940 Sherman Rd, N Hollywood, CA, 91605
Vintage and Contemporary 4 - 10 person Dining and Dinette Sets, mix and
match. Serving and barware.
sales@wearelittlebohemia.com * www.wearelittlebohemia.com

Modernica Props (323) 664-2322

NEST Studio Rentals, Inc. (818) 942-0339

Old N Country Prop Shop, LLC (818) 423-2599
We have a variety of Dining Room furniture - Tables, chairs, china cabinets,
and all the dishes, etc. to dress it.

Omega/Cinema Props (323) 466-8201

Prop Services West (818) 503-2790
Kitchen furniture and dining room furniture for rent

A Royal Suite Home Furinishings (661) 259-7000
26536 Carl Boyer Dr, Santa Clarita, CA, 91350
A Royal Suite, family-owned since 1978, Features AMERICAN-MADE
Furniture, and the Finest Furniture at the Greatest Value
norb@ars-email.com * www.aroyalsuite.com

Sony Pictures Studios-Prop House (Off Lot) (310) 244-5999

Warner Bros. Studios Property Department (818) 954-2181
Kitchen & Dining room tables, side chairs, ottomans, sofas, cabinets, dressers,
corner cabinets, display cabinets

Furniture, Medical

See: Medical Equip/Furniture, Graphics/Supplies* Exam Room

Furniture, Mexican

Arte De Mexico (818) 769-5090
5356 Riverton Ave, N Hollywood, CA, 91601
Mexican Furniture for rent and purchase.
www.artedemexico.com

C. P. Two (323) 466-8201

A Royal Suite Home Furinishings (661) 259-7000
26536 Carl Boyer Dr, Santa Clarita, CA, 91350
A Royal Suite, family-owned since 1978, Features AMERICAN-MADE
Furniture, and the Finest Furniture at the Greatest Value
norb@ars-email.com * www.aroyalsuite.com

Furniture, Mid-Century Modern

Advanced Liquidators Office Furniture   (818) 763-3470

Alpha Companies - Spellman Desk Co.   (818) 504-9090
Eames Furniture, Le Corbusier Furniture, Barcelona Furniture, Haller Furniture, Aeron Furniture, Danish Modern Furniture

Blueprint Furniture   (310) 657-4315
8600 Pico Blvd. Los Angeles, CA, 90035
Modern furniture lighting accessories early classic bauhaus mid-century contemporary design. Good studio rental history.
www.blueprintfurniture.com

Castle Antiques & Design   (818) 765-5000
11924 Vose St, N Hollywood, CA, 91605
All styles and types of Mid-Century Modern and Vintage furniture (1940's-1970's) for rent and purchase.
info@castleantiques.net * www.castleprophouse.com

Chez Camille   (213) 703-1706
By Appointment
chairs, tables, sofas, light fixtures & lamps, accessories
www.chezcamille.1stdibs.com

Clifford Antiques   (747) 283-1272
3429 Magnolia Blvd, Burbank, CA, 91505
British Antiques shipped from Scotland we're a family run business with over 40 years experience
wfcliffordantiques@yahoo.com * www.cliffordantiques.com

Faux Library Studio Props, Inc.   (818) 765-0096
mid century modern furniture, Danish modern furniture

huge collection • 60,000 sq ft • furniture • accessories • modern • antiques
Mid-century Modern • Antiques
PHOTOS BY DEBBIE @ DEBBIES BOOK

Faux Library Studio Props

FormDecor, Inc.   (310) 558-2582
America's largest event rental supplier of 20th Century furniture and accessories for Modern and Mid-Century styles.

formDecor
furniture rental

Galerie Sommerlath - French 50s 60s   (310) 838-0102
9608 Venice Blvd, Culver City, CA, 90232
Over 10,000 sq ft of Mid-Century, 70's & 80's furniture, lighting, accessories, home decor, art, sculptures, paintings.
info@galeriesommerlath.com * www.galeriesommerlath.com

Little Bohemia Rentals   (818) 853-7506
11940 Sherman Rd, N Hollywood, CA, 91605
American, European, Danish and Scandinavian designs of the 50s, 60s and 70s.
sales@wearelittlebohemia.com * www.wearelittlebohemia.com

MidcenturyLA   (818) 509-3050
5333 Cahuenga Blvd, N Hollywood, CA, 91601
Original vintage mid century furniture, lighting, rugs, pottery, beds, mirrors & large scale photos - rental & purchase.
www.midcenturyla.com

MIDCENTURYLA
5333 CAHUENGA BLVD NORTH HOLLYWOOD 91601
818.509.3050 WWW.MIDCENTURYLA.COM
7 DAYS A WEEK 10-5
FURNITURE, LIGHTING, & MORE
RENTALS & PURCHASES

Modern Props   (323) 934-3000
Midcentury Modern furniture & Midcentury Modern accessories
Modernica Props   (323) 664-2322
wide range of colors, classic items, accents; mid-century
Old N Country Prop Shop, LLC   (818) 423-2599
We have a variety of Mid-Century Modern furniture: night stands, Wakefield Bookcase style headboard
Omega/Cinema Props   (323) 466-8201
Pasadena Antique Center and Annex   (626) 449-7706
480 South Fair Oaks Ave, Pasadena, CA, 91105
Home, office, and outdoor furnishings
pasadenaantiqecenterandannex@gmail.com * bit.ly/PasadenaAntiqueCenter
Pasadena Antiques & Design   (626) 389-3938
330 S Fair Oaks Avenue, Pasadena, CA, 91105
Mid Century Modern Furniture and Mid Century Modern Accessories.
roy@antiquesofpasadena.com * www.antiquesofpasadena.com
Picture Start Props   (818) 255-5472
Big selection of mid-century chairs, mid-century couches, mid-century smalls and fixtures.
Prop Services West   (818) 503-2790
RC Vintage, Inc.   (818) 765-7107
furniture to household items, more
Universal Studios Property & Hardware Dept   (818) 777-2784
Mid-century furniture; Mid-century chairs, Mid-century tables, Mid-century artwork and more for rent.
Warner Bros. Studios Property Department   (818) 954-2181
Chairs, sofas, tables, styles from 1940's, 1950's & 1960's
Warner Bros. Studios The Collection   (818) 954-2181
4000 Warner Blvd Bldg 30, Burbank, CA, 91522
wbsfproperty@warnerbros.com * www.wbpropertydept.com
ZG04 DECOR   (818) 853-8040

12224 Montague St, Pacoima, CA 91331
818.853.8040 310.775.4042 www.zg04decor.com

Furniture, Middle Eastern

Badia Design, Inc.   (818) 762-0130
5420 Vineland Ave, N Hollywood, CA, 91601
Hanging wall lamps, ceiling lanterns, camel bone metal horn mirror,
info@badiadesign.com * www.badiadesign.com
Omega/Cinema Props   (323) 466-8201
Universal Studios Property & Hardware Dept   (818) 777-2784
Middle Eastern furniture; Middle Eastern chairs, Middle Eastern tables, Middle Eastern artwork and more for rent.
Warner Bros. Studios Property Department   (818) 954-2181

Furniture, Moroccan

See Also: African/Oceanic Decorative Items
Badia Design, Inc.   (818) 762-0130
5420 Vineland Ave, N Hollywood, CA, 91601
Badia Design Inc. offers a wide variety of Moroccan Furniture Los Angeles, home decor, chandeliers, tables and much more.
info@badiadesign.com * www.badiadesign.com

Importer & Distributor of Moroccan Fine Arts & Crafts
Custom Handmade Furnishings
Rentals & Sales
Wholesale & Retail
www.badiadesign.com
Badia Design
5034 Vineland St., N. Hollywood, CA 91601 • 818.761.2910
Warehouse: 5440 Vineland St., N. Hollywood, CA 91601 • 818.762.0130

Design Mix Furniture   (323) 939-7500
442 S La Brea Ave, Los Angeles, CA, 90036
Global imports of Indian, Indonesian, Chinese, African, Moroccan art, acc., antiques, reprod. & Industrial Furniture
alyssashah@earthlink.net * www.mixfurniture.com
Little Bohemia Rentals   (818) 853-7506
11940 Sherman Rd, N Hollywood, CA, 91605
Antique furnishings of Morocco.
sales@wearelittlebohemia.com * www.wearelittlebohemia.com
Warner Bros. Studios Property Department   (818) 954-2181

Furniture, Office

See: Office Furniture

Furniture, Outdoor/Patio

See Also: Cafe Tables/Chairs/Umbrellas* Garden/Patio

AIR Designs (818) 768-6639
Tables, Benches, Umbrella Tables, Lawn Chairs, Fast Food, 50's to Modern

All Patio (818) 361-2440
12863 Foothill Blvd, Sylmar, CA, 91342
restoration/repair, new/used, umbrellas, glass tops, vintage, relacing, restrapping, powder coating
www.allpatiofurniture.com

Alley Cats Studio Rentals (818) 982-9178
metal shell-back chairs, picnic tables w/metal umbrellas, folding chairs and beach chairs

C. P. Two (323) 466-8201
Outdoor furniture from porch swings to patio furniture.

Design Mix Furniture (323) 939-7500
442 S La Brea Ave, Los Angeles, CA, 90036
Global imports of Indian, Indonesian, Chinese, African, Moroccan art, acc., antiques, reprod. & Industrial Furniture
alyssashah@earthlink.net * www.mixfurniture.com

E.C. Prop Rentals (818) 764-2008
Aluminum & fiberglass table/bench units, aluminum/fiberglass/wood benches, and plastic chairs

Fishbecks (626) 796-9255
150 S. Raymond, Pasadena, CA, 91105
In Pasadena since 1899
www.fishbecks.com

FormDecor, Inc. (310) 558-2582
America's largest event rental supplier of 20th Century furniture and accessories for Modern and Mid-Century styles.

L. A. Party Works (888) 527-2789
9712 Alpaca St, S El Monte, CA, 91733
Outdoor furniture including benches, patio chairs/patio furniture, picnic tables for adults/kids and more.
partyworks@aol.com * www.partyworksinteractive.com

LCW Props (818) 243-0707
Outdoor Kitchen BBQ, Chairs, Tables

Lux Lounge EFR (888) 247-4411
106 1/2 Judge John Aiso St #318, Los Angeles, CA, 90012
Outdoor Furniture including Patio Sets & Umbrellas
info@luxloungeefr.com * www.luxloungeefr.com

Martin Iron Design (818) 760-3636
10750 Cumpston St, N Hollywood, CA, 91601
Patio furniture & Garden furniture available in various combinations, settings, and sizes. Contact for more information.
martinirondesign@yahoo.com * www.martinirondesign.com

Ob-jects (818) 351-4200
Complete sets of patio furniture/outdoor furniture and patio decorations including pots, plants and more.

Old N Country Prop Shop, LLC (818) 423-2599
A wide variety of outdoor furniture.

The Patio Collection (818) 772-5100
9000 Winnetka Ave, Northridge, CA 91324
Aluminum Furniture, Stainless Steel Furniture, Wicker Furniture, Wood Furniture, Resin Furniture, Wrought Iron Furniture
www.patiocollection.com

Prop Services West (818) 503-2790

RC Vintage, Inc. (818) 765-7107
Vintage Folding Chairs. BBQ's Ice Chests. Patio sets

Sony Pictures Studios-Prop House (Off Lot) (310) 244-5999
multiples, period/present, lawn chairs, picnic tables, furniture

Universal Studios Property & Hardware Dept (818) 777-2784
Outdoor furniture/patio furniture; patio chairs, patio tables, picnic tables and more for rent.

Warner Bros. Studios Property Department (818) 954-2181
Outdoor furniture, garden furniture, bamboo furniture, flags, gardening tools, hand trucks

Furniture, Pine

Clifford Antiques (747) 283-1272
3429 Magnolia Blvd, Burbank, CA, 91505
British Antiques shipped from Scotland we're a family run business with over 40 years experience
wfcliffordantiques@yahoo.com * www.cliffordantiques.com

Omega/Cinema Props (323) 466-8201

Prop Services West (818) 503-2790

A Royal Suite Home Furinishings (661) 259-7000
26536 Carl Boyer Dr, Santa Clarita, CA, 91350
A Royal Suite, family-owned since 1978, Features AMERICAN-MADE Furniture, and the Finest Furniture at the Greatest Value
norb@ars-email.com * www.aroyalsuite.com

Furniture, Plexi/Lucite

FormDecor, Inc. (310) 558-2582
America's largest event rental supplier of 20th Century furniture and accessories for Modern and Mid-Century styles.

Little Bohemia Rentals (818) 853-7506
11940 Sherman Rd, N Hollywood, CA, 91605
Charles Hollis Jones and Karl Springer designs.
sales@wearelittlebohemia.com * www.wearelittlebohemia.com

Lux Lounge EFR (888) 247-4411
106 1/2 Judge John Aiso St #318, Los Angeles, CA, 90012
Plastic Furniture and Decoration: Custom Bars, LED Furniture and more.
info@luxloungeefr.com * www.luxloungeefr.com

Omega/Cinema Props (323) 466-8201

Universal Studios Property & Hardware Dept (818) 777-2784
Lucite furniture/plexi furniture; lucite chairs, lucite tables, plexi chairs, plexi tables and more for rent.

ZG04 DECOR (818) 853-8040

Furniture, Rattan & Wicker

C. P. Two (323) 466-8201
Rattan chairs and wicker chairs, rattan baskets and wicker baskets, and more.

Clifford Antiques (747) 283-1272
3429 Magnolia Blvd, Burbank, CA, 91505
British Antiques shipped from Scotland we're a family run business with over 40 years experience
wfcliffordantiques@yahoo.com * www.cliffordantiques.com

Lux Lounge EFR (888) 247-4411
106 1/2 Judge John Aiso St #318, Los Angeles, CA, 90012
Wicker Furniture and Rattan Furniture rentals.
info@luxloungeefr.com * www.luxloungeefr.com

Old N Country Prop Shop, LLC (818) 423-2599
A wide variety of rattan and wicker furniture.

Omega/Cinema Props (323) 466-8201

Pier 1 Imports (Hollywood) (323) 466-3443
5711 Hollywood Blvd, Hollywood, CA, 90028
www.pier1.com

Prop Services West (818) 503-2790

Sony Pictures Studios-Prop House (Off Lot) (310) 244-5999

Universal Studios Property & Hardware Dept (818) 777-2784
Rattan furniture & wicker furniture; wicker chairs, wicker tables, rattan chairs, rattan tables and more for rent.

Warner Bros. Studios Property Department (818) 954-2181
Tables, chairs, cabinets, sofas, ottomans, bars and hand props

Furniture, Restaurant

See: Restaurant Furniture & Dressing

Furniture, Rustic

C. P. Two (323) 466-8201

Clifford Antiques (747) 283-1272
3429 Magnolia Blvd, Burbank, CA, 91505
British Antiques shipped from Scotland we're a family run business with over 40 years experience
wfcliffordantiques@yahoo.com * www.cliffordantiques.com

Evans Family Barrels (818) 523-8174
7918 Fairchild Ave, Canoga Park, CA, 91306
Solid oak wine barrel furniture: tables, chairs, cabinets, pet furniture, home & business decor, swings, vintage barrels
evansbarrels@gmail.com * www.EvansFamilyBarrels.com

Martin Iron Design (818) 760-3636
10750 Cumpston St, N Hollywood, CA, 91601
Rustic wrought iron furniture
martinirondesign@yahoo.com * www.martinirondesign.com

Old N Country Prop Shop, LLC (818) 423-2599
We have a variety of Rustic furniture: handmade tool benches, farm benches, tree stump end tables, etc.

Omega/Cinema Props (323) 466-8201

Prop Services West (818) 503-2790

A Royal Suite Home Furinishings (661) 259-7000
26536 Carl Boyer Dr, Santa Clarita, CA, 91350
A Royal Suite, family-owned since 1978, Features AMERICAN-MADE Furniture, and the Finest Furniture at the Greatest Value
norb@ars-email.com * www.aroyalsuite.com

Sony Pictures Studios-Prop House (Off Lot) (310) 244-5999

Universal Studios Property & Hardware Dept (818) 777-2784
Rustic furniture; rustic chairs, rustic tables and more for rent.

Warner Bros. Studios Property Department (818) 954-2181
Rustic tables, chairs, ottomans, desks, decorative items

ZG04 DECOR (818) 853-8040

Furniture, Southwest

Little Bohemia Rentals	(818) 853-7506

11940 Sherman Rd, N Hollywood, CA, 91605
Southwest style furniture
sales@wearelittlebohemia.com * www.wearelittlebohemia.com

Old N Country Prop Shop, LLC	(818) 423-2599

We have a variety of Southwest furniture (see above)

Omega/Cinema Props	(323) 466-8201
Pasadena Antique Center and Annex	(626) 449-7706

480 South Fair Oaks Ave, Pasadena, CA, 91105
Home, office, and outdoor furnishings
pasadenaantiqecenterandannex@gmail.com * bit.ly/PasadenaAntiqueCenter

Pasadena Antiques & Design	(626) 389-3938

330 S Fair Oaks Avenue, Pasadena, CA, 91105
California Rancho & Rustic Furnishings.
roy@antiquesofpasadena.com * www.antiquesofpasadena.com

A Royal Suite Home Furinishings	(661) 259-7000

26536 Carl Boyer Dr, Santa Clarita, CA, 91350
A Royal Suite, family-owned since 1978, Features AMERICAN-MADE
Furniture, and the Finest Furniture at the Greatest Value
norb@ars-email.com * www.aroyalsuite.com

Sony Pictures Studios-Prop House (Off Lot)	(310) 244-5999

Furniture, Spanish

Castle Antiques & Design	(818) 765-5000

11924 Vose St, N Hollywood, CA, 91605
A wide variety of Spanish furniture for rent and purchase.
info@castleantiques.net * www.castleprophouse.com

Omega/Cinema Props	(323) 466-8201
Pasadena Antique Center and Annex	(626) 449-7706

480 South Fair Oaks Ave, Pasadena, CA, 91105
Home, office, and outdoor furnishings
pasadenaantiqecenterandannex@gmail.com * bit.ly/PasadenaAntiqueCenter

Pasadena Antiques & Design	(626) 389-3938

330 S Fair Oaks Avenue, Pasadena, CA, 91105
Spanish Revival & Colonial Furniture & Accessories. Iron & Wood.
roy@antiquesofpasadena.com * www.antiquesofpasadena.com

A Royal Suite Home Furinishings	(661) 259-7000

26536 Carl Boyer Dr, Santa Clarita, CA, 91350
A Royal Suite, family-owned since 1978, Features AMERICAN-MADE
Furniture, and the Finest Furniture at the Greatest Value
norb@ars-email.com * www.aroyalsuite.com

Warner Bros. Studios Property Department	(818) 954-2181

Furniture, Tenement Tacky Motel

C. P. Two	(323) 466-8201

Tenement furniture and dressing from chairs to sconces.

Picture Start Props	(818) 255-5472

Big print couches, cheesy arm chairs and tons of fun smalls

Prop Services West	(818) 503-2790
Sony Pictures Studios-Prop House (Off Lot)	(310) 244-5999
Universal Studios Property & Hardware Dept	(818) 777-2784

Tenement tacky furniture; tenement tacky chairs, tenement tacky tables,
tenement tacky artwork and more for rent.

Warner Bros. Studios Property Department	(818) 954-2181

Distressed furniture pieces

Furniture, Traditional

Advanced Liquidators Office Furniture	(818) 763-3470
Alpha Companies - Spellman Desk Co.	(818) 504-9090

Chippendale, Queen Anne, Regency, Sheraton

Bridge Furniture & Props Los Angeles	(818) 433-7100

We carry modern & traditional furniture, lighting, accessories, art, & rugs. Items
are online for easy shopping.

Castle Antiques & Design	(818) 765-5000

11924 Vose St, N Hollywood, CA, 91605
Traditional furniture of different styles, types, countries, and period for rent and
purchase.
info@castleantiques.net * www.castleprophouse.com

CASTLE ANTIQUES & DESIGN
www.CastleAntiques.net
11924 Vose Street
North Hollywood, CA 91605
info@castleantiques.net
(818) 765-5000
The largest selection of authentic Antique and Mid-Century Modern pieces to choose from! 20,000 Square Feet
We are open to decorators and the general public Monday - Friday from 9am to 5pm

Dozar Office Furnishings	(310) 559-9292

9937 Jefferson Blvd, Culver City, CA, 90232
Rentals X22. Traditional furniture for the home and office.
dozarrents@aol.com * www.dozarrents.com

Ob-jects	(818) 351-4200

Traditional furniture rentals

Old N Country Prop Shop, LLC	(818) 423-2599

A wide variety of traditional furniture.

Omega/Cinema Props	(323) 466-8201

Antique furniture, vintage furniture, rustic furniture, wicker furniture, chairs,
stools, tables

Picture Start Props	(818) 255-5472

Traditional furniture including dining tables, chairs, shelving

**LISTINGS FOR THIS CATEGORY CONTINUE ON THE
FOLLOWING PAGE**

Prop Services West   (818) 503-2790

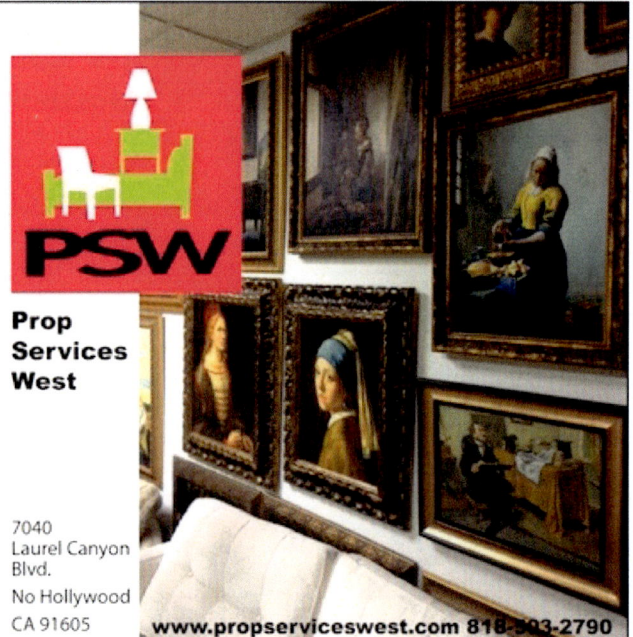

Prop Services West

7040 Laurel Canyon Blvd.

No Hollywood CA 91605

www.propserviceswest.com 818-503-2790

A Royal Suite Home Furinishings   (661) 259-7000
26536 Carl Boyer Dr, Santa Clarita, CA, 91350
A Royal Suite, family-owned since 1978, Features AMERICAN-MADE Furniture, and the Finest Furniture at the Greatest Value
norb@ars-email.com * www.aroyalsuite.com
Sony Pictures Studios-Prop House (Off Lot)   (310) 244-5999
Universal Studios Property & Hardware Dept   (818) 777-2784
Traditional furniture; traditional chairs, traditional tables, traditional artwork and more for rent.
Warner Bros. Studios Property Department   (818) 954-2181
Traditional tables, chairs, end tables, cabinets

Furniture, Transitional

See: Furniture, Contemporary* Furniture, Traditional* Furniture, English/French Country* Furniture, Eclectic* Asian Antiques, Furniture, Art & Artifacts

Furniture, Unfinished

See Also: Furniture, Custom-made/Reproduction
Burbank Unpainted Furniture   (818) 845-5975
3803 W Magnolia Blvd, Burbank, CA, 91505
Solid wood furniture: chairs, tables, stools, desks, office, armoires, bookcases, beds, kitchen, custom-built.
info@burbankunpaintedfurniture.com * www.burbankunpaintedfurniture.com
Clifford Antiques   (747) 283-1272
3429 Magnolia Blvd, Burbank, CA, 91505
British Antiques shipped from Scotland we're a family run business with over 40 years experience
wfcliffordantiques@yahoo.com * www.cliffordantiques.com

Furniture, Used/Second Hand

See Also: Thrift Shops
Advanced Liquidators Office Furniture   (818) 763-3470
chairs / desk / filing cabs / partitions / executive sets / package deals
Castle Antiques & Design   (818) 765-5000
11924 Vose St, N Hollywood, CA, 91605
Quality Used and Second Hand Furniture in many different styles and types available for rent or purchase.
info@castleantiques.net * www.castleprophouse.com

Clifford Antiques   (747) 283-1272
3429 Magnolia Blvd, Burbank, CA, 91505
British Antiques shipped from Scotland we're a family run business with over 40 years experience
wfcliffordantiques@yahoo.com * www.cliffordantiques.com
LCW Props   (818) 243-0707
Large Selection. Hoarder Houses, Debris, Junk Yards
Sony Pictures Studios-Prop House (Off Lot) (310) 244-5999
Universal Studios Property & Hardware Dept (818) 777-2784
Used furniture; used chairs, used tables, second hand chairs, second hand tables and more for rent.

Furniture, Victorian

Clifford Antiques   (747) 283-1272
3429 Magnolia Blvd, Burbank, CA, 91505
British Antiques shipped from Scotland we're a family run business with over 40 years experience
wfcliffordantiques@yahoo.com * www.cliffordantiques.com
Omega/Cinema Props   (323) 466-8201
Pasadena Antique Center and Annex   (626) 449-7706
480 South Fair Oaks Ave, Pasadena, CA, 91105
Home, office, and outdoor furnishings
pasadenaantiqecenterandannex@gmail.com * bit.ly/PasadenaAntiqueCenter
A Royal Suite Home Furnishings   (661) 259-7000
26536 Carl Boyer Dr, Santa Clarita, CA, 91350
A Royal Suite, family-owned since 1978, Features AMERICAN-MADE Furniture, and the Finest Furniture at the Greatest Value
norb@ars-email.com * www.aroyalsuite.com
Universal Studios Property & Hardware Dept (818) 777-2784
Victorian furniture; Victorian chairs, Victorian tables, Victorian artwork and more for rent.

Furniture, Western

C. P. Two   (323) 466-8201
antique furniture, vintage furniture, rustic furniture, wicker furniture, chairs, stools, tables
Old N Country Prop Shop, LLC   (818) 423-2599
We have a variety of Western furniture: Southwest carved back wood chairs, southwest design couch, wall carvings.
A Royal Suite Home Furnishings   (661) 259-7000
26536 Carl Boyer Dr, Santa Clarita, CA, 91350
A Royal Suite, family-owned since 1978, Features AMERICAN-MADE Furniture, and the Finest Furniture at the Greatest Value
norb@ars-email.com * www.aroyalsuite.com
Sony Pictures Studios-Prop House (Off Lot) (310) 244-5999
Universal Studios Property & Hardware Dept (818) 777-2784
Western furniture; Western chairs, Western tables, Western artwork and more for rent.

Futons & Bean Bag Chairs

Futon Factory L.A., Inc.   (310) 838-9261
10203 Venice Blvd, Los Angeles, CA, 90034
Futons, bean bags, foam furniture, screens, custom available
www.futonfactoryla.com
Omega/Cinema Props   (323) 466-8201
bean bag chairs
Prop Services West   (818) 503-2790
bean bag chairs
RC Vintage, Inc.   (818) 765-7107
bean bag chairs in many colors
A Royal Suite Home Furinishings   (661) 259-7000
26536 Carl Boyer Dr, Santa Clarita, CA, 91350
A Royal Suite, family-owned since 1978, Features AMERICAN-MADE Furniture, and the Finest Furniture at the Greatest Value
norb@ars-email.com * www.aroyalsuite.com
Sony Pictures Studios-Prop House (Off Lot) (310) 244-5999
bean bag chairs

Futuristic Furniture, Props, Decorations

See Also: Aliens* Fantasy Props, Costumes, or Decorations*
Printing, Graphics, Digital & Large Format* NASA Dressing*
Paintings/Prints* Space Shuttle/Space Hardware* Space Suits*
Spaceship Computer Panel

The Hand Prop Room LP.	(323) 931-1534
LCW Props	(818) 243-0707

Our Specialty. We Have A Large Selection Of Many Kinds. Rigged, Large &
Small Futuristic Props

Modern Props	(323) 934-3000

Futuristic furniture, futuristic props and futuristic decorations; lamps,
art/sculptures, accessories, futuristic tubes

Omega/Cinema Props	(323) 466-8201
ZG04 DECOR	(818) 853-8040

Futuristic Themed Parties

See: Costume Rental Houses* Costumes* Events, Decorations,
Supplies & Services* Events, Design/Planning/Production* Fantasy
Props, Costumes, or Decorations* Prop Houses

Gambling Equipment

See Also: Game Tables & Equipment* Poker Tables

C. P. Two	(323) 466-8201

Poker tables

Dealer Dolls	(866) 96-Dolls

#258 / 20058 Ventura Blvd, Woodland Hills, CA, 91364
info@dealerdolls.com * www.dealerdolls.com

The Hand Prop Room LP.	(323) 931-1534
It's A Deal Casino Rentals	(310) 379-DEAL

1805 Armour Lane, Redondo Beach, CA, 90278
All of our tables are casino quality, camera ready and easily broken down for
quick transport.
info@itsadealcasino.com * www.itsadealcasino.com

L. A. Party Works	(888) 527-2789

9712 Alpaca St, S El Monte, CA, 91733
in Vancouver tel. 604-589-4101, casino tables, black jack tables, poker tables
partyworks@aol.com * www.partyworksinteractive.com

Lennie Marvin Enterprises, Inc. (Prop Heaven)	(818) 841-5882

Gambling equipment including slot machines and card tables.

RC Vintage, Inc.	(818) 765-7107

Vintage Poker Tables, Craps, Roulette, Wheel Of Fortune, Large Selection:
Stools Casino Signs Blazing 777 and more.

Sony Pictures Studios-Prop House (Off Lot)	(310) 244-5999

casino equipment, playing cards, cribbage equipment, dice cups, dice,
dominoes case, lotto games, poker chips, raffle equipment

Universal Studios Property & Hardware Dept	(818) 777-2784

Poker tables for rent.

Game Booths

See Also: Carnival Games & Rides

Amusement Svcs/Candyland Amusements	(818) 266-4056

18653 Ventura Blvd Ste 235, Tarzana, CA, 91356
Games, rides, food stands, ticket booths. We are the owner, no middleman.
dunk tanks, machine gun alley, basketball, water race, game tents
raymond@candylandamusements.com * www.candylandamusements.com

L. A. Party Works	(888) 527-2789

9712 Alpaca St, S El Monte, CA, 91733
in Vancouver tel. 604-589-4101
partyworks@aol.com * www.partyworksinteractive.com

Game Show Electronics & Equipment

CBS Electronics   (323) 575-2645
7800 Beverly Blvd Rm M162, Los Angeles, CA, 90036
our specialty; custom, arbitrarily complicated

L. A. Party Works   (888) 527-2789
9712 Alpaca St, S El Monte, CA, 91733
in Vancouver tel. 604-589-4101
partyworks@aol.com * www.partyworksinteractive.com

888-527-2789
partyworksusa.com

CUSTOM GAME SHOWS / STAGING / CUSTOM SOFTWARE / CUSTOM BRANDING

PARTYWORKS
I N T E R A C T I V E

Game Tables & Equipment

See Also: Poker Tables Pool/Billiard Tables & Accessories*
Amusement Svcs/Candyland Amusements   (818) 266-4056
18653 Ventura Blvd Ste 235, Tarzana, CA, 91356
Games, rides, food stands, ticket booths. We are the owner, no middleman.
Many game booths, game exhibits and game kiosks
raymond@candylandamusements.com * www.candylandamusements.com
Lennie Marvin Enterprises, Inc. (Prop Heaven)   (818) 841-5882
blackjack, roulette, baccarat, craps, poker tables, Texas Hold'em, per-mod.
A Royal Suite Home Furinishings   (661) 259-7000
26536 Carl Boyer Dr, Santa Clarita, CA, 91350
A Royal Suite, family-owned since 1978, Features AMERICAN-MADE
Furniture, and the Finest Furniture at the Greatest Value
norb@ars-email.com * www.aroyalsuite.com

Games

See: Arcade Equipment, Games & Rides Events, Entertainment*
Sporting Goods & Services* Sports & Games Themed Events* Toys
& Games*

Garage Dressing

See: Automotive/Garage Equip. & Parts Motorcycles*

Garden/Patio

See Also: Canopies, Tents, Gazebos, Cabanas Fountains,
Decorative & Garden* Furniture, Outdoor/Patio* Greens* Heaters,
Outdoor* Lawn Mowers* Statuary*
Alley Cats Studio Rentals   (818) 982-9178
tools, lawnmowers, hoes
Bear Forest Products, Inc   (951) 727-1767
4685 Brookhollow Circle, Riverside, CA, 92509
Wood lattices and plastic lattices.
matto@bearfp.com * www.bearfp.com
Bridge Furniture & Props Los Angeles   (818) 433-7100
We carry modern & traditional furniture, lighting, accessories, art, & rugs. Items
are online for easy shopping.
E.C. Prop Rentals   (818) 764-2008
Tools, lawn mowers, garden "Vermont" carts, tool carts, chainsaws, hoses &
chairs
Evans Family Barrels   (818) 523-8174
7918 Fairchild Ave, Canoga Park, CA, 91306
Solid oak wine barrel furniture: tables, chairs, cabinets, pet furniture, home &
business decor, swings, vintage barrels
evansbarrels@gmail.com * www.EvansFamilyBarrels.com
Green Set, Inc.   (818) 764-1231
Baskets, Brass Planters, Ceramic Pots, Faux Pots, Planter Boxes, Terra Cotta
History For Hire, Inc.   (818) 765-7767
garden tools, whirligigs
Jackson Shrub Supply, Inc.   (818) 982-0100
8'-12' Japanese style garden bridges, garden decorations, fencing, fountains,
and more.
LCW Props   (818) 243-0707
Umbrellas, Tables & Chairs
Little Bohemia Rentals   (818) 853-7506
11940 Sherman Rd, N Hollywood, CA, 91605
Faux and Live succulents and indoor/house plants. Potted outdoor plants.
Hanging plants.
sales@wearelittlebohemia.com * www.wearelittlebohemia.com
Ob-jects   (818) 351-4200
Garden furniture, patio furniture, garden decorations
Potted   (323) 665-3801
3158 Los Feliz Blvd, Los Angeles, CA, 90039
Decorative garden accessories, furniture, fountains, statues and pots
info@pottedstore.com * www.pottedstore.com
Prop Services West   (818) 503-2790
Sony Pictures Studios-Prop House (Off Lot)   (310) 244-5999
tools, mowers, furniture, bird baths, chainsaws, garden tools, lawnmowers,
patio torches, power tools, rakes, and more
Universal Studios Property & Hardware Dept   (818) 777-2784
Gardening tools, patio furniture, lawn mowers, bird baths, and more for rent.
ZG04 DECOR   (818) 853-8040
Garden dressing and patio dressing including plants, tables and more.

Gargoyles

See: Architectural Pieces & Artifacts

Garment Racks

Acme Display Fixture & Packaging   (888) 411-1870
3829 S Broadway St, Los Angeles, CA, 90037
Complete store setups: garment racks, displays/display cases, counters,
packaging, shelving, hangers, mannequins
sales@acmedisplay.com * www.acmedisplay.com
Castex Rentals   (323) 462-1468
1044 N Cole Ave, Hollywood, CA, 90038
rolling collapsible wardrobe racks, steamers, irons, hangers, schmere kits, top
stick, sewing supplies, garment racks
service@castexrentals.com * www.castexrentals.com
History For Hire, Inc.   (818) 765-7767
empty/full rolling racks, period
ZG04 DECOR   (818) 853-8040
Many garment racks for rent.

Gas & Electric Meters

Alley Cats Studio Rentals   (818) 982-9178
gas, different styles
E.C. Prop Rentals   (818) 764-2008
residential/commercial several types
LCW Props   (818) 243-0707
Both Gas & Electric Meters, Period - Present, Residential, Commercial
Universal Studios Property & Hardware Dept   (818) 777-2784
Prop gas meters and prop electric meters for rent.

Gas Cans

AIR Designs	**(818) 768-6639**
1920's to Present, Vintage Gas Cans, Modern Gas Cans	
Alley Cats Studio Rentals	**(818) 982-9178**
E.C. Prop Rentals	**(818) 764-2008**
wide selection	
The Hand Prop Room LP.	**(323) 931-1534**
period-present, asst. styles/sizes	
History For Hire, Inc.	**(818) 765-7767**
all types	
LCW Props	**(818) 243-0707**
Large Selection	
Sony Pictures Studios-Prop House (Off Lot)	**(310) 244-5999**
ZG04 DECOR	**(818) 853-8040**
Large quantity of gas cans	

Gas Furnaces

See: Furnaces

Gas Logs

See: Fireplaces & Mantels/Screens/Tools/Andirons

Gas Pumps/Islands, Gas Station

See Also: Automotive/Garage Equip. & Parts

AIR Designs	**(818) 768-6639**
1920's-Present, signage, Gas Station & Mini Mart, Full Dressing	
Alley Cats Studio Rentals	**(818) 982-9178**
20s to present day (digital) large selection, service station props	
LCW Props	**(818) 243-0707**
Electric car chargers	

Gates

See: Fences Steel Folding Gates & Roll-Up Doors*

Gators

See: Grip Equipment

Gauges

Alley Cats Studio Rentals	**(818) 982-9178**
huge selection!	
E.C. Prop Rentals	**(818) 764-2008**
wide selection	
History For Hire, Inc.	**(818) 765-7767**
LCW Props	**(818) 243-0707**
Huge Selection, Military, Airplane, Industrial, PSI, MPH, Weather	
Universal Studios Property & Hardware Dept	**(818) 777-2784**
All kinds of prop gauges for rent.	

Geiger Counter

See: Mining & Prospecting Equipment

Gems, Minerals & Crystals

See Also: Jewelry, Fine/Reproduction

Little Bohemia Rentals	**(818) 853-7506**
11940 Sherman Rd, N Hollywood, CA, 91605	
Various polished and raw minerals and crystals.	
sales@wearelittlebohemia.com * www.wearelittlebohemia.com	
Sword & Stone	**(818) 562-6548**
Gemstones and jewelry	
Wonders of the World & Beyond	**(310) 393-4700**
1460 Lincoln Blvd, Santa Monica, CA, 90401	
4-8 pm Mon-Sat, but appt preferred; real fossils, minerals lrg crystals, reprod. ancient jewelry, lrg insect specimens	
www.worldsbestnaturestore.com	

General Store

See Also: Cash Registers Counters* Display Cases, Racks & Fixtures (Store)*

AIR Designs	**(818) 768-6639**
Counters, Coolers, Racks, Produce, Food, Signs, Hardware	
History For Hire, Inc.	**(818) 765-7767**
lots of products	
Old N Country Prop Shop, LLC	**(818) 423-2599**
Large "Bean or Dry Goods Counter" with beveled glass, display cases for spools, tools, sewing notions, scales, etc.	
RC Vintage, Inc.	**(818) 765-7107**
General Store Dressing, Pawnshop Dressing, many cases, shelving and racks, general store smalls, shelf fillers, cash registers	
Sony Pictures Studios-Prop House (Off Lot)	**(310) 244-5999**
Universal Studios Property & Hardware Dept	**(818) 777-2784**
General store dressing and general store props for rent.	

Generators

See Also: Power Generation/Distribution

Astro Audio Video Lighting, Inc.	**(818) 549-9915**
6615 San Fernando Rd, Glendale, CA, 91201	
Power generators of various sizes for rent.	
www.astroavl.com	
E.C. Prop Rentals	**(818) 764-2008**
non-working prop, portable	
Filmmaker Prod. Svcs-Atlanta @ Tyler Perry Studios	**(404) 450-1968**
2115 Sylvan Road, Atlanta, GA, 30344	
Grip & rigging equip. & services, lighting & sound	
chad.garcia@nbcuni.com * www.filmmakerproductionservices.com	
Filmmaker Prod. Svcs-Chicago @ Cinespace Chicago	**(678) 628-1997**
2558 W 16th Street Dock #4, Chicago, IL, 60608	
Grip & rigging equip. & services, lighting & sound	
patrick.flanagan@nbcuni.com * www.filmmakerproductionservices.com	
LCW Props	**(818) 243-0707**
Industrial, Residential, Commercial, Back Up	

Genetic Lab

See: Lab Equipment

German Themed Parties

See: Events, Decorations, Supplies & Services Events, Design/Planning/Production* Travel (City/Country) Themed Events*

40 YEARS OF DEBBIES BOOK

Princess Diana, Mother Theresa and John Denver died, 'Harry Potter' was first published in the UK. **'Ally McBeal', 'Dharma and Greg', 'Just Shoot Me'** and **'The Practice'** were popular on T.V. and on the big screen **'Men In Black',** and **'Air Force One'. AOL announces 10 million users online.**

Most connections are dial-up, very slow, not good for graphics only for text so our new website is designed mainly for speed and built around the Book's directory structure. We put directions on the book tabs to show people how to navigate our new website.

Gift Wrapping

See Also: Boxes* Packing/Packaging Supplies, Services* Wrapped Prop Gift Packages

Acme Display Fixture & Packaging (888) 411-1870
3829 S Broadway St, Los Angeles, CA, 90037
Complete store setups: garment racks, displays/display cases, counters, packaging, shelving, hangers, mannequins
sales@acmedisplay.com * www.acmedisplay.com

History For Hire, Inc. (818) 765-7767
also mfg.

Mail Boxes & Accessories (818) 843-5803
827 Hollywood Way, Burbank, CA, 91505
P.O. Box rentals, UPS, Fed-X, notary, bus cards, supplies, prop boxes, prop gift wrapping

Gilding Materials & Services

See: Metal Plating, Coating, Polishing

Glass & Mirrors

See Also: Breakaways (Glass, Props, Scenery)* Fun House Mirrors* Mirrors, Framed Decorative Furnishings

Acme Display Fixture & Packaging (888) 411-1870
3829 S Broadway St, Los Angeles, CA, 90037
Complete store setups: garment racks, displays/display cases, counters, packaging, shelving, hangers, mannequins
sales@acmedisplay.com * www.acmedisplay.com

Angelus Block Co., Inc (818) 767-8576
11374 Tuxford St, Sun Valley, CA, 91352
mfg. glass block
www.angelusblock.com

Antiqued Mirrors (818) 767-6188
12970 Branford St, Unit L, Arleta, CA, 91331
re-silver old mirrors & mfg new antiqued mirrors
www.antiquedmirrors.com

Castle Antiques & Design (818) 765-5000
11924 Vose St, N Hollywood, CA, 91605
We offer different styles and sizes of mirror, glass and crystal furniture and decor.
info@castleantiques.net * www.castleprophouse.com

Clifford Antiques (747) 283-1272
3429 Magnolia Blvd, Burbank, CA, 91505
British Antiques shipped from Scotland we're a family run business with over 40 years experience
wfcliffordantiques@yahoo.com * www.cliffordantiques.com

E.C. Prop Rentals (818) 764-2008
Castered dance studio mirrors and stainless steel restroom mirrors

Hollywood Glass (323) 661-7774
5119 Hollywood Blvd, Los Angeles, CA, 90027
www.hollywood-glass.com

Knickerbocker Plate Glass (212) 247-8500
79 New York Ave, Westbury, NY, 11590
furnish & install commercial & residential

Lux Lounge EFR (888) 247-4411
106 1/2 Judge John Aiso St #318, Los Angeles, CA, 90012
Mirror decorations, Vanity Mirrors, Mirrored Furniture, Glass tables
info@luxloungeefr.com * www.luxloungeefr.com

Manhattan Shade & Glass (212) 288-5616
14 E 38th St 5th floor, New York City, NY, 10021
www.manhattanshade.com

Motion Picture Glass (818) 885-8700
18135 Napa St, Northridge, CA, 91325
Wholesale glass supply, custom design, engineering & installation
www.motionpictureglass.com

Prop Services West (818) 503-2790

A Royal Suite Home Furinishings (661) 259-7000
26536 Carl Boyer Dr, Santa Clarita, CA, 91350
A Royal Suite, family-owned since 1978, Features AMERICAN-MADE Furniture, and the Finest Furniture at the Greatest Value
norb@ars-email.com * www.aroyalsuite.com

Ruben's Glass & Mirrors (323) 937-7519
616 S La Brea Ave, Los Angeles, CA, 90036
shower doors to store front windows
www.rubens-glass.com

Superior Glass Service (323) 663-1165
3923 W Sunset Blvd, Los Angeles, CA, 90029
custom frameless glass projects
www.superiorglassservice.com

ZG04 DECOR (818) 853-8040

Glass Door Coolers

AIR Designs (818) 768-6639
Single, Double, Triple, Mini-Mart, Period-Present

Modern Props (323) 934-3000
Glass door coolers

Glass Tinting

See: Glass & Mirrors, Art/Finishing/Etching/Etc.

Glasses

See: Eyewear, Glasses, Sunglasses, 3D

Glassware/Dishes

See Also: Bottles* Crystal Stemware* Fiesta Dinnerware* Pewter & Pewterware* Prop Houses* Restaurant Kitchens/Equip./Supplies

AIR Designs (818) 768-6639

Bargain Fair (Mid-City) (323) 965-2227
4635 W Pico Blvd, Los Angeles, CA, 90019
corner of Fairfax; dinnerware, glassware, silverware, cookware & more at unbelievable prices, open 7 days
sheida@bargainfair.com * www.bargainfair.com

Clifford Antiques (747) 283-1272
3429 Magnolia Blvd, Burbank, CA, 91505
British Antiques shipped from Scotland we're a family run business with over 40 years experience
wfcliffordantiques@yahoo.com * www.cliffordantiques.com

The Dish Factory, Inc. (213) 687-9500
310 S Los Angeles St, Los Angeles, CA, 90013
California's #1 source for restaurant supplies, dishes and equipment.
www.dishfactory.com

The Hand Prop Room LP. (323) 931-1534
Baccarat crystal glasses, cut glass, crystal glasses, rock glasses, bar glasses, high ball glasses, brandy snifters

History For Hire, Inc. (818) 765-7767

Little Bohemia Rentals (818) 853-7506
11940 Sherman Rd, N Hollywood, CA, 91605
Vintage glassware/vintage dishes and contemporary glassware/contemporary dishes.
sales@wearelittlebohemia.com * www.wearelittlebohemia.com

Modern Props (323) 934-3000
Contemporary/futuristic glassware and dishes, multiples

Ob-jects (818) 351-4200
Glassware and dishes

Omega/Cinema Props (323) 466-8201

Picture Start Props (818) 255-5472
Assortment of matching dishes, bowls, glasses/glassware and large assortment of mugs as well

Prop Services West (818) 503-2790

RC Vintage, Inc. (818) 765-7107
diner dressing to household, crystal cups, glass cups, glass mugs, vintage restaurant dishes,

A Royal Suite Home Furnishings (661) 259-7000
26536 Carl Boyer Dr, Santa Clarita, CA, 91350
A Royal Suite, family-owned since 1978, Features AMERICAN-MADE Furniture, and the Finest Furniture at the Greatest Value
norb@ars-email.com * www.aroyalsuite.com

Sony Pictures Studios-Prop House (Off Lot) (310) 244-5999
multiples, lg. selection pewter to ceramic

The Surface Library (323) 546-9314
A curated prop house specializing in surfaces and table top props for food, product, and lifestyle shoots.

Universal Studios Property & Hardware Dept (818) 777-2784
All kinds of glassware and dishware for rent.

Warner Bros. Studios Property Department (818) 954-2181
Large variety and styles of glassware & dishes, crystal stemware, restaurant supplies, multiples

ZG04 DECOR (818) 853-8040

Glitter

See: Hobby & Craft Supplies

Globes, World Map

See Also: Maps

The Hand Prop Room LP.	(323) 931-1534

table & floor, Old World, universe

History For Hire, Inc.	(818) 765-7767
Modern Props	(323) 934-3000

desk & floor-standing, oversized metallic cage globes. armillary globes, brass planet systems, ringed systems.

Picture Start Props	(818) 255-5472

Many vintage world globes and modern world globes of various sizes.

Prop Services West	(818) 503-2790
RC Vintage, Inc.	(818) 765-7107
Sony Pictures Studios-Prop House (Off Lot)	(310) 244-5999

world globes

ZG04 DECOR	(818) 853-8040

World map globes of various sizes from tiny to large

Gloves

See: Protective Apparel* Sporting Goods & Services* Wardrobe, Accessories

Glue

See: Expendables

Gold Leaf

See: Metal Plating, Coating, Polishing

Golf

See: Sporting Goods & Services

Gondolas

See: Boats & Water Sport Vehicles* Ski Equipment* Nautical/Marine Services & Charters* Market Equipment/Fixtures* Display Cases, Racks & Fixtures (Store)* Balloon (Hot Air) Gondolas

Goth/Punk/Bondage/Fetish/Erotica Etc.

See Also: Leather (Clothing, Accessories, Materials)* Occult/Spiritual/Metaphysical* Special Effects, Make-up/Prosthetics* Tattoo & Body Piercing Equipment & Supplies* Steampunk

665 Leather	(310) 854-7276

8722 Santa Monica Blvd, W Hollywood, CA, 90069
Leather & fetish clothing & access., erotica, on-site manufacturing, repairs, alterations
www.665leather.com

The Costume House	(818) 508-9933

club wear

Dapper Cadaver	(818) 771-0818

Gothic and punk decor: decorative skulls, oddities, dark statues, etc. Bondage furniture: restraint chairs, beds, etc.

GoodGoth.com	(818) 771-0818

Web Based Business
Gothic clothing & accessories, Hrs: M-F 10-4:30 EST
www.goodgoth.com

Hoss International	(213) 744-1364

1030 S. Los Angeles St, 2nd Floor, Los Angeles, CA, 90015
specialty corsets & waist cinchers; custom & bridal too, corsetry in plus sizes
www.hossinternational.com

Necromance	(323) 934-8684

7222 Melrose Ave, Los Angeles, CA, 90046
Goth jewelry & nasty looking access. some from real insects, incl. freeze dried rodents/bats, animals preserved in jars
www.necromance.com

The Pleasure Chest	(323) 650-1022

7733 Santa Monica Blvd, W Hollywood, CA, 90046
Erotic goods, S&M items, toys, lubes, DVDs, over 10,000 items; also stores in NYC & Chicago
www.thepleasurechest.com

Sony Pictures Studios-Wardrobe	(310) 244-5995

alterations, call (310) 244-7260

Sword & Stone	(818) 562-6548

aluminum, steel, leather & chainmail chastity belts & corsets

Gourds

See: Pumpkins & Gourds

Gowns

See: Clerical, Judicial, Academic Gowns/Apparel* Formal Wear* Wedding Attire

Graphics, Digital & Large Format Printing

See: Printing, Graphics, Digital & Large Format

Grass Mats

See Also: Greens

Green Set, Inc.	(818) 764-1231

Artificial Grasses & Artificial Turf, Grass Mats. Fake Grass, Fake Turf

Jackson Shrub Supply, Inc.	(818) 982-0100

all sizes, as well as artificial grass, grassmats

Linoleum City, Inc.	(323) 469-0063

4849 Santa Monica Blvd, Hollywood, CA, 90029
Astro turf, indoor/outdoor carpet, grass turf, walk off mats, coco brush, green turf, blue turf, black turf, white turf, grass tex.
sales@linocity.com * www.linoleumcity.com

Universal Studios Property & Hardware Dept	(818) 777-2784

Grass mats, golf mats and tatamis for rent.

Grass, Sisal

See: Carpet & Flooring

Grating, Grated Flooring, Catwalks

E.C. Prop Rentals	(818) 764-2008

steel & plastic floor grate sections

Grating Pacific, Inc.	(800) 321-4314

3651 Sausalito St, Los Alamitos, CA, 90720
Steel, aluminum, fiberglass gratings. Fabricated or stock sizes.
www.gratingpacific.com

Grave Markers

See: Cemetery Dressing

Gravel

See: Concrete Block, Brick, Gravel, Sand, Rocks, Etc.* Greens

Grease Boards

See: Office Equipment & Dressing* School Supplies, Desks & Dressing

Great Room

See: Antiques & Antique Decorations* Decorative Accessories* Furniture, Eclectic* Prop Houses* Rugs* Taxidermy, Hides/Heads/Skeletons

Grecian Themed Parties

See: Costume Rental Houses* Events, Decorations, Supplies & Services* Events, Design/Planning/Production* Events, Entertainment* Events Historical Era Themed Events* Wardrobe, Antique/Historical

Green Beds

See: Grip Equipment* Scenery/Set Rentals* Stages, Portable & Steel Deck

Green Rooms/Stage Client Areas

See: Office Furniture

Green Screens, Blue Screens

See Also: Backings* Light Fixtures* Sewing Services, Industrial

Composite Components Co.	(323) 257-1163

134 N. Avenue 61, Ste 103, Los Angeles, CA, 90042
screens, costumes, fabric, paint, fluorescent lights
info@digitalgreenscreen.com * www.digitalgreenscreen.com

Global Backings	(323) 769-0650

11970 Borden Ave, San Fernando, CA, 91340
backings: solids, muslins, nets, gridcloths, grip equip., chromakey fabric, paint, tape; truss frames w/rigging
www.globalbackings.com

LCW Props	(818) 243-0707

Blue, Green, White. Stands & Lighting Too

The Rag Place, Inc.	(818) 765-3338

13160 Raymer St, N Hollywood, CA, 91605
fabrics, grip backings, nets, silks, solid muslin, chromakey, grip
www.theragplace.com

Warner Bros. Studios Grip Department	(818) 954-1590

4000 Warner Blvd Bldg 43, Burbank, CA, 91522
Production, rigging & construction grip equipment, canvas shop, steel scaffolding rentals/services
www.wbgripdept.com

Greenhouses

See Also: Greens* Marijuana Plants, Dispensary Dressing & Hydroponics

Santa Barbara Greenhouses (800) 544-5276
721 Richmond Ave, Oxnard, CA, 93030
Greenhouses supplier and DIY greenhouses
robsbg@aol.com * www.sbgreenhouse.com

Turner Greenhouses (800) 672-4770
PO Box 1260, Goldsboro, NC, 27533
catalog sales; hobby greenhouses & related accessories
www.turnergreenhouses.com

Greens

See Also: Cactus, Live & Artificial* Concrete Block, Brick, Gravel, Sand, Rocks, Etc.* Dirt Skins* Florists/Floral Design* Flowers, Dried* Fountains, Decorative & Garden* Grass Mats* Pumpkins & Gourds* Pumpkins/Gourds, Artificial & Real* Marijuana Plants, Dispensary Dressing & Hydroponics

American Foliage & Design Group, Inc. (212) 741-5555
47 Ann St, New York NY, 10038
greens, trees, dirt, sand, rocks, snow, fountains, special EFX, fiberglass
www.americanfoliagedesign.com

Breaux's Arts (323) 221-8071
2222 Foothill Blvd E154, La Canada, CA, 91011
Call for Appt. Unusual, hard to find plant & natural materials, horticultural & botanical research
breauxarts@sbcglobal.net * fb.me/BreauxArts12

Flower Art (323) 935-6800
5859 West 3rd Street, Los Angeles, CA, 90036
Award-winning, full-service floral design for movie/television sets. Located near The Grove. SDSA members since 1994
info@flowerartla.com * www.flowerartla.com

Green Set, Inc. (818) 764-1231
Collected Materials, Cut Brush, Moss, Straw & Hay, Vines. live & artificial, full nursery facilities

Jackson Shrub Supply, Inc. (818) 982-0100
giant Sequoias, Cypress tropical, live/custom made palms, bushes

LCW Props (818) 243-0707
dirt skins, lots

Make Be Leaves (800) 634-1402
5311 Derry Ave Unit C, Agoura Hills, CA, 91301
Artificial trees, plants and floral designs
www.makebe-leaves.com

NatureMaker (800) 872-1889
6225 El Camino Real Ste 110, Carlsbad, CA, 92009
custom fabricators of steel art trees
www.naturemaker.com

Oceanic Arts (562) 698-6960
bamboo poles, 3/4" to 6" dia., bamboo fencing, thatch, mattings

Pacific Earth Resources (800) 942-5296
305 W Hueneme Rd, Camarillo, CA, 93012
sod farm
www.pacificsod.com

Picture Start Props (818) 255-5472
clean potted silk house plants, palms, ferns, and succulents.

Rainforest Flora, Inc. (310) 370-8044
19121 Hawthorne Blvd, Torrance, CA, 90503
largest supplier of exotic tropicals, bromeliads, and air plants
www.rainforestflora.com

ZG04 DECOR (818) 853-8040
Large selection of hedges, hedge walls, side wall hedges and kentia palms along with faux greens.

Grip Equipment

See Also: Expendables* Lighting & Sound, Concert/Theatrical/DJ/VJ* Rigging, Equipment or Services* Stage Lighting, Film/Video/TV

Alan Gordon Enterprises, Inc. (323) 466-3561
5625 Melrose Ave, Los Angeles, CA, 90038
grip, lighting, camera & audio equip.
www.alangordon.com

Bill Ferrell Co. (818) 767-1900
10556 Keswick St, Sun Valley, CA, 91352
Camera risers, Steel Deck and Ferrellel Decks.
www.billferrell.com

Birns & Sawyer, Inc. (323) 466-8211
5275 Craner Ave, N Hollywood, CA, 91601
film & video cameras, accessories, lighting/grip, expendables, for lighting & grip rental call (818) 766-2525
www.birnsandsawyer.com

Castex Rentals   **(323) 462-1468**
1044 N Cole Ave, Hollywood, CA, 90038
full line of grip equipment, boom arms, lights, reflectors, steel deck
service@castexrentals.com * www.castexrentals.com

Cineworks Lighting & Grip   **(818) 252-0001**
8125 Lankershim Blvd, N Hollywood, CA, 91605
Hot lighting, grip equipment, grip trucks, car mounts, specialty items,
expendables, kinoflos
cineworks@cineworksinc.com * www.cineworksinc.com

Filmmaker Prod. Svcs-Atlanta @ Tyler Perry   **(404) 450-1968**
Studios
2115 Sylvan Road, Atlanta, GA, 30344
Grip & rigging equip. & services, lighting & sound
chad.garcia@nbcuni.com * www.filmmakerproductionservices.com

Filmmaker Prod. Svcs-Chicago @ Cinespace   **(678) 628-1997**
Chicago
2558 W 16th Street Dock #4, Chicago, IL, 60608
Grip & rigging equip. & services, lighting & sound
patrick.flanagan@nbcuni.com * www.filmmakerproductionservices.com

Global Backings   **(323) 769-0650**
11970 Borden Ave, San Fernando, CA, 91340
backings: solids, muslins, nets, gridcloths, grip equip., chromakey fabric, paint,
tape; truss frames w/rigging
www.globalbackings.com

Highline Stages   **(212) 206-8280**
440 W. 15th Street, New York City, NY, 10011
expendables, lighting, generators, grip equip.
www.highlinestages.com

History For Hire, Inc.   **(818) 765-7767**
period

MBSE Burbank   **(818) 303-9464**
10616 Lanark St, Sun Valley, CA, 91352
grip & lighting, power generators, power & climate control

New Mexico Lighting & Grip Co.   **(505) 506-6564**
I-25 Studios 9201 Pan American Fwy NE, Albuquerque, NM, 87113
Grip & rigging equip. & services, lighting & sound
colin.pearman@nmlgc.com * www.newmexicolightingandgrip.com

Paladin Group, Inc.   **(323) 874-7758**
7351 Santa Monica Blvd, Hollywood, CA, 90046
grip equipment & stage lighting
www.paladinhollywood.com

Paskal Lighting   **(818) 896-5233**
12685 Van Nuys Blvd, Pacoima, CA, 91321
grip/lighting equip. & expendables
www.paskal.com

Source Lighting & Grip Rentals, Inc.   **(323) 463-5555**
1111 N Beachwood Dr, Hollywood, CA, 90038
Grip trucks, generators, lighting equipment, stages
www.sourcefilmstudio.com

Universal Studios Grip Dept   **(818) 777-2291**
100 Universal City Plaza, Universal City, CA, 91608
Extensive inventory of quality grip equipment incl. digital screens, steel deck &
more
universal.grip@nbcuni.com * http://universalstudioslot.com/grip

Warner Bros. Studios Grip Department   **(818) 954-1590**
4000 Warner Blvd Bldg 43, Burbank, CA, 91522
Production, rigging & construction grip equipment, canvas shop, steel
scaffolding rentals/services
www.wbgripdept.com

Grocery Check-out Stands (Complete)

AIR Designs   **(818) 768-6639**
Supermarket Dual Conveyor, Matching Pair

Lennie Marvin Enterprises, Inc. (Prop Heaven)   **(818) 841-5882**

Grocery Store

See: Market Equipment/Fixtures Prop Houses* Prop Products &
Packages* Scales* Shopping Bags (Silent)*

Grocery Store Produce Scales

See: Scales

Grooming

See: Make-up & Hair, Supplies & Services Shaving, Old Fashion,
Non-Electric*

Ground & Floor Protection

See: Floor, Ground & Surface Protection

Guard Shacks

See Also: Street Dressing

AIR Designs   **(818) 768-6639**
Clean/Rustic, Electric Toll Gate Mech. Arms, Lights, Pylons, Signage

E.C. Prop Rentals   **(818) 764-2008**
multiple styles, castered, lighted, practical parking arms

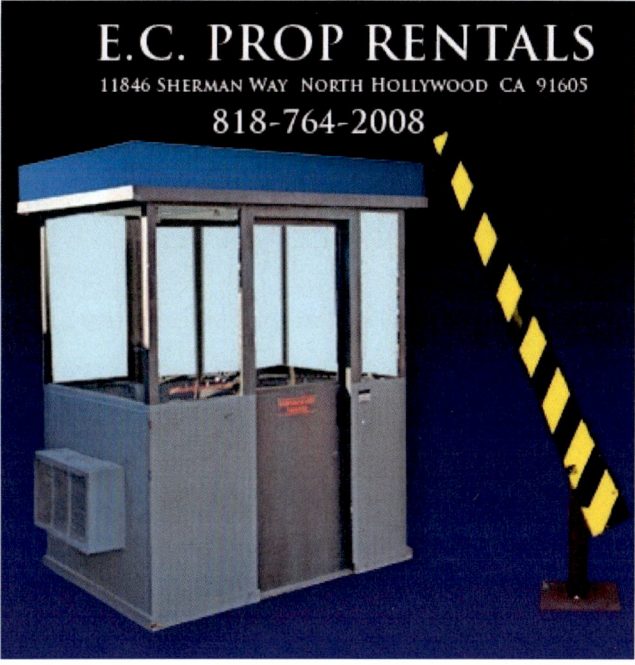

E.C. PROP RENTALS
11846 SHERMAN WAY NORTH HOLLYWOOD CA 91605
818-764-2008

Guillotines

Dapper Cadaver   **(818) 771-0818**
Guillotines. Severed heads, decapitated bodies and blood. More torture
equipment: gibbets, stocks, etc.

History For Hire, Inc.   **(818) 765-7767**

Sword & Stone   **(818) 562-6548**
Mini guillotine

Universal Studios Property & Hardware Dept   **(818) 777-2784**
Guillotine with wooden frame and fake blade, magician's guillotine and
miniature guillotines for rent.

Gumball Machines

See: Vending Machines

Gun Choreography

See Also: Guns & Firearms

I.T.T.S.   **(310) 446-1390**
12651 Little Tujunga Canyon Rd, Lake View Terrace, CA, 91342
technical consulting, weapons choreography
www.internationaltactical.com

Tactical Edge Group   **(706) 638-8499**
382 Beard Dr, Trion, GA, 30753
weapons specialists for film, TV; tech advisors military, law enforcement in
Georgia.
www.propguys.com

Guns & Firearms

See Also: Civil War Era* Non-Guns & Non-Pyro Flashes* Weaponry, Historical* Weapons* Western Wear* Gun Choreography

Caravan West Productions   (661) 268-8300
35660 Jayhawker Rd, Aqua Dulce, CA, 91390
Old West, exact reproduction all types, plain & fancy, gunsmiths too. Over 1000 guns from 1820s-1900s. 650 gun belts.
caravanwest@earthlink.net * www.caravanwest.com

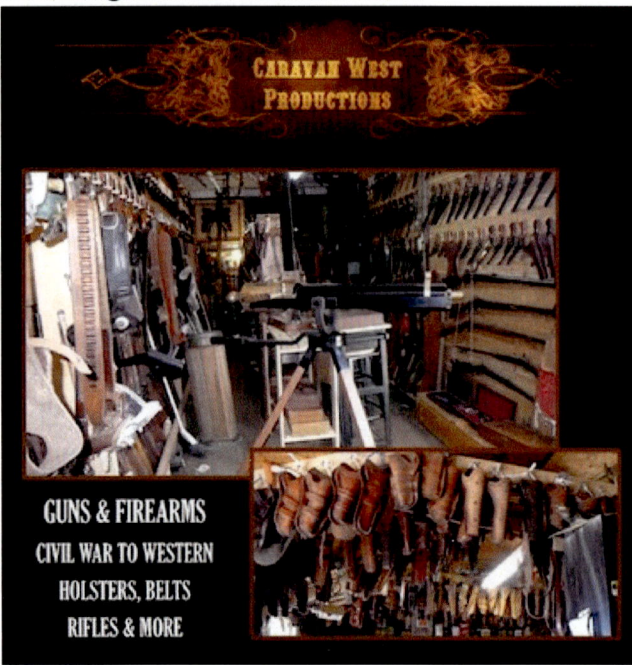

The Hand Prop Room LP.   (323) 931-1534
weapons, arsenal, handguns, rifles, fully automatic weapons, semi automatic weapons, antique handguns, six shooters
History For Hire, Inc.   (818) 765-7767
replicas only, flintlock to M-16
Independent Studio Services, Inc   (818) 951-5600
LCW Props   (818) 243-0707
Period - Present, Fake Guns, Futuristic Guns
Old N Country Prop Shop, LLC   (818) 423-2599
Variety of Non-guns available, shotguns, automatic, pistols, armor, etc.
RJR Props   (404) 349-7600
Prop guns; prop handguns, prop AK47s, prop M4 assault rifles, prop M16 assault rifles, plastic guns & realistic guns.
Target Props LLC   (818) 768-8499
7100 Fair Ave, North Hollywood, CA, 91605
Prop guns, rubber guns, gun replicas, and more.
targetprops@gmail.com * www.targetprops.com

Guns/Gunsmith

See: Guns & Firearms* Non-Guns & Non-Pyro Flashes* Weapons* Western Wear

Gurneys

See Also: Hospital Equipment* Military Props & Equipment* Intensive Care Unit / NICU (Natal Intensive Care Unit)* Emergency Room
A-1 Medical Integration   (818) 753-0319
Medical devices for Set Decoration & Property, from minor procedures to detailed hospital units.
Alpha Companies - Spellman Desk Co.   (818) 504-9090
period to contemporary from the #1 source for medical equipment in the Industry.
Dapper Cadaver   (818) 771-0818
Hospital gurneys and ambulance gurneys.
The Hand Prop Room LP.   (323) 931-1534
History For Hire, Inc.   (818) 765-7767
period, hospital, ambulance
LCW Props   (818) 243-0707
Stainless Steel, Morgue Dressing, Hospital
Universal Studios Property & Hardware Dept   (818) 777-2784
Medical gurneys, emergency gurneys and morgue gurneys for rent.

Gym & Tumbling Mats

See: Fall Pads & Crash Pads* Gymnasium & Gymnastic Equipment

Gym Equipment

See: Exercise & Fitness Equipment* Gymnasium & Gymnastic Equipment

Gym Floors

See: Carpet & Flooring* Gymnasium & Gymnastic Equipment

Gym Lights

See Also: Egg Crate Bottom Fluorescents* Light Fixtures* Lighting, Industrial
Alley Cats Studio Rentals   (818) 982-9178
working, goosenecks, poles, single
E.C. Prop Rentals   (818) 764-2008
working, many china hat & high bay styles

LCW Props   (818) 243-0707
Overhead, Fire, Exit, Industrial
Sony Pictures Studios-Fixtures   (310) 244-5996
5933 W Slauson Ave, Culver City, CA, 90230
period to present day
www.sonypicturesstudios.com

Gymnasium & Gymnastic Equipment

See Also: Ballet Barres & Dance Mirrors* Boxing, Wrestling, Mixed Martial Arts (MMA)* Exercise & Fitness Equipment* Fall Pads & Crash Pads* Lockers* Weightlifting Equipment
C. P. Two   (323) 466-8201
Gym mats and gym chairs
Curtis Gym Equipment   (818) 897-2804
10275 Glenoaks Blvd Ste #7, Pacoima, CA, 91331
Prop Rentals and Servicing. Complete Setups. Fitness Machines, Gymnastics & Weightlifting. Fake & Real Weights
curtisgymequipment@hotmail.com
E.C. Prop Rentals   (818) 764-2008
lights, lockers, benches, towel carts, basketball scoreboard etc
The Hand Prop Room LP.   (323) 931-1534
Pommel horse, jump rope, basketball hoops, basketball backboards, spring boards, wall clocks, countdown timers
Hollywood Gym Rentals   (310) 663-6161
200 West Chevy Chase Drive Unit B, Glendale, CA, 91204
Hollywood Gym Rentals specializes in short and long term rentals of fitness equipment in the Los Angeles area.
chris@hollywoodgymrentals.com * www.hollywoodgymrentals.com
Norbert's Athletic Products   (800) 779-1904
431 Figueroa St, Wilmington, CA, 90744
We specialize in matting and equipment for gymnastics, cheer, dance, yoga, stunt and martial arts.
info@norberts.net * www.norberts.net

Gypsy Wagon

L. A. Circus   **(323) 751-3486**
Call for Appt, Los Angeles, CA, 90047
Many gypsy wagons
circusinc@aol.com * www.lacircus.com
Universal Studios Property & Hardware Dept   **(818) 777-2784**
Wagons for rent, perfect for all your gypsy needs!

Hair

See: Beauty Salon* Make-up & Hair, Supplies & Services* Wigs

Hair Dryers

See: Beauty Salon

Hair Ornaments

See: Wardrobe, Accessories

Hairpieces

See: Wigs

Halliburton Cases

See: Futuristic Furniture, Props, Decorations

Halloween Dressing & Accessories

See Also: Haunted House* Holiday Costumes* Horror/Monster
Dressing* Pumpkins & Gourds* Pumpkins/Gourds, Artificial & Real
AA Surplus Sales Co., Inc.   **(323) 526-3622**
2940 E Olympic Blvd, Los Angeles, CA, 90023
Military Uniforms, Ghillie Suits, Footware and Accesories for the whole family in
used and new condition
surplusking@hotmail.com * www.aasurplus.com
Dapper Cadaver   **(818) 771-0818**
Halloween prop central. Monsters, gore, skeletons, tombstones, caskets,
candelabras & decor. Haunted mansion to zombie.
Gorygirl Halloween Event Staging and Prop   **(818) 912-6902**
Rental
Halloween Party staging by appointment only please call for availability
Green Set, Inc.   **(818) 764-1231**
skeletons, tombstones, scarecrows and many other scary figures and evil
figures, even gargoyles
Halloween Town   **(818) 848-3642**
2921 W Magnolia Bl, Burbank, CA, 91505
Halloween props, Halloween costumes, Halloween dressing and Halloween
accessories
Halloweentown7@aol.com * http://www.halloweentownstore.com
The Hand Prop Room LP.   **(323) 931-1534**
skeletons, skulls, cauldrons, chains, masks
History For Hire, Inc.   **(818) 765-7767**
vampire stakes, witches brooms
Jackson Shrub Supply, Inc.   **(818) 982-0100**
Halloween dressing and Halloween accessories
L. A. Party Works   **(888) 527-2789**
9712 Alpaca St, S El Monte, CA, 91733
in Vancouver tel. 604-589-4101
partyworks@aol.com * www.partyworksinteractive.com
Picture Start Props   **(818) 255-5472**
Vintage and contemporary Halloween and haunted house dressing.
Universal Studios Property & Hardware Dept   **(818) 777-2784**
Halloween props, Halloween dressing, and Halloween accessories for rent.

Halloween Make-up

See: Special Effects, Make-up/Prosthetics

Halloween Themed Parties

See: Events, Decorations, Supplies & Services* Events,
Design/Planning/Production* Holiday Theme Events

Hampers, Theatrical

iWeiss Theatrical Solutions   **(888) 325-7192**
815 Fairview Ave #10, Fairview, NJ 07022
info@iweiss.com * www.iweiss.com
Universal Studios Property & Hardware Dept   **(818) 777-2784**
Theatrical hampers, commercial hampers for rent.

Hand Bags

See: Leather (Clothing, Accessories, Materials)* Wardrobe,
Accessories

Hand Lettering

See: Calligraphy* Signs

Hand Trucks

See: Furniture Dollies, Pads & Hand Trucks

Handrails

See: Audience Seating* Moulding, Wood* Scenery/Set Construction

Hangar

See: Locations, Airport Dressing & Hangars

Hangers

See: Display Cases, Racks & Fixtures (Store)

Hard Hats

See: Headwear - Hats, Bonnets, Caps, Helmets Etc.* Traffic/Road
Signs, Lights, Safety Items* Uniforms, Trades/Professional/Sports

Hardware Store Dressing

See Also: Cash Registers* Counters* Credit Card Imprint Machine*
Display Cases, Racks & Fixtures (Store)* Shopping Bags (Silent)
Acme Display Fixture & Packaging   **(888) 411-1870**
3829 S Broadway St, Los Angeles, CA, 90037
Complete store setups: garment racks, displays/display cases, counters,
packaging, shelving, hangers, mannequins
sales@acmedisplay.com * www.acmedisplay.com
History For Hire, Inc.   **(818) 765-7767**
LCW Props   **(818) 243-0707**
A Huge Selection Of Hardware Store, Shelves With Product, Tools, POS
Systems, Security
Lennie Marvin Enterprises, Inc. (Prop Heaven)   **(818) 841-5882**
product/fixtures, period to modern, signage too
Old N Country Prop Shop, LLC   **(818) 423-2599**
A variety of antique tools, products, and more.

Hardware, Construction

See: Building Supply, Lumber, Hardware, Etc.

Hardware, Decorative

See Also: Expendables
Atlas Homewares   **(818) 240-3500**
1310 Cypress Ave, Los Angeles, CA, 90065
decorative hardware, knobs, pulls, knockers, house numbers
www.atlashomewares.com
The Craftsmen Hardware Co.   **(660) 376-2481**
P.O. Box 161, Marceline, MO, 64658
Hand-hammered copper hardware in the Arts & Crafts style
www.craftsmenhardware.com
Design Hardware   **(323) 930-1330**
6053 West 3rd St, Los Angeles, CA, 90036
all types of hardware, will do custom
www.designhardware.com
Designer Door & Window   **(818) 841-3181**
1037 N Victory Place, Burbank, CA 91502
decorative hardware & moldings
www.designerdoorandwindow.com
History For Hire, Inc.   **(818) 765-7767**
LCW Props   **(818) 243-0707**
Very large selection of marine hardware.

LISTINGS FOR THIS CATEGORY CONTINUE ON THE
FOLLOWING PAGE

Liz's Antique Hardware   (323) 939-4403
453 S La Brea Ave, Los Angeles, CA, 90036
All kinds of vintage and contemporary hardware & lighting from Victorian through to modern.
shop@lahardware.com * www.lahardware.com

Majestic Vent Covers Inc.   (888) 797-3808
19011 Parthenia St Unit E, Northridge, CA, 91324
Manufacturer of resin decorative grilles and registers for HVAC and decor. Custom sizes and designs also available.
sales@majesticventcovers.com * www.majesticventcovers.com

Ohio Travel Bag   (800) 800-1941
6481 Davis Industrial Pkwy, Solon, OH, 44139
luggage, purse, trunk, case, saddlery, etc. all components
info@ohiotravelbag.com * www.ohiotravelbag.com

Omega/Cinema Props   (323) 466-8201
door & window hardware, registers

Omnia   (800) 310-7960
5 Cliffside Dr PO Box 330, Cedar Grove, NJ, 07009
ornate brass & S.S. architectural trim, bath & cabinet, locks & latches
www.omniaindustries.com

The Reggio Register Co.   (800) 880-3090
31 Jytek Rd, Leominster, MA, 01453
catalog sales; cast iron, brass, alum., zinc & wood grills & registers for contemp. & traditional homes
www.reggioregister.com

Restoration Hardware   (626) 795-7234
127 W Colorado Blvd, Pasadena, CA, 91105
www.restorationhardware.com

Rompage Hardware   (323) 467-2129
1801 N Western Ave, Los Angeles, CA, 90027
http://ww3.truevalue.com/rompagetruevalue/

Sword & Stone   (818) 562-6548
Custom made decorative hardware

Universal Studios Property & Hardware Dept   (818) 777-2784
Decorative hardware for rent.

Van Dyke's Restorers   (800) 237-8833
PO Box 52, Louisiana, MO, 63353
catalog sales; woodworking and antique restoration supplies. antique reprod. hardware, locks
www.vandykes.com

Warner Bros. Studios Hardware Rentals   (818) 954-1335
4000 Warner Blvd Bldg 30, Burbank, CA, 91522
Door Knobs & Plates, Hinges, Window Fixtures, Elevator Panels, Train & Boat Accessories
wbsfproperty@warnerbros.com * www.wbpropertydept.com

Harness Carriage

See: Carriages, Horse Drawn* Horses, Horse Equipment, Livestock

Harpoons

See: Nautical Dressing & Props

Hat Blocks & Hat Boxes

California Millinery Supply Co.   (213) 622-8746
721 S. Spring St, Los Angeles, CA, 90014
hat blocks, hat boxes, hat frames & hat-making supplies
www.californiamillinery.net

The Hand Prop Room LP.   (323) 931-1534

History For Hire, Inc.   (818) 765-7767
hat boxes

Universal Studios Property & Hardware Dept   (818) 777-2784
Hat blocks & hat boxes for rent.

Western Costume Co.   (818) 760-0900

Hat Pins

See: Wardrobe, Accessories

Hat Racks

See Also: Display Cases, Racks & Fixtures (Store)* Hat Blocks & Hat Boxes* Headwear - Hats, Bonnets, Caps, Helmets Etc.* Store Shelf Units & Shelving

History For Hire, Inc.   (818) 765-7767
wall & floor

Omega/Cinema Props   (323) 466-8201

Prop Services West   (818) 503-2790

Sony Pictures Studios-Prop House (Off Lot)   (310) 244-5999
hat racks and coat stands, wall hooks

Universal Studios Property & Hardware Dept   (818) 777-2784
Hat racks from different time periods and styles for rent.

Hats

See: Headwear - Hats, Bonnets, Caps, Helmets Etc.

Haunted House

See Also: Cemetery Dressing* Halloween Dressing & Accessories* Horror/Monster Dressing* Special Effects, Equipment & Supplies

CONFETTI & FOG FX Special Effects Company   (877) 576-4239
1085 W 21st Pl, Hialeah, FL, 33010
Let us design the best haunted house for your Halloween event
Info@confettiandfogfx.com * www.caffx.com

Dapper Cadaver   (818) 771-0818
Haunted house prop central. Monsters, zombies, bodies, gore, skeletons, tombstones & decor. Custom fabrication & FX.

Gorygirl Halloween Event Staging and Prop Rental   (818) 912-6902
Haunted house small set dressing and staging service by appt only. Props subject to availability during month of October

History For Hire, Inc.   (818) 765-7767

LM Treasures   (626) 252-7354
Halloween props & statues; SoulTaker, Frankenstein, Vampire Statue, Witches, Bats, etc perfect for haunted houses.

Old N Country Prop Shop, LLC   (818) 423-2599
Lots of stuff to make that Haunted House Creepy: dolls, stuffed animals, old costumes, etc.

Universal Studios Property & Hardware Dept   (818) 777-2784
Haunted house dressing for rent, haunted house props.

Hawaiian Dressing

See Also: Carved Figures* Costume Rental Houses* Events, Decorations, Supplies & Services* Greens* Jungle Dressing* Light Fixtures, South Seas* Prop Houses* Tikis & Tropical Dressing

Frank's Cane & Rush Supply   (714) 847-0707
7252 Heil Avenue, Huntington Beach, CA, 92647
Natural bamboo, fences, mats, thatch, caning, unique materials
www.franksupply.com

History For Hire, Inc.   (818) 765-7767

LCW Props   (818) 243-0707
Nets, Shells, Surf Boards, Nautical

Oceanic Arts   (562) 698-6960
Raincape thatching - 7 sizes, Bamboo Poles 3/4" to 6" diameter, Mattings, Tikis, Tropical Lights, and more.

Hay

See: Greens

Hazardous Waste Removal

See: Sanitation, Waste Disposal

Headdresses

American Plume	**(800) 521-1132**

11 Skyine Drive East, Unit 2, Clarks Summit, PA 18411
Boas/jackets/theatrical division in NYC; (800) 962-8544. Vegas showgirl, wild natural
apff@epix.net * www.americanplume.com

The Hand Prop Room LP.	**(323) 931-1534**
Western Costume Co.	**(818) 760-0900**

Headstones

See: Cemetery Dressing

Headwear - Hats, Bonnets, Caps, Helmets Etc.

See Also: Formal Wear* Military Surplus/Combat Clothes, Field Gear* Sporting Goods & Services* Uniforms, Trades/Professional/Sports

AIR Designs	**(818) 768-6639**

Racing Helmets, Hard Hats

California Millinery Supply Co.	**(213) 622-8746**

721 S. Spring St, Los Angeles, CA, 90014
www.californiamillinery.net

CBS Costume Rental	**(323) 575-2666**

modern ladies', 1880s western M/F

The Costume House	**(818) 508-9933**

1870s-1970s, top hats, bonnets, derby, fedoras

Lynda Burdick Millinery	**(323) 662-7612**

By Appt. Only
baby & children's hats
www.lyndahats.com

Sony Pictures Studios-Wardrobe	**(310) 244-5995**

alterations, call (310) 244-7260. wide variety sizes, styles, periods

Sword & Stone	**(818) 562-6548**

Helmets of all styles & materials and headpieces including crowns.

Tarpy Tailors	**(310) 645-4694**

9100 S Sepulveda Blvd Ste 103, Los Angeles, CA, 90045
airline pilot, all airlines
www.tarpytailors.com

Universal Studios Costume Dept	**(818) 777-2722**

Rental, mfg., & alterations

Health Club Equipment/Dressing

See: Exercise & Fitness Equipment* Gymnasium & Gymnastic Equipment

Hearses

See: Vehicles/Picture Vehicles

Heat Suits

See: Environmental (Cool/Heat) Suits

Heaters, Indoor

See Also: Furnaces

Castex Rentals	**(323) 462-1468**

1044 N Cole Ave, Hollywood, CA, 90038
electric dish heaters, propane blower heaters, indoor heaters
service@castexrentals.com * www.castexrentals.com

E.C. Prop Rentals	**(818) 764-2008**

overhead and floor models, radiators

LCW Props	**(818) 243-0707**

Space Heaters, Wall Heaters

RC Vintage, Inc.	**(818) 765-7107**

Faux Radiators Wall type

Universal Studios Property & Hardware Dept	**(818) 777-2784**

Indoor heaters for rent from wall mounted to portable.

ZG04 DECOR	**(818) 853-8040**

Heaters, Outdoor

Castex Rentals	**(323) 462-1468**

1044 N Cole Ave, Hollywood, CA, 90038
propane dolly heaters, blower heaters, umbrella heaters, outdoor heaters
service@castexrentals.com * www.castexrentals.com

E.C. Prop Rentals	**(818) 764-2008**

contemp. propane

LCW Props	**(818) 243-0707**

Space Heaters, Wall Heaters, Patio Style

Universal Studios Property & Hardware Dept	**(818) 777-2784**

Outdoor heaters and outdoor space heaters.

ZG04 DECOR	**(818) 853-8040**

Heavy Machinery, Equipment & Specialists

See: Construction Site Equipment* Machine Shop & Machinery* Welding Equipment/Stations

Helicopters

See: Aircraft, Charters & Aerial Services

Helium Equipment

See: Balloons & Balloon Sculptures

Helmets

See: Headwear - Hats, Bonnets, Caps, Helmets Etc.* Military Surplus/Combat Clothes, Field Gear* Sporting Goods & Services* Uniforms, Trades/Professional/Sports

Hides

See: Costume/Wardrobe/Sewing Supplies* Leather (Clothing, Accessories, Materials)* Taxidermy, Hides/Heads/Skeletons

High Chairs

See: Children/Baby Accessories & Bedroom

Highway Safety Items

See: Barricades* Crowd Control: Barricades, Turnstiles Etc.* Traffic/Road Signs, Lights, Safety Items

Hip Hop

See: Bling

Historical & Antique Reproductions

See: Civil War Era* Egyptian Dressing* Prop Reproduction & Fabrication* Weaponry, Historical* Weaponry, Medieval

Historical Era Themed Events

See: Costume Rental Houses* Events, Backings & Scenery* Events, Decorations, Supplies & Services* Events, Design/Planning/Production* Wardrobe, Antique/Historical

Hoarder Dressing

See: Furniture, Used/Second Hand* Salvage, Rubble, Clutter & Trash (Prop)* Salvage, Architectural* Paperwork, Documents & Letters, Office* Newspapers (Prop)* Boxes* Bag Lady Carts

Hobby & Craft Supplies

See Also: Art, Supplies & Stationery* Model Ships/Planes/Trains/Autos Etc.* Scrapbooks

Burbank's House of Hobbies   (818) 848-3674
911 South Victory Blvd, Burbank, CA 91502
Plastic model kits, built up display airplanes (military and commercial), automobiles in all scales, pinewood derby kits
www.houseofhobbies.com

The Caning Shop   (800) 544-3373
926 Gilman St (at 8th), Berkeley, CA, 94710
caning/basketry/gourd crafting supplies, tools, books
www.caning.com

Craft Depot   (213) 627-5232
401 East 7th St, Los Angeles, CA, 90014

Kit Kraft, Inc.   (818) 509-9739
12109 Ventura Pl, Studio City, CA, 91604
crafts, models, art materials
www.kitkraft.com

Moskatels   (213) 689-4590
733 S San Julian St, Los Angeles, CA, 90014

Repro-Graphic Supply   (818) 771-9066
9838 Glenoaks Blvd, Sun Valley, CA, 91352
Hobby Craft Supplies/Sundry Supplies, Kroy Supplies, Sprays/Tapes/Adhesives, Pens/Markers/Leads, templates, rules, etc.
info@reprographicsupply.com * www.reprographicsupply.com

ShopWildThings   (928) 855-6075
2880 Sweetwater Ave, Lake Havasu City, AZ, 86406
Event Decor, Beaded Curtains, Chain Curtains, String Curtains & Columns, Crystal Columns. Reliable service & delivery.
help@shopwildthings.com * www.shopwildthings.com

Stats Floral Supply   (626) 795-9308
120 S Raymond Ave, Pasadena, CA, 91105
www.statsfloral.com

Utrecht Manufacturing Corp.   (310) 479-1416
11531 Santa Monica Blvd, Los Angeles, CA, 90025
art supply, 30+ stores in US, call (800) 223-9132
www.utrechtart.com

Hockey Equipment

See: Ice Skating Surfaces* Sporting Goods & Services

Holiday Costumes

See Also: Costume Rental Houses

The Costume House   (818) 508-9933
Mardi Gras costumes, Halloween costumes, Christmas Costumes, Christmas Tree Costume, Santa Claus Costume

Halloween Club   (714) 367-0859
14447 Firestone Blvd, La Mirada, CA 90638
Costumes, masks, props, make-up & all related accessories
www.halloweenclub.com

Sony Pictures Studios-Wardrobe   (310) 244-5995
alterations, call (310) 244-7260

Warner Bros. Studios Costume Dept   (818) 954-1297
Santa Suits, Elves, Patriotic, Bunnies, Valentine, St. Patricks Day

Holiday Theme Events

See Also: Christmas* Events, Decorations, Supplies & Services* Events, Design/Planning/Production* Events, Entertainment* Halloween Dressing & Accessories* Holiday Costumes

FROST   (310) 704-8812
Call for Appointment - 21405 Madrona Ave, Torrance, CA, 90503
Holiday decor, specializing in large scale trees, Santa sets, ornaments. Professional installations.
mdisplay@yahoo.com * www.frostchristmasprops.com

The Hand Prop Room LP.   (323) 931-1534

LM Treasures   (626) 252-7354
We specialize in high quality statues and decor for any season of the year.

ShopWildThings   (928) 855-6075
2880 Sweetwater Ave, Lake Havasu City, AZ, 86406
Event Decor, Beaded Curtains, Chain Curtains, String Curtains & Columns, Crystal Columns. Reliable service & delivery.
help@shopwildthings.com * www.shopwildthings.com

ZEdonk ART   (818) 693-1082
5330 Derry Ave Ste P, Agoura Hills, CA, 91301
ZEdonk Art offers a unique collection of handcrafted decorations for all occasions!
kelly@zedonkart.com * www.ZEdonkART.com

Hollywood Themed Parties

See: Events, Decorations, Supplies & Services* Events, Design/Planning/Production* Travel (City/Country) Themed Events

Holsters

See: Wardrobe, Accessories* Western Wear

Home Office Furniture

See: Office Furniture

Homeland Security

See: Research, Advisors, Consulting & Clearances* Security Devices or Services* Security Walk-Through & Baggage Alarms* Surveillance Equipment

Honeywagon Waste Removal

See: Production Vehicles/Trailers* Sanitation, Waste Disposal

Hoop Skirts

See: Wardrobe, Antique/Historical

Horror/Monster Dressing

Dapper Cadaver   (818) 771-0818
Horror prop central. Crime to supernatural. Bodies, gore, blood, fake weapons, bones, torture & oddities. Custom FX.

Gorygirl Halloween Event Staging and Prop Rental   (818) 912-6902
Subject to availability during the month of October. Staging service available for special events.

The Hand Prop Room LP.   (323) 931-1534
Horror Dressing and Monster Dressing

LCW Props   (818) 243-0707
Frankenstein Lair, Steam Punk, Van Helsing, Dracula's Castle, Torture Equipment

Universal Studios Property & Hardware Dept   (818) 777-2784
Horror props and monster props for rent.

Horror/Monster Make-up

See: Special Effects, Make-up/Prosthetics

Horse Drawn Carriages

See: Carriages, Horse Drawn

Horse Saddles & Tack

See Also: Western Dressing* Western Wear

Broken Horn Saddlery   (626) 337-4088
1022 Leorita St, Baldwin Park, CA, 91706
10-6 Wed.- Sat. 10-5 Sun. Closed Mon & Tues. feed, tack, saddles,
clothing-English & Western
www.brokenhornsaddlery.com

C. P. Two   (323) 466-8201

Caravan West Productions   (661) 268-8300
35660 Jayhawker Rd, Aqua Dulce, CA, 91390
Old West, historically accurate & museum quality.
caravanwest@earthlink.net * www.caravanwest.com

Da Moor's Tack & Feed   (818) 242-2841
1532 Riverside Dr, Glendale, CA, 91201
feed, clothing, tack
stableshoppepromo@gmail.com * www.damoorstackandfeed.com

The Hand Prop Room LP.   (323) 931-1534
saddles, saddlebags, bedrolls, tack, feedbags

History For Hire, Inc.   (818) 765-7767
Western & military saddles & tack, saddle bags, vintage

Sony Pictures Studios-Prop House (Off Lot)   (310) 244-5999

Weaver Leather   (800) 932-8371
PO Box 68, Mt Hope, OH, 44660-0068
catalog sales; leather, leather working tools, machinery. tack & saddle
making/repair supplies & tools
www.weaverleather.com

Horses, Horse Equipment, Livestock

See Also: Animals (Live), Services, Trainers & Wranglers Blacksmith
Shop/Foundry* Carriages, Horse Drawn* Horse Saddles & Tack*
Wagons* Western Dressing* Western Wear*

Caravan West Productions   (661) 268-8300
35660 Jayhawker Rd, Aqua Dulce, CA, 91390
horses, rolling stock, accurate recreations back to Civil War
caravanwest@earthlink.net * www.caravanwest.com

Harry Patton Horseshoeing Supplies   (626) 359-8018
223 W. Maple Ave, Monrovia, CA, 91016
blacksmith shop avail. as location; horseshoeing supplies, can locate farriers
harrypattonhorseshoes@gmail.com * www.harrypatton.com

Movin' On Livestock   (661) 252-8654
20527 Soledad St, Canyon Country, CA, 91351
livestock, many wagons & stagecoaches, jail wagon too
www.movinonlivestock.com

Horticulturalists

See: Greens

Hoses

Alley Cats Studio Rentals   (818) 982-9178

E.C. Prop Rentals   (818) 764-2008
Stainless braid, fire, water, air, industrial

History For Hire, Inc.   (818) 765-7767

LCW Props   (818) 243-0707
Large Selection, Any Size, Color, Style

Universal Studios Property & Hardware Dept   (818) 777-2784
All kinds of hoses; fire hoses, garden hoses, pneumatic hoses, aquarium
hoses, welding hose for rent.

Western Hose & Gasket   (310) 355-1500
12600 Chadron Ave, Hawthorne, CA, 90250
www.westflex.com

Hosiery

The Costume House   (818) 508-9933
men's tights, seamed hose

Sony Pictures Studios-Wardrobe   (310) 244-5995
alterations, call (310) 244-7260

Hospital Equipment

See Also: Ambulance/Paramedic Anesthesia Equipment* Gurneys*
Lab Equipment* Medical Equip/Furniture, Graphics/Supplies*
Morgue* MRI (Magnetic Resonance Imaging)* Uniforms,
Trades/Professional/Sports* Wheelchairs*

A-1 Medical Integration   (818) 753-0319
Medical devices for Set Decoration & Property, from minor procedures to
detailed hospital units.

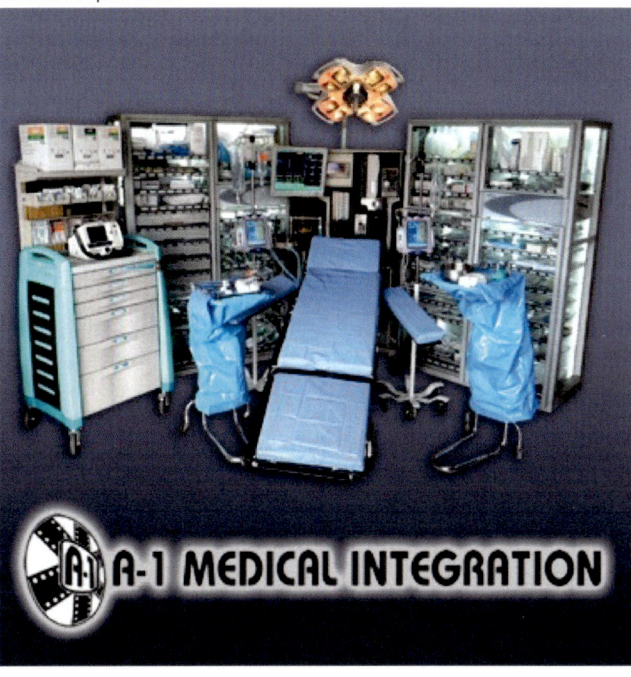

Alpha Companies - Spellman Desk Co.   (818) 504-9090
Period hospital equipment to contemporary hospital equipment, from the #1
source for medical equipment in the industry.

Angelus Medical & Optical Co., Inc. (310) 769-6060
13007 S Western Ave, Gardena, CA, 90249
O.R., surgery tables, lights, cabinets
www.angelusmedical.com

MEDICAL PROPS & INSTRUMENTS
NEW AND VINTAGE

ANGELUS MEDICAL & OPTICAL Co; Inc.

The Hand Prop Room LP. (323) 931-1534
past-present, gurney
History For Hire, Inc. (818) 765-7767
Period hospital equipment/Vintage hospital equipment
LCW Props (818) 243-0707
Whole Hospital Room Setup, Linen Carts, Gurneys, Graphics, Heart Monitors,
IV Poles
McBain Systems (805) 581-6800
1650 Voyager Ave, Simi Valley, CA, 93063
Rentals of All Types of Microscopes, Histology, Imaging and other Scientific
Lab Equipment
sales@mcbainsystems.com * www.mcbainsystems.com
RJR Props (404) 349-7600
Exam room, hospital sets, ER/OR hospital beds, hospital curtains, hospital
furniture, hospital props and more.
Universal Studios Property & Hardware Dept (818) 777-2784
All things hospital equipment and hospital dressing for rent.

Hot Dog Carts

See: Vendor Carts & Concession Counters

Hotel, Motel, Inn, Lodge

See Also: Furniture, Tenement Tacky Motel Prop Houses*
C. P. Two (323) 466-8201
The Hand Prop Room LP. (323) 931-1534
luggage, carts, signs, phones, electr. devices
History For Hire, Inc. (818) 765-7767
maid carts, keys, keywall, switchboards
Hollywood Studio Gallery (323) 462-1116
signage
Hotel Surplus Outlet (818) 787-7807
16625 Saticoy Ave, Van Nuys, CA, 91406
Hotel surplus
info@hotelsurplus.com * www.hotelsurplus.com
Omega/Cinema Props (323) 466-8201
Prop Services West (818) 503-2790
RC Vintage, Inc. (818) 765-7107
40s-60s fixtures to signage, Bad Art
Universal Studios Property & Hardware Dept (818) 777-2784
Hotel props & motel props; hotel keys, hotel signage, hotel pouf and more for
rent. Many multiples.

Hotspots, Wireless

See: Wi-Fi Boxes

Hub Caps

See: Automotive/Garage Equip. & Parts

Human Anatomy

See: Anatomical Charts & Models Bones, Skulls & Skeletons*
Medical Equip/Furniture, Graphics/Supplies*

Hurdles

See: Track & Field Equipment

Hypodermics

See: Medical Equip/Furniture, Graphics/Supplies

Ice Chests

See Also: Refrigerators Sporting Goods & Services*
Alley Cats Studio Rentals (818) 982-9178
period, modern
The Hand Prop Room LP. (323) 931-1534
period-present
History For Hire, Inc. (818) 765-7767
period, modern, rigged
Picture Start Props (818) 255-5472
Large selection of different sized coolers and ice chests.
Sony Pictures Studios-Prop House (Off Lot) (310) 244-5999

Ice Cream Carts & Bikes

See: Vendor Carts & Concession Counters

Ice Cubes, Plastic

See Also: Ice Chests Ice Sculpture*
The Hand Prop Room LP. (323) 931-1534
prop ice cubes, acrylic prop ice cubes, acrylic ice cubes, prop broken glass,
prop ice blocks, silicone glass
Universal Studios Property & Hardware Dept (818) 777-2784
Prop ice cubes/plastic ice cubes for rent.

Ice Delivery

See Also: Special Effects, Equipment & Supplies Snow, Artificial &
Real* Ice Sculpture*
Acton Ice Delivery (661) 269-2093
3932 Sourdough Rd, Acton, CA, 93510
Ice delivery and catering ice from Santa Clarita North to Mojave.
meltheiceman@gmail.com * www.actonice.com
Carving Ice & Big on Snow (714) 224-1455
900 S Placentia Ave Ste B, Placentia, CA, 92870
You're the best at what you do & so are we. Carving Ice & Blowing Snow for
the TV & film industries for over 20 years.
info@carvingice.com * www.carvingice.com
Newhall Ice Company (661) 259-0893
22502 5th St, Newhall, CA, 91321
Bulk ice & dry ice, ice sculpture, machine made snow at your site
http://newhallicecompany.com

Ice Machines

See Also: Snow, Artificial & Real Special Effects, Equipment &
Supplies*
AIR Designs (818) 768-6639
Outdoor & Indoor Machines, Ice Machines, Bar
Alley Cats Studio Rentals (818) 982-9178
C. P. Two (323) 466-8201
ice machines for rent
RC Vintage, Inc. (818) 765-7107
Bad Condition, restaurant ice machines, bar ice machines, industrial ice
machines for business
Universal Studios Property & Hardware Dept (818) 777-2784
Prop ice machines, commercial ice machines and restaurant ice machines for
rent.

Ice Sculpture

See Also: Ice Delivery* Special Effects, Equipment & Supplies* Snow, Artificial & Real

Carving Ice & Big on Snow (714) 224-1455
900 S Placentia Ave Ste B, Placentia, CA, 92870
You're the best at what you do & so are we. Carving Ice & Blowing Snow for the TV & film industries for over 20 years.
info@carvingice.com * www.carvingice.com

714 - 224 - 1455

Union Ice Co. / Arctic Glacier (323) 826-1914
2970 East 50th St, Vernon, CA, 90058
Van Nuys store (888) 830-8383; 24X7, M.P. catering, cubes custom carving, crushed ice, dry ice, real snow FX
www.unionice.com

Ice Skates

See: Sporting Goods & Services

Ice Skating Surfaces

See Also: Carpet & Flooring
Willy Bietak Productions, Inc (310) 576-2400
1404 3rd Street Promenade #200, Santa Monica, CA, 90401
portable, plastic, any size, luge tracks, hockey & curling rinks
bietakice.com

Independence Day

See: Holiday Costumes* Holiday Theme Events* Pyrotechnics

Indian Clubs

See: Gymnasium & Gymnastic Equipment

Indian Rugs, Furniture, Artifacts

See: Asian Antiques, Furniture, Art & Artifacts* Native American* Rugs* Western Dressing

Industrial Dressing

See: Break Room* Factory/Industrial* Grating, Grated Flooring, Catwalks* Scales

Industrial Lighting

See: Lighting, Industrial

Inflatable People

See: Audience Cutouts & Inflatables

Inflatables, Custom

Big Events, Inc. (760) 477-2655
1613 Ord Way, Oceanside, CA, 92056
giant custom shapes made, helium & cold-air inflatables
info@bigeventsonline.com * www.bigeventsonline.com
Creative Inflatables (626) 579-4454
9872 Rush St, South El Monte, CA, 91733
largest inventory, most unique sel. in U.S., we manufacture. from 8' up to 35' multitude of fabrics
www.creativeinflatables.com
Interactive Inflatables, Inc. (858) 622-6610
10427 Roselle St, San Diego, CA, 92121
Custom inflatables for movie premiers, promotional tours, set decor & more.
http://www.interactiveinflatables.com

Insects

See: Animals (Live), Services, Trainers & Wranglers* Insects, Artificial

Insects, Artificial

See Also: Animals (Live), Services, Trainers & Wranglers
Dapper Cadaver (818) 771-0818
Fake insects/fake bugs including leeches, parasites mounted insects, mounted specimens and more
LM Treasures (626) 252-7354
At Lm Treasures we have a variety of over size animals and insects statues for sale or for rent.

Insert Stages

See: Locations, Insert Stages & Theatres

Instant Rust

See: Paint & Painting Supplies

Instrument Cases

See: Musical Instrument Cases

Instrument Panels

See Also: Control Boards* Control Panels/Boxes* Electrical/Electronic Supplies & Services* Electronic Equipment (Dressing)* Space Shuttle/Space Hardware* Spaceship Computer Panel
E.C. Prop Rentals (818) 764-2008
industrial, stainless
LCW Props (818) 243-0707
Working, Large Selection, Period - Present
Modern Props (323) 934-3000
Fabricated contemporary electronic racks, futuristic electronic racks, instrument panels and sci-fi equipment.

Instruments

See: Dentist Equipment* Lab Equipment* Medical Equip/Furniture, Graphics/Supplies* Musical Instruments* Nautical Dressing & Props* Science Equipment* Surveying Equipment

Insulators

Alley Cats Studio Rentals (818) 982-9178
ceramic, glass, all sizes
E.C. Prop Rentals (818) 764-2008
Also power pole transformers, crossbars, and 12' 8" and 16' tall utility power poles
History For Hire, Inc. (818) 765-7767
w/posts
Universal Studios Property & Hardware Dept (818) 777-2784
Prop insulators, electrical insulators and more for rent.

Insurance

Abacus Insurance Brokers   (424) 214-3700
2512 Wilshire Blvd, Santa Monica, CA, 90403
entertainment industry products, special event coverage
www.abacus.net

Heffernan Insurance Brokers   (213) 622-6500
811 Wilshire Blvd Ste 810, Los Angeles, CA, 90017
www.heffins.com

Insurance West Corp. / NFP   (805) 579-1900
2450 Tapo St, Simi Valley, CA, 93063
40 years of motion picture insurance excellence. From cameras, sound equip,
cranes to post-production & pyrotechnics.
bob.sulzinger@nfp.com * www.insurancewest.com

INSURANCE WEST AGENTS & BROKERS

Entertainment Insurance

Specialized Industries:

Special Effects • Transportation • Lighting & Grip
Stages • Wardrobe • Sets • Post Production
Props • Miniatures / Mechanicals • Commercials
Music Videos • Video Duplication • Broadcasting
Audio, Sound, Video

P.E.R.A Member • A.I.C.P. Member • ASEPO

Looking Forward

United Agencies Inc., Insurance   (800) 800-5880
100 N 1st Street Ste 301, Burbank, CA, 91502
entertainment industry coverage; also in Las Vegas
www.unitedagencies.com

Wells Fargo Insurance Services   (818) 464-9300
333 S Grand Ave 20th floor, Los Angeles CA, 90071
custom-designed packages for production & special events
http://wfis.wellsfargo.com

Intensive Care Unit / NICU (Natal Intensive Care Unit)

See Also: Hospital Equipment* Medical Equip/Furniture,
Graphics/Supplies* Stretchers* Emergency Room

A-1 Medical Integration   (818) 753-0319
Medical devices for Set Decoration & Property, from minor procedures to
detailed hospital units.

Alpha Companies - Spellman Desk Co.   (818) 504-9090
The #1 source for medical equipment in the industry.

Interactive Equipment

See: Video Games

Intercoms

E.C. Prop Rentals   (818) 764-2008
wall-mount & free standing, apartment style & entrance keypads

History For Hire, Inc.   (818) 765-7767
period

LCW Props   (818) 243-0707
Large Selection, Emergency, Video, Phone

RJR Props   (404) 349-7600
Prop intercoms; apartment intercoms, parking deck intercoms, security
intercoms, vintage intercoms, antique intercoms

Sony Pictures Studios-Fixtures   (310) 244-5996
5933 W Slauson Ave, Culver City, CA, 90230
period to present day
www.sonypicturesstudios.com

Universal Studios Property & Hardware Dept   (818) 777-2784
Many kinds of intercoms for rent, from period to modern.

Investigation

See: Private Investigations* Research, Advisors, Consulting &
Clearances

Irish, All Things Irish

See Also: Pub Signs

Lennie Marvin Enterprises, Inc. (Prop Heaven)   (818) 841-5882
Irish pub signage, equip., neon, glassware & more

NEST Studio Rentals, Inc.   (818) 942-0339

Ironwork & Iron Furniture

See: Bedroom Furniture & Decorations* Furniture, Outdoor/Patio*
Furniture, Rustic* Metalworking, Decorative* Wrought Iron Furniture
& Decorations

Jacks

See: Automotive/Garage Equip. & Parts

Jacuzzis, Spas & Pools

Lifestyle Outdoor   (818) 997-3255
5830 Sepulveda Blvd, Van Nuys, CA, 91411
full showroom, all makes/models pools & spas in stock
http://lifestyleoutdoor.com

Janitorial Supplies

See Also: Expendables* Vacuum Cleaners

E.C. Prop Rentals   (818) 764-2008
carts, cleaning tools & supplies & clutter

The Hand Prop Room LP.   (323) 931-1534
complete setups, carts, fully outfitted

History For Hire, Inc.   (818) 765-7767
vintage

LCW Props   (818) 243-0707
Janitor Carts, Tools, Mops

Sony Pictures Studios-Prop House (Off Lot)   (310) 244-5999
janitorial equipment, janitorial carts, laundry baskets, janitorial cleaning
supplies

Universal Studios Property & Hardware Dept   (818) 777-2784
Janitor props; janitor carts, housekeeping carts and utility carts for rent.

Japanese Antiques

See: Asian Antiques, Furniture, Art & Artifacts

Jet Skis

See: Boats & Water Sport Vehicles* Sporting Goods & Services

Jewelry Display Cases

See: Display Cases, Racks & Fixtures (Store)

Jewelry Store

The Hand Prop Room LP.   (323) 931-1534

RC Vintage, Inc.   (818) 765-7107
Jewelry Display Cases stocked with Jewelry, Jewelry Neons & more. See our
Website

Jewelry, Costume

See Also: Bling* Goth/Punk/Bondage/Fetish/Erotica Etc.* Wardrobe,
Accessories

10 Karat Rentals   (818) 635-4124
7100 Tujunga (At RC Vintage), N Hollywood, CA, 91605
10karatrentals@gmail.com

Catherine Nash's Closet   (520) 620-6613
1102 W. Huron St, Tucson, AZ, 85745
wholesale to Industry only: costume jewelry 1860s-1970s
cnash@wvcnet.com

CBS Costume Rental   (323) 575-2666
1980s trendy earrings galore

The Costume House   (818) 508-9933
1900s to 1980s, necklaces, pins, earrings, bracelets

The Hand Prop Room LP.   (323) 931-1534
costume jewelry, vintage costume jewelry, fake pearls, pearl necklaces,
costume jewelry pins, rhinestone jewelry, rhinestone broaches

Hollywood Cinema Arts   (818) 504-7333
For costume jewelry that looks real, situated in a completely rentable jewelry
store.

K. Walters at the Sign of the Gray Horse　　**(703) 269-7126**
12131 Derriford Court, Woodbridge, VA, 22192
Historically accurate reproduction and inspired jewelry based on original examples, portraits, and prints.
kimberlywalters@comcast.net * www.kwaltersatthesignofthegrayhorse.com

Palace Costume & Prop Co.　　**(323) 651-5458**
11th to 20th C. & ethnic

Pasadena Antique Center and Annex　　**(626) 449-7706**
480 South Fair Oaks Ave, Pasadena, CA, 91105
Extensive assortment of affordable costume jewelry for purchase from a wide array of styles and eras.
pasadenaantiqecenterandannex@gmail.com * bit.ly/PasadenaAntiqueCenter

Playclothes　　**(818) 557-8447**
3100 W Magnolia Blvd, Burbank, CA, 91505
Men & Women's-1940s-1980s w/ original displays
www.vintageplayclothes.com

RC Vintage, Inc.　　**(818) 765-7107**
Large Selection of Costume Jewelry!

Repeat Performance　　**(323) 938-0609**
Web Based Business
www.rpvintage.com

Sony Pictures Studios-Prop House (Off Lot)　　**(310) 244-5999**
necklaces, bracelets, earrings, crystal drops, crystal chains, african jewelry, brooch pins, cameo, change purse, and more

Sony Pictures Studios-Wardrobe　　**(310) 244-5995**
alterations, call (310) 244-7260

Universal Studios Costume Dept　　**(818) 777-2722**
Rental, mfg., & alterations

Universal Studios Property & Hardware Dept　　**(818) 777-2784**
Lots of costume jewelry/prop jewelry for rent.

Warner Bros. Studios Costume Dept　　**(818) 954-1297**
Necklaces, Bracelets, Earrings, Rings, Beads, Cuffs, Vintage, Chokers, Tiaras, Clips

Western Costume Co.　　**(818) 760-0900**

Jewelry, Fine/Reproduction

See Also: Bling Gems, Minerals & Crystals* Jewelry, Costume* Prop Design & Manufacturing*

10 Karat Rentals　　**(818) 635-4124**
7100 Tujunga (At RC Vintage), N Hollywood, CA, 91605
10karatrentals@gmail.com

1928 Jewelry Company　　**(818) 841-1928**
3412 W Magnolia Blvd, Burbank, CA, 91505
fashion jewelry, custom antiq. reprod., open to public
www.1928.com

The Costume House　　**(818) 508-9933**
reproductions

The Hand Prop Room LP.　　**(323) 931-1534**
designer watches, reproduction designer jewelry, reproduction designer diamond necklaces, velvet jewelry boxes

Harry Winston Jewelers　　**(310) 271-8554**
310 N Rodeo Dr, Beverly Hills, CA, 90210
also salons in NY, Europe, Japan
www.harrywinston.com

K. Walters at the Sign of the Gray Horse　　**(703) 269-7126**
12131 Derriford Court, Woodbridge, VA, 22192
Historically accurate reproduction and inspired jewelry based on original examples, portraits, and prints.
kimberlywalters@comcast.net * www.kwaltersatthesignofthegrayhorse.com

www.kwaltersatthesignofthegrayhorse.com

L. Wilmington & Co.　　**(213) 624-8314**
611 Wilshire Blvd #1116, Los Angeles, CA, 90017
Jewelry mfg, numerous Industry credits; custom designs, able to copy most anything, military/championship/class rings
lwilco@pacbell.net * www.lwilmington.com

Martin Katz, Ltd　　**(310) 276-7200**
9540 Brighton Way, Beverly Hills, CA, 90210
ready-made, custom, estate & fine jewelry, will design to suit, all pieces made in Paris
www.martinkatz.com

Regency Jewelry Co., Inc.　　**(323) 655-2573**
8129 W 3rd St, Los Angeles, CA, 90048
Jewelry & jewelry repair
www.regencyjewelry.com

Sword & Stone　　**(818) 562-6548**
custom-made, silver, gold, bronze, gem cutting

Judaica

See: Religious Articles

Judge/Jury Props

See: Courtroom Furniture & Dressing

Judging Systems

See: Game Show Electronics & Equipment Scoreboards & Scoring Systems*

Juggling

See: Carnival Dressing/Supplies Clowns* Magicians & Props, Supplies, Dressing* Toys & Games*

Jukeboxes, Music/Dance Machines

See Also: Bars, Nightclubs, Barware & Dressing
AIR Designs	**(818) 768-6639**
40's-Now, Table & Floor Models	
C. P. Two	**(323) 466-8201**
Jukeboxes from many time periods.	
The Hand Prop Room LP.	**(323) 931-1534**
floor, tabletop	
RC Vintage, Inc.	**(818) 765-7107**
Working/Nonworking 40s-present/ CD Jukebox, variety, vintage jukeboxes, disco balls	
Sony Pictures Studios-Prop House (Off Lot)	**(310) 244-5999**

Jungle Dressing

See Also: Animals (Live), Services, Trainers & Wranglers* Greens* Tikis & Tropical Dressing
History For Hire, Inc.	**(818) 765-7767**
Oceanic Arts	**(562) 698-6960**
thatch & hut roofing, bamboo, alligators, birds, shields, masks	

Jungle Gym

See: Playground Equipment

Jungle Themed Parties

See: Events, Decorations, Supplies & Services* Events, Design/Planning/Production* Greens* Jungle Dressing* Taxidermy, Hides/Heads/Skeletons* Themed Environment Construction* Tikis & Tropical Dressing* Travel (City/Country) Themed Events

Junk Removal

See: Sanitation, Waste Disposal

Junkyard

See: Architectural Pieces & Artifacts* Salvage, Rubble, Clutter & Trash (Prop)

Kayaks

See: Boats & Water Sport Vehicles

Key Boxes & Racks

AIR Designs	**(818) 768-6639**
Valet & Industrial	
E.C. Prop Rentals	**(818) 764-2008**
Wall-Mounted Boxes & Wall-Mounted Boards with Keys, Valet Stands	
LCW Props	**(818) 243-0707**
Valet Stands, Locking Key Boxes	
Universal Studios Property & Hardware Dept	**(818) 777-2784**
Key boxes, key racks, valet boxes and valet racks for rent.	

Keyboards

See: Pianos & Keyboard Instruments

Keying Backgrounds

See: Fabrics* Paint & Painting Supplies

Keys & Locks

See Also: Lockers
Antrim's Security Co.	**(626) 795-8661**
2051 E Foothill Blvd, Pasadena, CA, 91107	
Door Keyper, Inc.	**(626) 794-6940**
942 N Amelia Ave, San Dimas, CA, 91773	
large master key systems	
www.doorkeyperinc.com	
History For Hire, Inc.	**(818) 765-7767**
Keedex Lock Museum	**(714) 630-0800**
1051 Grove St, Anaheim, CA 92806	
By Appt. Only, Mon-Thurs, lock & key museum, extensive collection for research	
www.keedex.com	
LCW Props	**(818) 243-0707**
Selection For Hardware Store, Hotel, Digital Locks, Safes	
Lockmasters Security Institute	**(866) 574-8724**
2101 John C Watts Dr, Nicholasville, KY, 40356	
Harry C. Miller lock collection (museum), items dating to 1300s, research source for covert entry methods/lock drilling	
www.lsieducation.com	
Sword & Stone	**(818) 562-6548**
Keys and locks, Medieval locks	
Universal Studios Property & Hardware Dept	**(818) 777-2784**
Many kinds of keys and locks for rent.	

Kids

See: Children's & Baby Clothing* Children/Baby Accessories & Bedroom* Game Tables & Equipment* Hobby & Craft Supplies* Sporting Goods & Services* Sportswear* Toys & Games* Video Games

Kilims

See: Rugs

Kiosks

See Also: Magazines & Magazine/Newspaper Racks* Newspapers (Prop)* Newsstands (Prop)
AIR Designs	**(818) 768-6639**
Newspaper, Food, Mall, Coffee, Flower	
Alley Cats Studio Rentals	**(818) 982-9178**
new, green wood, dressed, newspaper kiosk	
E.C. Prop Rentals	**(818) 764-2008**
park/college courtyard style kiosks	
LCW Props	**(818) 243-0707**
Large & Small. Mall, Merchandise, Airport Kiosks, Information, Video Kiosks	
Lennie Marvin Enterprises, Inc. (Prop Heaven)	**(818) 841-5882**
mall directory, mall vending, phone, etc.	
Modern Props	**(323) 934-3000**
ATM, airport or bus terminal, e-ticket, security entry, shopping mall directory, fabricate universal kiosks	
RC Vintage, Inc.	**(818) 765-7107**
ticket counters, mini bars, ticket kiosks, food kiosks, beverage kiosks, nameless kiosks, with chair sets, public buffet lines	

Kitchen Appliances

See: Appliances* Cooking Equipment* Kitchen Dressing* Refrigerators* Stoves

Kitchen Counters & Cabinets

C. P. Two	**(323) 466-8201**
The Kitchen Store	**(310) 839-5215**
6322 W Slauson Ave, Culver City, CA, 90230	
Our Studio Division provides expedited delivery of residential and commercial building materials for your design needs.	
www.studiosupplier.com	
RC Vintage, Inc.	**(818) 765-7107**
Kitchen Counters and Stoves and Fridges	
The ReUse People	**(818) 244-5635**
3015 Dolores St, Los Angeles, CA, 90065	
Contemporary, vintage and antique.	
JeffCockerell@TheReUsePeople.org * www.TheReUsePeople.org	
Warner Bros. Studios Cabinet & Furniture Shop	**(818) 954-1339**
Custom manufacturing and installation of cabinets, built-ins countertops. Wood & laminate finishes.	

Kitchen Dressing

See Also: Appliances* Cooking Equipment* Food, Artificial Food*
Glassware/Dishes* Linens, Household

C. P. Two	(323) 466-8201
The Hand Prop Room LP.	(323) 931-1534
period-present	
History For Hire, Inc.	(818) 765-7767
period	
Hollywood Studio Gallery	(323) 462-1116
wall dressing only	
LCW Props	(818) 243-0707
Large Quantity, Appliances, Pots & Pans, Outdoor Kitchen BBQ, Utensils	
Modern Props	(323) 934-3000
Contemporary/futuristic kitchen dressing, appliances, dishes & more	
Modern-Aire Ventilating Corp.	(818) 765-9870
7319 Lankershim Blvd, N Hollywood, CA, 91605	
Range hoods only, many styles/materials	
www.modernaire.com	
NEST Studio Rentals, Inc.	(818) 942-0339
household, large sel., gourmet to family	
Ob-jects	(818) 351-4200
dressing for gourmet kitchen, countertops/appliances "Kitchenaid"	
Old N Country Prop Shop, LLC	(818) 423-2599
A wide range of vintage kitchen appliances, antique kitchenware, silverware and more.	
Omega/Cinema Props	(323) 466-8201
Picture Start Props	(818) 255-5472
Small appliances, kitchen pots, kitchen pans, kitchen linens and containers, vintage cookies jars and canisters.	
Prop Services West	(818) 503-2790
Kitchen dressing and kitchen props	
RC Vintage, Inc.	(818) 765-7107
40s, 50s & 60s Flatware,and Wall Art, Blenders, Toasters, Sink Units Cookie Jars!	
Sony Pictures Studios-Prop House (Off Lot)	(310) 244-5999
large bowls, bread plates, butter plates, butter dishes w cover, cake plates, centerpieces, coffee server, dessert bowls	
Universal Studios Property & Hardware Dept	(818) 777-2784
All kinds of kitchen props and kitchen dressing for rent.	
Warner Bros. Studios Property Department	(818) 954-2181
Appliances, faux food, linens, table dressing, cooking equipment, toasters, kitchen smalls, table linens	
ZG04 DECOR	(818) 853-8040
Dishes, Cookware, Flatware	

Kites

See: Hobby & Craft Supplies* Sporting Goods & Services* Toys & Games* Windsocks

Kludge Dressing

See: Control Panels/Boxes* Foam* Futuristic Furniture, Props, Decorations* Lab Equipment* Pallets* Plastics, Materials & Fabrication* Science Equipment

Knick-knacks (Nick-nacks)

See: Prop Houses* Decorative Accessories

Knickers

See Also: Wardrobe, Antique/Historical

The Costume House	(818) 508-9933
colonial & 1930s golfing	
Sony Pictures Studios-Wardrobe	(310) 244-5995
alterations, call (310) 244-7260	
Western Costume Co.	(818) 760-0900

Knitting Supplies

See: Costume/Wardrobe/Sewing Supplies

Knives

See Also: Kitchen Dressing* Swords & Swordplay* Weaponry, Historical* Weaponry, Medieval* Weapons

Dapper Cadaver	(818) 771-0818
Plastic knives and foam knives. Machetes, cleavers, etc. More fake weapons.	

Emerson Knives   (310) 539-5633
1234 254th St, Harbor City, CA, 90710
Emerson Knives are the only choice of Elite Military and U.S. Covert Units.
They are truly, "Famous In the Worst Places"
eknives@aol.com * www.emersonknives.com

The Hand Prop Room LP.	(323) 931-1534
period-present, custom manufacturing	
History For Hire, Inc.	(818) 765-7767
period, all types	
Prop Services West	(818) 503-2790
Sony Pictures Studios-Prop House (Off Lot)	(310) 244-5999
Sword & Stone	(818) 562-6548
custom-made swords, knives & axes	

Lab Equipment

See Also: Cryogenic Equipment* Electron Microscope* Hospital Equipment* Scales* Science Equipment

A-1 Medical Integration (818) 753-0319
Medical devices for Set Decoration & Property, from minor procedures to detailed hospital units. Various lab equipment

Alpha Companies - Spellman Desk Co. (818) 504-9090
Complete hi-end lab dressing: tables, clean room, microscopes, refrigeration, fume hoods, cryogenics, analyzers and more

Dapper Cadaver (818) 771-0818
Period to modern. Laboratory glassware, specimen jars, lab instruments & scientific models. Forensic to high school lab.

E.C. Prop Rentals (818) 764-2008
Electron microscope, stainless steel tables, racks, carts, server towers

The Hand Prop Room LP. (323) 931-1534
beakers, Bunson burners, beaker racks, glass jars, formaldehyde jars, formaldehyde jars with specimens, lab tools, lab trays, lab utensils

History For Hire, Inc. (818) 765-7767
period

Kinemetrics, Inc. (626) 795-2220
222 Vista Ave, Pasadena, CA, 91107
mfr. seismic equip., will rent/repair, equip & software
www.kinemetrics.com

LCW Props (818) 243-0707
Our Specialty, Glassware, Equipment, DNA, Analyzers, Desks, Cryogenic, Any Kind; Microscopes, Large & Small

Machinery & Equipment Co., Inc. (909) 599-3916
115 N Cataract Ave, San Dimas, CA, 91773
Used lab equipment for sale and rent including bench top equipment, ovens, cabinets, hoods, freezers, screens and more.
sherri@machineryandequipment.com * www.machineryandequipment.com

McBain Systems (805) 581-6800
1650 Voyager Ave, Simi Valley, CA, 93063
Rentals of All Types of Microscopes, Histology, Imaging and other Scientific Lab Equipment
sales@mcbainsystems.com * www.mcbainsystems.com

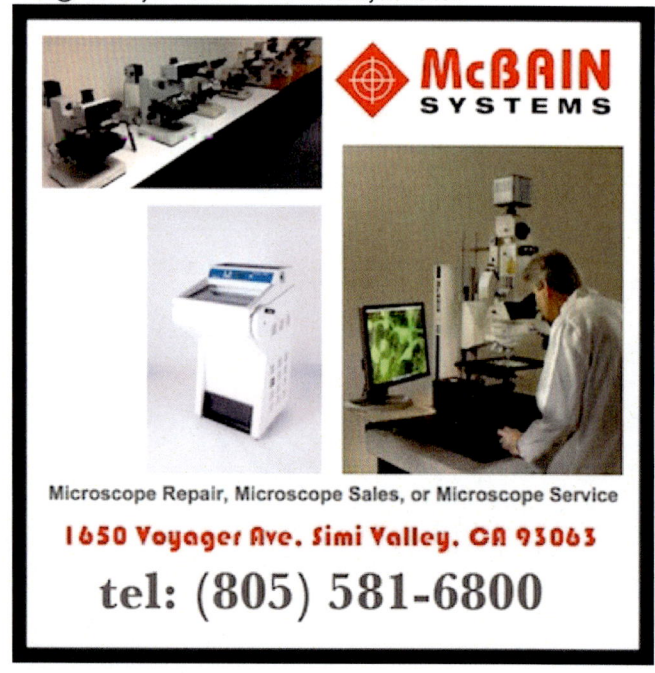

Modern Props (323) 934-3000
Lab equipment including; flumed hooded cabinets on casters, contemporary/futuristic-beakers to microscopes and much more

Universal Studios Property & Hardware Dept (818) 777-2784
Prop lab equipment for rent.

Lab Wear

See: Protective Apparel

Labels

See: Printing, Graphics, Digital & Large Format* Product Labels

Laces & Trims

See: Costume/Wardrobe/Sewing Supplies

Ladders

See Also: Scaffolding/Lighting Towers

Alley Cats Studio Rentals (818) 982-9178
wood, metal, fire escape

E.C. Prop Rentals (818) 764-2008
Rooftop Access Ladders, Wood Ladders, Metal Ladders, A-Frame Ladders, Extension Ladders, Warehouse Ladders, Rolling Ladders.

LCW Props (818) 243-0707
Rolling Industrial, Step Ladders, Construction, Extension

Universal Studios Property & Hardware Dept (818) 777-2784
All kinds of ladders for all your laddering needs.

Laminates

See: Paneling, Veneers & Laminates

Laminating & Mounting

See Also: Art & Picture Framing Services

Beyond Image Graphics (818) 547-0899
1853 Dana St, Glendale, CA, 91201
rafi@beyondimagegraphics.com * www.beyondimagegraphics.com

D'ziner Sign Co. (323) 467-4467
801 Seward Street, Los Angeles, CA, 90038
various backgrounds & laminating material up to 60" wide
sales@dzinersign.com * www.dzinersign.com

Dennis Bolton Enterprises, Inc. (818) 982-1800
7285 Coldwater Cyn Ave, N.Hollywood, CA, 91605
www.printingbydbe.com

Warner Bros. Studios Scenic Art & Sign Shop (818) 954-1815
4000 Warner Blvd Bldg 44, Burbank, CA, 91522
graphic design and production studio for signs & scenic art; digital printing to hand-painted
wbsigns@warnerbros.com * www.wbsignandscenic.com

Lamp Posts & Street Lights

See Also: Billboards & Billboard Lights* Bulkhead Lights* China Hat Lights* Lanterns* Light Fixtures* Light Fixtures, Period* Neon Lights & Signs* Searchlights/Skytrackers, Architectural Lights* Street Dressing* Street Dressing, Exterior Signs

AIR Designs (818) 768-6639
Street, Parking Lot, Traffic, Acorn, Cobras, Railroad

Alley Cats Studio Rentals (818) 982-9178
extra tall cobra head lights, acorn lights, billboard lights, Victorian, parking lot lamp posts

E.C. Prop Rentals (818) 764-2008
alum. cobra head poles, candy cane china hats, acorn, mushroom top

Green Set, Inc. (818) 764-1231
party lights & lot lights, street lamp posts, and street light sets. high end to period to modern, for any street

Jackson Shrub Supply, Inc. (818) 982-0100
Victorian lamp posts, single globe lamp posts, multiple globe lamp posts, poles, street lamps

LCW Props (818) 243-0707
Period - Present, Mercury Vapors, Cobra Heads

Lennie Marvin Enterprises, Inc. (Prop Heaven) (818) 841-5882
per-mod., practical lamp posts, traffic lights, large qty avail.

Omega/Cinema Props (323) 466-8201
Lamp posts and street lights

RC Vintage, Inc. (818) 765-7107
traditional lamp posts to wharf dock lights

Sony Pictures Studios-Prop House (Off Lot) (310) 244-5999
lamp posts

Universal Studios Property & Hardware Dept (818) 777-2784
Prop street lamps and street light dressing from many periods and styles for rent.

Lamp Shades

See Also: China Hat Lights* Lamps

The Hand Prop Room LP.	(323) 931-1534

LCW Props (818) 243-0707
futuristic, ultra modern, period

Old N Country Prop Shop, LLC (818) 423-2599
Large variety of lamp shades (of course you need one of our lamps to put it on!)

Prop Services West (818) 503-2790

Sony Pictures Studios-Prop House (Off Lot) (310) 244-5999

Warner Bros. Studios Property Department (818) 954-2181
Assorted lamp shades, fabric, metal, glass, wood shades

Lamps

See Also: Lamp Posts & Street Lights* Lamp Shades* Lanterns* Light Fixtures* Restaurant Table Lamps

Badia Design, Inc. (818) 762-0130
5420 Vineland Ave, N Hollywood, CA, 91601
brass chandelier, Moroccan hanging lamps, Henna lamps, metal and bones lamps, copper lamps, brass lamps
info@badiadesign.com * www.badiadesign.com

Blueprint Furniture (310) 657-4315
8600 Pico Blvd. Los Angeles, CA, 90035
Modern furniture lighting accessories early classic bauhaus mid-century contemporary design. Good studio rental history.
www.blueprintfurniture.com

Bridge Furniture & Props Los Angeles (818) 433-7100
We carry modern & traditional furniture, lighting, accessories, art, & rugs. Items are online for easy shopping.

Castle Antiques & Design (818) 765-5000
11924 Vose St, N Hollywood, CA, 91605
We offer lamps of different styles and sizes for rent or purchase.
info@castleantiques.net * www.castleprophouse.com

Dozar Office Furnishings (310) 559-9292
9937 Jefferson Blvd, Culver City, CA, 90232
Rentals X22. Goose neck table lamps, desk lamps, floor lamps, modern lamps, lamp shades, adjustable lamps & more.
dozarrents@aol.com * www.dozarrents.com

Faux Library Studio Props, Inc. (818) 765-0096
variety of desk and floor lamps, vintage floor lamps, vintage table lamps, retro floor lamps, many shapes sizes and colors

FormDecor, Inc. (310) 558-2582
America's largest event rental supplier of 20th Century furniture and accessories for Modern and Mid-Century styles.

Fortune Trading Co & Import Bazaar (323) 222-6287
483 Gin Ling Way (Old Chinatown), Los Angeles, CA, 90012
1000s of copies of many styles of paper lanterns, masks. Costumes, lions, dragons, gongs, scrolls, Oriental gift items
fortunetradingco@gmail.com

The Hand Prop Room LP. (323) 931-1534
all periods

Hollywood Cinema Arts (818) 504-7333
From standard lamps to one of a kind lamps. HCA has them all.

Little Bohemia Rentals (818) 853-7506
11940 Sherman Rd, N Hollywood, CA, 91605
Vintage and Contemporary lighting. Table and floor lamps.
sales@wearelittlebohemia.com * www.wearelittlebohemia.com

Lux Lounge EFR (888) 247-4411
106 1/2 Judge John Aiso St #318, Los Angeles, CA, 90012
Event Lamps and Decorations.
info@luxloungeefr.com * www.luxloungeefr.com

Modern Props (323) 934-3000
contemporary/futuristic lamps, wall sconces and floor, sculptural lamps.

Modernica Props (323) 664-2322
floor & table styles from the 20th century

NEST Studio Rentals, Inc. (818) 942-0339
large sel. of contemp. shaded pairs, desk & floor lamps: many cleared items

Ob-jects (818) 351-4200
designer lamps/contemporary lamps/traditional lamps

Old N Country Prop Shop, LLC (818) 423-2599
LARGE variety of vintage and traditional lamps and shades. Hanging globes, pole, industrial, table, art deco, 60s, etc.

Omega/Cinema Props (323) 466-8201
Decorative vintage, antique, and historical to modern sconces.

Pasadena Antiques & Design (626) 389-3938
330 S Fair Oaks Avenue, Pasadena, CA, 91105
Lamps , Sconces & Chandeliers.
roy@antiquesofpasadena.com * www.antiquesofpasadena.com

Picture Start Props (818) 255-5472
Many lamps of all styles from all periods.

Prop Services West (818) 503-2790

RC Vintage, Inc. (818) 765-7107
40s, 50s & 60s Large selection of lighting. Desk,Table Floor, Sconces, Check web site ..rcvintage.com

A Royal Suite Home Furnishings (661) 259-7000
26536 Carl Boyer Dr, Santa Clarita, CA, 91350
A Royal Suite, family-owned since 1978, Features AMERICAN-MADE Furniture, and the Finest Furniture at the Greatest Value
norb@ars-email.com * www.aroyalsuite.com

ShopWildThings (928) 855-6075
2880 Sweetwater Ave, Lake Havasu City, AZ, 86406
Event Decor, Beaded Curtains, Chain Curtains, String Curtains & Columns, Crystal Columns. Reliable service & delivery.
help@shopwildthings.com * www.shopwildthings.com

Sony Pictures Studios-Fixtures (310) 244-5996
5933 W Slauson Ave, Culver City, CA, 90230
period to present day, all styles,wall,floor
www.sonypicturesstudios.com

Sony Pictures Studios-Prop House (Off Lot) (310) 244-5999
gothic style lamp, hurricane lamp, lanterns, light bulb, light wheel, night light, novelty lamp, oil lamp, and MORE

Universal Studios Property & Hardware Dept (818) 777-2784
Prop lamps, sconces and lamp shades for rent.

Warner Bros. Studios Property Department (818) 954-2181
Table, desk, standing, floor, hanging, metal, wood, ornate, overhead, eclectic

ZG04 DECOR (818) 853-8040

Landscaping/Plants

See: Greens

Lanterns

See Also: Candelabras Candles* Lamps*
Badia Design, Inc. (818) 762-0130
5420 Vineland Ave, N Hollywood, CA, 91601
Moroccan hanging lanterns, Henna lanterns, metal and bones lanterns, copper lanterns, brass lanterns,
info@badiadesign.com * www.badiadesign.com
E.C. Prop Rentals (818) 764-2008
Kerosene Lanterns, Battery Operated Lanterns, Construction Lanterns, Vintage 'Ball-Shaped' Lanterns.
FormDecor, Inc. (310) 558-2582
America's largest event rental supplier of 20th Century furniture and accessories for Modern and Mid-Century styles.
Fortune Trading Co & Import Bazaar (323) 222-6287
483 Gin Ling Way (Old Chinatown), Los Angeles, CA, 90012
1000s of copies of many styles of paper lanterns, masks. Costumes, lions, dragons, gongs, scrolls, Oriental gift items
fortunetradingco@gmail.com
The Hand Prop Room LP. (323) 931-1534
nautical, railroad, barns, camping, gas, kerosene, rigged
History For Hire, Inc. (818) 765-7767
multiples, vintage
LCW Props (818) 243-0707
Large Selection Of Lighting
Omega/Cinema Props (323) 466-8201
Sony Pictures Studios-Fixtures (310) 244-5996
5933 W Slauson Ave, Culver City, CA, 90230
period to present day
www.sonypicturesstudios.com
Universal Studios Property & Hardware Dept (818) 777-2784
Lanterns from different styles, countries, and periods for rent.
Warner Bros. Studios Property Department (818) 954-2181
Table lanterns, hanging lanterns, camping lanterns, metal lanterns, outdoor lanterns, Asian lanterns

Large Format Printing
See: Printing, Graphics, Digital & Large Format

Large Screen Displays
See: Video Equipment

Las Vegas Themed Parties
See: Events, Decorations, Supplies & Services Events, Design/Planning/Production* Gambling Equipment* Game Tables & Equipment* Travel (City/Country) Themed Events*

Lasers
See: Lab Equipment Light Fixtures* Lighting & Sound, Concert/Theatrical/DJ/VJ* Special Effects, Lighting & Lasers* Ultraviolet Products*

Latex Make-up
See: Make-up & Hair, Supplies & Services Special Effects, Make-up/Prosthetics*

Lattices
See: Garden/Patio Greens*

Laundromat
See: Dry Cleaners (Dressing) Laundry Carts* Vending Machines* Washing Machines/Dryers*

Laundry Carts
C. P. Two (323) 466-8201
Laundry carts, white canvas laundry carts
E.C. Prop Rentals (818) 764-2008
canvas, vinyl, multiple sizes
History For Hire, Inc. (818) 765-7767
canvas

Lava Lamps
See: Lamps Light Fixtures* Light Fixtures, Period*

Law Books
See: Books, Real/Hollow & Faux Books Courtroom Furniture & Dressing* Prop Houses*

Lawn Chairs
See: Furniture, Outdoor/Patio

Lawn Mowers
Alley Cats Studio Rentals (818) 982-9178
gas, pushers, edgers
E.C. Prop Rentals (818) 764-2008
gas, weed whackers
The Hand Prop Room LP. (323) 931-1534
History For Hire, Inc. (818) 765-7767
push & power
Sony Pictures Studios-Prop House (Off Lot) (310) 244-5999
Universal Studios Property & Hardware Dept (818) 777-2784
Various lawn mowers for rent.

Layout Board
See: Expendables Floor, Ground & Surface Protection*

Leather (Clothing, Accessories, Materials)
See Also: Fabrics Fur Garments* Fur, Artificial & Real* Native American* Western Wear*
CBS Costume Rental (323) 575-2666
Trendy 80s & 90s, also 1880s western, Indian buckskin
gbb Custom Leather (818) 749-4944
P.O. Box 311, McDonald, Ohio 44437
Specializing in Film & Television prop & wardrobe pieces. Also, doubles, back-ups; fast turnaround.
www.gbbleather.com
The Hide House (800) 453-2847
595 Monroe St PO Box 509, Napa, CA 94995
all type leathers, findings, tools, thread, no finished items, "hair on" rugs, will rent for set dressing
www.hidehouse.com
MacPherson Custom Leather (818) 260-0091
519 N Victory Blvd, Burbank, CA, 91502
Leather makes custom leather items for the Movies, TV and Commercials and we meet your deadlines.
alan@macphersonla.com * www.mcpcustomleather.com
Montana Leather Company (800) 527-0227
2015 1st Ave North, Billings, MT, 59101
catalog sales; footwear components & leathers
www.montanaleather.com
The Rational Past (310) 476-6277
By Appointment, West Los Angeles, CA
In coordination with C & J Goods LA we create custom leather items.
info@therationalpast.com * www.therationalpast.com
Sword & Stone (818) 562-6548
custom made wardrobe, masks, accessories
Western Costume Co. (818) 760-0900
ZG04 DECOR (818) 853-8040

Leaves
See: Flowers, Dried Greens*

Lecterns
See: Podiums & Lecterns

LED Screens, Displays & Panels

See Also: Video Equipment* Lighting, LED, Fiber Optic & Specialty

EFX- Event Special Effects **(626) 888-2239**
125 Railroad Ave, Monrovia, CA, 91016
LED screens and LED displays
info@efxla.com * www.efxla.com

L. A. Party Works **(888) 527-2789**
9712 Alpaca St, S El Monte, CA, 91733
LED Screens and LED Displays for rent.
partyworks@aol.com * www.partyworksinteractive.com

Mandex LED Displays **(805) 497-8006**
3248 Jessica St, Newbury Park, CA, 91320
LED Seamless flexible or linear tickers, twist video tiles, message signs, LED tickers, LED Ribbons, LED screens
info@ledsignage.com * www.ledsignage.com

LED's, LED Color Changers

See: Lighting, LED, Fiber Optic & Specialty

Legal Documents

See: Courtroom Furniture & Dressing* Research, Advisors, Consulting & Clearances

Leis

See: Events, Decorations, Supplies & Services* Tikis & Tropical Dressing

Lemonade Fountains

See: Soda Fountain Dressing

Lettering

See: Calligraphy* Printing, Graphics, Digital & Large Format* Signs

Letters

See: Printing, Graphics, Digital & Large Format* Mail & Mail Room* Paperwork, Documents & Letters, Office* Signs

Library Books

See: Books, Real/Hollow & Faux Books* Prop Houses* Research, Advisors, Consulting & Clearances* Search Tools, Directories, Libraries

License Plates

AIR Designs **(818) 768-6639**
California & Out-of-State, Metal & Plastic
Alley Cats Studio Rentals **(818) 982-9178**
variety state and era, metal
The Hand Prop Room LP. **(323) 931-1534**
made-to-order
HPR Graphics **(323) 556-2694**
5674 Venice Blvd, Los Angeles, CA, 90019
Government license plates, metal plates, vacuum forming, foreign license plates, commercial license plates, and more.
hprcan@earthlink.net * www.hprgraphics.net
LCW Props **(818) 243-0707**
Period - Present
Sony Pictures Studios-Prop House (Off Lot) **(310) 244-5999**
cardboard set license plates, metal set license plates, license plate tags
Universal Studios Property & Hardware Dept **(818) 777-2784**
License plate rentals from many locations, time periods, and vehicles.

Life Vests, Jackets & Rings

See: Locations, Airport Dressing & Hangars* Nautical Dressing & Props

Lifts

See: Construction Site Equipment* Ladders* Scaffolding/Lighting Towers

Light Bulbs

See: Candelabras* Candles* Chandeliers* Chase Lights* Egg Crate Bottom Fluorescents* Expendables* Gym Lights* Lamp Posts & Street Lights* Lamp Shades* Lamps* Lanterns* Light Fixtures* Light Fixtures, Period* Light Fixtures, South Seas* Light Strings* Lighting & Sound, Concert/Theatrical/DJ/VJ* Lighting, Industrial* Lighting, LED, Fiber Optic & Specialty* Neon Lights & Signs* Special Effects, Lighting & Lasers* Stage Lighting, Film/Video/TV* Ultraviolet Products

Light Fixtures

See Also: Billboards & Billboard Lights* Bulkhead Lights* Caged Vapor Proof Lights* Candelabras* Candles* Chandeliers* Chase Lights* China Hat Lights* Egg Crate Bottom Fluorescents* Gym Lights* Lamp Posts & Street Lights* Lamp Shades* Lamps* Lanterns* Light Fixtures, Period* Light Fixtures, South Seas* Light Strings* Lighting & Sound, Concert/Theatrical/DJ/VJ* Lighting Control Boards* Lighting, Industrial* Lighting, LED, Fiber Optic & Specialty* Disco Balls/Mirror Balls & Drivers* Neon Lights & Signs* Restaurant Table Lamps* Searchlights/Skytrackers, Architectural Lights* Special Effects, Lighting & Lasers* Stage Lighting, Film/Video/TV* Ultraviolet Products

AIR Designs **(818) 768-6639**
China Hats, Warehouse Lights, Restaurant Lights, Pendants
Alley Cats Studio Rentals **(818) 982-9178**
china hats & vapor lights, cobra lights, fluorescents, street light poles
Alpha Companies - Spellman Desk Co. **(818) 504-9090**
Desk Lamps, Table Lamps, Floor Lamps, Office Lighting
Architectural Lighting & Design **(213) 742-8800**
1933 S Broadway Ste 1204, Los Angeles, CA, 90007
Open to the Trade only
http://lamartdirectory.com/directory/search/showrooms/1098
Badia Design, Inc. **(818) 762-0130**
5420 Vineland Ave, N Hollywood, CA, 91601
Moroccan Lighting Fixtures are elegantly designed from a combination of brass, metal, copper, glass and tin.
info@badiadesign.com * www.badiadesign.com
Bridge Furniture & Props Los Angeles **(818) 433-7100**
We carry modern & traditional furniture, lighting, accessories, art, & rugs. Items are online for easy shopping.
Castle Antiques & Design **(818) 765-5000**
11924 Vose St, N Hollywood, CA, 91605
We offer light fixtures of different styles and sizes for rent or purchase.
info@castleantiques.net * www.castleprophouse.com
Davis Fluorescent Lighting **(310) 836-4860**
8530 Venice Blvd (in rear), Los Angeles, CA, 90034
Fluorescent & HID light fixtures, fluorescent bulbs/fluorescent light bulbs for indoor/outdoor, rentals and purchases.
davisfluorescent@sbcglobal.net
E.C. Prop Rentals **(818) 764-2008**
fluorescents, wall sconces, china hats, ext. lighting, industrial

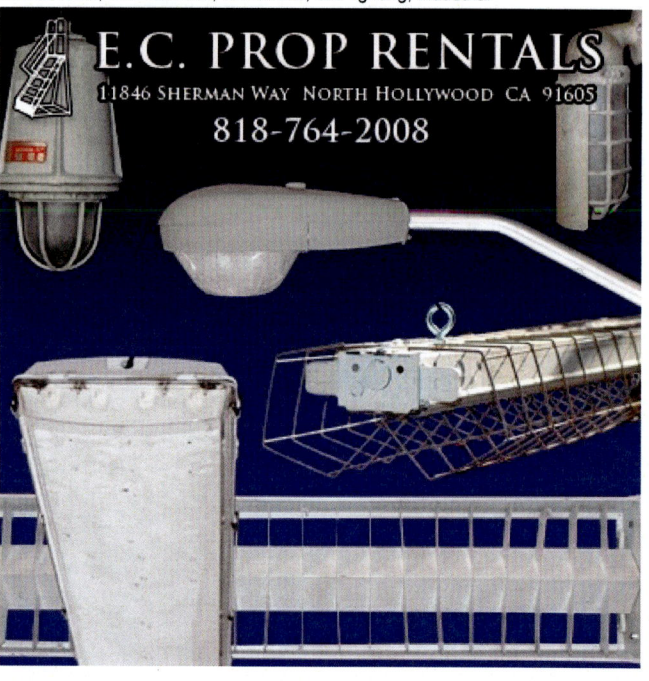

E.C. PROP RENTALS
11846 SHERMAN WAY NORTH HOLLYWOOD CA 91605
818-764-2008

Flix FX Inc. **(818) 765-3549**
7327 Lankershim Blvd #4, N Hollywood, CA, 91605
Custom light fixture fabrication
info@flixfx.com * www.flixfx.com
FormDecor, Inc. **(310) 558-2582**
America's largest event rental supplier of 20th Century furniture and accessories for Modern and Mid-Century styles.

Galerie Sommerlath - French 50s 60s   (310) 838-0102
9608 Venice Blvd, Culver City, CA, 90232
Over 10,000 sq ft of Mid-Century, 70's & 80's furniture, lighting, accessories, home decor, art, sculptures, paintings.
info@galeriesommerlath.com * www.galeriesommerlath.com

LCW Props   (818) 243-0707
Large Selection, Industrial, Residential, Commercial

Modern Props   (323) 934-3000
Contemporary light fixtures and futuristic light fixtures, lighting from chandeliers to lamps

RC Vintage, Inc.   (818) 765-7107
large selection 40s to present, huge sel. contemporary lighting

7100 TUJUNGA AVE
North Hollywood, 91605
E-MAIL
rcvintage@aol.com

California USA
Telephone: 818.765.7107
Fax: 818.765.7197
www.rcvintage.com

Sony Pictures Studios-Fixtures   (310) 244-5996
5933 W Slauson Ave, Culver City, CA, 90230
period to present day, all styles, wall, floor, commercial, drag racing lights, fluorescent, fake fire machine
www.sonypicturesstudios.com

Sony Pictures Studios-Prop House (Off Lot)   (310) 244-5999
vapor lights, light bulb socket extensions, sign lights, work lights, security lights, sconces

Universal Studios Property & Hardware Dept   (818) 777-2784
Light fixtures from all time periods, styles, and sizes.

Warner Bros. Studios Property Department   (818) 954-2181
Vapor lights, street lights, disco lights, decorative lights, coach lights, pole lights, security lights

ZG04 DECOR   (818) 853-8040
Modern Contemporary Lighting, Traditional Eclectic Lighting, Mid Century Lighting, Vintage Lighting

Light Fixtures, Period

See Also: Antiques & Antique Decorations

Alley Cats Studio Rentals   (818) 982-9178
ornate carriage street lights, vintage street lights

Castle Antiques & Design   (818) 765-5000
11924 Vose St, N Hollywood, CA, 91605
We offer light fixtures of different styles, eras, and sizes for rent or purchase.
info@castleantiques.net * www.castleprophouse.com

E.C. Prop Rentals   (818) 764-2008
working, industrial, incandescent & fluorescent, many types

Sony Pictures Studios-Fixtures   (310) 244-5996
5933 W Slauson Ave, Culver City, CA, 90230
period to present day
www.sonypicturesstudios.com

Sword & Stone   (818) 562-6548
Period sconces, candelabras

Universal Studios Property & Hardware Dept   (818) 777-2784
Period light fixture rentals

Warner Bros. Studios Property Department   (818) 954-2181

Light Fixtures, South Seas

See Also: Lamp Posts & Street Lights Lanterns*

Oceanic Arts   (562) 698-6960
pufferfish lights, glass floats in nets, tapa cloth & more

Universal Studios Property & Hardware Dept   (818) 777-2784
South sea light fixture rentals.

Warner Bros. Studios Property Department   (818) 954-2181

NEST Studio Rentals, Inc.   (818) 942-0339
wall sconces, contemp. hanging styles

Ob-jects   (818) 351-4200
contemporary light fixtures/traditional designer sconces

Old N Country Prop Shop, LLC   (818) 423-2599
A large selection of table lamps, desk lamps, hanging lamps, antique lamps, and more.

Omega/Cinema Props   (323) 466-8201

Pasadena Antique Center and Annex   (626) 449-7706
480 South Fair Oaks Ave, Pasadena, CA, 91105
Wide array of lighting from table top and floor lamps to sconces and ceiling fixtures. Representing all eras and styles.
pasadenaantiqecenterandannex@gmail.com * bit.ly/PasadenaAntiqueCenter

Practical Props Rentals   (818) 982-3198
11754 Vose St, N Hollywood, CA, 91605
Hours 8:30-4:30 M-F. new/vintage lamps, sconces, pendants, chandeliers
www.practicalprops.com

Prop Services West   (818) 503-2790

Light Strings

See Also: Chase Lights* Lighting, LED, Fiber Optic & Specialty*
Neon Lights & Signs

Amusement Svcs/Candyland Amusements (818) 266-4056
18653 Ventura Blvd Ste 235, Tarzana, CA, 91356
raymond@candylandamusements.com * www.candylandamusements.com

E.C. Prop Rentals (818) 764-2008
construction, carnival, Christmas tree lot, some cages & shades

RC Vintage, Inc. (818) 765-7107
String lights, motion animated. Strip Club. Carnival Lights. Flashing & preset,
exterior string lights, in many Colors!

ShopWildThings (928) 855-6075
2880 Sweetwater Ave, Lake Havasu City, AZ, 86406
Event Decor, Beaded Curtains, Chain Curtains, String Curtains & Columns,
Crystal Columns. Reliable service & delivery.
help@shopwildthings.com * www.shopwildthings.com

Sony Pictures Studios-Fixtures (310) 244-5996
5933 W Slauson Ave, Culver City, CA, 90230
period to present day
www.sonypicturesstudios.com

Universal Studios Property & Hardware Dept (818) 777-2784
Light string rentals, Christmas lights and more.

Warner Bros. Studios Property Department (818) 954-2181

ZG04 DECOR (818) 853-8040
Large bulb light strings, carnival light strings

Lighters

See: Smoking Products

Lighting & Sound, Concert/Theatrical/DJ/VJ

See Also: Events, Design/Planning/Production* Events,
Entertainment* Lighting Control Boards* Disco Balls/Mirror Balls &
Drivers* Rock 'n' Roll Lighting & Sound* Scaffolding/Lighting Towers*
Searchlights/Skytrackers, Architectural Lights* Special Effects,
Lighting & Lasers* Stage Lighting, Film/Video/TV* Stages, Portable &
Steel Deck

Astro Audio Video Lighting, Inc. (818) 549-9915
6615 San Fernando Rd, Glendale, CA, 91201
Sound & lighting, all sizes, concert/stage/club/church/school/DJ equipment and
staging
www.astroavl.com

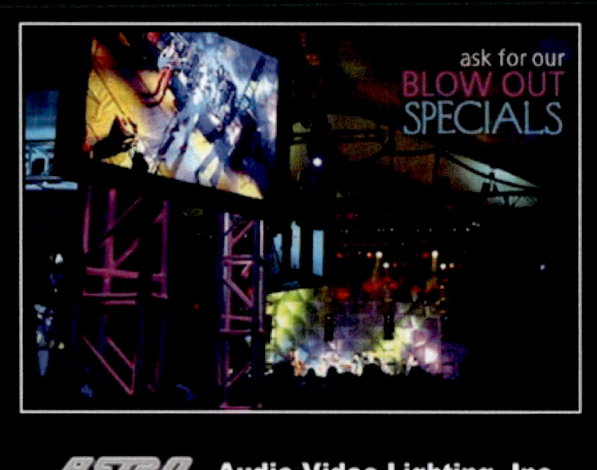

Barbizon Lighting Co. (866) 502-2724
8269 E 23rd Ave Suite 111, Denver CO, 80238
catalog sales; lighting & rigging equipment, see web site for locations
www.barbizon.com

Coast Recording Audio Props (818) 755-4692
10715 Magnolia Blvd, N Hollywood, CA, 91601
DJ Setup, Sound Board for Concert and Theatre.
props@coastrecording.com * www.coastrecordingprops.com

Derksen USA, Inc. (916) 903-7515
4934 Pathway Ct. Fair Oaks, CA 95528
custom gobos delivered anywhere in 14 days or less
www.derksen.com

EFX- Event Special Effects (626) 888-2239
125 Railroad Ave, Monrovia, CA, 91016
Stage Lighting- LED Screens- Event Lighting
info@efxla.com * www.efxla.com

History For Hire, Inc. (818) 765-7767
vintage lighting, dimmers

Musson Theatrical TV Film (800) 843-2837
890 Walsh Avenue, Santa Clara, CA, 95050
catalog sales; lighting, sound, expendables
www.musson.com

NBCUniversal LightBlade LED Lighting (818) 777-1671
Uses 30-70% less power than equivalent conventional production lighting -
Superior quality of light for stage & location
brandon.rensvold@nbcuni.com * www.lightbladeled.com

New Mexico Lighting & Grip Co. (505) 506-6564
I-25 Studios 9201 Pan American Fwy NE, Albuquerque, NM, 87113
Grip & rigging equip. & services, lighting & sound
colin.pearman@nmlgc.com * www.newmexicolightingandgrip.com

Strong International, Inc. (402) 453-4444
11422 Miracle Hill Dr Suite 300, Omaha NE, 68154
Digital lighting, entertainment lighting, cinema projection equipment
http://ballantynestrong.com

TLS Productions, Inc. (855) 515-8577
78 Jackson Plaza, Ann Arbor, MI, 48103
installation too
www.tlsproductionsinc.com

Universal Studios Set Lighting Dept (818) 777-1459
100 Universal City Plaza, Universal City, CA, 91608
Extensive inventory of quality stage & location lighting
sean.buckler@nbcuni.com * universalstudioslot.com/set-lighting

Lighting Control Boards

See Also: Control Boards* Electronic Equipment (Dressing)

Astro Audio Video Lighting, Inc. (818) 549-9915
6615 San Fernando Rd, Glendale, CA, 91201
Lighting control boards, lighting control systems, DMX lighting controllers, light
control boards and more.
www.astroavl.com

E.C. Prop Rentals (818) 764-2008
props-2 castered Mole Richardson units

History For Hire, Inc. (818) 765-7767
period, motion picture & theatrical

LCW Props (818) 243-0707
A Specialty Of Ours, Rigged, Period - Present

Lighting, Industrial

See Also: Caged Vapor Proof Lights* China Hat Lights* Egg Crate Bottom Fluorescents* Light Fixtures

AIR Designs (818) 768-6639
Warehouse Lights, Yard Lights, Work Lights
Alley Cats Studio Rentals (818) 982-9178
Fluorescents, Egg Crate Fluorescents, and more
E.C. Prop Rentals (818) 764-2008
7000 incandescent & fluorescent, many styles/multiples

E.C. PROP RENTALS
11846 SHERMAN WAY NORTH HOLLYWOOD CA 91605
818-764-2008

LCW Props (818) 243-0707
Large Selection Of Industrial Lighting, mercury Vapor, HPS, Flourescent

Lighting, LED, Fiber Optic & Specialty

See Also: Gobos/Projection* Lighting & Sound, Concert/Theatrical/DJ/VJ

Astro Audio Video Lighting, Inc. (818) 549-9915
6615 San Fernando Rd, Glendale, CA, 91201
LED lighting and specialty lighting for concerts, festivals and events.
www.astroavl.com
Charisma Design Studio, Inc. (818) 252-6611
8414 San Fernando Road, Sun Valley, CA, 91352
custom LED & fiber optic lights
info@charismadesign.com * www.charismadesign.com
EFX- Event Special Effects (626) 888-2239
125 Railroad Ave, Monrovia, CA, 91016
LED Stage Lighting- LED Screens- Event Lighting
info@efxla.com * www.efxla.com
Filmmaker Prod. Svcs-Atlanta @ Tyler Perry Studios (404) 450-1968
2115 Sylvan Road, Atlanta, GA, 30344
Grip & rigging equip. & services, lighting & sound
chad.garcia@nbcuni.com * www.filmmakerproductionservices.com
Filmmaker Prod. Svcs-Chicago @ Cinespace Chicago (678) 628-1997
2558 W 16th Street Dock #4, Chicago, IL, 60608
Grip & rigging equip. & services, lighting & sound
patrick.flanagan@nbcuni.com * www.filmmakerproductionservices.com

Lazarus Lighting Design, Inc (800) 553-5554
14701 Arminta St, Van Nuys, CA, 91402
custom fiber optic signs systems. no LEDs.
www.lldco.com
Mandex LED Displays (805) 497-8006
3248 Jessica St, Newbury Park, CA, 91320
LEDIT-Flex long scrolling full color LED tickers. Entertain, create themed memorable info. at your next event.
info@ledsignage.com * www.ledsignage.com
NBCUniversal LightBlade LED Lighting (818) 777-1671
Uses 30-70% less power than equivalent conventional production lighting - Superior quality of light for stage & location
brandon.rensvold@nbcuni.com * www.lightbladeled.com
Set Masters (818) 982-1506
24853 Avenue Rockefeller, Valencia, CA, 91355
Off the shelf purchases
info@setmasters.com * www.setmasters.com
ShopWildThings (928) 855-6075
2880 Sweetwater Ave, Lake Havasu City, AZ, 86406
Event Decor, Beaded Curtains, Chain Curtains, String Curtains & Columns, Crystal Columns. Reliable service & delivery.
help@shopwildthings.com * www.shopwildthings.com
Universal Studios Set Lighting Dept (818) 777-1459
100 Universal City Plaza, Universal City, CA, 91608
Extensive inventory of quality stage & location lighting
sean.buckler@nbcuni.com * universalstudioslot.com/set-lighting

Lime Wash

See: Paint & Painting Supplies

Limousine Service

AM-PM Limousine Service (800) 995-AMPM
W. Hollywood, CA, 90046
flat rates to all airports, beautiful cars & great rates
www.am-pmlimo.com
Ascot Limousine Service (310) 559-5959
375 E. Beach Ave., Inglewood, CA 90302
Limos, sedans, SUVs, vans
info@ascotlimousine.com * www.ascotlimousine.com
Avalon Transportation (800) 528-2566
5534 Westlawn Ave, Los Angeles, CA 90066
Flat rate airport service, sedans, limos
www.avalontrans.com
Limousine Connection (818) 766-4311
5118 Vineland Ave, N Hollywood, CA, 91601
Flat rate airport service, limos, sedans & stretches
reservations@limousineconnection.com * www.limousineconnection.com

Linens, Household

See Also: Slipcovers

Badia Design, Inc. (818) 762-0130
5420 Vineland Ave, N Hollywood, CA, 91601
Moroccan kilim pillows also, traditional designs
info@badiadesign.com * www.badiadesign.com

GBS Linens (714) 778-6448
305 N. Muller, Anaheim, CA, 92801
Wholesale specialty linens.
www.gbslinens.com

History For Hire, Inc. (818) 765-7767
huge selection of blankets, also quilts

International Down & Linen (310) 657-8243
8687 Melrose Ave B368, Los Angeles, CA, 90069
luxury linens, custom sewing & embroidery, custom sized pillows & comforters,
silk bedding
www.internationaldownandlinen.com

Little Bohemia Rentals (818) 853-7506
11940 Sherman Rd, N Hollywood, CA, 91605
Blankets, throws, tablecloths.
sales@wearelittlebohemia.com * www.wearelittlebohemia.com

Ob-jects (818) 351-4200
Household linens; antique/Aubusson contemp/country pillows; Beacon/chenille
throws, fine sel American quilts

Old N Country Prop Shop, LLC (818) 423-2599
Assorted blankets, quilts, cloths, and more.

Omega/Cinema Props (323) 466-8201
lrg sel bedding, blankets, quilts, decorative pillows, will also fabricate

Pier 1 Imports (Hollywood) (323) 466-3443
5711 Hollywood Blvd, Hollywood, CA, 90028
www.pier1.com

Prop Services West (818) 503-2790
decorative pillows

Sony Pictures Studios-Linens, Drapes, Rugs (310) 244-5999
5933 W Slauson Ave, Culver City, CA, 90230
tablecloths, napkins, decorative pillows, bedding/pillows, bedroom dress,
kitchen, and bath
www.sonypicturesstudios.com

Sony Pictures Studios-Prop House (Off Lot) (310) 244-5999
bedspreads for queen, king, twin, and full; airplane blankets, period blankets,
prison blankets, dust comforter, and more

Universal Studios Property & Hardware Dept (818) 777-2784
Household linens from different time period for rent.

Warner Bros. Drapery, Upholstery & Flooring (818) 954-1831
4000 Warner Bros Bldg 30, Burbank, CA, 91522
Bedding; Comforters; Pillows; Duvets; Table cloths; Napkins; Runners; Picnic;
Towels; Blankets
wbsfdrapery@warnerbros.com * www.wbdrapery.com

Warner Bros. Studios Property Department (818) 954-2181
Table linens, towels, sheets, napkins, see WBSF Drapery Department

ZG04 DECOR (818) 853-8040
Bedding, Bathroom Linens, Kitchen linens, Blankets

Linens, Tabletop & Events

See Also: Events, Decorations, Supplies & Services Linens,*
Household

Omega/Cinema Props (323) 466-8201

Resource One (818) 343-3451
6900 Canby Ave Ste 106, Reseda, CA, 91325
upscale table linens, unusual combinations, custom fabr.
http://resourceoneinc.com

ZG04 DECOR (818) 853-8040

Lingerie

See: Underwear & Lingerie, Bloomers, Corsets, Etc.

Linoleum

See: Carpet & Flooring

Liquid Iron

See: Paint & Painting Supplies

Liquor Bottles

AIR Designs (818) 768-6639
Liquor, Wine, Beer, Champagne, Large Quantity, Multiples of Cleared

The Hand Prop Room LP. (323) 931-1534
period-modern, breakaway, cust. labels

History For Hire, Inc. (818) 765-7767
all periods

LCW Props (818) 243-0707
New, Old, We Own The Recycling Center Next Door. Unlimited Quantity,
Cleared

Modern Props (323) 934-3000
contemporary liquor bottles, multiples

Omega/Cinema Props (323) 466-8201
Decanters of many kinds, scotch bottles, rye bottles, bourbon bottles and
more.

RC Vintage, Inc. (818) 765-7107
Large Assortment, faux liquor bottles, bar shelf liquor bottles, oversized
bottles/oversized liquor bottles

Sony Pictures Studios-Prop House (Off Lot) (310) 244-5999

Universal Studios Property & Hardware Dept (818) 777-2784
Liquor bottle rentals from all time periods and locales.

Liquor Store

See: Drugstore/Apothecary

Livestock

See: Animals (Live), Services, Trainers & Wranglers Horses, Horse*
Equipment, Livestock Western Dressing*

Loading Dock Dressing

See Also: Barrels & Drums, Wood/Metal/Plastic Crates/ Vaults**
Furniture Dollies, Pads & Hand Trucks Nautical Dressing & Props**
Pallets Warehouse Dressing*

Alley Cats Studio Rentals (818) 982-9178
pallets, drums, hand carts, coastal signage

E.C. Prop Rentals (818) 764-2008
1-stop shop for crates, drums, dollies, pallets, jacks, signage

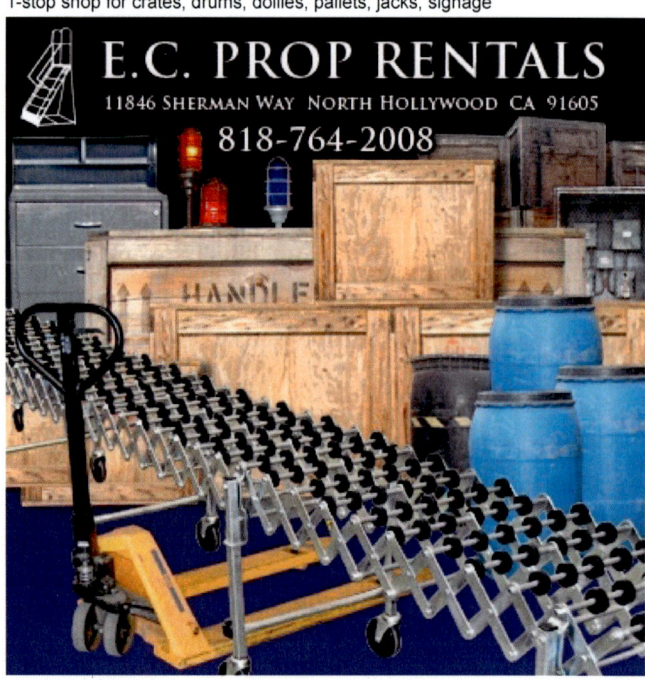

The Hand Prop Room LP. (323) 931-1534
drums, crates, pallets, dollies, carts

LCW Props (818) 243-0707
Crates, Drums, Pallet Jacks, Forklifts, Dollies, Signage

Lobby Cards

See: Posters, Art/Movie/Travel/Wanted Etc. Signs*

Lobby Seating

See Also: Dentist Equipment* Hotel, Motel, Inn, Lodge* Medical
Equip/Furniture, Graphics/Supplies
Alpha Companies - Spellman Desk Co. (818) 504-9090
medical office seating, dentists office seating, hotel lobby seating
ZG04 DECOR (818) 853-8040
Benches, Club-chairs, Sofas, Multiples

Lobster/Fish Traps

Alley Cats Studio Rentals (818) 982-9178
wood, metal, slat, also have cargo nets
History For Hire, Inc. (818) 765-7767

Locations

See: Locations, Airport Dressing & Hangars* Locations, Homes &
Residential* Locations, Outdoor Ranches/Fields/Exterior* Locations,
Businesses & Shops* Locations, Backlots/Standing Sets* Locations,
Stages/Studios, Film/TV/Events* Locations, Insert Stages &
Theatres* Locations, Events Destinations

Locations, Airport Dressing & Hangars

See Also: Model Ships/Planes/Trains/Autos Etc.* Security
Walk-Through & Baggage Alarms* Aerospace
Aero Mock-Ups (888) 662-5877
Aviation prop house. Complete airplane & airport dressing, service area gallery,
airports/airport terminals and jetways.
E.C. Prop Rentals (818) 764-2008
Int. Hangar, Ext. Ramp, Terminal Seats, Runway Lights, Stanchions, Rolling
Ladders
LCW Props (818) 243-0707
Terminal Seating, Baggage X-Ray Machines, Security Wands & Walk Through
Metal Detectors, Kiosks, Stewardess Carts
Modern Props (323) 934-3000
x-ray, walk-thru detectors, hand held metal detectors, seating, counters, Airport
Bench units, hand held metal detectors
RC Vintage, Inc. (818) 765-7107
Airport Seating, airport seats, modern airport seats, vintage airport seats,
stanchions, airport phone booths.
RJR Props (404) 349-7600
Airport dressing including x-ray baggage scanners, metal detector wands,
walkthrough metal detectors and more.

Locations, Backlots/Standing Sets

See Also: Locations, Insert Stages & Theatres
20th Century Fox Stages & Exteriors (310) 369-2786
10201 W Pico Blvd, Los Angeles, CA, 90067
www.foxstudios.com
The Studios At Paramount New York Streets (323) 956-8811
5555 Melrose Ave, Hollywood, CA, 90038
www.thestudiosatparamount.com
Universal Studios Stages & Backlot (818) 777-3000
100 Universal City Plaza, Universal City, CA, 91608
Universal Studios backlot
universal.locations@nbcuni.com *
http://universalstudioslot.com/stages-and-backlot
The Walt Disney Studios (818) 560-7450
500 S Buena Vista St, Burbank, CA, 91505
www.stu-ops.disney.com
Warner Bros. Studios Backlot (818) 954-2577
4000 Warner Blvd Bldg 34, Burbank, CA, 91522
Everything from a Midwest town center to a jungle lagoon are on the Studio's
backlot.
wbsfoperations@warnerbros.com * studiofacilities.warnerbros.com

Locations, Businesses & Shops

AIR Designs (818) 768-6639
Middleton Ranch, 120 Acre Filming Location, 30's Gas Station, Modern Gas
Station, Diner, Convenience Store
Altadena Ale & Wine House (626) 354-3562
2329 Fair Oaks Ave, Altadena, CA, 91001
Local pub location/bar location for filming. In addition to the bar and lounge
there's an outdoor patio on the premises.
info@AltadenaAleHouse.com * www.altadenaalehouse.com
Fortune Trading Co & Import Bazaar (323) 222-6287
483 Gin Ling Way (Old Chinatown), Los Angeles, CA, 90012
1000s of copies of many styles of paper lanterns, masks. Costumes, lions,
dragons, gongs, scrolls, Oriental gift items
fortunetradingco@gmail.com
International Printing Museum (714) 529-1832
315 Torrance Blvd, Carson, CA, 90745
antique printing/office equipment 1450-1980. old presses, machines, complete
shops
mail@printmuseum.org * www.printmuseum.org
Koch's Movie Ranch (661) 268-1341
7650 Soledad Canyon Road, Acton, CA, 93510
Locations: House, Cabin, Mineshaft, Cave, Barn, Outhouse, Restaurant,
70,000 gallon pond w/ waterfall & gazebo, Church
customerservice@kochs.com * www.kochsmovieranch.com
Living Art Aquatic Design, Inc. (310) 822-7484
2301 South Sepulveda Blvd, Los Angeles, CA, 90064
One of a kind 2000 sq ft aquarium showroom and aquarium store for saltwater
fish and freshwater fish.
ron@aquatic2000.com * www.aquatic2000.com
MorguePropRentals.com (818) 957-2178
5134 Valley Blvd, Los Angeles, CA, 90032
set-up for lighting/cameras, morgue location, period medical lab
info@1800autopsy.com * www.morgueproprentals.com
Mountain View Cemetery & Mausoleum (626) 794-7133
2400 N Fair Oaks Ave, Altadena, CA, 91001
Cemetery and mausoleum filming locations
www.mtn-view.com
Pro Boxing Supplies (818) 760-9500
4405 Laurel Canyon Blvd, Studio City, CA, 91607
Boxing studio and martial arts studio location for rent.
proboxingsupplies@yahoo.com * www.proboxingsupplies.com
Sword & Stone (818) 562-6548
medieval rooms & blacksmith workshop location

Locations, Events Destinations

See Also: Locations, Insert Stages & Theatres* Locations,
Stages/Studios, Film/TV/Events
Aquarium of the Pacific (562) 590-3100
100 Aquarium Way, Long Beach, CA, 90802
call Group Sales for location shoots, (562) 951-1684
www.aquariumofpacific.org
Cabrillo Marine Aquarium (310) 548-7562
3720 Stephen M White Dr, San Pedro, CA, 90731
www.cabrilloaq.org
Castle Park (951) 785-3000
3500 Polk St, Riverside, CA, 92505
miniature golf, arcade, haunted house, etc.
www.castlepark.com
Descanso Gardens (818) 949-4200
1418 Descanso Dr, La Canada, CA, 91011
contact "filming/rentals dept"
www.descansogardens.org
Disneyland (714) 781-4565
1313 Disneyland Dr, Anaheim, CA, 92802
www.disneyland.com
Disney's California Adventure (714) 781-4636
1313 Disneyland Dr, Anaheim, CA, 92803
www.disneyland.com
The Hollywood Museum (323) 464-7776
1660 N. Highland Ave, Hollywood, CA, 90028
events & location space
www.thehollywoodmuseum.com

**LISTINGS FOR THIS CATEGORY CONTINUE ON THE
FOLLOWING PAGE**

The Japanese Garden   (818) 756-8166
6100 Woodley Ave, Van Nuys, CA, 91406
www.thejapanesegarden.com

Knott's Berry Farm   (714) 220-5200
8039 Beach Blvd, Buena Park, CA, 90620
www.knotts.com

Legoland California   (760) 918-5346
1 Legoland Drive, Carlsbad, CA, 92008
www.legoland.com

Monterey Bay Aquarium   (831) 648-4800
886 Cannery Row, Monterey, CA, 93940
www.montereybayaquarium.org

Raging Waters   (909) 802-2200
111 Raging Waters Dr, San Dimas, CA, 91773
www.ragingwaters.com

RMS Queen Mary   (562) 499-1771
1126 Queens Hwy, Long Beach, CA, 90802
End of the 710 Fwy, in the water
www.queenmary.com

San Diego Zoo Safari Park   (760) 747-8702
15500 San Pasqual Valley Rd, Escondido, CA, 92027
www.sdzsafaripark.org

Sea World San Diego   (619) 226-3901
500 Sea World Dr, San Diego, CA, 92109
www.seaworld.com

Six Flags Hurricane Harbor   (661) 255-4100
26101 Magic Mountain Pkwy, Valencia, CA, 91355
www.sixflags.com/hurricaneharborla

Six Flags Magic Mountain   (661) 255-4100
26101 Magic Mountain Pkwy, Valencia, CA, 91355
www.sixflags.com/magicmountain

Sony Pictures Studios-Events   (310) 244-4456
10202 W Washington Blvd, Los Angeles, CA, 90232
www.sonypicturesstudios.com

Universal Studios Hollywood   (800) 892-1979
100 Universal City Plaza, Universal City, CA, 91608
www.filmmakersdestination.com

Universal Studios Special Events   (818) 777-9466
100 Universal City Plaza, Universal City, CA, 91608
universal.specialevents@nbcuni.com * universalstudioslot.com/special-events

Locations, Homes & Residential

Caravan West Productions   (661) 268-8300
35660 Jayhawker Rd, Aqua Dulce, CA, 91390
1890s house & 1950s house, 8-building frontier town. 2,488 acres in the 30 mile zone. Miles of dirt roads.
caravanwest@earthlink.net * www.caravanwest.com

Check The Gate Productions   (818) 903-4035
18616 Ingomar St, Reseda, CA, 91335
4,000 sqft. ranch style event space & filming location w/ 30,000 gallon Koi pond with waterfall and indoor viewing area.
joemayjoemay@gmail.com * www.40palmtrees.com

Koch's Movie Ranch   (661) 268-1341
7650 Soledad Canyon Road, Acton, CA, 93510
Locations: House, Cabin, Mineshaft, Cave, Barn, Outhouse, Restaurant, 70,000 gallon pond w/ waterfall & gazebo, Church
customerservice@kochs.com * www.kochsmovieranch.com

Locations, Insert Stages & Theatres

See Also: Locations, Airport Dressing & Hangars* Locations, Events Destinations* Locations, Stages/Studios, Film/TV/Events* Locations, Backlots/Standing Sets* Locations, Businesses & Shops* Locations, Outdoor Ranches/Fields/Exterior* Locations, Homes & Residential

Aero Mock-Ups   (888) 662-5877
Full service aviation prop house. airplane cabins onsite. Airline sets, ticketing area, TSA Security, boarding area, etc

Ahmanson Theater   (213) 628-2772
135 N Grand, Los Angeles, CA, 90012
for admin office, see Dorothy Chandler Pavillion, Filming (213) 972-7334, Rentals (213) 972-7478
www.centertheatregroup.org

AIR Designs   (818) 768-6639
Middleton Ranch, 120 Acre Filming Location, 30's Gas Station, Modern Gas Station, Diner, Convenience Store

California Theatre of Performing Arts   (909) 885-5152
562 W 4th St, San Bernardino, CA, 92402
www.californiatheatre.net

Caravan West Productions   (661) 268-8300
35660 Jayhawker Rd, Aqua Dulce, CA, 91390
8-building frontier town for print works. 2,488 acres in the 30 mile zone. Miles of dirt roads.
caravanwest@earthlink.net * www.caravanwest.com

WESTERN LOCATION
IN THE 30 MILE ZONE
PARKING FOR BASECAMP
MILES OF DIRT ROAD

Dolby Theater   (323) 308-6300
6801 Hollywood Blvd Ste 180 Admin, Hollywood, CA, 90028
www.dolbytheatre.com

Dorothy Chandler Pavilion   (213) 972-7211
135 N Grand Ave, Los Angeles, CA, 90012
venue for Music Center, Opera, Master Chorale admin office for Ahmanson & Mark Taper
www.musiccenter.org

El Capitan Theater   (323) 467-7674
6838 Hollywood Blvd, Hollywood, CA, 90028
www.elcapitantheatre.com

The Fonda Theater   (323) 464-0808
6126 Hollywood Blvd, Hollywood, CA, 90028
www.fondatheatre.com

Fortune Trading Co & Import Bazaar   (323) 222-6287
483 Gin Ling Way (Old Chinatown), Los Angeles, CA, 90012
1000s of copies of many styles of paper lanterns, masks. Costumes, lions, dragons, gongs, scrolls, Oriental gift items
fortunetradingco@gmail.com

The Forum   (310) 330-7300
3900 W Manchester Blvd, Inglewood, CA, 90305
www.fabulousforum.com

Greek Theatre   (844) 524-7335
2700 N Vermont Ave, Los Angeles, CA, 90027
www.lagreektheatre.com

Hollywood Bowl   (323) 850-2000
2301 N Highland Ave, Los Angeles, CA, 90078
www.hollywoodbowl.com

Hollywood Palladium   (323) 962-7600
6215 Sunset Blvd, Hollywood, CA, 90028
www.thehollywoodpalladium.com

International Printing Museum   (714) 529-1832
315 Torrance Blvd, Carson, CA, 90745
antique printing/office equipment 1450-1980. old presses, machines, complete shops
mail@printmuseum.org * www.printmuseum.org

John Anson Ford Theaters   (323) 856-5793
2580 Cahuenga Blvd E, Los Angeles, CA, 90068
box office (323) 461-3673
www.fordtheatres.org

Living Art Aquatic Design, Inc. (310) 822-7484
2301 South Sepulveda Blvd, Los Angeles, CA, 90064
One of a kind 2000 sq ft aquarium showroom and aquarium store for saltwater fish and freshwater fish.
ron@aquatic2000.com * www.aquatic2000.com

Local # 399 Studio Transportation Drivers (818) 985-7374
4747 Vineland Ave, N Hollywood, CA, 91602
Teamsters Local 399. Hire an experienced and knowledgeable location manager!
www.ht399.org

Los Angeles Memorial Coliseum (213) 747-7111
3911 S Figueroa St, Los Angeles, CA, 90037
www.lacoliseum.com

Mark Taper Forum (213) 628-2772
135 N Grand Ave, Los Angeles, CA, 90012
for admin office, see Dorothy Chandler Pavilion
www.centertheatregroup.org

Microsoft Theater (213) 763-6030
777 Chick Hearn Court, Los Angeles, CA, 90015
www.microsofttheater.com

MorguePropRentals.com (818) 957-2178
5134 Valley Blvd, Los Angeles, CA, 90032
set-up for lighting/cameras, morgue, period medical lab
info@1800autopsy.com * www.morgueproprentals.com

Pantages Theatre (323) 468-1700
6233 Hollywood Blvd, Hollywood, CA, 90028
www.hollywoodpantages.com

The Pasadena Playhouse (626) 356-7529
39 S El Molino Ave, Pasadena, CA, 91101
www.pasadenaplayhouse.org

Rancho Santa Ana Botanic Garden (909) 625-8767
1500 N College Ave, Claremont, CA, 91711
86 acre garden, native Cal. plants, herbarium, call X251 for visit info
www.rsabg.org

Repro-Graphic Supply (818) 771-9066
9838 Glenoaks Blvd, Sun Valley, CA, 91352
Bar Location, Restaurant Location, and House Location.
info@reprographicsupply.com * www.reprographicsupply.com

Saban Theatre (888) 645-5006
8440 Wilshire Blvd, Beverly Hills, CA, 90211
www.sabantheatre.org

San Gabriel Mission Playhouse (626) 308-2865
320 S Mission Drive, San Gabriel, CA, 91776
Location, Sound Stage, Venue, Rehearsal Space, Theater, Spanish style, wurlitzer organ
swilkinson@missionplayhouse.org * www.missionplayhouse.org

San Manuel Amphitheater (909) 880-6500
2575 Glen Helen Pkwy, San Bernardino, CA, 92407
www.sanmanuelamphitheater.net

Shrine Auditorium (213) 748-5116
665 W Jefferson Blvd, Los Angeles, CA, 90007
www.shrineauditorium.com

Sketch Paper Design (818) 442-0284
7771 Lemona Ave, Van Nuys, CA, 91405
White Cyc stage that can be painted depending on production's needs, stage for rent
info@sketchpaperdesign.com * www.sketchpaperdesign.com

Sword & Stone (818) 562-6548
medieval rooms & blacksmith workshop location

The Walt Disney Concert Hall (213) 972-7211
135 N Grand Ave, Los Angeles, CA, 90012
http://www.wdch.com/

The Wiltern (213) 388-1400
3790 Wilshire Blvd, Los Angeles, CA, 90010
call (213) 380-5005 for box office
www.thewiltern.com

Locations, Outdoor Ranches/Fields/Exterior

AIR Designs (818) 768-6639
Middleton Ranch, 120 Acre Filming Location, 30's Gas Station, Modern Gas Station, Diner, Convenience Store

The Brig Parking Lot (310) 709-3540
1515 Abbot Kinney Blvd #200, Venice, CA, 90291
6700 sf 30 cars, Only large surface lot in the heart of Abbot Kinney for parking catering craft wardrobe. Vintage mural.
pariswst@gte.net

Caravan West Productions (661) 268-8300
35660 Jayhawker Rd, Aqua Dulce, CA, 91390
2,488 acre land & a 23 acre horse ranch in the 30 mile zone; covered arena, modern bunk house, access to Vasquez Rocks.
caravanwest@earthlink.net * www.caravanwest.com

Koch's Movie Ranch (661) 268-1341
7650 Soledad Canyon Road, Acton, CA, 93510
Locations: House, Cabin, Mineshaft, Cave, Barn, Outhouse, Restaurant, 70,000 gallon pond w/ waterfall & gazebo, Church
customerservice@kochs.com * www.kochsmovieranch.com

Locations, Stages/Studios, Film/TV/Events

See Also: Locations, Insert Stages & Theatres

ABC 7 Broadcast Center (818) 560-7450
500 Circle Seven Dr, Glendale, CA, 91201

Ahmanson Theater (213) 628-2772
135 N Grand, Los Angeles, CA, 90012
for admin office, see Dorothy Chandler Pavillion, Filming (213) 972-7334, Rentals (213) 972-7478
www.centertheatregroup.org

Albuquerque Studios (505) 227-2000
5650 University Blvd SE, Albuquerque, NM, 87106
www.abqstudios.com

Anaheim Convention Center (714) 765-8950
800 W Katella Ave, Anaheim, CA, 92802
www.anaheimconventioncenter.com

Anaheim Grove (714) 712-2700
2200 E Katella Ave, Anaheim, CA, 92806
event inquiries: (714) 712-2703
www.citynationalgroveofanaheim.com

Angel Stadium of Anaheim (714) 940-2000
2000 Gene Autry Way, Anaheim, CA, 92806
http://losangeles.angels.mlb.com/ana/ballpark/index.jsp

The Barker Hangar Santa Monica Air Center (310) 390-9071
3021 Airport Ave Ste 203, Santa Monica, CA, 90405
Large clearspan interior, high ceilings
www.barkerhangar.com

Ben Kitay Studios (323) 466-9015
1015 N Cahuenga Blvd, Hollywood, CA, 90038
www.benkitay.com

The Burbank Studios (818) 840-3000
3000 W Alameda Ave, Burbank, CA, 91523
www.theburbankstudios.com

California Theatre of Performing Arts (909) 885-5152
562 W 4th St, San Bernardino, CA, 92402
www.californiatheatre.net

CBS Studio Center (818) 655-5000
4024 Radford Ave, Studio City, CA, 91604
Residential streets, central park, new york street, and subway car mock up and subway station mock up.
www.cbssc.com

CBS Television City (323) 575-2676
7800 Beverly Blvd, Los Angeles, CA, 90036
www.cbstelevisioncity.com

Cerritos P.A.C. (562) 916-8510
12700 Center Court Dr, Cerritos, CA, 90703
www.cerritoscenter.com

Chandler Valley Center Studios (818) 424-4551
13927 Saticoy St, Van Nuys, CA, 91402
Commercials & music videos, TV/Movies
www.cvcstudios.com

The Culver Studios (310) 202-1234
9336 W Washington Blvd, Culver City, CA, 90232
www.theculverstudios.com

Delfino Studios (818) 361-2421
12501 Gladstone Ave, Sylmar, CA, 91342
www.delfinostudios.com

depict (323) 222-1001
1460 Naud St, Los Angeles, CA, 90012
info@depict33.com * www.depict33.com

Dodger Stadium (866) 363-4377
1000 Elysian Park Ave, Los Angeles, CA, 90012
http://losangeles.dodgers.mlb.com

Dolby Theater (323) 308-6300
6801 Hollywood Blvd Ste 180 Admin, Hollywood, CA, 90028
www.dolbytheatre.com

Dorothy Chandler Pavilion (213) 972-7211
135 N Grand Ave, Los Angeles, CA, 90012
venue for Music Center, Opera, Master Chorale admin office for Ahmanson & Mark Taper
www.musiccenter.org

El Capitan Theater (323) 467-7674
6838 Hollywood Blvd, Hollywood, CA, 90028
www.elcapitantheatre.com

Empire Studio (818) 840-1400
1845 Empire Ave, Burbank, CA, 91504
www.lbimedia.com

LISTINGS FOR THIS CATEGORY CONTINUE ON THE FOLLOWING PAGE

ENOX Filming & Concert Location   (323) 770-4822
4550-4560 Worth St, Los Angeles, CA, 90063
Warehouse location complete with large parking lot, loading dock and high
ceiling.
catx4046@gmail.com * www.enoxevents.com

The Fonda Theater   (323) 464-0808
6126 Hollywood Blvd, Hollywood, CA, 90028
www.fondatheatre.com

The Forum   (310) 330-7300
3900 W Manchester Blvd, Inglewood, CA, 90305
www.fabulousforum.com

Glendale Production Center   (818) 550-6000
1239 S Glendale Ave, Glendale, CA, 91205
www.glendalestudios.com

GMT Studios   (310) 649-3733
5751 Buckingham Pkwy, Culver City, CA, 90230
www.gmtstudios.com

Greek Theatre   (844) 524-7335
2700 N Vermont Ave, Los Angeles, CA, 90027
www.lagreektheatre.com

Historic Hudson Studios   (323) 461-1044
1106 N Hudson Ave, Hollywood, CA, 90038
Boutique photo studio: wifi, meeting area, prep kitchen, set kitchen,
diffused/black out curtains & addl. equipment.
info@historichudsonstudios.com * www.historichudsonstudios.com

Historic Hudson Studios
www.historichudsonstudios.com
323.461.1044

Hollywood Bowl   (323) 850-2000
2301 N Highland Ave, Los Angeles, CA, 90078
www.hollywoodbowl.com

Hollywood Center Studios   (323) 860-0000
1040 N Las Palmas Ave, Los Angeles, CA, 90038
see floor plans, lighting/grip & tech dept on our website
www.hollywoodcenter.com

Hollywood Palladium   (323) 962-7600
6215 Sunset Blvd, Hollywood, CA, 90028
www.thehollywoodpalladium.com

The Honda Center, AKA Arrowhead Pond   (714) 704-2400
2695 E. Katella Ave, Anaheim, CA, 92806
www.hondacenter.com

John Anson Ford Theaters   (323) 856-5793
2580 Cahuenga Blvd E, Los Angeles, CA, 90068
box office (323) 461-3673
www.fordtheatres.org

KCAL TV Studios   (818) 655-2000
4200 Radford Ave, Studio City, CA, 91604
http://losangeles.cbslocal.com/station/cbs-kcal/

KCBS TV Studios   (818) 655-2000
4200 Radford Ave, Studio City, CA, 91604
http://losangeles.cbslocal.com/station/cbs-kcal/

KCET TV Studios   (747) 201-5258
2900 W Alameda Ave, Burbank, CA, 91505
contact@kcet.org * www.kcet.org

KLCS TV Studios   (213) 241-4000
1061 W Temple St, Los Angeles, CA, 90012
http://klcs.org/

KMEX TV Studios (Univision)   (310) 216-3434
5999 Center Drive, Los Angeles, CA, 90045
losangeles.univision.com

Koch's Movie Ranch   (661) 268-1341
7650 Soledad Canyon Road, Acton, CA, 93510
Locations: House, Cabin, Mineshaft, Cave, Barn, Outhouse, Restaurant,
70,000 gallon pond w/ waterfall & gazebo, Church
customerservice@kochs.com * www.kochsmovieranch.com

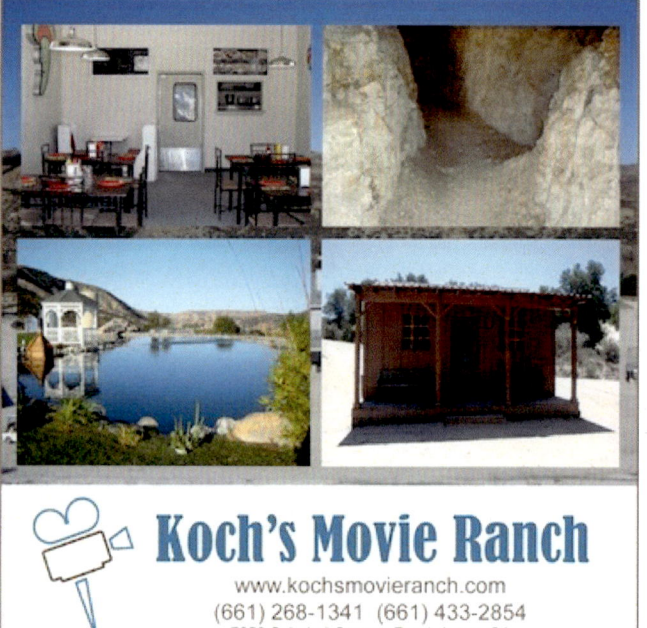

Koch's Movie Ranch
www.kochsmovieranch.com
(661) 268-1341 (661) 433-2854
7650 Soledad Canyon Road, Acton, CA

KTLA TV Studios   (323) 460-5500
5800 Sunset Blvd, Los Angeles, CA, 90028
www.ktla.com

KTTV TV Fox 11 Studios   (310) 584-2000
1999 S Bundy Dr, Los Angeles, CA, 90025
www.myfoxLA.com

The L. A. Lofts   (323) 462-5880
6442 Santa Monica Blvd Ste 203, Los Angeles, CA, 90038
www.thelalofts.com

Lacy Street Production Center   (323) 222-8872
2630 Lacy St, Los Angeles, CA, 90031
standing sets, music videos, commercials
www.lacystreet.com

Long Beach Convention Center   (562) 436-3636
300 E Ocean Blvd, Long Beach, CA, 90802
www.longbeachcc.com

Los Angeles Center Studios   (213) 534-3000
1201 W 5th Street Ste T-110, Los Angeles, CA, 90017
www.lacenterstudios.com

Los Angeles Convention Center   (213) 741-1151
1201 S Figueroa St, Los Angeles, CA, 90015
Event Services X5360
www.lacclink.com

Los Angeles Memorial Coliseum   (213) 747-7111
3911 S Figueroa St, Los Angeles, CA, 90037
www.lacoliseum.com

Los Angeles Sports Arena   (213) 747-7111
3939 S Figueroa St, Los Angeles, CA, 90037
www.lacoliseumlive.com

The Lot (323) 850-3180
1041 N Formosa Ave, W Hollywood, CA, 90046
www.thelotstudios.com

Mack Sennett Studios (323) 660-8466
1215 Bates Ave, Los Angeles, CA, 90029
www.macksennettstudios.net

Mark Taper Forum (213) 628-2772
135 N Grand Ave, Los Angeles, CA, 90012
for admin office, see Dorothy Chandler Pavilion
www.centertheatregroup.org

Microsoft Theater (213) 763-6030
777 Chick Hearn Court, Los Angeles, CA, 90015
www.microsofttheater.com

Occidental Studios (213) 384-3331
201 N Occidental Blvd, Los Angeles, CA, 90026
12 locations, stages from 1,000 to 43,000 sq. ft., lighting, grip, offices, props, etc.
www.occidentalentertainment.com

Panavision (Woodland Hills) (818) 316-1000
6101 Variel Ave, Woodland Hills, CA, 91367
Cameras & film. Commercials, music videos, hair & make-up test, trailers
www.panavision.com

Pantages Theatre (323) 468-1700
6233 Hollywood Blvd, Hollywood, CA, 90028
www.hollywoodpantages.com

Pasadena Civic Auditorium (626) 793-2122
300 E Green St, Pasadena, CA, 91101
Also, Pasadena Convention Center.
www.thepasadenacivic.com

The Pasadena Playhouse (626) 356-7529
39 S El Molino Ave, Pasadena, CA, 91101
www.pasadenaplayhouse.org

The Production Group (323) 469-8111
1626 N Wilcox Ave Ste 281, Hollywood, CA, 90028
www.productiongroup.tv

Prospect Studios (323) 671-4022
4151 Prospect Ave, Los Angeles, CA, 90027
http://studioservices.go.com/prospectstudios/index.html

Quixote Studios (323) 851-5030
1011 N Fuller Ave, W Hollywood, CA, 90046
trucks and stages, greenrooms, production stages
www.quixotestudios.com

Raleigh Studios (323) 960-3456
5300 Melrose Ave, Hollywood, CA, 90038
www.raleighstudios.com

Red Studios Hollywood (323) 463-0808
846 Cahuenga Blvd, Los Angeles, CA, 90038
http://www.redstudio.com/

Rose Bowl (626) 577-3100
1001 Rose Bowl Dr, Pasadena, CA, 91103
www.rosebowlstadium.com

Saban Theatre (888) 645-5006
8440 Wilshire Blvd, Beverly Hills, CA, 90211
www.sabantheatre.org

San Gabriel Mission Playhouse (626) 308-2865
320 S Mission Drive, San Gabriel, CA, 91776
Location, Sound Stage, Venue, Rehearsal Space, Theater, Spanish style, wurlitzer organ
swilkinson@missionplayhouse.org * www.missionplayhouse.org

San Manuel Amphitheater (909) 880-6500
2575 Glen Helen Pkwy, San Bernardino, CA, 92407
www.sanmanuelamphitheater.net

Santa Barbara Bowl (805) 962-7411
1122 N Milpas St, Santa Barbara, CA, 93103
www.sbbowl.com

Santa Clarita Studios (661) 294-2000
25135 Anza Dr, Santa Clarita, CA, 91355
www.santaclaritastudios.com

Santa Monica Civic Auditorium (310) 458-8551
1855 Main St, Santa Monica, CA, 90401
www.santamonicacivic.org

Schmidli Backdrops LA (323) 938-2098
5830 W Adams Blvd, Culver City, CA, 90232
Providing hand painted Textured and Scenic backdrops to the commercial, film, and fashion industry for over 20 years.
backdrops@schmidli.com * www.schmidli.com

Segerstrom Center (714) 556-2121
600 Town Center Dr, Costa Mesa, CA, 92626
Five performing arts & event venues
www.scfta.org

Shrine Auditorium (213) 748-5116
665 W Jefferson Blvd, Los Angeles, CA, 90007
www.shrineauditorium.com

Sony Pictures Studios (310) 244-6926
10202 W Washington Blvd, Culver City, CA, 90232
www.sonypicturesstudios.com

Stage 1001 (323) 876-1001
1001 N Poinsettia Pl, Los Angeles, CA, 90046
www.stage1001.com

Staples Center (213) 742-7100
1111 S Figueroa St, Los Angeles, CA, 90015
www.staplescenter.com

The Studios At Paramount (323) 956-5000
5555 Melrose, Hollywood, CA, 90038
Call (323) 956-8811 for booking stages.
www.thestudiosatparamount.com

Sunset Gower Studios (323) 467-1001
1438 North Gower Box 21, Hollywood, CA, 90028
Call (323) 315-9460 for new inquiries
www.sgsandsbs.com

Thunder Studios (310) 762-1360
20434 S Santa Fe Ave, Long Beach, CA, 90810
15 stages, hard cycs, fisher boxes/flats
www.thunderstudios.com

Twentieth Century Fox (310) 369-1000
10201 W Pico Blvd, Los Angeles, CA, 90035
www.foxstudios.com

Universal Studios Stages & Backlot (818) 777-3000
100 Universal City Plaza, Universal City, CA, 91608
universal.locations@nbcuni.com *
http://universalstudioslot.com/stages-and-backlot

The Walt Disney Concert Hall (213) 972-7211
135 N Grand Ave, Los Angeles, CA, 90012
http://www.wdch.com/

The Walt Disney Studios (818) 560-7450
500 S Buena Vista St, Burbank, CA, 91505
www.stu-ops.disney.com

Warner Bros. Studios (818) 954-6000
4000 Warner Blvd, Burbank, CA, 91522
For facilities, call (818) 954-3000
www.warnerbros.com

The Wiltern (213) 388-1400
3790 Wilshire Blvd, Los Angeles, CA, 90010
call (213) 380-5005 for box office
www.thewiltern.com

Locations, Underwater Sets & Filming Tanks

Aquavision (562) 433-2863
3708 E 4th St, Long Beach, CA, 90814
picture & camera boats/crews, scouting, stunts, set medics lifeguards, safety divers, marine prop fab., underwater sets
www.aquavision.net

Warner Bros. Studios Backlot (818) 954-2577
4000 Warner Blvd Bldg 34, Burbank, CA, 91522
Swimming pools w/ ports and film tanks, heated and filtered optional
wbsfoperations@warnerbros.com * studiofacilities.warnerbros.com

WaterHole Ranch (435) 669-0106
Call for Appt, Big Water, UT, 84741
Underwater film tank built by contractor that made tanks for Bay Watch and remodeled Warner Bro Ranch's tank.
dstewartw@gmail.com

Lockers

See Also: School Supplies, Desks & Dressing

Alley Cats Studio Rentals (818) 982-9178
locker room, locker row units, blue, silver etc

C. P. Two (323) 466-8201
School lockers, gym lockers, footlockers, hallway lockers, wood lockers, metal lockers, public lockers, coin-op lockers

E.C. Prop Rentals (818) 764-2008
School Lockers, Gym Lockers, Locker Room, Pro-Sports, Coin-Op, Iarport Lockers, Bus Station, Multiples, Some Castered.

E.C. PROP RENTALS
11846 SHERMAN WAY NORTH HOLLYWOOD CA 91605
818-764-2008

FormDecor, Inc. (310) 558-2582
America's largest event rental supplier of 20th Century furniture and accessories for Modern and Mid-Century styles.

LCW Props (818) 243-0707
Large Selection, School, Industrial, Wood, Metal, Military

L.C.W. PROPS
INDUSTRIAL LOCKERS
POLICE LOCKERS
AIRPORT LOCKERS   SCHOOL LOCKERS
6439 San Fernando Rd. Glendale, CA 91201
Phone: 818-243-0707 - www.lcwprops.com

Lennie Marvin Enterprises, Inc. (Prop Heaven) (818) 841-5882
Lockers of many kinds; gym lockers, school lockers, display lockers and more.

RJR Props (404) 349-7600
High school lockers, gym lockers for rent.

Sony Pictures Studios-Prop House (Off Lot) (310) 244-5999
small, bus depot, locker room dressing

Warner Bros. Studios Property Department (818) 954-2181
Gym lockers, school lockers, storage lockers, Doctors lounge lockers, metal and office lockers, multiples of lockers

Locks & Locksmith

See: Keys & Locks

Lodge

See: Hotel, Motel, Inn, Lodge

Logo Design

See: Printing, Graphics, Digital & Large Format* Signs

Lubricants

See: Expendables

Luggage

See Also: Briefcases* Steamer Trunks* Trunks

The Hand Prop Room LP. (323) 931-1534

History For Hire, Inc. (818) 765-7767
huge selection, custom made luggage, period luggage, carpet bags

Innerspace Cases Unltd. (818) 767-3030
11555 Cantara St, N. Hollywood, CA, 91605
custom protective cases for film, music, video, medical, sports equipment
www.innerspacecases.com

LCW Props (818) 243-0707
Period, Cases & Crates

Old N Country Prop Shop, LLC (818) 423-2599
Large variety of sizes and styles of vintage luggage: beautiful to distressed suitcases with lining, locks, straps, etc.

Picture Start Props (818) 255-5472
Various types of luggage from trunks and suitcases to carry-on pieces including vintage suitcases & more.

Sony Pictures Studios-Prop House (Off Lot) (310) 244-5999
backpacks, briefcases, garment bags, gun cases, messenger bags, shoulder bags

Universal Studios Property & Hardware Dept (818) 777-2784
Luggage rentals; from period to modern.

Warner Bros. Studios Property Department (818) 954-2181
Assorted Suitcases, Briefcase, Luggage Caddy, Carry On luggage, Garment Bags, luggage racks, trunks

Luggage Carts

C. P. Two (323) 466-8201
Luggage carts available

E.C. Prop Rentals (818) 764-2008
several styles

The Hand Prop Room LP. (323) 931-1534
airport, hotel, train station

History For Hire, Inc. (818) 765-7767
train, plane, airport

LCW Props (818) 243-0707
We Have Clean Cleared Luggage Carts

Sony Pictures Studios-Prop House (Off Lot) (310) 244-5999

Universal Studios Property & Hardware Dept (818) 777-2784
Hotel luggage carts and airport luggage carts for rent.

Lumber

See: Building Supply, Lumber, Hardware, Etc.

Lunch Boxes

The Hand Prop Room LP. (323) 931-1534
period-present

History For Hire, Inc. (818) 765-7767
vintage

RC Vintage, Inc. (818) 765-7107
40s, 50s & 60s striped, metal, kids, big, small and locked lunch boxes. with art, or plain for work

Sony Pictures Studios-Prop House (Off Lot) (310) 244-5999
metal, plastic

Universal Studios Property & Hardware Dept (818) 777-2784
Adult lunchboxes and kids lunchboxes from period to modern.

Lunch Counters

AIR Designs (818) 768-6639
Diner Restaurant, Cafeteria
C. P. Two (323) 466-8201
assortment & period
RC Vintage, Inc. (818) 765-7107
40s, 50s & 60s diner and restaurant counters, break room counters, wall pieces
with counters

Machine Shop & Machinery

See Also: Automotive/Garage Equip. & Parts Factory/Industrial*
Tools* Welding Equipment/Stations* Heavy Machinery, Equipment &
Specialists*
E.C. Prop Rentals (818) 764-2008
power & hand tools, tables, cabinets, signage
Machinery & Equipment Co., Inc. (909) 599-3916
115 N Cataract Ave, San Dimas, CA, 91773
Used industrial processing & packaging equipment. Over 5000 items available
in our inventory. Stainless steel equipment.
sherri@machineryandequipment.com * www.machineryandequipment.com
Sword & Stone (818) 562-6548
Anvils, power hammers, belt grinders and much more.

Magazines & Magazine/Newspaper Racks

See Also: Comic Books & Comic Book Racks Display Cases, Racks
& Fixtures (Store)* Newspapers (Prop)* Newsstands* Newsstands
(Prop)* Store Shelf Units & Shelving*
AIR Designs (818) 768-6639
Stands, Racks, Dressed, Indoor & Outdoor, Bundled Newspaper, Crates of
Magazines
Alley Cats Studio Rentals (818) 982-9178
period, modern magazine racks
The Hand Prop Room LP. (323) 931-1534
History For Hire, Inc. (818) 765-7767
magazines & racks, custom, vintage periodicals
LCW Props (818) 243-0707
Unlimited Quantity Of Newspaper & Magazines
Prop Services West (818) 503-2790
Sony Pictures Studios-Prop House (Off Lot) (310) 244-5999
magazines & racks
Warner Bros. Studios Property Department (818) 954-2181
Magazine stands, metal newspaper racks, period/vintage racks, standing
magazine racks & stands

Magicians & Props, Supplies, Dressing

See Also: Occult/Spiritual/Metaphysical
The Hand Prop Room LP. (323) 931-1534
magic cases, ventriloquist dummies
L. A. Party Works (888) 527-2789
9712 Alpaca St, S El Monte, CA, 91733
in Vancouver tel. 604-589-4101. custom built medium to large scale illusions
partyworks@aol.com * www.partyworksinteractive.com

Owen Magic Supreme (626) 969-4519
734 N McKeever Ave, Azusa, CA, 91702
magic effects, consulting techniques, props, spec. effects
alanz@owenmagic.com * www.owenmagic.com
ShowFx, Inc. (562) 903-7285
10024 Romandel Ave, Santa Fe Springs, CA, 90670
stock magic illusions & custom build
www.showfx.net
The Society of American Magicians (303) 362-0575
4927 S Oak Court, Littleton, CO, 80127
advances magic as a performing art, contact performers via links to local
chapters on their website
www.magicsam.com
Universal Studios Property & Hardware Dept (818) 777-2784
Magician props, magician supplies, and magician dressing for rent.

Mail & Mail Room

See Also: Post Office* Scales
Advanced Liquidators Office Furniture (818) 763-3470
Wide variety of office dressing, and office furniture fit to satisfy the look of any
type of business office.
E.C. Prop Rentals (818) 764-2008
canvas & wire carts, sorting units, tables, racks, shelving
Faux Library Studio Props, Inc. (818) 765-0096
Mail room dressing and faux mail dressing for rent.
History For Hire, Inc. (818) 765-7767
stamps, stamp machines
LCW Props (818) 243-0707
Mail Sorters, Mailboxes, Cleared Mail, Postage Scales
Universal Studios Property & Hardware Dept (818) 777-2784
Mail only for rent.

Mailboxes

AIR Designs (818) 768-6639
USPS Mailboxes, Storage Boxes, Package Drop Off
Alley Cats Studio Rentals (818) 982-9178
Blue U.S. Mail, green relay, rural boxes on posts
E.C. Prop Rentals (818) 764-2008
rural & apartment type, several styles, multiples
History For Hire, Inc. (818) 765-7767
home & street
Jackson Shrub Supply, Inc. (818) 982-0100
mail boxes
LCW Props (818) 243-0707
Large Selection. Apartment, Office, Slots, Hotel, Mail Sorters
RC Vintage, Inc. (818) 765-7107
Modern US POST OFFICE DROP BOX!
Sony Pictures Studios-Prop House (Off Lot) (310) 244-5999
Universal Studios Property & Hardware Dept (818) 777-2784
Mailboxes from different time periods and styles for rent.
Warner Bros. Studios Property Department (818) 954-2181
Outdoor mailboxes, rural mail boxes, wood & metal mail boxes, standing
mailboxes, rustic mailboxes

Make-up & Hair, Supplies & Services

See Also: Expendables* Production Vehicles/Trailers* Salon & Spa Equipment* Special Effects, Make-up/Prosthetics* Tattoos (Temporary) Body/Face Painting* Wigs

Alcone Co. (718) 361-8373
5-45 49th Avenue, Long Island City, NY, 11101
technical supply catalog for animal glue, paints, etc. & make-up catalog for theatrical make-up & supplies
www.alconeco.com

Ball Beauty Supply (323) 655-2330
1535 S La Cienega Blvd, Los Angeles, CA, 90035
beauty supply shop
www.ballbeauty.com

Ben Nye Co. Inc. (310) 839-1984
3655 Lenawee Ave, Los Angeles, CA, 90016
Mfg., call for local dealer referral
www.bennye.com

Bobbe Joy Make-up Studio (310) 275-3505
350 N. Bedford Dr, Beverly Hills, CA 90210
Bobbe Joy make-up, custom made cosmetics
www.bobbejoycosmetics.com

Cinema Secrets, Inc. (818) 846-0579
4400 Riverside Dr #110, Burbank, CA, 91505
huge sel.
info@cinemasecrets.com * www.cinemasecrets.com

Frends Beauty Supply (818) 769-3834
5244 Laurel Canyon Blvd, N. Hollywood, CA, 91607
theatrical & special FX make-up
www.frendsbeauty.com

GlenPro Beauty Center (818) 244-1776
717 E. California Ave, Glendale, CA, 91206
beauty supply shop

The Hand Prop Room LP. (323) 931-1534
period-present

History For Hire, Inc. (818) 765-7767
most eras through 1970s

IM Hair Studio (818) 562-1858
3913 W Riverside Dr, Burbank, CA, 91505
Hair only, no make-up
imhairstudio.com

Kryolan Corporation (800) 579-6526
134 9th St, 1st floor, San Francisco, CA, 94103
catalog sales; make-up supplies
www.kryolan.com

Larchmont Beauty Supply (323) 461-0162
208 N Larchmont Blvd, Los Angeles, CA, 90004
beauty supply shop
www.larchmontbeauty.com

Lorac Cosmetics, Inc (818) 678-3939
29025 Avenue Penn, Valencia, CA, 91355
ask for Product Placement
www.loraccosmetics.com

M.A.C. (310) 659-9161
8507 Melrose Ave West Hollywood CA, 90069
M.A.C. make-up
www.maccosmetics.com

Make-Up Center (212) 977-9494
Web Based Business
Mail order & web services only. cosmetics & theatrical make-up
www.make-up-center.com

Melrose Beauty Center (323) 852-6910
7617 Melrose Ave, Los Angeles, CA, 90046
beauty supply shop
www.melroseavela.com/item/melrose-beauty-center

Naimie's Beauty Supply (818) 655-9933
12640 Riverside Dr, Valley Village, CA, 91607
Studio services (818) 655-9922
www.naimies.com

Party Plus (909) 335-2811
1801 Orange Tree Lane, Redlands, CA, 92374
Ben Nye dealer-Moulage
info@partyplus.net * http://partyplus.net

Senna Cosmetics (661) 257-3662
28042 Avenue Stanford Ste A, Valencia, CA, 91355
www.sennacosmetics.com

Ursula's Costumes, Inc. (310) 582-8230
2516 Wilshire Blvd, Santa Monica, CA, 90403
www.ursulascostumes.com

Wilshire Beauty Supply (213) 910-6464
5401 Wilshire Blvd, Los Angeles, CA, 90036
wilshirebeauty.com

Make-up Schools

Dinair Airbrush Make-up & Institute (818) 780-4777
6215 Laurel Canyon Blvd, N. Hollywood, CA, 91606
www.airbrushmakeup.com

The Joe Blasco Make-up Center (407) 363-1234
461 Sandy Creek Suite 4129, Fayetteville GA, 30214
customerservice@joeblasco.com * www.joeblasco.com

Make-Up Designory (MUD) (818) 729-9420
129 S San Fernando Blvd, Burbank, CA, 91502
Los Angeles School of Make-Up, Inc.
www.mud.edu

Make-up Tables & Mirrors

Castex Rentals (323) 462-1468
1044 N Cole Ave, Hollywood, CA, 90038
portable wood/metal make-up tables, make-up mirrors and full length mirrors, salon chairs, portable dressing rooms
service@castexrentals.com * www.castexrentals.com

History For Hire, Inc. (818) 765-7767
lots

Lennie Marvin Enterprises, Inc. (Prop Heaven) (818) 841-5882
quantities avail.

Prop Services West (818) 503-2790

Universal Studios Property & Hardware Dept (818) 777-2784
Makeup tables and makeup tables with mirrors for rent.

ZG04 DECOR (818) 853-8040

Mall Carts

See: Vendor Carts & Concession Counters

Man Hole Covers

See: Alley Dressing* Street Dressing

Manicure & Pedicure Stations

See: Beauty Salon

Mannequins

See Also: Anatomical Charts & Models Dress Forms* Puppets, Marionettes, Automata, Animatronics* Robots*

Acme Display Fixture & Packaging (888) 411-1870
3829 S Broadway St, Los Angeles, CA, 90037
Complete store setups: garment racks, displays/display cases, counters, packaging, shelving, hangers, mannequins
sales@acmedisplay.com * www.acmedisplay.com

Cheertie Display Fixtures (626) 579-9001
9906 Gidley St, El Monte, CA, 91731
We carry a wide assortment of high-end and affordable mannequins in ultra-realistic and abstract forms.

LCW Props (818) 243-0707
White Store Mannequins, Limbs Too

Lennie Marvin Enterprises, Inc. (Prop Heaven) (818) 841-5882
per-mod., full body & torso, child/adult w/clothing

The Mannequin Gallery (818) 834-5555
12350 Montague St, Pacoima, CA, 91331
www.mannequingallery.com

Modern Props (323) 934-3000
traditional mannequins, fantasy, real people, exotic humans, futuristic, hi-tech, modern, conventional, small collection

RC Vintage, Inc. (818) 765-7107
50s & 60s, and new ones too, can change position, flesh colored, cloth colored, bust only, full figured mannequins

Rubens Display World (909) 923-5671
1482 E Francis St, Ontario, CA, 91761
In house sculptor, superior craftsmanship, and fast turnaround. In house inventory of flexible, articulated mannequins.
www.rubensdisplay.com

Sony Pictures Studios-Prop House (Off Lot) (310) 244-5999
base mannequins, dummy mannequins, display mannequins

Sword & Stone (818) 562-6548
Mannequins; women mannequins, men mannequins

Universal Studios Property & Hardware Dept (818) 777-2784
Different kinds of mannequins, mannequin parts and sizes for rent from different time periods.

Mantels

See: Fireplaces & Mantels/Screens/Tools/Andirons

Maps

See Also: Globes, World Map

Clearedart.com/El Studio Granados (818) 240-4421
958 Verdugo Circle Dr, Glendale, CA, 91206
"Age of Exploration" ancient-styled maps and charts. Period treasure maps, and hand-props. Custom work.
fineart@elstudiogranados.com * www.clearedart.com

D'ziner Sign Co. (323) 467-4467
801 Seward Street, Los Angeles, CA, 90038
print mockups of any kind
sales@dzinersign.com * www.dzinersign.com

Faux Library Studio Props, Inc. (818) 765-0096
globes and wall maps, some cleared

The Hand Prop Room LP. (323) 931-1534
antique-present, standing, wall, desk, book, travel, academic

History For Hire, Inc. (818) 765-7767
rental & custom

Hollywood Studio Gallery (323) 462-1116
rental only

Old Maps Online (323) 462-1116
Web Based Business
OldMapsOnline.org indexes over 400,000 maps from across time, old maps to new maps.
info@oldmapsonline.org * www.oldmapsonline.org

Omega/Cinema Props (323) 466-8201
Various maps

Rand McNally (800) 275-7263
9855 Woods Dr, Skokie, IL, 60077
mfg. of maps, atlas, travel videos. Truck GPS, RV GPS, more
www.randmcnally.com

Sony Pictures Studios-Prop House (Off Lot) (310) 244-5999
maps, wall maps

Universal Studios Property & Hardware Dept (818) 777-2784
Maps from different time periods, countries and styles for rent.

Marble

See: Tile, Marble, Granite, Etc.

Mardi Gras

See: Carnival Dressing/Supplies Events, Decorations, Supplies & Services* Events, Design/Planning/Production* Holiday Costumes* Holiday Theme Events* Masks* Travel (City/Country) Themed Events*

Marijuana Plants, Dispensary Dressing & Hydroponics

See Also: Greenhouses Greens*

Jackson Shrub Supply, Inc. (818) 982-0100
Marijuana field set with bamboo, silk marijuana bush, silk marijuana bush on bamboo pole

LCW Props (818) 243-0707
Marijuana, Nutrients, Lights, Tables, Scales, Jars, Bags of Marijuana, Containers, Counters, Signage, Edibles

Marine

See: Nautical Dressing & Props* Nautical/Marine Services & Charters* Tikis & Tropical Dressing

Marionettes

See: Puppets, Marionettes, Automata, Animatronics

Market Equipment/Fixtures

See Also: Bakery* Cash Registers* Credit Card Imprint Machine* Delicatessen Equipment* Display Cases, Racks & Fixtures (Store)* Printing, Graphics, Digital & Large Format* Grocery Check-out Stands (Complete)* Produce Carts* Produce Crates* Produce Stands* Prop Houses* Prop Products & Packages* Shopping Bags (Silent)* Shopping Carts* Signs* Store Shelf Units & Shelving

AIR Designs (818) 768-6639
Shelving, Racks, Counters, Coolers, Freezers, Large Selection, Period to Present
Lennie Marvin Enterprises, Inc. (Prop Heaven) (818) 841-5882
gondolas, shelving, signage, fixtures, products, foods, more

Marquees

See Also: Canopies, Tents, Gazebos, Cabanas* Neon Lights & Signs* Signs

AIR Designs (818) 768-6639
Marquee signs
Alley Cats Studio Rentals (818) 982-9178
theater marquee sign, seating
Lennie Marvin Enterprises, Inc. (Prop Heaven) (818) 841-5882
Church marquees, theater marquees/movie theater marquees, letter board marquees

Martial Arts

See: Boxing, Wrestling, Mixed Martial Arts (MMA)

Mascot Character

See: Animal Costumes & Walk Around Characters

Mascots

See: Animal Costumes & Walk Around Characters

Masks

See Also: Art, Tribal & Folk* Leather (Clothing, Accessories, Materials)

American Plume (800) 521-1132
11 Skyine Drive East, Unit 2, Clarks Summit, PA 18411
Boas/jackets/theatrical division in NYC; (800) 962-8544. highest quality feather masks
apff@epix.net * www.americanplume.com
Clearedart.com/El Studio Granados (818) 240-4421
958 Verdugo Circle Dr, Glendale, CA, 91206
100s of multi-media masks, from miniature to large-sized, in Native American, Guatemalan, and contemporary styles.
fineart@elstudiogranados.com * www.clearedart.com
Fortune Trading Co & Import Bazaar (323) 222-6287
483 Gin Ling Way (Old Chinatown), Los Angeles, CA, 90012
1000s of copies of many styles of paper lanterns, masks. Costumes, lions, dragons, gongs, scrolls, Oriental gift items
fortunetradingco@gmail.com
The Hand Prop Room LP. (323) 931-1534
tribal, paper mache, porcelain
Hollywood Studio Gallery (323) 462-1116
Asian, South American, African
Make-up Effects Laboratories (818) 982-1483
7110 Laurel Canyon Blvd Bldg E, N Hollywood, CA, 91605
latex, silicone, foam, cast from your choice of model
www.melefx.com
Oceanic Arts (562) 698-6960
Carved Wood masks, 22 Authentic styles and some one of a kind. South Pacific, New Guinea, and African.
Omega/Cinema Props (323) 466-8201
Prop Services West (818) 503-2790
ethnic decorative masks
Sony Pictures Studios-Prop House (Off Lot) (310) 244-5999
Sony Pictures Studios-Wardrobe (310) 244-5995
alterations, call (310) 244-7260
Sword & Stone (818) 562-6548
leather, feather, aluminum, steel, bronze

The Theater Maskery (360) 297-4160
PO Box 421, Indianola, WA, 98342
mask makers & mask theater instructors
www.themaskery.com
Universal Studios Property & Hardware Dept (818) 777-2784
Many prop masks for different time periods and cultures for rent.
Warner Bros. Studios Costume Dept (818) 954-1297
Mardi Gras, Feathered, Jeweled, Venetian, Masquerade, Opera

Massage Rollers

See: Exercise & Fitness Equipment* Gymnasium & Gymnastic Equipment

Massage Tables

See Also: Physical Therapy* Medical Equip/Furniture, Graphics/Supplies

E.C. Prop Rentals (818) 764-2008
several styles
I-Rep Therapy Products, Inc. (800) 828-0852
508 Chaney St Ste B, Lake Elsinore, CA, 92530
Contact i-REP for all of your equipment and set dressing needs for massage, therapy, and spa.
btwilhelm@gmail.com * www.i-reptherapyproducts.com
L. A. Party Works (888) 527-2789
9712 Alpaca St, S El Monte, CA, 91733
Multiple massage tables and masseuse talent for rent.
partyworks@aol.com * www.partyworksinteractive.com
Modern Props (323) 934-3000
contemporary massage tables
Picture Start Props (818) 255-5472
Contemporary table with light wood frame and black vinyl pads
Universal Studios Property & Hardware Dept (818) 777-2784
Massage chairs and massage tables for rent.

Mats

See: Fall Pads & Crash Pads* Gymnasium & Gymnastic Equipment

Mechanic Shop

See: Automotive/Garage Equip. & Parts

Mechanical Bull (Riding Simulators)

See Also: Western Dressing

L. A. Party Works (888) 527-2789
9712 Alpaca St, S El Monte, CA, 91733
in Vancouver tel. 604-589-4101
partyworks@aol.com * www.partyworksinteractive.com
Party Pals (858) 622-6613
10427 Roselle St, San Diego, CA, 92121
www.partypals.com

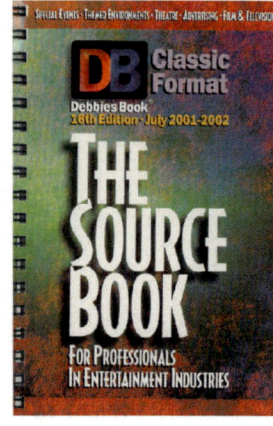

Mechanical Effects

Action Sets and Props / WonderWorks, Inc.   (818) 992-8811
Space shuttle & station, space suit, specialty props, miniatures, mechanical effects, cityscape, miniature buildings

Bill Ferrell Co.   (818) 767-1900
10556 Keswick St, Sun Valley, CA, 91352
Turntables, lifts, winches, conveyors; moving props, sets. Simple or automated. We design, fabricate, install, operate.
www.billferrell.com

Charisma Design Studio, Inc.   (818) 252-6611
8414 San Fernando Road, Sun Valley, CA, 91352
custom mechanical effects & fabrication
info@charismadesign.com * www.charismadesign.com

CONFETTI & FOG FX Special Effects Company   (877) 576-4239
1085 W 21st Pl, Hialeah, FL, 33010
Specialize in a variety of mechanical special effects. Refer to our website!
Info@confettiandfogfx.com * www.caffx.com

EFX- Event Special Effects   (626) 888-2239
125 Railroad Ave, Monrovia, CA, 91016
Snow- Confetti- Cryo- Bubbles- Fog- Foam- Fluid- Lighting- Fabrication
info@efxla.com * www.efxla.com

Flix FX Inc.   (818) 765-3549
7327 Lankershim Blvd #4, N Hollywood, CA, 91605
Custom mechanical EFX fabrication-motorized, pneumatic, hydraulic, RC
info@flixfx.com * www.flixfx.com

The Hand Prop Room LP.   (323) 931-1534
HPR Custom   (323) 931-1534
5700 Venice Blvd, Los Angeles, CA, 90019
Remote control, wireless, electronics, digital, fabrication, and mechanical effect manufacturing
www.hprcustom.com

Rando Productions, Inc   (818) 982-4300
11939 Sherman Rd, N Hollywood, CA, 91605

Special Effects Unlimited, Inc.   (323) 466-3361
1005 N Lillian Way, Hollywood, CA, 90038
turntables, gimbals, special purpose rigging
www.specialeffectsunlimited.com

Ultra Prototypes LLC   (818) 292-1906
Call for Appointment
We specialize in Mechanical Effects and Props.
jeff@ultraprototypes.com * www.ultraprototypes.com

Warner Bros. Studios Special Effects & Prop Shop (818) 954-1365
4000 Warner Blvd Bldg 44, Burbank, CA, 91522
Consultation, Script Break-down, Equipment Rentals, Expendable Sales, Picture Car Prep, Action Props
www.wbspecialeffects.com

Medical Equip/Furniture, Graphics/Supplies

See Also: Physical Therapy* Lobby Seating* Exam Room* Radiology* Emergency Room* Intensive Care Unit / NICU (Natal Intensive Care Unit)* Birthing Room* Waiting Room* Nurses Station* X-rays & X-ray Viewers* Wheelchairs* Uniforms,Trades/Professional/ Sports* Stretchers* Scales* Morgue* Lab Equipment* Hospital Equipment* Doctor's Bags* Dentist Equipment* Bones, Skulls & Skeletons* Anesthesia Equipment* Ambulance/Paramedic

A-1 Medical Integration   (818) 753-0319
Medical devices for Set Decoration & Property, from minor procedures to detailed hospital units.

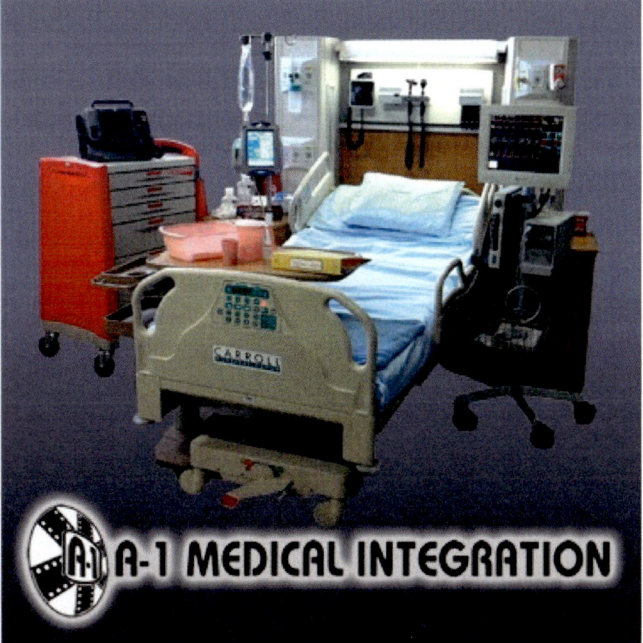

AA Surplus Sales Co., Inc.   (323) 526-3622
2940 E Olympic Blvd, Los Angeles, CA, 90023
Military field operating tables, field nurse stations, military hospital beds, scrubs, field hospital beds & stretchers
surplusking@hotmail.com * www.aasurplus.com

Alpha Companies - Spellman Desk Co.   (818) 504-9090
The #1 source for medical equipment in the industry; from vintage medical equipment to contemporary medical equipment.

the**alpha**companies
motion picture rentals

Hospital and Medical Props
Equipment • Tools • Furniture • Supplies

alphaprops.com (818) 504-9090

Angelus Medical & Optical Co., Inc.   (310) 769-6060
13007 S Western Ave, Gardena, CA, 90249
emergency equipment, physical therapy, opthalmic, etc.
www.angelusmedical.com

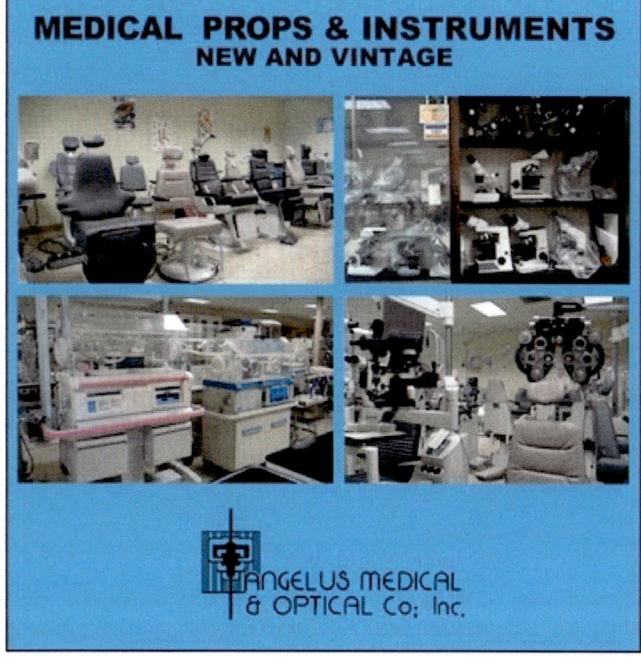

MEDICAL PROPS & INSTRUMENTS
NEW AND VINTAGE

ANGELUS MEDICAL & OPTICAL Co; Inc.

LISTINGS FOR THIS CATEGORY CONTINUE ON THE FOLLOWING PAGE

Dapper Cadaver (818) 771-0818
Medical equipment: gurneys, mayo stands & autopsy equipment. Stainless steel instruments & trays. Anatomical models.

E.C. Prop Rentals (818) 764-2008
first aid kits & signage

The Hand Prop Room LP. (323) 931-1534
stretchers, gurney, first aid, doctor's bags, no furniture

History For Hire, Inc. (818) 765-7767
prosthetics, crutches, amputation kits, oxygen tanks, stethoscopes and more

I-Rep Therapy Products, Inc. (800) 828-0852
508 Chaney St Ste B, Lake Elsinore, CA, 92530
Contact i-REP for all of your equipment and set dressing needs for medical & therapy equipment, furniture and supplies.
btwilhelm@gmail.com * www.i-reptherapyproducts.com

LCW Props (818) 243-0707
Large Selection Of Medical Files, Equipment, Supplies, Custom Graphics

Modern Props (323) 934-3000
contemp./futuristic medical equipment, medical furniture & medical dressing

RJR Props (404) 349-7600
Medical props, ER props, ICU props and OR props for rent.

Sony Pictures Studios-Prop House (Off Lot) (310) 244-5999
xray viewers, bandages, bio hazard container, blood pressure equipment, bones, medical bottles, patient charts, and more

Universal Studios Property & Hardware Dept (818) 777-2784
A lot of prop medical equipment for rent.

Warner Bros. Studios Property Department (818) 954-2181
Medical equipment, Aspirator, Newborn Hospital Bed, rolling bedside trays, bladder pumps, x-ray machines

Medical Examiner

See: Morgue* Exam Room

Medical Library

See: Books, Real/Hollow & Faux Books

Medicine Balls

See: Gymnasium & Gymnastic Equipment

Medieval

See Also: Armor, Chainmail, Suits of Armor* Blacksmith Shop/Foundry* Goth/Punk/Bondage/Fetish/Erotica Etc.* Historical Era Themed Events* Lanterns* Leather (Clothing, Accessories, Materials)* Swords & Swordplay* Torture Equipment* Wardrobe, Antique/Historical* Weaponry, Historical* Weaponry, Medieval

The Hand Prop Room LP. (323) 931-1534
armor, swords, shields, custom mfg.

Historic Enterprises, Inc. (760) 789-2299
19722 Casner Rd, Ramona, CA, 92065
custom fab, replicas, specialty/stunt props, horse equip, tents
www.historicenterprises.com

History For Hire, Inc. (818) 765-7767
good selection

Hollywood Studio Gallery (323) 462-1116
swords, shields, armor

LM Treasures (626) 252-7354
Medieval statues; we have several life size medieval Knights & medieval armors available for rent and for sale.

Omega/Cinema Props (323) 466-8201

Sony Pictures Studios-Prop House (Off Lot) (310) 244-5999
medieval swords, medieval shields, medieval knives, medieval cauldrons, lanterns

Sword & Stone (818) 562-6548
iron maiden, ball & chain, shackles, dungeon dressing

Universal Studios Property & Hardware Dept (818) 777-2784
Medieval props of various kinds for rent.

Megaphones

The Hand Prop Room LP. (323) 931-1534

History For Hire, Inc. (818) 765-7767
all types

LCW Props (818) 243-0707
Handheld, Police, Cheerleader, Working

Universal Studios Property & Hardware Dept (818) 777-2784
Prop megaphones for rent.

Memorabilia & Novelties

See Also: Coca Cola Memorabilia* Collectibles* Promotional Items & Materials* Prop Houses* Sports Fan Items, Memorabilia, Photographs

History For Hire, Inc. (818) 765-7767

LCW Props (818) 243-0707
Sporting, Old Periodicals, Photos

RC Vintage, Inc. (818) 765-7107
period to present Toys, Sports Memorabilia and TV items from the past

Universal Studios Property & Hardware Dept (818) 777-2784
Prop novelties and prop memorabilia for rent.

Menus

See Also: Printing, Graphics, Digital & Large Format

AIR Designs (818) 768-6639
Restaurant, Bakery, Diner, Coffee Shop, Neon's, Menu Boards

C. P. Two (323) 466-8201
Chalkboard menus, vinyl menus, menu racks, menu holders, vintage menu signs, standing menu boards, french menu sign

The Hand Prop Room LP. (323) 931-1534
custom design

History For Hire, Inc. (818) 765-7767
rental & custom

Kater-Crafts Bookbinders (562) 692-0665
4860 Gregg Rd, Pico Rivera, CA, 90660
Custom menu covers. Industry credits. any size/style binding.
sales@katercrafts.com * www.katercrafts.com

LCW Props (818) 243-0707
Selection Of Restaurant Menus For Indoor & Outdoor

RC Vintage, Inc. (818) 765-7107
40s, 50s & 60s Diner style. Drive Thru Menu Signs w speaker box

Sony Pictures Studios-Prop House (Off Lot) (310) 244-5999

Universal Studios Graphic Design & Sign Shop (818) 777-2350
custom

Universal Studios Property & Hardware Dept (818) 777-2784
Prop menus for various restaurants for rent.

Mercury Glass

See: Antiques & Antique Decorations* Decorative Accessories

Merry-go-round

See: Carnival Games & Rides* Carousel Horses* Playground Equipment

Messenger & Courier Services

See Also: Walkie-Talkies

LA Messenger (818) 789-5121
13351-D Riverside Dr #672, Sherman Oaks, CA, 91423
24 By 7 delivery, online realtime delivery tracking
www.lamessenger.com

Lightning Messenger Express (818) 754-1234
5435 Cahuenga Blvd Suite C, North Hollywood, 91601
Pickup & delivery for greater LA area, plus Orange Cty, San Diego
info@lightningme.com * www.lightningmessengerexpress.com

Pacific Couriers (714) 278-6100
1706 Orangethorpe, Fullerton, CA, 92833
Messenger svcs for entire LA studio zone
info@pacificcouriers.com * http://pacificcouriers.com

Metal Detectors

See Also: Mining & Prospecting Equipment* Police Equipment*
Security Walk-Through & Baggage Alarms
Faux Library Studio Props, Inc. (818) 765-0096
Metal detectors for rent
The Hand Prop Room LP. (323) 931-1534
LCW Props (818) 243-0707
Our Specialty. We Have A Large Selection Of Many Kinds. Rigged, Large & Small

Metal Plating, Coating, Polishing

See Also: Paint & Painting Supplies
Artcraft Plating & Finishing (818) 845-9292
76 E Santa Anita Ave, Burbank, CA, 91502
on metals or non-metallic props, electroforming
www.artcraftplating.com
Astro Plating (818) 781-1463
8136 Lankershim Blvd, North Hollywood CA, 91605
www.astroplating.com
Barry Avenue Plating Co. (310) 478-0078
2210 Barry Ave, Los Angeles, CA, 90064
www.barryavenueplating.com
Charisma Design Studio, Inc. (818) 252-6611
8414 San Fernando Road, Sun Valley, CA, 91352
custom fabrication, metal plating & polishing
info@charismadesign.com * www.charismadesign.com
F & H Plating (818) 765-1221
12023 Vose St, N. Hollywood, CA, 91605
nickle, brass, copper, gold, silver, tin, small items
www.fandhplating.com
General Plating (323) 263-7593
1313 Mirasol St, Los Angeles, CA, 90023
plating & polishing, many finishes, jewelry, automotive, lighting, electronics + more, many film credits, studio friendl
alanolick@aol.com * www.generalplating.com
LNL Anodizing (818) 768-9224
9900 Glenoaks Blvd, Unit 3, Sun Valley, CA, 91352
plating, antiquing, anodizing, sand blasting
www.lnlanodizing.net
Pyramid Powder Coating (818) 768-5898
12251 Montague St, Pacoima, CA, 91331
custom colors, production runs, sandblasting, powder coating
www.pyramidpowder.com
Sepp Leaf Products (212) 683-2840
381 Park Avenue South #1301, New York City, NY, 10016
Metal leaf materials & brushes. Edible gold & silver leaf.
www.seppleaf.com
Sword & Stone (818) 562-6548
Metal plating and metal coating services

Metal Shop

See Also: Factory/Industrial* Tools
E.C. Prop Rentals (818) 764-2008
power & hand tools, welding equipment, tables, cabinets, signage
Sword & Stone (818) 562-6548
Working metal shop
Warner Bros. Studios Metal Shop (818) 954-1265
4000 Warner Blvd Bldg 44, Burbank, CA, 91522
Custom metal fabrication creating anything from structural steel elements to intricate custom furniture
WBDS@warnerbros.com * www.wbmetalshop.com

Metal Suppliers

See Also: Grating, Grated Flooring, Catwalks
Alameda Pipe (310) 532-7911
14500 Avalon Blvd, Gardena, CA, 90248
new/used steel/non-ferrous, wide variety of forms
www.alamedapipe.com
Bobco Metals (888) 304-5927
2000 S. Alameda St, Los Angeles, CA, 90058
steel, brass, copper, aluminum, power tools, welding supplies
www.bobcometal.com
Borrmann Metal Center (818) 846-7171
110 W. Olive Ave, Burbank, CA, 91502
www.borrmannmetals.com
Burbank Metal Supply (818) 846-4333
3207 N. San Fernando Blvd, Burbank, CA, 91504
aluminum distributors

Coast Aluminum and Architectural (562) 946-6061
10628 Fulton Wells Ave, Santa Fe Springs, CA 90670
aluminum, brass, stainless, custom shapes
www.coastaluminum.com
Hadco Aluminum (800) 221-0344
120 Spagnoli Rd., Melville, NY 11747
plate, sheet, wire, rod, bar, extrusions, tube, pipe, fittings
www.hadco-metal.com
Industrial Metal Supply Co. (818) 729-3333
8300 San Fernando Rd, Sun Valley, CA, 91352
ferrous/non-ferrous, speedrail products
www.imsmetals.com
M & K Metal (310) 327-9011
14400 S Figueroa St, Gardena, CA, 90248
ferrous/non-ferrous, variety of stock
www.mkmetal.net
McNichols (562) 921-3344
14108 Arbor Pl, Cerritos, CA, 90703
www.mcnichols.com
Metal Depot (562) 921-2524
1509 S. Bluff Road, Montebello, CA 90640
www.metaldepot.com
Phillip's Steel (562) 435-7571
1368 W Anaheim St, Long Beach, CA, 90813
Since 1915. steel, aluminum, stainless, brass, sheet, plate, angle, channel, tubing, beams, tools, fabrication
www.phillipssteel.com
Premier Steel (800) 220-9940
1330 N Knollwood Circle, Anaheim, CA, 92801
structural steel, stainless, aluminum
www.premiersteel.com
Totten Tubes (800) 882-3748
500 Danlee St, Azusa, CA, 91702
steel distributor, wide variety tubing & finishing svcs
www.tottentubes.com
Tube Service (800) 776-8823
9351 S Norwalk Blvd, Santa Fe Springs, CA, 90670
alum. & steel pipe/tubing
www.tubeservice.com

Metalworking, Decorative

See Also: Prop Design & Manufacturing* Sculpture* Wrought Iron
Furniture & Decorations
Charisma Design Studio, Inc. (818) 252-6611
8414 San Fernando Road, Sun Valley, CA, 91352
custom all metals, functional art & arch. pcs, water jet cutting
info@charismadesign.com * www.charismadesign.com
KIHL STUDIOS (818) 812-9594
9701 Owensmouth Ave Unit 1, Chatsworth, CA, 91311
Decorative metalworking, welded art, plasma and laser cut steel.
design@kihlstudios.com * www.kihlstudios.com
Martin Iron Design (818) 760-3636
10750 Cumpston St, N Hollywood, CA, 91601
Custom made wrought iron furniture, wrought iron decorations and chandeliers by your design.
martinirondesign@yahoo.com * www.martinirondesign.com
Set Masters (818) 982-1506
24853 Avenue Rockefeller, Valencia, CA, 91355
Custom Manufacturing; Architectural; Structural and Creative; 3D Renderings Available
info@setmasters.com * www.setmasters.com
Sword & Stone (818) 562-6548
wrought iron, sheet metal fab, etching, plating, embossing
Universal Studios Property & Hardware Dept (818) 777-2784
Decorative metalworking and decorative metal items for rent.
Warner Bros. Studios Metal Shop (818) 954-1265
4000 Warner Blvd Bldg 44, Burbank, CA, 91522
Custom metal fabrication creating anything from structural steel elements to intricate custom furniture
WBDS@warnerbros.com * www.wbmetalshop.com

Metalworking, Welding & Structural

See Also: Welding Equipment/Stations

Alameda Pipe (310) 532-7911
14500 Avalon Blvd, Gardena, CA, 90248
cutting, beveling, straightening, buffing, welding
www.alamedapipe.com

Centerline Scenery (818) 252-7467
8238 Lankershim Blvd, N Hollywood, CA, 91605
meredyth@centerlinescenery.com

Chamber Sheet Metal (818) 346-5685
7026 Deering Ave, Canoga Park, CA, 91303
only sheet metal fabrication & A/C ducts

EFX- Event Special Effects (626) 888-2239
125 Railroad Ave, Monrovia, CA, 91016
Custom Fabrication- CNC- Plasma Table- Pipe & Ring Benders- 3D
Renderings
info@efxla.com * www.efxla.com

Flix FX Inc. (818) 765-3549
7327 Lankershim Blvd #4, N Hollywood, CA, 91605
Machining, tube & pipe bending, cutting & finishing, welding (certified)
info@flixfx.com * www.flixfx.com

The Hand Prop Room LP. (323) 931-1534

HPR Custom (323) 931-1534
5700 Venice Blvd, Los Angeles, CA, 90019
Steel fabrication, MIG welding, TIG welding, ARC welding, water jet cutting,
and CNC machining.
www.hprcustom.com

Pipeworks Fabrication (562) 432-6826
1471 Cota Ave, Long Beach, CA, 90813
www.pipeworksfabrication.com

Scenic Highlights (818) 252-7760
10830 Cantara St, Sun Valley, CA, 91352
scenichighlights.com

Set Masters (818) 982-1506
24853 Avenue Rockefeller, Valencia, CA, 91355
Custom Manufacturing; Architectural; Structural and Creative; 3D renderings
Available
info@setmasters.com * www.setmasters.com

Sword & Stone (818) 562-6548
sheet metal, wrought iron, & welding

Tractor Vision Scenery & Rentals (323) 235-2885
340 E Jefferson Blvd, Los Angeles, CA, 90011
Specializing in entertainment, trade shows, & events, we bring your projects to
life with precision, speed & personality
sets@tractorvision.com * www.tractorvision.com

Warner Bros. Studios Metal Shop (818) 954-1265
4000 Warner Blvd Bldg 44, Burbank, CA, 91522
Custom metal fabrication creating anything from structural steel elements to
intricate custom furniture
WBDS@warnerbros.com * www.wbmetalshop.com

Metaphysical

See: Astrological Occult/Spiritual/Metaphysical*

Meters

See: Electronic Equipment (Dressing) Gas & Electric Meters*

Mexican Decorations

See Also: Pottery

The Hand Prop Room LP. (323) 931-1534
period-present

History For Hire, Inc. (818) 765-7767
period

Lennie Marvin Enterprises, Inc. (Prop Heaven) (818) 841-5882
street vendor carts

Omega/Cinema Props (323) 466-8201
Mexican decor from folk art and pottery to rugs and chairs.

Universal Studios Property & Hardware Dept (818) 777-2784
Many Mexican themed decorations available for rent.

Mexican Pottery

See: Pottery

Mexican Themed Parties

See: Costume Rental Houses Events, Decorations, Supplies &
Services* Events, Design/Planning/Production* Mexican
Decorations* Travel (City/Country) Themed Events*

Microphones

See Also: Audio Equipment Radio/TV Station*

Astro Audio Video Lighting, Inc. (818) 549-9915
6615 San Fernando Rd, Glendale, CA, 91201
Wireless microphones and wired microphones, handheld microphones and
microphone receivers.
www.astroavl.com

C. P. Two (323) 466-8201

Coast Recording Audio Props (818) 755-4692
10715 Magnolia Blvd, N Hollywood, CA, 91601
Microphones from the 20s to the present. Prop microphones
props@coastrecording.com * www.coastrecordingprops.com

The Hand Prop Room LP. (323) 931-1534
period-present, hand-held, stand, personal

History For Hire, Inc. (818) 765-7767
biggest selection there is

LCW Props (818) 243-0707
DJ, Boom, Radio, Stage, Headsets

Modern Props (323) 934-3000
Microphones for non-functional set dressing only

Sony Pictures Studios-Prop House (Off Lot) (310) 244-5999

Universal Studios Property & Hardware Dept (818) 777-2784
Many kinds of microphones from different time periods and uses for rent.

ZG04 DECOR (818) 853-8040
Various microphones for rent

Microscopes

See: Electron Microscope Lab Equipment* Medical Equip/Furniture,
Graphics/Supplies*

Mid-Century Furnishings

See: Furniture, Mid-Century Modern

Military Props & Equipment

See Also: Camouflage Nets Canopies, Tents, Gazebos, Cabanas*
Civil War Era* Police Car, Police Motorcycle* Police Equipment*
Stretchers* Weapons*

AA Surplus Sales Co., Inc. (323) 526-3622
2940 E Olympic Blvd, Los Angeles, CA, 90023
U.S. military tents, clothing, footwear & field gear, military shipping containers,
bunk beds, ammo cans
surplusking@hotmail.com * www.aasurplus.com

American Military Museum (626) 442-1776
1918 N. Rosemead Blvd, S. El Monte, CA, 91733
www.tankland.com

At The Front Militaria (270) 384-1965
430 Rose Ln, Columbia, KY, 42728
WW II re-enactor uniforms/equip. web site has extensive links to related
resources
www.atthefrontshop.com

E.C. Prop Rentals (818) 764-2008
Missile containers, ammo boxes, checkpoint barricades, guard shacks, tarps

Emerson Knives (310) 539-5633
1234 254th St, Harbor City, CA, 90710
Emerson Knives are the only choice of Elite Military and U.S. Covert Units.
They are truly, "Famous In the Worst Places"
eknives@aol.com * www.emersonknives.com

Fall Creek Corporation (765) 482-1861
PO Box 92, Whitestown, IN, 46075
Civil War era, military & civilian. Civil War era reproductions
ajfulks@fcsutler.com * www.fcsutler.com

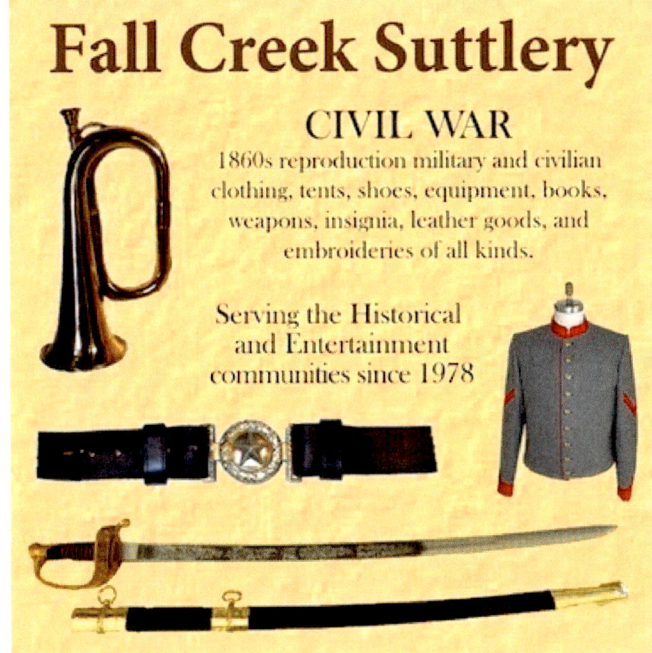

Fall Creek Suttlery

CIVIL WAR

1860s reproduction military and civilian
clothing, tents, shoes, equipment, books,
weapons, insignia, leather goods, and
embroideries of all kinds.

Serving the Historical
and Entertainment
communities since 1978

The Hand Prop Room LP. (323) 931-1534
History For Hire, Inc. (818) 765-7767
Large accurate selection of military leather work
Hollywood Studio Gallery (323) 462-1116
framed medals, photos, posters only
Landser Outfitters, LLC (877) 499-1939
26741 Portola Pkwy Ste 1E411, Foothill Ranch, CA, 92610
WW II German Third Reich / uniforms equipment & medals
sales@landser.com * www.landser.com
LCW Props (818) 243-0707
A Specialty Of Ours, Rigged, Period - Present, Camo, Weapons, Field Gear,
Cases & Ammo Crates, Missiles, Bombs & Marine
LM Treasures (626) 252-7354
We have several types of life size life size army men statues including the
famous fallen soldier statue.
RDD U.S.A. Inc. (213) 742-0666
4638 E Washington Blvd, Commerce, CA, 90040
field gear, military equipment, tents
www.rddusa.com
RJR Props (404) 349-7600
Military electronics, military communications sets,military tactical electronics,
military telemetry units and more.
Supply Sergeant (323) 849-3744
503 N Victory Blvd, Burbank, CA, 91502
Military movie props including ancient Greek/Roman armor & helmets as well
as modern military surplus & military gear.
david@jacksgt.com * www.supplysergeantshop.com
Surplus City (530) 534-9956
4514 Pacific Heights Rd, Oroville, CA, 95965
Military museum rentals
www.surpluscity.com
Sword & Stone (818) 562-6548
Military swords, military daggers, military guns for rent
Universal Studios Property & Hardware Dept (818) 777-2784
Military equipment and military props for rent.

Military Surplus/Combat Clothes, Field Gear

See Also: Civil War Era* Costume Rental Houses* Uniforms, Military
AA Surplus Sales Co., Inc. (323) 526-3622
2940 E Olympic Blvd, Los Angeles, CA, 90023
US military tents, military bunk beds, stretchers, clothing, footwear & field gear,
camping equipment, knives, children
surplusking@hotmail.com * www.aasurplus.com
At The Front Militaria (270) 384-1965
430 Rose Ln, Columbia, KY, 42728
WW II re-enactor uniforms/equip. web site has extensive links to related
resources
www.atthefrontshop.com

California Surplus Mart (323) 465-5525
6263 Santa Monica Blvd, Los Angeles, CA, 90038
Army/Navy & camping gear & work clothes & boots
www.californiasurplusmart.com
The Duffle Bag (845) 878-7106
1270 Route 311, Patterson, NY, 12563
U.S./foreign WW I-current, clothes/insignia/gear, 10-5 M-F or by appt
info@thedufflebaginc.com * www.thedufflebaginc.com
History For Hire, Inc. (818) 765-7767
"surplus" items, no clothing
KSI NYC (212) 757-5670
319 West 42nd Street, New York City, NY, 10036
a real military surplus store, well stocked, good sel., American & German, some
British WWII
www.kaufmansarmynavy.com
LCW Props (818) 243-0707
Camo Nets, Artillery, Field Radios
Omaha's Original Surplus (817) 332-1493
2412 Whitmore St, Fort Worth, TX 76107
your source for original Vietnam gear, vast inventory of genuine military
surplus, an authentic Army/Navy store
www.omahas.com
RDD U.S.A. Inc. (213) 742-0666
4638 E Washington Blvd, Commerce, CA, 90040
military clothing & equipment, field gear, tents
www.rddusa.com

MILITARY SURPLUS NEW & USED SINCE 1985

Tents & Tarps Military Clothing & Props Camouflage Nets Field Gear
www.rdusa.com
www.americawear.com

Supply Sergeant (323) 849-3744
503 N Victory Blvd, Burbank, CA, 91502
Army surplus, military clothes, army clothes, navy surplus, navy clothes,
military gear, camping gear, camping equipment
david@jacksgt.com * www.supplysergeantshop.com

Milk Bottles & Cans

The Hand Prop Room LP. (323) 931-1534
bottles & cans
History For Hire, Inc. (818) 765-7767
cans & bottles
LCW Props (818) 243-0707
Unlimited Quantity, We Own The Recycling Center Next Door
Sony Pictures Studios-Prop House (Off Lot) (310) 244-5999
cans & bottles
Universal Studios Property & Hardware Dept (818) 777-2784
Prop milk bottles and prop milk cans for rent.

Milk Crates

See: Expendables

Milk Paint

See: Paint & Painting Supplies

Mini-mart

See: Cash Registers* Counters* Credit Card Imprint Machine* Display Cases, Racks & Fixtures (Store)* Food, Artificial Food* General Store* Printing, Graphics, Digital & Large Format* Steel Folding Gates & Roll-Up Doors* Store Shelf Units & Shelving* Surveillance Equipment

Miniatures/Models

See Also: Dollhouses* Dolls* Model Ships/Planes/Trains/Autos Etc.* Prop Design & Manufacturing* Puppets, Marionettes, Automata, Animatronics

Action Sets and Props / WonderWorks, Inc.　　(818) 992-8811
Space shuttle & station, space suit, specialty props, miniatures, mechanical effects, cityscape, miniature buildings

Culver Architects Inc.　　(310) 721-9867
Call for Appointment, Playa del Rey, CA, 90293
Rentals of architecture models & landscape/interior design renderings, drawings, material samples, drafting tools, art.
ron@culverarchitects.com * www.carcinc.com/C_ARC/model_rentals.html

History For Hire, Inc.　　(818) 765-7767
tract houses, model houses

IDF Studio Scenery　　(818) 982-7433
6844 Lankershim Blvd, North Hollywood, CA, 91605
Custom fabrication of miniatures & props
info@idfstudioscenery.com * www.idfstudioscenery.com

LCW Props　　(818) 243-0707
Anatomical Models, DNA, Elements

Merritt Productions, Inc.　　(818) 760-0612
10845 Vanowen St, North Hollywood, CA, 91605
specialty props, miniatures, sculpture, mech effects, set const. A whole city of miniature buildings.
www.merrittproductions.com

My Doll's House　　(310) 320-4828
1218 El Prado Ave Ste 136, Torrance, CA 90501
Dollhouses, Dollhouse Kits, Room Boxes, Miniatures, Collectibles, Accessories, Tools and Supplies
margiesminiatures@gmail.com * www.mydollshouse.com

Sketch Paper Design　　(818) 442-0284
7771 Lemona Ave, Van Nuys, CA, 91405
Custom Designed Miniature Scenery, Faux facade installation and removal
info@sketchpaperdesign.com * www.sketchpaperdesign.com

Tractor Vision Scenery & Rentals　　(323) 235-2885
340 E Jefferson Blvd, Los Angeles, CA, 90011
Specializing in entertainment, trade shows, & events, we bring your projects to life with precision, speed & personality
sets@tractorvision.com * www.tractorvision.com

Mining & Prospecting Equipment

Black Cat Mining　　(541) 622-8225
By Appointment Only
everything for prospecting & rock hounding
www.blackcatmining.com

Keene Engineering, Inc.　　(818) 993-0411
20201 Bahama St, Chatsworth CA, 91311
Dredges, hydraulic systems, and related mining equip., website lists dealer network
www.keeneeng.com

Machinery & Equipment Co., Inc.　　(909) 599-3916
115 N Cataract Ave, San Dimas, CA, 91773
Used industrial mining equipment from lab to major production.
sherri@machineryandequipment.com * www.machineryandequipment.com

Universal Studios Property & Hardware Dept　　(818) 777-2784
Gold mining pans, mining ore buckets and more for rent.

Mirrors, Framed Decorative Furnishings

See Also: Ballet Barres & Dance Mirrors* Bathroom Fixtures* Fun House Mirrors* Glass & Mirrors* Make-up Tables & Mirrors

Acme Display Fixture & Packaging　　(888) 411-1870
3829 S Broadway St, Los Angeles, CA, 90037
Complete store setups: garment racks, displays/display cases, counters, packaging, shelving, hangers, mannequins
sales@acmedisplay.com * www.acmedisplay.com

Bridge Furniture & Props Los Angeles　　(818) 433-7100
We carry modern & traditional furniture, lighting, accessories, art, & rugs. Items are online for easy shopping.

Castle Antiques & Design　　(818) 765-5000
11924 Vose St, N Hollywood, CA, 91605
We offer many decorative and framed mirrors available for rent and purchase.
info@castleantiques.net * www.castleprophouse.com

Clifford Antiques　　(747) 283-1272
3429 Magnolia Blvd, Burbank, CA, 91505
British Antiques shipped from Scotland we're a family run business with over 40 years experience
wfcliffordantiques@yahoo.com * www.cliffordantiques.com

The Hand Prop Room LP.　　(323) 931-1534

Lux Lounge EFR　　(888) 247-4411
106 1/2 Judge John Aiso St #318, Los Angeles, CA, 90012
Mirror Furniture/Mirrored Furniture Rentals
info@luxloungeefr.com * www.luxloungeefr.com

Ob-jects　　(818) 351-4200
Decorative mirrors

Omega/Cinema Props　　(323) 466-8201

Prop Services West　　(818) 503-2790

Sony Pictures Studios-Prop House (Off Lot)　　(310) 244-5999
dance studio mirrors, standing mirrors, studio makeup mirrors, tabletop mirrors, wall mounted mirrors

U-Frame It Gallery　　(818) 781-4500
6203 Lankershim Blvd, N Hollywood, CA, 91606
Framed mirrors, wide variety, custom framing
uframit@aol.com * www.uframeitgallery.com

Universal Studios Property & Hardware Dept　　(818) 777-2784
Decorative mirrors and framed mirrors for rent.

ZG04 DECOR　　(818) 853-8040
Wall Mirrors, Cheval Mirror, Bathroom - Mirrors, Standing, Hanging

Mission Control Consoles

See Also: Control Boards* Electronic Equipment (Dressing)

LCW Props　　(818) 243-0707
Large Selection Of Aerospace Panels, Rigged, Consoles, Boxes & Graphics

Woody's Electrical Props　　(818) 503-1940
period to futuristic. Apollo 13 is one of our successes! Fantasy sets, military sets, industrial sets, electrical panels

Model Makers

See: Miniatures/Models* Prop Design & Manufacturing* Puppets, Marionettes, Automata, Animatronics

Model Ships/Planes/Trains/Autos Etc.

See Also: Dollhouses* Hobby & Craft Supplies* Miniatures/Models* Prop Houses

Action Sets and Props / WonderWorks, Inc.　　(818) 992-8811
Space shuttle & station, space suit, specialty props, miniatures, mechanical effects, cityscape, miniature buildings

The Hand Prop Room LP.　　(323) 931-1534

History For Hire, Inc.　　(818) 765-7767
model trains

Modern Props　　(323) 934-3000
variety of models including architectural buildings.

Pacmin　　(714) 447-4478
2021 Raymer Ave, Fullerton, CA, 92833
lrg sel aircraft, 10"-20' or more, airline, military, corporate custom build; NYC office (585) 226-8540
www.pacmin.com

Prop Services West　　(818) 503-2790

Sony Pictures Studios-Prop House (Off Lot)　　(310) 244-5999
model airplanes, model bicycles, model canoes, model helicopters, model lighthouses, model motorcycles, model rockets, and more

The Train Shack　　(818) 842-3330
1030 N Hollywood Way, Burbank, CA, 91505
www.trainshack.com

Universal Studios Property & Hardware Dept　　(818) 777-2784
Many kinds of models for rent.

ZG04 DECOR　　(818) 853-8040
Scale Models: Speed Boat Models, Sail Boat Ship Models, Car Models, Airplane Models, Architectural Models

Modular Work Stations

See: Office Furniture

Mold Making

See Also: Prop Design & Manufacturing* Sculpture* Statuary

Flix FX Inc. (818) 765-3549
7327 Lankershim Blvd #4, N Hollywood, CA, 91605
info@flixfx.com * www.flixfx.com

The Hand Prop Room LP. (323) 931-1534

HPR Custom (323) 931-1534
5700 Venice Blvd, Los Angeles, CA, 90019
Roto casting, 3D rapid prototyping, silicone molding, fiberglass molding, spin casting, and 3D modeling.
www.hprcustom.com

KIHL STUDIOS (818) 812-9594
9701 Owensmouth Ave Unit 1, Chatsworth, CA, 91311
Mold making & casting services.
design@kihlstudios.com * www.kihlstudios.com

Reynolds Advanced Materials: Smooth-On (818) 358-6000
Distributor
10856 Vanowen St, N Hollywood, CA, 91605
Hollywood's F/X source for Liquid Rubbers, and Plastics. Lifecasting, F/X Makeup, Dragon Skin, Eco Flex and more.
LA@reynoldsam.com * www.moldmakingmaterials.com

Warner Bros. Studios Staff Shop (818) 954-2269
Manufacturer of exterior & interior details used for the creation of sets in all architectural styles & eras.

Money (Prop)

See Also: Bank Dressing

The Earl Hays Press (818) 765-0700
10707 Sherman Way, Sun Valley, CA, 91352
prop money/fake money
ehp@la.twcbc.com * www.theearlhayspress.com

The Hand Prop Room LP. (323) 931-1534

History For Hire, Inc. (818) 765-7767
paper money, coins, gold bricks, real period currency

LCW Props (818) 243-0707
Large Quantites, Fake Money, Coin, Bundles, Pallets Of Money, Gold Bars, Treasure, cash cannons/cash guns

RJR Props (404) 349-7600
Prop money/stage money/fake money; legal fake money in all denominations and amounts including bags of cash & stacks.

Sony Pictures Studios-Prop House (Off Lot) (310) 244-5999
fake money, fake gold bars, fake silver bars

Universal Studios Property & Hardware Dept (818) 777-2784
Prop money, money bags, money bundles, money clips, money molds, prop gold ingots and more for rent.

Money Belts

See: Underwear & Lingerie, Bloomers, Corsets, Etc.

Monkey Cages

See: Animal Cages

Monsters

See: Aliens* Horror/Monster Dressing* Special Effects, Make-up/Prosthetics

Morgue

See Also: Cemetery Dressing* Mortuary

A-1 Medical Integration (818) 753-0319
Medical devices for Set Decoration & Property, from minor procedures to detailed hospital units.

Alpha Companies - Spellman Desk Co. (818) 504-9090
The #1 source for medical equipment in the industry.

Dapper Cadaver (818) 771-0818
Autopsy tables and instruments. Autopsy bodies with organs. Embalming tables and pumps. Body bags, toe tags, etc.

LCW Props (818) 243-0707
Morgue Tables, Doors, Tools & Equipment

MorguePropRentals.com (818) 957-2178
5134 Valley Blvd, Los Angeles, CA, 90032
surg/pathology instrument props, set dressing, shooting loc.
info@1800autopsy.com * www.morgueproprentals.com

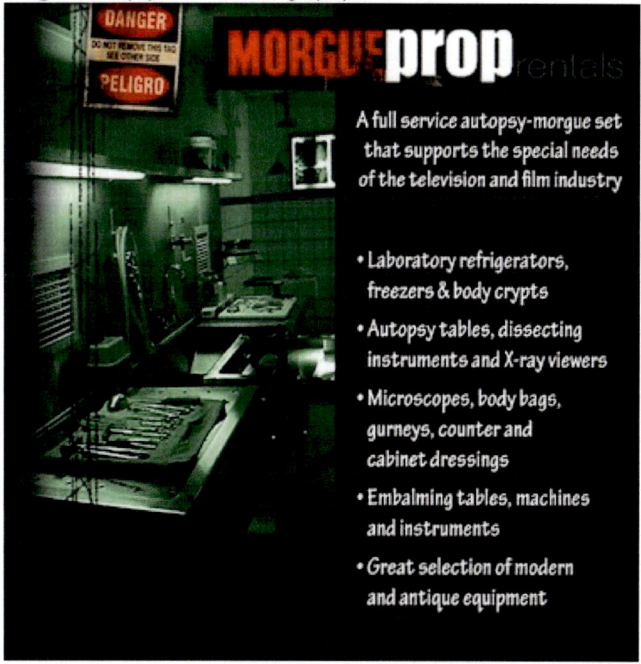

Mortuary

See Also: Caskets* Cemetery Dressing* Florists/Floral Design
Dapper Cadaver (818) 771-0818
Embalming tables, embalming pumps and instruments like trocars. Caskets and lecterns.
MorguePropRentals.com (818) 957-2178
5134 Valley Blvd, Los Angeles, CA, 90032
prep room/embalming equip. & instruments
info@1800autopsy.com * www.morguepoprentals.com

Motel

See: Furniture, Tenement Tacky Motel* Hotel, Motel, Inn, Lodge

Motion Control

See Also: Mechanical Effects* Rigging, Equipment or Services
Bill Ferrell Co. (818) 767-1900
10556 Keswick St, Sun Valley, CA, 91352
Turntables, lifts, winches, conveyors; moving props, ramps, sets. Simple or automated positioning and speed controls.
www.billferrell.com
General Lift (310) 414-0717
111 Maryland St. El Segundo, CA 90245
variety of portable motion control systems for camera filming
www.general-lift.com
Skjonberg Controls, Inc. (805) 650-0877
1363 Donlon St Ste 6, Ventura, CA, 93003
www.skjonberg.com

Motion Picture Camera Equipment

See Also: Camera Equipment* Video 24fps / Sync System / D.D.I.* Video Camera Equipment & Services* Video Equipment
Birns & Sawyer, Inc. (323) 466-8211
5275 Craner Ave, N Hollywood, CA, 91601
film & video cameras, accessories, lighting/grip, expendables, for lighting & grip rental call (818) 766-2525
www.birnsandsawyer.com
Panavision (Woodland Hills) (818) 316-1000
6101 Variel Ave, Woodland Hills, CA, 91367
Cameras & film. Commercials, music videos, hair & make-up test, trailers
www.panavision.com
Panavision (Hollywood) (323) 464-3800
6735 Selma Ave, Hollywood, CA, 90028
expendables, plus camera equip., HD 900R, F23, Varicam. 16mm, 35mm, HD900
www.panavision.com
Slow Motion Inc.-Film & Digital (818) 982-4400
7211 Clybourn Ave, Sun Valley, CA, 91352
high speed cameras/lenses, underwater, sound cameras, carry many brands/models
www.slowmotioninc.com

Motion Picture Production Equip., Period

See Also: Camera Equipment* Motion Picture Projectors
History For Hire, Inc. (818) 765-7767
most comprehensive selection of period motion picture production equipment there is
Universal Studios Property & Hardware Dept (818) 777-2784
Vintage and period motion picture equipment for rent.

Motion Picture Projectors

See Also: Camera Equipment* Film Reels
The Hand Prop Room LP. (323) 931-1534
period-present
History For Hire, Inc. (818) 765-7767
8mm, 16mm, 35mm, all levels
LCW Props (818) 243-0707
8mm, 16mm, 35mm Projectors

Motor Homes

See: RV Vehicles & Travel Trailers, Equip & Parts

Motorcycles

See Also: Police Car, Police Motorcycle* Vehicles/Picture Vehicles
Alley Cats Studio Rentals (818) 982-9178
parts only, not complete cycles
Bartel's Harley Davidson (310) 823-1112
4141 Lincoln Blvd, Marina Del Rey, CA, 90292
motorcycles, clothing, collectibles, parts
www.bartelsharley.com
Cornwell & Sheridan Picture Vehicles (310) 217-9060
15700 S Broadway, Gardena, CA, 90248
Convertibles, Coupes, Sedans, Limos, Motorcycles
davesimoncars@yahoo.com * www.old-cars.net
Laidlaw's Harley-Davidson (626) 851-0412
1919 Puente Ave, Baldwin Park, CA, 91706
Sales, service & rentals
www.laidlawsharley.com
MovieMoto.com (626) 359-0016
16015 Adelante St, Irwindale, CA, 91702
Rare, Odd, Classic, Exotic, Unknown MOTORCYCLE RENTALS. Specializing in Italian marks.
www.MovieMoto.com

Picture Mopeds & Motorcycles (626) 818-3519
Call for an Appointment
We deliver and offer on location assistance for our vehicles/equip ensuring 100% reliability so you get the right shot.
kdoogie69@yahoo.com * www.pasadenamoped.com
Route 66 Riders (310) 578-0112
4161 Lincoln Blvd, Marina Del Rey, CA, 90292
Only Harleys
www.route66riders.com

Moulding, Wood

See Also: Staff Shops

American Wood Column Corp.   **(718) 782-3163**
913 Grand St, Brooklyn, NY, 11211-2785
catalog sales; large sel. of millwork, architectural/decorative small finials to tall columns, plain to ornate, custom t
www.americanwoodcolumncorp.com

Diamond Hardwoods   **(559) 264-4888**
2534 San Benito, Fresno, CA 93721
millwork, mouldings, casings, and plywood.
http://diamondhardwoods.net

Moulding Center   **(818) 985-5376**
6501 Lankershim Blvd, N Hollywood, CA, 91606
www.mouldingcenter.squarespace.com

National Hardwood Flooring & Moulding   **(818) 988-9663**
14959 Delano St, Van Nuys, CA, 91411
Flooring, moulding, custom milling, stains, finishes, abrasives, sundries, tools, fireplace mantels & stair components
www.nationalhardwood.com

Stock Mill   **(818) 842-8139**
161 W Cypress Ave, Burbank, CA, 91502
custom milling
www.buildwithbmc.com

Sunland Wood Products   **(818) 982-3110**
11929 Vose St, North Hollywood CA, 91605
custom, spindles, railings, std/cust doors & windows, etc.
www.sunlandwood.com

Vintage Woodworks   **(903) 356-2158**
9195 Highway 34 S PO Box 39, Quinlan, TX, 75474
catalog sales; + online sales, old-fashioned interior/exterior details, mouldings, Victorian gingerbread, doors, porch p
www.vintagewoodworks.com

Warner Bros. Studios Paint Department   **(818) 954-1817**
4000 Warner Blvd Bldg 47, Burbank, CA, 91522
Production expendables & supplies to the entertainment community at great prices
www.wbpaintdept.com

Mounted Heads

See: Taxidermy, Hides/Heads/Skeletons

Mounting Services

See: Art & Picture Framing Services

Movie Lobby

See: Crowd Control: Barricades, Turnstiles Etc.* Display Cases, Racks & Fixtures (Store)* Posters, Art/Movie/Travel/Wanted Etc.* Stanchions & Rope* Vendor Carts & Concession Counters

Movie Posters

See: Memorabilia & Novelties* Posters, Art/Movie/Travel/Wanted Etc.

MRI (Magnetic Resonance Imaging)

See Also: X-ray Machine* X-rays & X-ray Viewers

Alpha Companies - Spellman Desk Co.   **(818) 504-9090**
various styles

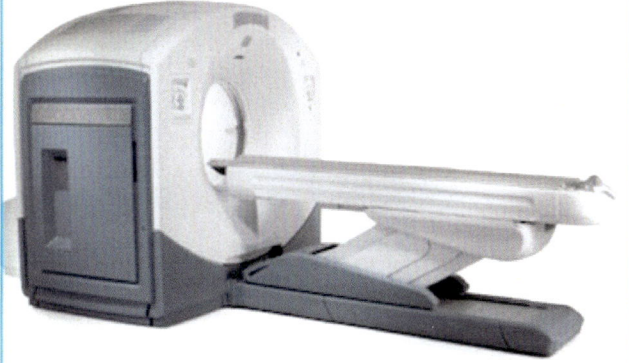
Muffler Man

See: Automotive/Garage Equip. & Parts

Mummies

See: Egyptian Dressing

Murals

See: Art, Artists For Hire* Backings* Scenic Artists* Wall Coverings

Music & Dance Machines

See: Jukeboxes, Music/Dance Machines

Music Boxes

Music Box Attic   **(818) 255-0871**
7346 Radford Ave, N Hollywood, CA, 91605
Music boxes, singing birds, dancing dolls, musical pocket watches, musical automata, watch cases, & antique music boxes.
www.musicboxattic.com

Omega/Cinema Props   **(323) 466-8201**
Music boxes of various kinds from decorative to toy.

Universal Studios Property & Hardware Dept   **(818) 777-2784**
Decorative music boxes to plain music boxes

Warner Bros. Studios Property Department   **(818) 954-2181**
Music boxes; childrens music boxes/kids music boxes, jewelry music boxes and more

Music Stands

See Also: Music, Sheet

C. P. Two	(323) 466-8201
The Hand Prop Room LP.	(323) 931-1534
History For Hire, Inc.	(818) 765-7767
choices	
RC Vintage, Inc.	(818) 765-7107
1930s Big Band style, band stands	
Sony Pictures Studios-Prop House (Off Lot)	(310) 244-5999
sheet music stands, guitar stands	
Universal Studios Property & Hardware Dept	(818) 777-2784

Wooden musics stands, metal music stands, modern music stands and vintage music stands for rent.

Music, Sheet

See Also: Music Stands

The Hand Prop Room LP.	(323) 931-1534
History For Hire, Inc.	(818) 765-7767
rental & custom	
Hollywood Sheet Music	(818) 567-4338

323 S Front St, Burbank, CA, 91502
Online sales only
www.hollywoodsheetmusic.com

Old N Country Prop Shop, LLC	(818) 423-2599

Large assortment of vintage sheet music. Collections, as well as individual songs.

Musical Instrument Cases

See Also: Prop Houses

C. P. Two	(323) 466-8201
History For Hire, Inc.	(818) 765-7767
Sony Pictures Studios-Prop House (Off Lot)	(310) 244-5999

Musical Instruments

See Also: Beatles Musical Instruments* Calliopes* Chimes & Bells* Pianos & Keyboard Instruments* Prop Houses* Rock 'n' Roll Instruments

The Auditorium   (877) 732-7733
7684 Clybourn Ave 2nd Fl Unit C, Sun Valley, CA, 91352
We specialize in musical prop rentals and set dressing for media production.
info@auditoriumprops.com * www.auditoriumprops.com

Badia Design, Inc.   (818) 762-0130
5420 Vineland Ave, N Hollywood, CA, 91601
Moroccan Musical Instrument including Moroccan ceramic drum, small iron castanets, Moroccan hand drum and more.
info@badiadesign.com * www.badiadesign.com

C. P. Two   (323) 466-8201
Wide range of instruments from rock and acoustic to traditional and classical incl upright pianos, grand pianos & more.

Doug Rowell, Sculptor   (818) 353-4607
Call for appt, Tujunga, CA, 91042
Wood, foam, metal, custom only, design/fabrication/any size job
doug@carverdoug.com * www.carverdoug.com

The Hand Prop Room LP.   (323) 931-1534
all instruments

History For Hire, Inc.   (818) 765-7767
Huge selection of instruments from all periods, rock 'n' roll our specialty including Beatles musical instruments!

LCW Props   (818) 243-0707
Guitars, Some Percussion, Violins, Wind Instruments, Music Trays

Los Angeles Percussion Rentals   (310) 666-8152
26450 Ruether Ave Unit 208, Santa Clarita, CA, 91350
Drums, guitars, bass, keyboards, percussion & orchestra instruments (modern or vintage). For performance or prop use.
dan@lapercussionrentals.com * www.lapercussionrentals.com

Music Depot LA   (951) 237-3521
11762 De Palma Rd Ste 1-C #63, Corona, CA, 92883
One-stop shop for name brand, unique or custom built musical instruments and music props. Music industry experts.
del@musicdepotla.com * www.MusicDepotLA.com

Norman's Rare Guitars   (818) 344-8300
18969 Ventura Blvd, Tarzana, CA, 91356
vintage guitars
www.normansrareguitars.com

Old N Country Prop Shop, LLC   (818) 423-2599
Variety of instruments - guitars, upright bass, drums, large vintage bass drum, keyboards, etc.

Omega/Cinema Props   (323) 466-8201
Pianos, church organs, mandolins and more.

Sony Pictures Studios-Prop House (Off Lot)   (310) 244-5999
Bagpipes, orchestral instruments, band instruments, folk instruments, pianos, organs percussion instruments and more

Universal Studios Property & Hardware Dept   (818) 777-2784
and cases

Muskets

See: Weaponry, Historical

Mutoscope

See: Arcade Equipment, Games & Rides

Name Badges

See: Badges, Patches & Buttons

Name Plates

See: Courtroom Furniture & Dressing* Bank Dressing* Desk Dressing* Engraving* Office Equipment & Dressing

NASA Dressing

See Also: Computers* Science Equipment* Space Shuttle/Space Hardware

Action Sets and Props / WonderWorks, Inc. (818) 992-8811
Space shuttle & station, space suit, specialty props, miniatures, mechanical effects, cityscape, miniature buildings

E.C. Prop Rentals (818) 764-2008
NASA 'worm font' brass letters
LCW Props (818) 243-0707
NASA dressing, including NASA CEV

NASCAR

See Also: Vehicles/Picture Vehicles
AIR Designs (818) 768-6639
Pit Carts, Equipment, Jacks, Tire Racks, Tires, & More
K4 Motorsports (818) 713-0552
PO Box 8902, Calabasas, CA, 91372
Full NASCAR Racing Resources for Production, Features, T.V., and Commercials; Race cars, haulers, pit equip., drivers.
www.k4motorsports.com

Native American

See Also: Archery Equipment, Training* Baskets* Leather (Clothing, Accessories, Materials)* Pottery* Rugs* Wardrobe, Antique/Historical* Western Dressing
Absaroka Western Designs (307) 455-2440
1414 Warm Springs Dr, Dubois, WY, 82513
Lodgepole furniture, raw costuming/prop materials, also tanning & some finished costumes
www.absarokawesterndesign.com
American Plume (800) 521-1132
11 Skyine Drive East, Unit 2, Clarks Summit, PA 18411
Boas/jackets/theatrical division in NYC; (800) 962-8544. war bonnet, spirit mask, dreamcatcher, mandela
apff@epix.net * www.americanplume.com

Autry National Center (323) 667-2000
4700 Western Heritage Way, Los Angeles, CA, 90027
Research room Ext 349, book, archival, artifact collection on the Native American & history of Amer. West
www.theautry.org
Caravan West Productions (661) 268-8300
35660 Jayhawker Rd, Aqua Dulce, CA, 91390
everything Native American, enough for a whole Indian village, trading post
caravanwest@earthlink.net * www.caravanwest.com
Clearedart.com/El Studio Granados (818) 240-4421
958 Verdugo Circle Dr, Glendale, CA, 91206
Contemporary-traditional native art, many mediums/styles. Fill your gallery w/ custom framed/professionally mounted art.
fineart@elstudiogranados.com * www.clearedart.com
Crazy Crow Trading Post (800) 786-6210
1801 N. Airport Dr, Pottsboro, TX 75076
Catalog; Native American & mountain man craft supplies, finished goods, catalog is $5.
www.crazycrow.com
The Hand Prop Room LP. (323) 931-1534
auth. antiques, headdresses, knives, beadwork, animal skins etc
History For Hire, Inc. (818) 765-7767
Authentic antiques; baskets, beadwork, blankets
Hollywood Studio Gallery (323) 462-1116
Western paintings, prints & masks
Indian Art Center (818) 763-3430
12666 Ventura Blvd, Studio City, CA, 91604
Rugs & blankets, artifacts, jewelry
www.indianartcenter.net
Indian Images (618) 664-3384
203 Asbury St, Greenville, IL, 62246
High quality made-to-order costumes, props & set decoration of planes, plateau, southwest & northeast woodlands indians.
b.k.brewer@knewwavecomm.net
The Indian Store (760) 639-5309
1950 Hacienda Dr, Vista, CA, 92081
beads, jewelry findings, fur, feather, leather, rawhide, pottery finished artifacts, many books on Indian lore/tribes
www.indianstore.org
LM Treasures (626) 252-7354
Native American statues & Native American themed statues

Nautical Dressing & Props

See Also: Boats & Water Sport Vehicles* Caged Vapor Proof Lights* Canvas* Chain & Rope* Fish, Artificial & Rubber* Pirate, Chests & Treasures* Seashells
Alley Cats Studio Rentals (818) 982-9178
Extensive/all sizes, everything from anchors to shark diving cage including bouys, wooden boats, and beach signage.
The Hand Prop Room LP. (323) 931-1534
ship parts & access., auth. artifacts
History For Hire, Inc. (818) 765-7767
anchors,fish/cargo nets,life jackets/rings,portholes, binnacles, ship's wheel
LCW Props (818) 243-0707
Large Selection, Russian Sub, Regular Sub, Nets, Rope, Anchors, Outboard Motors, Ship, Yacht & Pilot House Interiors
Lennie Marvin Enterprises, Inc. (Prop Heaven) (818) 841-5882
netting, fenders, ropes, lights, anchors, life jackets, portholes, lifeguard towers etc.
LM Treasures (626) 252-7354
Assorted Sand Dollars, starfish, & anchors are just a few items sold to help recreate any type beach like theme in mind.
Oceanic Arts (562) 698-6960
Rope Rigging, Belaying Pins, Cleats, Dead Eyes, Wood Block Pulleys, Barrels, Used fish nets.
Prop Services West (818) 503-2790
Sony Pictures Studios-Prop House (Off Lot) (310) 244-5999
nautical bells, boat bumpers, boat hooks, boat motors, buoys, anchors, life jackets/rings, portholes, etc.

LISTINGS FOR THIS CATEGORY CONTINUE ON THE FOLLOWING PAGE

Tally Ho Marine Salvage & Decor   (310) 548-5273
406 22nd St, San Pedro, CA, 90731
If we don't have it & can't find it, we can build it. anchors, fish nets, dock cleats, lanterns, cargo & safety nets

Universal Studios Property & Hardware Dept   (818) 777-2784
Nautical props and nautical dressing for rent; cargo nets, fish nets, life jacket/rings, portholes, ship's wheel
Warner Bros. Studios Hardware Rentals   (818) 954-1335
4000 Warner Blvd Bldg 30, Burbank, CA, 91522
Door Knobs & Plates, Hinges, Window Fixtures, Elevator Panels, Train & Boat Accessories
wbsfproperty@warnerbros.com * www.wbpropertydept.com

Nautical Themed Events

See: Events, Backings & Scenery Events, Decorations, Supplies & Services* Events, Design/Planning/Production* Prop Houses*

Nautical/Marine Services & Charters

See Also: Wetsuits, Diving/Surfing
Aquavision   (562) 433-2863
3708 E 4th St, Long Beach, CA, 90814
picture & camera boats/crews, scouting, stunts, set medics lifeguards, safety divers, marine prop fab., underwater sets
www.aquavision.net
Cinema Rentals, Inc   (661) 222-7342
25876 The Old Rd #174, Stevenson Ranch, CA, 91381
picture boats/ships, marine filming equip., underwater cameras, unmanned aerial filming equip.
ocxinc@gmail.com * www.cinemarentals.com
Executive Yacht Management, Inc.   (310) 306-2555
644 Venice Blvd, Marina Del Rey, CA, 90291
power & sail yachts, camera boats, marine coordination, technical advisors
info@yacht-management.com * www.yacht-management.com
HEF Pool Service Corp   (818) 439-6234
6632 Hesperia Ave, Reseda, CA, 91335
Portable filtration units, any size tank. Surface skimmers. Chemical balance to Health Board specs. Onsite maintenance.
www.hefpool.com
Hornblower Cruises & Events   (310) 301-6000
13755 Fiji Way, Marina Del Rey, CA, 90292
also loc in San Francisco, Berkeley, Newport Beach, San Diego
mdr@hornblower.com * www.hornblower.com
Living Art Aquatic Design, Inc.   (310) 822-7484
2301 South Sepulveda Blvd, Los Angeles, CA, 90064
Water tanks.
ron@aquatic2000.com * www.aquatic2000.com
Nautical Film Services   (310) 729-6920
PO Box 50066, Long Beach, CA, 90815
comprehensive marine services for film, TV, print ad photography, special events
www.nauticalfilmservices.com
Offshore Grip Marine   (310) 547-3515
22631 Pacific Coast Hwy #764, Malibu, CA, 90265
comprehensive svcs from picture & camera boats, to underwater services (diving, rigging for stunts, etc.)
Outerside   (615) 720-7011
Call for Appointment.
Environmental & underwater photography
www.outerside.com

Neglige

See: Underwear & Lingerie, Bloomers, Corsets, Etc.

Neon Lights & Signs

See Also: Bars, Nightclubs, Barware & Dressing Carnival Dressing/Supplies* Light Fixtures* Signs* Special Effects, Lighting & Lasers*

AIR Designs   **(818) 768-6639**
Large Selection, Auto, Bar, Diner, Restaurant, Ice Cream, Coffee

Alley Cats Studio Rentals   **(818) 982-9178**
including night club decorations, coastal signage

American Sign Museum   **(513) 541-6366**
1330 Monmouth Ave, Cincinnati, OH, 45225
Most of our signs are electric, incandescent to neon. Some still new in the box. Goldleaf signs from the 1890s to 1910.
info@americansignmuseum.org * www.americansignmuseum.org

C. P. Two   **(323) 466-8201**

The Hand Prop Room LP.   **(323) 931-1534**
lrg sel., creative, commercial

Heaven or Las Vegas Neon   **(818) 949-2677**
7740 Lemona Ave, Van Nuys, CA, 91405
Thousands of neon signs & neon props. Custom mfg, install, strike & delivery services. CA Electric Sign Lic#931962
mail@rentneon.com * www.rentneon.com

Hollywood Neon, Inc   **(323) 227-6208**
Call for Appt.
custom neon design
www.hollywoodneon.com

Lennie Marvin Enterprises, Inc. (Prop Heaven)   **(818) 841-5882**
wide variety, commercial to art piece

Nights of Neon   **(818) 756-4791**
13815 Saticoy St, Van Nuys, CA, 91402
Over 2,000 neon props in stock. Custom neon lighting and neon fabrication done onsite.
contact@nightsofneon.com * www.nightsofneon.com

RC Vintage, Inc.   **(818) 765-7107**
large selection of neon signs, Neon Clocks, and more

Sony Pictures Studios-Prop House (Off Lot)   **(310) 244-5999**
neon dimmer switch, neon signs, neon transformer, neon lights, misc neon supplies, neon shipping crate

Universal Studios Property & Hardware Dept   **(818) 777-2784**
Bar, restaurant, hotel and clubs neon signs for rent.

Nets

See: Camouflage Nets Cargo Nets* Military Surplus/Combat Clothes, Field Gear* Nautical Dressing & Props* Sporting Goods & Services*

New Orleans/Mardi Gras Themed Parties

See: Costume Rental Houses Events, Decorations, Supplies & Services* Events, Design/Planning/Production* Masks* Travel (City/Country) Themed Events*

New York City Set Dressing & Props

AIR Designs   **(818) 768-6639**
Trash Cans, Subway Entrance, Signage & More

Alley Cats Studio Rentals   **(818) 982-9178**
newsracks, kiosks, subway & street signs, NY park bench, street vendors, food carts, vendor carts, and much more.

E.C. Prop Rentals   **(818) 764-2008**
Orange/White Steam Vents, Newspaper Machines, Street Signage, Subway Signage, Blue Police Barricades.

The Hand Prop Room LP.   **(323) 931-1534**
vendor carts, taxi, police, firemen, set-ups

History For Hire, Inc.   **(818) 765-7767**
police, etc.

Lennie Marvin Enterprises, Inc. (Prop Heaven)   **(818) 841-5882**
lights, benches, trash cans, parking pods, Central Park benches

Picture Start Props   **(818) 255-5472**
Many New York street and subway signs. Also a subway station bench.

Universal Studios Property & Hardware Dept   **(818) 777-2784**
New York city set dressing and New York city props for rent.

New York Themed Parties

See: Events, Decorations, Supplies & Services* Events, Design/Planning/Production* Statue Of Liberty* Travel (City/Country) Themed Events

News Vans & Broadcast Trucks

See: Newsroom* Vehicles/Picture Vehicles

Newspapers (Prop)

History For Hire, Inc.	**(818) 765-7767**
custom & stock items for sale	
Timothy Hughes Rare & Early Newspapers	**(570) 326-1045**
PO Box 3636, Williamsport, PA, 17701	
buy/sell historic newspapers, 1600s to 1991, over 2 million original & historic issues	
www.rarenewspapers.com	

Newsroom

E.C. Prop Rentals	**(818) 764-2008**
desk & smalls, chairs, phones	
History For Hire, Inc.	**(818) 765-7767**
teletypes, typewriters, phones, etc.	
LCW Props	**(818) 243-0707**
News Desk, Monitors, Lighting, Paperwork	
RJR Props	**(404) 349-7600**
Newsroom cameras, newsroom pedestals, news crew cameras, ENV cameras	
Universal Studios Property & Hardware Dept	**(818) 777-2784**
Newsroom props, news anchor desks and newsroom dressing for rent.	
Warner Bros. Studios Property Department	**(818) 954-2181**
News desks/anchor desks for rent. More in The Collection!	

Newsstands

Above The Fold	**(323) 464-6397**
226 N Larchmont Blvd, Los Angeles, CA, 90004	
RC Vintage, Inc.	**(818) 765-7107**
Newspaper stands	
Robertson Magazine	**(310) 205-8956**
1414 S Robertson Blvd, Los Angeles, CA, 90035	
Sherman Oaks Newsstand	**(818) 995-0632**
14500 Ventura Blvd, Sherman Oaks, CA, 91403	

Newsstands (Prop)

See Also: Kiosks* Magazines & Magazine/Newspaper Racks

AIR Designs	**(818) 768-6639**
Full Size, Boxes, Books, Newspaper, Lottery Stands, Wall Units	
Alley Cats Studio Rentals	**(818) 982-9178**
magazine stands, newspaper racks	
E.C. Prop Rentals	**(818) 764-2008**
Newspaper Machines	
History For Hire, Inc.	**(818) 765-7767**
full or empty	
LCW Props	**(818) 243-0707**
Newspapers, Magazines, News Racks, Kiosks	
Universal Studios Property & Hardware Dept	**(818) 777-2784**
Prop newsstands, vending newsstands, and newsstand displays for rent.	
Warner Bros. Studios Property Department	**(818) 954-2181**
Outdoor newsstands, metal newsstands, vintage/period newsstands	

Nightclubs

See: Banquets/Booths (Seating)* Bars, Nightclubs, Barware & Dressing* Chairs* Liquor Bottles* Tables

Nightgowns

See: Sleepwear - Pajamas, Nightgowns, Etc.

Nodders

Modern Props	**(323) 934-3000**
good selection of bobbleheads/nodders	
RC Vintage, Inc.	**(818) 765-7107**
lots! baseball, football, dogs, cats, aliens, ducks, hula dancers, boxers, and many more bobble heads!	

Non-Guns & Non-Pyro Flashes

See: Guns & Firearms

Notions

See: Costume/Wardrobe/Sewing Supplies* Fabrics* Trims, Fringe, Tassels, Beading Etc.

Novelties

See: Magicians & Props, Supplies, Dressing* Memorabilia & Novelties

Nursery, Baby

See: Children/Baby Accessories & Bedroom* Hospital Equipment

Nurses Station

See Also: Medical Equip/Furniture, Graphics/Supplies

A-1 Medical Integration	**(818) 753-0319**
Medical devices for Set Decoration & Property, from minor procedures to detailed hospital units.	
Alpha Companies - Spellman Desk Co.	**(818) 504-9090**
The #1 source for medical equipment in the industry.	

Obstacle Courses

See: Fall Pads & Crash Pads* Ramps: Skateboard, BMX, Freestyle, etc.* Sports & Games Themed Events

Occult/Spiritual/Metaphysical

See Also: Astrological* Crystal Balls* Goth/Punk/Bondage/Fetish/Erotica Etc.* Tarot Cards

Psychic Eye Book Shops, Inc.	**(818) 906-8263**
13435 Ventura Blvd, Sherman Oaks, CA, 91423	
new age, metaphysical, self help, occult, astrology, also several other stores in LA area	
www.pebooks.com	
Dapper Cadaver	**(818) 771-0818**
Occult oddities. Witch & vampire props. Supernatural props. Egyptian, Voodoo & Dia De Los Muertos. Apothecary props.	
History For Hire, Inc.	**(818) 765-7767**
good selection, including tarot cards and more	
Sony Pictures Studios-Prop House (Off Lot)	**(310) 244-5999**
Universal Studios Property & Hardware Dept	**(818) 777-2784**
Voodoo dolls, voodoo props, witch props, spiritual props and more for rent.	

Office Equipment & Dressing

See Also: Bulletin Boards* Business Machines* Certificates* Computers* Copy Machines* Desk Dressing* Drafting Equipment & Supplies* Fans-Table, Floor or Ceiling* Filing Cabinets* Fountains, Drinking (Wall & Stand)* Globes, World Map* Paperwork, Documents & Letters, Office* Safes/Vaults* Trash Cans & Waste Baskets* Typewriters* Water Coolers

Advanced Liquidators Office Furniture	**(818) 763-3470**
selection of used equipment, professional office furniture designer sets, many qualities, full range of office dressing	
Copyrite Solutions	**(818) 503-0015**
12945 Sherman Way Ste 4, N Hollywood, CA, 91605	
copiers, fax m/cs, typewriters, all supplies	
Dozar Office Furnishings	**(310) 559-9292**
9937 Jefferson Blvd, Culver City, CA, 90232	
Rentals X22: desks, tables, chairs, cabinets, office dressing, office accessories, office dressing, office smalls & more	
dozarrents@aol.com * www.dozarrents.com	
E.C. Prop Rentals	**(818) 764-2008**
Industrial tables, smalls, computer monitors/keyboards, chairs	
Faux Library Studio Props, Inc.	**(818) 765-0096**
Home Office Dressing, Furniture Home Office, retro office dressing, vintage office dressing, period office dressing	
The Hand Prop Room LP.	**(323) 931-1534**
History For Hire, Inc.	**(818) 765-7767**
all the smalls, desk sets, coat racks	
LCW Props	**(818) 243-0707**
Desk Setups, Printers, Faxes, Copiers, Desks, Chairs, Large Selection Of Computers & Monitors	

Modern Props (323) 934-3000
contemporary/futuristic-furniture & accessories, including cleared photos, models, full sets, hi-tech, and other office amenities.

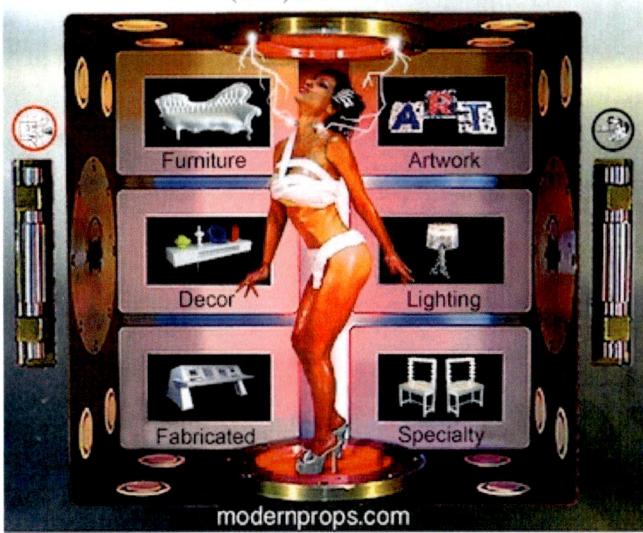

NEST Studio Rentals, Inc. (818) 942-0339
home office/exec. furniture, lighting, desk sets, accessories
Old N Country Prop Shop, LLC (818) 423-2599
Vintage to current office equipment of various sizes - everything from staplers and file holders to desks.
Omega/Cinema Props (323) 466-8201
executive boardroom desks, office desks
Picture Start Props (818) 255-5472
Office printers, office scanners and large assortment of smalls.
Prop Services West (818) 503-2790
Repro-Graphic Supply (818) 771-9066
9838 Glenoaks Blvd, Sun Valley, CA, 91352
Office equipment and office dressing of all kinds including office supplies
info@reprographicsupply.com * www.reprographicsupply.com
RJR Props (404) 349-7600
Office dressing for up to 400 person bull pen/office; computers, phones, fax machines, copy machines, projectors & more.
Sony Pictures Studios-Prop House (Off Lot) (310) 244-5999
paper cup dispenser, gooseneck desk fixture, memo holder, blueprint holder, map holder, brochure stand
Universal Studios Property & Hardware Dept (818) 777-2784
Office dressing, office equipment, office props and more for rent.
Warner Bros. Studios Property Department (818) 954-2181
Phones, partitions, desk dressing, smalls, assorted computer monitors & CPUs, fax machines, printers, grease board
ZG04 DECOR (818) 853-8040

Office Furniture

See Also: Business Machines* Filing Cabinets* Office Equipment & Dressing* Office Supplies
Advanced Liquidators Office Furniture (818) 763-3470
New/used: chairs, desks, filing cabinets, partitions executive sets. High end office furniture for every job and person

Alpha Companies - Spellman Desk Co. (818) 504-9090
desks, chairs, tables, sofas, traditional to contemporary. Hi-End office furnishings.
Blueprint Furniture (310) 657-4315
8600 Pico Blvd. Los Angeles, CA, 90035
Modern furniture lighting accessories early classic bauhaus mid-century contemporary design. Good studio rental history.
www.blueprintfurniture.com
Dozar Office Furnishings (310) 559-9292
9937 Jefferson Blvd, Culver City, CA, 90232
Rentals X22: desks, tables, chairs, cabinets, office dressing, office accessories, office dressing, office smalls & more
dozarrents@aol.com * www.dozarrents.com
E.C. Prop Rentals (818) 764-2008
office utility tables, chairs, phones, lighting, water coolers

Faux Library Studio Props, Inc. (818) 765-0096
conference room to executive desks, vintage office furniture, retro office furniture, mid century office furniture

huge collection • 60,000 sq ft • furniture • accessories • modern • antiques

Office Furniture • Props • Desk Dressing

Faux Library Studio Props

FormDecor, Inc. (310) 558-2582
America's largest event rental supplier of 20th Century furniture and accessories for Modern and Mid-Century styles.
LCW Props (818) 243-0707
Chairs, Desks, File Cabinets
Modern Props (323) 934-3000
contemporary/futurisitic, desks, shelfs, cabinets, chairs, dividers, tables, counters, executive and hi-tech, realistic to innovative.
Omega/Cinema Props (323) 466-8201
Picture Start Props (818) 255-5472
Office desks, office chairs, office filing cabinets and office tables.
A Royal Suite Home Furinishings (661) 259-7000
26536 Carl Boyer Dr, Santa Clarita, CA, 91350
A Royal Suite, family-owned since 1978, Features AMERICAN-MADE Furniture, and the Finest Furniture at the Greatest Value
norb@ars-email.com * www.aroyalsuite.com
Sony Pictures Studios-Prop House (Off Lot) (310) 244-5999
childrens desks, pedestal desks, reception desks, roll top desks, office desks, laptop desks, and more
TR Trading Company (310) 329-9242
15604 S Broadway, Gardena, CA, 90248
85,000 sq/ft of items, selection and inventory changes weekly. extensive!
sales@trtradingcompany.com * trtradingcompany.com
Universal Studios Property & Hardware Dept (818) 777-2784
Executive office furniture and regular office furniture for rent.
ZG04 DECOR (818) 853-8040

Office Supplies

See Also: Art, Supplies & Stationery Expendables*
Repro-Graphic Supply (818) 771-9066
9838 Glenoaks Blvd, Sun Valley, CA, 91352
Pens/Rulers/Markers/Leads Clearprint/Vellums/Diazo Film Graphic/Sketch Paper/Title Block Cutting Supplies/Tools/Boards
info@reprographicsupply.com * www.reprographicsupply.com

Oil Cans & Drums

AIR Designs	(818) 768-6639
1 Quart to 55 Gallon Drum, Metal & Plastic	
Alley Cats Studio Rentals	(818) 982-9178
street propane tanks, yellow barrel containers	
C. P. Two	(323) 466-8201
Oil cans/oil drums	
E.C. Prop Rentals	(818) 764-2008
large sel., multiples	
History For Hire, Inc.	(818) 765-7767
LCW Props	(818) 243-0707
55 Gallon Drums, 25 Gallon, Handheld, Garage, Industrial	
Sony Pictures Studios-Prop House (Off Lot)	(310) 244-5999
Universal Studios Property & Hardware Dept	(818) 777-2784
Period oil cans to modern oil cans for rent.	

On-Air Signs

C. P. Two	(323) 466-8201
On the air signs, on air signs	
History For Hire, Inc.	(818) 765-7767
lots, choices	
LCW Props	(818) 243-0707
Selection Of On-Air Signs, Rigged	
Modern Props	(323) 934-3000
On-air signs for rent	
RC Vintage, Inc.	(818) 765-7107
Universal Studios Property & Hardware Dept	(818) 777-2784
Prop On Air signs for rent.	

Opera Chairs

C. P. Two	(323) 466-8201
Omega/Cinema Props	(323) 466-8201
Universal Studios Property & Hardware Dept	(818) 777-2784
Opera chairs/opera audience chairs for rent.	
Warner Bros. Studios Property Department	(818) 954-2181

Operating Room & Equipment

See Also: Hospital Equipment
A-1 Medical Integration   (818) 753-0319
Medical devices for Set Decoration & Property, from minor procedures to detailed hospital units.
Alpha Companies - Spellman Desk Co.   (818) 504-9090
The #1 source for medical equipment in the industry.
Universal Studios Property & Hardware Dept (818) 777-2784
Operating room props and operating room equipment for rent.

Ophthalmic Equipment

See: Hospital Equipment Medical Equip/Furniture, Graphics/Supplies*

Optical Lab Equipment

See: Eyewear, Glasses, Sunglasses, 3D Hospital Equipment* Lab Equipment* Medical Equip/Furniture, Graphics/Supplies*

Orchid Plants

See: Greens

Organs

See: Body Parts Musical Instruments*

Oriental Dressing

See: Asian Antiques, Furniture, Art & Artifacts Rickshaws*

Oriental Themed Parties

See: Events, Decorations, Supplies & Services Events, Design/Planning/Production* Travel (City/Country) Themed Events*

Outdoor Advertising

See: Billboards & Billboard Lights

Outer Space Themed Parties

See: Aliens Costume Rental Houses* Costumes* Events, Decorations, Supplies & Services* Events, Design/Planning/Production* Fantasy Props, Costumes, or Decorations* Special Effects, Make-up/Prosthetics*

Outerwear

The Costume House   (818) 508-9933
men's & women's period coats & jackets, period furs
Sony Pictures Studios-Wardrobe   (310) 244-5995
alterations, call (310) 244-7260
Universal Studios Costume Dept   (818) 777-2722
Rental, mfg., & alterations
Western Costume Co.   (818) 760-0900

Outrigger Canoes

See: Boats & Water Sport Vehicles

Oversized Props

Flix FX Inc.   (818) 765-3549
7327 Lankershim Blvd #4, N Hollywood, CA, 91605
Oversized prop fabrication
info@flixfx.com * www.flixfx.com
GreatBigStuff.com   (800) 773-8832
Web Based Business
Website with large selection of oversized props for sale.
http://www.greatbigstuff.com
The Hand Prop Room LP.   (323) 931-1534
crayons, pencils, etc.
History For Hire, Inc.   (818) 765-7767
also undersized

L. A. Party Works   (888) 527-2789
9712 Alpaca St, S El Monte, CA, 91733
in Vancouver tel. 604-589-4101. for film, advertising, events, visual merchandising
partyworks@aol.com * www.partyworksinteractive.com

LCW Props   (818) 243-0707
Planets, Giant Pot, Chess Pieces, Getting New Stuff All The Time
Lennie Marvin Enterprises, Inc. (Prop Heaven) (818) 841-5882
teddy bears, baby pins, crayons, pens, large fake cake/popout cake/pop out cake etc.
LM Treasures   (626) 252-7354
8ft silver back gorillas & 13ft long pre-historic fish are some examples of how we range from small to very large items.
Modern Props   (323) 934-3000
Oversized props including oversized crayons, oversized combs, oversized toys more
Prop Services West   (818) 503-2790
RC Vintage, Inc.   (818) 765-7107
We have lots of oversize props!
Set Masters   (818) 982-1506
24853 Avenue Rockefeller, Valencia, CA, 91355
Oversized Prop Fabrication
info@setmasters.com * www.setmasters.com
ShopWildThings   (928) 855-6075
2880 Sweetwater Ave, Lake Havasu City, AZ, 86406
Event Decor, Beaded Curtains, Chain Curtains, String Curtains & Columns, Crystal Columns. Reliable service & delivery.
help@shopwildthings.com * www.shopwildthings.com
Sony Pictures Studios-Prop House (Off Lot) (310) 244-5999
oversized corn, oversized apple, oversized fork, oversized spoon, oversized pencil, and many more oversized props, more
Universal Studios Property & Hardware Dept (818) 777-2784
Oversized props for rent and fabrication.

Packaging Design

See: Printing, Graphics, Digital & Large Format* Product Labels

Packing/Packaging Supplies, Services

See Also: Boxes* Crates/ Vaults* Expendables* Gift Wrapping*
Wrapped Prop Gift Packages

Absolute Packaging   **(818) 557-2697**
11940 Sherman Road, N Hollywood, CA, 91605
std/custom, boxes, wardrobe, custom foam, bubble wrap, tape. gift bags,
shipping boxes

Banner Packing & Crating   **(310) 276-0804**
344 N La Cienega, Los Angeles, CA, 90048
www.bannerpackingandcrating.com

Basaw Manufacturing, Inc.   **(818) 765-6650**
7300 Varna, N Hollywood, CA, 91605
Basaw builds crates to order, large inventory in stock. domestic & export
packaging, standard & specialized
fredy@basaw.com * www.basaw.com

Delta Packaging Co.   **(310) 538-8700**
14110 S. Broadway, Los Angeles, CA, 90061
EPS foam boxes, liners, packing expendables esp. for produce, floral, biotech
www.deltapackaging.com

Imperial Paper Co.   **(818) 769-4400**
5733-37 Cahuenga Blvd, N Hollywood, CA, 91601
Wardrobe, tape, cushioning, foam, bubblewrap, custom & stock shipping
boxes.
www.imperialpaper.com

Paint & Painting Supplies

See Also: Expendables* Prop & Set Design Supplies, Parts, Tools*
Ultraviolet Products

Burbank Paint   **(818) 845-2684**
548 S. San Fernando Blvd, Burbank, CA, 91502
specialty industrial paints

Day-Glo Corp.   **(800) 289-3294**
4515 St. Clair Ave, Cleveland, OH, 44103
mfg. of Day-Glo paints, inks, plastics, coated papers/fabrics
dayglo@dayglo.com * www.dayglo.com

Dunn Edwards   **(800) 735-4632**
7064 W. Sunset Blvd., Hollywood, CA 90028
www.dunnedwards.com

G & M Paint & Supply   **(818) 771-0608**
8011 Webb Ave, N. Hollywood, CA, 91605
automotive & industrial paints
www.gmpaint.com

Mann Brothers   **(323) 936-5168**
758 N La Brea Ave, Los Angeles, CA, 90038
www.mannbrothers.com

Mark's Paint Store   **(818) 766-3949**
4830 Vineland Ave, N Hollywood, CA, 91601
special purpose paint store catering to the Industry
www.markspaint.com

Newhall Paint Store, Inc.   **(661) 259-3454**
24401 Main St, Newhall, CA, 91321
general purpose paint store in good location
http://wtpecsi3.wix.com/newhallpaint

North Hollywood Hardware, Inc.   **(818) 980-2453**
11847 Ventura Blvd, Studio City, CA, 91604
Paint, stains, faux & spray finishes, computerized color matching. Grass paint
now available in wide range of sizes.
nohohardware@gmail.com * www.ehardware2go.com

Nova Color Artists Acrylic Paint   **(310) 204-6900**
5894 Blackwelder St, Culver City, CA, 90232
mfr/retail special purpose acrylics, 80 colors, free price list & color chart, ship to
USA & Canada
www.novacolorpaint.com

Portola Paint & Glazes   **(323) 655-2211**
8213 West 3rd St, Los Angeles, CA, 90048
Lime wash, Roman Clay, Wrought Iron, Royal Satin, Florentine glaze
www.portolapaints.com

Warner Bros. Studios Paint Department   **(818) 954-1817**
4000 Warner Blvd Bldg 47, Burbank, CA, 91522
Supplier of all major paint, stain & finish brands, tools, brushes, rollers,
adhesives, tapes & more
www.wbpaintdept.com

Paint Removal

See: Sanitation, Waste Disposal

Paintball

See: Sporting Goods & Services

Paintings/Prints

See Also: Art For Rent (Cleared Art)* Art, Artists For Hire* Art, Tribal
& Folk* Art & Picture Framing Services* Posters,
Art/Movie/Travel/Wanted Etc.* Prop Houses

Art Dimensions Inc.   **(310) 433-8934**
Web Based Business
Cleared contemporary art for lease including paintings, prints, sculptures and
photography by more than 80 artists.
info@artdimensionsonline.com * www.artdimensionsonline.com

ART PIC   **(818) 503-5999**
6826 Troost Ave, N Hollywood, CA, 91605
Contemporary Art Rental and Sales. All mediums ALL ART CLEARED. Open
M-F 9-5. We ship worldwide.
artpicla@mac.com * www.artpic2000.com

Artspace Warehouse   **(323) 936-7020**
7358 Beverly Blvd, Los Angeles, CA, 90036
Huge selection of cleared original art in stock for same day rent or sale at
affordable prices.
info@artspacewarehouse.com * www.artspacewarehouse.com

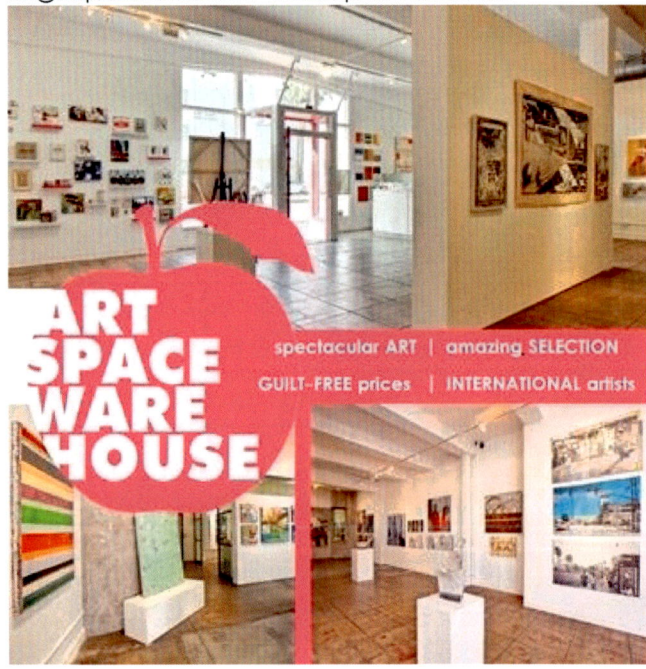

Bridge Furniture & Props Los Angeles　　　(818) 433-7100
We carry modern & traditional furniture, lighting, accessories, cleared art, & rugs. Items are online for easy shopping.

Clearedart.com/El Studio Granados　　　(818) 240-4421
958 Verdugo Circle Dr, Glendale, CA, 91206
Multi-media variety of original paintings and prints in a multitude of styles and techniques.
fineart@elstudiogranados.com * www.clearedart.com

Collins Visual Media　　　(818) 686-6581
10518 Johanna Ave, Shadow Hills, CA, 91040
Our artists and technicians are skilled at creating or reproducing your files and art.
www.collinsvisualmedia.com

Dina Art Co.　　　(323) 469-4073
6433 W Sunset Blvd, Los Angeles, CA, 90028
Cleared art, art posters, custom framing, hand colored prints & more. Over 3,000 images in 22 categories available.
dina@dinaart.com * www.dinaart.com

FILM ART LA　　　(323) 461-4900
Culver City Warehouse at Jefferson & Hauser. Call for address.
Film Art LA rents cleared art and creates digital, painted reproductions, specialty prop art, portraits and paintings.
filmartla@gmail.com * www.filmartla.com

Ghettogloss Cleared Art　　　(323) 871-8100
Web Based Business
Cutting edge contemporary paintings & photography 100% Cleared. Street Art, Graffiti, Outsider Art, Low Brow & Pop.
www.ghettogloss.com

The Hand Prop Room LP.　　　(323) 931-1534
1,000 cleared pcs

Hollywood Cinema Arts　　　(818) 504-7333
Nobody has more cleared painting/prints than HCA

Hollywood Studio Gallery　　　(323) 462-1116
neo-classical to contemporary

LCW Props　　　(818) 243-0707
Paintings, Photos, Sketches

Modern Props　　　(323) 934-3000
cleared paintings and cleared prints, contemporary/futuristic large selection

NEST Studio Rentals, Inc.　　　(818) 942-0339
cleared original paintings & prints in stock

Ob-jects　　　(818) 351-4200
Paintings and prints; sets of architectural, floral & portraits

Omega/Cinema Props　　　(323) 466-8201

Pasadena Antique Center and Annex　　　(626) 449-7706
480 South Fair Oaks Ave, Pasadena, CA, 91105
Artwork from all eras and in various styles and mediums.
pasadenaantiqecenterandannex@gmail.com * bit.ly/PasadenaAntiqueCenter

Prop Services West　　　(818) 503-2790
Cleared paintings and cleared prints from many genres including Masters

Sony Pictures Studios-Prop House (Off Lot)　　　(310) 244-5999

Universal Studios Property & Hardware Dept　　　(818) 777-2784
Framed and unframed paintings and prints for rent.

Wallspace　　　(323) 930-0471
607 N La Brea, Los Angeles, CA, 90036
Contemporary abstract art gallery and photography. Available for rent and sale with permission to use on tv film & print
art@wallspacela.com * www.wallspacela.com

ZG04 DECOR　　　(818) 853-8040
Abstract, Portrait, Landscape, Seascape, Botanical, Nude, Portraits, Figurative Drawings, Floral, Shadowboxes

Pallets

Alley Cats Studio Rentals　　　(818) 982-9178
wood & metal style, modern, crates

Basaw Manufacturing, Inc.　　　(818) 765-6650
7300 Varna, N Hollywood, CA, 91605
Basaw builds crates to order, large inventory in stock. machinery/electronic crates
fredy@basaw.com * www.basaw.com

E.C. Prop Rentals　　　(818) 764-2008
wood & plastic pallets, also pallet jacks, good multiples, pallet racks

LCW Props　　　(818) 243-0707
Large Selection, Wood, Metal, Plastic, Warehouse Dressing

Universal Studios Property & Hardware Dept　　　(818) 777-2784
Pallets and pallet jacks for rent.

Paneling, Veneers & Laminates

See Also: Building Supply, Lumber, Hardware, Etc. Floor, Ground & Surface Protection*

Architectural Plywood　　　(818) 255-1900
7104 Case Ave, N Hollywood, CA, 91605
wholesale & retail; custom veneers only, lumber, plywood

Bear Forest Products, Inc　　　(951) 727-1767
4685 Brookhollow Circle, Riverside, CA, 92509
Plywood, veneer, and wood paneling.
matto@bearfp.com * www.bearfp.com

California Panel & Veneer　　　(562) 926-5834
14055 Artesia Blvd, Cerritos, CA, 90703
panel, veneer, laminates
www.calpanel.com

General Veneer Manufacturing Co.　　　(323) 564-2661
8652 Otis St, South Gate, CA, 90280
Breakaway balsa wood sheets & boards
balsasales@generalveneer.com * www.generalveneer.com

MacBeath Hardwood　　　(877) 499-7350
2648 Teepee Dr, Stockton CA, 95205
hardwood veneers, paneling, hardwood stock
www.macbeath.com

Manhattan Laminates　　　(800) 762-2929
481 Washington St, New York, NY 10013
laminates
www.manhattanlaminates.com

Phillips Plywood　　　(818) 897-7736
13599 Desmond St, Pacoima, CA, 91331
wholesaler of plywood, laminates & laminated panels
www.phillipsplywood.com

Wurth Louis and Company　　　(800) 422-4389
895 Columbia St, Brea, CA, 92821
distribute Chemetal, metal laminates, solid metals, treefrog veneers, Nevamar laminates
www.wurthlac.com

Panty Hose

See: Hosiery

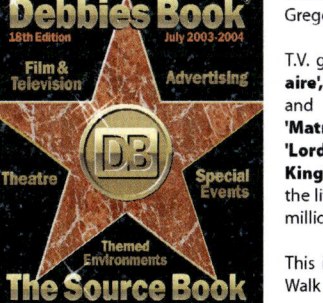

Paper

See Also: Art, Supplies & Stationery

188 Galerie (800) 809-9880
188 Lafayette St, New York, NY, 10013
paper goods; 5 stores in NY
galerie@188lafayette.com * www.188galerie.com

Flax Art & Design (510) 867-2324
1501 Martin Luther King Jr Way, Oakland, CA 94612
catalog sales; fine papers, printed, natural, textured, machine-milled,
chiyogami, tissue & lace, many varieties/colors
www.flaxart.com

Hiromi Paper, Inc. (310) 998-0098
9469 Jefferson Blvd, Culver City CA, 90232
conservation, framing, art, decorative, stationary, acid-free, Japanese papers,
book/paper making supplies, spec. orders
www.hiromipaper.com

Repro-Graphic Supply (818) 771-9066
9838 Glenoaks Blvd, Sun Valley, CA, 91352
Ink Jet Paper, Xerographic Paper (Xerox Paper), Plotting Paper, Copy Paper,
Toner Cartridges, Ink Cartridges & much more
info@reprographicsupply.com * www.reprographicsupply.com

Paper, Seamless

See: Expendables

Paperwork, Documents & Letters, Office

Advanced Liquidators Office Furniture (818) 763-3470
Faux Library Studio Props, Inc. (818) 765-0096
desk plates, glass plaques, glass inscribed awards, over sized dollar bills,
many colored file folders

The Hand Prop Room LP. (323) 931-1534
letters, paperwork

History For Hire, Inc. (818) 765-7767
anything done custom, paperwork to rent

HPR Graphics (323) 556-2694
5674 Venice Blvd, Los Angeles, CA, 90019
Law enforcement files, letterheads, business cards, identification, newspapers,
certificates, diplomas, stocks and more.
hprcan@earthlink.net * www.hprgraphics.net

LCW Props (818) 243-0707
Our Specialty. Huge Quantities Of Any Kind. Medical, Legal, Office, Blueprints,
Binders, Custom

L.C.W. PROPS

6439 San Fernando Rd. Glendale, CA 91201
Phone: 818-243-0707 - www.lcwprops.com

Omega/Cinema Props (323) 466-8201
paperwork & letters

Universal Studios Property & Hardware Dept (818) 777-2784
Prop office paperwork, prop documents, prop letters, prop office documents,
prop paperwork; all for rent.

Parades

See: Events, Decorations, Supplies & Services* Events,
Design/Planning/Production* Events, Entertainment

Paramedic Equipment

See: Ambulance/Paramedic

Parasols

See: Umbrellas, Hand & Parasols

Park Benches

See: Benches

Park Playground

See: Playground Equipment

Parking Meters & Sign Poles

AIR Designs (818) 768-6639
Large Selection of Single & Double Meter, Sign Poles 4'-10'

Alley Cats Studio Rentals (818) 982-9178
Parking meters mounted on self-standing poles as well as new digital meters.
Coin and credit card parking meters

E.C. Prop Rentals (818) 764-2008
poles with bases, lrg multiples

The Hand Prop Room LP. (323) 931-1534

History For Hire, Inc. (818) 765-7767
quantity in matching

LCW Props (818) 243-0707
Singles & Doubles

Lennie Marvin Enterprises, Inc. (Prop Heaven) (818) 841-5882
period/modern meters, parking poles/signs, NYC parking pods

RC Vintage, Inc. (818) 765-7107
free standing Digital, coin operated parking meters, vintage parking meters,
period parking meters, multiple sizes

Universal Studios Property & Hardware Dept (818) 777-2784
Freestanding parking meters & coin operated parking meters from different
periods and many street signs/sign poles for rent.

Partitions

See: Office Furniture

Party Decorations & Design

See: Events, Decorations, Supplies & Services* Events,
Design/Planning/Production* Events, Entertainment* Trade Shows &
Conventions

Party Food Props

See: Food, Artificial Food

Patches

See: Badges, Patches & Buttons

Patio & Outdoor Furniture

See: Cafe Tables/Chairs/Umbrellas* Furniture, Outdoor/Patio

Patterns

See Also: Fabrics* Stage Lighting, Film/Video/TV* Lighting & Sound,
Concert/Theatrical/DJ/VJ

Amazon Drygoods (812) 852-1780
3788 Wilson St, Osgood, IN 47037
catalog sales; 19 C. wardrobe/patterns, home access., books
kevin@amazondrygoods.com * www.amazondrygoods.com

Edinburgh Imports (800) 334-6274
58406 Joshua Ln, Yucca Valley CA, 92284
1000+ plush fabrics: 1/16"-3" pile. patterns, kits & hardware
www.edinburghimports.com

PDAs (Personal Digital Assistant)

See: Computers

Peanut Carts

See: Vendor Carts & Concession Counters

Pedal Cars/Toys

See: Toys & Games

Pedestals

See Also: Architectural Pieces & Artifacts* Columns

C. P. Two	(323) 466-8201
Castle Antiques & Design	(818) 765-5000

11924 Vose St, N Hollywood, CA, 91605
We off various styles and sizes of pedestals available for rent or purchase.
info@castleantiques.net * www.castleprophouse.com

depict	(323) 222-1001

1460 Naud St, Los Angeles, CA, 90012
info@depict33.com * www.depict33.com

The Hand Prop Room LP.	(323) 931-1534
Modern Props	(323) 934-3000

contemporary pedestals and futuristic pedestals

Omega/Cinema Props	(323) 466-8201
Prop Services West	(818) 503-2790
Sony Pictures Studios-Prop House (Off Lot)	(310) 244-5999
Universal Studios Property & Hardware Dept	(818) 777-2784

Pedestals of various time periods and sizes for rent.

Warner Bros. Studios Property Department	(818) 954-2181

Pedestal bases, column pedestals, classic pedestals, commode pedestals, figural pedestals, Asian, Syrian

Pennants

See: Badges, Patches & Buttons* Flags/Banners

Penny Arcade

See: Arcade Equipment, Games & Rides* Vendor Carts & Concession Counters

Pens, Fountain

See Also: Art, Supplies & Stationery

The Hand Prop Room LP.	(323) 931-1534

antique, period pcs, lrg sel.

History For Hire, Inc.	(818) 765-7767

all working

Sony Pictures Studios-Prop House (Off Lot)	(310) 244-5999
Universal Studios Property & Hardware Dept	(818) 777-2784

Fountain pens of different time periods and styles for rent.

Pepsi Memorabilia

AIR Designs	(818) 768-6639

Signage, Vending Machine

History For Hire, Inc.	(818) 765-7767

Perfume Bottles

Badia Design, Inc.	(818) 762-0130

5420 Vineland Ave, N Hollywood, CA, 91601
info@badiadesign.com * www.badiadesign.com

The Hand Prop Room LP.	(323) 931-1534

period-contemp

History For Hire, Inc.	(818) 765-7767

many

Modern Props	(323) 934-3000

contemporary perfume bottles, many sizes & styles

Ob-jects	(818) 351-4200

Perfume bottles for rent

Prop Services West	(818) 503-2790
Sony Pictures Studios-Prop House (Off Lot)	(310) 244-5999
Universal Studios Property & Hardware Dept	(818) 777-2784

Contemporary perfume bottles, period perfume bottles, decorative perfume bottles and more for rent.

Periscopes

See: Military Props & Equipment

Personal Care

See: Make-up & Hair, Supplies & Services* Shaving, Old Fashion, Non-Electric

Pet Cemetery & Cremated Services

See Also: Cemetery Dressing* Mortuary* Taxidermy, Hides/Heads/Skeletons

Cal Pet Crematory	(818) 983-2313

9595 Glenoaks Blvd, P.O. Box 488, Sun Valley, CA 91353-0488
Pet cremation services for small to medium pets as well as decorative urns and memorial stones.
www.calpet.com

Pet Furniture, Houses, Clothing

Alley Cats Studio Rentals	(818) 982-9178

1 dog house

Animal Stars	(661) 424-1700

16787 Sierra Hwy, Santa Clarita, CA, 91351
Luxury pet accessories, Swarovski crystal tags, collars, jewelry, clothing
www.animalstars.com

Evans Family Barrels	(818) 523-8174

7918 Fairchild Ave, Canoga Park, CA, 91306
Solid oak wine barrel furniture: tables, chairs, cabinets, pet furniture, home & business decor, swings, vintage barrels
evansbarrels@gmail.com * www.EvansFamilyBarrels.com

The Retro Kats	(818) 834-5022

Located in Sylmar, CA, 91342
Luxury & Rustic Style Pet Products - Dog & Cat Beds, Cat Trees, Cat Scratchers, Lush Dog & Cat Mats, Dog & Cat Pillows, Unique Cat Toys
TheRetroKats@gmail.com * www.TheRetroKats.com

Universal Studios Property & Hardware Dept	(818) 777-2784

Cat scratching poles, cat scratching pads, dog houses and dog beds for rent.

Worldwise, Inc.	(415) 721-7400

6 Hamilton Landing Ste 150, Novato, CA, 94949
pet furniture, plush toys, pet jewelry, pet beds, collars & leads
www.worldwise.com

Pews

See: Church, Chapel, Synagogue, Mosque

Pewter & Pewterware

Gibson Pewter	(603) 464-3410

26 N Main St., Washington NH, 03280
Lead-free reproduction pewterware, tankards, plates, bowls, porringers, etc.
www.gibsonpewter.com

The Hand Prop Room LP.	(323) 931-1534
History For Hire, Inc.	(818) 765-7767

pewter plates, bowls, cups, good selection

Omega/Cinema Props	(323) 466-8201
Prop Services West	(818) 503-2790
Sword & Stone	(818) 562-6548

Pewter vases, pewter vases and more

Pharmacy

See: Drugstore/Apothecary

Phonograph Records

See Also: Record/Video Store

Amoeba Music	(323) 245-6400

6400 Sunset Blvd, Hollywood, CA, 90028
big, changing sel. of hard-to-find collectible disks/records, also new & vintage rock posters & memorabilia
www.amoeba.com

Astro Audio Video Lighting, Inc.	(818) 549-9915

6615 San Fernando Rd, Glendale, CA, 91201
Time code and control vinyl for DJ software including Serato systems and Traktor systems
www.astroavl.com

The Hand Prop Room LP.	(323) 931-1534
History For Hire, Inc.	(818) 765-7767

from wax cylinders to 78s, 45s, 33s as well as record players

Omega/Cinema Props	(323) 466-8201

Phonograph record players, period and vintage.

Sony Pictures Studios-Prop House (Off Lot)	(310) 244-5999
Universal Studios Property & Hardware Dept	(818) 777-2784

Phonograph records for rent.

Phonographs

See Also: Audio Equipment* Victrolas/Gramophones

Astro Audio Video Lighting, Inc.   (818) 549-9915
6615 San Fernando Rd, Glendale, CA, 91201
Phonographs/record players for rent or purchase including DJ turntables;
Technics, Pioneer & Numark.
www.astroavl.com

The Hand Prop Room LP.   (323) 931-1534
all periods

History For Hire, Inc.   (818) 765-7767
most eras

LCW Props   (818) 243-0707
Period - Present

Omega/Cinema Props   (323) 466-8201

RC Vintage, Inc.   (818) 765-7107
40s, 50s, 60s & 70s, vintage brass phonographs, vintage record players, horn
phonographs

Universal Studios Property & Hardware Dept   (818) 777-2784
Phonographs, victrolas, gramophones and more for rent.

Photo Albums

See: Scrapbooks

Photo Blow-ups

See Also: Printing, Graphics, Digital & Large Format

D'ziner Sign Co.   (323) 467-4467
801 Seward Street, Los Angeles, CA, 90038
standees
sales@dzinersign.com * www.dzinersign.com

Warner Bros. Studios Photo Lab   (818) 954-7118
4000 Warner Blvd, Burbank, CA, 91522
A complete imaging resource serving the needs of the entertainment industry
for over 85 years.
photolab@warnerbros.com * www.wbphotolab.com

Photo Booths

L. A. Party Works   (888) 527-2789
9712 Alpaca St, S El Monte, CA, 91733
in Vancouver tel. 604-589-4101
partyworks@aol.com * www.partyworksinteractive.com

888-527-2789
partyworksusa.com

VARIETY OF PHOTO BOOTHS / PROPS / CUSTOM BRANDING & MESSAGE ON UNIT & PHOTO PRINTS

Lennie Marvin Enterprises, Inc. (Prop Heaven)   (818) 841-5882
coin-op. photo booths (non-op.)

RC Vintage, Inc.   (818) 765-7107
arcade, period, coin-operated, 25 cent photo booths

Photographic Equipment

See: Camera Equipment

Photographs

See Also: Memorabilia & Novelties* Paintings/Prints* Art & Picture
Framing Services* Sports Fan Items, Memorabilia, Photographs

ART PIC   (818) 503-5999
6826 Troost Ave, N Hollywood, CA, 91605
Contemporary Art Rental and Sales. All mediums ALL ART CLEARED. Open
M-F 9-5. We ship worldwide.
artpicla@mac.com * www.artpic2000.com

Bridge Furniture & Props Los Angeles   (818) 433-7100
We carry modern & traditional furniture, lighting, accessories, art, & rugs. Items
are online for easy shopping.

Faux Library Studio Props, Inc.   (818) 765-0096
Art photos, cleared family photos and cleared police photos, framed and
unframed

FILM ART LA   (323) 461-4900
Culver City Warehouse at Jefferson & Hauser. Call for address.
Large Inventory of cleared art rentals 19th Century to Present. All types Art,
Photography and Sculpture High Rez images
filmartla@gmail.com * www.filmartla.com

The Hand Prop Room LP.   (323) 931-1534

Hollywood Studio Gallery   (323) 462-1116
cleared photos (b/w & color) large selection

LCW Props   (818) 243-0707
Period - Present

Little Bohemia Rentals   (818) 853-7506
11940 Sherman Rd, N Hollywood, CA, 91605
Cleared family photos, vintage and modern.
sales@wearelittlebohemia.com * www.wearelittlebohemia.com

Modern Props   (323) 934-3000
large collection of cleared modern photographs and cleared contemporary
photographs

NEST Studio Rentals, Inc.   (818) 942-0339
cleared, framed art photos, framed family photos

Ob-jects   (818) 351-4200
Cleared photography/photographs

Pasadena Antique Center and Annex   (626) 449-7706
480 South Fair Oaks Ave, Pasadena, CA, 91105
All types of photographic images and accessories in a wide range of eras
pasadenaantiqecenterandannex@gmail.com * bit.ly/PasadenaAntiqueCenter

Sony Pictures Studios-Prop House (Off Lot)   (310) 244-5999
Old black and white photographs, black and white photos

Superstock   (800) 828-4545
6620 Southpoint Dr South Ste 501, Jacksonville, FL, 32216
stock photography & fine art, licensing or royalty-free. Email
tom@superstock.com for contract information.
www.superstock.com

Universal Studios Property & Hardware Dept   (818) 777-2784
Framed photographs, unframed photographs, cleared photographs and more
for rent.

Wallspace   (323) 930-0471
607 N La Brea, Los Angeles, CA, 90036
Contemporary abstract art gallery and photography. Available for rent and sale
with permission to use on tv film & print
art@wallspacela.com * www.wallspacela.com

Warner Bros. Studios Photo Lab   (818) 954-7118
4000 Warner Blvd, Burbank, CA, 91522
A complete imaging resource serving the needs of the entertainment industry
for over 85 years.
photolab@warnerbros.com * www.wbphotolab.com

Photographs, Digital Processing

Warner Bros. Studios Photo Lab   (818) 954-7118
4000 Warner Blvd, Burbank, CA, 91522
A complete imaging resource serving the needs of the entertainment industry
for over 85 years.
photolab@warnerbros.com * www.wbphotolab.com

Physical Therapy

See Also: Exercise & Fitness Equipment* Massage Tables* Medical
Equip/Furniture, Graphics/Supplies* Traction Equipment*
Weightlifting Equipment

A-1 Medical Integration   (818) 753-0319
Medical devices for Set Decoration & Property, from minor procedures to
detailed hospital units.

Alpha Companies - Spellman Desk Co.   (818) 504-9090
The #1 source for medical equipment in the industry.

Angelus Medical & Optical Co., Inc.   (310) 769-6060
13007 S Western Ave, Gardena, CA, 90249
Physical therapy props
www.angelusmedical.com

I-Rep Therapy Products, Inc.   (800) 828-0852
508 Chaney St Ste B, Lake Elsinore, CA, 92530
Contact i-REP for all of your weightlifting equipment and set dressing needs for
physical therapy, exercise and fitness.
btwilhelm@gmail.com * www.i-reptherapyproducts.com

Pianos & Keyboard Instruments

C. P. Two	**(323) 466-8201**
Upright pianos and grand pianos	
History For Hire, Inc.	**(818) 765-7767**
electric, upright, large selection	
Hollywood Piano Rental Company	**(818) 954-8500**
323 S Front Street, Burbank, CA, 91502	
Over 700 pianos in stock, all colors, sizes, periods. Tuning, piano services & repairs, Piano moving (insured/bonded)	
tims@hollywoodpiano.com * www.hollywoodpiano.com	
Universal Studios Property & Hardware Dept	**(818) 777-2784**
Many pianos of all styles for rent.	

Picnic Tables

See: Furniture, Outdoor/Patio

Picture Frames

See Also: Photographs

The Hand Prop Room LP.	**(323) 931-1534**
selection in stock, custom framing	
Hollywood Studio Gallery	**(323) 462-1116**
ornate, ready made or custom	
Little Bohemia Rentals	**(818) 853-7506**
11940 Sherman Rd, N Hollywood, CA, 91605	
Tabletop and Wall with Cleared photos and/or art.	
sales@wearelittlebohemia.com * www.wearelittlebohemia.com	
Ob-jects	**(818) 351-4200**
Pictures and picture frames	
Omega/Cinema Props	**(323) 466-8201**
Picture Start Props	**(818) 255-5472**
Small and medium picture frames (most with cleared photos and art inside).	
Prop Services West	**(818) 503-2790**
A Royal Suite Home Furnishings	**(661) 259-7000**
26536 Carl Boyer Dr, Santa Clarita, CA, 91350	
A Royal Suite, family-owned since 1978, Features AMERICAN-MADE Furniture, and the Finest Furniture at the Greatest Value	
norb@ars-email.com * www.aroyalsuite.com	
Sony Pictures Studios-Prop House (Off Lot)	**(310) 244-5999**
framed drawing, framed paintings, framed photographs, picture plaques, print / litho, shadow box picture, picture stands	
U-Frame It Gallery	**(818) 781-4500**
6203 Lankershim Blvd, N Hollywood, CA, 91606	
classic frames to modern, laminating, restorations and more	
uframit@aol.com * www.uframeitgallery.com	

Universal Studios Property & Hardware Dept	**(818) 777-2784**
Different picture frames from styles and time periods for rent.	
ZG04 DECOR	**(818) 853-8040**
Framed Art & Tabletop Frames	

Picture Framing Services

See: Picture Frames Art & Picture Framing Services*

Picture Vehicles

See: Aircraft, Charters & Aerial Services Ambulance/Paramedic* Jet Skis* Motorcycles* Nautical/Marine Services & Charters* Police Car, Police Motorcycle* RV Vehicles & Travel Trailers, Equip & Parts* Trains* Vehicle Preparation Services* Vehicles/Picture Vehicles*

Pictures

See: Paintings/Prints Photographs* Posters, Art/Movie/Travel/Wanted Etc.* Sports Fan Items, Memorabilia, Photographs*

Pilings

See: Nautical Dressing & Props

Pillows, Decorative

See Also: Linens, Household Prop Houses*

Little Bohemia Rentals	**(818) 853-7506**
11940 Sherman Rd, N Hollywood, CA, 91605	
African Mud Cloth, Japanese Shibori, Indigo, Embroidered, Kilim, Vintage and Contemporary.	
sales@wearelittlebohemia.com * www.wearelittlebohemia.com	
Lux Lounge EFR	**(888) 247-4411**
106 1/2 Judge John Aiso St #318, Los Angeles, CA, 90012	
Decorative Pillows: Assorted Colored Pillows, Couch Throw Pillows, Sequin Pillows, Custom Design Pillows & More.	
info@luxloungeefr.com * www.luxloungeefr.com	
NEST Studio Rentals, Inc.	**(818) 942-0339**
large selection	
Picture Start Props	**(818) 255-5472**
Big selection of decorative pillows arranged my color.	
Prop Services West	**(818) 503-2790**
A Royal Suite Home Furnishings	**(661) 259-7000**
26536 Carl Boyer Dr, Santa Clarita, CA, 91350	
A Royal Suite, family-owned since 1978, Features AMERICAN-MADE Furniture, and the Finest Furniture at the Greatest Value	
norb@ars-email.com * www.aroyalsuite.com	
ZG04 DECOR	**(818) 853-8040**
Modern, Contemporary, Traditional, Vintage	

Pinata

See: Mexican Decorations

Pinball Machines

See Also: Arcade Equipment, Games & Rides

L. A. Party Works	**(888) 527-2789**
9712 Alpaca St, S El Monte, CA, 91733	
in Vancouver tel. 604-589-4101	
partyworks@aol.com * www.partyworksinteractive.com	
LCW Props	**(818) 243-0707**
Modern & High End Gaming Systems	
RC Vintage, Inc.	**(818) 765-7107**
arcade, modern to period, coin-operated Cleared, many models, large assortment	

Pipe & Bases

See: Rigging, Equipment or Services Theatrical Draperies, Hardware & Rigging*

Pipes (Metal & Plastic)

Alley Cats Studio Rentals	(818) 982-9178
PVC, metal w/valves, rooftop	
E.C. Prop Rentals	(818) 764-2008
large sel w/gate valves, many sizes & diameters	
LCW Props	(818) 243-0707
Large Selection Of Industrial, Plastic, Steel, Basement, Conduit	

Pipes, Smoking

See: Smoking Products* Marijuana Plants, Dispensary Dressing & Hydroponics

Pirate, Chests & Treasures

Dapper Cadaver	(818) 771-0818
Pirate props & pirate themed decorations. Mummies & skeletons. Stocks, gallows & gibbets. Monkeys & parrots.	
The Hand Prop Room LP.	(323) 931-1534
fully dressed	
History For Hire, Inc.	(818) 765-7767
outfitted	
Lennie Marvin Enterprises, Inc. (Prop Heaven)	(818) 841-5882
large/small chests, treasure, nautical dressing & more	
LM Treasures	(626) 252-7354
Life size pirates to cannons and treasure chests are all fun ways to spice up any dull room or yard.	
Sword & Stone	(818) 562-6548
Pirate chests available for rent	

Pitching Machine, Baseball

See: Baseball Pitching Machine

Pizza Ovens & Boxes

AIR Designs	(818) 768-6639
Ovens, Signage, Paddles, Neon, Kitchen Equipment	
Lennie Marvin Enterprises, Inc. (Prop Heaven)	(818) 841-5882
boxes, pizza scoops, rotating pizza display oven countertop	

Planters

See: Pottery

Plants

See: Greens

Plaques

See: Badges, Patches & Buttons* Engraving* Trophies/Trophy Cases

Plaster, Ornamental

See: Staff Shops

Plastic Food

See: Food, Artificial Food

Plastic Ice Cubes

See: Ice Cubes, Plastic

Plastic Snow

See: Snow, Artificial & Real

Plastics, Materials & Fabrication

See Also: Clear Vinyl* Flowers, Silk, Plastic & Dried* Foam* Ice Cubes, Plastic* Rubber & Foam Rubber

Canal Plastic Center	(212) 925-1032
345 Canal St, New York, NY, 10013	
supply plastics	
www.canalplastic.com	
depict	(323) 222-1001
1460 Naud St, Los Angeles, CA, 90012	
info@depict33.com * www.depict33.com	
Gavrieli Plastic Supply	(818) 982-0000
11733 Sherman Way, N Hollywood, CA, 91605	
small sheet form plastics	
www.gavrieli.com	
Harrington Industrial Plastics	(818) 781-7826
15000 Keswick St, Suite B, Van Nuys, CA, 91405	
sheet form, tanks, pipes, grating, industrial shapes	
www.hipco.com	
LCW Props	(818) 243-0707
Huge Selection Of Tubes, Tanks, Spheres	
Living Art Aquatic Design, Inc.	(310) 822-7484
2301 South Sepulveda Blvd, Los Angeles, CA, 90064	
Custom acrylic work, forming, aquariums, Point of Purchase displays, ReadyReef, nano cubes.	
ron@aquatic2000.com * www.aquatic2000.com	

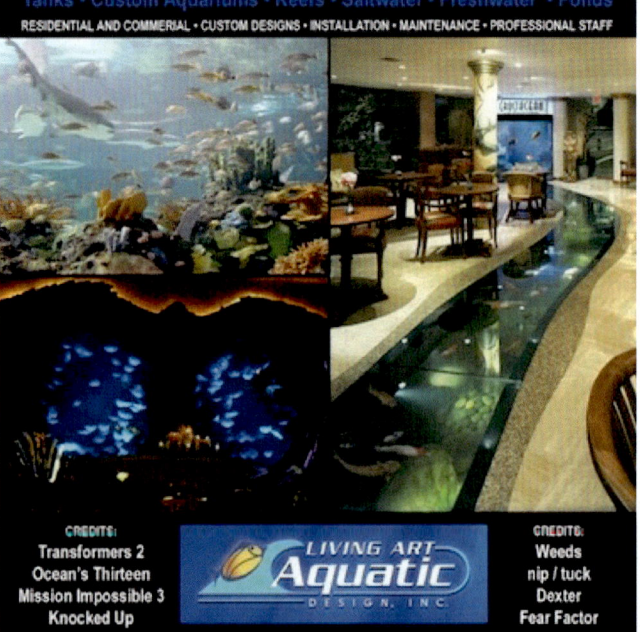

Tanks • Custom Aquariums • Reefs • Saltwater • Freshwater • Ponds
RESIDENTIAL AND COMMERIAL • CUSTOM DESIGNS • INSTALLATION • MAINTENANCE • PROFESSIONAL STAFF

CREDITS:
Transformers 2
Ocean's Thirteen
Mission Impossible 3
Knocked Up

LIVING ART Aquatic
DESIGN, INC.

CREDITS:
Weeds
nip / tuck
Dexter
Fear Factor

M.A.S. Plastics	(818) 997-8064
14229 Oxnard St, Van Nuys, CA, 91401	
sheet plastic & display case fabrication, custom acrylic fabrication svcs.	
www.acrylicfabricationlosangeles.com	
Orange County Industrial Plastics	(714) 632-9450
4811 E La Palma, Anaheim, CA, 92807	
wide sel. sheet/rod/block; design & fabrication too	
www.ocip.com	
Plastic Depot	(818) 843-3030
2907 N San Fernando Blvd, Burbank, CA, 91504	
Fiberglass resins & cloths, silicone mold making materials	
www.plasticdepotofburbank.com	

Plastic Mart (800) 200-4228
43535 Gadsen Ave Ste F113, Lancaster, CA, 93534
We stock material from .020" to 4.0"
www.theplasticmart.com
Plastifab/Leed Plastics (909) 596-1927
1425 Palomares Ave, La Verne, CA, 91750
sheets, rods, tubes
www.plastifabonline.com
PSI-Plastic Sales South (800) 257-7747
17622 Metzler Ln, Huntington Beach, CA, 92647
raw materials
Reynolds Advanced Materials: Smooth-On (818) 358-6000
Distributor
10856 Vanowen St, N Hollywood, CA, 91605
Hollywood's F/X source for Liquid Rubbers, Plastics & more
LA@reynoldsam.com * www.moldmakingmaterials.com
Sabic Polymershapes (562) 942-9381
9905 Pioneer Blvd, Santa Fe Springs, CA, 90670
sheets, rods, tubes, films
www.sabicpolymershapes.com
Solter Plastics (310) 473-5115
12016 W Pico Blvd, Los Angeles, CA, 90064
sheet materials, unique colors & textures
www.solterplastics.com
Vinyl Technology, Inc. (626) 443-5257
200 Railroad Ave, Monrovia, CA, 91016
plastic fabr., thermoforming, vacuum forming, berm liners very large
environmental protection shipping containers
www.vinyltechnology.com
Walco Materials Group/Fiberlay San Diego (619) 692-3888
5304 Custer St, San Diego, CA, 92110
liquid plastics, silicones
www.fiberlay.com

Platforms

See: Audience Seating Stages, Portable & Steel Deck*

Playground Equipment

Alley Cats Studio Rentals (818) 982-9178
jungle gym, swings, slides, monkey bars, merry-go-round, kids geo domes,
metal basketball rims, bicycle racks, benches
L. A. Steelcraft Products, Inc. (626) 798-7401
1975 N Lincoln Ave, Pasadena, CA, 91103
jungle gym, merry-go-round, slides, play barrels, teeter-totter, arch climbers,
hoppy animals, swings, etc.
www.lasteelcraft.com
Lennie Marvin Enterprises, Inc. (Prop Heaven) (818) 841-5882
Playground equipment including playground playset, spring animals, outdoor
gym equipment, and ball pit balls
Sunland Creations (818) 521-0053
Call for Appointment Only. Facility in North Hills.
We supply both Swing Sets, Play Houses, Slides and Trampolines for T.V. -
Film Productions and Photography Shoots.
sunlandcreations@mac.com * www.swingsetsolutions.com
Universal Studios Property & Hardware Dept (818) 777-2784
Jungle gyms, slides, swings, swing set, tether balls, school benches, etc. for
rent.
Worlds of Wow (817) 380-4215
1800 Shady Oaks Drive, Denton, TX, 76205
Custom contained playgrounds, 3D sculptures, safety surfacing, parent seating,
modular play features, airbrushed murals
www.worldsofwow.com

Plexi-Lucite Furniture

See: Furniture, Plexi/Lucite

Plexiglass

See: Plastics, Materials & Fabrication

Plotters & Plotting Services

See Also: Blueprint Equipment & Supplies Computers* Printing,
Graphics, Digital & Large Format*
The Hand Prop Room LP. (323) 931-1534
Nights of Neon (818) 756-4791
13815 Saticoy St, Van Nuys, CA, 91402
over 2,000 neon props in stock. plotting services
contact@nightsofneon.com * www.nightsofneon.com
Repro-Graphic Supply (818) 771-9066
9838 Glenoaks Blvd, Sun Valley, CA, 91352
equipment & service, all Ind.'s. OCE & HP wide format plotters. See Display Ad
in Blueprint Equipment
info@reprographicsupply.com * www.reprographicsupply.com
Steven Enterprises (800) 491-8785
17952 Skypark Circle Unit E, Irvine, CA, 92614
Wide Format Printers. Rent/Buy. Authorized Dealer: HP, KIP, Canon, Oce,
Epson. We service & supply everything we install
sales@plotters.com * www.plotters.com

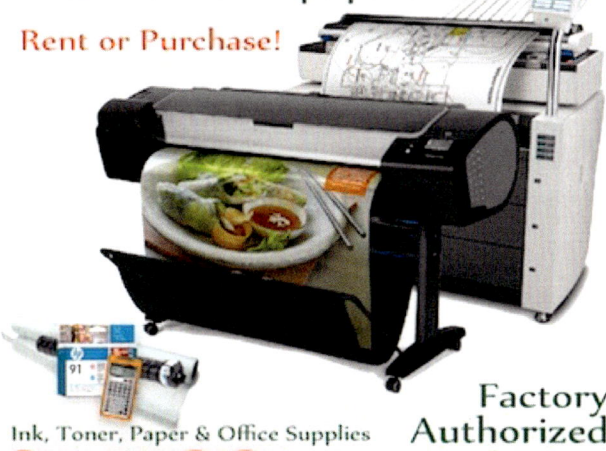

Plumbing Fixtures, Heating/Cooling Appliances

See Also: Air Conditioning & Heating, Production/Event* Bathroom Fixtures* Factory/Industrial* Furnaces* Heaters, Indoor* Prison Dressing/Jail Cell Dressing* Plastics, Materials & Fabrication* Sinks

Alley Cats Studio Rentals (818) 982-9178
Swamp coolers, plastic & metal valves, stainless steel sink, stainless steel prison toilet and prison sink unit

E.C. Prop Rentals (818) 764-2008
rooftop & window units, furnace/boiler, ducting/vents, fire sprinklers

LCW Props (818) 243-0707
Appliances, Parts, Tools, Empty Air Conditioners, Heaters, etc.

Mike Green Fire Equipment Co. (818) 989-3322
11916 Valerio St, N Hollywood, CA, 91605
Fire Sprinkler Systems; Fire Sprinkler design, Fire Sprinkler installation, Fire Sprinkler parts.
info@mgfire.com * www.Mgfire.com

The ReUse People (818) 244-5635
3015 Dolores St, Los Angeles, CA, 90065
Kitchen and bath sinks, faucets, toilets, bidets, both tubs, Jacuzzis, and more.
JeffCockerell@TheReUsePeople.org * www.TheReUsePeople.org

Studio Plumbing Rentals (323) 829-9339
7373 Atoll Ave, N Hollywood, CA, 91605
studioplumbingrentals@gmail.com * www.studioair.com

Universal Studios Property & Hardware Dept (818) 777-2784
Prop plumbing fixtures for rent.

Universal Studios Special Effects Equip. (818) 777-3333
portable water heaters, water pumps

Pocket Watches

See: Watches & Pocket Watches

Podiums & Lecterns

See Also: Furniture, Plexi/Lucite* Game Show Electronics & Equipment* Teleprompting

C. P. Two (323) 466-8201
Podiums and lecterns from presidential to lecture hall and valet parking podium.

The Hand Prop Room LP. (323) 931-1534

History For Hire, Inc. (818) 765-7767

L. A. Party Works (888) 527-2789
9712 Alpaca St, S El Monte, CA, 91733
in Vancouver tel. 604-589-4101. game show/party
partyworks@aol.com * www.partyworksinteractive.com

LCW Props (818) 243-0707
Futuristic, Lighting, Award Ceremony, Custom, Contemporary

Lennie Marvin Enterprises, Inc. (Prop Heaven) (818) 841-5882
business & church, acrylic lecterns

Modern Props (323) 934-3000
Podiums and lecterns made of wood, metal, acrylic

Omega/Cinema Props (323) 466-8201
Podiums and lecterns from presidential to lecture hall.

Prop Services West (818) 503-2790

Sony Pictures Studios-Prop House (Off Lot) (310) 244-5999
custom podiums, library podiums, office podiums, presidential podiums, lecterns,

Universal Studios Property & Hardware Dept (818) 777-2784
Podiums of different styles and time periods for rent.

Used Church Items, Religious Rentals (412) 220-2272
115 East Barr Street, Mcdonald, PA, 15057
Walk in and Free Standing Podiums, Pulpits, Lecterns, Baptismals, Wood and Metal, Large and Small, Old to Modern.
www.religiousrentals.com

ZG04 DECOR (818) 853-8040

Poker Tables

See: Gambling Equipment

Police Barricades

See: Traffic/Road Signs, Lights, Safety Items

Police Car, Police Motorcycle

See Also: Siren Lights* Vehicles/Picture Vehicles

The Hand Prop Room LP. (323) 931-1534
interior dressing, skins, vizbaps

Universal Studios Property & Hardware Dept (818) 777-2784
Police car rentals and police motorcycle rentals, contact Universal Studios Transportation.

Police Equipment

See Also: Badges, Patches & Buttons* Printing, Graphics, Digital & Large Format* Military Props & Equipment* Military Surplus/Combat Clothes, Field Gear* Police Car, Police Motorcycle* Uniforms, Trades/Professional/Sports* Walkie-Talkies* Police Office Dressing

E.C. Prop Rentals (818) 764-2008
squadroom & locker room dressing, lighted POLICE sign

The Hand Prop Room LP. (323) 931-1534
SWAT gear, arsenal, communication, fully outfitted

History For Hire, Inc. (818) 765-7767
Lots of police uniforms, hand cuffs, hard hats. 1880's - present police dressing and uniforms.

Hollywood Studio Gallery (323) 462-1116
pre-dressed bulletin boards posters,certificates,signs,maps

LCW Props (818) 243-0707
Helmets, Belts, Fake Guns, Taser, Batons, Handcuffs

RJR Props (404) 349-7600
Prop police equipment; police radios, police computers, police car consoles, police lights and much more.

Shomer-Tec (360) 733-6214
PO Box 28070, Bellingham, WA, 98228
catalog sales; badges/patches, handcuffs, metal detectors, covert ops equip. & SWAT gear; no guns
www.shomer-tec.com

Sony Pictures Studios-Prop House (Off Lot) (310) 244-5999
Tasers, shotguns, police badges, police id holder, police belts, police belt accessories, body bags, radios more!

Universal Studios Property & Hardware Dept (818) 777-2784
All kinds of police gear, police props and police equipment for rent.

Police Expendable Supplies

See: Expendables

Police Office Dressing

See Also: Books, Real/Hollow & Faux Books* Courtroom Furniture & Dressing* Filing Cabinets* Office Furniture* Paperwork, Documents & Letters, Office* Police Equipment

Faux Library Studio Props, Inc. (818) 765-0096
desktop and cleared photos, police station dressing

The Hand Prop Room LP. (323) 931-1534

On Set Graphics (661) 233-6786
Web Based Business
Police Office Dressing including Coroners Office documents, Crime Scene Photos, Police Records, Missing Person and more.
info@onsetgraphics.com * www.onsetgraphics.com

RJR Props (404) 349-7600
Police office dressing including computers, phones, copiers, water coolers and police desk dressing.

Police Uniforms

See: Badges, Patches & Buttons* Police Car, Police Motorcycle* Police Equipment* Uniforms, Trades/Professional/Sports

Political Campaign Memorabilia

See: Memorabilia & Novelties

Polyester Fiber

See: Upholstery Materials/Services

Polynesian Dressing

See: Hawaiian Dressing* Jungle Dressing* Tikis & Tropical Dressing

Pom Pons

The Hand Prop Room LP.	(323) 931-1534
History For Hire, Inc.	(818) 765-7767

period & contemporary

National Spirit	(800) 527-4366

6745 Lenox Center Court Ste 300, Memphis, TN, 38115
custom, standard, small to large, metallic, streamers, etc.
www.varsity.com

Team Leader	(877) 365-7555

Call for Appt
Online uniform catalog. Will make custom pom pons.
www.teamleader.com

Universal Studios Property & Hardware Dept	(818) 777-2784

Various pom poms/pom pons for rent of many sizes and colors.

Pool/Billiard Tables & Accessories

See Also: Game Tables & Equipment

Adler Pool Tables	(310) 676-5331

3155 W El Segundo Blvd, Hawthorne, CA, 90250
pool table rental, billiard table rental, accessories, lamps, moving, restoring, sales
www.adlerpooltables.com

AIR Designs	(818) 768-6639

Tables, Lights, Signs, Racks & Props

C. P. Two	(323) 466-8201
The Hand Prop Room LP.	(323) 931-1534

cues, racks, rubber pool balls

RC Vintage, Inc.	(818) 765-7107

Pool Tables w Pool Cues Stands, pool ball signs, billiard light fixtures

Universal Studios Property & Hardware Dept	(818) 777-2784

Pool tables and pool table accessories for rent.

Pools

See: Swimming Pools

Popcorn & Machines

See: Vendor Carts & Concession Counters

Porcelain/Ceramics

See: Decorative Accessories* Pottery* Prop Houses* Urns

Portable Studio Lighting

See: Stage Lighting, Film/Video/TV

Portable Toilets

See: Production Vehicles/Trailers* Toilets, Portable Prop

Portapotty

See: Construction Site Equipment* Production Vehicles/Trailers* Toilets, Portable Prop

Portfolios

See: Book Covers & Bookbinding

Portholes

See: Nautical Dressing & Props

Post Office

See Also: Mail & Mail Room* Prop Houses

History For Hire, Inc.	(818) 765-7767

hampers, bags, letter carrier bags, period maiboxes

LCW Props	(818) 243-0707

Postal Scales, Bins, Cleared Mail

Posters, Art/Movie/Travel/Wanted Etc.

See Also: Art For Rent (Cleared Art)* Printing, Graphics, Digital & Large Format* Paintings/Prints* Signs

Artery Props	(877) 732-7733

7684 Clybourn Ave 2nd Floor Unit C, Sun Valley, CA, 91352
100% cleared & owned artwork: posters, stickers, flyers, gold records, signs, CDs, DVDs, albums, mic flags & more.
info@arteryprops.com * www.arteryprops.com

CANADIAN ART PRINTS & WINN DEVON ART GROUP	(800) 663-1166

UNIT 110 - 6311 Westminster Hwy, Richmond, BC, Canada, V7C 4V4
Clearable stocked posters with a wide variety of images. Printed canvas, and a selection framed art is available too.
sales@capandwinndevon.com * www.capandwinndevon.com

Collins Visual Media	(818) 686-6581

10518 Johanna Ave, Shadow Hills, CA, 91040
Best source for custom posters. Any size or quantity, unmounted or mounted on your choice of substrate, in any finish.
www.collinsvisualmedia.com

Dina Art Co.	(323) 469-4073

6433 W Sunset Blvd, Los Angeles, CA, 90028
Cleared art, art posters, custom framing, hand colored prints & more. Over 3,000 images in 22 categories available.
dina@dinaart.com * www.dinaart.com

Eddie Brandt's Saturday Matinee	(818) 506-4242

5006 Vineland Ave, N Hollywood, CA, 91601
Tues.-Fri. 1:00-6:00 pm Sat. 8:30am - 5:00 pm. video rentals, vintage & hard to find photos, no posters

Faux Library Studio Props, Inc.	(818) 765-0096

large variety of art to travel posters, cleared

FILM ART LA	(323) 461-4900

Culver City Warehouse at Jefferson & Hauser. Call for address.
art posters & poster research. ORDER ARTWORK ONLINE: Address for pick ups and returns only.
filmartla@gmail.com * www.filmartla.com

History For Hire, Inc.	(818) 765-7767

manufacturing, period, contemporary

Hollywood Studio Gallery	(323) 462-1116

travel, many places, framed & unframed

Omega/Cinema Props	(323) 466-8201
On Set Graphics	(661) 233-6786

Web Based Business
Law enforcement paperwork, family photos, hotel paperwork, restaurant dressing, wanted posters and more.
info@onsetgraphics.com * www.onsetgraphics.com

Sony Pictures Studios-Prop House (Off Lot)	(310) 244-5999

foreign,govt.,movie,transportation,school,travel (many places)

Universal Studios Property & Hardware Dept	(818) 777-2784

Framed posters and unframed posters for rent.

Pot Belly Stoves

See: Stoves

Pottery

See Also: Statuary* Urns

Asian Ceramics, Inc.	(626) 449-6800

2800 Huntington Dr, Duarte, CA, 91010
Thailand, Vietnam, China, large & unique jars etc., planters, urns in stoneware, rustic & glazed finishes
sales@asian-ceramics.com * www.asian-ceramics.com

Badia Design, Inc.	(818) 762-0130

5420 Vineland Ave, N Hollywood, CA, 91601
Badia Design Inc. has a large selection of Moroccan clay pots that can be used for plants or any of your design needs.
info@badiadesign.com * www.badiadesign.com

C. P. Two	(323) 466-8201
The Hand Prop Room LP.	(323) 931-1534

American, Asian, African, Mexican, Egyptian, American Indian

LISTINGS FOR THIS CATEGORY CONTINUE ON THE FOLLOWING PAGE

History For Hire, Inc. (818) 765-7767
Mexican, Egyptian, archaeology, pottery shards

Jackson Shrub Supply, Inc. (818) 982-0100
pots 4"-44" diameter, contemporary pottery, classical pottery, plastic pottery, fiberglass pottery

Little Bohemia Rentals (818) 853-7506
11940 Sherman Rd, N Hollywood, CA, 91605
Danish modern pottery, Japanese pottery, Art pottery, Studio pottery. Vintage pottery and Contemporary pottery.
sales@wearelittlebohemia.com * www.wearelittlebohemia.com

Omega/Cinema Props (323) 466-8201
pottery from around the world

Pasadena Antique Center and Annex (626) 449-7706
480 South Fair Oaks Ave, Pasadena, CA, 91105
Pottery of all kinds from around the globe ranging from Pre-Colombian to Mid-Century in a variety of styles and sizes
pasadenaantiqecenterandannex@gmail.com * bit.ly/PasadenaAntiqueCenter

Picture Start Props (818) 255-5472
Big and small pots from various periods.

Pottery Manufacturing & Distributing Inc. (310) 323-7754
18881 S Hoover St, Gardena, CA, 90248
gotpots@potterymfg.com * www.potterymfg.com

Prop Services West (818) 503-2790

Sony Pictures Studios-Prop House (Off Lot) (310) 244-5999
large assortment styles & sizes

Universal Studios Property & Hardware Dept (818) 777-2784
Pottery from multiple styles & sizes for rent.

The Village Art Project Ceramic Studio (818) 985-9357
11602 Ventura Blvd, Studio City, CA, 91604
Custom ceramics, props, pottery & clay supplies. Classes and consulting as well.
www.villageartproject.com

Westmoore Pottery (910) 464-3700
4622 Busbee Rd, Seagrove, NC, 27341
17th, 18th, early 19th Century replicas
www.westmoorepottery.com

ZG04 DECOR (818) 853-8040
Vases, Vessels, Bowls, Arts & Crafts Pottery, Dishware

Pouffe (Hotel)

See: Hotel, Motel, Inn, Lodge

Power Generation/Distribution

See Also: Floor, Ground & Surface Protection Generators*

Ace Rentals (818) 255-5995
11950 Sherman Rd, N Hollywood, CA, 91605
up to 500 KW generators, service, fueling, 24 Hrs.
www.acegenerators.com

Aggreko Event Services (818) 767-7288
13230 Cambridge St, Santa Fe Springs, CA 90670
big, quiet power, heating & HVAC systems, over 130 locations globally for filming, tours, events
www.aggreko.com

Astro Audio Video Lighting, Inc. (818) 549-9915
6615 San Fernando Rd, Glendale, CA, 91201
Power cords of many sizes, surge protectors of all types, and power generators available; Power Distro 3kw-50kva
www.astroavl.com

Castex Rentals (323) 462-1468
1044 N Cole Ave, Hollywood, CA, 90038
portable Honda generators 9 amp-60 amp, ac cords
service@castexrentals.com * www.castexrentals.com

Presentation Books

See: Research, Advisors, Consulting & Clearances

Press Equipment

The Hand Prop Room LP. (323) 931-1534

History For Hire, Inc. (818) 765-7767
all eras thru present day, biggest sel.

Press Room

See: Newsroom

Press Walls

See: Printing, Graphics, Digital & Large Format

Pretzel Cart/Machines

See: Vendor Carts & Concession Counters

Primates

See: Animals (Live), Services, Trainers & Wranglers

Printing Presses

International Printing Museum (714) 529-1832
315 Torrance Blvd, Carson, CA, 90745
antique printing/office equipment 1450-1980. period printing, resource books, period advertising, period artwork
mail@printmuseum.org * www.printmuseum.org

Printing, 3-D, 3-Dimensional Printing

See Also: Prop & Set Design Supplies, Parts, Tools Prop Design & Manufacturing* Prop Reproduction & Fabrication*

depict (323) 222-1001
1460 Naud St, Los Angeles, CA, 90012
info@depict33.com * www.depict33.com

Kapow! 3D, LLC (310) 591-2964
1636 19th St, Santa Monica, CA, 90404
Kapow! 3D is a Santa Monica-based shop providing 3D Printing, Scanning, and Modeling.
info@kapow3d.com * www.kapow3d.com

Printing, Graphics, Digital & Large Format

See Also: Calligraphy Embroidery, Screen Printing, Etc.* Medical Equip/Furniture, Graphics/Supplies* Printing Presses* Promotional Items & Materials* Prop Houses* Signs*

ARC Imaging Resources (800) 950-3729
616 Monterey Pass Rd, Monterey Park, CA, 91754
CAD/Graphics Printers/Copiers/Scanners. Oce, Xerox, HP, Canon. We service & supply what we place.
mike.timchenko@e-arc.com * www.arcsupplies.com

Art, Signs & Graphics (818) 503-7997
6939 Farmdale Ave, N Hollywood, CA, 91605
props, banners, vinyl graphics, vehicle graphics, 3D router cut letters & logos, DVDs and CD cases
jessee@artsignsandgraphics.com * www.artsignsandgraphics.com

Artery Props (877) 732-7733
7684 Clybourn Ave 2nd Floor Unit C, Sun Valley, CA, 91352
100% cleared & owned artwork: posters, stickers, flyers, gold records, signs, CDs, DVDs, albums, mic flags & more.
info@arteryprops.com * www.arteryprops.com

Beyond Image Graphics (818) 547-0899
1853 Dana St, Glendale, CA, 91201
Large Format Imaging, Canvas Printing, Canvas Stretching, Trade Show Graphics, Exhibit Graphics, Custom Decals
rafi@beyondimagegraphics.com * www.beyondimagegraphics.com

Collins Visual Media (818) 686-6581
10518 Johanna Ave, Shadow Hills, CA, 91040
Grand-format supergraphics, both front-lit and backlit, seamless and non-glare for event backdrops, media walls, etc.
www.collinsvisualmedia.com

D'ziner Sign Co. (323) 467-4467
801 Seward Street, Los Angeles, CA, 90038
graphics design & 8' wide digital printing in house, rush orders
sales@dzinersign.com * www.dzinersign.com

depict (323) 222-1001
1460 Naud St, Los Angeles, CA, 90012
info@depict33.com * www.depict33.com
The Earl Hays Press (818) 765-0700
10707 Sherman Way, Sun Valley, CA, 91352
services the Industry only. lrg sel & custom creation
ehp@la.twcbc.com * www.theearlhayspress.com
EFX- Event Special Effects (626) 888-2239
125 Railroad Ave, Monrovia, CA, 91016
Step & Repeat Printing- Large Format- Decals- Signage- Poster- Mounting
info@efxla.com * www.efxla.com
Flix FX Inc. (818) 765-3549
7327 Lankershim Blvd #4, N Hollywood, CA, 91605
Vinyl graphics and 3D vacuum formed signs
info@flixfx.com * www.flixfx.com
The Hand Prop Room LP. (323) 931-1534
in-house graphics dept.
History For Hire, Inc. (818) 765-7767
Full service graphic shop for signs, labels, event tickets, and more.
HPR Graphics (323) 556-2694
5674 Venice Blvd, Los Angeles, CA, 90019
Product labels, certificates, magazine covers, newspapers, antique graphics, thermo printing, inkjet printing, and more.
hprcan@earthlink.net * www.hprgraphics.net
JP Graphics Design+Print (747) 230-6840
5354 Denny Ave, N Hollywood, CA, 91601
We Provide the Highest Quality Turn Key Solutions from Design to Completion.
signs@jp-dp.com * www.jp-dp.com
L. A. Party Works (888) 527-2789
9712 Alpaca St, S El Monte, CA, 91733
Large Format Printing, Vehicle Printing & Wrapping, Canvas Printing, Trade Show Graphics, Step & Repeats, Custom Decals
partyworks@aol.com * www.partyworksinteractive.com

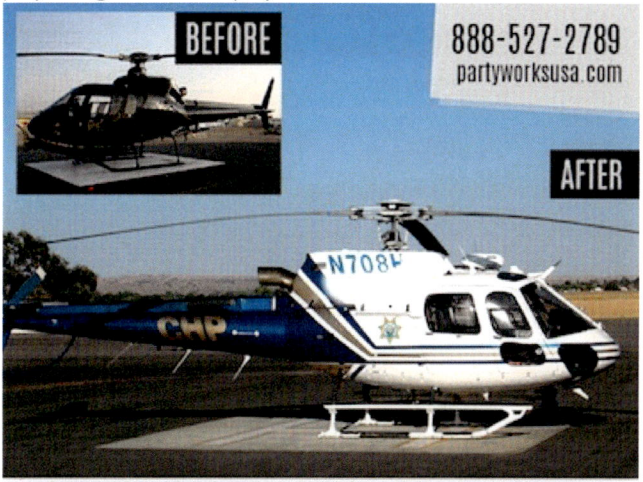

LCW Props (818) 243-0707
Custom Graphics Department. We Make Any Video Files Needed & Have A Huge Stock
Nights of Neon (818) 756-4791
13815 Saticoy St, Van Nuys, CA, 91402
Full service sign shop, digital imaging, vinyl graphics, sheet graphics, metal/posters
contact@nightsofneon.com * www.nightsofneon.com

LISTINGS FOR THIS CATEGORY CONTINUE ON THE FOLLOWING PAGE

Repro-Graphic Supply   (818) 771-9066
9838 Glenoaks Blvd, Sun Valley, CA, 91352
drafting & engineering supplies, equipment & service, all Ind.'s. large format xerographics printing
info@reprographicsupply.com * www.reprographicsupply.com

Step and Repeat LA   (818) 434-7591
10518 Johanna Ave, Shadow Hills, CA, 91040
We specialize in step and repeat backdrops and media walls for all events, especially red carpet.
Services@StepandRepeatLA.com * StepandRepeatLA.com

Steven Enterprises   (800) 491-8785
17952 Skypark Circle Unit E, Irvine, CA, 92614
Wide Format Printers. Rent/Buy. Authorized Dealer: HP, KIP, Canon, Oce, Epson. We service & supply everything we install
sales@plotters.com * www.plotters.com

Tractor Vision Scenery & Rentals   (323) 235-2885
340 E Jefferson Blvd, Los Angeles, CA, 90011
Specializing in entertainment, trade shows, & events, we bring your projects to life with precision, speed & personality
sets@tractorvision.com * www.tractorvision.com

Universal Studios Graphic Design & Sign Shop   (818) 777-2350
design, large format printing to 100" wide, & full service sign

Warner Bros. Studios Production Sound & Video   (818) 954-2511
4000 Warner Blvd Bldg 43, Burbank, CA, 91522
A/V Equipment Rental, Design, Presentations, Install & Support; Visual Display Creation; Communication
wbsfproductionsound@warnerbros.com * www.wbsoundandvideo.com

Warner Bros. Studios Property Department   (818) 954-2181
2 LF 16', any size matl, backlit, see-through, seaming, design/install

Warner Bros. Studios Scenic Art & Sign Shop   (818) 954-1815
4000 Warner Blvd Bldg 44, Burbank, CA, 91522
graphic design and production studio for signs & scenic art; digital printing to hand-painted
wbsigns@warnerbros.com * www.wbsignandscenic.com

Prints

See: Paintings/Prints

Prison Dressing

See: Electric Chairs Prison Dressing/Jail Cell Dressing*

Prison Dressing/Jail Cell Dressing

Alley Cats Studio Rentals　　　　　(818) 982-9178
sinks, toilets, beds, tables, benches with handcuff bar

Alley Cats Props
(818) 982-9178 alleycatsprops@gmail.com

Alpha Companies - Spellman Desk Co.　　(818) 504-9090
Prison dressing and jail dressing
C. P. Two　　　　　　　　　　　　　(323) 466-8201
Prison beds/prison bunkbeds, prison toilets, prison mattresses, custody
benches and more.
E.C. Prop Rentals　　　　　　　　　(818) 764-2008
wall-mounted bunks, stools/tables, jail & prison signage, sink/toilet unit, jail
bars

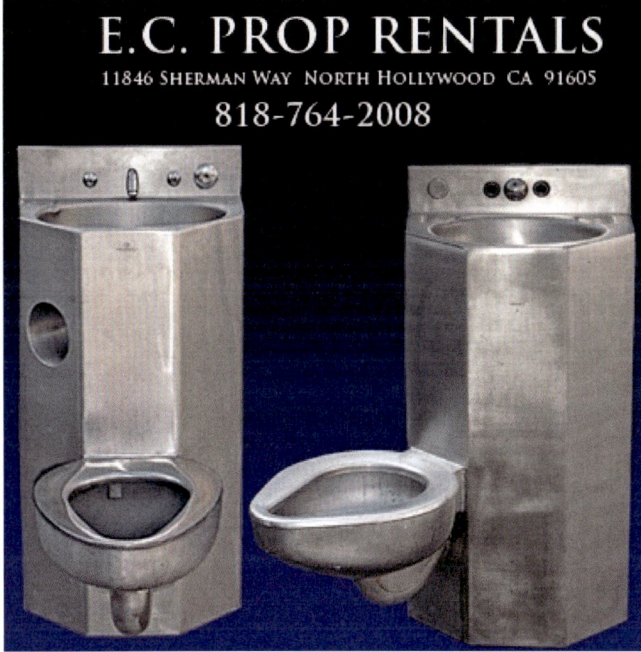

E.C. PROP RENTALS
11846 SHERMAN WAY NORTH HOLLYWOOD CA 91605
818-764-2008

Lennie Marvin Enterprises, Inc. (Prop Heaven)　(818) 841-5882
Prison props/jail props
RC Vintage, Inc.　　　　　　　　　(818) 765-7107
Prison Cell Dressing; Prison Beds, Prison Toilets, Prison Sinks, Prison
Benches and other Prison Dressing

RJR Props　　　　　　　　　　　　(404) 349-7600
Prison beds, prison toilets, prison phones, prison cameras, and more.
Sony Pictures Studios-Prop House (Off Lot)　(310) 244-5999
prison tables, prison toilets, jail bathrooms
Universal Studios Property & Hardware Dept　(818) 777-2784
Props for jail cell dressing, prison dressing for rent.
Warner Bros. Studios Property Department　(818) 954-2181
Prison toilets, prison beds, prison visiting room phones and a few wall mounted
prison bunkbeds

Private Investigations

Westside Detectives Inc.　　　　　(323) 583-8660
6230 Wilshire Blvd #59, Los Angeles, CA, 90048
Investigations, trademark infringement, intellectual property investigations,
polygraph, bodyguards, background checks
www.westsidedetectives.com

Produce Carts

See Also: Produce Stands
AIR Designs　　　　　　　　　　　(818) 768-6639
Vegetable, Fruit, Flower, Farmers Market
Alley Cats Studio Rentals　　　　　(818) 982-9178
Produce crates w/artificial produce, wood
Universal Studios Property & Hardware Dept　(818) 777-2784
Produce carts from different time periods available for rent.

Produce Crates

See: Food, Artificial Food* Grocery Check-out Stands (Complete)*
Produce Carts* Produce Stands* Food, Food Stylists

Produce Stands

AIR Designs　　　　　　　　　　　(818) 768-6639
Vegetable, Fruit, Signage, Farmers Market, Grocery Store
Alley Cats Studio Rentals　　　　　(818) 982-9178
variety of food stands as well, with crates, fake food and umbrella tops.
Lennie Marvin Enterprises, Inc. (Prop Heaven)　(818) 841-5882
period & modern, wide variety, product too
Sony Pictures Studios-Prop House (Off Lot)　(310) 244-5999
Universal Studios Property & Hardware Dept　(818) 777-2784
Contemporary produce stand, produce crates & produce carts for rent.

Product Labels

See Also: Printing, Graphics, Digital & Large Format* Prop Houses
Collins Visual Media　　　　　　　(818) 686-6581
10518 Johanna Ave, Shadow Hills, CA, 91040
We design, print and create labels and removable or permanent decals of any
dimension.
www.collinsvisualmedia.com
D'ziner Sign Co.　　　　　　　　　(323) 467-4467
801 Seward Street, Los Angeles, CA, 90038
labels & packaging
sales@dzinersign.com * www.dzinersign.com
The Earl Hays Press　　　　　　　(818) 765-0700
10707 Sherman Way, Sun Valley, CA, 91352
services the Industry only. knockoff/real, custom design
ehp@la.twcbc.com * www.theearlhayspress.com
The Hand Prop Room LP.　　　　　(323) 931-1534
in stock & custom
History For Hire, Inc.　　　　　　　(818) 765-7767
custom graphics
HPR Graphics　　　　　　　　　　(323) 556-2694
5674 Venice Blvd, Los Angeles, CA, 90019
Beverage labels, food labels, food boxes, media packaging, cigarette
packaging, liquor labels, beer labels and more.
hprcan@earthlink.net * www.hprgraphics.net
I Communications　　　　　　　　(404) 596-5311
2135 Defoor Hills Rd NW Suite H, Atlanta, GA, 30318
paper, foam, fabric; cust. logos, layouts, drawings, etc.
graphics@icommnetwork.net * http://icommrentals.net
Universal Studios Graphic Design & Sign Shop　(818) 777-2350
package design & point of sale display signage
Warner Bros. Studios Scenic Art & Sign Shop　(818) 954-1815
4000 Warner Blvd Bldg 44, Burbank, CA, 91522
graphic design and production studio for signs & scenic art; digital printing to
hand-painted
wbsigns@warnerbros.com * www.wbsignandscenic.com

Product Placement

AIM Productions (718) 729-9288
34-12 36th Street, Suite 228, Astoria, NY, 11106
an entertainment marketing company
www.aimproductionsinc.com
LCW Props (818) 243-0707
Let Us Help You Find Anything You Need

Production Vehicles/Trailers

See Also: Vehicles/Picture Vehicles
D. Aguiar Production Vehicles (310) 925-0967
PO Box 1473, Chino Hills, CA, 91709
talent, wardrobe, production, make-up/hair trailers & motorhomes
www.daequipment.com
Easy Rider Productions, Inc. (818) 822-8782
23919 Newhall Ave, Newhall, CA 91321
trailers: 2 room talent, 6 & 8 station make-up/wardrobe, 4, 5 & 8 room
honeywagons, generators, work vehicles.
www.easyriderprod.com
Hollywood Honeywagon & Prod. Vehicles (818) 763-1966
11160 Victory Blvd, N. Hollywood, CA, 91606
Prod. trailers & motorhomes, 2 & 3 room star trailers, 4-9 room honeywagons,
make-up/wardrobe, upscale portable toilets
www.hollywoodhoneywagon.com
Star Waggons Production Trailers (818) 367-5946
Los Angeles, New Orleans, Atlanta, Albuquerque
dressing room trailers
www.starwaggons.com
Stardeck Industries (951) 270-0015
1275 Railroad St, Carona, CA, 92882
Prod. trailers with pop-outs & skydecks, honeywagons, motorhomes
www.stardeckrvs.com
Touring Video, Inc. (818) 504-3500
827 Hollywood Way Ste 424, Burbank, CA, 91505
studio recording, corp. production, webcasting, concert tours
www.touringvideo.com
Universal Studios Transportation (818) 777-2966
100 Universal City Plaza, Universal City, CA, 91608
Production vehicles, trailers, SUVs, vans & more
universalstudioslot.com/transportation
Western Studio Service, Inc. (818) 842-9272
4561 Colorado Blvd, Los Angeles, CA, 90039
We have the largest fleet of custom trailers to transport scenery of all sizes and
heights. All trailers for rent too!
www.westernstudioservice.com

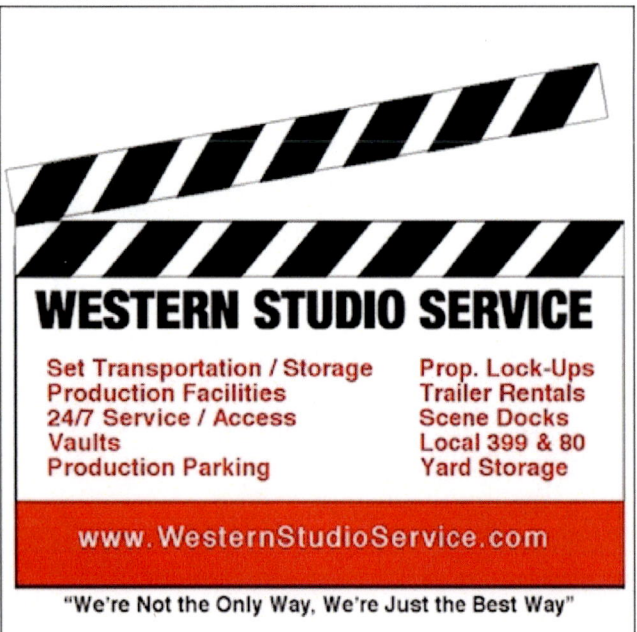

Projectors

See: Motion Picture Projectors

Promotional Items & Materials

See Also: Badges, Patches & Buttons Embroidery, Screen Printing,
Etc.* Printing, Graphics, Digital & Large Format*
Aah-Inspiring Balloons (562) 494-7605
Call for an Appointment.
After 14 years in the TV and Film Industry, Aah-Inspiring Balloon Decor has
been seen in over 200 TV shows and Films.
aahinspiring1@aol.com * www.aahinspiringballoons.com
Kater-Crafts Bookbinders (562) 692-0665
4860 Gregg Rd, Pico Rivera, CA, 90660
Custom work. Presentation binders, folders, portfolios, boxes, foil stamping.
sales@katercrafts.com * www.katercrafts.com

Prompting

See: Teleprompting

Prop & Set Design Supplies, Parts, Tools

See Also: CNC Router & Laser Etching Services Metal Plating,
Coating, Polishing* Paint & Painting Supplies* Plastics, Materials &
Fabrication* Scenery/Set Construction* Special Effects,
Make-up/Prosthetics* Ultraviolet Products* Water Jet CNC Services*
E. B. Bradley (800) 533-3030
5602 Bickett St, Vernon, CA 90058
6 Loc., B2B, don't sell to general public, tools & hardware, carry Wilsonart
metallic finish laminates
www.ebbradley.com
Flanders Control Cables (626) 303-0700
859 Meridian St, Duarte, CA 91010
small dia. cables, housings, fittings for wire control mechanisms
www.flanderscables.com
General Veneer Manufacturing Co. (323) 564-2661
8652 Otis St, South Gate, CA, 90280
Breakaway balsa wood sheets & boards
balsasales@generalveneer.com * www.generalveneer.com

Grainger (800) 472-4643
570 S. Alameda St, Los Angeles CA, 90013
catalog sales; industrial supplies, tools, etc.
www.grainger.com
Heatshrink.com (801) 621-1501
2752 South 1900 West, Ogden, UT, 84401
heatshrink tubing
www.heatshrink.com

Konica Minolta Sensing Americas, Inc. (888) 473-2656
101 Williams Dr, Ramsey, NJ, 07446
Non-contact 3D digitizing scanners
www.konicaminolta.com

Krayden Inc. (714) 549-1343
2655 S Orange Ave, Santa Ana, CA, 92707
mold making materials & tools, several locations
www.krayden.com

LCW Props (818) 243-0707
huge sel machine parts, great prop starters

Leica Geosystems HDS, Inc. (925) 790-2300
4550 Norris Canyon Rd, San Ramon, CA, 94586
Scene, structure & site scanning hardware & software
hds.leica-geosystems.us

LM Treasures (626) 252-7354
Life Size & Oversized Fiberglass Resin Statues of Many Kinds

Mike Green Fire Equipment Co. (818) 989-3322
11916 Valerio St, N Hollywood, CA, 91605
Large inventory of new and used fire alarm cabinets & fire protection devices.
info@mgfire.com * www.Mgfire.com

Montroy Supply (800) 666-8769
1601 S Maple Ave, Montebello, CA, 90640 x1000
sign & graphics mfg. materials, supplies, equip.
www.montroy.com

My Doll's House (310) 320-4828
1218 El Prado Ave Ste 136, Torrance, CA 90501
Dollhouses, Dollhouse Kits, Room Boxes, Miniatures, Collectibles,
Accessories, Tools and Supplies
margiesminiatures@gmail.com * www.mydollshouse.com

Ohio Travel Bag (800) 800-1941
6481 Davis Industrial Pkwy, Solon, OH, 44139
1000s of hard-to-find fasteners & decorative hdw parts
info@ohiotravelbag.com * www.ohiotravelbag.com

Prop Masters, Inc. (818) 846-3915
2721 Empire Ave, Burbank, CA, 91504
casting & mold making materials
www.propmastersinc.com

Quixote (504) 266-2297
10289 Airline Hwy, St Rose, LA, 70087
Set building, gloves, Construction, glues, tape, expendables, lumber, power
tools, delivers, online orders.
nola@quixote.com * www.quixote.com

Reynolds Advanced Materials: Smooth-On (818) 358-6000
Distributor
10856 Vanowen St, N Hollywood, CA, 91605
Hollywood's F/X source for Liquid Rubbers, Plastics & more
LA@reynoldsam.com * www.moldmakingmaterials.com

Roland DGA Corp. (800) 542-2307
15363 Barranca Pkwy, Irvine, CA, 92618
A business resource. Special purpose 2D/3D scanning, milling, engraving,
printing devices; use web site to locate nearest dealer
www.rolanddga.com

Sculptural Arts Coating, Inc. (800) 743-0379
PO Box 10546, Greensboro, NC, 27404
Mfg. of "Sculpt or Coat" nontoxic plastic cream for making props, scenery,
puppets, masks, costumes, arch. elements
www.sculpturalarts.com

ShopWildThings (928) 855-6075
2880 Sweetwater Ave, Lake Havasu City, AZ, 86406
Event Decor, Beaded Curtains, Chain Curtains, String Curtains & Columns,
Crystal Columns. Reliable service & delivery.
help@shopwildthings.com * www.shopwildthings.com

Specialty Coatings & Chemicals (818) 983-0055
4677 Worth St, Los Angeles CA, 90063
special coatings, paints & dyes
www.special-tcoatings.com

Wurth Louis and Company (800) 422-4389
895 Columbia St, Brea, CA, 92821
distribute Chemetal, metal laminates, solid metals, treefrog veneers, Nevamar
laminates
www.wurthlac.com

Prop Breakaways

See: Breakaways (Glass, Props, Scenery)

Prop Builders

See: Architectural Pieces & Artifacts Fiberglass
Products/Fabrication* Prop Design & Manufacturing* Prop
Reproduction & Fabrication* Scenery/Set Construction*
Vacu-forms/Vacu-forming*

Prop Design & Manufacturing

See Also: Animal Costumes & Walk Around Characters Art, Artists
For Hire* CNC Router & Laser Etching Services* Fiberglass
Products/Fabrication* Food, Artificial Food* Metalworking,
Decorative* Metalworking, Welding & Structural* Miniatures/Models*
Prop Reproduction & Fabrication* Robots* Scenery/Set Construction*
Sculpture* Staff Shops* Vacu-forms/Vacu-forming* Water Jet CNC
Services*

Action Sets and Props / WonderWorks, Inc. (818) 992-8811
Space shuttle & station, space suit, specialty props, miniatures, mechanical
effects, cityscape, miniature buildings

Arteffex/Dann O'Quinn (818) 506-5358
911 Mayo St, Los Angeles, CA, 90042
acfx@att.net * www.acfxo.com

CBS Electronics (323) 575-2645
7800 Beverly Blvd Rm M162, Los Angeles, CA, 90036
Complete carpentry shop and fabrication shop.

The Character Shop (805) 306-9441
4735 Industrial St #4B-G, Simi Valley, CA, 93063
Extraordinary Custom Animatronic Animals & Creatures, Puppets, Marionettes,
Replicas, Robots, Props, Art Installations
lazzwaldo@mac.com * www.character-shop.com

Charisma Design Studio, Inc. (818) 252-6611
8414 San Fernando Road, Sun Valley, CA, 91352
metal/glass/wood/stone, 12'X6' CNC water jet cutter, custom art
info@charismadesign.com * www.charismadesign.com

Charisma Design Studio, Inc.
CNC WATERJET CUTTING
GLASS ETCHING   SIGN FABRICATION
PROP FABRICATION
www.charismadesign.com

LISTINGS FOR THIS CATEGORY CONTINUE ON THE
FOLLOWING PAGE

Collins Visual Media   (818) 686-6581
10518 Johanna Ave, Shadow Hills, CA, 91040
Our team of designers, fabricators and installers will help you with any project from sign props to trade show booths.
www.collinsvisualmedia.com

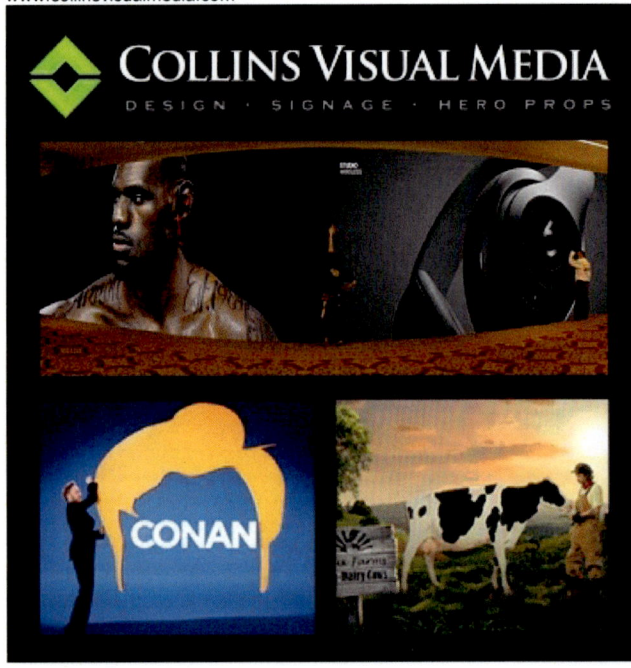

Dapper Cadaver   (818) 771-0818
Custom bodies, stunt dummies, horror & supernatural characters, body parts, mummies, skeletons & fake animals.

Decker Studios Art Foundry   (818) 503-9913
7400 Ethel Ave, N. Hollywood, CA, 91605
Open 11-3; fine arts & sculpture casting, mold making, restorations, small scale to large public space pieces
www.deckerstudios.com

depict   (323) 222-1001
1460 Naud St, Los Angeles, CA, 90012
info@depict33.com * www.depict33.com

EFX- Event Special Effects   (626) 888-2239
125 Railroad Ave, Monrovia, CA, 91016
Custom Fabrication- CNC- Plasma Table- Pipe & Ring Benders- 3D Renderings
info@efxla.com * www.efxla.com

Elden Designs   (323) 550-8922
2767 W. Broadway, Eagle Rock, CA, 90041
custom props for TV/film & commercials & print advertising
cargocollective.com/eldendesign

Flix FX Inc.   (818) 765-3549
7327 Lankershim Blvd #4, N Hollywood, CA, 91605
Mechanical EFX, CNC routing, sculpting, vacuforming & Prop Making
info@flixfx.com * www.flixfx.com

FormDecor, Inc.   (310) 558-2582
America's largest event rental supplier of 20th Century furniture and accessories for Modern and Mid-Century styles.

FXperts, Inc.   (818) 767-0883
11352 Goss St, Sun Valley, CA, 91352
custom props, sets, special visual effects
www.fxpertsinc.com

Global Entertainment Industries, Inc.   (818) 567-0000
2948 N. Ontario St, Burbank, CA, 91504
molds, sculpting, miniatures
www.globalentind.com

The Hand Prop Room LP.   (323) 931-1534
in-house, custom, mfg. & design, leather, wood, metal

HPR Custom   (323) 931-1534
5700 Venice Blvd, Los Angeles, CA, 90019
3D modeling, woodworking, CNC machining, CAD drawings, water jet cutting, metal working, custom electronics and more.
www.hprcustom.com

J & M Special Effects, Inc.   (718) 875-0140
524 Sackett St, Brooklyn, NY, 11217
Formerly Jauchem & Meeh. effects design
info@jmfx.net * www.jmfx.net

KIHL STUDIOS   (818) 812-9594
9701 Owensmouth Ave Unit 1, Chatsworth, CA, 91311
Custom prop design & fabrication services. Sci-fi/fantasy, historical, functional electrical & mechanical props, etc.
design@kihlstudios.com * www.kihlstudios.com

L. A. Party Works   (888) 527-2789
9712 Alpaca St, S El Monte, CA, 91733
in Vancouver tel. 604-589-4101
partyworks@aol.com * www.partyworksinteractive.com

Merritt Productions, Inc.   (818) 760-0612
10845 Vanowen St, North Hollywood, CA, 91605
specialty props, miniatures, sculpture, mech effects, set const.
www.merrittproductions.com

MovieMoto.com   (626) 359-0016
16015 Adelante St, Irwindale, CA, 91702
A manufacturer of Model Airplane Engines, a mechanical engineering company, and can design and make anything, literally.
www.MovieMoto.com

New Deal Studios, Inc.   (310) 578-9929
15392 Cobalt St, Sylmar, CA, 91342
Design miniatures, photography, digital & visual effects & stage rental
www.newdealstudio.com

New Rule FX   (818) 387-6450
7751 Densmore Ave, Van Nuys, CA, 91406
Breakaway props-all types & categories Custom prop & FX design & construction, 3D printing Prototypes, Molding & Casting
ryan@newrulefx.com * www.NewRuleFX.com

Nights of Neon   (818) 756-4791
13815 Saticoy St, Van Nuys, CA, 91402
over 2,000 neon props in stock. custom neon prop design
contact@nightsofneon.com * www.nightsofneon.com

RJR Props   (404) 349-7600
Can design props and manufacture props including printing fake money.

Scenic Highlights   (818) 252-7760
10830 Cantara St, Sun Valley, CA, 91352
scenichighlights.com

Set Masters   (818) 982-1506
24853 Avenue Rockefeller, Valencia, CA, 91355
Our team of Designers and Fabricators will help you with any project big or small.
info@setmasters.com * www.setmasters.com

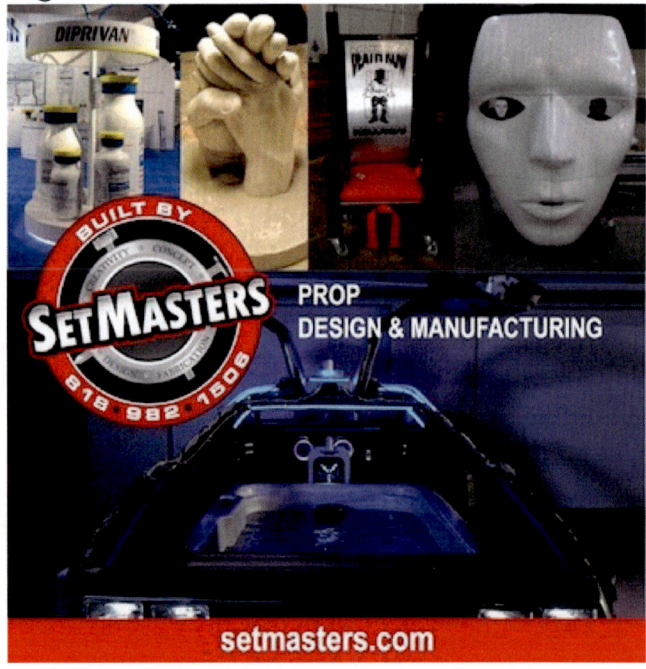

Sets, Etc.-Bob Pinkos Services   **(925) 432-1083**
270 E 15th St, Pittsburg, CA, 94565
cust. sets, displays, props, 3-D signs, models, prototypes, backdrops, illusions, quality prof. corp. art svcs since 198
www.setsetc.com

Sword & Stone   **(818) 562-6548**
metal, wood, glass, wrought iron, 1-day custom etching

Tech Works FX Studios   **(504) 722-1504**
13405 Seymour Meyers Blvd #5, Covington, LA, 70433
Specializes in Mechanical Props, Fabrication and Design, Molding and casting and Robotics.
info@techworksstudios.com * www.techworksstudios.com

Tractor Vision Scenery & Rentals   **(323) 235-2885**
340 E Jefferson Blvd, Los Angeles, CA, 90011
Specializing in entertainment, trade shows, & events, we bring your projects to life with precision, speed & personality
sets@tractorvision.com * www.tractorvision.com

Ultra Prototypes LLC   **(818) 292-1906**
Call for Appointment
We build your ideas!
jeff@ultraprototypes.com * www.ultraprototypes.com

2005
40 YEARS OF DEBBIES BOOK

YouTube is launched, The Group of 8 nations pledges aid to Africa, we have the Terry Schiavo case, and the Michael Jackson trial begins. **Scooter Libby** is indicted, **Hurricane Katrina** hits the Gulf Coast.

T.V. brings us **'Grey's Anatomy'**, **'Medium'**, **'Lost'**, and **'Survivor: Palau'**. **'Million Dollar Baby'** and **'Aviator'** do well at the Oscars.

Universal Studios Graphic Design & Sign Shop   **(818) 777-2350**
the complete range of materials & applications for graphics work

Universal Studios Staff Shop   **(818) 777-2337**

Warner Bros. Studios Special Effects & Prop Shop   **(818) 954-1365**
4000 Warner Blvd Bldg 44, Burbank, CA, 91522
Consultation, Script Break-down, Equipment Rentals, Expendable Sales, Picture Car Prep, Action Props
www.wbspecialeffects.com

Woody's Electrical Props   **(818) 503-1940**
period to futuristic. design/build panels, consoles, sound mix boards more

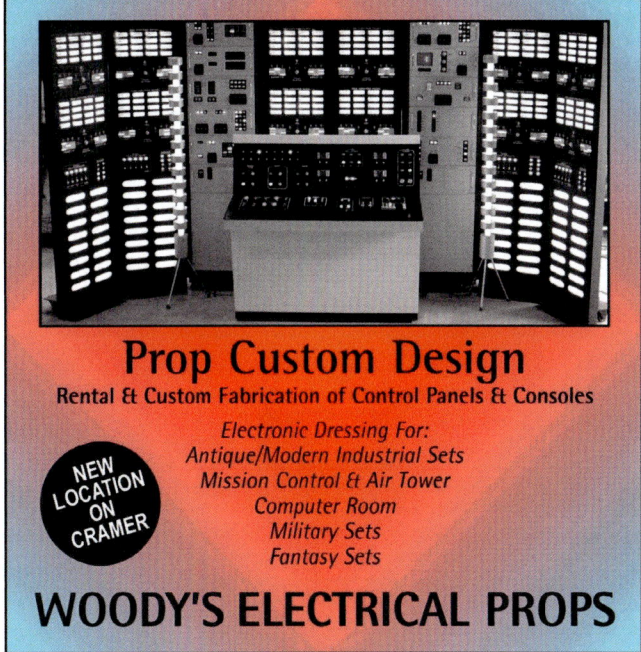

Prop Custom Design
Rental & Custom Fabrication of Control Panels & Consoles

NEW LOCATION ON CRAMER

Electronic Dressing For:
Antique/Modern Industrial Sets
Mission Control & Air Tower
Computer Room
Military Sets
Fantasy Sets

WOODY'S ELECTRICAL PROPS

Worlds of Wow   **(817) 380-4215**
1800 Shady Oaks Drive, Denton, TX, 76205
Custom foam designed, hard-coated, painted, and finished environments.
www.worldsofwow.com

Prop Food

See: Food, Artificial Food Food, Food Stylists*

Debbies Book Always at your fingertips

DB Debbies Book
CELEBRATING 40 YEARS

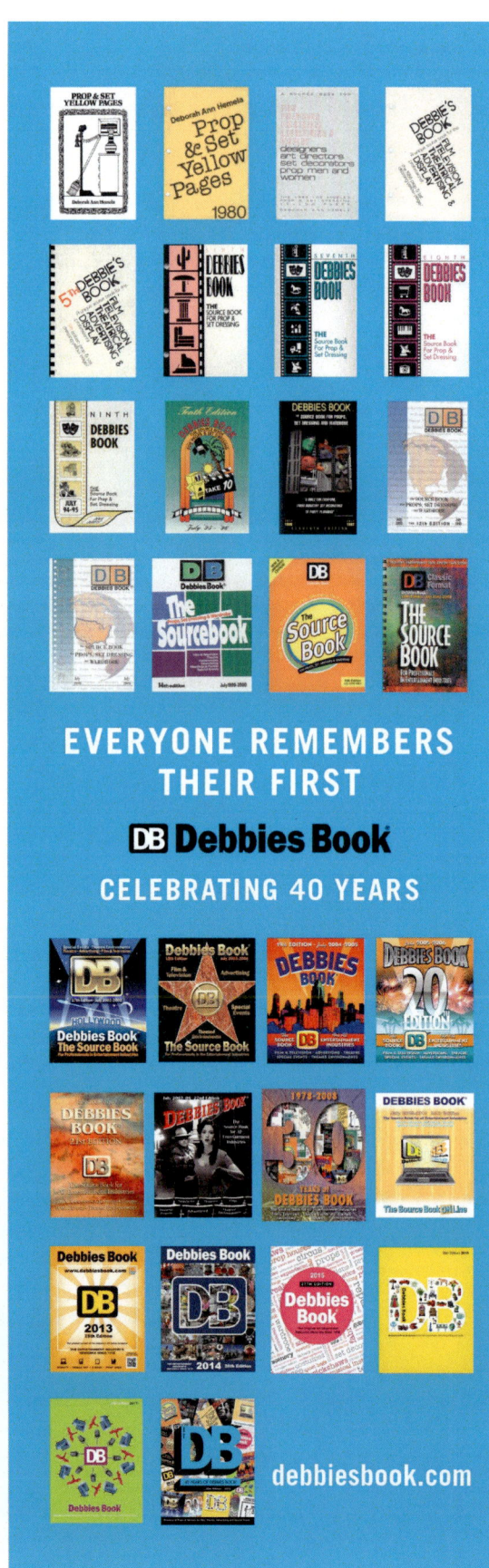

EVERYONE REMEMBERS
THEIR FIRST

DB Debbies Book

CELEBRATING 40 YEARS

debbiesbook.com

Prop Houses

See Also: Prop & Set Design Supplies, Parts, Tools Prop Design &
Manufacturing* Prop Reproduction & Fabrication* Scenery/Set
Construction*

A-1 Medical Integration   (818) 753-0319
7344 Laurel Canyon Blvd, N Hollywood, CA, 91605
Medical devices for Set Decoration & Property, from minor procedures to
detailed hospital units.
a1medwarehouse@aol.com * www.a1props.com

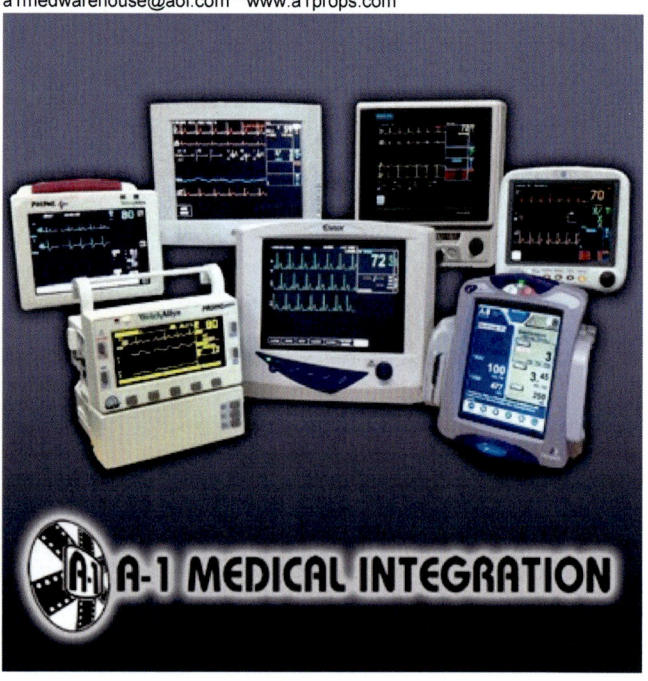

Advanced Liquidators Office Furniture   (818) 763-3470
11151 Vanowen St, N Hollywood, CA, 91605
Specializes in new and used office furniture as well as studio rentals.
rentals@advancedliquidators.com * www.advancedliquidators.com

Aero Mock-Ups   (888) 662-5877
13126 Saticoy St, N Hollywood, CA, 91605
Aviation prop house. Complete airplane interiors & airport dressing, model
airplanes, jet engines, and airline costumes.
info@aeromockups.com * www.aeromockups.com

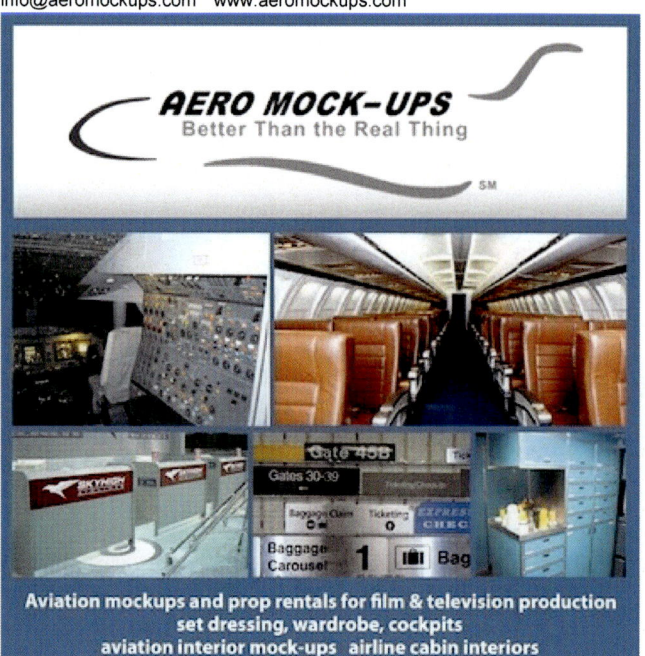

Aviation mockups and prop rentals for film & television production
set dressing, wardrobe, cockpits
aviation interior mock-ups   airline cabin interiors

AIR Designs　　　　　　　　　　　　　(818) 768-6639
11900 Wicks St, Sun Valley, CA, 91352
Auto, Gas, Racing, Fast Food, Coffee, Diner, Cafeteria, Store, Street, Vendor Carts
info@airdesigns.net * www.airdesigns.net

Alley Cats Studio Rentals　　　　　　　(818) 982-9178
7101 Case Ave, N Hollywood, CA, 91605
alleycatsprops@gmail.com * www.alleycatsprops.com

Alpha Companies - Spellman Desk Co.　　(818) 504-9090
7990 San Fernando Rd, Sun Valley, CA, 91352
The #1 source for medical equipment in the industry.
rentals@alphaprops.com * www.alphaprops.com

Arenson Prop Center　　　　　　　　　(917) 210-2562
1115 Broadway, 6th Floor, New York, NY 10010
info@aof.com * www.aof.com/p/props

Artkraft Taxidermy Rentals　　　　　　(818) 505-8425
10847 Vanowen St, N Hollywood, CA, 91605
Taxidermied animals of all kinds: birds, fish, mammals, and much more from Africa, North America, and exotic locales.
info@artkrafttaxidermy.com * www.artkrafttaxidermy.net

MUSEUM QUALITY TAXIDERMIED ANIMALS - FROM ANTELOPES TO ZEBRAS
ESTABLISHED 1969 HOLLYWOOD, CA

DB Debbies Book®
CELEBRATING 40 YEARS

Mobile App　　　　**Desktop Website**　　　　**Blog**

Print Book　　　　**Mobile Web**　　　　**eBook**

Bridge Furniture & Props Los Angeles (818) 433-7100
3210 Vanowen St, Burbank, CA, 91505
We carry modern & traditional furniture, lighting, accessories, cleared art, & rugs. Items are online for easy shopping.
la@bridgeprops.com * la.bridgeprops.com

E.C. Prop Rentals (818) 764-2008
11846 Sherman Way, N Hollywood, CA, 91605
Factory, Industrial, Loading Dock, Warehouse, Locker Room, Garage, Street/Alley, Shipping Yard
ecprops@aol.com * www.ecprops.com

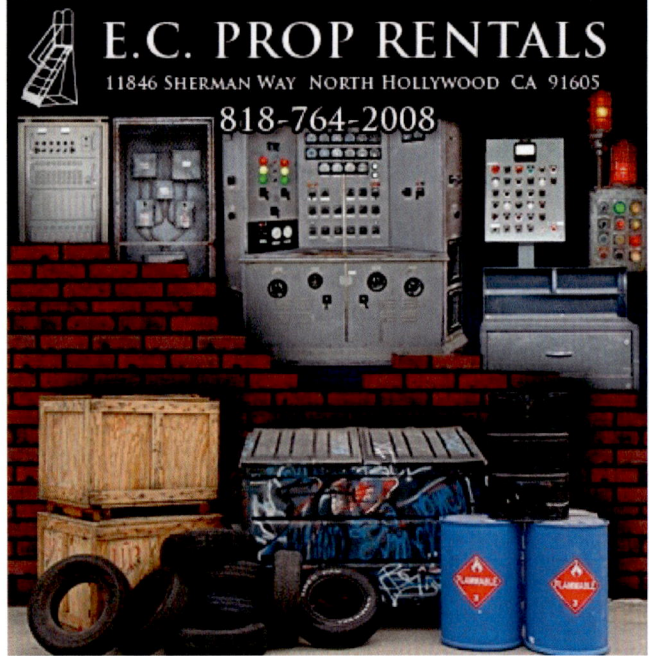

E.C. PROP RENTALS
11846 SHERMAN WAY NORTH HOLLYWOOD CA 91605
818-764-2008

C. P. Two (323) 466-8201
5755 Santa Monica Blvd, Los Angeles, CA, 90038
www.omegacinemaprops.com

Central Atlanta Props & Sets (470)-225-6709
675 Metropolitan Parkway SW Ste 5121, Atlanta, GA, 30310
Atlanta prop house with industrial, office, rustic, exterior or classic furnishing needs.
capsga@outlook.com * http://capsga.com

Dapper Cadaver (818) 771-0818
7648 San Fernando Rd, Sun Valley, CA, 91352
Specializes in horror, science, medical, crime, oddity & Halloween props. Custom fabrication & FX. Rent & buy online.
info@dappercadaver.com * www.dappercadaver.com

Eccentric Trading Company Ltd. 011 44 20 8453-1125
Unit 2 Frogmore Estate, Acton Lane, London NW10 7NQ
www.eccentrictrading.com

Eclectic/Encore Props (212) 645-8880
47-51 33rd St, Long Island City, NY 11101
sbieler@eclecticprops.com * www.eclecticprops.com

The Farley Group 011 44 20 8749-9925
1-17 Brunel Rd, London, W3 7XR UK
props@farley.co.uk * www.farley.co.uk

Faux Library Studio Props, Inc. (818) 765-0096
7100 Case Avenue, N Hollywood, CA, 91605
large selection of hollow books, office furniture, desk dressing, decorative accessories and of course books
fauxlibrary@sbcglobal.net * fb.me/fauxlibrary

huge collection • 60,000 sq ft • furniture • accessories • modern • antiques
Furniture • Prop Books • Libraries • Desk Dressing

Faux Library Studio Props

FormDecor, Inc. (310) 558-2582
5600 Argosy Circle Ste 200, Huntington Beach, CA, 92649
America's largest event rental supplier of 20th Century furniture and
accessories for Modern and Mid-Century styles.
info@formdecor.com * www.formdecor.com

Gorygirl Halloween Event Staging and Prop (818) 912-6902
Rental
5330 Derry Ave Unit G, Agoura Hills, CA, 91301
Halloween themed prop house renting the creepy, crawly and spooky
gorygirlevents@gmail.com * gorygirl.com

Green Set, Inc. (818) 764-1231
11617 Dehougne St, N Hollywood, CA, 91605
www.greenset.com
5700 Venice Blvd, Los Angeles, CA, 90019
Large Prop House for prop rentals, prop weapons, custom graphic design &
custom graphic printing, expendables and more.
info@hpr.com * www.hpr.com

History For Hire, Inc. (818) 765-7767
7149 Fair Ave, N Hollywood, CA, 91605
info@historyforhire.com * www.historyforhire.com

Hollywood Cinema Arts (818) 504-7333
8110 Webb Ave, N Hollywood, CA, 91605
Hollywood Cinema Arts, "The Pro's Prop House."
hollywoodcinemaarts@gmail.com * www.hcarts.com

Hollywood Cinema Production Resources (310) 258-0123
9700 S. Sepulveda Blvd, Los Angeles, CA, 90045
props@hollywoodcpr.org * www.hollywoodcpr.org

Hollywood Studio Gallery (323) 462-1116
1035 Cahuenga Blvd, Hollywood, CA, 90038
hsginfo@hollywoodstudiogallery.com * www.hollywoodstudiogallery.com

Independent Studio Services, Inc (818) 951-5600
9545 Wentworth St, Sunland, CA, 91040
www.issprops.com

Jackson Shrub Supply, Inc. (818) 982-0100
11505 Vanowen St, N Hollywood, CA, 91605
Plant rentals, shrub rentals, tree rentals. Christmas decorations and Halloween
decorations and more.
gary@jacksonshrub.com * www.jacksonshrub.com

LCW Props (818) 243-0707
6439 San Fernando Rd, Glendale, CA, 91201
LCW Is Your 1-Stop Shop For Almost Anything. We Work With Any Budget.
props@lcwprops.com * www.lcwprops.com

6439 San Fernando Rd. Glendale, CA 91201
Phone: 818-243-0707 - www.lcwprops.com

Lennie Marvin Enterprises, Inc. (Prop Heaven) (818) 841-5882
3110 Winona Ave, Burbank, CA, 91504
catering to the entertainment industry
info@propheaven.com * www.propheaven.com

LM Treasures (626) 252-7354
10557 Juniper Ave Unit A, Fontana, CA, 92337
Statue rentals of many types: movie props, lamps, prop rentals, figurines
rentals, prop store, prop showroom
lmtreasures.ll@gmail.com * www.lifesizestatues.net

Modern Props (323) 934-3000
972 Griswold Ave, San Fernando, CA, 91340
Modern Props, Contemporary Props, Futuristic Props, & Electronic Props
ken@modernprops.com * www.modernprops.com

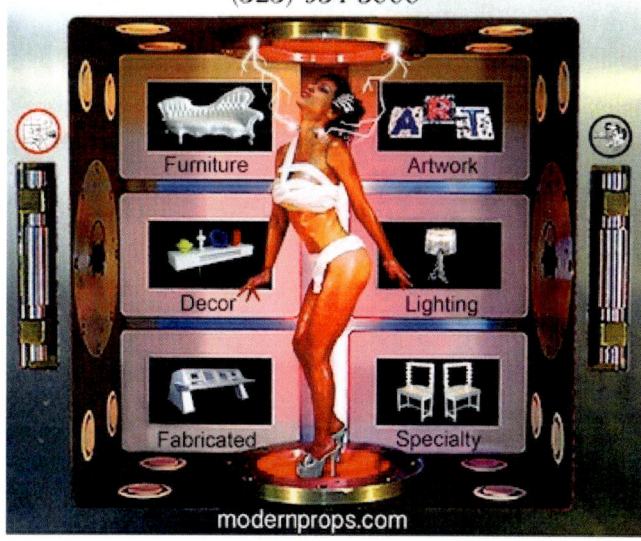

"WHERE OUR THINGS ARE" **MODERN PROPS** BRING YOUR CREATIVE IMAGINATION TO LIFE
(323) 934-3000
Furniture   Artwork
Decor   Lighting
Fabricated   Specialty
modernprops.com

Modernica Props   (323) 664-2322
2805 Gilroy Street, Los Angeles, CA, 90039
huge inventory 50s-70s furniture & decor. From couches to record players,
multiples up to 500 for many
www.modernicaprops.net

NEST Studio Rentals, Inc.   (818) 942-0339
7007 Lankershim Blvd, N Hollywood, CA, 91605
contemporary furniture, rugs, lighting, art, drapery, smalls
sales@neststudiorentals.net * www.neststudiorentals.net

Ob-jects   (818) 351-4200
10623 Keswick St, Sun Valley, CA, 91352
Upscale props and furniture, wide variety in clean, large warehouse.
fred@ob-jects.com * www.ob-jects.com

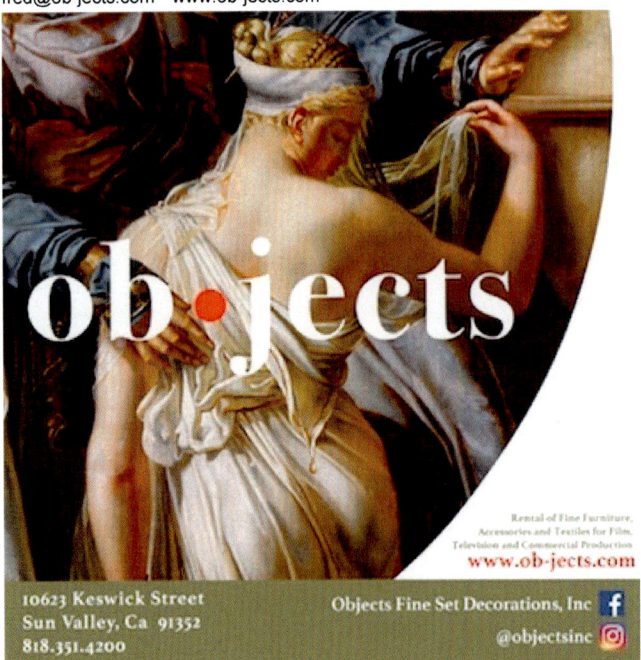

Oceanic Arts   (562) 698-6960
12414 Whittier Blvd, Whittier, CA, 90602-1017
We Rent and We Sell Hawaiian, Polynesian, Tropical, and Nautical Decor.
oceanicarts56@gmail.com * www.oceanicarts.net

Old N Country Prop Shop, LLC   (818) 423-2599
12007 Vose St, Los Angeles, CA, 91605
We are a family owned prop house specializing in Americana and hard to find
antiques from the East Coast, and MUCH more!
propshop@oldncountry.com * www.oldncountry.com

Omega/Cinema Props   (323) 466-8201
5857 Santa Monica Blvd, Los Angeles, CA, 90038
www.omegacinemaprops.com

Picture Start Props   (818) 255-5472
7040 Laurel Canyon Blvd UNIT B, N Hollywood, CA, 91605
jennifer@picturestartprops.com * www.picturestartprops.com

Pinacoteca Picture Props   (818) 764-2722
7120 Case Ave, N Hollywood, CA, 91605
art rentals, linens, furniture & custom framing
sales@pinaprops.com * www.pinaprops.com

Premiere Props.   (818) 768-3800
11500 Sheldon St, Sun Valley, CA, 91352
www.premiereprops.net

Prop Mart, Inc.   (773) 772-7775
2343 W St Paul Ave, Chicago, IL, 60647
table top, mainly commercials; dishes, linens, flatware, more

Prop Services West   (818) 503-2790
7040 Laurel Canyon Blvd, North Hollywood, CA, 91605
www.propserviceswest.com

Propabilities   (773) 278-2384
1517 N Elston, Chicago, IL, 60642
hand props, set dressing, furniture, smalls, park benches, photo surfaces
www.propabilitiesonline.com

propNspoon / Props for Today   (212) 244-9600
32-00 Skillman Ave, 3rd Floor, Long Island City, NY, 11101
www.propsfortoday.com

RC Vintage, Inc.   (818) 765-7107
7100 Tujunga Ave, N Hollywood, CA, 91605
specializing in 40s, 50s, 60s & 70s
rcvintage@aol.com * www.rcvintage.com

RJR Props   (404) 349-7600
5300 Westpark Drive SW Ste B, Atlanta, CA, 30336
RJR Props can provide working realistic Props for your feature film, show,
commercial, music video, or event.
rjrelectronics@aol.com * www.rjrprops.com

Seasons Textiles Ltd   011 44 20
9 Gorst Road, London NW10 6LA   8965-6161
enquiries@seasonstextiles.net * www.seasonstextiles.co.uk

Sony Pictures Studios-Prop House (Off Lot)   (310) 244-5999
5933 W Slauson Ave, Culver City, CA, 90230
www.sonypicturesstudios.com

Sony Pictures Studios-Wardrobe   (310) 244-5995
5933 W Slauson Ave, Culver City, CA, 90230
alterations, call (310) 244-7260
www.sonypicturesstudios.com

Studio Plumbing Rentals   (323) 829-9339
7373 Atoll Ave, N Hollywood, CA, 91605
studioplumbingrentals@gmail.com * www.studioair.com

Studio Props, Inc.   (661) 775-1655
21170 Centre Pointe Parkway #200, Santa Clarita, CA, 91350
Police Equip, SWAT, Replica Weapons, Press and Media, Cameras, EMT
Equip.
actionprops@yahoo.com * http://www.studioprops.net

The Surface Library   (323) 546-9314
1106 N Hudson Ave 2nd Floor, Los Angeles, CA, 90038
A curated prop house specializing in surfaces and table top props for food,
product, and lifestyle shoots.
info@thesurfacelibrary.com * www.thesurfacelibrary.com

Sword & Stone   (818) 562-6548
1100 W Isabel St, Burbank, CA, 91506
medieval & fantasy props
tony@swordandstone.com * www.swordandstone.com

Technical Props, Inc   (818) 761-4993
6811 Farmdale Ave, N Hollywood, CA, 91605
techpropsinc@rr.com * www.techpropsinc.com

Trading Post Ltd.   011 44 20 8903-3727
1-3 Beresford Avenue, Wembley, Middlesex, HA0 1NU
info@tradingposthire.co.uk * www.tradingposthire.co.uk
Trevor Howsam Ltd   011 44 20 8838-6166
182 Acton Lane, Park Royal, London NW10 7NH
props@trevorhowsam.co.uk * www.retrowallpaper.co.uk
Universal Studios Drapery Dept   (818) 777-2761
100 Universal City Plaza, Universal City, CA, 91608
universal.property@nbcuni.com * http://universalstudioslot.com/drapery
Universal Studios Graphic Design & Sign Shop   (818) 777-2350
100 Universal City Plaza, Universal City, CA, 91608
universal.signshop@nbcuni.com *
http://universalstudioslot.com/graphic-design-and-sign-shop
Universal Studios Property & Hardware Dept   (818) 777-2784
100 Universal City Plaza, Universal City, CA, 91608
One of the oldest prop houses with departments for everything from
conceptualizing to finalizing your project.
universal.property@nbcuni.com * universalstudioslot.com/property
Universal Studios Special Effects Equip.   (818) 777-3333
100 Universal City Plaza, Universal City, CA, 91608
universal.property@nbcuni.com * http://universalstudioslot.com/property
Universal Studios Staff Shop   (818) 777-2337
100 Universal City Plaza, Universal City, CA, 91608
staff.shop@nbcuni.com * http://universalstudioslot.com/staff-shop
Warner Bros. Studios Cabinet & Furniture Shop   (818) 954-1339
4000 Warner Blvd Bldg 44, Burbank, CA, 91522
Custom Cabinetry & Furniture, Furniture Repair & Refinishing, Special Set
Construction Antique Restoration.
www.wbcabinetshop.com
Warner Bros. Studios Property Department   (818) 954-2181
4000 Warner Blvd Bldg 30, Burbank, CA, 91522
wbsfproperty@warnerbros.com * www.wbpropertydept.com

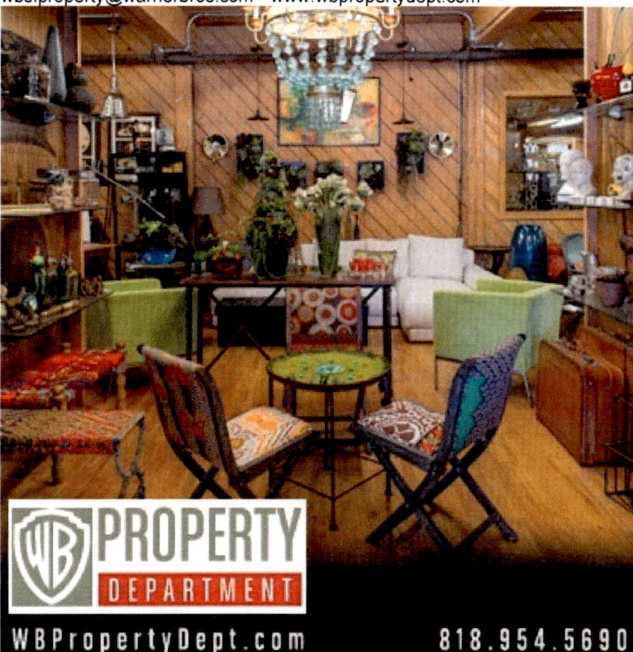

Warner Bros. Studios Staff Shop   (818) 954-2269
4000 Warner Blvd Bldg 44, Burbank, CA, 91522
Manufacturer of exterior & interior details used for the creation of sets in all
architectural styles & eras.
wbds@warnerbros.com * www.wbstaffshop.com
Woody's Electrical Props   (818) 503-1940
5323 Craner Ave, N Hollywood, CA, 91601-3313
Period to futuristic. Electronic equipment. Custom built to specifications.
Electrical paneling
woody@woodysprops.com * www.woodysprops.com
Zap Props   (773) 376-2278
3611 S Loomis Pl, Chicago, IL, 60609
hand props, set dressing, street dressing, big & small
www.zapprops.com
ZG04 DECOR   (818) 853-8040
12224 Montague St, Sun Valley, CA, 91331
Rental & Sale
saul@zg04decor.com * www.zg04decor.com

Prop Locators

See: Research, Advisors, Consulting & Clearances

Prop Products & Packages

See Also: Product Labels
The Hand Prop Room LP.   (323) 931-1534
in stock & custom
History For Hire, Inc.   (818) 765-7767
big selection, also custom
Warner Bros. Studios Scenic Art & Sign Shop   (818) 954-1815
4000 Warner Blvd Bldg 44, Burbank, CA, 91522
graphic design and production studio for signs & scenic art; digital printing to
hand-painted
wbsigns@warnerbros.com * www.wbsignandscenic.com

Prop Reproduction & Fabrication

See Also: Fiberglass Products/Fabrication Furniture,
Custom-made/Reproduction* Metalworking, Decorative*
Metalworking, Welding & Structural* Prop Design & Manufacturing*
Scenery/Set Construction* Staff Shops* Vacu-forms/Vacu-forming*
Centerline Scenery   (818) 252-7467
8238 Lankershim Blvd, N Hollywood, CA, 91605
meredyth@centerlinescenery.com
Charisma Design Studio, Inc.   (818) 252-6611
8414 San Fernando Road, Sun Valley, CA, 91352
metal/glass/wood/stone
info@charismadesign.com * www.charismadesign.com
Dapper Cadaver   (818) 771-0818
Custom fabrication and prop making. Specializing in bodies and body parts.
Animals and taxidermy.
depict   (323) 222-1001
1460 Naud St, Los Angeles, CA, 90012
info@depict33.com * www.depict33.com
EFX- Event Special Effects   (626) 888-2239
125 Railroad Ave, Monrovia, CA, 91016
Custom Fabrication- CNC- Plasma Table- Pipe & Ring Benders- 3D
Renderings
info@efxla.com * www.efxla.com
Fall Creek Corporation   (765) 482-1861
PO Box 92, Whitestown, IN, 46075
Civil War era, military & civilian. Civil War era reproductions, rifles, muskets,
civil war clothing
ajfulks@fcsutler.com * www.fcsutler.com
Flix FX Inc.   (818) 765-3549
7327 Lankershim Blvd #4, N Hollywood, CA, 91605
Sculpting, molding, casting, digitizing & vacuum forming up to 5' x 10'
info@flixfx.com * www.flixfx.com
The Hand Prop Room LP.   (323) 931-1534
History For Hire, Inc.   (818) 765-7767
the best for vintage
Hollywood Elevators/ Red Truck INC   (562) 896-6070
4707 Exposition Blvd, Los Angeles, CA, 90016
redtruck321@sbcglobal.net * hollywoodelevators.com
HPR Custom   (323) 931-1534
5700 Venice Blvd, Los Angeles, CA, 90019
Machining, woodworking, CNC machining, CAD drawings, water jet cutting,
welding, metal working and more.
www.hprcustom.com
KIHL STUDIOS   (818) 812-9594
9701 Owensmouth Ave Unit 1, Chatsworth, CA, 91311
Custom prop design & fabrication services. Sci-fi/fantasy, historical, functional
electrical & mechanical props, etc.
design@kihlstudios.com * www.kihlstudios.com
LA Fabricators   (323) 264-8763
1630 Miller Ave, Los Angeles, CA, 90063
Art Fabrication, prop fabrication
www.LAFabricators.com
LM Treasures   (626) 252-7354
Our products can vary in many different ways from casual items for your house
to extravagant pieces to help a business.

**LISTINGS FOR THIS CATEGORY CONTINUE ON THE
FOLLOWING PAGE**

Modern Props   (323) 934-3000
Prop fabrication and fabricated props, fabricated electronic dressing, prop fabricators

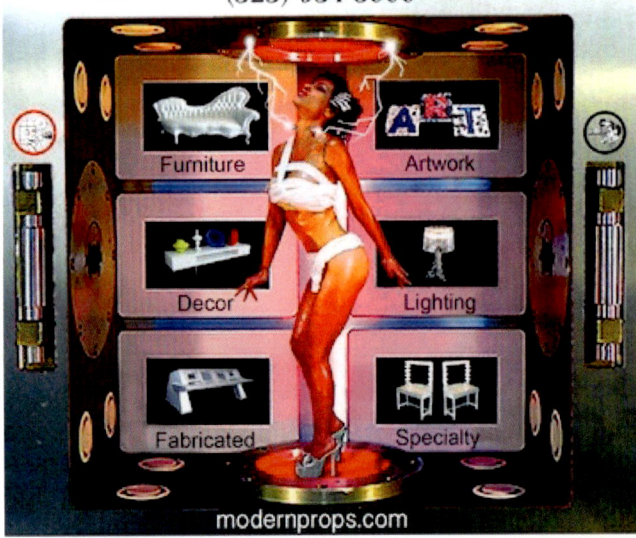

New Rule FX   (818) 387-6450
7751 Densmore Ave, Van Nuys, CA, 91406
Breakaway props-all types & categories Custom prop & FX design & construction, 3D printing Prototypes, Molding & Casting
ryan@newrulefx.com * www.NewRuleFX.com

Nights of Neon   (818) 756-4791
13815 Saticoy St, Van Nuys, CA, 91402
over 2,000 neon props in stock. custom neon props
contact@nightsofneon.com * www.nightsofneon.com

Set Masters   (818) 982-1506
24853 Avenue Rockefeller, Valencia, CA, 91355
Custom fabrication and prop making from period to futuristic and everything in-between
info@setmasters.com * www.setmasters.com

Sword & Stone   (818) 562-6548
Prop weapon fabrication, weapon reproduction and more

Warner Bros. Studios Metal Shop   (818) 954-1265
4000 Warner Blvd Bldg 44, Burbank, CA, 91522
Custom metal fabrication creating anything from structural steel elements to intricate custom furniture
WBDS@warnerbros.com * www.wbmetalshop.com

Woody's Electrical Props   (818) 503-1940
Period to futuristic. Design & build panels, consoles, sound mix boards and more

July 2006-2007
DEBBIES BOOK
21st EDITION

The Source Book for All Entertainment Industries
Film & Television • Advertising • Theatre
Special Events • Themed Environments

2006
40 YEARS OF DEBBIES BOOK

Property Master Storage Rooms

Independent Studio Services, Inc   (818) 951-5600
Western Studio Service, Inc.   (818) 842-9272
4561 Colorado Blvd, Los Angeles, CA, 90039
personal lockups to store kits, supplies, ladders, tools, etc. with 24/7 access.
www.westernstudioservice.com

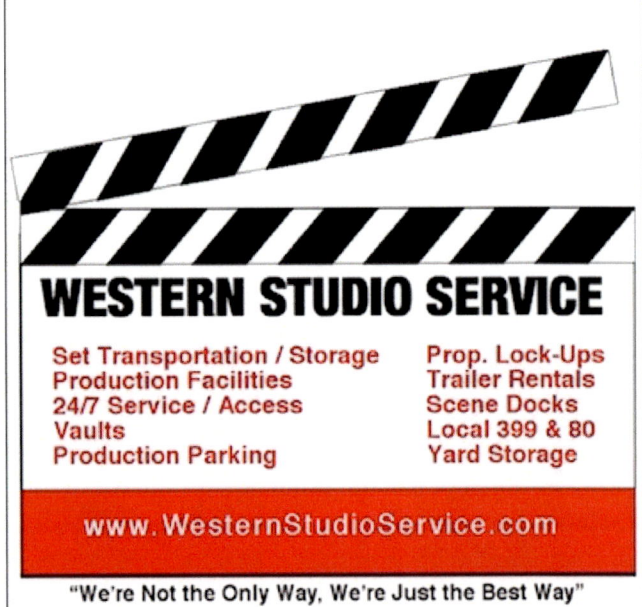

Prosthetics

See: Medical Equip/Furniture, Graphics/Supplies Special Effects, Make-up/Prosthetics*

Protective Apparel

See Also: Duvetyne Flameproofing*
Allstar Fire Equipment, Inc.   (626) 652-0900
12328 Lower Azusa Rd, Arcadia, CA, 91006
fireman & hazmat apparel & gear
www.allstarfire.com

CBS Costume Rental   (323) 575-2666
flesh color wet suits

E.C. Prop Rentals   (818) 764-2008
industrial gloves, glasses, goggles, aprons, facemasks

LCW Props   (818) 243-0707
Fire Suits, Radiation Suits

R. S. Hughes   (818) 686-9111
10639 Glenoaks Blvd Ste 1, Pacoima, CA, 91331
industrial suits, hats, gloves, shoes
www.rshughes.com

Warner Bros. Studios Costume Dept   (818) 954-1297
HazMat suits from "Outbreak"

Pub Signs

Collins Visual Media   (818) 686-6581
10518 Johanna Ave, Shadow Hills, CA, 91040
We've designed, created and installed many English pub and tavern signs as permanent displays or temporary for filming.
www.collinsvisualmedia.com

Lennie Marvin Enterprises, Inc. (Prop Heaven) (818) 841-5882
neon & old, vast selection

Universal Studios Property & Hardware Dept   (818) 777-2784
Pub signs for rent for pub dressing.

Pulleys

See: Rigging, Equipment or Services

Pumping Services

See: Sanitation, Waste Disposal

Pumpkins/Gourds, Artificial & Real

See Also: Greens Halloween Dressing & Accessories*

Gorygirl Halloween Event Staging and Prop Rental   (818) 912-6902
Fake pumpkins and related dressing for rent.

Green Set, Inc.   (818) 764-1231
Artificial Fruits and Artificial Vegetables

Jackson Shrub Supply, Inc.   (818) 982-0100
small artificial pumpkins & large artificial pumpkins, plain artificial pumpkins, carved artificial pumpkins, & lighted

The Pumpkin Patch   (909) 795-8733
32335 Live Oak Canyon Rd, Redlands, CA, 92373
seasonal, pumpkins, gourds, Xmas trees, kid rides, live entertainment
http://pumpkins.liveoakcanyon.com

Universal Studios Property & Hardware Dept   (818) 777-2784
Artificial pumpkins/fake pumpkins from jack-o-lanterns to gourds for rent.

Puppets, Marionettes, Automata, Animatronics

See Also: Mannequins Robots* Special Effects, Make-up/Prosthetics*

Amalgamated Dynamics, Inc.   (818) 882-8638
20100 Plummer St, Chatsworth, CA, 91311
design & build custom animatronics/creatures
www.studioadi.com

Anatomorphex/The Sculpture Studio   (818) 768-2880
8210 Lankershim Blvd Ste 14, N. Hollywood, CA, 91605
design/build realistic animals, creatures, body doubles
www.anatomorphex.com

Animal Firm   (830) 324-6578
By appointment only.
Call for information. custom built realistic & fantasy animals, animal costumes
information@animalfirm.com * www.animalfirm.com

AnimatronicBear.com   (714) 768-5809
765 South James Rd, Unit A8, Columbus, OH, 43227
Photo-realistic animal doubles for hire for film & live events
info@animatronicbear.com * www.animatronicbear.com

Bob Baker Marionettes   (213) 250-9995
1345 W First St, Los Angeles, CA, 90026
marionette performer, plus lrg collection marionettes
www.bobbakermarionettetheater.com

The Character Shop   (805) 306-9441
4735 Industrial St #4B-G, Simi Valley, CA, 93063
Extraordinary Custom Animatronic Animals & Creatures, Puppets, Marionettes, Replicas, Robots, Props, Special Makeup FX
lazzwaldo@mac.com * www.character-shop.com

THE · CHARACTER · SHOP

(805) 306-9441 www.character-shop.com (805) 306-9444 FAX

Chiodo Bros Productions, Inc   (818) 842-5656
511 5th St, Suite A, San Fernando, CA, 91340
animatronix, puppets, special effects for TV/film
klowns@chiodobros.com * www.chiodobros.com

Flix FX Inc.   (818) 765-3549
7327 Lankershim Blvd #4, N Hollywood, CA, 91605
Puppet & animatronic construction & SAG puppeteers
info@flixfx.com * www.flixfx.com

Folkmanis Puppets   (800) 654-8922
1219 Park Ave, Emeryville, CA, 94608
Original, innovative, heirloom-quality puppets featuring animals and characters inspired by nature and literature.
www.folkmanis.com

The Fratello Marionettes   (925) 984-3401
696 San Ramon Valley Blvd, Ste 200, Danville, CA, 94526
cust marionettes, Pelham puppet collection, performance company
www.fratellomarionettes.com

The Frisch Marionette Co.   (513) 451-8875
P.O. Box 58505, Cincinatti, OH, 45258
custom build marionettes, performance company
www.frischmarionettes.com

Grey Seal Puppets, Inc.   (704) 521-2878
814 Pinckney St, McClellanville, SC, 29458
puppet character design, performance company, contact via web site
www.greysealpuppets.com

Handemonium   (301) 257-5135
Washington D.C. area
in-stock & custom celebrity look-alike hand puppets
barry@handemonium.com * www.handemonium.com

Hollywood Baby Nursery   (818) 645-6513
Call for Appt.
Various baby doubles/fake babies for rent
hollywoodbabynursery@gmail.com

Jim Henson's Creature Shop   (323) 802-1500
1416 N. La Brea Ave, Hollywood, CA, 90028
puppets & animatronics, also HQ, NY & London loc.
www.creatureshop.com

Legacy Effects   (818) 782-0870
340 Parkside Drive, San Fernando, CA, 91340
www.legacyefx.com

LifeFormations   (419) 352-2101
2029 Woodbridge Blvd, Bowling Green, OH, 43402
Characters, scenery, props & support media, for exhibits & theme parks
www.lifeformations.com

Masters FX, Inc.   (818) 834-3000
10316 Norris Ave Unit C, Arleta, CA, 91331
animatronic & rod puppets, realistic animals, demons, aliens
www.mastersfx.com

Michael Curry Design   (503) 543-4010
50759 Dike Rd, Scappoose, OR, 97056
design/build/perform puppets, costume mechanics, effects for theater, theme park, film, exhibits, live performance
www.michaelcurrydesign.com

Puppet Studio   (818) 506-7374
10903 Chandler Blvd, N Hollywood, CA, 91601
character design, hand/rod/animatronic, motion FX, live shows
www.puppetstudio.com

Puppeteers Of America   (612) 821-2382
310 East 38th St, Suite 127, Minneapolis, MN, 55409
Website links to many resources, incl. local/regional guilds, (like LA, OC, NYC) which in turn lists puppet performers.
fb.me/PuppeteersOfAmerica

Rene and His Artists Productions   (818) 848-6809
707 S Main St, Burbank, CA, 91506
vent puppets, marionettes, animatronics, walkaround characters
renesmarionettes.com

Sally Corporation   (904) 355-7100
745 W Forsyth St, Jacksonville, FL, 32204
custom animatronics: human, animal, fantasy, plus animated shows & dark ride adventures
www.sallycorp.com

Tech Works FX Studios   (504) 722-1504
13405 Seymour Meyers Blvd #5, Covington, LA, 70433
Specializes in Animatronic Animals, Creatures, Robots, Puppets, Costumes and Special FX Make Up.
info@techworksstudios.com * www.techworksstudios.com

Ultra Prototypes LLC   (818) 292-1906
Call for Appointment
We specialize in Robots and Automata.
jeff@ultraprototypes.com * www.ultraprototypes.com

UNIMA-USA   (404) 873-3089
1404 Spring St NW, Atlanta, GA, 30309
Has Puppetry Yellow Pages resource directory & Puppetry International, nationally dist. periodical
www.unima-usa.org

Wayne Martin Puppets   (617) 733-9418
24 Pine Ridge Way, Carver, MA, 02330
Entertainment performance company; also design/build for TV, film & commercials
www.waynemartinpuppets.com

Purses

See: Wardrobe, Accessories

Pyrotechnics

See Also: Non-Guns & Non-Pyro Flashes* Special Effects, Equipment & Supplies* Special Effects, Lighting & Lasers

Atlas Pyrovision Productions (603) 532-8324
PO Box 498, Jaffrey, NH, 03452
fireworks productions
sales@atlaspyro.com * www.atlaspyro.com

CONFETTI & FOG FX Special Effects Company (877) 576-4239
1085 W 21st Pl, Hialeah, FL, 33010
Many pyrotechnic services and equipment available. For fireworks refer to FuegoWorks Miami Inc.
Info@confettiandfogfx.com * www.caffx.com

Fireworks America (800) 464-7976
P.O. Box 488, Lakeside, CA, 92040
indoor/outdoor displays & effects, pull permits, insurance, prof. technicians
www.fireworksamerica.com

J & M Special Effects, Inc. (718) 875-0140
524 Sackett St, Brooklyn, NY, 11217
Formerly Jauchem & Meeh. torches & flash equip., pyro supplies, licensed pyrotechnicians
info@jmfx.net * www.jmfx.net

Lantis Fireworks & Lasers (800) 443-3040
P.O. Box 491, Draper, UT, 84020
fireworks displays & technicians, multimedia spectaculars, indoor/outdoor & close proximity
www.lantisfireworks.com

Phantom Fireworks (775) 537-1737
921 South Highway 160, Pahrump, NV, 89048
wholesale fireworks suppliers, many locations in U.S.
www.fireworks.com

Pyro Spectaculars by Souza (888) 477-7976
3196 N Locust, Rialto, CA, 92377
fireworks choreography & effects, mfg custom effects for stage, film, TV, events
www.pyrospec.com

Spectrum Effects, Inc. (661) 510-5633
Call for Appt.
www.spectrumeffects.com

Zambelli Fireworks Internationale (800) 322-7142
PO Box 986, Shafter, CA, 93263
www.zambellifireworks.com

Quiet Bags

See: Grocery Check-out Stands (Complete)

Quilts

See: Linens, Household

Racks

See: Display Cases, Racks & Fixtures (Store)* Warehouse Dressing

Radiators (Household)

C. P. Two (323) 466-8201
Prop radiators for rent
E.C. Prop Rentals (818) 764-2008
NYC apartment style, heater panels, large sel.
History For Hire, Inc. (818) 765-7767
lightweight
LCW Props (818) 243-0707
Large Selection Of Real & Fake Radiators
RC Vintage, Inc. (818) 765-7107
40s, 50s & 60s Wallmount Faux, stand up radiators, many styles, vintage heaters,
Sony Pictures Studios-Prop House (Off Lot) (310) 244-5999
Universal Studios Property & Hardware Dept (818) 777-2784
Many kinds of radiators from fiberglass radiators to functional radiators for rent.

Radio/TV Station

See Also: Audio Equipment* Microphones* On-Air Signs* Video Camera Equipment & Services

Coast Recording Audio Props (818) 755-4692
10715 Magnolia Blvd, N Hollywood, CA, 91601
Everything for a complete Radio Station - One stop shopping! Radio station dressing, tv station dressing, station props
props@coastrecording.com * www.coastrecordingprops.com

History For Hire, Inc. (818) 765-7767
the most complete selection there is

LCW Props (818) 243-0707
Desks, Signs, Mixing Boards, Microphones, Media, AV Server Racks, etc

Modern Props (323) 934-3000
Radio station props/TV Station props including consoles, racks of tape machines, large selection

Omega/Cinema Props (323) 466-8201
RJR Props (404) 349-7600
TV station dressing and radio station dressing available for rent.

Woody's Electrical Props (818) 503-1940
Period to futuristic. Digital counters & dressing.

Radiology

See: MRI (Magnetic Resonance Imaging)* X-ray Machine* X-rays & X-ray Viewers* Waiting Room

Radios

See Also: Audio Equipment* Televisions* Walkie-Talkies

Antique Radio Store (858) 268-4155
8280 Clairmont Mesa Blvd #114, San Diego, CA, 92111
Sales & repair of antique radios - 1920-1960 vintage, hours M & W 5-7 PM, Sat 9-4
www.oldradiosrus.com

C. P. Two (323) 466-8201
Prop radios: Period radios to contemporary radios.

Ham Radio Outlet (800) 854-6046
1525 West Magnolia Blvd, Burbank, CA, 91506
Various radios including amateur radios, shortwave radios and more.
www.hamradio.com

The Hand Prop Room LP. (323) 931-1534
period-present

History For Hire, Inc. (818) 765-7767
antique to present

LCW Props (818) 243-0707
Military, Transistor, Boom Box, Period - Present

Ob-jects (818) 351-4200
Radios for rent

Old N Country Prop Shop, LLC (818) 423-2599
Vintage and antique radios in a range of different sizes and styles, from CB, art deco, stereos, transistor radios, etc.

Picture Start Props (818) 255-5472
Eclectic collection of radios from the forties to today including boomboxes, walkmans and transistor radios.

Prop Services West (818) 503-2790
40s-70s

RC Vintage, Inc. (818) 765-7107
period, 30s to 60s, tabletop & floor Large Selection Vintage Wooden, boom boxes, transistor radios, stereos

RJR Props (404) 349-7600
Handheld radios, car radios, military radios and more for rent.

Sony Pictures Studios-Prop House (Off Lot) (310) 244-5999
antique to present

Universal Studios Property & Hardware Dept (818) 777-2784
Prop radios from period to present for rent.

Warner Bros. Studios Property Department (818) 954-2181
Portable radios, shortwave radios, clock radios, 2-way radios, transistor radios Period radios, radio cabinets

Railroad Crossing Signal

AIR Designs (818) 768-6639
Matching Crossing Signals
Alley Cats Studio Rentals (818) 982-9178
lights, signs

Railroads

See: Trains

Ramps, Automobile

E.C. Prop Rentals (818) 764-2008
drive-up ramps, bottle jacks, hydraulic jacks, large sel.

Ramps: Skateboard, BMX, Freestyle, etc.

See Also: Scenery/Set Construction

Keen Ramps   (562) 715-8643
3914 Cherry Ave Unit D, Long Beach, CA, 90807
Skateboard/BMX/bike/scooter ramp rentals: half pipe, mini ramp, quarter pipe,
rail, launch, grind box & custom obstacles
info@keenramps.com * www.keenramps.com

Skate & Action Sports Ramps
Quarter Pipes • Half Pipes • Boxes • Custom

Spohn Ranch, Inc.   (626) 330-5803
6824 S Centinela Ave, Los Angeles, CA, 90230
Bike & skateboard performance ramps. Skate equipment and BMX equipment.
www.spohnranch.com

Ranch

See: Horse Saddles & Tack Horses, Horse Equipment, Livestock*
Locations, Insert Stages & Theatres* Wagons* Western Dressing*

Ranges

See: Stoves

Rapper Jewelry

See: Bling

Read-outs

See Also: Game Show Electronics & Equipment
CBS Electronics   (323) 575-2645
7800 Beverly Blvd Rm M162, Los Angeles, CA, 90036
variety; bulb, video, etc.
L. A. Party Works   (888) 527-2789
9712 Alpaca St, S El Monte, CA, 91733
in Vancouver tel. 604-589-4101
partyworks@aol.com * www.partyworksinteractive.com
LCW Props   (818) 243-0707
Digital, LED, Analog, Medical, Office, etc

Record/Video Store

See: Video Rental/Sales Store Video Store Dressing*

Recording Studio (Prop)

See Also: Audio Equipment
Coast Recording Audio Props   (818) 755-4692
10715 Magnolia Blvd, N Hollywood, CA, 91601
Everything for a Complete Recording Studio - One stop shopping! used and
new sound studio props
props@coastrecording.com * www.coastrecordingprops.com
The Hand Prop Room LP.   (323) 931-1534
History For Hire, Inc.   (818) 765-7767
the best selection

Records Management

See: Archiving Media/Records Management

Records, Phonograph

See: Phonograph Records

Recycling Services

See Also: Charities & Donations Sanitation, Waste Disposal*
EcoSet ReDirect   (323) 669-0697
3423 Casitas Ave, Los Angeles, CA, 90039
One-stop drop-off solution for reusable production and event discards. We
specialize in scenic builds and custom pieces.
www.ecosetconsulting.com/redirect
L. A. Recycling Center   (323) 221-9188
1000 N Main St, Los Angeles, CA, 90012
Don't take electronics. Mon-Fri, 7:30-4:30, Sat 7:30-3:00
Westside Metal Recycling   (818) 243-6965
6449 San Fernando Rd, Glendale, CA, 91201
Since 1946, full recycling, hauling, clean-up, buyer all metal. Ewaste/computer
disposal, equipment, machinery.
www.westsidemetalrecycling.com

Red Carpeting, Events/Premiers

Astro Audio Video Lighting, Inc.   (818) 549-9915
6615 San Fernando Rd, Glendale, CA, 91201
Event red carpeting, rope & stanchions, step & repeats and lighting
www.astroavl.com
Collins Visual Media   (818) 686-6581
10518 Johanna Ave, Shadow Hills, CA, 91040
Your best source and fastest turnaround for events and exhibitions. Use our
team of designers, creators and installers.
www.collinsvisualmedia.com
EFX- Event Special Effects   (626) 888-2239
125 Railroad Ave, Monrovia, CA, 91016
Step & Repeat Printing- Carpet- Lighting- Stanchion & Rope- Printing
info@efxla.com * www.efxla.com
Linoleum City, Inc.   (323) 469-0063
4849 Santa Monica Blvd, Hollywood, CA, 90029
Largest selection and always in stock. Red carpet runners, solid carpet
runners, premier red carpet.
sales@linocity.com * www.linoleumcity.com

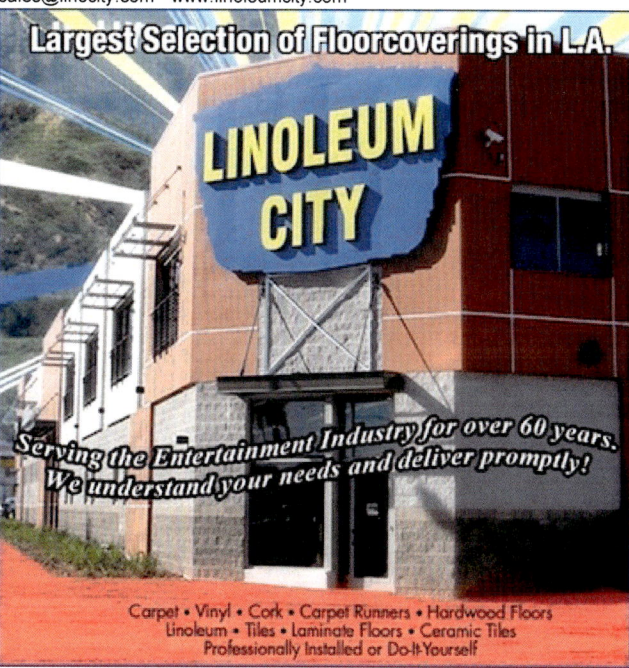

Largest Selection of Floorcoverings in L.A.

LINOLEUM CITY

Serving the Entertainment Industry for over 60 years.
We understand your needs and deliver promptly!

Carpet • Vinyl • Cork • Carpet Runners • Hardwood Floors
Linoleum • Tiles • Laminate Floors • Ceramic Tiles
Professionally Installed or Do-It-Yourself

Step and Repeat LA   (818) 434-7591
10518 Johanna Ave, Shadow Hills, CA, 91040
We specialize in step and repeat backdrops for red carpet events. We are a
one-stop shop for a red-carpet display!
Services@StepandRepeatLA.com * StepandRepeatLA.com
ZG04 DECOR   (818) 853-8040

Refrigerators

AIR Designs	**(818) 768-6639**
Single Door Units Period to Present, Home Industrial, Mini Bar, Commercial	
Alley Cats Studio Rentals	**(818) 982-9178**
C. P. Two	**(323) 466-8201**
Period refrigerators to modern residential refrigerators; Commercial refrigerators, double door refrigerators & more.	
LCW Props	**(818) 243-0707**
Commercial, Industrial, Laboratory	
Modern Props	**(323) 934-3000**
contemporary/commercial refrigerators	
Ob-jects	**(818) 351-4200**
Sub Zero (gourmet refrigerators only)	
RC Vintage, Inc.	**(818) 765-7107**
40s, 50s & 60s Asst Colors, vintage home refrigerators, diner refrigerators, bar refrigerators, display refrigerators, coolers	
Sony Pictures Studios-Prop House (Off Lot)	**(310) 244-5999**
Universal Studios Property & Hardware Dept	**(818) 777-2784**
Prop refrigerators from period to modern for rent.	

Registers

See: Hardware, Decorative

Religious Articles

See Also: Church, Chapel, Synagogue, Mosque* Clerical, Judicial, Academic Gowns/Apparel

Abi's Judaica & Gifts	**(818) 705-4573**
18369 Ventura Blvd, Tarzana, CA, 91356	
Cotter Church Supplies	**(213) 385-3366**
1701 James M. Wood Blvd, Los Angeles, CA, 90015	
Also, church & chapel, statuary	
www.cotters.com	
The Hand Prop Room LP.	**(323) 931-1534**
period-present, worldwide sel.	
History For Hire, Inc.	**(818) 765-7767**
prayer books, bibles, religious statues	
Hollywood Studio Gallery	**(323) 462-1116**
stations of the cross	
LCW Props	**(818) 243-0707**
Bibles, Hymnal Books, Crosses, Urns, Candelabras, Pews, Chalice, Caskets	
Ob-jects	**(818) 351-4200**
Religious props including candle votive stands and more.	
Omega/Cinema Props	**(323) 466-8201**
Sony Pictures Studios-Prop House (Off Lot)	**(310) 244-5999**
religious crosses, religious shrines, religious wall decorations	
Universal Studios Property & Hardware Dept	**(818) 777-2784**
Many religious articles and pieces for rent.	
Used Church Items, Religious Rentals	**(412) 220-2272**
115 East Barr Street, Mcdonald, PA, 15057	
Statues, Lights, Chandeliers, Podiums, Lecterns, Votive Stands, Crucifixes, Kneelers, Vestments, Chalices, Altars	
www.religiousrentals.com	
Warner Bros. Studios Property Department	**(818) 954-2181**
Alters, candle holders, crucifixs, statues, kneelers, menorahs, candelabras, incense holders	

Relocation Services

See: Transportation, Trucking and/or Storage

Renaissance Themed Parties

See: Costume Rental Houses* Events, Decorations, Supplies & Services* Events, Design/Planning/Production* Events, Entertainment* Historical Era Themed Events* Wardrobe, Antique/Historical

Reproductions

See: Prop Reproduction & Fabrication

Reptiles

See: Animals (Live), Services, Trainers & Wranglers

Research, Advisors, Consulting & Clearances

See Also: Art, Artists For Hire* Private Investigations* Search Tools, Directories, Libraries

Act One Script Clearance, Inc.	**(818) 240-2416**
230 N Maryland Ave Ste 201, Glendale, CA, 91206	
Script research. clearances	
www.actonescript.com	
Brand Library & Art Center	**(818) 548-2051**
1601 W. Mountain St, Glendale, CA, 91201	
info@brandlibrary.org * www.brandlibrary.org	
Burbank Central Library	**(818) 238-5600**
110 N. Glenoaks Blvd, Burbank, CA, 91502	
Warner Research Library	
www.burbank.lib.ca.us	
Caravan West Productions	**(661) 268-8300**
35660 Jayhawker Rd, Aqua Dulce, CA, 91390	
Old West back to Civil War and trained Old West crew	
caravanwest@earthlink.net * www.caravanwest.com	
The Costume House	**(818) 508-9933**
books, magazines, patterns, photo collection	
Front Sight Firearms Training Institute	**(800) 987-7719**
1 Front Sight Road, Pahrump, NV, 89061	
firearms, firearm choreography, location filming, actor training	
www.frontsight.com	
The Hand Prop Room LP.	**(323) 931-1534**
on-site research library	
History For Hire, Inc.	**(818) 765-7767**
research & consulting, no clearances	
Kansas Cosmosphere & Space Center	**(800) 397-0330**
1100 N Plum, Hutchinson, KS, 67501-1499	
U.S. Space Program equipment	
www.cosmo.org	
Michael Dempsey	**(805) 345-0006**
296 Mountain View Dr, Santa Maria CA, 93455	
27 years experience as historical re-enactor, clothing, housewares, arms, camp goods, mid-1600s to Civil War	
dempseyscenic2@gmail.com	
MorguePropRentals.com	**(818) 957-2178**
5134 Valley Blvd, Los Angeles, CA, 90032	
script writing assist., autopsy, mortuary, crime scene, etc.	
info@1800autopsy.com * www.morgueproprentals.com	
SCA Marketplace	**(800) 789-7486**
P.O. Box 360789, Milpitas, CA, 95036	
catalog sales; books/patterns for historical clothing, artifacts from around the world, website has useful links	
www.sca.org/links/shopping.html	
Smithsonian Institution	**(202) 633-1000**
PO Box 37012, SI Bldg. Room 153 MRC 010, Washington, DC, 20013	
all museum info; image research, printing & photographic svcs.	
www.si.edu	
Sony Pictures Studios-Wardrobe	**(310) 244-5995**
alterations, call (310) 244-7260	
Sword & Stone	**(818) 562-6548**
medieval period, over 5,000 reference books in our library	

Resource Books

See: Search Tools, Directories, Libraries

Restaurant Bar

See: Bars, Nightclubs, Barware & Dressing* Cafe Tables/Chairs/Umbrellas* Jukeboxes, Music/Dance Machines* Liquor Bottles

Restaurant Furniture & Dressing

See Also: Banquets/Booths (Seating)* Bars, Nightclubs, Barware & Dressing* Cafe Tables/Chairs/Umbrellas* Counters* Salad Bars

AIR Designs	**(818) 768-6639**
Complete Dressing for Restaurant, Diner, Fast Food, Coffee Shop, Pizzeria, Salad Bars, Salsa Bars	
C. P. Two	**(323) 466-8201**
Period to modern restaurant chairs and restaurant tables.	
History For Hire, Inc.	**(818) 765-7767**
period	
Hollywood Studio Gallery	**(323) 462-1116**
signage, wall food/beverage pictures	
LCW Props	**(818) 243-0707**
Commercial, Industrial, Tables, Appliances, Chairs, Menus, POS Systems	
Lennie Marvin Enterprises, Inc. (Prop Heaven)	**(818) 841-5882**
all furniture/dressing/equip. for complete diner/restaurant	
LM Treasures	**(626) 252-7354**
We carry an extensive assortment of Restaurant furnishings including menu board holders, butler statues, and wall decor.	

Modern Props (323) 934-3000
contemp/futuristic restaurant furniture and restaurant dressing including cabinets & more
RC Vintage, Inc. (818) 765-7107
40s, 50s & 60s, Chairs, Tables, Booths, Stools, Bar sets, Diner Counters & wide variety Contemporary Lamps!
Sony Pictures Studios-Prop House (Off Lot) (310) 244-5999
Restaurant Lamp, cash caddy, waitress tray, waitress station rail, cafeteria tray, change dispenser, coffee bean dispenser
Universal Studios Property & Hardware Dept (818) 777-2784
Restaurant furniture, restaurant props and dressing for rent.

Restaurant Kitchens/Equip./Supplies

See Also: Bars, Nightclubs, Barware & Dressing* Cafeteria Counter/Line* Cooking Equipment* Credit Card Imprint Machine* Deep Fryer* Food, Artificial Food* Glass Door Coolers* Glassware/Dishes* Lunch Counters* Menus* Pizza Ovens & Boxes* Restaurant Furniture & Dressing* Vendor Carts & Concession Counters* Food, Food Stylists
AIR Designs (818) 768-6639
Complete Dressing for Restaurant, Diner, Fast Food, Coffee Shop, Pizzeria
Bargain Fair (Beverly/Fairfax) (323) 655-2227
7901 Beverly Blvd, Los Angeles, CA, 90048
corner of Fairfax; dinnerware, glassware, silverware, cookware & more at unbelievable prices, open 7 days
sheida@bargainfair.com * www.bargainfair.com
Bargain Fair (Mid-City) (323) 965-2227
4635 W Pico Blvd, Los Angeles, CA, 90019
located in Mid-City; dinnerware, glassware, silverware, cookware & more at unbelievable prices, open 7 days
sheida@bargainfair.com * www.bargainfair.com
C. P. Two (323) 466-8201
Restaurant sinks, restaurant counters, restaurant workspaces, restaurant dishware, meat grinders and cookware.
E.C. Prop Rentals (818) 764-2008
stainless sinks & tables, freezer barrier curtain, exhaust fan
History For Hire, Inc. (818) 765-7767
LCW Props (818) 243-0707
Commercial, Industrial, Tables, Appliances, Chairs, Menus, POS Systems
Machinery & Equipment Co., Inc. (909) 599-3916
115 N Cataract Ave, San Dimas, CA, 91773
Used commercial restaurant equipment including kettles, mixers, ovens, fryers, braising pans, cookers and more.
sherri@machineryandequipment.com * www.machineryandequipment.com
Prop Services West (818) 503-2790
RC Vintage, Inc. (818) 765-7107
40s, 50s & 60s, large sel., & fast food equipment Drive Up Window order Menu Board.....
Universal Studios Property & Hardware Dept (818) 777-2784
Restaurant kitchen dressing and commercial kitchen dressing for rent.
ZG04 DECOR (818) 853-8040

Restaurant Table Lamps

See: Restaurant Furniture & Dressing

Restoration & Repair

See: Furniture & Art, Repair & Restoration

Retractable Syringes

See: Medical Equip/Furniture, Graphics/Supplies

Retractable Tape Posts

See: Crowd Control: Barricades, Turnstiles Etc.* Stanchions & Rope

Rickshaws

History For Hire, Inc. (818) 765-7767
Universal Studios Property & Hardware Dept (818) 777-2784
Rickshaws for rent.
Warner Bros. Studios Property Department (818) 954-2181
Wicker rickshaws, rickshaws

Rigging, Equipment or Services

See Also: Motion Control* Nautical Dressing & Props* Theatrical Draperies, Hardware & Rigging
A1-STUNTWORLD inc (310) 666-3004
Hollywood, CA 90028
stunt coordinators, stunt performers, master stunt riggers, stunt equipment rental (large inventory), skydivers & more.
www.stuntworldinc.com
Action Specialists (661) 775-8530
25620 Rye Canyon Rd Unit E, Valencia, CA, 91355
stunt rigging, coordination, setup, rig rentals, fire gel sales, cell (818) 915-4691
www.actionspecialists.com
Astro Audio Video Lighting, Inc. (818) 549-9915
6615 San Fernando Rd, Glendale, CA, 91201
Trusses, truss bases, box trusses, rigging trick lines, pipe and bases, cheesebrough clamps and more available.
www.astroavl.com
Beckman Rigging/BRS Rigging (310) 532-3933
13516 Mariposa Ave, Gardena, CA, 90247
24/7 services for rigging, mobile fab. show design, stunt coordination, motion control, robotics, stages & decking
rigyou@mac.com * www.brsrigging.com
Branam Enterprises (818) 885-6474
9152 Independence Ave., Chatsworth, CA 91311
flying, rigging & truss systems provider/fabricator
www.branament.com
Filmmaker Prod. Svcs-Atlanta @ Tyler Perry Studios (404) 450-1968
2115 Sylvan Road, Atlanta, GA, 30344
Grip & rigging equip. & services, lighting & sound
chad.garcia@nbcuni.com * www.filmmakerproductionservices.com
Filmmaker Prod. Svcs-Chicago @ Cinespace Chicago (678) 628-1997
2558 W 16th Street Dock #4, Chicago, IL, 60608
Grip & rigging equip. & services, lighting & sound
patrick.flanagan@nbcuni.com * www.filmmakerproductionservices.com
Flying By Foy (702) 454-3500
3275 E. Patrick Lane, Las Vegas, NV, 89120
live performance, theatrical flying effects
www.flybyfoy.com
Leavittation, Inc. (661) 252-7551
25982 Sand Canyon Rd, Santa Clarita, CA, 91387
extensive stunt equipment/rigging,crash & stunt pad rentals
www.stuntrev.com
Lowy Enterprises (310) 763-1111
1970 E Gladwick St, Rancho Dominguez, CA, 90220
webbing, fasteners, Velcro, cord, soft goods, parachutes
www.lowyusa.com
Matt Sweeney Special Effects, Inc. (818) 902-9354
14201 Bessemer St, Van Nuys, CA 91401
stunt equip, sheaves, pulleys, snatch blocks, flying rigs
www.sweeney-special-effects.com
New Mexico Lighting & Grip Co. (505) 506-6564
I-25 Studios 9201 Pan American Fwy NE, Albuquerque, NM, 87113
Grip & rigging equip. & services, lighting & sound
colin.pearman@nmlgc.com * www.newmexicolightingandgrip.com
Peak Trading Corporation (800) 952-7325
1 Tomsons Rd #100, Saugerties, NY 12477
catalog sales; cable, chain, rope, hardware, hoists, harnesses, tools
www.peaktrading.com
Sapsis Rigging, Inc. (800) 727-7471
3883 Ridge Ave, Philadelphia, PA, 19132
www.sapsis-rigging.com
Universal Studios Grip Dept (818) 777-2291
100 Universal City Plaza, Universal City, CA, 91608
Extensive inventory of quality grip equipment incl. digital screens, steel deck & more
universal.grip@nbcuni.com * http://universalstudioslot.com/grip
Ver Sales (818) 567-3000
2509 N Naomi St, Burbank, CA, 91504
rigging for rafting, mountain climbing, hang gliding, sailing; also safety items, fall protection equipment & classes
www.versalestore.com
Warner Bros. Studios Grip Department (818) 954-1590
4000 Warner Blvd Bldg 43, Burbank, CA, 91522
Production, rigging & construction grip equipment, canvas shop, steel scaffolding rentals/services
www.wbgripdept.com
West EFX, Inc. (818) 762-1059
11635 Sheldon St, Sun Valley, CA, 91352
equip. rentals, lrg scale cust. FX, flying/rigging, crash & burn
www.westefx.com
ZFX Inc. (502) 637-2500
611 Industry Rd, Louisville, KY, 40208
Flying effects for live performance, film & TV; equipment, choreography
www.zfxflying.com

Risers

See: Audience Seating* Stages, Portable & Steel Deck

Road Signs

See: Railroad Crossing Signal* Traffic/Road Signs, Lights, Safety Items

Robes

See: Clerical, Judicial, Academic Gowns/Apparel* Costume Rental Houses* Costumes

Robots

See Also: Factory/Industrial* Mannequins* Puppets, Marionettes, Automata, Animatronics

Advanced Animations (802) 746-8974
P.O. Box 34, Route 107, Stockbridge, VT, 05772
rentals for trade shows, cust. design for theme parks
www.advancedanimations.com

E.C. Prop Rentals (818) 764-2008
robotic arms, battery powered

Flix FX Inc. (818) 765-3549
7327 Lankershim Blvd #4, N Hollywood, CA, 91605
Radio controlled robots & robotic arms & SAG puppeteers
info@flixfx.com * www.flixfx.com

Florida Robotics (407) 568-6146
24123 Peachland Blvd C-4 #226, Port Charlotte, FL, 33954
"live" robots for events, trade shows, road shows, animatronic characters available

LCW Props (818) 243-0707
Large Selection Of Rigged Robotics. Arms, Battle Bots, Large & Small

Tech Works FX Studios (504) 722-1504
13405 Seymour Meyers Blvd #5, Covington, LA, 70433
Specializes in Robots for Rental, Custom Robots, Robot Suits and Costumes and Animatronics.
info@techworksstudios.com * www.techworksstudios.com

Ultra Prototypes LLC (818) 292-1906
Call for Appointment
If you need a Robot, we can design and build it.
jeff@ultraprototypes.com * www.ultraprototypes.com

Rock 'n' Roll Instruments

See Also: Musical Instruments

History For Hire, Inc. (818) 765-7767
all periods-the biggest selection!

LCW Props (818) 243-0707
call for styles and latest models

Music Depot LA (951) 237-3521
11762 De Palma Rd Ste 1-C #63, Corona, CA, 92883
One-stop shop for name brand, unique or custom built musical instruments and music props. Music industry experts.
del@musicdepotla.com * www.MusicDepotLA.com

Rock 'n' Roll Lighting & Sound

See: Lighting & Sound, Concert/Theatrical/DJ/VJ

Rock Climbing Walls

See: Events, Entertainment

Rocking Chairs

See: Chairs

Rocks

See: Concrete Block, Brick, Gravel, Sand, Rocks, Etc.* Greens

Roll-Up Doors

See: Steel Folding Gates & Roll-Up Doors

Roman Themed Parties

See: Columns* Costume Rental Houses* Events, Decorations, Supplies & Services* Locations, Events Destinations* Events, Entertainment* Wardrobe, Antique/Historical

Rooftop Dressing

See Also: Satellite Dishes* Weather Vanes

Alley Cats Studio Rentals (818) 982-9178
vents, turbines, rooftop A/C, skylights, swamp coolers, antennas, satellite dishes, signs

E.C. Prop Rentals (818) 764-2008
gutted castered swamp coolers & AC units, vents, ducting, ladders, lighting

LCW Props (818) 243-0707
Large Selection, Vents, AC's, Roof Antennas, High Voltage, Transistors

Rope

See: Chain & Rope* Expendables* Nautical Dressing & Props

Rope Ladders

See: Nautical Dressing & Props

Rowboats & Oars

See: Boats & Water Sport Vehicles

Rowing Machines

See: Exercise & Fitness Equipment

Rubber & Foam Rubber

See Also: Plastics, Materials & Fabrication* Special Effects, Make-up/Prosthetics

American Rubber & Supply Co. (818) 782-8234
P. O. Box 7398, Van Nuys CA, 91409
sheet, sponge, matting & mats, extrusion, tubing, foam, all rainwear, and some other finished products
www.americanrubberandsupply.com

Canal Rubber Supply Co. (800) 444-6483
329 Canal Street, New York City, NY, 10013
wide variety, sheet, foam, mats, flooring, hoses, tubing, sponge
www.canalrubber.com

Reynolds Advanced Materials: Smooth-On Distributor (818) 358-6000
10856 Vanowen St, N Hollywood, CA, 91605
Hollywood's F/X source for Liquid Rubbers, Plastics & more
LA@reynoldsam.com * www.moldmakingmaterials.com

Rubber Stamps

See Also: Art, Supplies & Stationery* Office Equipment & Dressing

North Hollywood Rubber Stamp Co. (323) 463-3111
5105 Cleon Ave, N Hollywood, CA, 91601
Custom rubber stamps including self inking stamps, pre inked stamps, wood handled stamps, stock stamps and more.
northhollywoodrubberstamp@gmail.com * www.hrsco.com

West Valley Rubber Stamp (800) 540-8881
3215 N California St Ste 1, Stockton, CA, 95204
Custom dies for molds for custom rubber stamps; Self-inking stamps and more
margaret.rawn@westvalleyrubberstamp.com * www.westvalleyrubberstamp.com

Rubble

See: Salvage, Rubble, Clutter & Trash (Prop)

Ruby Dressing

See: Alley Dressing

Rugs

See Also: Art Deco Carpet & Rugs* Carpet & Flooring* Red Carpeting, Events/Premiers* Sono Tubes

Bridge Furniture & Props Los Angeles   **(818) 433-7100**
We carry modern & traditional furniture, lighting, accessories, art, & rugs. Items are online for easy shopping.

David's Rug Gallery   **(310) 657-4623**
505 N La Cienega Blvd, Los Angeles, CA, 90048
new/old/antiques, Persian Rugs, Chinese Rugs, Pakistani Rugs, Indian Rugs, Turkish Rugs
davidsrug@yahoo.com * http://bit.ly/DavidsRugGallery

FormDecor, Inc.   **(310) 558-2582**
America's largest event rental supplier of 20th Century furniture and accessories for Modern and Mid-Century styles.

Linoleum City, Inc.   **(323) 469-0063**
4849 Santa Monica Blvd, Hollywood, CA, 90029
Area rugs, carpet runners, custom area rugs, sisal rugs, seagrass rugs, binding, serging, many custom sizes and styles.
sales@linocity.com * www.linoleumcity.com

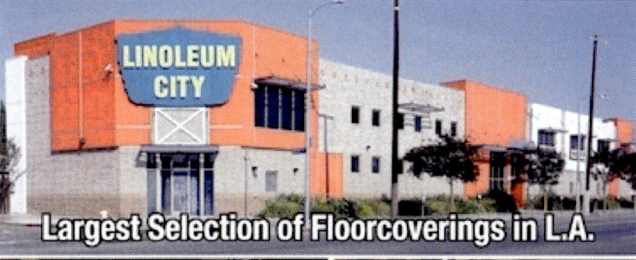

Serving the Entertainment Industry for over 65 years.
We understand your needs and deliver promptly!

Carpet • Vinyl • Cork • Carpet Runners • Hardwood Floors
Linoleum • Tiles • Laminate Floors • Ceramic Tiles
Window Treatments • Wall Coverings

Little Bohemia Rentals   **(818) 853-7506**
11940 Sherman Rd, N Hollywood, CA, 91605
Kilims, Flatweaves, Flokatis, Persians. Vintage rugs and Contemporary rugs.
sales@wearelittlebohemia.com * www.wearelittlebohemia.com

Mehraban Rugs   **(310) 657-4400**
545 N La Cienega Ave, Los Angeles, CA, 90048
antique/reprod. ethnic, kilims, Oriental, Persian, Iran, Gabbehs
www.mehraban.com

Modernica Props   **(323) 664-2322**
over 200 50s-70s pop, period & shag rugs

Monarch Carpet   **(213) 388-0148**
3021 West Temple St, Los Angeles, CA, 90026
Onsite plant can finish area rugs to your specifications. Can finish rug with a bound, serge, leather or specialty edge.
monarchcar@aol.com * www.monarchcarpet.com

NEST Studio Rentals, Inc.   **(818) 942-0339**
contemporary, traditional, sizes to 9' by 12'

Ob-jects   **(818) 351-4200**
Americana rugs, ethnic rugs, Aubusson rugs, needlepoint, modern rugs, Navajo rugs, Oriental rugs

Old N Country Prop Shop, LLC   **(818) 423-2599**
A selection of antique, Persian, and modern rugs in different sizes and colors.

Omega/Cinema Props   **(323) 466-8201**
Oriental rugs & more

Pasadena Antique Center and Annex   **(626) 449-7706**
480 South Fair Oaks Ave, Pasadena, CA, 91105
Antique Rugs from all over the world
pasadenaantiqecenterandannex@gmail.com * bit.ly/PasadenaAntiqueCenter

Picture Start Props   **(818) 255-5472**
Small and large contemporary rugs in a variety of styles and colors.

Prop Services West   **(818) 503-2790**
braided/rag/hooked,ethnic tribal,Oriental,Persian,Navajo,runners

A Royal Suite Home Furinishings   **(661) 259-7000**
26536 Carl Boyer Dr, Santa Clarita, CA, 91350
A Royal Suite, family-owned since 1978, Features AMERICAN-MADE Furniture, and the Finest Furniture at the Greatest Value
norb@ars-email.com * www.aroyalsuite.com

Sony Pictures Studios-Linens, Drapes, Rugs   **(310) 244-5999**
5933 W Slauson Ave, Culver City, CA, 90230
Throw rungs, runner rugs, and area rugs
www.sonypicturesstudios.com

Sony Pictures Studios-Prop House (Off Lot)   **(310) 244-5999**
runner rugs, doormats, floor matting, throw rugs, bath mats

Universal Studios Drapery Dept   **(818) 777-2761**
area rugs

Universal Studios Property & Hardware Dept   **(818) 777-2784**
Many rugs for rent; period-modern, Oriental to European, kilims, handmade/hooked

Warner Bros. Drapery, Upholstery & Flooring   **(818) 954-1831**
4000 Warner Blvd Bldg 30, Burbank, CA, 91522
Commercial; Plush & composite: Binding; Cleaning & Repair
wbsfdrapery@warnerbros.com * www.wbdrapery.com

Warner Bros. Studios Property Department   **(818) 954-2181**
Area rugs, Persian rugs, shag rugs, outdoor rugs, tiger rugs, rug beaters

Woven Accents   **(310) 652-6520**
8674 Melrose Ave, West Hollywood, CA, 90069
With our collection of 4,500 Antique, New, Vintage & Modern Rugs & Tapestries, you will find the right rug within budget
sam@wovenonline.com * www.wovenonline.com

Y & B Bolour   **(310) 274-6719**
321 S Robertson Blvd, Los Angeles, CA, 90048
European, handmade/hooked, kilims, Oriental, Persian
www.ybbolour.com

ZG04 DECOR   **(818) 853-8040**
Area Rugs, Runners, Modern Rugs, Contemporary Rugs, Traditional Rugs, Antique Rugs

Runners

See: Rugs

RV Vehicles & Travel Trailers, Equip & Parts

L. A. Circus (323) 751-3486
Call for Appt, Los Angeles, CA, 90047
Airstream trailers only
circusinc@aol.com * www.lacircus.com

Silver Trailer - Vintage Airstream Rentals & Props (530) 295-9299
California / Las Vegas
Silver Trailer is a vintage trailer rental company specializing in Airstream trailers and props.
studio@silvertrailer.com * www.SilverTrailer.com

Vita Motus (408) 679-1781
2148 1/2 W Sunset Blvd, Los Angeles, CA, 90026
2016 Airstream 28ft available for shoots (music, magazine, television, commercial, etc). Tow in / out services provided.
sam@vitamotus.com * http://vitamotus.com

Sacks

See: Expendables* Packing/Packaging Supplies, Services

Saddles

See: Horse Saddles & Tack

Safes/Vaults

1st Security Safe Co. (800) 400-7675
901 South Hill St, Los Angeles, CA, 90015
Come visit the largest showroom you can find filled with both new and used safes.
info@firstsecuritysafe.com * www.firstsecuritysafe.com

C. P. Two (323) 466-8201
Real safes/real vaults & prop safes/prop vaults

Dean Safe Company (818) 997-1234
6020 Laurel Canyon Blvd, N Hollywood, CA, 91606
large selection of safes
info@deansafe.com * www.deansafe.com

Dozar Office Furnishings (310) 559-9292
9937 Jefferson Blvd, Culver City, CA, 90232
Rentals X22. Fire safes, combination safes/combo safes, sandstone safes, key safes, fire safes. Dimensions chart online.
dozarrents@aol.com * www.dozarrents.com

Faux Library Studio Props, Inc. (818) 765-0096
Safe boxes only, hidden books, hidden money, book boxes, book safes

History For Hire, Inc. (818) 765-7767
vintage

LCW Props (818) 243-0707
Large Selection Of Large & Small Safes, Military, Rigged Safe Doors, Vault Doors

RJR Props (404) 349-7600
Prop safes and prop vaults; giant vaults, lock dials and more.

Santa Monica Lock & Safe Company, Inc (310) 450-5101
2208 Pico Blvd, Santa Monica, CA, 90405
www.santamonicalockandsafe.com

Sony Pictures Studios-Prop House (Off Lot) (310) 244-5999
safe front, home style safe, rolling safe, coin banks, combination locks

Universal Studios Property & Hardware Dept (818) 777-2784
Many kinds of prop safes for rent.

Safety

See: Floor, Ground & Surface Protection* Nautical Dressing & Props* Protective Apparel* Research, Advisors, Consulting & Clearances* Traffic/Road Signs, Lights, Safety Items* Uniforms, Trades/Professional/Sports

Sails & Sail Makers

See: Boats & Water Sport Vehicles* Canvas* Nautical Dressing & Props

Saint Patrick's Day

See: Events, Decorations, Supplies & Services* Events, Entertainment* Holiday Costumes* Holiday Theme Events* Irish, All Things Irish

Salon & Spa Equipment

See Also: Barber Shop* Beauty Salon* Jacuzzis, Spas & Pools

Lennie Marvin Enterprises, Inc. (Prop Heaven) (818) 841-5882
full salon & manicure stations

Modern Props (323) 934-3000
Salon equipment and spa equipment for rent

Salvage, Architectural

See: Architectural Pieces & Artifacts

Salvage, Rubble, Clutter & Trash (Prop)

See Also: Alley Dressing* Sanitation, Waste Disposal

AIR Designs (818) 768-6639
Auto, Drums, Tires, Junkyard Dressing, etc.

E.C. Prop Rentals (818) 764-2008
shapes, textures galore, pipe, tires, drums, spools, carts etc.

LCW Props (818) 243-0707
Our Specialty! Large Selections Of Any Kind of clean trash, Own A Recyling Center, Our Inventory Cannot Be Matched

6439 San Fernando Rd. Glendale, CA 91201
Phone: 818-243-0707 - www.lcwprops.com

Tally Ho Marine Salvage & Decor (310) 548-5273
406 22nd St, San Pedro, CA, 90731
If we don't have it & can't find it, we can build it. marine

Universal Studios Property & Hardware Dept (818) 777-2784
Prop trash for rent.

Warner Bros. Studios Property Department (818) 954-2181
Pallets of faux rubble/fake rubble at The Ranch.

Sand

See: Concrete Block, Brick, Gravel, Sand, Rocks, Etc.* Greens

Sandbags

See: Greens

Sandwich Board Store Sign

AIR Designs (818) 768-6639
Assorted Sizes, Types, Curb Signs

D'ziner Sign Co. (323) 467-4467
801 Seward Street, Los Angeles, CA, 90038
sandwich signs, directional signs
sales@dzinersign.com * www.dzinersign.com

Sanitation, Waste Disposal

See Also: Charities & Donations* Recycling Services

Andy Gump Temporary Site Services　　　(800) 992-7755
26954 Ruether Ave, Santa Clarita, CA, 91351
State of the art equipment to meet all your sanitation needs, incl. trailers that productions can take along with them
www.andygump.com

BCS Recycling Specialists　　　(818) 341-4820
8745 Remmet Ave, Canoga Park, CA, 91304
Call first: computer parts, scrap metals, cellular phones
www.scrapdr.com

EcoSet ReDirect　　　(323) 669-0697
3423 Casitas Ave, Los Angeles, CA, 90039
One-stop drop-off solution for reusable production and event discards. We specialize in scenic builds and custom pieces.
www.ecosetconsulting.com/redirect

L & M Stripping　　　(818) 983-1200
14232 Aetna St, Van Nuys, CA, 91401
paint & rust removal from metal, but not wood
www.lmstripping.com

LCW Props　　　(818) 243-0707
Trash bins, Roll-Off Containers, Recycling Bins, Yard Waste

Patriot Environmental Services　　　(800) 624-9136
508 East E Street, Wilmington, CA 90744
will come to stage or location, assist with permits, emergency response service
www.patriotenvironmental.com

Waste Management, Inc　　　(713) 512-6200
1001 Fannin St Ste 4000, Houston, TX, 77002
Phone number is main office, call for local numbers
www.wm.com

Santa Sleigh

See: Sleighs

Santa Thrones

See: Christmas

Sash Cord

See: Expendables

Sashes, Window

See: Window Treatments

2007

40 YEARS OF DEBBIES BOOK

First female Speaker of the House: Nancy Pelosi. **Writer's Strike** lasts until 2/14/08. Polar Bears designated as threatened. CA Supreme Court rules in favor of **gay marriage**; human rights protesters target the Olympic torch relay, **mortgage meltdown.**

By now, if you've read through all of these Book pages, I'm sure you found some arguable details in a fact or two, or some news event more important than one given. Don't bother to let me know what it is because by this time I'm too old, just be glad my mind still works. I still own an electric typewriter (even though we have more computers than I ever wanted) and I answer my own phone – just a breed from the old school.

Satellite Dishes

E.C. Prop Rentals　　　(818) 764-2008
prop only, multiple sizes, wall mount and pole mount

LCW Props　　　(818) 243-0707
Large Selection. From 12" To 16', All Kinds

L.C.W. PROPS
MANY DIFFERENT STYLES, SIZES & SHAPES

6439 San Fernando Rd. Glendale, CA 91201
Phone: 818-243-0707 - www.lcwprops.com

Modern Props　　　(323) 934-3000
8' diameter satellite dishes

Universal Studios Property & Hardware Dept　　　(818) 777-2784
Different satellite dishes, commercial to residential for rent.

Woody's Electrical Props　　　(818) 503-1940
Period to futuristic. Large & small.

Satellites

See: Space Shuttle/Space Hardware

Scaffolding/Lighting Towers

See Also: Ladders* Lighting & Sound, Concert/Theatrical/DJ/VJ* Rigging, Equipment or Services

E.C. Prop Rentals　　　(818) 764-2008
Castered painter's scaffolds

Mike Brown Grandstands　　　(800) 266-2659
2300 Pomona Blvd, Pomona, CA, 91768
and camera towers/platforms
www.mbgs.com

Scale Models

See: Dollhouses* Miniatures/Models* Model Ships/Planes/Trains/Autos Etc.* Prop Design & Manufacturing* Toys & Games

Scales

AIR Designs　　　(818) 768-6639
Grocery Store Scales, Deli Scales, Vending Vending Scales, Industrial Scales

Alley Cats Studio Rentals　　　(818) 982-9178
contemporary scales, antique scales, grocery store scales, produce scales, and carnival scales

E.C. Prop Rentals　　　(818) 764-2008
several styles; lollipop, desktop & floor models

The Hand Prop Room LP.　　　(323) 931-1534
period-present

History For Hire, Inc.　　　(818) 765-7767

LCW Props　　　(818) 243-0707
Postal, Industrial, Commercial, Part Scales, Gram Scales, Platform Scales

Old N Country Prop Shop, LLC　　　(818) 423-2599
Large variety of scales, for whatever need weighing.

Universal Studios Property & Hardware Dept　　　(818) 777-2784
Prop scales; period and antique for rent.

Scenery Trailer Rentals

See: Production Vehicles/Trailers

Scenery/Set Construction

See Also: Architectural Pieces & Artifacts* Backings* CNC Router & Laser Etching Services* Columns* Events, Backings & Scenery* Fiberglass Products/Fabrication* Printing, Graphics, Digital & Large Format* Hardware, Decorative* Moulding, Wood* Prop & Set Design Supplies, Parts, Tools* Staff Shops* Themed Environment Construction* Water Jet CNC Services

41 Sets　　　　　　　　　　　　　　**(323) 860-2442**
1040 N Los Palmas Ave Bldg 42, Los Angeles, CA, 90038
Full service Art Department, set creation and design for your production
info@41sets.com * www.41sets.com

From Concept to Design to Reality... We are your source.

(323) 860-2442 www.41sets.com info@41sets.com

A & D Scenery　　　　　　　　　　　**(702) 362-9404**
3200 Sirius Ave, Ste F, Las Vegas, NV, 89102
fabrication, scenic & exhibit design, staging, turntables
www.adscenery.com

California Theaming, Inc.　　　　　　**(626) 303-2349**
404 W. Evergreen Ave, Monrovia, CA, 91016
themed architectural facades, set pieces

Carthay Set Services　　　　　　　　**(818) 762-3566**
5539 Riverton Ave, N Hollywood, CA, 91601
sets, props, billboards, small to large scale
www.carthay.com

Centerline Scenery　　　　　　　　　**(818) 252-7467**
8238 Lankershim Blvd, N Hollywood, CA, 91605
meredyth@centerlinescenery.com

CENTERLINE SCENERY

8238 Lankershim Blvd. North Hollywood, CA 91605

Chris G TV inc.　　　　　　　　　　　**(917) 969 8443**
11930 Wicks St, Sun Valley, CA, 91352
Providing Scenery Rentals, set construction and custom work to the Film and TV industry. Delivery available.
chrisg@chrisg.tv * www.chrisg.tv

Continental Scenery　　　　　　　　**(818) 404-3418**
Call for Appt
film, TV, theater, outdoor themed environments

depict　　　　　　　　　　　　　　　**(323) 222-1001**
1460 Naud St, Los Angeles, CA, 90012
info@depict33.com * www.depict33.com

Global Entertainment Industries, Inc.　**(818) 567-0000**
2948 N. Ontario St, Burbank, CA, 91504
indoor/outdoor themed displays & facades, set building
www.globalentind.com

Hollywood Elevators/ Red Truck INC　**(562) 896-6070**
4707 Exposition Blvd, Los Angeles, CA, 90016
redtruck321@sbcglobal.net * hollywoodelevators.com

IDF Studio Scenery　　　　　　　　　**(818) 982-7433**
6844 Lankershim Blvd, North Hollywood, CA, 91605
Custom Construction, Scenic Painting, welding & extensive rental inventory, architectural details and pieces
info@idfstudioscenery.com * www.idfstudioscenery.com

Ironwood (818) 265-2055
1514 Flower St, Glendale, CA, 91201
small set pcs to very large metal fab & arch. pcs, sculptures
www.ironwoodfabrication.com

Jet Sets (818) 764-5644
6910 Farmdale Ave, N Hollywood, CA, 91605
set construction, custom props, scenic painting, special effects, set illustration,
research library for clients
dougmorris@jetsets.com * www.jetsets.com

KIHL STUDIOS (818) 812-9594
9701 Owensmouth Ave Unit 1, Chatsworth, CA, 91311
We build worlds, from film and stage sets to marketing event & trade show
environments.
design@kihlstudios.com * www.kihlstudios.com

Merritt Productions, Inc. (818) 760-0612
10845 Vanowen St, North Hollywood, CA, 91605
specialty props, miniatures, sculpture, mech effects, set const.
www.merrittproductions.com

Pizzazz Scenic Contractors, Inc. (904) 641-1239
1354 Wigmore St, Jacksonville, FL, 32206
Design & build themed environments, scenic art, sculptures, signage, &
architectural elements
www.pizzazzscenic.com

Sally Corporation (904) 355-7100
745 W Forsyth St, Jacksonville, FL, 32204
custom animatronics: human, animal, fantasy, plus animated shows & dark ride
adventures
www.sallycorp.com

Scenic Express (323) 254-4351
3019 Andrita St, Los Angeles, CA, 90065
Specialize in scenics, prop/set construction, displays and production.
www.scenicexpress.net

Scenic Highlights (818) 252-7760
10830 Cantara St, Sun Valley, CA, 91352
scenichighlights.com

Schmidli Backdrops LA (323) 938-2098
5830 W Adams Blvd, Culver City, CA, 90232
Providing hand painted Textured and Scenic backdrops to the commercial, film,
and fashion industry for over 20 years.
backdrops@schmidli.com * www.schmidli.com

Set Masters (818) 982-1506
24853 Avenue Rockefeller, Valencia, CA, 91355
Concept; Design; Custom; Specialty; Interior & Exterior; Live Events; Exhibits;
Road Shows; Special Effects
info@setmasters.com * www.setmasters.com

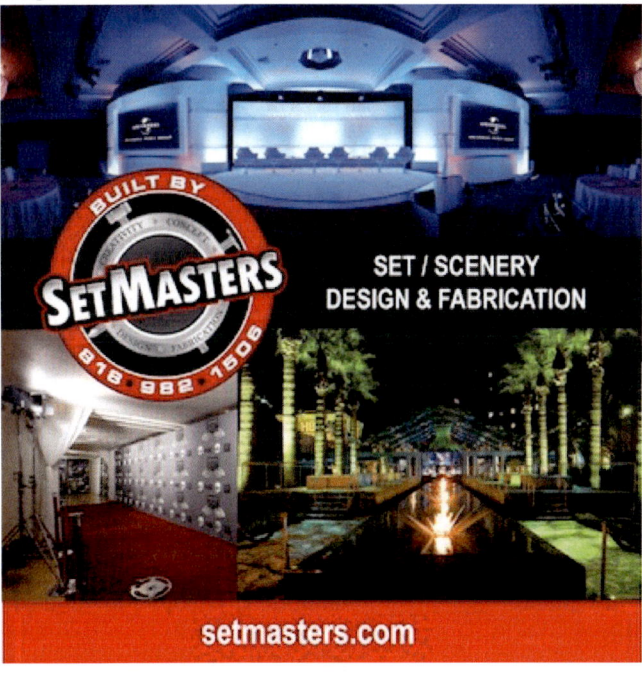

Tractor Vision Scenery & Rentals (323) 235-2885
340 E Jefferson Blvd, Los Angeles, CA, 90011
Specializing in entertainment, trade shows, & events, we bring your projects to
life with precision, speed & personality
sets@tractorvision.com * www.tractorvision.com

Tribal Scenery (818) 558-4045
3216 Vanowen St, Burbank, CA, 91505
scenic painting, set design & construction
www.tribalscenery.com

Universal Studios Graphic Design & Sign Shop (818) 777-2350
dimensional set pieces & architectural elements

Universal Studios Staff Shop (818) 777-2337

Vision Scenery (818) 567-2818
12450 Foothill Blvd, Sylmar, CA, 91342
Set construction and design
projects@visionscenery.com * http://visionscenery.com

Warner Bros. Design Studio (818) 954-4430
4000 Warner Blvd Bldg 44, Burbank, CA, 91522
Concept, Design, Fabrication of Interior & Exterior Standing Sets, Facades,
Exhibits, Road Shows
wbds@warnerbros.com * www.warnerbrosdesignstudio.com

Worlds of Wow (817) 380-4215
1800 Shady Oaks Drive, Denton, TX, 76205
Concept, design, custom themes, custom scenic fabrication, prop design &
manufacturing
www.worldsofwow.com

Scenery/Set Rentals

See Also: Architectural Pieces & Artifacts* Backings* Columns* Scenery/Set Construction

Chris G TV inc.   **(917) 969 8443**
11930 Wicks St, Sun Valley, CA, 91352
Providing Scenery Rentals and custom work to the Film and TV industry.
Delivery available.
chrisg@chrisg.tv * www.chrisg.tv

depict   **(323) 222-1001**
1460 Naud St, Los Angeles, CA, 90012
info@depict33.com * www.depict33.com

Hollywood Elevators/ Red Truck INC   **(562) 896-6070**
4707 Exposition Blvd, Los Angeles, CA, 90016
redtruck321@sbcglobal.net * hollywoodelevators.com

IDF Studio Scenery   **(818) 982-7433**
6844 Lankershim Blvd, North Hollywood, CA, 91605
Extensive rental inventory of set walls, windows, doors, fireplaces, etc.
info@idfstudioscenery.com * www.idfstudioscenery.com

LCW Props   **(818) 243-0707**
Backdrops, Some Set Walls

Merritt Productions, Inc.   **(818) 760-0612**
10845 Vanowen St, North Hollywood, CA, 91605
specialty props, miniatures, sculpture, mech effects, set const.
www.merrittproductions.com

NBCUniversal Television Asset Center   **(818) 777-5163**
11625 Hart St, N Hollywood, CA, 91605
Hundreds of complete sets and open stock pieces available for rent from our expanding inventory.
nbcutvassetcenter.com

Schmidli Backdrops LA   **(323) 938-2098**
5830 W Adams Blvd, Culver City, CA, 90232
Providing hand painted Textured and Scenic backdrops to the commercial, film, and fashion industry for over 20 years.
backdrops@schmidli.com * www.schmidli.com

Tractor Vision Scenery & Rentals   **(323) 235-2885**
340 E Jefferson Blvd, Los Angeles, CA, 90011
Specializing in entertainment, trade shows, & events, we bring your projects to life with precision, speed & personality
sets@tractorvision.com * www.tractorvision.com

Warner Bros. Studios Scenic Art & Sign Shop   **(818) 954-1815**
4000 Warner Blvd Bldg 44, Burbank, CA, 91522
hand-painted art to grand-format digital printing for backings, billboards, murals and portraits
wbsigns@warnerbros.com * www.wbsignandscenic.com

Scenery/Set Storage

Bill Ferrell Co.   **(818) 767-1900**
10556 Keswick St, Sun Valley, CA, 91352
www.billferrell.com

Centerline Scenery   **(818) 252-7467**
8238 Lankershim Blvd, N Hollywood, CA, 91605
meredyth@centerlinescenery.com

depict   **(323) 222-1001**
1460 Naud St, Los Angeles, CA, 90012
info@depict33.com * www.depict33.com

Scenic Expressions   **(818) 409-3354**
8238 Lankershim Blvd, N Hollywood, CA, 91605
mark@scenicexpressions.com * www.scenicexpressions.com

Scenic Highlights   **(818) 252-7760**
10830 Cantara St, Sun Valley, CA, 91352
scenichighlights.com

Tractor Vision Scenery & Rentals   **(323) 235-2885**
340 E Jefferson Blvd, Los Angeles, CA, 90011
Specializing in entertainment, trade shows, & events, we bring your projects to life with precision, speed & personality
sets@tractorvision.com * www.tractorvision.com

Western Studio Service, Inc.   **(818) 842-9272**
4561 Colorado Blvd, Los Angeles, CA, 90039
Full service set storage using union crews to properly store stock sets and set dec. safely & securely.
www.westernstudioservice.com

Scenic Artists

See Also: Backings* Guilds, Unions, Societies, Associations

Tractor Vision Scenery & Rentals   **(323) 235-2885**
340 E Jefferson Blvd, Los Angeles, CA, 90011
Specializing in entertainment, trade shows, & events, we bring your projects to life with precision, speed & personality
sets@tractorvision.com * www.tractorvision.com

Warner Bros. Studios Scenic Art & Sign Shop   **(818) 954-1815**
4000 Warner Blvd Bldg 44, Burbank, CA, 91522
hand-painted art to grand-format digital printing for backings, billboards, murals and portraits
wbsigns@warnerbros.com * www.wbsignandscenic.com

School Lockers

See: Lockers

School Supplies, Desks & Dressing

See Also: Bulletin Boards* Chalk Boards* Lockers* Playground Equipment

Advanced Liquidators Office Furniture   **(818) 763-3470**
Large sel. used tanker desks, lockers, package deals available.

Alley Cats Studio Rentals   **(818) 982-9178**
student desks, school desks, student lockers, school lockers

Art By Kidz   **(818) 625-1477**
Call for Appt, Glendale, CA, 91207
100s of ORIGINAL CHILDRENS 2D & 3D ARTWORKS for rent at low flat rates based on size. Cleared copyright, located in Glendale.
artbykidz@gmail.com * www.artbykidz.com

E.C. Prop Rentals   **(818) 764-2008**
hallway, shop, gym & locker room dressing

The Hand Prop Room LP.   **(323) 931-1534**
period-present dressing

History For Hire, Inc.   **(818) 765-7767**
supplies & dressing

Lakeshore Learning Materials   **(310) 559-9630**
8888 Venice Blvd, Los Angeles, CA, 90034
toys, furniture, school supplies
www.lakeshorelearning.com

LCW Props   **(818) 243-0707**
School Desks, Chairs, Science Projects, Chalk & White Boards

On Set Graphics   **(661) 233-6786**
Web Based Business
100% cleared kids artwork, school tests, college flyers, and more.
info@onsetgraphics.com * www.onsetgraphics.com

Prop Services West   **(818) 503-2790**

RJR Props   **(404) 349-7600**
School props and dressing for rent

Universal Studios Property & Hardware Dept   **(818) 777-2784**
School lockers, desks, maps, flags and more for rent.

Warner Bros. Studios Property Department   **(818) 954-2181**
School chairs, blackboards, school lockers, cubbies, school desks & desk dressing, kids toys and art supplies en masse.

ZEdonk ART   **(818) 693-1082**
5330 Derry Ave Ste P, Agoura Hills, CA, 91301
ZEdonk ART has over 5000 pieces of cleared school aged artwork, reports & projects, a decorator's dream!
kelly@zedonkart.com * www.ZEdonkART.com

Science Equipment

See Also: Lab Equipment

Dapper Cadaver   **(818) 771-0818**
Period to modern. Specimen jars, fossils & dinosaurs. Lab equipment, instruments & medical props.

E.C. Prop Rentals   **(818) 764-2008**
lots of stainless shapes, racks, tables, cabinets, lights, smalls

The Hand Prop Room LP.   **(323) 931-1534**
lab glassware

History For Hire, Inc.   **(818) 765-7767**
vintage

Jadis   **(310) 396-3477**
2701 Main St, Santa Monica, CA, 90405
Period laboratory dressing, Tesla coils, vintage quack medical and optical equipment.
jadis1@gmail.com * www.jadisprops.com

LCW Props   **(818) 243-0707**
Glassware, Test Equipment, DNA, Analyzers, Microscopes, Instrumentation

Lynn Harding Antique Instruments   **(805) 646-0204**
103 W Aliso St, Ojai, CA, 93023
lab, medical, pharmacy, nautical, surveyor, models, planetarium, natural history

McBain Systems   **(805) 581-6800**
1650 Voyager Ave, Simi Valley, CA, 93063
Rentals of All Types of Microscopes, Histology, Imaging and other Scientific Lab Equipment
sales@mcbainsystems.com * www.mcbainsystems.com

Modern Props   **(323) 934-3000**
Science equipment; contemporary/futuristic-beakers to microscopes, petri dishes, glass jars, vials, vial holders, more

The Rational Past   **(310) 476-6277**
By Appointment, West Los Angeles, CA
Authentic science, industrial, technical antiques & collectibles. Many professions & eras represented. See web site.
info@therationalpast.com * www.therationalpast.com

Universal Studios Property & Hardware Dept   **(818) 777-2784**
Science equipment and science props for rent.

Science Fiction

See: Aliens* Costumes* Fantasy Props, Costumes, or Decorations* Futuristic Furniture, Props, Decorations* Goth/Punk/Bondage/Fetish/Erotica Etc.* Prop Design & Manufacturing* Space Shuttle/Space Hardware* Space Suits* Spaceship Computer Panel* Special Effects, Electronic* Special Effects, Equipment & Supplies* Special Effects, Make-up/Prosthetics

Sconces

See: Lamps* Light Fixtures

Scoreboards & Scoring Systems

See Also: Clocks, Analog & Residential* Game Show Electronics & Equipment

Athletic Room   **(818) 764-9801**
12750 Raymer St, N Hollywood, CA, 91605
Sports scoreboards, vintage football scoreboards, golf scoreboards, electronic basketball scoreboards
athleticroom@mac.com * www.athleticroomprops.net

CBS Electronics   **(323) 575-2645**
7800 Beverly Blvd Rm M162, Los Angeles, CA, 90036
Custom electronics only.

E.C. Prop Rentals   **(818) 764-2008**
Practical working wall-mounted indoor basketball scoreboard

L. A. Party Works   **(888) 527-2789**
9712 Alpaca St, S El Monte, CA, 91733
Working shot clocks, working scoreboards, working timing devices and more.
partyworks@aol.com * www.partyworksinteractive.com

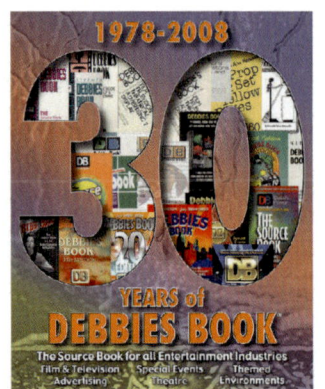

SCOREBOARDS & SHOTCLOCKS
FOR ALL SPORTS & EVENTS
CALL TODAY 888-527-2789

LCW Props   **(818) 243-0707**
Working Scoreboards, Just About Any Sport

Modern Props   **(323) 934-3000**
8' long scoreboards and 12' long scoreboards, for set dressing only.

RC Vintage, Inc.   **(818) 765-7107**
Basketball, and Baseball, shot clocks, full display score boards, electrical scoreboards

Scrapbooks

See Also: Hobby & Craft Supplies* Prop Houses

The Hand Prop Room LP.   **(323) 931-1534**
will fabricate

History For Hire, Inc.   **(818) 765-7767**
outfitted & empty

Kater-Crafts Bookbinders   **(562) 692-0665**
4860 Gregg Rd, Pico Rivera, CA, 90660
Custom work. Scrapbooks, albums, portfolios, binders, journals, foil stamping.
sales@katercrafts.com * www.katercrafts.com

Universal Studios Property & Hardware Dept   **(818) 777-2784**
Prop scrapbooks for rent.

Screens, Folding

Badia Design, Inc.   **(818) 762-0130**
5420 Vineland Ave, N Hollywood, CA, 91601
info@badiadesign.com * www.badiadesign.com

Bridge Furniture & Props Los Angeles   **(818) 433-7100**
We carry modern & traditional furniture, lighting, accessories, art, & rugs. Items are online for easy shopping.

Modern Props   **(323) 934-3000**
Chinese folding screens, Deco folding screens, futuristic folding screens & more

Ob-jects   **(818) 351-4200**
Folding screens; antique, contemporary

Omega/Cinema Props   **(323) 466-8201**

Prop Services West   **(818) 503-2790**

Sony Pictures Studios-Prop House (Off Lot)   **(310) 244-5999**
divider screens, dressing screens, hanging panels, medical screens, paneled screens, Oriental screens, decorative screens

Universal Studios Property & Hardware Dept   **(818) 777-2784**
Various prop folding screens for rent.

Warner Bros. Studios Property Department   **(818) 954-2181**
1 Panel Screens, 2 Panel Screens, 3 Panel Screens, Asian screens, Moroccan screens, rolling screens

ZG04 DECOR   **(818) 853-8040**

Scuba & Wetsuits

See: Wetsuits, Diving/Surfing

30 years of Debbies Book…whew!
From 1977 to 2009 who would of guessed that we would be the 'go to resource for the odd and unusual for over 30 years. Since our original internet database was put into place in 1997 and therefore designed for dial up, it became apparent it was time to upgrade. We were also getting closer (along with our programmers) to making the move to putting the book on the Internet full time. This would make Debbies Book an online source book with the capability of making changes for our users on a regular basis, guaranteeing accuracy.

1978-2008
30 YEARS of DEBBIES BOOK
The Source Book for all Entertainment Industries
Film & Television * Special Events * Themed
Advertising * Theatre * Environments

2008 40 YEARS OF DEBBIES BOOK

Sculpture

See Also: Art For Rent (Cleared Art) Art, Artists For Hire* Balloons &
Balloon Sculptures* Carved Figures* Decorative Accessories* Ice
Sculpture* Mold Making* Prop Design & Manufacturing* Statuary*

ART PIC (818) 503-5999
6826 Troost Ave, N Hollywood, CA, 91605
Contemporary Art Rental and Sales. All mediums ALL ART CLEARED. Open
M-F 9-5. We ship worldwide.
artpicla@mac.com * www.artpic2000.com

Charisma Design Studio, Inc. (818) 252-6611
8414 San Fernando Road, Sun Valley, CA, 91352
metal/glass/wood/stone, esthetic & functional
info@charismadesign.com * www.charismadesign.com

Clearedart.com/El Studio Granados (818) 240-4421
958 Verdugo Circle Dr, Glendale, CA, 91206
Multi-media sculptures and carvings in many styles and mediums,
works-in-progress
fineart@elstudiogranados.com * www.clearedart.com

Cope Studios: The Haven (818) 913-7187
926 Western Ave Ste A & B, Glendale, CA, 91201
Our studio creates high end realistic figurative sculpture for purchase or rental.
figurativesculptor@hotmail.com * www.copestudios.com

DeRouchey Foam (888) 959-4852
13618 Vaughn Street, San Fernando, CA, 91340
We offer a full line of foam sculpting materials and services. Urethane, EPS,
HardCoat, Foam Adhesive. 24/7 Service.
info@derofoam.com * www.derofoam.com

Designers Views (323) 463-1818
1028 N La Brea Ave, W Hollywood, CA, 90038
Botanical sculptures and organic art sculptures
info@designersviews.com * www.designersviews.com

Doug Rowell, Sculptor (818) 353-4607
Call for appt, Tujunga, CA, 91042
Wood, foam, metal, custom only, design/fabrication/any size job
doug@carverdoug.com * www.carverdoug.com

FILM ART LA (323) 461-4900
Culver City Warehouse at Jefferson & Hauser. Call for address.
Small & Large Sculpture. Cleared Art spans 16th century to Contemporary. We
custom print to all sizes. Ship worldwide.
filmartla@gmail.com * www.filmartla.com

The Hand Prop Room LP. (323) 931-1534
art pcs, theme, busts

KIHL STUDIOS (818) 812-9594
9701 Owensmouth Ave Unit 1, Chatsworth, CA, 91311
Original dimensional artwork and decor created by sculptor and designer
Brandon Kihl.
design@kihlstudios.com * www.kihlstudios.com

Merritt Productions, Inc. (818) 760-0612
10845 Vanowen St, North Hollywood, CA, 91605
specialty props, miniatures, sculpture, mech effects, set const.
www.merrittproductions.com

Modern Props (323) 934-3000
all periods of sculptures for rent

Ob-jects (818) 351-4200
Sculpture

Omega/Cinema Props (323) 466-8201

Prop Services West (818) 503-2790

Sculpture by Bruce Gray (323) 223-4059
688 South Avenue 21, Los Angeles, CA, 90031
standing sculptures, wall sculptures, abstract, figurative, modern art, kinetic art,
mobiles, rolling ball machines, rub
bruce@brucegray.com * www.brucegray.com

Sword & Stone (818) 562-6548
Sculpture and custom work available

Universal Studios Property & Hardware Dept (818) 777-2784
Many sculptures and fake sculptures for rent. Sculpture fabrication also
available.

Warner Bros. Studios Property Department (818) 954-2181
Animal sculptures, Black moor Sculptures, Bronze & wood Sculpture, Buddha
Sculpture, Eiffel Tower Sculpture

ZG04 DECOR (818) 853-8040
Bronzes, Steel, Wood Carvings & Stone Carvings

Seagrass Floor Covering

See: Carpet & Flooring

Search Tools, Directories, Libraries

Corbin Ball Associates (360) 734-8756
506 14th St, Bellingham, WA, 98225
Hosts web's most comprehensive site about meeting planning and events
technology
www.corbinball.com

Directory of Major Malls (800) 898-MALL
P.O. Box 837, Nyack, NY, 10960
Details, contacts, tenants lists for the major shopping centers and malls in the
US and Canada.
www.ShoppingCenters.com

Entertainment Resources & Marketing Association (310) 452-0426
2315 28th Street Ste 204, Santa Monica, CA, 90405
ERMA is an association of marketing, product placement, and brand integration
professionals.
michael@erma.org * www.erma.org

The Internet Movie Database (206) 266-4064
web directory of movie/TV history, facts, news and also sales of DVDs, tickets,
showtimes & more
www.imdb.com

L. A. Public Library (213) 228-7000
630 W 5th St, Los Angeles, CA, 90071
Also, website has links to contact info for all neighborhood libraries
www.lapl.org

Library of Congress (202) 707-5000
101 Independence Ave SE Washington, DC 20540
Phone # is for general information
www.loc.gov

New York Production Guide (203) 299-1330
50 Washington St Ste 703, South Norwalk, CT, 06854
best New York area production resource reference
www.nypg.com

ProductionHUB.com (877) 629-4122
Web Based Business
Guide, directory and jobs for film and video
www.productionhub.com

Productionville SF (415) 531-3019
Web Based Business
Best Northern California resource for Film & Video, Photography, & Experential
marketing production.
www.productionvillesf.com

Thomas Industrial Network (800) 699-9822
5 Penn Plaza, New York, NY, 10001
Web directory of 1000s of manufacturers
www.thomasnet.com

Variety 411 (646) 359-5571
11175 Santa Monica Blvd Ste 8, Los Angeles, CA, 90025
resources for preproduction & postproduction. LA411 (So. California) & NY411
(NYC region)
411update@variety.com * http://variety411.com

Visual Profile Books (212) 279-7000 ex 319
389 5th Avenue Ste 1105, New York City, NY, 10016
from outside U.S., call (212) 279-7000. Books on Interior Design, Architecture,
Visual Merchandising
www.visualprofilebooks.com

World Wide Arts Resources (646) 455-1425
PO Box 150, Granville, OH, 43023
Art marketplace, art news & research, links to art museums & galleries
worldwide
help@absolutearts.com * www.absolutearts.com

Searchlights/Skytrackers, Architectural Lights

See: Special Effects, Lighting & Lasers

Seashells

See Also: Nautical Dressing & Props* Tikis & Tropical Dressing

Alley Cats Studio Rentals (818) 982-9178
large selection

The Hand Prop Room LP. (323) 931-1534

History For Hire, Inc. (818) 765-7767

Oceanic Arts (562) 698-6960
shells, pufferfish, fish nets & related items

Omega/Cinema Props (323) 466-8201

Prop Services West (818) 503-2790

Universal Studios Property & Hardware Dept (818) 777-2784
Prop seashells and natural seashells for rent.

Seating

See: Audience Seating* Benches* Chairs* Theater Seating

Security Devices or Services

See Also: Metal Detectors* Police Equipment* Private Investigations* Security Walk-Through & Baggage Alarms* Surveillance Equipment

Andrews International (818) 487-4060
455 N. Moss St. Burbank, CA 91502
Full service security company specializing in the Entertainment Industry.
www.andrewsinternational.com
LCW Props (818) 243-0707
Wide Selection, Homeland Security, High Tech Devices Of All Kinds

Security Fencing

See: Fences

Security Walk-Through & Baggage Alarms

AIR Designs (818) 768-6639
Walk-Through & Baggage Security Detectors
E.C. Prop Rentals (818) 764-2008
Walk-through security metal detectors
LCW Props (818) 243-0707
Large Selection Of Walk Through Metal Detectors. Beautiful Baggage X-Ray Machines
Modern Props (323) 934-3000
security walk-through, baggage alarms, metal detectors, baggage X-ray/conveyor & more

Seismic Equipment

See: Lab Equipment

Septic Tank Pumping

See: Sanitation, Waste Disposal

Serving Tables & Serving Carts

AIR Designs (818) 768-6639
Hot & Cold, Many Sizes/Types
Lennie Marvin Enterprises, Inc. (Prop Heaven) (818) 841-5882
Serving tables and serving carts

Set Boxes & Taco Carts (Propmaster & Set)

Backstage Studio Equipment (818) 504-6026
8052 Lankershim Blvd, N Hollywood, CA, 91605
taco carts, magliners, set boxes, all kinds of carts & dollies
www.backstageweb.com
Universal Studios Property & Hardware Dept (818) 777-2784
Set boxes of various sizes and types for rent.

Set Construction

See: Scenery/Set Construction* Scenic Artists

Sewing Equipment & Workrooms

Jaeil, Inc. (818) 577-8280
12106 Sherman Way, N Hollywood, CA, 91605
Costume workroom

Sewing Machines

History For Hire, Inc. (818) 765-7767
Sewing machines & spinning wheels
Kato's Sewing Machine Co. (213) 626-6026
604 E 1st St, Los Angeles, CA, 90012
Commercial/domestic sales/repair, by appt. only
alvinkato@yahoo.com
Old N Country Prop Shop, LLC (818) 423-2599
Many different antique and vintage sewing machines, sewing tables, and an assortment sewing equipment.
Omega/Cinema Props (323) 466-8201
Antique and modern sewing machines.
Universal Studios Property & Hardware Dept (818) 777-2784
Many sewing machines from all time periods for rent.
Weaver Leather (800) 932-8371
PO Box 68, Mt Hope, OH, 44660-0068
catalog sales; leather, leather working tools, machinery. leather working
www.weaverleather.com

Sewing Services, Industrial

See: Tarps, Covers, Custom Sewing

Sewing Supplies

See: Costume/Wardrobe/Sewing Supplies

Shackles

The Hand Prop Room LP. (323) 931-1534
fake, real, rigged, custom mfg.
History For Hire, Inc. (818) 765-7767
real, fake, rigged
LCW Props (818) 243-0707
Handcuffs, Iron Shackles
Sword & Stone (818) 562-6548
ball & chain, shackles, dungeon dressing
Universal Studios Property & Hardware Dept (818) 777-2784
Prop shackles of different time periods for rent.

Shark Diving Cage

See: Nautical Dressing & Props

Shaving, Old Fashion, Non-Electric

The Hand Prop Room LP. (323) 931-1534
History For Hire, Inc. (818) 765-7767
vintage

Sheet Music

See: Music, Sheet

Shelving

See: Display Cases, Racks & Fixtures (Store)* Store Shelf Units & Shelving* Warehouse Dressing

Ship Models

See: Model Ships/Planes/Trains/Autos Etc.

Ship Wheels

See: Nautical Dressing & Props

Shipping

See: Packing/Packaging Supplies, Services* Transportation, Trucking and/or Storage

Shipping Supplies

See: Boxes* Expendables* Packing/Packaging Supplies, Services* Transportation, Trucking and/or Storage

Shoe Boxes

History For Hire, Inc. (818) 765-7767
big selection
Universal Studios Property & Hardware Dept (818) 777-2784
Prop shoe boxes for rent from different time periods.

Shoe Lifts, Men's

See: Shoes, Boots & Footwear

Shoe Shine Boxes, Chairs & Stands

AIR Designs (818) 768-6639
Open & Covered Units, Period to Present, Vending & Buffing Machine
C. P. Two (323) 466-8201
Shoe shine stands, shoe shine boxes
The Hand Prop Room LP. (323) 931-1534
period
History For Hire, Inc. (818) 765-7767
RC Vintage, Inc. (818) 765-7107
Period shoe shine stations, shoe shine signs
Universal Studios Property & Hardware Dept (818) 777-2784
Prop shoe polish, shoe shine brushes, shoe shine kits, shoe shine stands and shoe shine boxes for rent.
Warner Bros. Studios Property Department (818) 954-2181

Shoe Store

See Also: Cash Registers* Counters* Credit Card Imprint Machine* Shoe Boxes* Shoes, Boots & Footwear* Shopping Bags (Silent)

Acme Display Fixture & Packaging   (888) 411-1870
3829 S Broadway St, Los Angeles, CA, 90037
Complete store setups: garment racks, displays/display cases, counters, packaging, shelving, hangers, mannequins
sales@acmedisplay.com * www.acmedisplay.com
History For Hire, Inc.   (818) 765-7767
Lennie Marvin Enterprises, Inc. (Prop Heaven)   (818) 841-5882
product, signage, fitting stools, Brannock device & displays
Universal Studios Property & Hardware Dept   (818) 777-2784
Shoe display stands, shoe forms, decorative shoe display boxes, shoe display feet and mannequin shoe stands for rent.

Shoe Stretchers

See: Shoes, Boots & Footwear

Shoes, Boots & Footwear

See Also: Military Surplus/Combat Clothes, Field Gear* Sportswear* Uniforms, Military* Uniforms, Trades/Professional/Sports* Western Wear

American Duchess Inc.   (775) 238-3674
Web Based Business
American Duchess offers fine ladies' historically accurate reproduction shoes & accessories based on original examples.
info@americanduchess.com * www.americanduchess.com

AMERICAN DUCHESS
HISTORICAL FOOTWEAR

Birkenstock USA, LP   (415) 884-3315
8171 Redwood Blvd, Novato, CA, 94945
product placement: ask for "PR"
www.birkenstockusa.com
CBS Costume Rental   (323) 575-2666
modern M/F, also 1880s western M/F, boots
Champion Dance Shoes   (323) 874-8704
3383 Barham Blvd, Los Angeles, CA, 90068
shoes for ballroom, ballet, swing, Latin, salsa, jazz, tango, tap
www.championdanceshoes.net
The Costume House   (818) 508-9933
repro lace-up 1890s woman's boots up to size 11 & men's knee-high boots
Early Halloween   (212) 691-2933
130 West 25th St, 11th Floor, New York, NY, 10001
vintage 1900-1970
www.earlyhalloween.com

Eastern Costume   (818) 982-3611
Full-service costume house, formal, casual, uniform, 1920's to present, military, police, civilian footwear
E.C. Prop Rentals   (818) 764-2008
rubber boots & boot racks
Glamour Uniform Shop   (323) 666-2122
4951 W. Sunset Blvd, Los Angeles, CA, 90027
nurses, restaurant, mechanics, maids uniforms
History For Hire, Inc.   (818) 765-7767
wooden shoes, shoe stretchers, for dressing
My Professional Uniforms   (818) 242-3404
1102 E Colorado St, Glendale, CA, 91205
nursing
www.myprofessionaluniforms.com
Re-Mix Vintage Shoes   (323) 936-6210
7384 Beverly Blvd, Los Angeles, CA, 90036
reproduction M/W styles, 30s to 70s, also unused deadstock
www.remixvintageshoes.com
Royal Vintage Shoes LLC   (775) 376-5845
Web Based Business
Vintage style shoes from the 1920s, 1930s, and 1940s chosen for their retro styling.
info@royalvintageshoes.com * www.RoyalVintageShoes.com

Royal Vintage SHOES
FOR WOMEN WHO INSIST ON VINTAGE STYLES—
ROYALVINTAGESHOES.COM

Screaming Mimi's   (212) 677-6464
240 West 14th St, New York NY, 10011
vintage clothing for men & women 1940s - 1980s
www.screamingmimis.com
Sony Pictures Studios-Wardrobe   (310) 244-5995
alterations, call (310) 244-7260. variety of styles/periods shoes/boots
Universal Studios Costume Dept   (818) 777-2722
Rental, mfg., & alterations
Warner Bros. Studios Costume Dept   (818) 954-1297
High Heels, Flats, Sneakers, Saddle Shoes, Open Toed, Sling Backs, Wedges, Business, Loafers, Boots
Western Costume Co.   (818) 760-0900
Willie's Shoe Service   (323) 463-5011
1174 S La Brea Ave, Los Angeles, CA, 90019
shoe lifts, shoe stretchers, shoe repairing & dyeing, shoe shines & custom-made shoes
www.williesshoeservice.com

Shoji Screens

See Also: Asian Antiques, Furniture, Art & Artifacts

L. A. Shoji & Decorative Products Inc.   (323) 732-9161
4848 W Jefferson Blvd, Los Angeles, CA, 90016
www.lashoji.com
Warner Bros. Studios Property Department   (818) 954-2181
tatami mats

Shopping Bags (Silent)

The Hand Prop Room LP.	(323) 931-1534

Shopping Carts

AIR Designs	(818) 768-6639
Large Quantity Carts, Corrals, Signage, Chrome & Plastic	
E.C. Prop Rentals	(818) 764-2008
assorted generic for alleyway	
History For Hire, Inc.	(818) 765-7767
old-style	
LCW Props	(818) 243-0707
Plastic, Metal, bag Lady, Debris, Recyclables	
Universal Studios Property & Hardware Dept	(818) 777-2784
Prop shopping carts of various kinds for rent.	

Shower Doors

See: Glass & Mirrors

Shower Trailers

See: Production Vehicles/Trailers

Showers

See: Bathroom Fixtures* Production Vehicles/Trailers

Shutters

See: Window Treatments

Sidewalk Dressing

See: Alarms* Alley Dressing* Bag Lady Carts* Billboards & Billboard Lights* Bus Shelter* Fences* Guard Shacks* Kiosks* Lamp Posts & Street Lights* Mailboxes* Marquees* Parking Meters & Sign Poles* Sandwich Board Store Sign* Signs* Steel Folding Gates & Roll-Up Doors* Street Dressing* Telephone Poles Prop* Traffic/Road Signs, Lights, Safety Items* Vendor Carts & Concession Counters

Sign Painters

Collins Visual Media	(818) 686-6581

10518 Johanna Ave, Shadow Hills, CA, 91040
Our fast and versatile sign painters are in fact old masters who can create any period look or design that you want.
www.collinsvisualmedia.com

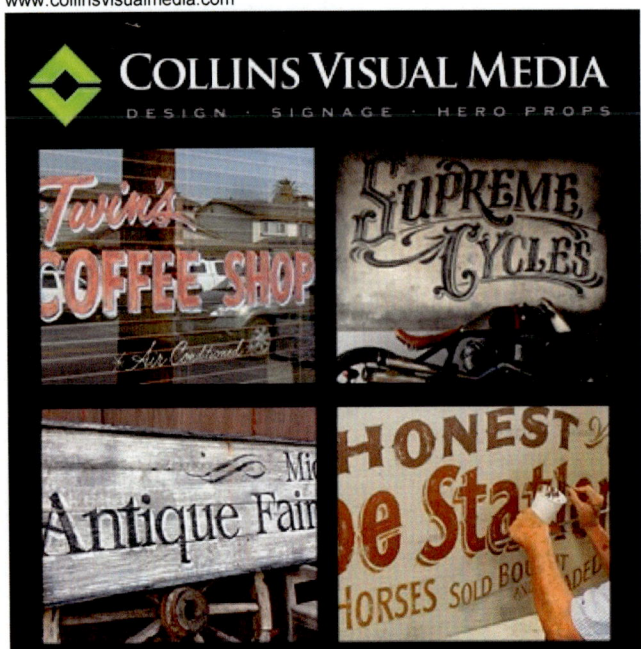

Warner Bros. Studios Scenic Art & Sign Shop	(818) 954-1815

4000 Warner Blvd Bldg 44, Burbank, CA, 91522
graphic design and production studio for signs & scenic art; digital printing to hand-painted
wbsigns@warnerbros.com * www.wbsignandscenic.com

Sign Posts

AIR Designs	(818) 768-6639
4' to 10' Multiples	
Alley Cats Studio Rentals	(818) 982-9178
metal, wood, self-standing, menu boards, traffic light poles	
Collins Visual Media	(818) 686-6581

10518 Johanna Ave, Shadow Hills, CA, 91040
Posts for road signs, real estate hanging displays or large sign panels; we can provide what you need.
www.collinsvisualmedia.com

E.C. Prop Rentals	(818) 764-2008
good multiples, various heights w/bases	

Signals

See: Nautical Dressing & Props* Traffic/Road Signs, Lights, Safety Items

Signs

See Also: Engraving* Flags/Banners* Printing, Graphics, Digital & Large Format* Laminating & Mounting* Lighting, LED, Fiber Optic & Specialty* Neon Lights & Signs* On-Air Signs* Paintings/Prints* Parking Meters & Sign Poles* Pub Signs* Read-outs* Sandwich Board Store Sign* Sign Painters* Signs, Foreign* Street Dressing, Exterior Signs* Traffic/Road Signs, Lights, Safety Items

AIR Designs	(818) 768-6639
Restaurant, Diner, Coffee Shop, Traffic, Directional, Period, Neon	
Alley Cats Studio Rentals	(818) 982-9178
street, hwy, gas station, produce, construction, hotel neon, coast signs, bus stop, bench ads, menu boards, men working etc	
American Sign Museum	(513) 541-6366

1330 Monmouth Ave, Cincinnati, OH, 45225
Most of our signs are electric, incandescent to neon. Some still new in the box. Goldleaf signs from the 1890s to 1910.
info@americansignmuseum.org * www.americansignmuseum.org

Artery Props	(877) 732-7733

7684 Clybourn Ave 2nd Floor Unit C, Sun Valley, CA, 91352
100% cleared & owned artwork: banners, lawn signs, mic flags, signs, flyers, posters, CDs, DVDs, albums, stickers & more
info@arteryprops.com * www.arteryprops.com

Beyond Image Graphics (818) 547-0899
1853 Dana St, Glendale, CA, 91201
Dimensional Signage, Custom Die-Cut Standees, Die Cut Standees, Backlit prints
rafi@beyondimagegraphics.com * www.beyondimagegraphics.com

Big Apple Visual Group (212) 629-3650
247 West 35th St, New York, NY, 10001
24-hour rush service available
www.bigapplegroup.com

Charisma Design Studio, Inc. (818) 252-6611
8414 San Fernando Road, Sun Valley, CA, 91352
high-end artistic metal/plastic/glass/neon/wood/stone
info@charismadesign.com * www.charismadesign.com

Collins Visual Media (818) 686-6581
10518 Johanna Ave, Shadow Hills, CA, 91040
130 years combined experience in sign painting, printing & creating any type of signage! Complete, custom versatility.
www.collinsvisualmedia.com

D'ziner Sign Co. (323) 467-4467
801 Seward Street, Los Angeles, CA, 90038
2000 fonts, symbols, aging, banners
sales@dzinersign.com * www.dzinersign.com

E.C. Prop Rentals (818) 764-2008
street, loading dock, warehouse, factory, military, lab, automotive, exit, no smoking

The Hand Prop Room LP. (323) 931-1534
neon, custom design

LISTINGS FOR THIS CATEGORY CONTINUE ON THE FOLLOWING PAGE

Heaven or Las Vegas Neon (818) 949-2677
7740 Lemona Ave, Van Nuys, CA, 91405
Thousands of neon signs & neon props. Custom mfg, install, strike & delivery services. CA Electric Sign Lic#931962
mail@rentneon.com * www.rentneon.com

History For Hire, Inc. (818) 765-7767
JP Graphics Design+Print (747) 230-6840
5354 Denny Ave, N Hollywood, CA, 91601
We Produce a Variety of Signage For all of Your Set Dressing Needs.
signs@jp-dp.com * www.jp-dp.com
LCW Props (818) 243-0707
Neon, Lighting Signs, Traffic, Lab, Medical, Foreign - Chinese, Arabic, German, Airport, Lots Of Others Too...
Metromedia Technologies (800) 999-4668
370 Amapola Ave, Torrance, CA, 90501
Outdoor signage
www.mmt.com
Nights of Neon (818) 756-4791
13815 Saticoy St, Van Nuys, CA, 91402
over 2,000 neon props in stock. neon, wood, foam, vinyl, sheet metal, computer table router, marquees & more
contact@nightsofneon.com * www.nightsofneon.com
RC Vintage, Inc. (818) 765-7107
signs & sign poles Highway Signs. Neon signs and A frame signs
Sign Comm (213) 383-2111
3214 Beverly Blvd, Los Angeles, CA, 90057
signs, banners, digital printing
http://signcomminc.com

Sony Pictures Studios-Prop House (Off Lot) (310) 244-5999
A-Frames, advertisement signage, airport signs, award signs, bulletin board signs, caution signs, certificates, more
Tractor Vision Scenery & Rentals (323) 235-2885
340 E Jefferson Blvd, Los Angeles, CA, 90011
Specializing in entertainment, trade shows, & events, we bring your projects to life with precision, speed & personality
sets@tractorvision.com * www.tractorvision.com
Universal Studios Graphic Design & Sign Shop (818) 777-2350
specialty prop signage, design, large fmt printing up to 100" wide
Universal Studios Property & Hardware Dept (818) 777-2784
Many signs for rent as well as sign fabrication.
Warner Bros. Studios Scenic Art & Sign Shop (818) 954-1815
4000 Warner Blvd Bldg 44, Burbank, CA, 91522
graphic design and production studio for signs & scenic art; digital printing - hand-painted; sign printing & graphics
wbsigns@warnerbros.com * www.wbsignandscenic.com
WestOn Letters (818) 503-9472
7259 N Atoll Ave, N Hollywood, CA, 91605
Serving the signage needs of the entertainment industry since the 1960s
sales@westonletters.com * www.WestonLetters.com

Serving the signage needs of the
entertainment industry since the 1960s
Custom Cut Acrylic Letters – SAME DAY
Thousands of letters IN STOCK
3D Letters – Foam, Plastic, Metal, etc
Changeable Letters, Marquee Letters
Large Format Digital Printing, Banners
Imitation Metal Plaques
All types of interior signs

Worlds of Wow (817) 380-4215
1800 Shady Oaks Drive, Denton, TX, 76205
Monument Signs and Custom 3D Signage - foam designed, hard-coated, painted, and finished signs.
www.worldsofwow.com
ZEdonk ART (818) 693-1082
5330 Derry Ave Ste P, Agoura Hills, CA, 91301
ZEdonk ART is the premier, one-stop shop for hand-painted, handcrafted signs, felt banners & printed graphic posters.
kelly@zedonkart.com * www.ZEdonkART.com

Signs, Foreign

Collins Visual Media (818) 686-6581
10518 Johanna Ave, Shadow Hills, CA, 91040
Any country, language or period, we design and create signage with valid and verifiable translations.
www.collinsvisualmedia.com

D'ziner Sign Co. (323) 467-4467
801 Seward Street, Los Angeles, CA, 90038
9 languages, any material, aging
sales@dzinersign.com * www.dzinersign.com

E.C. Prop Rentals (818) 764-2008
Chinese, Spanish, European road signage

Universal Studios Property & Hardware Dept (818) 777-2784
Many signs available for different countries for rent.

Silk Screening

See: Embroidery, Screen Printing, Etc. Fabric Dyeing/Tie Dyeing/Painting/Aging*

Silverware, Silver Serving Pieces

See Also: Prop Houses Tableware/Flatware*

Badia Design, Inc. (818) 762-0130
5420 Vineland Ave, N Hollywood, CA, 91601
info@badiadesign.com * www.badiadesign.com

The Hand Prop Room LP. (323) 931-1534
period-present, incredible collection

History For Hire, Inc. (818) 765-7767

LCW Props (818) 243-0707
Period - Present

Omega/Cinema Props (323) 466-8201

Prop Services West (818) 503-2790

Sony Pictures Studios-Prop House (Off Lot) (310) 244-5999
Assorted flatware, butter knife, dinner knife, salad fork, dessert fork, silver sets, silver flatware sets, soup spoons and more

Universal Studios Property & Hardware Dept (818) 777-2784
Large selection of silver and silverware for rent.

ZG04 DECOR (818) 853-8040

Single/Double Drop Trailers

See: Production Vehicles/Trailers

Sinks

Alley Cats Studio Rentals (818) 982-9178
period ceramic pedestal styles, metal janitor sink, stainless steel, prison toilet sink combo, fountain sink

E.C. Prop Rentals (818) 764-2008
Stainless steel lab, wash fountain sinks, utility/work sinks

LCW Props (818) 243-0707
Pedestal Sinks, Kitchen, Bathroom

Modern Props (323) 934-3000
modern, hi-tech, stainless steel sinks/prop sinks

Universal Studios Property & Hardware Dept (818) 777-2784
Prop sinks for rent.

Studio Plumbing Rentals (323) 829-9339
7373 Atoll Ave, N Hollywood, CA, 91605
studioplumbingrentals@gmail.com * www.studioair.com

Siren Lights

E.C. Prop Rentals	**(818) 764-2008**
110v red/amber/green/blue/clear with mounts, also some 12 VDC	
History For Hire, Inc.	**(818) 765-7767**
LCW Props	**(818) 243-0707**
Sirens, Bells, Police Bars, Revolving Flashing Lights	

Sisal

See: Carpet & Flooring

Skate Ramps

See: Ramps: Skateboard, BMX, Freestyle, etc. Scenery/Set Construction*

Skeletons

See: Bones, Skulls & Skeletons Fossils*

Ski Equipment

See Also: Prop Houses Sporting Goods & Services*

C. P. Two	**(323) 466-8201**
Ski equipment for rent	
Doc's Ski Haus	**(310) 828-3492**
3101 Santa Monica Blvd, Santa Monica, CA, 90404	
pro shop, also fly fishing	
www.docskiandsports.com	
The Hand Prop Room LP.	**(323) 931-1534**
History For Hire, Inc.	**(818) 765-7767**
vintage	
Jackson Shrub Supply, Inc.	**(818) 982-0100**
Ski lift gondola	
LCW Props	**(818) 243-0707**
Skis, Snow Shoes, Boots & Mountain Gear	
Universal Studios Property & Hardware Dept	**(818) 777-2784**
All kinds of ski equipment and ski props for rent.	

Ski Machines

See: Exercise & Fitness Equipment

Skulls & Skeletons

See: Bones, Skulls & Skeletons Dinosaurs* Fossils* Taxidermy, Hides/Heads/Skeletons*

Sky Lights (Rooftop)

See: Rooftop Dressing Searchlights/Skytrackers, Architectural Lights*

Slates/Clapboards

C. P. Two	**(323) 466-8201**
The Hand Prop Room LP.	**(323) 931-1534**
History For Hire, Inc.	**(818) 765-7767**
period	
Hollywood Clapperboards	**(818) 275-7048**
Web based business.	
Custom clapperboards/clapboards	
hollywoodclapperboards.com	
Universal Studios Property & Hardware Dept	**(818) 777-2784**
Prop slates and prop clapboards for rent.	

Sleds

The Hand Prop Room LP.	**(323) 931-1534**
period-present, toboggans to horse drawn	
History For Hire, Inc.	**(818) 765-7767**
vintage	
LCW Props	**(818) 243-0707**
Dog Sled, 1-4 Man Sleds, Period - Present	
Universal Studios Property & Hardware Dept	**(818) 777-2784**
Prop sleds/prop snow sleds for rent.	

Sleepwear - Pajamas, Nightgowns, Etc.

CBS Costume Rental	**(323) 575-2666**
sexy soap opera lingerie, silk robes	
The Costume House	**(818) 508-9933**
pj's, nightgowns/baby dolls	
Sony Pictures Studios-Wardrobe	**(310) 244-5995**
alterations, call (310) 244-7260	
Universal Studios Costume Dept	**(818) 777-2722**
Rental, mfg., & alterations	
Western Costume Co.	**(818) 760-0900**

Sleighs

See Also: Carriages, Horse Drawn

FROST	**(310) 704-8812**
Call for Appointment - 21405 Madrona Ave, Torrance, CA, 90503	
Traditional full size Holiday Sleighs	
mdisplay@yahoo.com * www.frostchristmasprops.com	
Green Set, Inc.	**(818) 764-1231**
many Xmas/Santa, regular/oversize, w/reindeer	
The Hand Prop Room LP.	**(323) 931-1534**
Jackson Shrub Supply, Inc.	**(818) 982-0100**
Santa sleigh + more	
Universal Studios Property & Hardware Dept	**(818) 777-2784**
Snow sleighs, toboggans and Stanta sleighs for rent.	
Warner Bros. Studios Property Department	**(818) 954-2181**
Santa clause sleighs, wood sleighs	

Slipcovers

See: Events, Decorations, Supplies & Services Upholstery Materials/Services*

Slot Machines

See: Gambling Equipment

Smalls

See: Decorative Accessories Prop Houses*

Smoking Products

See Also: Marijuana Plants, Dispensary Dressing & Hydroponics

Badia Design, Inc. (818) 762-0130
5420 Vineland Ave, N Hollywood, CA, 91601
info@badiadesign.com * www.badiadesign.com

The Cigar Warehouse (818) 784-1391
15141 Ventura Blvd, Sherman Oaks, CA, 91403
large sel. cigars, cutters, pipes, tobacco, leather cases, humidors

The Hand Prop Room LP. (323) 931-1534

History For Hire, Inc. (818) 765-7767
vintage cigars, cigar boxes, cigarettes, tobacco, etc.

LCW Props (818) 243-0707
full cigar shop, humidors

RC Vintage, Inc. (818) 765-7107
40s, 50s & 60s Ashtrays

Snow Blankets

See: Greens

Snow Shoes

C. P. Two (323) 466-8201

Snow, Artificial & Real

See Also: Ice Sculpture Special Effects, Equipment & Supplies*

Carving Ice & Big on Snow (714) 224-1455
900 S Placentia Ave Ste B, Placentia, CA, 92870
You're the best at what you do & so are we. Carving Ice & Blowing Snow for the TV & film industries for over 20 years.
info@carvingice.com * www.carvingice.com

714-224-1455

CONFETTI & FOG FX Special Effects Company (877) 576-4239
1085 W 21st Pl, Hialeah, FL, 33010
Anything from a snowy pack shot in a studio to a winter landscape w/ falling snow & a light flurry to a severe blizzard.
Info@confettiandfogfx.com * www.caffx.com

EFX- Event Special Effects (626) 888-2239
125 Railroad Ave, Monrovia, CA, 91016
Snow Machines, Snow Blankets, Evaporative Snow, Real Snow
info@efxla.com * www.efxla.com

WWW.EFXLA.COM 626.888.2239

Green Set, Inc. (818) 764-1231
snow props, including snowballs, icicles, glacier ice walls

Jackson Shrub Supply, Inc. (818) 982-0100
snow blankets, plastic snowflakes

L. A. Party Works (888) 527-2789
9712 Alpaca St, S El Monte, CA, 91733
Snow machines, confetti cannons, cryo and much more.
partyworks@aol.com * www.partyworksinteractive.com

LCW Props (818) 243-0707
blowers and flake

Reliable Snow Service (661) 269-2093
3932 Sourdough Rd, Acton, CA, 93510
We make snow at your location and deliver ice from Santa Clarita North to Mojave!
meltheiceman@gmail.com * www.reliablesnowservice.com

Special Effects Unlimited, Inc. (323) 466-3361
1005 N Lillian Way, Hollywood, CA, 90038
buy it, or have us do the whole job (including cleanup)
www.specialeffectsunlimited.com

Snowboards

See: Ski Equipment* Sporting Goods & Services

Snowmobiles

See: Sporting Goods & Services

Soccer Goals & Balls

See: Sporting Goods & Services

Societies

See: Guilds, Unions, Societies, Associations

Soda Fountain Dressing

AIR Designs	**(818) 768-6639**
Complete Dressing, Dishes to Signage, Counters, Equipment	
C. P. Two	**(323) 466-8201**
Soda fountain signs and accessories, soda fountain dispensers, soda fountain machines.	
History For Hire, Inc.	**(818) 765-7767**
period soda fountain equipment, milk shake machines	
RC Vintage, Inc.	**(818) 765-7107**
40s, 50s & 60s Counters, Ice Cream Chairs, Freezers, Soda Jerks, Lemonade dispensers, etc	
Universal Studios Property & Hardware Dept	**(818) 777-2784**
Soda fountain dressing, soda dispensers, soda machines, soda fountain signs, soda fountains and more for rent.	

Soda Guns

See: Bars, Nightclubs, Barware & Dressing* Soda Fountain Dressing

Soldier Toys & Drums

See Also: Christmas

History For Hire, Inc.	**(818) 765-7767**
period	
Universal Studios Property & Hardware Dept	**(818) 777-2784**
Prop toy soldiers, Christmas toy soldiers, toy soldier lawn ornament, Toy soldier nutcrackers and more for rent.	

Sono Tubes

Linoleum City, Inc.	**(323) 469-0063**
4849 Santa Monica Blvd, Hollywood, CA, 90029	
Cardboard tubes. 6 foot sono tubes, 12 foot sono tubes.	
sales@linocity.com * www.linoleumcity.com	
Superior-Studio Specialties	**(323) 278-0100**
2239 Yates, Commerce, CA, 90040	
3" up to 60" dia.	
http://superiorstudio.com/en	

Sound Equipment

See: Audio Equipment* Lighting & Sound, Concert/Theatrical/DJ/VJ* Recording Studio (Prop)* Rock 'n' Roll Lighting & Sound

Sound Stages

See: Locations, Stages/Studios, Film/TV/Events

South Seas Decorative Items

See: Light Fixtures, South Seas* Seashells* Tikis & Tropical Dressing

Souvenirs

See: Memorabilia & Novelties* Statue Of Liberty

Spa Equipment & Dressing

See: Beauty Salon* Salon & Spa Equipment

Space Shuttle/Space Hardware

See Also: Space Suits* Spaceship Computer Panel

Action Sets and Props / WonderWorks, Inc.   **(818) 992-8811**
Space shuttle & station, space suit, specialty props, miniatures, mechanical effects, cityscape, miniature buildings

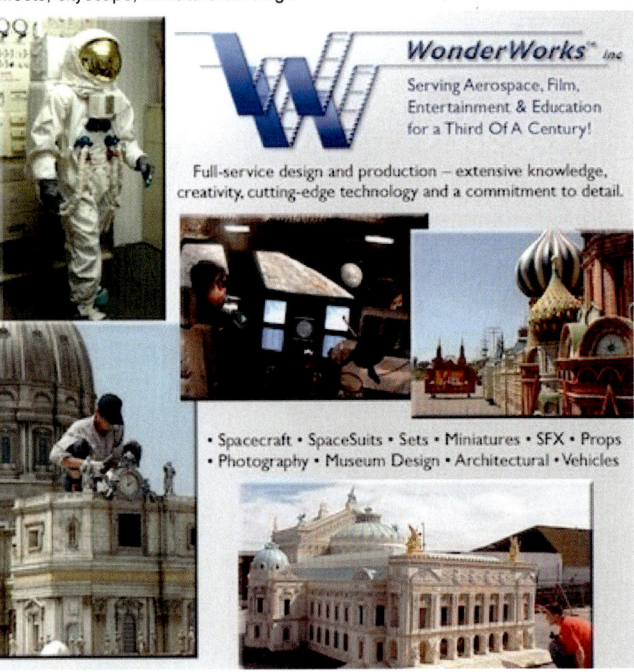

WonderWorks Inc
Serving Aerospace, Film, Entertainment & Education for a Third Of A Century!

Full-service design and production — extensive knowledge, creativity, cutting-edge technology and a commitment to detail.

• Spacecraft • SpaceSuits • Sets • Miniatures • SFX • Props • Photography • Museum Design • Architectural • Vehicles

Kansas Cosmosphere & Space Center	**(800) 397-0330**
1100 N Plum, Hutchinson, KS, 67501-1499	
U.S. Space Program equipment	
www.cosmo.org	
Modern Props	**(323) 934-3000**
Space hardware including electronic racks for space shuttles	

Space Suits

See Also: Space Shuttle/Space Hardware

Action Sets and Props / WonderWorks, Inc.   **(818) 992-8811**
Space shuttle & station, space suit, specialty props, miniatures, mechanical effects, cityscape, miniature buildings

Global Effects, Inc.   **(818) 503-9273**
7115 Laurel Canyon Blvd, N Hollywood, CA, 91605
Space suit rentals, both custom spaces suits and rental space suits.
office@globaleffects.com * www.globaleffects.com

Spaceship Computer Panel

See Also: Control Panels/Boxes* Space Shuttle/Space Hardware

Action Sets and Props / WonderWorks, Inc.   **(818) 992-8811**
Space shuttle & station, space suit, specialty props, miniatures, mechanical effects, cityscape, miniature buildings

Kansas Cosmosphere & Space Center   **(800) 397-0330**
1100 N Plum, Hutchinson, KS, 67501-1499
U.S. Space Program equipment
www.cosmo.org

LCW Props   **(818) 243-0707**
Large Quantity, Wall Dressing, Futuristic, Blinking Eye Candy, etc.

Modern Props   **(323) 934-3000**
futuristic/electronic spaceship computer panels, spaceship consoles, wall units & more

Speakers

See: Audio Equipment* Lighting & Sound, Concert/Theatrical/DJ/VJ* Stereo Equipment

Special Effects, Electronic

See Also: Special Effects, Equipment & Supplies* Special Effects, Lighting & Lasers

Astro Audio Video Lighting, Inc. (818) 549-9915
6615 San Fernando Rd, Glendale, CA, 91201
Including lighting, lasers, fog machines, confetti machines, black lights, foam machines and bubble machines.
www.astroavl.com

EFX- Event Special Effects (626) 888-2239
125 Railroad Ave, Monrovia, CA, 91016
Snow- Confetti- Cryo- Bubbles- Fog- Foam- Fluid- Lighting- Fabrication
info@efxla.com * www.efxla.com

Flix FX Inc. (818) 765-3549
7327 Lankershim Blvd #4, N Hollywood, CA, 91605
Electronic & lighted props, design & fabrication
info@flixfx.com * www.flixfx.com

Gilderfluke & Company, Inc (818) 840-9484
205 S Flower St, Burbank, CA, 91502
cust. computerized animation show control systems & components
www.gilderfluke.com

LCW Props (818) 243-0707
Custom Graphics Department. We Make Any Video Files Needed & Have A Huge Stock

Set Masters (818) 982-1506
24853 Avenue Rockefeller, Valencia, CA, 91355
Electronic Props; Lighting; Period to Futuristic and Everything In-between.
info@setmasters.com * www.setmasters.com

Ultra Prototypes LLC (818) 292-1906
Call for Appointment
We build your Electronic ideas.
jeff@ultraprototypes.com * www.ultraprototypes.com

Woody's Electrical Props (818) 503-1940
period to futuristic

Special Effects, Equipment & Supplies

See Also: Audio/Visual Film Equipment* Backings* Breakaways (Glass, Props, Scenery)* Bubble Machines* Confetti* Conveyor Equipment* Expendables* Fog Machines* Lighting & Sound, Concert/Theatrical/DJ/VJ* Lighting, LED, Fiber Optic & Specialty* Mechanical Effects* Motion Control* Prop Design & Manufacturing* Puppets, Marionettes, Automata, Animatronics* Pyrotechnics* Rigging, Equipment or Services* Robots* Scenery/Set Construction* Snow, Artificial & Real* Special Effects, Electronic* Special Effects, Lighting & Lasers* Special Effects, Make-up/Prosthetics* Stage Lighting, Film/Video/TV

Astro Audio Video Lighting, Inc. (818) 549-9915
6615 San Fernando Rd, Glendale, CA, 91201
Special effects equipment and special effects supplies; visual effects and theatrical special effects.
www.astroavl.com

Bill Ferrell Co. (818) 767-1900
10556 Keswick St, Sun Valley, CA, 91352
Motion FX turntables, winches, scissor lifts, conveyors, treadmills. Computer automation. Sets, props. Confetti effects.
www.billferrell.com

Castex Rentals (323) 462-1468
1044 N Cole Ave, Hollywood, CA, 90038
effects fans, foggers, bubble machines, special effects, special fx
service@castexrentals.com * www.castexrentals.com

CONFETTI & FOG FX Special Effects Company (877) 576-4239
1085 W 21st Pl, Hialeah, FL, 33010
Air canons, air compressors, blacklights, bubbles, confetti, lasers, snow, tshirt launchers, wind and much more.
Info@confettiandfogfx.com * www.caffx.com

EFX- Event Special Effects (626) 888-2239
125 Railroad Ave, Monrovia, CA, 91016
Snow- Confetti- Cryo- Bubbles- Fog- Foam- Fluid- Lighting- Fabrication
info@efxla.com * www.efxla.com

Flix FX Inc. (818) 765-3549
7327 Lankershim Blvd #4, N Hollywood, CA, 91605
Foggers, fans, turntables, specialty equipment & rigs
info@flixfx.com * www.flixfx.com

Full Scale Effects (818) 760-0875
6875 Tujunga Ave, N Hollywood, CA, 91605
We have the ability to fabricate a variety of mechanical effects. We can fabricate: Fog machines, varied Ritter fans & more
admin@fullscalefx.com * www.fullscalefx.com

J & M Special Effects, Inc. (718) 875-0140
524 Sackett St, Brooklyn, NY, 11217
Formerly Jauchem & Meeh. breakaway glass, atmospheric, weapons, pyro, show packages
info@jmfx.net * www.jmfx.net

Jet Effects (818) 764-5644
6910 Farmdale Ave, N Hollywood, CA, 91605
atmospheric & mechanical effects for film & TV
tito@jeteffects.net * www.jeteffects.net

L. A. Party Works (888) 527-2789
9712 Alpaca St, S El Monte, CA, 91733
Special effects equipment including fog machines, bubble machines, foam machines, misting fans, confetti cannons & more.
partyworks@aol.com * www.partyworksinteractive.com

LCW Props (818) 243-0707
Custom Graphics Department. We Make Any Video Files Needed & Have A Huge Stock

Mee Industries Inc. (626) 359-4550
16021 Adelante St, Irwindale, CA, 91702
Mfg. custom, turnkey large scale devices for pure water, ultra fine fog droplet effects
www.meefog.com

NAC Effects & Prop Animation (805) 376-0206
1772-J E Avenida de los Arboles #396, Thousand Oaks, CA, 91362
Flying rigs, motion bases, misc. special effects, hydraulic pumps
www.naceffects.com

Rando Productions, Inc (818) 982-4300
11939 Sherman Rd, N Hollywood, CA, 91605
turntables, lifts, rolling rooms, gimbals, hydraulics & custom
www.randoproductions.com

Reel EFX, Inc (818) 762-1710
5539 Riverton Ave, N Hollywood, CA, 91601
atmospheric, fire, wind, rain, green screen treadmill etc. & cust. tabletop effect illusions
www.reelefx.com

Reynolds Advanced Materials: Smooth-On Distributor (818) 358-6000
10856 Vanowen St, N Hollywood, CA, 91605
Hollywood's F/X source for Liquid Rubbers, Plastics, lifecasting, rubber and plastic breakaway glass, and more.
LA@reynoldsam.com * www.moldmakingmaterials.com

Roger George Rentals (818) 994-3049
14525 Bessemer St, Van Nuys, CA, 91411
Special effects equipment rentals
sales@rogergeorge.com * www.rogergeorge.com

Set Stuff Rentals (323) 993-9500
1105 N Sycamore Ave, Hollywood, CA, 90038
rent/operate fire/rain/smoke/wind, canopies, comm equip.
www.setstuffrentals.com

Special Effects Unlimited, Inc. (323) 466-3361
1005 N Lillian Way, Hollywood, CA, 90038
A complete line of rental equipment & expendables, along with custom special effects services.
www.specialeffectsunlimited.com

Technifex, Inc. (661) 294-3800
25261 Rye Canyon Rd, Valencia, CA, 91355
Design, mfg. mechanical, fluid, video & optical special effects, turnkey shows, themed environments
www.technifex.com

Universal Studios Special Effects Equip. (818) 777-3333
wind, wave, rain, snow, fog, bubble, cobweb machines/supplies

Warner Bros. Studios Special Effects & Prop Shop (818) 954-1365
4000 Warner Blvd Bldg 44, Burbank, CA, 91522
Consultation, Script Break-down, Equipment Rentals, Expendable Sales, Picture Car Prep, Action Props
www.wbspecialeffects.com

Special Effects, Lighting & Lasers

See Also: Lighting & Sound, Concert/Theatrical/DJ/VJ* Lighting, LED, Fiber Optic & Specialty* Searchlights/Skytrackers, Architectural Lights* Stage Lighting, Film/Video/TV

Astro Audio Video Lighting, Inc. (818) 549-9915
6615 San Fernando Rd, Glendale, CA, 91201
Special effects lighting, special effects lasers; machines, production and design.
www.astroavl.com

CONFETTI & FOG FX Special Effects Company (877) 576-4239
1085 W 21st Pl, Hialeah, FL, 33010
These lasers are simple, low output DJ lasers and do not require any special permits.
Info@confettiandfogfx.com * www.caffx.com

EFX- Event Special Effects (626) 888-2239
125 Railroad Ave, Monrovia, CA, 91016
High powered lasers- laser lighting- skywriters- concert lasers & more!
info@efxla.com * www.efxla.com

Luminys Systems Corp (800) 321-3644
11961 Sherman Rd, N Hollywood, CA, 91605
see web site for dealers. mfg. lightning simulators
www.luminyscorp.com

Strong Lighting (714) 237-9270
2780 East Regal Park Dr, Anaheim, CA, 92806
automated Xenon lighting systems, skylights
www.syncrolite.com

Universal Studios Special Effects Equip. (818) 777-3333

Special Effects, Make-up/Prosthetics

See Also: Animal Costumes & Walk Around Characters* Blood*
Make-up & Hair, Supplies & Services* Tattoos (Temporary)
Body/Face Painting

Amalgamated Dynamics, Inc.   (818) 882-8638
20100 Plummer St, Chatsworth, CA, 91311
make-up, design & build prosthetics & creature effects
www.studioadi.com

The Character Shop   (805) 306-9441
4735 Industrial St #4B-G, Simi Valley, CA, 93063
Extraordinary Custom Animatronic Animals & Creatures, Puppets, Marionettes,
Replicas, Robots, Props, Special Makeup FX
lazzwaldo@mac.com * www.character-shop.com

Chiodo Bros Productions, Inc   (818) 842-5656
511 5th St, Suite A, San Fernando, CA, 91340
animatronix, puppets, special effects for TV/film
klowns@chiodobros.com * www.chiodobros.com

Creative Character Engineering   (818) 901-0507
16110 Hart St, Van Nuys, CA, 91406
Baby Doubles, Makeup Prosthetics and More
www.creativecharacter.com

Dinair Airbrush Make-up & Institute   (818) 780-4777
6215 Laurel Canyon Blvd, N. Hollywood, CA, 91606
www.airbrushmakeup.com

Make-Up Designory (MUD)   (818) 729-9420
129 S San Fernando Blvd, Burbank, CA, 91502
Los Angeles School of Make-Up, Inc.
www.mud.edu

Make-up Effects Laboratories   (818) 982-1483
7110 Laurel Canyon Blvd Bldg E, N Hollywood, CA, 91605
prosthetic pieces
www.melefx.com

Masters FX, Inc.   (818) 834-3000
10316 Norris Ave Unit C, Arleta, CA, 91331
demons, aliens, age, fat, gore, etc.
www.mastersfx.com

Premiere Products Inc.   (800) 346-4774
10312 Norris Ave, Ste C, Pacoima, CA, 91331
make-up/prosthetic adhesives & removal solvents
www.ppipremiereproducts.com

Professional Vision Care Assoc.   (818) 789-3311
14607 Ventura Blvd, Sherman Oaks, CA, 91043
special FX lenses for film/TV/theatre
www.provisioncare.com

Reel Creations, Inc.   (818) 346-7335
7831 Alabama Ave Ste 21, Canoga Park, CA, 91304
reel blood, temp. tattoos, airbrush/body paint, prosthetic inks
www.reelcreations.com

Tech Works FX Studios   (504) 722-1504
13405 Seymour Meyers Blvd #5, Covington, LA, 70433
Specializes in Special Make Up FX, Creature Suit Design, Monsters, Costumes
and Gore FX.
info@techworksstudios.com * www.techworksstudios.com

Special Events

See: Events, Decorations, Supplies & Services* Events,
Design/Planning/Production* Events, Entertainment

Spinning Wheels

See: Sewing Machines

Spittoons

AIR Designs   (818) 768-6639
Bar Dressing, Brass

History For Hire, Inc.   (818) 765-7767

LCW Props   (818) 243-0707
Brass, Silver Plated

Universal Studios Property & Hardware Dept   (818) 777-2784
Prop brass spitoons, antique spitoons, decorative spitoons and metal spitoons
for rent.

Sporting Goods & Services

See Also: Archery Equipment, Training* Baseball Pitching Machine*
Basketball Court & Backboards* Bicycles & Bicycling Supplies*
Bowling Equipment* Boxing, Wrestling, Mixed Martial Arts (MMA)*
Camping Equipment* Exercise & Fitness Equipment* Fall Pads &
Crash Pads* Fishing Equipment & Tackle* Gymnasium & Gymnastic
Equipment* Nets* Prop Houses* Rigging, Equipment or Services* Ski
Equipment* Snow Shoes* Surfboard, Wakeboard* Track & Field
Equipment* Uniforms, Trades/Professional/Sports* Volleyball Setup

Above It All Kites   (360) 665-5483
312 Pacific Blvd S, Long Beach, WA, 98631
Kites, stunt kites, windsocks, also custom orders
www.aboveitallkites.com

Athletic Room   (818) 764-9801
12750 Raymer St, N Hollywood, CA, 91605
Golf, Camping, Surf, Baseball, Soccer, Football, Basketball, Hockey, Yoga,
Boxing, Water Sports, Variety of Sports Props
athleticroom@mac.com * www.athleticroomprops.net

Best Buy Figure Skating   (714) 518-3240
300 W Lincoln Ave, Anaheim, CA, 92805
ice & roller skates, sticks, protective equip.
www.bestbuyfigureskating.com

C. P. Two   (323) 466-8201
Sports related items from gear and equipment to trophies and posters.

Dick's Sporting Goods   (626) 351-1843
3359 E. Foothill Blvd, Pasadena, CA, 91107
multiple stores, sporting goods, esp. good sel. apparel
www.dickssportinggoods.com

Escalade Sports   (812) 467-1200
817 Maxwell Avenue, Evansville, IN 47711
Accudart darts, Stiga, Goalrilla, Harvard, Bear archery, Woodplay playsets,
Atomic game table
www.escaladesports.com

Fold-A-Goal   (800) 542-4625
4856 W Jefferson Blvd, Los Angeles, CA, 90016
everything for soccer; goals, nets & balls, uniforms, and field lining equipment &
service
www.fold-a-goal.com

The Hand Prop Room LP.   (323) 931-1534
lrg sel, all sports

History For Hire, Inc.   (818) 765-7767
Vintage baseball equipment, ice skates, roller skates, sports graphics, sport
ticket fabrication & more!

I & I Sports Supply, Inc.   (310) 715-6800
19751 S Figueroa St, Carson, CA, 90745
multiple stores; martial arts, boxing, paintball
www.iisports.com

Into The Wind   (800) 541-0314
1408 Pearl St, Boulder, CO, 80302
Kites, windsocks, wind art
www.intothewind.com

LCW Props   (818) 243-0707
Balls, Equipment, Scoreboards, Memorabilia

Roger Dunn Golf Shop   (818) 763-3622
5445 Lankershim Blvd, N Hollywood, CA, 91601
a wide array of golf products
www.worldwidegolfshops.com

Ski Net Sports   (818) 505-1294
11378 Ventura Blvd, Studio City, CA, 91604
Closed on Wed. inline skates, hiking/walking boots/shoes, foldup go boards
www.skinetsports.com

Soccer Plus Sports Shop   (800) 945-7291
1640 E Washington Blvd, Pasadena, CA, 91104
only soccer
www.soccerplus.net

Soccer Stores Inc.   (818) 243-7790
520 S Brand Blvd, Glendale, CA, 91204
only soccer
www.soccerstoresinc.com

Sony Pictures Studios-Prop House (Off Lot)   (310) 244-5999
Cricket sticks, volleyballs, air hockey, badminton racket, baseball equipment,
basketball equipment, bicycles, billiard equipment

Universal Studios Property & Hardware Dept   (818) 777-2784
Prop sports equipment and goods for rent.

Val-Surf   (818) 769-6977
4810 Whitsett Ave, Valley Village, CA, 91607
skateboards, surfboards, snowboards, wakeboards
www.valsurf.com

Warner Bros. Studios Property Department   (818) 954-2181
Weight & exercise machines, assorted sports equipment, skis, bowling
equipment, bikes, surf boards

Sports & Games Themed Events

See Also: Arcade Equipment, Games & Rides* Events, Decorations, Supplies & Services* Events, Design/Planning/Production* Events, Entertainment* Scoreboards & Scoring Systems

L. A. Party Works   **(888) 527-2789**
9712 Alpaca St, S El Monte, CA, 91733
Obstacle Courses, Scoreboards, Bleachers, sports related games and more.
Vancouver tel. 604-589-4101
partyworks@aol.com * www.partyworksinteractive.com

LARGE INVENTORY OF PRO EQUIPMENT IN STOCK
PARTYWORKS
INTERACTIVE
888-527-2789
partyworksusa.com

Sports Bar Dressing

AIR Designs	**(818) 768-6639**
Unique Items, Pictures, Signs, Games, Memorabilia	
History For Hire, Inc.	**(818) 765-7767**
Lots!	
LCW Props	**(818) 243-0707**
TV's, Kegs, Taps, Seating, Tables, Memorabilia	
Lennie Marvin Enterprises, Inc. (Prop Heaven)	**(818) 841-5882**
signs, memorabilia, counter, glassware, etc.	
RC Vintage, Inc.	**(818) 765-7107**
Sports bar dressing including sports bar neon signs, old photographs, beer taps, decanters and more.	
Universal Studios Property & Hardware Dept	**(818) 777-2784**
Sports bar dressing, sports bar props and sports bar menus for rent.	

Sports Fan Items, Memorabilia, Photographs

See Also: Collectibles* Memorabilia & Novelties

Athletic Room	**(818) 764-9801**
12750 Raymer St, N Hollywood, CA, 91605	
Framed Jerseys, Sports Art, Trophies, Tailgate Dressing, Fan Props, Vintage Memorabilia, Furniture, Banners, Beach.	
athleticroom@mac.com * www.athleticroomprops.net	
History For Hire, Inc.	**(818) 765-7767**
Hollywood Studio Gallery	**(323) 462-1116**
LCW Props	**(818) 243-0707**
Balls, Equipment, Scoreboards, Memorabilia	
Universal Studios Property & Hardware Dept	**(818) 777-2784**
Many kinds of sports memorabilia for rent.	

Sports Lockers

See: Lockers

Sports/Athletic Field Lining/Graphics

See: Sporting Goods & Services

Sportswear

See Also: Knickers* Uniforms, Trades/Professional/Sports

CBS Costume Rental	**(323) 575-2666**
modern M/F	
Dick's Sporting Goods	**(626) 351-1843**
3359 E. Foothill Blvd, Pasadena, CA, 91107	
multiple stores, sporting goods, esp. good sel. apparel	
www.dickssportinggoods.com	
Fila U.S.A., Inc.	**(212) 726-5937**
1411 Broadway 30th Flr, New York, NY, 10018	
Fila product placement	
www.fila.com	
Sony Pictures Studios-Wardrobe	**(310) 244-5995**
alterations, call (310) 244-7260	
Team Leader	**(877) 365-7555**
Call for Appt	
Online uniform catalog. Will make custom pom pons.	
www.teamleader.com	
Universal Studios Costume Dept	**(818) 777-2722**
Rental, mfg., & alterations	
Warner Bros. Studios Costume Dept	**(818) 954-1297**
Collection of period & contemporary costumes for rent categorized by era, decade and style	

Spray Paint Booth

See: Paint & Painting Supplies

Sprinklers, Fire Protection

See: Plumbing Fixtures, Heating/Cooling Appliances

Spy Items

See: Surveillance Equipment

Squadroom

See: Police Equipment

Squawk Boxes

See: Military Props & Equipment

Stadium Seats

See: Audience Seating

Staff Shops

American Wood Column Corp.	**(718) 782-3163**
913 Grand St, Brooklyn, NY, 11211-2785	
catalog sales; large sel. of millwork, architectural/decorative small finials to tall columns, plain to ornate, custom t	
www.americanwoodcolumncorp.com	
The Decorators Supply Corporation	**(773) 847-6300**
3610 South Morgan St, Chicago, IL, 60609	
catalog sales; 15,000 cast plaster & wood carved ornaments for woodwork & furniture, also custom mantels, custom work	
www.decoratorssupply.com	
Universal Studios Staff Shop	**(818) 777-2337**
Warner Bros. Studios Staff Shop	**(818) 954-2269**
Manufacturer of exterior & interior details used for the creation of sets in all architectural styles & eras.	

Stage Lighting Equipment

See: Lighting & Sound, Concert/Theatrical/DJ/VJ* Stage Lighting, Film/Video/TV

Stage Lighting, Film/Video/TV

See Also: Chase Lights* Lighting & Sound, Concert/Theatrical/DJ/VJ* Lighting Control Boards* Special Effects, Lighting & Lasers

Astro Audio Video Lighting, Inc.   **(818) 549-9915**
6615 San Fernando Rd, Glendale, CA, 91201
wash, concert, followspot, intelligent, control, video, screen
www.astroavl.com

Blue Feather Lighting & Design   **(818) 701-5404**
19630 Lanark St, Reseda, CA, 91335
West Coast Unilux technician; stroboscopic lights to shoot things that pour, spritz or splash
www.unilux.com

Castex Rentals   **(323) 462-1468**
1044 N Cole Ave, Hollywood, CA, 90038
HMIs, Kino Flos, Fresnels, Source 4s, stage lighting
service@castexrentals.com * www.castexrentals.com

Serving the Motion Picture & Photography Industries Since 1955

Production, Grip, Lighting Expendables & More...

1044 Cole Avenue, Hollywood, CA 90038
Tel: 323.462.1468 · Fax: 323.462.3719

www.castexrentals.com

EFX- Event Special Effects   **(626) 888-2239**
125 Railroad Ave, Monrovia, CA, 91016
Stage Lighting- Event Lighting
info@efxla.com * www.efxla.com

Filmmaker Prod. Svcs-Atlanta @ Tyler Perry Studios   **(404) 450-1968**
2115 Sylvan Road, Atlanta, GA, 30344
Grip & rigging equip. & services, lighting & sound
chad.garcia@nbcuni.com * www.filmmakerproductionservices.com

Filmmaker Prod. Svcs-Chicago @ Cinespace Chicago   **(678) 628-1997**
2558 W 16th Street Dock #4, Chicago, IL, 60608
Grip & rigging equip. & services, lighting & sound
patrick.flanagan@nbcuni.com * www.filmmakerproductionservices.com

High End   **(800) 890-8989**
2105 Gracy Farms Ln, Austin, Tx 78758
mfg. lighting equip., also office in NYC, TX, Europe
www.highend.com

History For Hire, Inc.   **(818) 765-7767**
vintage

Luminys Systems Corp   **(800) 321-3644**
11961 Sherman Rd, N Hollywood, CA, 91605
see web site for dealers. mfg. Softsun special purpose lighting
www.luminyscorp.com

NBCUniversal LightBlade LED Lighting   **(818) 777-1671**
Uses 30-70% less power than equivalent conventional production lighting - Superior quality of light for stage & location
brandon.rensvold@nbcuni.com * www.lightbladeled.com

New Mexico Lighting & Grip Co.   **(505) 506-6564**
I-25 Studios 9201 Pan American Fwy NE, Albuquerque, NM, 87113
Grip & rigging equip. & services, lighting & sound
colin.pearman@nmlgc.com * www.newmexicolightingandgrip.com

Pacific Northwest Theatre Associates   **(800) 622-7850**
2414 SW Andover C100, Seattle, WA, 98106
catalog sales; theatrical supplies, make-up, expendables, rigging, drops, lighting, sound, effects
www.pnta.com

Radiance Lightworks, Inc.   **(818) 879-1516**
4607 Lakeview Canyon Rd, Ste 500, Westlake Village, CA, 91361
full svc. lighting design for film/video, special events, architecture, themed environments & theatre systems
www.radiancelightworks.com

TLS Productions, Inc.   **(855) 515-8577**
78 Jackson Plaza, Ann Arbor, MI, 48103
installation too
www.tlsproductionsinc.com

Universal Studios Grip Dept   **(818) 777-2291**
100 Universal City Plaza, Universal City, CA, 91608
Extensive inventory of quality grip equipment incl. digital screens, steel deck & more
universal.grip@nbcuni.com * http://universalstudioslot.com/grip

Universal Studios Set Lighting Dept   **(818) 777-1459**
100 Universal City Plaza, Universal City, CA, 91608
Extensive inventory of quality stage & location lighting
sean.buckler@nbcuni.com * universalstudioslot.com/set-lighting

Stage Turntables

Bill Ferrell Co.   **(818) 767-1900**
10556 Keswick St, Sun Valley, CA, 91352
Turntables 4"-40'; simple or computer-automated. Surrounds, guardrails, stairs, ramps, lifts, winches. Set construction.
www.billferrell.com

Flix FX Inc.   **(818) 765-3549**
7327 Lankershim Blvd #4, N Hollywood, CA, 91605
3" (product) to 8' motorized tables, 5' glass top lazy susan
info@flixfx.com * www.flixfx.com

Stages, Portable & Steel Deck

See Also: Audience Seating* Bleachers & Grandstand Seating

Accurate Staging　　　　　　　　　　　　(310) 324-1040
1820 W 135th Street, Gardena, CA, 90249
rolling risers, platforms
www.accuratestaging.com

Astro Audio Video Lighting, Inc.　　　　　(818) 549-9915
6615 San Fernando Rd, Glendale, CA, 91201
Temporary stages and portable stages custom in any size, height; stairs, rails, etc.
www.astroavl.com

Bill Ferrell Co.　　　　　　　　　　　　　(818) 767-1900
10556 Keswick St, Sun Valley, CA, 91352
Steel Deck, Ferrellels, rounds, ramps, triangles, rollers, risers. Sets, props.
Turntables, winches, lifts, conveyors.
www.billferrell.com

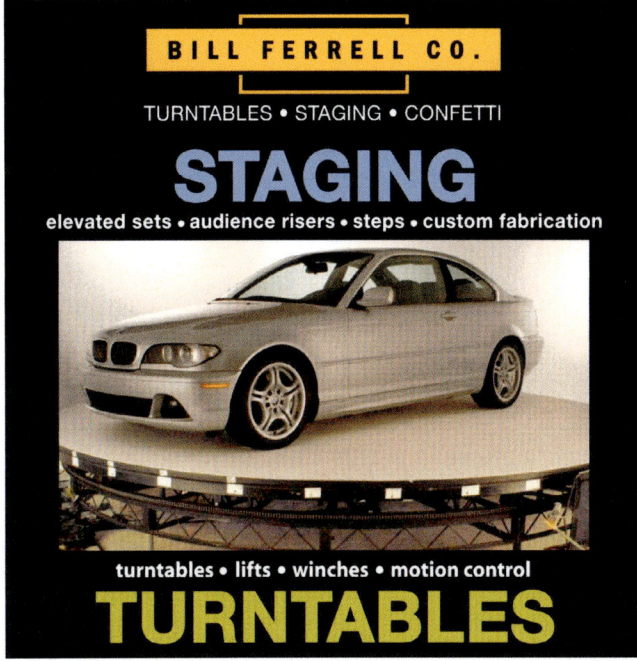

EFX- Event Special Effects　　　　　　　(626) 888-2239
125 Railroad Ave, Monrovia, CA, 91016
Steel Deck- Stage- Drape- Carpet- Back Drop- Steps- Railing
info@efxla.com * www.efxla.com

L. A. Party Works　　　　　　　　　　　(888) 527-2789
9712 Alpaca St, S El Monte, CA, 91733
Portable staging/temporary staging for rent
partyworks@aol.com * www.partyworksinteractive.com

Scenic Highlights　　　　　　　　　　　(818) 252-7760
10830 Cantara St, Sun Valley, CA, 91352
scenichighlights.com

Steeldeck, Inc.　　　　　　　　　　　　(323) 290-2100
3339 Exposition Place, Los Angeles, CA, 90018
rentals@steeldeck.com * www.steeldeck.com

Upstage Rentals Inc.　　　　　　　　　　(818) 247-1149
8238 Lankershim Blvd, N Hollywood, CA, 91605
Steel Deck Platform Rental - steps and truss rental
www.upstagerentals.com

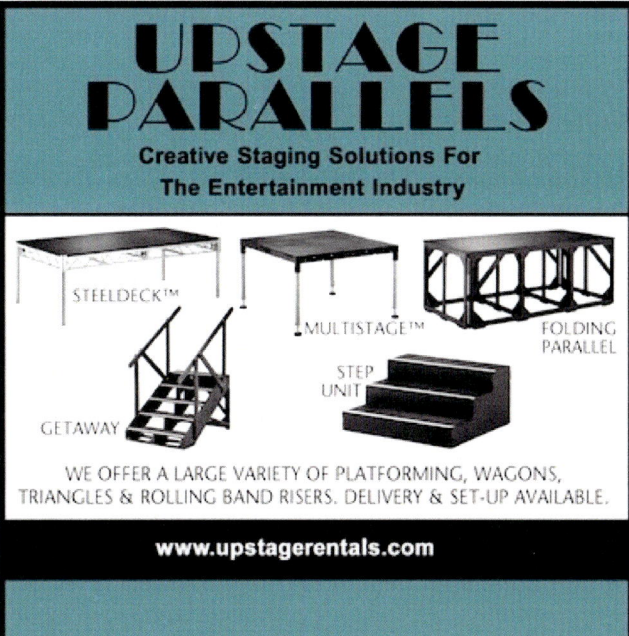

Stained Glass

See: Glass & Mirrors, Art/Finishing/Etching/Etc.

Stair Climbers

See: Exercise & Fitness Equipment

Stanchions & Rope

See Also: Audience Seating* Crowd Control: Barricades, Turnstiles Etc.

AIR Designs　　　　　　　　　　　　　(818) 768-6639
Airport, Car Lot, Traffic Delineators, Bar & Club, Tape, & Rope

Astro Audio Video Lighting, Inc.　　　　　(818) 549-9915
6615 San Fernando Rd, Glendale, CA, 91201
Stanchions and rope dividers for rent.
www.astroavl.com

C. P. Two　　　　　　　　　　　　　　(323) 466-8201
Stanchion ropes, stanchion signs, stanchion carts, stanchion tape, vinyl
stanchions and retractable stanchions.

Collins Visual Media　　　　　　　　　　(818) 686-6581
10518 Johanna Ave, Shadow Hills, CA, 91040
We provide a variety of stanchions and ropes for crowd control and red carpet glamour.
www.collinsvisualmedia.com

The Hand Prop Room LP.　　　　　　　　(323) 931-1534
bank, theatre, airport

History For Hire, Inc.　　　　　　　　　(818) 765-7767

Lennie Marvin Enterprises, Inc. (Prop Heaven)　(818) 841-5882
period to modern-bank, theatre, airport

RC Vintage, Inc.　　　　　　　　　　　(818) 765-7107
rope, velvet rope & ribbon for stanchions

Sony Pictures Studios-Linens, Drapes, Rugs　(310) 244-5999
5933 W Slauson Ave, Culver City, CA, 90230
Chrome stanchions and black ropes
www.sonypicturesstudios.com

Sony Pictures Studios-Prop House (Off Lot)　(310) 244-5999
Black wire stanchions, brass stanchions, chrome stanchions, black retractable
stanchions, chrome retractable stanchions

Step and Repeat LA　　　　　　　　　　(818) 434-7591
10518 Johanna Ave, Shadow Hills, CA, 91040
We are a resource for Retractable Belt Barrier Stanchions & Rope Stanchion
Rentals for all kinds of events & productions.
Services@StepandRepeatLA.com * StepandRepeatLA.com

Universal Studios Property & Hardware Dept　(818) 777-2784
Prop stanchions and stanchion ropes for rent.

ZG04 DECOR　　　　　　　　　　　　(818) 853-8040
Many stanchions and retractable belt head stanchions

Stand-Ups

See: Audience Cutouts & Inflatables

Stationery

See: Art, Supplies & Stationery

Statuary

See Also: Mold Making* Sculpture

Green Set, Inc.	**(818) 764-1231**
fountains, waterfalls, garden statuary, Greek statuary	
The Hand Prop Room LP.	**(323) 931-1534**
bronze pcs, assorted styles	
Jackson Shrub Supply, Inc.	**(818) 982-0100**
garden statues, garden monuments, bird baths, giant Venus clam shell	
LM Treasures	**(626) 252-7354**
All our items are hand painted and crafted to provide each customer with their own personally unique piece.	
Ob-jects	**(818) 351-4200**
Omega/Cinema Props	**(323) 466-8201**
Statuary	
Sony Pictures Studios-Prop House (Off Lot)	**(310) 244-5999**
abstract statuary, animal statuary, bust statuary, human statuary, bird baths, carousel horse, columns, decorative statuary, more	
Universal Studios Property & Hardware Dept	**(818) 777-2784**
Many prop statues and statuettes for rent.	
Used Church Items, Religious Rentals	**(412) 220-2272**
115 East Barr Street, Mcdonald, PA, 15057	
400 Religious Statues, Angels, Patron Saints, Jesus, Joseph, Mary, Crucifixes, Stations of the Cross, Stands, Altars. www.religiousrentals.com	
Warner Bros. Studios Property Department	**(818) 954-2181**

Statue Of Liberty

Green Set, Inc.	**(818) 764-1231**
7' tall, full figure	
History For Hire, Inc.	**(818) 765-7767**
desk-top size	
Modern Props	**(323) 934-3000**
6 ft Statue of Liberty statue	
RC Vintage, Inc.	**(818) 765-7107**
multiples & various sizes	
Universal Studios Property & Hardware Dept	**(818) 777-2784**
Prop statue of liberty and fiberglass statue of liberty for rent.	

Steam Cabinets

See: Exercise & Fitness Equipment* Gymnasium & Gymnastic Equipment

Steamer Trunks

The Hand Prop Room LP.	**(323) 931-1534**
period-present, antique Louis Vuitton	
History For Hire, Inc.	**(818) 765-7767**
dozens	
Universal Studios Property & Hardware Dept	**(818) 777-2784**
Vintage steamer trunks, antique steamer trunks, wooden steamer trunks, old steamer trunks and more for rent.	

Steampunk

See Also: Carriages, Horse Drawn* Eyewear, Glasses, Sunglasses, 3D* Fantasy Props, Costumes, or Decorations* Western Dressing* Western Wear* Furniture, Industrial

Faux Library Studio Props, Inc.	**(818) 765-0096**
Steampunk themed items and steam punk desk dressing	

huge collection • 60,000 sq ft • furniture • accessories • modern • antiques
Office Furniture • Props • Desk Dressing
Faux Library Studio Props

History For Hire, Inc.	**(818) 765-7767**
Jadis	**(310) 396-3477**
2701 Main St, Santa Monica, CA, 90405	
Motorized gear units, control panels with vintage switches and gauges, Tesla coils, Van de Graaff generators. jadis1@gmail.com * www.jadisprops.com	
LCW Props	**(818) 243-0707**
Our Specialty. We Have A Large Selection Of Many Items. Rigged, Large & Small. Check Us Out Online.	
Lux Lounge EFR	**(888) 247-4411**
106 1/2 Judge John Aiso St #318, Los Angeles, CA, 90012	
Steampunk Furniture Collection, Steampunk Sofa, Steampunk Chairs, Steampunk Banquete, Steampunk Chandelier info@luxloungeefr.com * www.luxloungeefr.com	
The Rational Past	**(310) 476-6277**
By Appointment, West Los Angeles, CA	
Authentic science, industrial, technical antiques & collectibles. Many professions & eras represented. See web site. info@therationalpast.com * www.therationalpast.com	
Sword & Stone	**(818) 562-6548**
Custom steam punk apparel and weapons fabrication.	
Universal Studios Property & Hardware Dept	**(818) 777-2784**
Steampunk/steam punk items including steam punk lamps and steam punk decorations	
Warner Bros. Studios Property Department	**(818) 954-2181**
Steam punk, Victorian copper and brass rolling control panels, consoles with gauges, levers and hand controls.	

Steel Deck Platforms

See: Stages, Portable & Steel Deck

Steel Folding Gates & Roll-Up Doors

E.C. Prop Rentals	**(818) 764-2008**
Store front scissor gates	
Lawrence Roll Up Doors	**(626) 869-0837**
4525 Littlejohn St, Baldwin Park, CA, 91706	
Sales, service, installation & mfg. of all types of doors, grills & gates, commercial & industrial www.lawrencedoors.com	
McMaster-Carr	**(562) 692-5911**
9630 Norwalk Blvd, Santa Fe Springs, CA, 90670	
Sales - (562) 695-2323; entry security gates www.mcmaster.com	

Stemware

See: Crystal Stemware

Stencils

See: Art, Supplies & Stationery* Printing, Graphics, Digital & Large Format* Signs

Step & Repeats

See: Printing, Graphics, Digital & Large Format* Signs

Stereo Equipment

See Also: Audio Equipment* Radios
Astro Audio Video Lighting, Inc.   **(818) 549-9915**
6615 San Fernando Rd, Glendale, CA, 91201
Speakers, stereo equipment and stereo systems for rent.
www.astroavl.com
C. P. Two   **(323) 466-8201**
Speakers, component stereos, portable stereos, stationary stereos. Antique to modern.
The Hand Prop Room LP.   **(323) 931-1534**
History For Hire, Inc.   **(818) 765-7767**
period, stereos, wall speakers, vox amplifiers
LCW Props   **(818) 243-0707**
DJ Equipment, Turntables, Speakers, Media, Recievers, Amplifiers
Old N Country Prop Shop, LLC   **(818) 423-2599**
Old Stereo Receivers, Vintage Reel-to-Reel, 8-track & Cassette Stereo systems, and variety of speakers
Rewind Audio   **(213) 273-8904**
1041 N Alvarado St, Los Angeles, CA, 90026
Turntables, record players, amps, speakers and more.
rewindaudiola@gmail.com * www.rewindaudio.com
Sony Pictures Studios-Prop House (Off Lot)   **(310) 244-5999**
Universal Studios Property & Hardware Dept   **(818) 777-2784**
Prop speakers, stereo equipment stereo systems for rent.

Stone

See: Architectural Pieces & Artifacts* Columns* Concrete Block, Brick, Gravel, Sand, Rocks, Etc.* Sculpture* Tile, Marble, Granite, Etc.

Stone Restoration

See: Sanitation, Waste Disposal

Stools

See Also: Chairs
Asian Art Imports   **(818) 778-0852**
16876 Stagg St, Van Nuys, CA, 91406
Asian Art Imports has the largest collection of carved and organic stools available.
asianartimports@yahoo.com * www.asianartimports.com
E.C. Prop Rentals   **(818) 764-2008**
Industrial/stainless steel/metal/wood
FormDecor, Inc.   **(310) 558-2582**
America's largest event rental supplier of 20th Century furniture and accessories for Modern and Mid-Century styles.
LCW Props   **(818) 243-0707**
Garage, Lab, Medical, Office
Lux Lounge EFR   **(888) 247-4411**
106 1/2 Judge John Aiso St #318, Los Angeles, CA, 90012
Bar Stools & High Chairs for rent
info@luxloungeefr.com * www.luxloungeefr.com
Modern Props   **(323) 934-3000**
contemporary stools, large selection, multiples
Old N Country Prop Shop, LLC   **(818) 423-2599**
A variety of antique, modern, and custom-made stools.
Picture Start Props   **(818) 255-5472**
Wooden bar stools, vintage metal shop stools and contemporary stools
Prop Services West   **(818) 503-2790**
A Royal Suite Home Furinishings   **(661) 259-7000**
26536 Carl Boyer Dr, Santa Clarita, CA, 91350
A Royal Suite, family-owned since 1978, Features AMERICAN-MADE Furniture, and the Finest Furniture at the Greatest Value
norb@ars-email.com * www.aroyalsuite.com
Sony Pictures Studios-Prop House (Off Lot)   **(310) 244-5999**
Bar stools, cafe stools, camp stools, counter stools, country stools, dinner stools, drafting stools, foot stool, more
Universal Studios Property & Hardware Dept   **(818) 777-2784**
Many kinds of stools for rent for all kinds of spaces and occasions
ZG04 DECOR   **(818) 853-8040**
Poofs, Ottomans, Stools, Barstools

Stop Signs

See: Railroad Crossing Signal* Traffic/Road Signs, Lights, Safety Items

Storage

See: Archiving Media/Records Management* Hampers, Theatrical* Property Master Storage Rooms* Scenery/Set Storage* Set Boxes & Taco Carts (Propmaster & Set)* Transportation, Trucking and/or Storage* Warehouse Dressing

Store Dressing

See: Bakery* Bookstores* Cash Registers* Counters* Credit Card Imprint Machine* Department Store* Display Cases, Racks & Fixtures (Store)* Drugstore/Apothecary* General Store* Printing, Graphics, Digital & Large Format* Grocery Check-out Stands (Complete)* Hardware Store Dressing* Jewelry Store* Market Equipment/Fixtures* Record/Video Store* Sandwich Board Store Sign* Security Walk-Through & Baggage Alarms* Shoe Store* Steel Folding Gates & Roll-Up Doors* Store Shelf Units & Shelving* Surveillance Equipment* Video Rental/Sales Store* Video Store Dressing

Store Front Folding Gates

See: Steel Folding Gates & Roll-Up Doors

Store Front Rental Location

See: Locations, Insert Stages & Theatres* Scenery/Set Rentals

Store Shelf Units & Shelving

See Also: Candy Racks* Display Cases, Racks & Fixtures (Store)* Garment Racks
Acme Display Fixture & Packaging   **(888) 411-1870**
3829 S Broadway St, Los Angeles, CA, 90037
Complete store setups: garment racks, displays/display cases, counters, packaging, shelving, hangers, mannequins
sales@acmedisplay.com * www.acmedisplay.com
Alley Cats Studio Rentals   **(818) 982-9178**
dressed or empty/gondola shelving
E.C. Prop Rentals   **(818) 764-2008**
Industrial Shelving & Racks, Warehouse Shelving & Racks, Many Styles, Many Castered
Faux Library Studio Props, Inc.   **(818) 765-0096**
Bookcases and book shelving units, library shelving
LCW Props   **(818) 243-0707**
Call For An Updated Listing
Modern Props   **(323) 934-3000**
contemporary/futuristic store shelf units/store shelving, multiples
Outwater Plastics Industries   **(800) 248-2067**
4720 W Van Buren, P.O. Box 18190, Phoenix, AZ, 85043
catalog sales; plastics. slatwall, gridwall, pegboard, hanging holders
www.outwater.com
Universal Studios Property & Hardware Dept   **(818) 777-2784**
Store shelving units and store display shelves for rent.

Stores, Retail

See: Barber Shop* Beauty Salon* Bookstores* Delicatessen Equipment* Department Store* Drugstore/Apothecary* General Store* Hardware Store Dressing* Jewelry Store* Record/Video Store* Shoe Store* Video Rental/Sales Store

Story Book Themed Parties

See: Costume Rental Houses* Costumes* Events, Decorations, Supplies & Services* Events, Design/Planning/Production* Fantasy Props, Costumes, or Decorations* Prop Houses

Storyboards, Illustrations

See: Art, Artists For Hire

Storyboards, Production Illustration

See: Art, Artists For Hire

Stools

See Also: Restaurant Kitchens/Equip./Supplies
AIR Designs (818) 768-6639
Restaurant, Ranges, Ovens, Pizza
Antique Stove Heaven (323) 298-5581
5414 Western Ave, Los Angeles, CA, 90062
Antique, early 1900s - 1950s, sales, restorations, service
www.antiquestoveheaven.com
C. P. Two (323) 466-8201
stoves and botbelly stoves
History For Hire, Inc. (818) 765-7767
potbelly stoves only
LCW Props (818) 243-0707
Appliances Of All Kinds. Period - Present.
Modern Props (323) 934-3000
30s to present day stoves
Ob-jects (818) 351-4200
industrial stoves
RC Vintage, Inc. (818) 765-7107
40s, 50s, 60s & 70s Assorted Colors; Pink, Yellow, Green, and Boring White.
Gas stoves & electric stoves
Sony Pictures Studios-Prop House (Off Lot) (310) 244-5999
stoves & potbellies too
Universal Studios Property & Hardware Dept (818) 777-2784
Stoves for rent from potbellies & period to modern stoves.
Warner Bros. Studios Property Department (818) 954-2181
Black Smith's Stove, camp stoves, kitchen stoves, restaurant stoves, cast iron stoves

Streaks 'N Tips

See: Expendables* Make-up & Hair, Supplies & Services

Street Dressing

See Also: Alarms* Alley Dressing* Antenna* Bag Lady Carts*
Billboards & Billboard Lights* Bus Shelter* Fences* Guard Shacks*
Kiosks* Lamp Posts & Street Lights* Mailboxes* Marquees* Parking
Meters & Sign Poles* Sandwich Board Store Sign* Signs* Steel
Folding Gates & Roll-Up Doors* Street Dressing, Exterior Signs*
Telephone Poles Prop* Traffic/Road Signs, Lights, Safety Items*
Vendor Carts & Concession Counters
AIR Designs (818) 768-6639
Mail Box, Parking Meters, Street Lamps, Street Signs, Trash Cans,
Newsstands, Coin-Ops, Construction
Alley Cats Studio Rentals (818) 982-9178
street signals/signs, manhole vents, period/modern hydrants, benches, street
vendors, parking meters, dirty mattresses
E.C. Prop Rentals (818) 764-2008
cobra head street lights, K-rails, signs/posts, trash cans, bus shelters/benches

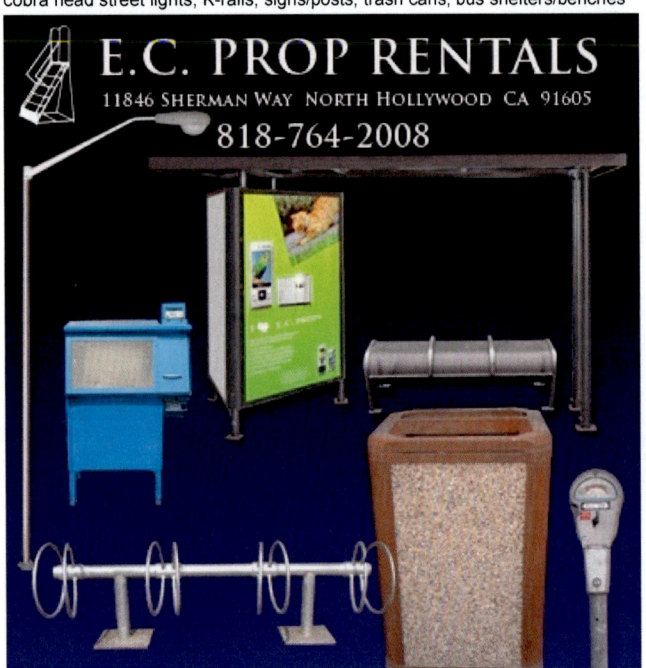

E.C. PROP RENTALS
11846 SHERMAN WAY NORTH HOLLYWOOD CA 91605
818-764-2008

The Hand Prop Room LP. (323) 931-1534
lrg sel.
History For Hire, Inc. (818) 765-7767
LCW Props (818) 243-0707
Trash bins, Roll-Off Containers, Recycling Bins, Yard Waste, Debris, Street
Lights, Cross Arms, Stop Lights
Lennie Marvin Enterprises, Inc. (Prop Heaven) (818) 841-5882
signage,trash cans,benches,fireplugs,traffic lights,hydrants
Omega/Cinema Props (323) 466-8201
Street lamps and more.
RC Vintage, Inc. (818) 765-7107
40s, 50s & 60s, signals, Period signals and Modern remote Control.
Universal Studios Property & Hardware Dept (818) 777-2784
All kinds of street dressing props for rent.

Street Dressing, European

Street Dressing, Exterior Signs

See Also: Billboards & Billboard Lights* Neon Lights & Signs
AIR Designs (818) 768-6639
Large Selection, Business, Location, Parking, Directional, Neon, Traffic,
Construction, Store Front
Collins Visual Media (818) 686-6581
10518 Johanna Ave, Shadow Hills, CA, 91040
We provide a wide range of street dressing products: storefront signage, media
walls & custom crowd control barricades.
www.collinsvisualmedia.com
D'ziner Sign Co. (323) 467-4467
801 Seward Street, Los Angeles, CA, 90038
illuminated & non-illuminated
sales@dzinersign.com * www.dzinersign.com
E.C. Prop Rentals (818) 764-2008
Parking Signs, Bus Stop Signs, Directional Signs, Speed Limit Signs, School
Signs, Alley Signs, Sign Posts
LCW Props (818) 243-0707
Trash bins, Roll-Off Containers, Recycling Bins, Yard Waste, Debris, Street
Lights, Cross Arms, Stop Lights
Sony Pictures Studios-Prop House (Off Lot) (310) 244-5999
street lights, post lamps, barriades
Universal Studios Property & Hardware Dept (818) 777-2784
Many exterior sign rentals for rent.
Warner Bros. Studios Property Department (818) 954-2181
Street signs, Emergency signs, exit signs, neon signs, cardboard signs, caution
signs

Street Lights

See: Lamp Posts & Street Lights

Street Scene

See: Locations, Insert Stages & Theatres* Locations,
Backlots/Standing Sets

Street Vendor Carts

See: Catering* Flower Carts* Gypsy Wagon* Produce Carts*
Produce Stands* Taco Carts (Propmaster & Set)* Vendor Carts &
Concession Counters

Stretchers

A-1 Medical Integration (818) 753-0319
Medical devices for Set Decoration & Property, from minor procedures to
detailed hospital units.
Alpha Companies - Spellman Desk Co. (818) 504-9090
The #1 source for medical equipment in the industry.
The Hand Prop Room LP. (323) 931-1534
period-present
History For Hire, Inc. (818) 765-7767
Civil War to modern
Supply Sergeant (323) 849-3744
503 N Victory Blvd, Burbank, CA, 91502
military stretchers, army stretchers, navy stretchers
david@jacksgt.com * www.supplysergeantshop.com

Strobe Lights

See: Bars, Nightclubs, Barware & Dressing* Light Fixtures* Lighting
& Sound, Concert/Theatrical/DJ/VJ

Studio Backlots

See: Locations, Insert Stages & Theatres

Studio Services

See: Wardrobe, Studio Services

Studio Tile Flooring

See Also: Carpet & Flooring
Linoleum City, Inc.   **(323) 469-0063**
4849 Santa Monica Blvd, Hollywood, CA, 90029
Studio tiles, stage floors, dance floors, solid color floors, solid color floors, shiny floors.
sales@linocity.com * www.linoleumcity.com

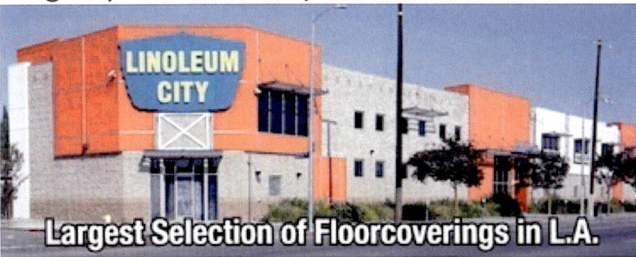

Studios

See: Locations, Stages/Studios, Film/TV/Events

Stuffed Animals

See: Taxidermy, Hides/Heads/Skeletons Toys & Games*

Stunts

See Also: Aircraft, Charters & Aerial Services Guilds, Unions, Societies, Associations* Nautical/Marine Services & Charters* Pyrotechnics* Rigging, Equipment or Services* Sporting Goods & Services* Swords & Swordplay* Vehicle Preparation Services* Vehicles/Picture Vehicles*
A1-STUNTWORLD inc   **(310) 666-3004**
Hollywood, CA 90028
stunt coordinators, stunt performers, master stunt riggers, stunt equipment rental (large inventory), skydivers & more.
www.stuntworldinc.com
CONFETTI & FOG FX Special Effects Company   **(877) 576-4239**
1085 W 21st Pl, Hialeah, FL, 33010
Stunt services and stunt equipment
Info@confettiandfogfx.com * www.caffx.com
L. A. Party Works   **(888) 527-2789**
9712 Alpaca St, S El Monte, CA, 91733
Free fall from up to 30' high on our 30ft square landing area. It's designed for the general public and for all ages.
partyworks@aol.com * www.partyworksinteractive.com

Styrofoam

See Also: Foam
DeRouchey Foam   **(888) 959-4852**
13618 Vaughn Street, San Fernando, CA, 91340
We offer a full line of foam sculpting materials and services. Urethane, EPS, HardCoat, Foam Adhesive. 24/7 Service.
info@derofoam.com * www.derofoam.com
Jackson Shrub Supply, Inc.   **(818) 982-0100**
garden styled foams, fluted column foam, foam blocks, foam rock clumps, foam wailing wall, giant garden foam clam shell

Sublimation Dye Printing

See: Printing, Graphics, Digital & Large Format

Suitcases

See: Luggage

Suits Of Armor

See: Armor, Chainmail, Suits of Armor

Sunglasses

See: Eyewear, Glasses, Sunglasses, 3D

Sunrise/Sunset Times

Old Farmer's Almanac   **(603) 563-8111**
1121 Main St, P.O. Box 520, Dublin, NH, 03444
North America's oldest, continuously published periodical.
www.almanac.com
Sunrise/Sunset Times   **(603) 563-8111**
This U.S. Navy site gives access to Sunrise/Sunset/Twilight times in U.S. & worldwide for 1000s of locations, past & fut
www.usno.navy.mil

Supermarket

See: Display Cases, Racks & Fixtures (Store) Food, Artificial Food* Grocery Check-out Stands (Complete)* Market Equipment/Fixtures* Prop Products & Packages* Shopping Bags (Silent)* Shopping Carts* Store Shelf Units & Shelving*

Surface Protection

See: Floor, Ground & Surface Protection

Surfaces

See: Surfaces, Tabletop Wall Coverings* Vacu-forms/Vacu-forming* Staff Shops* Scenery/Set Construction* Prop Reproduction & Fabrication* Plastics, Materials & Fabrication* Paneling, Veneers & Laminates* Paint & Painting Supplies* Moulding, Wood* Fiberglass Products/Fabrication* Fabrics*

Surfaces, Tabletop

The Surface Library   **(323) 546-9314**
A curated prop house specializing in surfaces and table top props for food, product, and lifestyle shoots.

Surfboard, Wakeboard

See Also: Sporting Goods & Services Wetsuits, Diving/Surfing*
C. P. Two   **(323) 466-8201**
Wood surfboards and fiberglass surfboards in long board and short board sizes.
The Hand Prop Room LP.   **(323) 931-1534**
period-present, long boards
LCW Props   **(818) 243-0707**
Some Styles, Call For An Updated Listing
Lennie Marvin Enterprises, Inc. (Prop Heaven)   **(818) 841-5882**
60s to present, surfboards, long boards & more
RC Vintage, Inc.   **(818) 765-7107**
surfboards; old long boards & modern, small surfboards too
Warner Bros. Studios Property Department   **(818) 954-2181**
Surfboards, wakeboards

Surgery Equipment & Lighting

See: Hospital Equipment Medical Equip/Furniture, Graphics/Supplies*

Surplus Stores

See: Military Props & Equipment Military Surplus/Combat Clothes, Field Gear*

Surveillance Equipment

See Also: Binoculars, Scopes & Telescopes* Police Equipment* Security Devices or Services

Bolide Technology   (909) 305-8889
468 S. San Dimas Ave, San Dimas, CA, 91773
security, spying & surveillance equipment
www.bolideco.com

E.C. Prop Rentals   (818) 764-2008
prop cameras, monitors, good multiples

Electronic City   (818) 632-4494
22287 Mulholland Highway #197, Calabasas, CA 91302
extensive variety of miniature components, consulting expertise
www.electroniccity.com

Gcom Consultants   011 44 20
42 Manchester St, London, England W1U7LW   355-4971
High-tech security, surveillance, protection equip.
www.gcomtech.com

The Hand Prop Room LP.   (323) 931-1534
LCW Props   (818) 243-0707
Large Selection Of Cameras, Van Interiors, Electronics, Graphics, etc.

Modern Props   (323) 934-3000
surveillance equipment including cameras, monitors, briefcases, consoles

Surveying Equipment

LCW Props   (818) 243-0707
Surveyors Kits, Tripods

Universal Studios Property & Hardware Dept   (818) 777-2784
Antique surveyor equipment/surveying equipment

Swamp Coolers

See: Rooftop Dressing

Swap Meets, Southern California

Canning Enterprises & Attractions   (323) 560-7469
4515 E 59th Pl, Maywood, CA 90270
Promoter of many different flea markets, select events & swap meets in So.
Cal. Call Mon-Fri 10AM-5PM

Long Beach Antique Market   (323) 655-5703
4901 E Conant Street, Long Beach, CA 90808
3rd Sunday of every month.
www.longbeachantiquemarket.com

Metropolitan Marketing   (818) 884-6430
6320 Canoga Ave, Suite 1630, Woodland Hills, CA, 91367
indoor swap meets & events

Pasadena City College Flea Market   (626) 585-7906
1570 E. Colorado Boulevard, Pasadena, CA 91106
1st Sunday of every month.
www.pasadena.edu/fleamarket

Rose Bowl Flea Market   (323) 560-7469
1001 Rose Bowl Dr, Pasadena, CA, 91103
2nd Sunday of every month.
mlrshowbiz@aol.com * www.rgcshows.com/RoseBowl.aspx

San Bernardino Out Door Flea Market   (323) 560-7469
689 S E St, San Bernardino, CA, 92408
Every Sunday.
www.rgcshows.com/SanBernardino.aspx

Topanga Vintage Market   (310) 422-1844
Victory Blvd & Mason Ave, Pierce College, Woodland Hills, CA, 91306
4th Sunday of every month.
info@topangavintagemarket.com * www.topangavintagemarket.com

Valley Indoor Swap Meet - Panorama City   (818) 892-0183
14650 Parthenia St, Panorama City, CA, 91402
Every day except Tuesdays.
info@indoorswap.com *
www.indoorswap.com/index2.php?location=PanoramaCity

Valley Indoor Swap Meet - Pomona   (909) 620-4792
1600 East Holt Blvd, Pomona, CA, 91767
Every day except Tuesdays.
info@indoorswap.com * www.indoorswap.com/index2.php?location=Pomona

Ventura County Fairgrounds Flea Market   (323) 560-7469
10 W Harbor Blvd, Ventura, CA, 93001
Held 7 times a year, see website for details.
www.rgcshows.com/Ventura.aspx

Swat Team

See: Police Car, Police Motorcycle* Police Equipment

Swim Wear

See: Bathing Suits, Swim & Beach Wear

Swimming Pool Dressing & Accessories

See Also: Jacuzzis, Spas & Pools* Locations, Underwater Sets & Filming Tanks* Sporting Goods & Services

Sony Pictures Studios-Prop House (Off Lot)   (310) 244-5999
Swimming pool equipment/swimming equipment and swimming accessories.

Universal Studios Property & Hardware Dept   (818) 777-2784
Swimming pool floats and toys

Swimming Pools

See: Jacuzzis, Spas & Pools

Swings

See: Furniture, Outdoor/Patio* Playground Equipment

Switchboards

History For Hire, Inc.   (818) 765-7767
some rigged, electrical walls

LCW Props   (818) 243-0707
Period - Present, Lighting, Rigged, Security, Police, Head sets

Universal Studios Property & Hardware Dept   (818) 777-2784
Telephone switchboard props with headphones and mics for rent. Vintage to contemporary.

Swords & Swordplay

See Also: Weapons

Academy of Theatrical Combat   (818) 364-8420
Call for appt, North Hollywood, CA 91605
on set choreographing/training for fencing, sword rental
www.theatricalcombat.com

Costume Armour Inc.   (845) 534-9120
2 Mill Street, Building 1 Suite 101, Cornwall, NY 12518
Medieval weapons
info@costumearmour.com * www.costumearmour.com

The Hand Prop Room LP.   (323) 931-1534
period-present rubber, foam, military, medieval, ninja, cust.

History For Hire, Inc.   (818) 765-7767
LCW Props   (818) 243-0707
Quanitities Of Swords, Period - Present

Society of American Fight Directors   (818) 243-0707
1350 E Flamingo Rd #25, Las Vegas, NV, 89119
contact regional rep. via their web site
www.safd.org

Sony Pictures Studios-Prop House (Off Lot)   (310) 244-5999
metal, rubber, leather & plastic

Sword & Stone   (818) 562-6548
all nations & periods, steel, aluminum, custom made

Swordplay LA   (818) 566-1777
416 S Victory Blvd, Burbank, CA, 91502
sword choreography/training for film & TV
www.swordplayla.com

Universal Studios Property & Hardware Dept   (818) 777-2784
All kinds of prop swords from all time periods for rent.

T-shirts

See: Embroidery, Screen Printing, Etc.* Fabric Dyeing/Tie Dyeing/Painting/Aging* Promotional Items & Materials* Wardrobe

Tablecloths

See: Linens, Household

Tables

See Also: Cafe Tables/Chairs/Umbrellas* Folding Chairs/Tables* Furniture, Outdoor/Patio* Furniture, Plexi/Lucite* Office Equipment & Dressing* Office Furniture* Prop Houses* Serving Tables & Serving Carts

Advanced Liquidators Office Furniture   (818) 763-3470
new, used, wide selection of office furniture, tables for any purpose in any size, design, model, and style.

AIR Designs   (818) 768-6639
Indoor, Outdoor, Restaurant, Diner, Fast Food, Bar, Coffee House, Auto

Asian Art Imports   (818) 778-0852
16876 Stagg St, Van Nuys, CA, 91406
Asian Art Imports stocks a variety of tables.
asianartimports@yahoo.com * www.asianartimports.com

Badia Design, Inc.   (818) 762-0130
5420 Vineland Ave, N Hollywood, CA, 91601
Badia Design Inc. imports many different types of Moroccan tables which include wood, wrought iron, metal and more.
info@badiadesign.com * www.badiadesign.com

Bridge Furniture & Props Los Angeles   **(818) 433-7100**
We carry modern & traditional furniture, lighting, accessories, art,& rugs. Items are online for easy shopping.

BRIDGE LA
FURNITURE & PROPS

3210 Vanowen St.   BridgeProps.com
Burbank, CA 91505   Tel: 818.433.7100

E.C. Prop Rentals   **(818) 764-2008**
Office, utility, workshop, lab, wood/metal/stainless steel
LCW Props   **(818) 243-0707**
Folding, Restaurant / Bar, Plastic, Wood, Metal
Lennie Marvin Enterprises, Inc. (Prop Heaven)   **(818) 841-5882**
variety of styles
Lux Lounge EFR   **(888) 247-4411**
106 1/2 Judge John Aiso St #318, Los Angeles, CA, 90012
Tables of Various Kinds in Multiples.
info@luxloungeefr.com * www.luxloungeefr.com
Modern Props   **(323) 934-3000**
conference tables, coffee tables, dining tables, end tables, cafe tables, consoles, drafting tables
Modernica Props   **(323) 664-2322**
NEST Studio Rentals, Inc.   **(818) 942-0339**
dining, occasional
Old N Country Prop Shop, LLC   **(818) 423-2599**
A large assortment of different shaped and sized antique and vintage tables. Dining, End Tables, etc.
Omega/Cinema Props   **(323) 466-8201**
Picture Start Props   **(818) 255-5472**
Dining, coffee tables, end tables, side tables, sofa tables and more
Prop Services West   **(818) 503-2790**
RC Vintage, Inc.   **(818) 765-7107**
Tables of all kinds from end tables and coffee tables to dining tables and patio tables.
A Royal Suite Home Furinishings   **(661) 259-7000**
26536 Carl Boyer Dr, Santa Clarita, CA, 91350
A Royal Suite, family-owned since 1978, Features AMERICAN-MADE Furniture, and the Finest Furniture at the Greatest Value
norb@ars-email.com * www.aroyalsuite.com
Sony Pictures Studios-Prop House (Off Lot)   **(310) 244-5999**
Coffee, computer, sewing, serving, all kinds of tables
Universal Studios Property & Hardware Dept   **(818) 777-2784**
All kinds of tables for rent for all occasions and themes.
Warner Bros. Studios Property Department   **(818) 954-2181**
Side tables & end tables, dining tables, console tables, buffet tables, cafe tables, work tables
ZG04 DECOR   **(818) 853-8040**
Modern Tables, Contemporary Tables, Traditional Tables, Transitional Tables, Vintage Tables, Eclectic Tables

Tableware/Flatware

See Also: Events, Decorations, Supplies & Services Fiesta Dinnerware* Kitchen Dressing* Pewter & Pewterware* Prop Houses* Silverware, Silver Serving Pieces*
Bargain Fair (Mid-City)   **(323) 965-2227**
4635 W Pico Blvd, Los Angeles, CA, 90019
corner of Fairfax; dinnerware, glassware, silverware, cookware & more at unbelievable prices, open 7 days
sheida@bargainfair.com * www.bargainfair.com
History For Hire, Inc.   **(818) 765-7767**
restaurant, Old West
LCW Props   **(818) 243-0707**
Stainless Steel, Silver, Antique
Old N Country Prop Shop, LLC   **(818) 423-2599**
A wide range of flat and tableware, in a variety of styles.
Omega/Cinema Props   **(323) 466-8201**
Prop Services West   **(818) 503-2790**
Replacements, Ltd   **(800) 737-5223**
1089 Knox Rd, McLeansville, NC, 27301
Enormous inventory of china, crystal, silverware, more than 300,000 patterns; matching, repairs, research
www.replacements.com
Universal Studios Property & Hardware Dept   **(818) 777-2784**
All kinds of tableware and flatware for rent.
Warner Bros. Studios Property Department   **(818) 954-2181**
Assorted patterns of flatware, silver flatware, serving flatware & utensils
ZG04 DECOR   **(818) 853-8040**
Serving utensils, Dish-sets, Barware, Platters, Carafe, silverware, flatware

Tackle

See: Fishing Equipment & Tackle

Taco (Food) Carts

See: Vendor Carts & Concession Counters

Taco Carts (Propmaster & Set)

See: Set Boxes & Taco Carts (Propmaster & Set)

Tanker Desks

See: Office Furniture

40 YEARS OF DEBBIES BOOK

Debbies Book
DB
2014   26th Edition
THE ENTERTAINMENT INDUSTRY'S RESOURCE SINCE 1978

The Tonight Show snagged **Jimmy Fallon**, climate changes moved faster around the world, and the **Ebola virus** became a frequent topic in the news. The Church of England voted on allowing women to become bishops, and we wondered if the Cold War was once again being waged.

Debbies Book was released in both print and e-Book editions again, and upgrades were made to the iTunes app to include live turn by turn driving instructions. Meanwhile, release of the **Android app** just before Valentine's Day made Android users happy.

Tanks

See Also: Aquariums & Tropical Fish* Barrels & Drums,
Wood/Metal/Plastic* Factory/Industrial* Wine Kegs

E.C. Prop Rentals (818) 764-2008
Large liquid storage, castered nitrogen tanks, propane, welding

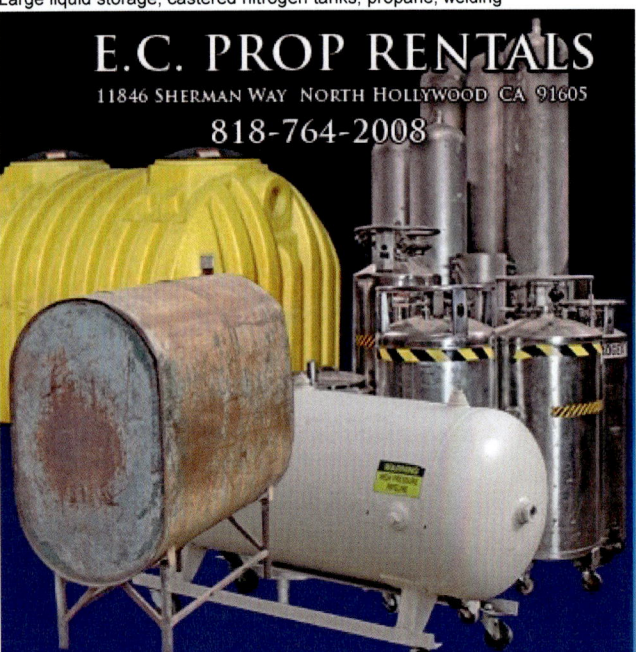

LCW Props (818) 243-0707
Our Specialty. Large Selection Of Any Style Tanks. Industrial, Safety, Cryo,
Nitrogen / Oxygen, Hi Vac, etc.

Machinery & Equipment Co., Inc. (909) 599-3916
115 N Cataract Ave, San Dimas, CA, 91773
Used tanks from 1 liter to 20,000 gallon, including stainless steel, carbon steel,
plastic, fiberglass and more.
sherri@machineryandequipment.com * www.machineryandequipment.com

Tape

See: Expendables

Tape Recorders

C. P. Two (323) 466-8201
Various models, sizes, and types of tape recorders.
The Hand Prop Room LP. (323) 931-1534
period-present
History For Hire, Inc. (818) 765-7767
most eras
LCW Props (818) 243-0707
Period - Present, Data Racks, Reel To Reel
Old N Country Prop Shop, LLC (818) 423-2599
A Variety of WORKING Reel-to-Reel, 8-Track, and Cassette Players and
Recorders. Tapes to go with them too!
Picture Start Props (818) 255-5472
Some vintage small and larger tape recorders

Tapestry Wall Hangings

Ob-jects (818) 351-4200
Tapestry wall hangings
Omega/Cinema Props (323) 466-8201
Sony Pictures Studios-Prop House (Off Lot) (310) 244-5999
Wall decorations, dream catchers, fabric wall decorations, floral wall
decorations, wall plaque, wicker wall decorations, more
Warner Bros. Drapery, Upholstery & Flooring (818) 954-1831
4000 Warner Blvd Bldg 30, Burbank, CA, 91522
Vintage; Modern
wbsfdrapery@warnerbros.com * www.wbdrapery.com
Warner Bros. Studios Property Department (818) 954-2181
Assorted wall hanging tapestries, see WBSF Drapery department
Y & B Bolour (310) 274-6719
321 S Robertson Blvd, Los Angeles, CA, 90048
www.ybbolour.com

Tarot Cards

See: Occult/Spiritual/Metaphysical

Tarps

See: Sewing Services, Industrial* Tarps, Covers, Custom Sewing

Tarps, Covers, Custom Sewing

AA Surplus Sales Co., Inc. (323) 526-3622
2940 E Olympic Blvd, Los Angeles, CA, 90023
U.S. military camouflage nets, army cargo parachutes and personnel
parachutes, desert OD tarps, etc.
surplusking@hotmail.com * www.aasurplus.com
EIDE Industries, Inc (562) 402-8335
16215 Piuma Ave, Cerritos, CA, 90703
Custom mfg. of awnings, canopies, tents, covers, cabanas, tension structures;
industrial sewing services
www.EIDEIndustries.com
ProtecTarps, Inc. (818) 771-1211
11176 Penrose St #10, Sun Valley, CA, 91352
Tarpaulins and custom covers. Onsite sewing fabrication, RF welding and
custom fabrics. Fast turn-around.
www.protectarps.com

Tattoo & Body Piercing Equipment & Supplies

See Also: Goth/Punk/Bondage/Fetish/Erotica Etc.
The Hand Prop Room LP. (323) 931-1534
History For Hire, Inc. (818) 765-7767
period tattoo equip & flesh art
RC Vintage, Inc. (818) 765-7107
Tattoo Guns and Signs Swatches Chairs. Vintage Tattoo Signs, A-Frames
Sony Pictures Studios-Prop House (Off Lot) (310) 244-5999
photos & samples of tattoos

Tattoos (Temporary) Body/Face Painting

See Also: Make-up & Hair, Supplies & Services* Special Effects, Make-up/Prosthetics

Faux Tattoo Studio (323) 332-2882
Call for appointment
Temporary tattoos and body art for production, music videos and photo shoots using the latest of cutting edge technology.
info@fauxtattoostudios.com * www.fauxtattoostudios.com

L. A. Party Works (888) 527-2789
9712 Alpaca St, S El Monte, CA, 91733
in Vancouver tel. 604-589-4101
partyworks@aol.com * www.partyworksinteractive.com

Reel Creations, Inc. (818) 346-7335
7831 Alabama Ave Ste 21, Canoga Park, CA, 91304
innovator of the original temporary tattoo process, stock/custom
www.reelcreations.com

TATS (310) 686-1956
Call for Appt
Mobile temp. airbrush tattoos, private parties, corp events, fundraisers, up to 5 artists.
tatstattoo.com

Tinsley Transfers (818) 767-4277
Web Based Business - Sun Valley, 91352
custom & in-stock SFX tattoos
www.tinsleytransfers.com

Tavern Dressing

See: Bars, Nightclubs, Barware & Dressing* Jukeboxes, Music/Dance Machines* Liquor Bottles* Paintings/Prints* Restaurant Furniture & Dressing

Taxidermy, Hides/Heads/Skeletons

See Also: Bones, Skulls & Skeletons* Fossils

Artkraft Taxidermy Rentals (818) 505-8425
Taxidermied birds, fish, mammals, and much more from Africa, North America, and exotic locales.

MUSEUM QUALITY TAXIDERMIED ANIMALS · FROM ANTELOPES TO ZEBRAS
ESTABLISHED 1969 HOLLYWOOD, CA

Bischoff's Animal EFX + Taxidermy (818) 843-7561
54 E Magnolia Blvd, Burbank, CA, 91502
life-size animals, animal fabrication & FX, hides, furs & head mounts
bischoffsanimals@gmail.com * http://www.bischoffsanimals.com

C. P. Two (323) 466-8201
Cow skulls, steer longhorns, deer heads, moose heads, coyote taxidermy, skunk taxidermy and more; Hunting lodge dressing.

Caravan West Productions (661) 268-8300
35660 Jayhawker Rd, Aqua Dulce, CA, 91390
Deer heads, buffalo heads, cow heads, horse heads, coyote heads, bear heads, antlers, hides and skins, furs.
caravanwest@earthlink.net * www.caravanwest.com

Dapper Cadaver (818) 771-0818
Fake lifelike & wounded animals. Butcher shop. Taxidermy, specimens, skeletons & rubber reptiles. Custom FX.

The Hand Prop Room LP. (323) 931-1534
lrg sel.

History For Hire, Inc. (818) 765-7767
animal hides, skulls, skeletons

Jonas Supply Company (800) 279-7985
PO Box 480, Granite Quarry, NC 28072
catalog sales; taxidermy supplies & tools.
www.jonas-supply.com

Lietzau Taxidermy (320) 877-7297
320 N Saturn, Cosmos, MN, 56228
Catalog; reproduction craft & costuming supplies. Native American dressing.

LM Treasures (626) 252-7354
We have animal heads ranging from life size tiger heads to moose heads, personally handcrafted to make each one unique.

Sony Pictures Studios-Prop House (Off Lot) (310) 244-5999
Stuffed animals from birds to camels and everything in between. Animal traps

Universal Studios Property & Hardware Dept (818) 777-2784
Many kinds of taxidermy of various animals for rent.

Tchotchkes

See: Children/Baby Accessories & Bedroom* Decorative Accessories* Miniatures/Models* Model Ships/Planes/Trains/Autos Etc.* Toys & Games

Tech Benches

LCW Props (818) 243-0707

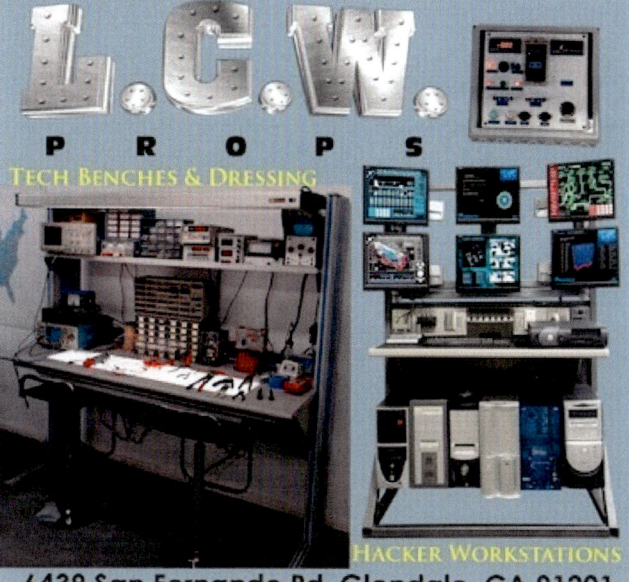

6439 San Fernando Rd. Glendale, CA 91201
Phone: 818-243-0707 - www.lcwprops.com

Modern Props (323) 934-3000
tech benches and dressing

RJR Props (404) 349-7600
Tech bench rentals; computers are our specialty so so we have a lot of tech bench dressing

Woody's Electrical Props (818) 503-1940

Teeter-Totter

See: Playground Equipment

Teeth

See: Dentist Equipment

Teeth & Braces

See: Special Effects, Make-up/Prosthetics

Telegrams (Prop)

History For Hire, Inc. (818) 765-7767
custom

Telephone Booths & Pay Telephones

AIR Designs	(818) 768-6639
Period to Present, USA Phone Booths, Pedestal Phones	
Alley Cats Studio Rentals	(818) 982-9178
New York, L.A., various styles	
C. P. Two	(323) 466-8201
Telephone booths from standing and walk in to British and wall mounted. Antique pay phones and modern.	
E.C. Prop Rentals	(818) 764-2008
pedestal-style booths, wall-mount payphones	
The Hand Prop Room LP.	(323) 931-1534
domestic, English	
History For Hire, Inc.	(818) 765-7767
LCW Props	(818) 243-0707
Wood, Metal, Period - Present	
Lennie Marvin Enterprises, Inc. (Prop Heaven)	(818) 841-5882
Many pay phones available w/ stands, kiosks and without.	
LM Treasures	(626) 252-7354
We offer different types of telephone booths including booths you can stand in and booths you can use as a cabinet.	
Modern Props	(323) 934-3000
contemporary/vintage, metallic pay phone sets, street pay phones, triple unit pay phones, airport phones, variety	
Omega/Cinema Props	(323) 466-8201
Telephone booths from standing and walk in to British and wall mounted. Antique pay phones and modern.	
RC Vintage, Inc.	(818) 765-7107
large selection Oak, and Aluminum phone booths. 1930's - 1990's	
Sony Pictures Studios-Prop House (Off Lot)	(310) 244-5999
telephone booths, telephone signs, telephone oedestaks	
Universal Studios Property & Hardware Dept	(818) 777-2784
Many kinds of prop pay phones/phone booths for rent from different time periods and regions.	

Telephone Directories

See: Telephones

Telephone Poles Prop

See Also: Electrical/Electronic Supplies & Services Insulators*

AIR Designs	(818) 768-6639
12' wooden poles, call box poles	
E.C. Prop Rentals	(818) 764-2008
Wooden poles, crossbars, transformer cans, and porcelain insulators	

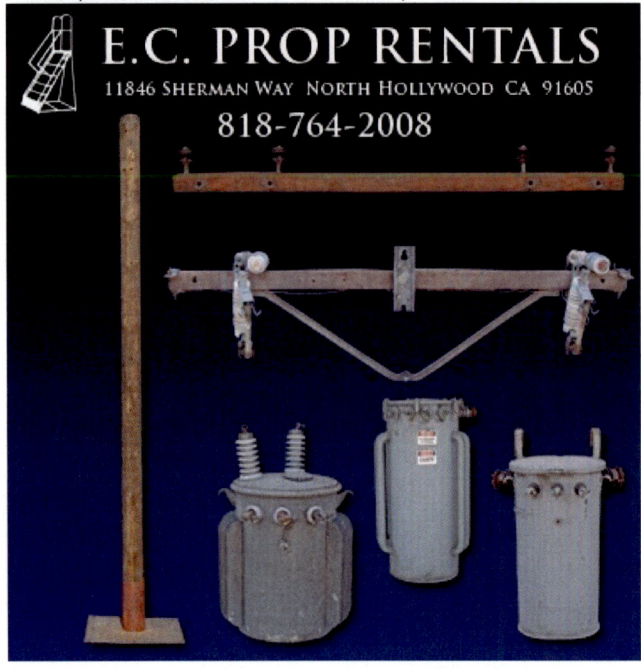

Telephones

See Also: Intercoms Switchboards* Telephone Booths & Pay Telephones* Telephones, Cellular*

Advanced Liquidators Office Furniture	(818) 763-3470
large sel. contemp. used desktop dressing	
Alley Cats Studio Rentals	(818) 982-9178
dial, push-button, period, modern & cell phones	
E.C. Prop Rentals	(818) 764-2008
Industrial telephone cabinets, freeway call box w/ optional sign/pole/base/solar panel	
The Hand Prop Room LP.	(323) 931-1534
period-present, lrg sel.	
History For Hire, Inc.	(818) 765-7767
big selection & colors, very good condition	
LCW Props	(818) 243-0707
Large Selection Of Office Phones, Some Rigged / Working	
Modern Props	(323) 934-3000
contemporary/futuristic, large selection, many colors, themes, purposes, and time periods	
Old N Country Prop Shop, LLC	(818) 423-2599
A variety of different colors and styles vintage phones. Dial, wall, push-button, trimline, etc.	
Omega/Cinema Props	(323) 466-8201
Office phones and desk phones antique to contemporary; residential phones from antique to modern.	
Picture Start Props	(818) 255-5472
Vintage rotary phones as well as large selection of vintage cell phones.	
Prop Services West	(818) 503-2790
RC Vintage, Inc.	(818) 765-7107
30s to 60s, period, modern, all colors	
Sony Pictures Studios-Prop House (Off Lot)	(310) 244-5999
cell phones, call boxes, grey command box, dialess phones, telephone intercom, military field phones, mobile telephone, more	
Universal Studios Property & Hardware Dept	(818) 777-2784
All kinds of phones with all kinds of functions from all kinds of periods for rent.	

Telephones, Cellular

See Also: Telephone Booths & Pay Telephones Telephones* Walkie-Talkies*

Airwaves Wireless	(818) 501-8200

13400 Riverside Dr # 103 Sherman Oaks, CA, 91423
Cell phones, Cell Service, Tablets, Laptops, POS Displays, Smart Watches, Credit Card Readers, Android, Windows, Apple.
sales@airwaveswireless.com * www.airwaveswireless.com

The Hand Prop Room LP.	(323) 931-1534
rigged	
LCW Props	(818) 243-0707
Large Selection Of Older Model Cell Phones	
Wireless for All	(818) 551-9191

919 S Glendale Ave Ste A1, Glendale, CA, 91205
Unlocked cell phones, used cell phones, and new cell phones. All brands and models available.
wirelessforallsocal@gmail.com * www.instagram.com/wirelessforall

Teleprompting

Cue Tech Teleprompting   (818) 487-2700
5527 Satsuma Ave, N Hollywood, CA, 91601
www.cue-tech.com
Vision Prompt, Inc.   (818) 223-8884
23958 Craftsman Rd, Calabasas, CA, 91302
Teleprompting services and equipment rental.
www.visionprompt.com
Vitec Video Com   (212) 929-7755
44 Progress Dr, Shelton CT, 06484
www.vitecvideocom.com

Telescopes

See: Binoculars, Scopes & Telescopes

Teletypes

History For Hire, Inc.   (818) 765-7767
some practical

Television Antennas

See: Rooftop Dressing

Television Lighting

See: Stage Lighting, Film/Video/TV

Television Stations

See: Locations, Stages/Studios, Film/TV/Events

Television Studio Dressing

See Also: Video Equipment
E.C. Prop Rentals   (818) 764-2008
assorted parts/switches & dimmer boards
The Hand Prop Room LP.   (323) 931-1534
History For Hire, Inc.   (818) 765-7767
huge inventory, TV cameras all eras many practical, control room
LCW Props   (818) 243-0707
AV Racks, Mics, Booms, Control Panels & Boards, Mixing, Cameras

Televisions

24Frame.com, Inc.   (213) 745-2411
944 Venice Blvd, Los Angeles, CA, 90015
TV sets for sync playback
info@24frame.com * www.24frame.com
Astro Audio Video Lighting, Inc.   (818) 549-9915
6615 San Fernando Rd, Glendale, CA, 91201
TVs 13" to 80" plasma TVs, LED TVs; video walls, projectors & projection
screens in all sizes.
www.astroavl.com
C. P. Two   (323) 466-8201
TVs/Televisions of carious periods
The Hand Prop Room LP.   (323) 931-1534
History For Hire, Inc.   (818) 765-7767
LCW Props   (818) 243-0707
LCD, Plasma, Computer Monitors Large & Small. Also Fake TV's As Well
Modern Props   (323) 934-3000
contemporary/futuristic televisions/TVs
Omega/Cinema Props   (323) 466-8201
RC Vintage, Inc.   (818) 765-7107
30s to 60s, floor models & portable
RJR Props   (404) 349-7600
Prop televisions/prop TV's for rent; antique to modern; many different sizes.
Universal Studios Property & Hardware Dept   (818) 777-2784
Many prop tvs/ prop television for rent.
Warner Bros. Studios Property Department   (818) 954-2181
Big Screen Television, Console Television, Converter Boxes, Flat Panel
Television, LCD televisions

Tennis Equipment

See: Prop Houses* Sporting Goods & Services

Tents

See: Canopies, Tents, Gazebos, Cabanas

Tepees

See: Native American

Text Books

See: Books, Real/Hollow & Faux Books* School Supplies, Desks &
Dressing

Textilene

See: Fabrics* Upholstery Materials/Services* Fabric Dyeing/Tie
Dyeing/Painting/Aging

Textiles

See: Fabrics

Theater Seating

See Also: Audience Seating
Alley Cats Studio Rentals   (818) 982-9178
multiple seats, theater seats sections of 2 and 4, cinema chairs
C. P. Two   (323) 466-8201
Vintage theatre seating to vinyl theatre seating and upholstered theatre seating
& theatre seats
Lennie Marvin Enterprises, Inc. (Prop Heaven)   (818) 841-5882
rows of seats
Universal Studios Property & Hardware Dept   (818) 777-2784
Theater seating for rent.

Theaters

See: Locations, Insert Stages & Theatres* Locations, Stages/Studios,
Film/TV/Events

Theatrical Draperies, Hardware & Rigging

See Also: Backings* Drapery & Curtains* Flameproofing* Rigging,
Equipment or Services
iWeiss Theatrical Solutions   (888) 325-7192
815 Fairview Ave #10, Fairview, NJ 07022
draperies, curtain track, hanging hdw, fabric
info@iweiss.com * www.iweiss.com
Lushes Curtains   (626) 453-0337
1855 Tyler Ave Unit C, S El Monte, CA, 91733
Your Direct Velvet Curtain Manufacture! Delivering Elegant and Quality
Curtains to Every Industry World Wide!
Joe@LushesCurtains.com * www.LushesCurtains.com
Omega/Cinema Props   (323) 466-8201
S & K Theatrical Draperies   (818) 503-0596
7313 Varna Ave, N Hollywood, CA, 91605
www.sktheatricaldraperies.com
Sapsis Rigging, Inc.   (800) 727-7471
3883 Ridge Ave, Philadelphia, PA, 19132
www.sapsis-rigging.com
ShopWildThings   (928) 855-6075
2880 Sweetwater Ave, Lake Havasu City, AZ, 86406
Event Decor, Beaded Curtains, Chain Curtains, String Curtains & Columns,
Crystal Columns. Reliable service & delivery.
help@shopwildthings.com * www.shopwildthings.com
Triangle Scenery Drapery Co.   (323) 662-8129
PO Box 29205, Los Angeles, CA, 90029
Theatrical fabrics - fabrication - rigging
tcmill@aol.com * www.tridrape.com
TRU-ROLL   (626) 599-8337
735 Los Angeles Ave, Monrovia, CA, 91016
Design and manufacture theatrical tracks, counterweight rigging systems, stage
and pipe grid hardware and stage drapery.
info@truroll.com * www.truroll.com
Universal Studios Drapery Dept   (818) 777-2761
Warner Bros. Drapery, Upholstery & Flooring   (818) 954-1831
4000 Warner Blvd Bldg 30, Burbank, CA, 91522
Theatrical; Beaded; Rope tie backs; Vintage fringed; Velour, damask, velvet &
Mylar; Pipe & Base
wbsfdrapery@warnerbros.com * www.wbdrapery.com

Theatrical Make-up

See: Make-up & Hair, Supplies & Services* Make-up Schools

Themed Environment Construction

See Also: Architectural Pieces & Artifacts* Audio/Visual Film
Equipment* Prop Design & Manufacturing* Scenery/Set
Construction* Special Effects, Electronic* Special Effects, Lighting &
Lasers* Stage Lighting, Film/Video/TV

Barry Howard Ltd   **(805) 966-6622**
420 E Carrillo St, Santa Barbara, CA, 93101
museum & themed attraction design, planning, development
www.barryhowardlimited.com

BRC Imagination Arts   **(818) 841-8084**
2711 Winona Ave, Burbank, CA, 91504
design, plan, produce themed attractions, educational attractions, brand
experiences
www.brcweb.com

BRPH Entertainment Design Studio   **(321) 254-7666**
5700 N Harbor City Blvd Ste 400, Melbourne, FL, 32940
architectural, civil, structural, mechanical, electrical, program mgmnt, design &
build services to the Industry
www.brph.com

Chicago Scenic Studios, Inc.   **(312) 274-9900**
955 W. Cermak Rd, Chicago IL, 60608
Design and/or build spaces for museums, amusement parks, special &
corporate events, broadcast, retail
info@chicagoscenic.com * www.chicagoscenic.com

Cost of Wisconsin, Inc.   **(800) 221-7625**
4201 Co Rd P, Jackson, WI, 53037
Themed facades, architectural panels, simulated trees, sculptures, rock &
water features, murals
www.costofwisconsin.com

Cuningham Group   **(310) 895-2200**
8665 Hayden Place, Culver City, CA 90232
full range of design svcs; feasibility studies, planning, architecture, interior
design & construction svcs
hello@cuningham.com * www.cuningham.com

David L. Manwarren Corp.   **(909) 989-5883**
3830 Wacker Dr, Mira Loma CA, 91752
Design & build aquarium, zoo, and museum exhibits, international clientele
www.manwarrenhabitats.com

Designage, Inc.   **(407) 647-2950**
311 Circle Dr, Maitland, FL, 32751
design, build themed environments for theme parks, resorts, entertainment
projects
www.designage.net

Dillon Works! Inc.   **(425) 493-8309**
11775 Harbour Reach Dr, Mukilteo, WA, 98275
interior/exterior dimensional and architectural elements, custom design &
fabrication
www.dillonworks.com

Duncan Design, Inc.   **(707) 636-2300**
48 Barham Ave, Santa Rosa, CA, 95407
design/fabricate/install museum exhibits, retail displays, themed sets, props &
backings
info@duncandesigninc.com * www.duncandesigninc.com

Huitt Zollars   **(407) 839-0414**
111N Magnolia Ave Suite 1600, Orlando, FL, 32801
design & master planning services for themed public facilities
www.morrisarchitects.com

KHS & S Contractors   **(714) 695-3670**
5109 E La Palma Ave Ste A, Anaheim, CA, 92807
Interior & exterior finishes, rockwork/water features, large-scale projects
www.khss.com

KIHL STUDIOS   **(818) 812-9594**
9701 Owensmouth Ave Unit 1, Chatsworth, CA, 91311
We build worlds! Permanent experiential decor, temporary pop-up installations,
photo ops, signage, and more.
design@kihlstudios.com * www.kihlstudios.com

The Nassal Company   **(407) 648-0400**
415 W Kaley St, Orlando, FL, 32806
Theming, exhibitory & rockwork fabrication, installation services provided
worldwide since 1984
www.nassal.com

Penwal Industries, Inc.   **(909) 466-1555**
10611 Acacia St, Rancho Cucamonga, CA, 91730
Design, engineering, proj. mgmnt., & construction of exhibits, and retail spaces
www.penwal.com

R. D. Olson Construction   **(949) 474-2001**
2955 Main Street, Third Floor, Irvine, CA, 92614
General construction for projects in entertainment, restaurant, retail &
hospitality industries, ask for Tim Cromwell
www.rdolson.com

Reynolds Advanced Materials: Smooth-On   **(818) 358-6000**
Distributor
10856 Vanowen St, N Hollywood, CA, 91605
Hollywood's F/X source for Liquid Rubbers, Plastics & more. NEW Smooth-0n
HABITAT Zoo Epoxy Putty and Fire Rated version.
LA@reynoldsam.com * www.moldmakingmaterials.com

Sparks Exhibits & Environments   **(562) 941-0101**
3143 S La Cienega Blvd, Los Angeles, CA, 90016
Design, construction, installation; extensive fabrication, special effects
capability, worldwide
wearesparks.com

ThemeWorks, Inc.   **(386) 454-7500**
17594 Main Street, High Springs FL, 32643
Design/build scenery, rockwork, architectural elements, sculpture, exhibits,
artificial animals
www.themeworks.com

Utopia Entertainment, Inc.   **(818) 980-9940**
4111 W Alameda Ave, Burbank CA, 91505
Full service, turnkey, design, fabrication, installation; permanent installations &
live shows
www.utopiaworldwide.com

Warner Bros. Design Studio   **(818) 954-4430**
4000 Warner Blvd Bldg 44, Burbank, CA, 91522
Concept, Design, Fabrication of Interior & Exterior Standing Sets, Facades,
Exhibits, Road Shows
wbds@warnerbros.com * www.warnerbrosdesignstudio.com

Themed Environments/Entertainment

See: Events, Decorations, Supplies & Services* Events,
Design/Planning/Production* Events, Entertainment* Prop Design &
Manufacturing* Prop Houses* Scenery/Set Construction

Thermometers, Wall

Alley Cats Studio Rentals   **(818) 982-9178**
antique, modern
E.C. Prop Rentals   **(818) 764-2008**
nice variety
LCW Props   **(818) 243-0707**
Stainless Steel, Industrial, & Old Factory

Thirties Theme Parties

See: Costume Rental Houses* Costumes* Events, Backings &
Scenery* Events, Decorations, Supplies & Services* Events,
Design/Planning/Production* Historical Era Themed Events*
Wardrobe, Vintage

Thrift Shops

See Also: Charities & Donations* Furniture, Used/Second Hand

American Way Thrift Store   **(818) 841-6013**
3226 W. Magnolia Blvd, Burbank, CA, 91505
www.americanwaythriftstores.com

Carriage "Hope" Children's Charity   **(818) 509-9515**
11311 Vanowen St, N Hollywood, CA, 91605
Thrift Store with 1000s of vintage, contemp. & antique household items,
clothing & collectibles; fine art, open 7 days.
hope@carriagehope.org * www.carriagehope.org

Children's Hospital Los Angeles Thrift Shop   **(818) 845-6606**
3301 W Burbank Blvd, Burbank, CA, 91505
(open T, W, Th, Sat; 10-4) benefits Children's Hospital of L.A.
ThriftShop@LaProvidenciaGuild.org *
www.laprovidenciaguild.org/Thrift_Shop.html

Goodwill Industries   **(818) 242-9399**
1622 W. Glenoaks Blvd, Glendale, CA, 91202
www.goodwillsocal.org

Habitat for Humanity of Greater Los Angeles   **(424) 246-3637**
8739 E Artesia Blvd, Bellflower, CA, 90706
Habitat's ReStores are home-improvement thrift stores, helping to fund our
mission. Free pick-up, tax-deductible.
www.ShopHabitat.org

Helping Hand Thrift Shop   **(323) 857-1191**
1033 South Fairfax Ave, Los Angeles, CA, 90019
We are a thrift store with a constantly changing inventory.
fairfaxhelpinghand@gmail.com * www.helpinghandthriftshop.com

Out of the Closet Thrift Store   **(323) 664-4394**
3160 Glendale Blvd, Glendale, CA, 90039
http://outofthecloset.org

Thrones

FROST   **(310) 704-8812**
Call for Appointment - 21405 Madrona Ave, Torrance, CA, 90503
Oversized Santa thrones for all your santa set needs. Check our website for
styles available!
mdisplay@yahoo.com * www.frostchristmasprops.com
History For Hire, Inc.   **(818) 765-7767**
Santa
Omega/Cinema Props   **(323) 466-8201**
Universal Studios Property & Hardware Dept   **(818) 777-2784**
Many kinds of thrones from all kinds of periods.

Tiaras

See: Crowns & Tiaras

Ticker Tape & Machines

History For Hire, Inc.   **(818) 765-7767**
Ticker tape machines
RC Vintage, Inc.   **(818) 765-7107**
Early 1920's Type Glass dome

Ticket Booths

See Also: Carnival Dressing/Supplies
AIR Designs   **(818) 768-6639**
Guard booth/ticket booth, Parking Lot booth, Toll Gate Arms, Ticket
Dispensers
Alley Cats Studio Rentals   **(818) 982-9178**
ornate deco ticket booths
Amusement Svcs/Candyland Amusements   **(818) 266-4056**
18653 Ventura Blvd Ste 235, Tarzana, CA, 91356
ticket vendors, Carnival entrance, Ticket carts, carnival booths, game booths,
stub booths, entry booths
raymond@candylandamusements.com * www.candylandamusements.com
E.C. Prop Rentals   **(818) 764-2008**
Ticket booths; large castered units & small "shack" style

E.C. PROP RENTALS
11846 SHERMAN WAY NORTH HOLLYWOOD CA 91605
818-764-2008

LCW Props   **(818) 243-0707**
Guard Shack, Ticket Machines, ticket booths

Tickets

See Also: Printing, Graphics, Digital & Large Format* Prop Houses
Collins Visual Media   **(818) 686-6581**
10518 Johanna Ave, Shadow Hills, CA, 91040
We create a wide variety of custom tickets, backstage passes, badges,
lanyards and name tags, etc., used for filming.
www.collinsvisualmedia.com
History For Hire, Inc.   **(818) 765-7767**
stock items & custom

Ties, Neckwear

See: Costumes* Uniforms, Trades/Professional/Sports* Wardrobe*
Wardrobe, Accessories

Tikis & Tropical Dressing

See Also: Carved Figures* Greens* Hawaiian Dressing* Jungle
Dressing* Light Fixtures, South Seas* Seashells
C. P. Two   **(323) 466-8201**
Tropical dressing and tiki themed dressing.
Green Set, Inc.   **(818) 764-1231**
facemasks, torches, figures, wide variety of tropical plants including many palm
tree styles real and faux
History For Hire, Inc.   **(818) 765-7767**
Tikis, bamboo, tropical dressing/tropical decorations
Jackson Shrub Supply, Inc.   **(818) 982-0100**
jungle vines, fantasy creations, Tiki heads, tropical decorations, tiki
decorations, tropical plants, tropical flowers
LCW Props   **(818) 243-0707**
Tiki Torches, Bamboo
Lennie Marvin Enterprises, Inc. (Prop Heaven)   **(818) 841-5882**
tikis, pictures, Hula Hoops, dolls, signage, nets, bars, chairs
Oceanic Arts   **(562) 698-6960**
Carved wood Tikis & Fiberglass Tikis, Roof Thatching, Bamboo Poles,
Mattings, South Sea Lights, and more.
Picture Start Props   **(818) 255-5472**
Island tables and chairs made of palm wood, tiki statues large and small.
Sony Pictures Studios-Prop House (Off Lot)   **(310) 244-5999**
Tropical decorations and tropical rentals

Tile, Marble, Granite, Etc.

See Also: Bathroom Decorations* Carpet & Flooring
American Marble & Onyx   **(310) 649-1355**
10321 S. La Cienega Blvd, Los Angeles, CA, 90045
only slab stone
www.americanmarble.us
Dal Tile   **(310) 559-8680**
3633 Lenawee Ave, Los Angeles, CA 90016
www.daltile.com
Emser International   **(323) 650-2010**
8431 Santa Monica Blvd, W. Hollywood, CA, 90069
www.emser.com
Firenze Ceramic Tile   **(818) 982-3961**
7283 Bellaire Ave, Unit A, N. Hollywood, CA, 91605
tile
www.firenzetilela.com
Formation Stone Surfaces   **(760) 773-1001**
74-824 42nd Ave, Palm Desert, CA, 92260
tile, large slab stone
info@formationstone.com * www.formationstone.com
Global Stone   **(818) 785-7900**
14533 Keswick St, Van Nuys, CA, 91405
tile & slab stone
www.marblewarehouse.com
Ground Floor   **(800) 540-3478**
15812 Arminta St, Van Nuys, CA 91406
Steam cleaning & stone restoration. No sales, stone, tile, grout, metal and
glass restoration only.
www.groundfloor.org
Ideal Tile   **(212) 759-2339**
405 East 51st Street, New York City, NY, 10022
web site has dealer locator. tile & pre-sized slab stone
www.idealtile.com
Impression   **(310) 618-1299**
22599 S Western Ave, Torrance, CA, 90501
limestone & terra cotta only
www.limestone.com
Marble/Unlimited, Inc.   **(818) 988-0100**
14554 Keswick St, Van Nuys, CA, 91405
wholesale only; slab stone
www.marbleunlimitedinc.com
Mission Tile West   **(626) 799-4595**
853 Mission St, S Pasadena, CA, 91030
www.missiontilewest.com
San Fernando Marble & Granite   **(818) 897-4033**
9803 San Fernando Rd, Pacoima, CA, 91331
tile & slab stone
http://onlinestonecatalog.com/wordpress1
Simply Tiles   **(310) 373-7781**
3968 Pacific Coast Hwy, Torrance, CA, 90505
tile & slab stone
www.simplytiles.com
Surfaces USA   **(818) 982-0069**
11501 Hart St, N Hollywood, CA, 91605
tile & slab stone
http://surfacesusa.com

Tile, Mile of Tile, Anaheim

Bedrosians-Tile-Marble (714) 778-8453
1235 S State College Blvd, Anaheim, CA, 92806
www.bedrosians.com
California Wholesale Tile (714) 937-0591
1656 S. State College Blvd, Anaheim, CA, 92806
imported tile
www.cwtile.com
Marmol Export, U.S.A. (714) 939-0697
1550 S State College Blvd, Anaheim, CA, 92806
tile, slab stone
www.marmolusa.com
Orion Tile & Marble (714) 772-2300
1301 S State College Blvd, Anaheim, CA, 92806
www.oriontile.com
Pacific Land Marble & Tile Corp. (714) 776-2424
1300 S State College Blvd, Anaheim, CA, 92806
tile, small precut slab stone
www.pacificlandtile.com
Porcelanosa (714) 772-3183
1301 S State College Blvd Ste E, Anaheim, CA, 92806
tile
www.porcelanosa-usa.com
SpecCeramics (714) 808-0134
851 Enterprise Way, Fullerton, CA, 92831
Summitville brand tile, thinbrick, tactile-tread
www.specceramics.com
Stone Age Tile (714) 704-9293
1701 S State College Blvd, Anaheim, CA, 92806
tile, small & large stone slabs
www.satile.com
Tile Expo (714) 635-0406
1360 S State College Blvd, Anaheim, CA, 92806
tile, pre-sized slab stone
http://tileexpoinc.com

Tinting

See: Make-up & Hair, Supplies & Services* Window Treatments

Tires

AIR Designs (818) 768-6639
Street Tires, Racing Tires, Tire Racks/Wheels, Displays, Period to Present & Bling
Alley Cats Studio Rentals (818) 982-9178
E.C. Prop Rentals (818) 764-2008
Large inventory used tires, auto/truck/tractor, castered tire racks
History For Hire, Inc. (818) 765-7767
period
LCW Props (818) 243-0707
Large & Small, With Or Without Rims

Tobacconist

See: Smoking Products

Toilets

See: Bathroom Fixtures* Production Vehicles/Trailers

Toilets, Portable Prop

See Also: Prop Houses
Alley Cats Studio Rentals (818) 982-9178
port-a-potties, jail cell toilets
Studio Plumbing Rentals (323) 829-9339
7373 Atoll Ave, N Hollywood, CA, 91605
studioplumbingrentals@gmail.com * www.studioair.com

Tombstones

See: Cemetery Dressing

Tool Boxes & Tool Carts

See: Automotive/Garage Equip. & Parts

Tools

See Also: Expendables
AIR Designs (818) 768-6639
Large Selection of Automotive Dressing, Carpentry Dressing and Workshop Dressing
E.C. Prop Rentals (818) 764-2008
Hand and power tools, for shop/factory/industrial

Grainger (800) 472-4643
570 S. Alameda St, Los Angeles CA, 90013
catalog sales; industrial supplies, tools, etc.
www.grainger.com
The Hand Prop Room LP. (323) 931-1534
period-present, rubber
History For Hire, Inc. (818) 765-7767
big selection
LCW Props (818) 243-0707
Construction, Industrial, Machine Shope, Garage, Medical, Dentistry
Lehman's Non-Electric Items (888) 438-5346
4779 Kidron Road, Dalton, OH, 44618
ship anywhere, all sales are final. non-electric hand tools
info@Lehmans.com * www.lehmans.com
Old N Country Prop Shop, LLC (818) 423-2599
Lots of vintage tools and tool boxes.
The Rational Past (310) 476-6277
By Appointment, West Los Angeles, CA
Authentic science, industrial, technical antiques & collectibles. Many professions & eras represented. See web site.
info@therationalpast.com * www.therationalpast.com
Sony Pictures Studios-Prop House (Off Lot) (310) 244-5999
Home tools, office tools, garage tools, automobile tools, more

Top Hats

See: Headwear - Hats, Bonnets, Caps, Helmets Etc.

Topiary/Hedges, Artificial

See: Greens

Torture Equipment

Dapper Cadaver (818) 771-0818
Dungeon equipment, fake weapons & steel instruments. Electric chair, guillotine, stocks, restraints & heads on spikes.
History For Hire, Inc. (818) 765-7767
LCW Props (818) 243-0707
Bed Of Nails, Iron Maiden, Water Boards, Guillotine, Shockers, Electric Chair
Sword & Stone (818) 562-6548
Rack Beds, Iron Maidens, Flays, Manacles, Locks, Spiked Chairs, Ball and Chains, Breast Rippers, Skull Crushers, etc.
Universal Studios Property & Hardware Dept (818) 777-2784
Many torture props for rent.

Totem Poles

The Hand Prop Room LP. (323) 931-1534
Native American Totems
Universal Studios Property & Hardware Dept (818) 777-2784
Totem poles and prop totem poles of various sizes for rent.

Towing Services

See Also: Automotive/Garage Equip. & Parts* Transportation, Trucking and/or Storage* Vehicles/Picture Vehicles
Gordy's Garage & Towing Service (626) 797-6591
843 W Woodbury Rd, Altadena, CA 91001
Larry's Towing Service (818) 365-7122
1900 1st St, San Fernando, CA, 91340

Toys & Games

See Also: Christmas* Dolls* Memorabilia & Novelties* Nodders* Prop Houses* School Supplies, Desks & Dressing* Soldier Toys & Drums
AIR Designs (818) 768-6639
Pedal Cars, Skill Games, Rides
B. Shackman & Co., Inc. (800) 221-7656
P.O. Box 247 Galesburg MI, 49503
mfr & importer; toys, novelties, paper dolls, decorations
www.shackman.com
Benjamin Pollock's Toyshop +44 (0) 207 379 7866
44 The Market, Covent Garden, London, UK, WC2E - 8RF
toy theatres & traditional European toys
info@pollocks-coventgarden.co.uk * www.pollocks-coventgarden.co.uk
Gann Memorials, LLC Custom Plush Toys (919) 692-5559
104 Tabor Industrial Park, Tabor City NC, 28463
We are a family owned US based custom toy company, who is able to source custom products through both U.S. and Chinese factories.
gannmemorials@aol.com * www.gannmemorials.com
The Hand Prop Room LP. (323) 931-1534
antique toys
History For Hire, Inc. (818) 765-7767
period toys, period games, pedal toys, stuffed animals and more
Hollywood Toys & Costumes (800) 554-3444
6600 Hollywood Blvd, Hollywood, CA, 90028
www.yourhollywoodcostumes.com

Modern Props   (323) 934-3000
contemporary toys and games, modern, small collection
Ob-jects   (818) 351-4200
Games and toys for rent
Omega/Cinema Props   (323) 466-8201
Prop Services West   (818) 503-2790
RC Vintage, Inc.   (818) 765-7107
rocking horses; lots of unusual, crazy little toys, board games, boardgames,
children's bedroom smalls
Sony Pictures Studios-Prop House (Off Lot)   (310) 244-5999
doll carriage, doll clothes, doll furniture, dollhouse, educational toys,
educational kit, dollhouse furniture
Stevenson Brothers   011 44 20
The Workshop, Ashford Road, Ashford TN26 3AP   3382-0363
Custom handcrafted rocking horses.
sue@stevensonbros.com * www.stevensonbros.com
Universal Studios Property & Hardware Dept   (818) 777-2784
Many toy props and game props for rent.
Warner Bros. Studios Property Department   (818) 954-2181
Games, stuffed animals, board games, puzzles, dolls, rubber toys, new and
used toys, sporting good toys

Toys, Oversize

See: Oversized Props

Track & Field Equipment

See Also: Prop Houses* Sporting Goods & Services
OnTrack and Field, Inc.   (800) 697-2999
2901 Winona Ave, Burbank, CA, 91504
Complete line of track & field athletic equipment & gear. Select vintage
equipment collection as well.
sales@ontrackandfield.com * www.ontrackandfield.com
VS Athletics   (800) 676-7463
1450 W 228th St Ste 8, Torrance, CA, 90501
www.vsathletics.com

Traction Equipment

See: Physical Therapy

Trade Associations

See: Guilds, Unions, Societies, Associations

Trade Shows & Conventions

See Also: Audience Seating* Backings* Events, Decorations,
Supplies & Services* Flags/Banners* Inflatables, Custom* Oversized
Props* Prop Design & Manufacturing* Prop Houses* Rigging,
Equipment or Services* Scenery/Set Construction* Scenery/Set
Rentals* Signs* Stage Lighting, Film/Video/TV* Stages, Portable &
Steel Deck* Stanchions & Rope* Transportation, Trucking and/or
Storage
Astro Audio Video Lighting, Inc.   (818) 549-9915
6615 San Fernando Rd, Glendale, CA, 91201
Video, screens, plasma, projectors, PA systems, podiums, pipe and drape,
power distribution and lighting.
www.astroavl.com
EFX- Event Special Effects   (626) 888-2239
125 Railroad Ave, Monrovia, CA, 91016
Custom Fabrication- CNC- Plasma Table- Pipe & Ring Benders- 3D
Renderings
info@efxla.com * www.efxla.com
Ultra Prototypes LLC   (818) 292-1906
Call for Appointment
Display design and construction.
jeff@ultraprototypes.com * www.ultraprototypes.com

Traffic Cones

See: Traffic/Road Signs, Lights, Safety Items

Traffic Management

See: Barricades* Crowd Control: Barricades, Turnstiles Etc.*
Traffic/Road Signs, Lights, Safety Items

Traffic/Road Signs, Lights, Safety Items

See Also: Barricades* Parking Meters & Sign Poles* Railroad
Crossing Signal
AIR Designs   (818) 768-6639
Practical Traffic Lights, Signage, Crosswalks, Call Box, Cones/Pylon
Barricades & More
Alley Cats Studio Rentals   (818) 982-9178
barricades, flashing lights/cones/arrows, stop signs on poles, men working,
construction traffic lights, bus stop, street lights & more
Collins Visual Media   (818) 686-6581
10518 Johanna Ave, Shadow Hills, CA, 91040
We design & fabricate road signs of any size, plus any type of traffic or subway
signs. Complete with aging as you wish.
www.collinsvisualmedia.com
D'ziner Sign Co.   (323) 467-4467
801 Seward Street, Los Angeles, CA, 90038
domestic & foreign made to your specs
sales@dzinersign.com * www.dzinersign.com
E.C. Prop Rentals   (818) 764-2008
barricades, lanterns, delineators, signage, good inv./multiples
The Hand Prop Room LP.   (323) 931-1534
signs, cones, road work barricades
LCW Props   (818) 243-0707
Cones, Guard Rails, Traffic Signs, Deliniators, etc.
Modern Props   (323) 934-3000
wall-mounted traffic lights
RC Vintage, Inc.   (818) 765-7107
Traffic lights, traffic signals
Sony Pictures Studios-Prop House (Off Lot)   (310) 244-5999
lights & signs
Statewide Traffic Safety & Sign   (714) 468-1919
13261 Garden Grove Blvd, Garden Grove, CA, 92840
signage, barricades, equipment, traffic control personnel many credits
www.statewidesafety.com
Sterndahl Enterprises, Inc.   (818) 834-8199
11861 Branford St, Sun Valley, CA, 91352
traffic control equipment, signage, barricades, striping, trucks & bobcats
www.sterndahl.com

Warner Bros. Studios Property Department   (818) 954-2181
Safety Barricade, emergency signs, assorted road signs

Trailers

See: Production Vehicles/Trailers* RV Vehicles & Travel Trailers, Equip & Parts

Trains

See Also: Bus Shelter* Model Ships/Planes/Trains/Autos Etc.

American Assn. of Private R.R. Car Owners　**(706) 326-6262**
311 E Main St Suite 512, Galesburg IL, 61401
website lists private cars nationwide, contacts for usage
aaprcodirector@aol.com * www.aaprco.com

California State Railroad Museum　**(916) 323-9280**
125 I Street, Sacramento, CA, 95814
Vintage trains & R.R. locations; Contact Paul Hammond, 2 sites, Old
Sacramento & Jamestown (in Sierra foothills)
www.csrmf.org

Fillmore & Western Railway Co.　**(805) 524-2546**
351 Santa Clara St, Fillmore, CA, 93015
Dinner trains, excursion rides, special events, holiday theme trains
www.fwry-blog.com

Grand Canyon Railway　**(800) 843-8724**
233 N. Grand Canyon Blvd, Williams, AZ, 86046
railroad/locations/excursions
www.thetrain.com

Pacific Harbor Line, Inc.　**(310) 984-5776**
705 North Henry Ford Ave, Wilmington, CA, 90744
Film location for scenes requiring RR tracks, equipment, and facilities
www.anacostia.com

Pacific Southwest Railway Museum Assn.　**(619) 465-7776**
4695 Nebo Dr, La Mesa, CA, 91941
Museums at La Mesa, CA & Campo, CA
www.psrm.org

Travel Town Museum　**(323) 662-5874**
5200 W Zoo Drive, Los Angeles, CA, 90027
access to equip. & locations owned by the city
www.traveltown.org

Verde Canyon Railroad　**(800) 582-7245**
300 N Broadway, Clarkdale, AZ, 86324
www.verdecanyonrr.com

Tramp Art

See: Paintings/Prints

Trampolines

See: Gymnasium & Gymnastic Equipment

Transformers

See: Electrical/Electronic Supplies & Services

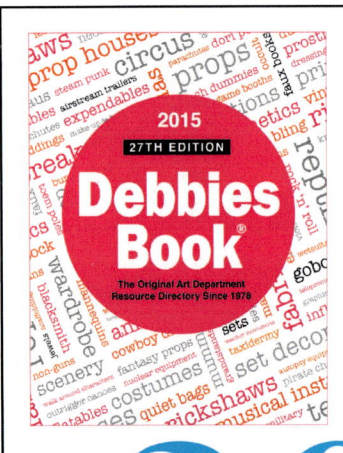

With the 20th anniversary of our website, we released yet another updated Debbies Book. The website has gone through it's ups and downs since it's debut, most notably in 2009 with our first makeover (required logins are NO MORE!) That bumpy road has brought us to now. A more streamlined web search alongside the release of our iPhone and Android apps without a login requirement. Don't forget to keep us posted on possible changes you want to see or new companies that would benefit from exposure in our database. As always we will continue to work for you getting the information you need, when you need, wherever you might be.

40 YEARS OF DEBBIES BOOK

2015

Transportation, Trucking and/or Storage

See Also: Limousine Service Property Master Storage Rooms*
Scenery/Set Storage* Vehicles/Picture Vehicles* Towing Services*

Bill Ferrell Co.　**(818) 767-1900**
10556 Keswick St, Sun Valley, CA, 91352
www.billferrell.com

Castex Rentals　**(323) 462-1468**
1044 N Cole Ave, Hollywood, CA, 90038
truck shelves, racks, dollies, magliners, pads, ratchets, rope, dollies, magliner
carts, furniture pads, super shelves
service@castexrentals.com * www.castexrentals.com

Centerline Scenery　**(818) 252-7467**
8238 Lankershim Blvd, N Hollywood, CA, 91605
meredyth@centerlinescenery.com

Clark Transfer, Inc.　**(800) 488-7585**
800 A Paxton St, Harrisburg, PA, 17104
domestic/global, air/ocean, specialized equip.
www.clarktransfer.com

depict　**(323) 222-1001**
1460 Naud St, Los Angeles, CA, 90012
info@depict33.com * www.depict33.com

Gilbert Production Service　**(323) 871-0006**
5540 Harbor St, Commerce, CA 90040
Strike it, truck it, store it
www.gilbertproduction.net

Green Set, Inc.　**(818) 764-1231**
crane service & brush hauling also available (no storage)

Jackson Shrub Supply, Inc.　**(818) 982-0100**

Portable Storage Corp.　**(800) 527-8673**
835 W State St, Ontario, CA, 91762
Portable storage containers for sale from 4ft to 40ft and more, including used.
http://www.storagecontainer.com

Production Storage Group　**(818) 512-8472**
110 Topsail Mall, Marina Del Rey, CA, 90292
Also in West LA. Call before visiting us; band & production storage, musical
equip., cartage & trucking
productionstoragegroup.com

Prop Transport Inc.　**(212) 594-2521**
34-18 Northern Blvd Suite 26B, Long Island City NY, 11101
24X7 service; equip. transportation for Film & Theatrical productions
www.proptransport.net

Scenic Expressions　**(818) 409-3354**
8238 Lankershim Blvd, N Hollywood, CA, 91605
All Production needs - Double Drop, Single drop, A-frame trailers and
Construction wall trailers
mark@scenicexpressions.com * www.scenicexpressions.com

Scenic Highlights (818) 252-7760
10830 Cantara St, Sun Valley, CA, 91352
scenichighlights.com

Silverado Coach Company, Inc. (818) 251-9700
Call for Service.
limousine production tranportation, LA, NYC, SF, Miami, Chicago, also picture cars
www.silveradocoach.com

Studio Express (818) 352-9402
10333 McVine Ave, Sunland, CA, 91040
studio trucking & storage
www.studioexpress.biz

Universal Studios Transportation (818) 777-2966
100 Universal City Plaza, Universal City, CA, 91608
range of vehicles available, SUVs to tractor trailers, no trucking or storage
universalstudioslot.com/transportation

Western Studio Service, Inc. (818) 842-9272
4561 Colorado Blvd, Los Angeles, CA, 90039
We have the largest fleet of custom trailers to transport scenery of all sizes and heights. All trailers for rent too!
www.westernstudioservice.com

Trash

See: Salvage, Rubble, Clutter & Trash (Prop)* Sanitation, Waste Disposal

Trash Cans & Waste Baskets

AIR Designs (818) 768-6639
Fast Food, Wire Gas Station, Park, Bus, Street, New York Style

Alley Cats Studio Rentals (818) 982-9178
galvanized, plastic, wire, flare-top, residential

E.C. Prop Rentals (818) 764-2008
Dumpsters, roll-out scoop trash bins, residential roll-out, interior/exterior, many styles, good multiples

FormDecor, Inc. (310) 558-2582
America's largest event rental supplier of 20th Century furniture and accessories for Modern and Mid-Century styles.

The Hand Prop Room LP. (323) 931-1534

History For Hire, Inc. (818) 765-7767

LCW Props (818) 243-0707
Huge Selection Of Trash Bins, Recycling, Yard Waste, Roll-Off Containers, etc.

Lennie Marvin Enterprises, Inc. (Prop Heaven) (818) 841-5882
wire mesh, galvanized, plastic, wood, stone, metal

Modern Props (323) 934-3000
modern, indoor, outdoor, silver, metal, gold, business, home, alley, heavy duty, professional, trash compactors

Omega/Cinema Props (323) 466-8201

RC Vintage, Inc. (818) 765-7107
many shapes, sizes and colors

Sony Pictures Studios-Prop House (Off Lot) (310) 244-5999
commercial trash cans, dumpsters, domestic trash cans, hospital trash cans, park trash cans, recycle bins, rubber maid bins

Universal Studios Property & Hardware Dept (818) 777-2784
Trash cans/wastebaskets of all kinds for all scenarios for rent.

ZG04 DECOR (818) 853-8040
Event trash cans of many types for rent

Travel (City/Country) Themed Events

See: Costume Rental Houses* Costumes* Events, Decorations, Supplies & Services* Events, Design/Planning/Production* Greens* Nautical Dressing & Props

Travel Posters

See: Posters, Art/Movie/Travel/Wanted Etc.

Travel Trailers

See: RV Vehicles & Travel Trailers, Equip & Parts

Treadmills

See: Conveyor Equipment* Exercise & Fitness Equipment* Special Effects, Equipment & Supplies

Treasure Chests

See: Pirate, Chests & Treasures

Trees

See: Greens

Trims, Fringe, Tassels, Beading Etc.

See Also: Costume/Wardrobe/Sewing Supplies* Fabrics* Theatrical Draperies, Hardware & Rigging* Upholstery Materials/Services

Cheep Trims   **(877) 289-8746**
3957 S. Hill St. 2nd Floor Los Angeles, CA 90037
www.cheeptrims.com

Palladia Passementerie   **(651) 488-1603**
Web Based Business
High quality trims, from Europe & Asia, 100s in stock & custom, blending past with present, wholesale
www.palladiapassementerie.com

ShopWildThings   **(928) 855-6075**
2880 Sweetwater Ave, Lake Havasu City, AZ, 86406
Event Decor, Beaded Curtains, Chain Curtains, String Curtains & Columns, Crystal Columns. Reliable service & delivery.
help@shopwildthings.com * www.shopwildthings.com

Trophies/Trophy Cases

AIR Designs   **(818) 768-6639**
Automotive, Boat, Awards, Flags

C. P. Two   **(323) 466-8201**
Sports trophies, army trophies, sports awards, army awards and more.

Charisma Design Studio, Inc.   **(818) 252-6611**
8414 San Fernando Road, Sun Valley, CA, 91352
glass, metal, marble awards, label etching to carving it out
info@charismadesign.com * www.charismadesign.com

E.C. Prop Rentals   **(818) 764-2008**
trophies & trophy cases

Faux Library Studio Props, Inc.   **(818) 765-0096**
large selection of trophies and awards, high school trophy case

The Hand Prop Room LP.   **(323) 931-1534**

History For Hire, Inc.   **(818) 765-7767**
trophies, ribbons

Hollywood Cinema Arts   **(818) 504-7333**
Over 4,600 trophies. You have to see it to believe it.

Hollywood Studio Gallery   **(323) 462-1116**
new & character (no cases)

LCW Props   **(818) 243-0707**
Misc. Trohpies Of All Styles, Large Wood Cases Multiple Styles

Omega/Cinema Props   **(323) 466-8201**
Trophy cups, trophy plaques, trophy stands, sports trophies, display cabinets and more.

Picture Start Props   **(818) 255-5472**
Many vintage trophies and modern trophies and plaques for a variety of sports and events.

Prop Services West   **(818) 503-2790**
trophies

RC Vintage, Inc.   **(818) 765-7107**
Asst Trophie Nice Oak Trophy Case Full Size

So. California Trophy Co., Inc.   **(818) 550-9144**
337 W Cerritos Ave, Glendale, CA, 91204
info@socaltrophy.com * www.socaltrophy.com

Sony Pictures Studios-Prop House (Off Lot)   **(310) 244-5999**
Medals, plaques, ribbons, taxidermy, trophies of many kinds, trophy parts. Only trophies

Universal Studios Property & Hardware Dept   **(818) 777-2784**
Many kinds of trophies for all kinds of occasions and trophy display cases for rent.

Tropical Dressing

See: Aquariums & Tropical Fish* Tikis & Tropical Dressing

Truck Rentals

See: Vehicles/Picture Vehicles

Trucking

See: Transportation, Trucking and/or Storage* Towing Services

Trunks

See Also: Steamer Trunks

Alley Cats Studio Rentals   **(818) 982-9178**

History For Hire, Inc.   **(818) 765-7767**
huge selection

LCW Props   **(818) 243-0707**
Period - Present, Antique

Old N Country Prop Shop, LLC   **(818) 423-2599**
A large variety of antique and vintage trunks, boxes, and crates of all sizes.

Prop Services West   **(818) 503-2790**

Sony Pictures Studios-Prop House (Off Lot)   **(310) 244-5999**

Universal Studios Property & Hardware Dept   **(818) 777-2784**
Prop storage trunks and travel trunks for rent.

Warner Bros. Studios Property Department   **(818) 954-2181**
Army Trunks, Leather Trunks, rustic trunks, steamer trunks, western trunks, trunks on wheels, metal trunks

Truss

See Also: Lighting & Sound, Concert/Theatrical/DJ/VJ* Stage Lighting, Film/Video/TV

Astro Audio Video Lighting, Inc.   **(818) 549-9915**
6615 San Fernando Rd, Glendale, CA, 91201
Everything truss; box trusses, circle trusses, truss tables, truss tool sets and truss bolts.
www.astroavl.com

EFX- Event Special Effects   **(626) 888-2239**
125 Railroad Ave, Monrovia, CA, 91016
Trussing- Arch- Cubes- Structures- Stage- Stands, Mount
info@efxla.com * www.efxla.com

LCW Props   **(818) 243-0707**
Square, Triangle, Aluminum, Steel, Quantities

Turbines

Alley Cats Studio Rentals   **(818) 982-9178**
small to extra large including roof top turbines.

E.C. Prop Rentals   **(818) 764-2008**
rooftop all sizes, exhaust

LCW Props   **(818) 243-0707**
Jet, Aero, Large Quantities

Turnstiles

See: Crowd Control: Barricades, Turnstiles Etc.

Turntables

See: Mechanical Effects* Phonographs* Stage Turntables

Tuxedo

See: Formal Wear

TV/Film Production Facilities

See: Locations, Stages/Studios, Film/TV/Events

Twenties Themed Parties

See: Costume Rental Houses* Events, Backings & Scenery* Events, Decorations, Supplies & Services* Events, Design/Planning/Production* Historical Era Themed Events* Prop Houses* Wardrobe, Vintage

Twentyfour Frame Video

See: Video 24fps / Sync System / D.D.I.

Typewriters

Anderson Business Technology (626) 793-2166
120 E. Colorado Blvd, Pasadena, CA, 91105
Repairs & Sales of copiers, fax, printers & other office equipment
www.andersonbt.com
Batchelor Business Machine (818) 222-2152
5169 Douglas Fir Rd Ste 6, Calabasas, CA, 91302
IBM compatible typewriters & supplies
www.ibmtypewriters.com
The Hand Prop Room LP. (323) 931-1534
period-present
History For Hire, Inc. (818) 765-7767
many practical, multiples
International Printing Museum (714) 529-1832
315 Torrance Blvd, Carson, CA, 90745
antique printing/office equipment 1450-1980. old typewriters, printing machines
mail@printmuseum.org * www.printmuseum.org
LCW Props (818) 243-0707
Electric, Manual, Mystery Writer's Typewriter
Old N Country Prop Shop, LLC (818) 423-2599
From the "Butterfly" typewriter, to L. C. Smith; Remington; Underwood; Corona,
ALL Manual; IBM Selectric, etc.
Omega/Cinema Props (323) 466-8201
Various typewriters
Picture Start Props (818) 255-5472
Great collection of vintage typewriters.
Universal Studios Property & Hardware Dept (818) 777-2784
Electric typewriters and manual typewriters from various time periods for rent.

UFOs

See: Aliens* Fantasy Props, Costumes, or Decorations* Futuristic Furniture, Props, Decorations

Ultraviolet Lights

See: Light Strings* Lighting & Sound, Concert/Theatrical/DJ/VJ* Lighting, LED, Fiber Optic & Specialty* Neon Lights & Signs* Ultraviolet Products

Ultraviolet Products

See Also: Lighting, LED, Fiber Optic & Specialty* Neon Lights & Signs
History For Hire, Inc. (818) 765-7767
Like, the 60s, can you dig it?
Shannon Luminous Materials, Inc. (800) 543-4485
304 A North Townsend St, Santa Ana, CA, 92703
fluorescent & phosphorescent materials, paints, dyes, black lights
www.blacklite.com

Umbrellas, Hand & Parasols

See Also: Canes* Headwear - Hats, Bonnets, Caps, Helmets Etc.* Protective Apparel* Wardrobe, Accessories
The Costume House (818) 508-9933
1890s parasols & umbrellas, 1940s umbrellas
The Hand Prop Room LP. (323) 931-1534
period-present
History For Hire, Inc. (818) 765-7767
period to present umbrellas & parasols
Lace-Parasols (915) 594-0878
9333 Shaver Drive, El Paso, TX, 79925
Unique cotton Battenburg lace parasols in various styles, sizes and colors.
Other lace accessories too.
lace@lace-parasols.com * www.lace-parasols.com
LCW Props (818) 243-0707
Omega/Cinema Props (323) 466-8201
umbrellas
Prop Services West (818) 503-2790
umbrellas
Sony Pictures Studios-Prop House (Off Lot) (310) 244-5999
Paper umbrellas, parasols, rain umbrellas, sun umbrellas
Universal Studios Property & Hardware Dept (818) 777-2784
Many parasols & umbrellas for rent.

Umbrellas, Patio

See: Furniture, Outdoor/Patio* Garden/Patio

Underwater Filming

See: Nautical/Marine Services & Charters

Underwear & Lingerie, Bloomers, Corsets, Etc.

CBS Costume Rental (323) 575-2666
modern sexy, also 1880s bustles, corsets, etc.
The Costume House (818) 508-9933
Victorian corsets, bloomers, slips, 1950s merry widows
Dark Garden Unique Corsetry (415) 431-7684
321 Linden St, San Francisco, CA, 94102
custom, made-to-order & ready-to-wear corsets
www.darkgarden.com
Universal Studios Costume Dept (818) 777-2722
Rental, mfg., & alterations
Warner Bros. Studios Costume Dept (818) 954-1297
Bras, Panties, Lace, Garters, Stockings, Nylons, Pantyhose, Slips, Tights, Negligees, Nightgowns

Uniforms, Military

See Also: Badges, Patches & Buttons* Civil War Era* Military Props & Equipment* Military Surplus/Combat Clothes, Field Gear* Wardrobe, Antique/Historical
AA Surplus Sales Co., Inc. (323) 526-3622
2940 E Olympic Blvd, Los Angeles, CA, 90023
US Military clothing, combat boots and accessories in used and new condition
surplusking@hotmail.com * www.aasurplus.com
American Costume Corp. (818) 764-2239
1750s to present for film & TV industries
CBS Costume Rental (323) 575-2666
1880s U.S. Cavalry
Costume Rentals Corporation (818) 753-3700
motion picture supplier & special order items
Eastern Costume (818) 982-3611
1920's to present, uniform & civilian wardrobe, military, alterations, hazmat, racks, ethnic costumes, NASA, and props.
Heritage Costumes (310) 320-6392
military uniforms & accessories
Lost Battalions (916) 221-2828
P.O. Box 478 Folsom, CA, 95763
WW I German & WW II German/Allied
www.lostbattalions.com
Motion Picture Costume Company (818) 557-1247
uniforms & civilian wardrobe, 1775 to present
OPFOR Solutions, Inc (747) 666-7367
8100 Remmet Ave Unit #6, Canoga Park, CA, 91304
Opfor Solutions, Inc. brings you ethnic/military apparel from countries such as - Afghanistan, Iraq, Libya & more.
moe@opforsolutions.com * www.opforsolutions.com
RDD U.S.A. Inc. (213) 742-0666
4638 E Washington Blvd, Commerce, CA, 90040
complete line of G. I. military uniforms & clothing
www.rddusa.com
The Russian Store/G & J Imports (818) 999-1257
7657 Winnetka Ave Ste 203, Canoga Park, CA, 91306
www.russianstore.net
Sony Pictures Studios-Wardrobe (310) 244-5995
alterations, call (310) 244-7260
Supply Sergeant (323) 849-3744
503 N Victory Blvd, Burbank, CA, 91502
Military clothing including army uniforms, military uniforms, navy uniforms
david@jacksgt.com * www.supplysergeantshop.com
Western Costume Co. (818) 760-0900
World War II Impressions (562) 946-6768
12025 E Florence Ave #402, Santa Fe Springs, CA, 90670
Reproductions - By Appt Only.
www.wwiiimpressions.com

Uniforms, Trades/Professional/Sports

See Also: Badges, Patches & Buttons* Clerical, Judicial, Academic Gowns/Apparel* Clowns* Costumes, International/Ethnic* Fireman Uniforms, Hats & Equipment* Sportswear* Uniforms, Military

Becnel Uniform Co. (213) 623-4522
758 S San Pedro, Los Angeles, CA, 90014
police, transportation, industrial - also accessories & shoes
www.becneluniforms.com

CBS Costume Rental (323) 575-2666
medical scrubs, lab coats

The Costume House (818) 508-9933
maid's, lab coats, nurses, waitresses, airline (60s, 70s)

Costume Rentals Corporation (818) 753-3700
motion picture supplier & special order items

Frank Bee Uniforms (800) 372-6523
Call for Appt.
school uniforms, grad caps & gowns, police & law enforcement, military & camo, scouts
www.frankbee.com

Glamour Uniform Shop (323) 666-2122
4951 W. Sunset Blvd, Los Angeles, CA, 90027
nurses, restaurant, mechanics, maids uniforms. sizes 3-56

LCW Props (818) 243-0707
school uniforms, others

Motion Picture Costume Company (818) 557-1247
uniforms & civilian wardrobe, 1775 to present

My Professional Uniforms (818) 242-3404
1102 E Colorado St, Glendale, CA, 91205
Medical
www.myprofessionaluniforms.com

National Spirit (800) 527-4366
6745 Lenox Center Court Ste 300, Memphis, TN, 38115
warm/cold weather cheerleader outfits, megaphones, pom-pons etc.
www.varsity.com

RDD U.S.A. Inc. (213) 742-0666
4638 E Washington Blvd, Commerce, CA, 90040
complete line of law enforcement and security uniforms & accessories
www.rddusa.com

Sony Pictures Studios-Wardrobe (310) 244-5995
alterations, call (310) 244-7260

Sports Studio (310) 559-3999
1831 W 208th St, Torrance, CA, 90501
Antique & contemporary sports uniforms
http://sportsstudio.net

Supply Sergeant (323) 849-3744
503 N Victory Blvd, Burbank, CA, 91502
david@jacksgt.com * www.supplysergeantshop.com

Tarpy Tailors (310) 645-4694
9100 S Sepulveda Blvd Ste 103, Los Angeles, CA, 90045
airline/corporate pilot, flight attendant, customer service
www.tarpytailors.com

Uniforms By Park Coats, Inc. (718) 499-1182
790 3rd Ave, Brooklyn, NY, 11232
police, fire, EMS, coats, pants, shirts, hats, outerwear
www.uniformsbypark.com

Western Costume Co. (818) 760-0900

Unions

See: Guilds, Unions, Societies, Associations

Upholstery Materials/Services

See Also: Fabrics* Furniture & Art, Repair & Restoration* Furniture, Custom-made/Reproduction* Hardware, Decorative* Rubber & Foam Rubber* Slipcovers

Diamond Foam & Fabric Co. (323) 931-8148
611 S La Brea Ave, Los Angeles, CA, 90036
decorative fabrics & foam for upholstery, drapery & slipcovers, custom sewing on premises
www.diamondfoamandfabric.com

Fine Custom Upholstery (310) 837-5541
8929 National Blvd, Los Angeles, CA, 90034
leather upholstering
info@clubchairinc.com * www.clubchairinc.com

Keystone Bros (818) 243-3222
1100 South Grove Ave, Ontario CA, 91761
vinyl, leather, fabrics or textiles for the automotive, marine, contract/hospitality industries
www.keystonbros.com

Larry St. John & Co. (310) 630-5828
17021 S Broadway, Gardena, CA, 90248
Custom, heavily discounted, locally made upholstery materials and upholstery services,
info@larrystjohn.com * www.larrystjohn.com

Leather Corral Inc (818) 764-7880
13052 Raymer St, N Hollywood, CA, 91605
Upholstery supplies extending from vinyls, poly foam, carpet, headliner, leather all the way to sewing threads.
leathercorral@yahoo.com * www.leathercorral.com

Lux Lounge EFR (888) 247-4411
106 1/2 Judge John Aiso St #318, Los Angeles, CA, 90012
Upholstery Materials and Custom Upholstery Services
info@luxloungeefr.com * www.luxloungeefr.com

Omega/Cinema Props (323) 466-8201

Universal Studios Drapery Dept (818) 777-2761
manufacturing

Warner Bros. Drapery, Upholstery & Flooring (818) 954-1831
4000 Warner Blvd Bldg 30, Burbank, CA, 91522
Custom Furniture Manufacturing; Re-upholstery; Repair; Slip Covers; Fabric, Vinyl & Leather Sales
wbsfdrapery@warnerbros.com * www.wbdrapery.com

Urinals

See: Bathroom Fixtures* Plumbing Fixtures, Heating/Cooling Appliances

Urns

See Also: Pottery

The Hand Prop Room LP. (323) 931-1534

Jackson Shrub Supply, Inc. (818) 982-0100
classic urns & contemporary urns, bontoc gourd urns, planter urns

Prop Services West (818) 503-2790

Sony Pictures Studios-Prop House (Off Lot) (310) 244-5999
burial urns, decorative urns, jardiniere urns, pottery urns, wall mounted urns

Universal Studios Property & Hardware Dept (818) 777-2784
Many urns and prop urns for rent.

Vacu-forms/Vacu-forming

See Also: Staff Shops

Flix FX Inc. (818) 765-3549
7327 Lankershim Blvd #4, N Hollywood, CA, 91605
Full vacuum forming services. Sculpting through trimming. Up to 5' x 10' and pre printed vacuum forming
info@flixfx.com * www.flixfx.com

Warner Bros. Studios Scenic Art & Sign Shop (818) 954-1815
4000 Warner Blvd Bldg 44, Burbank, CA, 91522
Thermal Former machine can pull up to 6'0 x 10'0 in plastic! We are ready for any of your large scale project needs!
wbsigns@warnerbros.com * www.wbsignandscenic.com

Warner Bros. Studios Staff Shop (818) 954-2269
Manufacturer of exterior & interior details used for the creation of sets in all architectural styles & eras.

Vacuum Cleaners

AIR Designs (818) 768-6639
Shop, Vintage, Gas Station, Car Wash

Omega/Cinema Props (323) 466-8201
Vacuum cleaners for rent, many periods.

Valves

See: Factory/Industrial* Plumbing Fixtures, Heating/Cooling Appliances

Vehicle Preparation Services

See Also: Special Effects, Equipment & Supplies
L. A. Prep, Inc.   (562) 595-8886
2700 Signal Pkwy, Signal Hill, CA, 90755
Complete vehicle preparation services
info@lapreinc.com * www.lapreinc.com
RZI Car Prep   (818) 786-9030
6911 Valjean Ave, Van Nuys, CA, 91406
Comprehensive car preparation facilities
www.rzicarprep.com
Shelly Ward Enterprises   (818) 255-5850
7255 Radford Ave, N Hollywood, CA, 91605
camera rigging, stunt construction, car prep, car fabrication
shellyward.com
Vehicle Effects   (818) 768-2343
7606 Clybourn Ave, Sun Valley, CA, 91352
Custom picture car modification and fabrication
www.vehicleeffects.com

Vehicle Wraps

See Also: Printing, Graphics, Digital & Large Format
Beyond Image Graphics   (818) 547-0899
1853 Dana St, Glendale, CA, 91201
Custom vehicle wrapping
rafi@beyondimagegraphics.com * www.beyondimagegraphics.com
Collins Visual Media   (818) 686-6581
10518 Johanna Ave, Shadow Hills, CA, 91040
We can create vehicle wraps for everything from helicopters, boats and trucks
to cars and vans.
www.collinsvisualmedia.com
D'ziner Sign Co.   (323) 467-4467
801 Seward Street, Los Angeles, CA, 90038
Vehicle wrapping
sales@dzinersign.com * www.dzinersign.com
JP Graphics Design+Print   (747) 230-6840
5354 Denny Ave, N Hollywood, CA, 91601
We offer Complete Color Changes, Full Printed Wraps, Cover Ups, Partial
Wraps and Die Cut Vehicle Logos.
signs@jp-dp.com * www.jp-dp.com
L. A. Party Works   (888) 527-2789
9712 Alpaca St, S El Monte, CA, 91733
Vehicle wrapping services
partyworks@aol.com * www.partyworksinteractive.com
Tractor Vision Scenery & Rentals   (323) 235-2885
340 E Jefferson Blvd, Los Angeles, CA, 90011
Specializing in entertainment, trade shows, & events, we bring your projects to
life with precision, speed & personality
sets@tractorvision.com * www.tractorvision.com

Vehicles/Picture Vehicles

See Also: Aircraft, Charters & Aerial Services* Ambulance/Paramedic* Children/Baby Accessories & Bedroom* Jet Skis* Limousine Service* Military Props & Equipment* Motorcycles* Nautical/Marine Services & Charters* Police Car, Police Motorcycle* Production Vehicles/Trailers* Ramps, Automobile* RV Vehicles & Travel Trailers, Equip & Parts* Transportation, Trucking and/or Storage* Window Treatments* Towing Services
1A Action Picture Cars   (818) 767-2355
11040 Olinda St, Sun Valley, CA, 91352
picture vehicles, classics, exotics, late models, contemporary cars, wrecked
and collision recreation
rent@actionpicturecars.com * www.actionpicturecars.com
Action Antique Period Picture Cars   (562) 693-5641
2684 Turnbull Canyon Rd, City of Industry, CA, 91745
antique and classic cars & trucks, parts & garage items
Action Sets and Props / WonderWorks, Inc. (818) 992-8811
Space shuttle & station, space suit, specialty props, miniatures, mechanical
effects, cityscape, miniature buildings
Advanced Fire & Rescue Services   (661) 299-4801
16654 Soledad Canyon Rd, #186 Canyon Country, 91387
Fire trucks, antique & modern, rescue trucks, onsite personnel, prof.
firefighters, EMTs, jaws of life
Eng12capt@yahoo.com * www.advancedfire.com
Cinema Vehicle Services   (818) 780-6272
12580 Saticoy St, N Hollywood, CA, 91605
On-camera rentals, car carriers, body/paint/graphics/upholstery/fabr/mech
contact@cinemavehicles.com * www.cinemavehicles.com

Cornwell & Sheridan Picture Vehicles   (310) 217-9060
15700 S Broadway, Gardena, CA, 90248
Convertibles, Coupes, Sedans, Limos, Motorcycles
davesimoncars@yahoo.com * www.old-cars.net

depict   (323) 222-1001
1460 Naud St, Los Angeles, CA, 90012
info@depict33.com * www.depict33.com
FamVans, Inc.   (714) 274-1144
10870 Kalama River Ave, Fountain Valley, CA, 92708
Suppliers of commercial van and trucks for the entertainment industry. Contact
Mike or Aziz for all general inquiries.
famvans.com
Fire In Motion   (661) 510-5771
27844 Ferguson Dr, Castaic, CA, 91384
Functional Pumpers, Ladder trucks, Ambulances, Suburban Battalion Chief and
Crown Vic.
jim@fireinmotion.net * www.fireinmotion.net
5-Star Military Vehicles   (310) 740-6931
Call for appt, Seal Beach, CA
Tanks, Humvees, Jeeps and Land Rovers, WW II to current day
info@militaryvehicles.com * www.militaryvehicles.com

LISTINGS FOR THIS CATEGORY CONTINUE ON THE FOLLOWING PAGE

Galpin Motors Studio Rentals   (323) 957-3333
1763 N Ivar Ave, Hollywood, CA, 90028
Trucks designed specifically for the Art & Prop department. Picture cars: specializing in ALL late model manufacturers.
lou@galpin.com * www.galpinstudiorentals.com

Mr. Vintage Machine   (213) 369-0281
Call for Appointment, Los Angeles, CA, 90027
Vintage vehicles, hot rods, custom classics, motorcycles, choppers, low riders, luxury & specialty cars
gabriel@mistervintagemachine.com * www.mistervintagemachine.com

K4 Motorsports   (818) 713-0552
PO Box 8902, Calabasas, CA, 91372
Full NASCAR Racing Resources for Production, Features, T.V., and Commercials; Race cars, haulers, pit equip., drivers.
www.k4motorsports.com

MovieMoto.com   (626) 359-0016
16015 Adelante St, Irwindale, CA, 91702
Rare, Odd, Classic, Exotic, Unknown MOTORCYCLE RENTALS. Specializing in Italian marks.
www.MovieMoto.com

Picture Vehicles Unlimited   (661) 295-7711
25111 Rye Canyon Loop, Santa Clarita, CA, 91355
all types, vintage-present, comprehensive services, incl. stunts
http://www.picturevehiclesunlimited.com

Sterndahl Enterprises, Inc.   (818) 834-8199
11861 Branford St, Sun Valley, CA, 91352
traffic control equipment, signage, barricades, striping, trucks & bobcats
www.sterndahl.com

Studio Picture Vehicles, Inc   (818) 765-1201
7502 Wheatland Ave, Sun Valley, CA, 91352
police, ambulance
office@studiopicturevehicles.com * www.studiopicturevehicles.com

Universal Studios Transportation   (818) 777-2966
100 Universal City Plaza, Universal City, CA, 91608
range of vehicles available, SUVs to tractor trailers
universalstudioslot.com/transportation

The Wood N' Carr   (562) 498-8730
2345 Walnut Ave, Signal Hill, CA, 90755
woodies from 30s-50s, restored old beach buggies
www.woodncarr.net

Vending Machines

AIR Designs (818) 768-6639
Soda, Sandwich, Coffee, Ice Cream Dispensers/Ice Cream Machines, Popcorn, Candy, Snack
Alley Cats Studio Rentals (818) 982-9178
candy, soda/beverage, snacks, cigarettes, subway/train ticket, gumball
E.C. Prop Rentals (818) 764-2008
newspaper, plastic & metal
History For Hire, Inc. (818) 765-7767
vintage
Lennie Marvin Enterprises, Inc. (Prop Heaven) (818) 841-5882
period-modern, gumballs, soda, snacks, tampons, condoms
Omega/Cinema Props (323) 466-8201
Condom machines, hygiene machines
RC Vintage, Inc. (818) 765-7107
gumball, beverage to food. Modern Cola, and cleared Snack artwork
Sony Pictures Studios-Prop House (Off Lot) (310) 244-5999
large selection, food, drink etc., candy vending machine, cigarette vending machine,

Vendor Carts & Concession Counters

See Also: Carnival Dressing/Supplies* Circus Equipment/Dressing/Costumes* Events, Decorations, Supplies & Services* Produce Carts* Taco Carts (Propmaster & Set)* Vending Machines* Food, Food Stylists

AIR Designs (818) 768-6639
Concession Counters, Popcorn, Flower, Espresso, Hot Dog, Taco, Mall
Alley Cats Studio Rentals (818) 982-9178
hot dog, coffee, candy, popcorn, churro, flower, mail, cell phone display
Amusement Svcs/Candyland Amusements (818) 266-4056
18653 Ventura Blvd Ste 235, Tarzana, CA, 91356
Candy applies, shaved ice, snow cones, cotton candy, Harry's diner, many carts, booths, vendors, kiosks, counters and themed tables
raymond@candylandamusements.com * www.candylandamusements.com
C. P. Two (323) 466-8201
Hot dog cars/New York Vendor Carts
The Hand Prop Room LP. (323) 931-1534
popcorn, hot dog, pretzel, cotton candy
History For Hire, Inc. (818) 765-7767
plain & fancy, chestnut carts
L. A. Party Works (888) 527-2789
9712 Alpaca St, S El Monte, CA, 91733
Hot dog carts, popcorn carts, cotton candy carts, lemonade carts, bear making carts & more. Vancouver tel. 604-589-4101.
partyworks@aol.com * www.partyworksinteractive.com

LCW Props (818) 243-0707
Multiple Styles
Lennie Marvin Enterprises, Inc. (Prop Heaven) (818) 841-5882
hot dog, popcorn, coffee, chestnut, ice cream, floral, cot. cand
RC Vintage, Inc. (818) 765-7107
Hot Dog Ice cream, popcorn, peanut, chestnut, cot. candy, 20s to present, mall carts
Sony Pictures Studios-Prop House (Off Lot) (310) 244-5999
Universal Studios Property & Hardware Dept (818) 777-2784
Prop vendor carts and prop concession counters/concession stands for rent.

Veneer

See: Paneling, Veneers & Laminates

Venetian & Vertical Blinds

See: Window Treatments

Ventriloquist Figures

See: Puppets, Marionettes, Automata, Animatronics

Vents

See: Plumbing Fixtures, Heating/Cooling Appliances

Victrolas/Gramophones

See Also: Phonographs
The Hand Prop Room LP. (323) 931-1534
antique period, lrg sel.
History For Hire, Inc. (818) 765-7767
RC Vintage, Inc. (818) 765-7107
Large Brass Horn, maroon flower victrolas, wind up gramophones

Video 24fps / Sync System / D.D.I.

See Also: Video Camera Equipment & Services
24Frame.com, Inc. (213) 745-2411
944 Venice Blvd, Los Angeles, CA, 90015
24Frame/24P sync playback of all video & computer
info@24frame.com * www.24frame.com

Hill Digital (818) 445-9211
By Appointment, Los Angeles, CA
Video syncing services
www.hilldigital.com
Inter Video (818) 843-3624
2000 N Lincoln St, Burbank, CA, 91504
Video sync playback services
intervideo.co
Warner Bros. Studios Production Sound & Video (818) 954-2511
4000 Warner Blvd Bldg 43, Burbank, CA, 91522
A/V Equipment Rental, Design, Presentations, Install & Support; Visual Display Creation; Communication
wbsfproductionsound@warnerbros.com * www.wbsoundandvideo.com

Video Camera Equipment & Services

See Also: Camera Equipment* Radio/TV Station* Video 24fps / Sync System / D.D.I.

24Frame.com, Inc. (213) 745-2411
944 Venice Blvd, Los Angeles, CA, 90015
televisions, monitors, decks, switchers, sync
info@24frame.com * www.24frame.com

Bexel (818) 565-4399
2701 N Ontario St, Burbank, CA, 91504
camera packages
www.bexel.com

CCI Digital (818) 562-6300
2921 W. Alameda Ave, Burbank, CA, 91505
post production rentals & services
www.ccidigital.com

Innovision Optics (310) 453-4866
2858 Colorado Ave, Santa Monica CA, 90404
camera motion control systems, special purpose lens systems
sales@innovisionoptics.com * www.innovisionoptics.com

Runway (310) 636-2000
1330 N Vine St, Hollywood, CA, 90028
camera packages
www.runway.com

Sim Digital (323) 978-9000
1017 N. Las Palmas Ave., Hollywood, California, 90038
camera packages
www.simdigital.com

Sweetwater (818) 902-9500
7635 Airport Business Parkway, Van Nuys, CA, 91406
video production truck package, video projection, flypacks
www.nepinc.com/welcome/sweetwater

VER Video Equipment Rentals (818) 502-8900
757 W California Ave, Glendale CA, 91201
Located nationwide, camera packages, hi-def, AV/audio
www.ver.com

Westcoast Video Productions, Inc. (818) 785-8033
14141 Covello St, Ste 9A, Van Nuys, CA, 91405
broadcast video remote facility, equip. & crew pkgs.
www.wvpinc.com

Wintech Video (818) 501-6565
7625 Hayvenhurst Ste 22, Van Nuys, CA, 91406
equip, rentals, production crew & equip. pkgs.
http://wintechvideo.com

World Wide Digital Services (818) 500-7559
1819 Dana St, Unit E, Glendale, CA, 91201
camera & recording packages
http://worldwidela.com

Video Equipment

See Also: Audio/Visual Film Equipment* Camera Equipment* Control Boards* Editing Equipment & Services* Press Equipment

24Frame.com, Inc. (213) 745-2411
944 Venice Blvd, Los Angeles, CA, 90015
televisions, monitors, decks, switchers, sync
info@24frame.com * www.24frame.com

Astro Audio Video Lighting, Inc. (818) 549-9915
6615 San Fernando Rd, Glendale, CA, 91201
High Def, projectors, recorders, players, screens, plasmas, LED video walls
www.astroavl.com

LCW Props (818) 243-0707
Large Selection, Monitors, Security, LCD / Plasma, Video Projection, Video Walls

Old N Country Prop Shop, LLC (818) 423-2599
Many vintage cameras, from 8mm, Polaroid, SLR, Brownie, etc.

Sony Pictures Studios-Prop House (Off Lot) (310) 244-5999
televisions, tape recorders, tape players, AV VCR player, video cassette recorders, AV Viewer, Video rewinder

Warner Bros. Studios Production Sound & Video (818) 954-2511
4000 Warner Blvd Bldg 43, Burbank, CA, 91522
All types of A/V Equipment Rental, Design, Presentations, Install & Support; Visual Display Creation; Communication
wbsfproductionsound@warnerbros.com * www.wbsoundandvideo.com

Woody's Electrical Props (818) 503-1940
Period to futuristic. Fantasy sets, military sets, industrial sets, air tower/mission control.

Video Games

See Also: Arcade Equipment, Games & Rides

Arcade Amusements (866) 576-8878
802 West Washington Ave Ste E, Escondido, CA, 92025-1644
Planning a Party? How about having some games there? How about 10? How about 20? How about... Well, you get the idea.
phil@arcadeamusements.com * www.arcadeamusements.com

L. A. Party Works (888) 527-2789
9712 Alpaca St, S El Monte, CA, 91733
in Vancouver tel. 604-589-4101. X-Box, PS3, & Wii, LaserTag, RockWall, V.R.,Gyros
partyworks@aol.com * www.partyworksinteractive.com

Lennie Marvin Enterprises, Inc. (Prop Heaven) (818) 841-5882
period to modern, arcade equip.

RC Vintage, Inc. (818) 765-7107
vintage/modern, practical, 1970s-1990s Cleared Video Game Art Selection. Sit Down Motorcycle and Race Car games

Video Rental/Sales Store

See Also: Cash Registers* Counters* Credit Card Imprint Machine* Steel Folding Gates & Roll-Up Doors* Store Shelf Units & Shelving

Cinefile (310) 312-8836
11280 Santa Monica Blvd, Los Angeles, CA, 90025
Euro-trash, Italian horror, big goofy monsters
www.cinefilevideo.com

Eddie Brandt's Saturday Matinee (818) 506-4242
5006 Vineland Ave, N Hollywood, CA, 91601
Tues.-Fri. 1:00-6:00 pm Sat. 8:30am - 5:00 pm. vintage & hard to find video

Video Store Dressing

See Also: Video Rental/Sales Store

AIR Designs (818) 768-6639
Wall Racks, Counters, Display Units, VCR Cases, CD's, Records, Signs

Alley Cats Studio Rentals (818) 982-9178
DVD store counters & racks, signs, DVDs, CDs, VHS Tapes, Cassette Tapes

LCW Props (818) 243-0707
Media, Shelving, Cases, POS System, Beta, VHS, DVD, CD, Video Games

Vintage Clothing

See: Jewelry, Costume* Jewelry, Fine/Reproduction* Wardrobe, Vintage

Vinyl

See: Clear Vinyl* Fabrics* Phonograph Records* Plastics, Materials & Fabrication

Vinyl Letters

See: Signs

Virtual Reality Games

See: Arcade Equipment, Games & Rides

Volleyball Setup

The Hand Prop Room LP. (323) 931-1534
Universal Studios Property & Hardware Dept (818) 777-2784
Volleyball set up for rent.

Voting

See Also: Game Show Electronics & Equipment

County of L.A. Registrar/Recorder (800) 815-2666
12400 Imperial Hwy, Norwalk, CA, 90650
Voting booth rentals
www.lavote.net

E.C. Prop Rentals (818) 764-2008
Electronic voting machine, in rolling case with monitor

LCW Props (818) 243-0707
Voting Booths, Stanchions, Swags, Flags, Desks

Wagons

See Also: Gypsy Wagon* Horses, Horse Equipment, Livestock*
Western Dressing
C. P. Two   (323) 466-8201
large wagon wheels, small wagon wheels; Hollywood's largest selection!
Caravan West Productions   (661) 268-8300
35660 Jayhawker Rd, Aqua Dulce, CA, 91390
historically accurate Western wagons, buckboards, chuckwagons, Covered
stagecoach
caravanwest@earthlink.net * www.caravanwest.com
Jackson Shrub Supply, Inc.   (818) 982-0100
wagons & buggies
Movin' On Livestock   (661) 252-8654
20527 Soledad St, Canyon Country, CA, 91351
livestock, many wagons & stagecoaches, jail wagon too
www.movinonlivestock.com
Universal Studios Property & Hardware Dept   (818) 777-2784
Western wagons, fancy wagons, beat up wagons, covered wagons and more
for rent.

Waiting Room

See Also: Lobby Seating
Alpha Companies - Spellman Desk Co.   (818) 504-9090
medical waiting room dressing, doctors office dressing, doctors office furniture

Wakeboard

See: Surfboard, Wakeboard

Walk Around Characters

See: Animal Costumes & Walk Around Characters* Prop Design &
Manufacturing

Walkie-Talkies

See Also: Radios* Telephones* Telephones, Cellular
Airwaves Wireless   (818) 501-8200
13400 Riverside Dr # 103 Sherman Oaks, CA, 91423
Walkie-talkies, Base Stations, Repeaters, Cell Signal Boosters, Mobile
Wireless Internet, Cell Phones, Satellite Phones.
sales@airwaveswireless.com * www.airwaveswireless.com
Castex Rentals   (323) 462-1468
1044 N Cole Ave, Hollywood, CA, 90038
Motorola CP200, headsets, surveillance kits, walkie-talkies
service@castexrentals.com * www.castexrentals.com
E.C. Prop Rentals   (818) 764-2008
police/security type w/charging stands/racks
The Hand Prop Room LP.   (323) 931-1534
military, police, civilian, real & prop
History For Hire, Inc.   (818) 765-7767
police, militiary, civilian
LCW Props   (818) 243-0707
Military, Security, Personal, CB Radios, Home Base
Picture Start Props   (818) 255-5472
Selection of vintage pairs of walkie talkies.
Warner Bros. Studios Production Sound &   (818) 954-2511
Video
4000 Warner Blvd Bldg 43, Burbank, CA, 91522
A/V Equipment Rental, Design, Presentations, Install & Support; Visual Display
Creation; Communication
wbsfproductionsound@warnerbros.com * www.wbsoundandvideo.com
ZG04 DECOR   (818) 853-8040
Practical walkie talkies for events, film, television productions and more

Walking Sticks

See: Canes

Wall "O" Fects

See: Masks

Wall Coverings

See Also: Tapestry Wall Hangings
Adelphi   (518) 284-9066
102 Main St, POB 135, Sharon Springs, NY, 13459
period wallpaper hand-made by wood blocks
www.adelphipaperhangings.com
Bradbury & Bradbury Art Wallpapers   (707) 746-1900
P.O. Box 155, Benicia, CA, 94510
Historic wallpapers from the Victorian, Arts & Crafts, Art Deco & Modern styles
www.bradbury.com
Collins Visual Media   (818) 686-6581
10518 Johanna Ave, Shadow Hills, CA, 91040
We can create for you any type of wall covering: permanent or removable,
seamless, wallpaper, canvas, fabric, etc.
www.collinsvisualmedia.com
Linoleum City, Inc.   (323) 469-0063
4849 Santa Monica Blvd, Hollywood, CA, 90029
Decorative wall cork, bulletin board cork. No wallpaper.
sales@linocity.com * www.linoleumcity.com

Oceanic Arts   (562) 698-6960
Native Tropical Mattings woven from Palm Leaves, Banana Leaves, Bamboo.
17 Varieties. Lauhala in 5 sizes.
Outwater Plastics Industries   (800) 248-2067
4720 W Van Buren, P.O. Box 18190, Phoenix, AZ, 85043
catalog sales; plastics. stamped steel, pressed tin, embossed vinyl
www.outwater.com
Prop Services West   (818) 503-2790
Pulp Art Surfaces   (818) 655-5804
4021 Radford Ave, Studio City, CA, 91604
Finished and unfinished wall skins
www.pulpartsurfaces.com
Secondhand Rose   (212) 393-9002
Call for Appt.
vintage wallpaper
www.secondhandrose.com
Wallpaper City & Flooring   (310) 393-9422
1758 Lincoln Blvd, Santa Monica, CA, 90404
especially vintage, American/European, also will fabricate
www.wallpapercityflooring.com
Worlds of Wow   (817) 380-4215
1800 Shady Oaks Drive, Denton, TX, 76205
Custom designed digital wall coverings, custom mural airbrushing
www.worldsofwow.com

Wall Hangings

See: Paintings/Prints* Photographs* Posters, Art/Movie/Travel/Wanted Etc.* Tapestry Wall Hangings* Wall Coverings

Wall Maps

See: Maps

Wallpaper

See: Wall Coverings

Wanted Posters

See: Police Equipment* Posters, Art/Movie/Travel/Wanted Etc.

Wardrobe

See Also: Costume Rental Houses* Costumes* Wardrobe, Accessories* Wardrobe, Antique/Historical* Wardrobe, Construction & Alterations* Wardrobe, Contemporary* Wardrobe, International/Ethnic* Wardrobe, Vintage

Action Sets and Props / WonderWorks, Inc. (818) 992-8811
Space shuttle & station, space suit, specialty props, miniatures, mechanical effects, cityscape, miniature buildings

Adele's of Hollywood (323) 663-2231

American Costume Corp. (818) 764-2239
1770s through 1970s for film & TV industries

CBS Costume Rental (323) 575-2666
Designer modern M/F, also western & Indian of 1880s

The Costume House (818) 508-9933
1880s-1980s civilian, men/women/children

Costume Rentals Corporation (818) 753-3700
motion picture supplier & special order items

Des Kohan (323) 857-0200
671 Cloverdale, Los Angeles, CA, 90036
designer clothing, vintage jewelry & home accessories, celebrity stylists available
www.deskohan.com

Eastern Costume (818) 982-3611
Full-service costume house, military, police & civilian wardrobe, 1920's to present, alterations & tailoring.

Gohn Bros. (574) 825-2400
105 S. Main St, P.O. Box 1110, Middlebury, IN, 46540
Fabrics and needs of the Amish community
www.gohnbrothers.com

History For Hire, Inc. (818) 765-7767
full racks, rented as set dressing only

LCW Props (818) 243-0707
Call For An Updated Listing

The New Mart (213) 627-0671
127 E 9th St, Los Angeles, CA, 90015
wholesale trade, 90+ agents rep 100s of directional manufacturers; call for tenant directory
www.newmart.net

RDD U.S.A. Inc. (213) 742-0666
4638 E Washington Blvd, Commerce, CA, 90040
military jackets, rain & cold weather clothing, dress jackets
www.rddusa.com

Roxy Deluxe (818) 487-7800
1860-1970 clothing accessories & jewelry

Sony Pictures Studios-Wardrobe (310) 244-5995
alterations, call (310) 244-7260

Syren (The Stockroom) (213) 989-0334
2121 W Sunset Blvd, Los Angeles, CA, 90026
M/W rubber clothing, variety of colors/styles
syrencouture.com

Universal Studios Costume Dept (818) 777-2722
Rental, mfg., & alterations

Used Church Items, Religious Rentals (412) 220-2272
115 East Barr Street, Mcdonald, PA, 15057
Catholic Church Priest Vestments, Religious Robe, Liturgical, Christian, Clergy Apparel, Chasuble, Stole, Cope, Dalmatic
www.religiousrentals.com

The Way We Wore, Inc. Retail (323) 937-0878
334 S La Brea Ave, Los Angeles, CA, 90036
huge sel. of women's clothing: access. from 1910-1979. hard-to-find items like bathing suits, stockings etc.
http://thewaywewore.com

Western Costume Co. (818) 760-0900

Wardrobe Racks

See: Garment Racks

Wardrobe Supplies

See: Costume/Wardrobe/Sewing Supplies

Wardrobe, Accessories

See Also: Archery Equipment, Training* Armor, Chainmail, Suits of Armor* Badges, Patches & Buttons* Bling* Crowns & Tiaras* Doctor's Bags* Environmental (Cool/Heat) Suits* Eyewear, Glasses, Sunglasses, 3D* Fabric Dyeing/Tie Dyeing/Painting/Aging* Feathers* Guns & Firearms* Fireman Uniforms, Hats & Equipment* Flameproofing* Fur, Artificial & Real* Headdresses* Headwear - Hats, Bonnets, Caps, Helmets Etc.* Jewelry, Costume* Jewelry, Fine/Reproduction* Keys & Locks* Knickers* Leather (Clothing, Accessories, Materials)* Lunch Boxes* Pom Pons* Trims, Fringe, Tassels, Beading Etc.* Umbrellas, Hand & Parasols* Underwear & Lingerie, Bloomers, Corsets, Etc.* Weaponry, Historical* Weaponry, Medieval* Weapons* Western Wear* Wigs* Steampunk

The Costume House	**(818) 508-9933**

hats, purses, jewelry, shoes, vintage purses, vintage shoes, vintage ties, vintage hats

Early Halloween	**(212) 691-2933**

130 West 25th St, 11th Floor, New York, NY, 10001
Neckties, etc.; old stock never worn 1940-50
www.earlyhalloween.com

The Hand Prop Room LP.	**(323) 931-1534**

period-present, jewelry, hair clips, hat pins

Helen Uffner Vintage Clothing LLC	**(718) 937-0220**

authentic 1860s to 1970s M/W/children

History For Hire, Inc.	**(818) 765-7767**

gloves, collars & cuffs, hair clips, etc.

Ob-jects	**(818) 351-4200**
Screaming Mimi's	**(212) 677-6464**

240 West 14th St, New York NY, 10011
vintage clothing for men & women 1940s - 1980s
www.screamingmimis.com

Sony Pictures Studios-Prop House (Off Lot)	**(310) 244-5999**
Universal Studios Costume Dept	**(818) 777-2722**

Rental, mfg., & alterations

Western Costume Co.	**(818) 760-0900**

Wardrobe, Antique/Historical

See Also: Native American

Amazon Drygoods	**(812) 852-1780**

3788 Wilson St, Osgood, IN 47037
catalog sales; 19 C. wardrobe/patterns, home access., books. clothing, access, footwear
kevin@amazondrygoods.com * www.amazondrygoods.com

American Costume Corp.	**(818) 764-2239**

1770s through 1970s for film & TV industry

Blockade Runner	**(931) 389-6294**

1027 Bell Buckle Wartrace Rd, Wartrace, TN, 37183
Antebellum, Southern US authentic uniforms & civilian wear, Civil War research center
www.blockaderunner.com

C & D Jarnagin Co.	**(662) 287-4977**

518 Wicks St, Corinth, MS, 38834
1750-1815 F & I, Rev, & 1812 Wars, Military/Civil.
www.jarnaginco.com

CBS Costume Rental	**(323) 575-2666**

western M/F 1880s

The Costume House	**(818) 508-9933**

clothes, 1870s to 1980's & medieval & colonial costumes

Fall Creek Corporation	**(765) 482-1861**

PO Box 92, Whitestown, IN, 46075
Civil War era, military & civilian. leather clothing, civil war uniforms, shoes, accessories
ajfulks@fcsutler.com * www.fcsutler.com

Jas. Townsend & Son, Inc.	**(574) 594-5852**

133 N 1st St, P.O. Box 415, Pierceton, IN, 46562
catalog sales; American Colonial period inspired reprod. of wardrobe & household items, books/patterns of Colonial perio
www.jas-townsend.com

Make Believe, Inc.	**(310) 396-6785**

We also sell masks, wigs, theatrical makeup & access. historical/biblical figures, Renaissance,18th-19th centuries

The Smoke & Fire Co.	**(800) 766-5334**

27 N River Rd, Waterville, OH, 43566
Supplies for Colonial re-enactors, patterns, clothes, books
www.smoke-fire.com

Sword & Stone	**(818) 562-6548**

Medieval tiaras, crowns, sceptres, boots, shoes

Used Church Items, Religious Rentals	**(412) 220-2272**

115 East Barr Street, Mcdonald, PA, 15057
Church Robes, Catholic Priest Vestments, Pope, Bishop, Pastor, Deacon, Minister, Vicar, Clergy, Vintage Clothing, Mitre.
www.religiousrentals.com

Western Costume Co.	**(818) 760-0900**

Wardrobe, Construction & Alterations

See Also: Costume Rental Houses* Costume/Wardrobe/Sewing Supplies* Costumes* Wardrobe* Wardrobe, Accessories

The Costume House	**(818) 508-9933**

work room, will built to your design, wardrobe alterations on site, fitting rooms available

Costume Rentals Corporation	**(818) 753-3700**

motion picture supplier & special order items

Eastern Costume	**(818) 982-3611**

Full-service, 1920's to present, alterations, tailoring, boots, footwear, uniform, military, police & civilian wardrobe.

JFF Uniforms-Costumes	**(310) 320-1327**

557 Van Ness Ave, Torrance, CA, 90501
Custom garments 1-10,000 pcs made from sketch or sample. Period, military, modern & more.
www.jffuniforms.com

Milt & Edie's	**(818) 846-4734**

4021 W Alameda at Pass, Burbank, CA, 91505
Tailoring & Alterations available 24/7/365. Instant alterations available at no extra charge.
info@miltandedies.com * www.miltandedies.com

Muto-Little Inc.	**(323) 469-1618**

519 North Larchmont Blvd, Los Angeles, CA, 90004
www.muto-little.com

SERJ Costumes & Tailoring	**(818) 845-2800**

1707 W Magnolia Blvd, Burbank, CA, 91506
http://serjcustomtailoring.com

Universal Studios Costume Dept	**(818) 777-2722**

Rental, mfg., & alterations

Warner Bros. Studios Costume Dept	**(818) 954-1297**

Made-to-order mens tailoring & ladies dressmaking, expert alterations, Custom manufacturing, Repairs

Western Costume Co.	**(818) 760-0900**

Wardrobe, Contemporary

See Also: Costume Rental Houses

American Rag Cie (323) 935-3154
150 S. La Brea, Los Angeles, CA, 90036
clothing, shoes, hats, accessories
www.amrag.com

California Market Center (213) 630-3600
110 E. 9th St, Los Angeles, CA, 90079
1,000+ wholesale showrooms for registered buyers, see web site for directory,
info desk (213) 630-3600
www.californiamarketcenter.com

CBS Costume Rental (323) 575-2666
designer suits, day wear, M/F

Garment District Alliance (212) 764-9600
209 W 38th St, 2nd Floor, New York, NY, 10018
promotes garment district, our website lists resources/contacts. Assists with
business Improvement.
info@garmentdistrictnyc.com * http://garmentdistrictnyc.com

Gemelli (310) 955-5819
By Appointment Only
When your character is closing a million $$ deal, starting a career, going out on
the town, or just likes to look sharp.
info@gemelliwear.com * www.gemelliwear.com

LCW Props (818) 243-0707
Call For An Updated Listing

Los Angeles Fashion District (213) 488-1153
110 E. 9th Street, Suite A-1175, Los Angeles, CA 90079
website/directory lists shops by types
www.fashiondistrict.org

Ravishing Resale (323) 655-8480
Call for Appt.
high quality & designer
www.ravishingresale.com

Sony Pictures Studios-Wardrobe (310) 244-5995
alterations, call (310) 244-7260

Warner Bros. Studios Costume Dept (818) 954-1297
Collection of period & contemporary costumes for rent categorized by era,
decade and style

Western Costume Co. (818) 760-0900

Wardrobe, International/Ethnic

See Also: Costumes, International/Ethnic

Alberene Royal Mail (800) 843-9078
5175 Alberene Rd, North Garden VA, 22959
catalog sales; books, clan tartans/prints/mugs, pub dressing
www.alberene.com

C & D Jarnagin Co. (662) 287-4977
518 Wicks St, Corinth, MS, 38834
1833-1865 Mexican War & Civil War, Military/Civil.
www.jarnaginco.com

CBS Costume Rental (323) 575-2666

The Costume House (818) 508-9933
Scottish, Japanese kimonos & obis

R.P. Blandford & Son, Ltd. (909) 483-1070
8439 White Oak Ave Ste 107, Rancho Cucamonga, CA, 91730
Scottish, clan tartans, accessories, bagpipes, etc.
www.blandfordimports.com

The Tartan Patch (714) 841-1860
18011 Sky Park Circle Ste P, Irvine, CA, 92614
Ethnic Scottish/Irish apparel
www.tartanpatch.com

Western Costume Co. (818) 760-0900

Wm. Glen & Son (415) 989-5458
360 Sutter St, San Francisco, CA, 94108
Retail sales; ethnic Scottish apparel for M/W/Children. Kilt wear and more for
all tartans and clans.
wmglenusa.com

Wardrobe, Studio Services

See Also: Expendables* Grip Equipment* Locations, Stages/Studios,
Film/TV/Events* Transportation, Trucking and/or Storage* Heavy
Machinery, Equipment & Specialists

Alandales (310) 838-5100
9705 Washington Blvd., Culver City, CA 90232
Men's apparel
www.alandales.com

American Rag Cie (323) 935-3154
150 S. La Brea, Los Angeles, CA, 90036
Men's & women's vintage & designer clothing
www.amrag.com

Barney's New York - Beverly Hills (310) 777-5709
9570 Wilshire Blvd., Beverly Hills, CA 90212
Men's & women's apparel, 4th floor
bhstudioservices@barneys.com

Barney's New York - New York (212) 833-2086
660 Madison Ave, New York, NY, 10021
Men's & women's apparel

Bloomingdale's - Beverly Center (310) 360-2714
8500 Beverly Blvd, Los Angeles, CA, 90048
Studio services for Beverly Center
http://fashion.bloomingdales.com/about-us/shopping/fashion-studio-styling-serv
ices

Bloomingdale's - Century City (310) 712-2234
10250 California Route 2, Los Angeles, CA, 90067
Studio services for Century City
http://fashion.bloomingdales.com/about-us/shopping/fashion-studio-styling-serv
ices

Bloomingdale's - Fashion Square (818) 325-2301
14060 Riverside Dr, Sherman Oaks, CA, 91423
Studio services for Sherman Oaks
http://fashion.bloomingdales.com/about-us/shopping/fashion-studio-styling-serv
ices

Bloomingdale's - Lenox Square (404) 495-2943
3393 Peachtree Road NE, Atlanta, GA, 30326
Studio services for Atlanta, Georgia
http://fashion.bloomingdales.com/about-us/shopping/fashion-studio-styling-serv
ices

Bloomingdale's - New York City (212) 705-3673
1000 Third Ave, New York, NY, 10022
Studio services for New York
http://fashion.bloomingdales.com/about-us/shopping/fashion-studio-styling-serv
ices

Carroll & Co. (310) 273-9060
425 N. Canon Dr., Beverly Hills, CA 90210

Emporio Armani (310) 271-7790
338 N Rodeo Dr, Beverly Hills, CA 90210

Ermenegildo Zegna (310) 247-8827
337 N Rodeo Dr, Beverly Hills, CA 90210
Men's apparel

Giorgio Armani (310) 271-5555
436 N. Rodeo Dr., Beverly Hills, CA 90210
Men's & women's apparel

Hugo Boss (310) 859-2888
414 N Rodeo Dr, Beverly Hills, CA, 90210
Ask for marketing contact. Studio services & product placement

Italian Fashion Group - di Stefano Suits (213) 622-7756
1414 Santee St, Los Angeles, CA, 90015
Ready made and custom men's wear; shirts, suits, tuxedos, contemporary &
period wardrobe.

Macy's - Beverly Center Mens Dept (310) 659-4752
8500 Beverly Blvd, Los Angeles, CA, 90048
Mens Studio Services - 1st Floor

Macy's - Beverly Center Womens Dept (310) 659-9660
8500 Beverly Blvd, Los Angeles, CA, 90048
Womens Studio Services - 7th Floor

Macy's - Fashion Square (818) 788-8350
14000 Riverside Dr., Sherman Oaks, CA 91423 Ext. 7855
Full line of apparel

Neiman Marcus (310) 975-4336
9700 Wilshire Blvd., Beverly Hills, CA 90212
Men's & women's apparel, also try (310) 550-5900 x4336

Nordstrom - Americana (818) 664-7030
102 Caruso Ave, Glendale, CA, 91210
Full line of apparel

Nordstrom - Santa Monica (310) 752-4170
220 Broadway, Santa Monica, CA, 90401
Full line of apparel

Nordstrom - The Grove (323) 900-1670
189 The Grove Dr, Los Angeles, CA, 90036
Full line of apparel

Nordstrom - Westfield Topanga (818) 592-4622
21725 Victory Blvd, Canoga Park, CA, 91303
Full line of apparel

Nordstrom - Westside Pavilion (310) 254-1690
10830 W Pico Blvd, Los Angeles, CA, 90064
Full line of apparel

Polo/Ralph Lauren (310) 281-7200
444 N Rodeo Dr, Beverly Hills, CA, 90210

Rochester Big & Tall (310) 274-9468
9737 Wilshire Blvd., Beverly Hills, CA 90212
Men's apparel, specializing in big & tall sizes

Ron Herman (323) 651-4129
8100 Melrose Ave, Los Angeles, CA 90046
Call to set up account first, extension 230

Saks Fifth Avenue - Beverly Hills (310) 271-6726
9600 Wilshire Blvd., Beverly Hills, CA 90212
Full line of apparel

Saks Fifth Avenue - New York (212) 940-4323
8 E 50th St, New York, NY 10022
Full line of apparel

Sy Devore (818) 783-2700
12930 Ventura Blvd. Ste 124, Studio City, CA 91604
Men's apparel
dannymarsh@sbcglobal.net

Wardrobe, Vintage

American Costume Corp. (818) 764-2239
1770s through 1970s for film & TV industry

American Rag Cie (323) 935-3154
150 S. La Brea, Los Angeles, CA, 90036
fashionable vintage men's & women's, 50s - 80s styles
www.amrag.com

Armani Wells (818) 985-5899
12404 Ventura Blvd, Studio City, CA, 91604
Men's high fashion at 60% to 90% below retail; new & vintage
http://www.armaniwells.com/aw

Buffalo Exchange (323) 938-8604
131 N. La Brea Ave, Los Angeles, CA, 90036
chic apparel recycler, buy, sell, trade, also Sherman Oaks location (818) 783-3420
www.buffaloexchange.com

Catherine Nash's Closet (520) 620-6613
1102 W. Huron St, Tucson, AZ, 85745
wholesale to Industry only: finest quality vintage clothing, 1860s-1970s
cnash@wvcnet.com

CBS Costume Rental (323) 575-2666
1940s to 1980s, day/evening

The Costume House (818) 508-9933
genuine & original, 1870s to 1880s/Renaissance, childrens vintage clothing,
womens vintage clothing

Decades (323) 655-0223
8214 Melrose Ave, Los Angeles, CA, 90046
designer 60s-80s; Decadestwo has contemp. couture resale
www.decadesinc.com

Early Halloween (212) 691-2933
130 West 25th St, 11th Floor, New York, NY, 10001
men/women/child 1900-1960
www.earlyhalloween.com

Helen Uffner Vintage Clothing LLC (718) 937-0220
authentic 1850-1973 M/W/children apparel & accessories

Heritage Costumes (310) 320-6392
men's & women's, full line of vintage clothing

Jet Rag (323) 939-0528
825 N La Brea Ave, Hollywood, CA, 90038

King Richards Antique & Vintage Center (562) 698-5974
12301 Whittier Blvd, Whittier, CA, 90602
Bettie Page Clothing: An exclusive retailer of BP retro/rockabilly clothing.
Located in the largest antique store in CA.
martha@kingrichardsantiques.com * www.kingrichardsantiques.com

Lily Et Cie (310) 724-5757
9044 Burton Way, Beverly Hills, CA, 90211
ladies designer vintage
info@lilyetcie.com * www.lilyetcie.com

Madison Ave Furs LTD (212) 594-5744
118 W 27th St Ground Floor, New York, NY, 10001
Madison Avenue Furs, LTD. in NYC is a 3rd generation, family owned,
multifaceted retail & wholesale fur business.
hcfurmatcher@msn.com * www.cowitfurs.com

Maxfield (310) 274-8800
8825 Melrose Ave, Los Angeles, CA, 90069
largest sel. of vintage Hermes items
www.maxfieldla.com

Meow (562) 438-8990
2210 E 4th St, Long Beach, CA, 90814
original "never worn" 1940s-80 men/women/kid apparel/accessories
www.meowvintage.com

Ozzie Dots - Vintage Clothing & Costumes (323) 663-2867
4637 Hollywood Blvd, Los Angeles, CA, 90027
Victorian to 70s, full line of access, open 7 days
www.ozziedots.com

Palace Costume & Prop Co. (323) 651-5458
men, women, children 1850s-1980s

The Paper Bag Princess, Inc. (310) 385-9036
8050 Melrose Ave, Los Angeles CA 90046
designer vintage, also construction/custom couture, red carpet design
www.thepaperbagprincess.com

Playclothes (818) 557-8447
3100 W Magnolia Blvd, Burbank, CA, 91505
men's, women's & children-1920s-1980s clothing & access.
www.vintageplayclothes.com

Polkadots and Moonbeams (323) 651-1746
8367 W 3rd St, Los Angeles, CA, 90048
Turn of century to 70s, plus new stock from latest designers
www.polkadotsandmoonbeams.com

Ragg Mopp Vintage (323) 666-0550
3816 Sunset Blvd, Los Angeles, CA, 90026
very reasonable "vintage" prices
www.raggmoppvintage.com

Ravishing Resale (323) 655-8480
Call for Appt.
ladies vintage
www.ravishingresale.com

Repeat Performance (323) 938-0609
Web Based Business
www.rpvintage.com

Resurrection (323) 651-5516
8006 Melrose Ave, Los Angeles, CA, 90046
designer vintage
www.resurrectionvintage.com

Screaming Mimi's (212) 677-6464
240 West 14th St, New York NY, 10011
vintage clothing, accessories for men & women 1940s - 1980s
www.screamingmimis.com

Squaresville (323) 669-8464
1800 N Vermont Ave, Los Angeles, CA, 90027
vintage clothing, low prices, clean/good merchandise, 30s to 80s,
buy/sell/trade
www.squaresvillevintage.com

Unique Vintage (818) 953-2877
2013 W Magnolia Ave, Burbank, CA, 91506
Vintage inspired clothing
www.unique-vintage.com

Universal Studios Costume Dept (818) 777-2722
Rental, mfg., & alterations

Warner Bros. Studios Costume Dept (818) 954-1297
Collection of period & contemporary costumes for rent categorized by era,
decade and style.

Wasteland, Inc. (323) 653-3028
7428 Melrose Ave, Los Angeles, CA, 90046
Mon-Sat 11-8, Sun 11-7
www.shopwasteland.com

Western Costume Co. (818) 760-0900

Warehouse Dressing

See Also: Barrels & Drums, Wood/Metal/Plastic* Conveyor Equipment* Grating, Grated Flooring, Catwalks* Lighting, Industrial* Pallets

AIR Designs (818) 768-6639
Shelving, Ladders, Dollies, Pallet Jacks, etc.

Alley Cats Studio Rentals (818) 982-9178
Barrels, pallets, crates, lighting

Basaw Manufacturing, Inc. (818) 765-6650
7300 Varna, N Hollywood, CA, 91605
Basaw builds crates to order, large inventory in stock. crates, boxes, railroad & ship containers too
fredy@basaw.com * www.basaw.com

E.C. Prop Rentals (818) 764-2008
Drums, Crates, Shelving, Containers, Pallets/Jacks, Signage

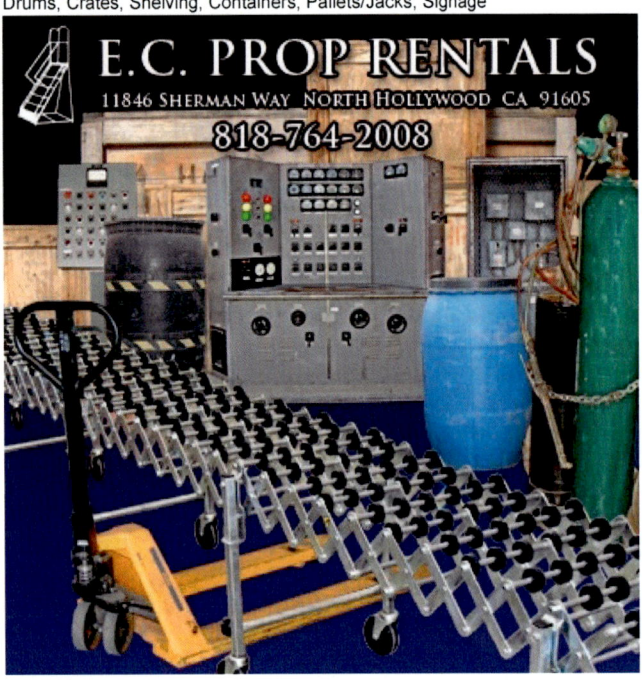

E.C. PROP RENTALS
11846 SHERMAN WAY NORTH HOLLYWOOD CA 91605
818-764-2008

History For Hire, Inc. (818) 765-7767

LCW Props (818) 243-0707
Pallets, Drums, Pallet Jacks, Forklifts, Rolling Ladders, Inventory Carts, Shipping / Receiving, Marine/Dock

Modern Props (323) 934-3000
Warehouse dressing including plastic shipping crates, lights, metro shelving, industrial dressing.

Omega/Cinema Props (323) 466-8201

Sony Pictures Studios-Prop House (Off Lot) (310) 244-5999

Wash Tubs

C. P. Two (323) 466-8201
Period wash tubs

Washing Machines/Dryers

See Also: Laundry Carts

C. P. Two (323) 466-8201
contemp./antique

LCW Props (818) 243-0707
Stock Of Different Styles & Colors. Call For An Updated Listing.

Sony Pictures Studios-Prop House (Off Lot) (310) 244-5999

Universal Studios Property & Hardware Dept (818) 777-2784
Prop washing machines & prop dryers for rent.

Waste Baskets

See: Trash Cans & Waste Baskets

Watches & Pocket Watches

See Also: Clocks, Analog & Residential

The Costume House (818) 508-9933
reproduction Victorian pocket watches

Feldmar Watch & Clock Center (310) 274-8016
9000 W. Pico Blvd, Los Angeles, CA, 90035
Repairs
www.feldmarwatch.com

The Hand Prop Room LP. (323) 931-1534
period-present, wristwatches, doubles, 18th-19th C. pocket

History For Hire, Inc. (818) 765-7767
vintage watches, chains, fobs

LCW Props (818) 243-0707
Silver, Gold, Modern, Timex, Antique, Fakes

Sony Pictures Studios-Prop House (Off Lot) (310) 244-5999
watches & pocket watches

Universal Studios Property & Hardware Dept (818) 777-2784
Prop watches, prop wristwatches & prop pocket watches for rent.

Warner Bros. Studios Property Department (818) 954-2181
Womens & mens watches, costume watches, high end watches, mens pocket watches, Wrist watches

Water Coolers

AIR Designs (818) 768-6639
Wall & Stand, Period & Present, Some Rigged

Alley Cats Studio Rentals (818) 982-9178

E.C. Prop Rentals (818) 764-2008
Period/Contemporary styles, wall-mounted and free-standing

History For Hire, Inc. (818) 765-7767

LCW Props (818) 243-0707
Large Selection

RC Vintage, Inc. (818) 765-7107
Water coolers

Sony Pictures Studios-Prop House (Off Lot) (310) 244-5999

Universal Studios Property & Hardware Dept (818) 777-2784
Office water coolers, ice chests and camping water containers for rent.

ZG04 DECOR (818) 853-8040
Water coolers of various sizes

Water Fountains

See: Fountains, Drinking (Wall & Stand)* Greens* Statuary

Water Jet CNC Services

See Also: CNC Router & Laser Etching Services* Prop Design & Manufacturing

Charisma Design Studio, Inc. (818) 252-6611
8414 San Fernando Road, Sun Valley, CA, 91352
waterjet can cut through 8" thickness of almost any material. 0,005" accuracy, smooth edging.
info@charismadesign.com * www.charismadesign.com

Charisma Design Studio, Inc.
CNC WATERJET CUTTING
GLASS ETCHING   SIGN FABRICATION
PROP FABRICATION
www.charismadesign.com

HPR Custom   (323) 931-1534
5700 Venice Blvd, Los Angeles, CA, 90019
Water jet cutting/water jet CNC services
www.hprcustom.com

TRU-ROLL   (626) 599-8337
735 Los Angeles Ave, Monrovia, CA, 91016
Small runs, proto typical work, both CNC & conventional machining. Waterjet is a Flow 30 hp Hyplex with 48"x96" capacity
info@truroll.com * www.truroll.com

Water Sports/Water Craft

See: Boats & Water Sport Vehicles* Ski Equipment* Sporting Goods & Services* Surfboard, Wakeboard* Vehicles/Picture Vehicles

Waterfalls

See: Greens* Mold Making* Statuary* Wedding Props

Watering Cans

See: Garden/Patio

Waterproofing

See: Floor, Ground & Surface Protection

Weaponry, Historical

See Also: Archery Equipment, Training* Armor, Chainmail, Suits of Armor* Civil War Era

Caravan West Productions   (661) 268-8300
35660 Jayhawker Rd, Aqua Dulce, CA, 91390
Old West, exact reprod. all types, plain & fancy, gunsmiths too
caravanwest@earthlink.net * www.caravanwest.com

The Hand Prop Room LP.   (323) 931-1534
great pcs; cust design & mfg

History For Hire, Inc.   (818) 765-7767
replica firearms, swords, muskets, bayonnets

Sword & Stone   (818) 562-6548
Ancient & Medieval to Futuristic; Swords, Knives, Armor & more.

Weaponry, Medieval

See Also: Archery Equipment, Training* Armor, Chainmail, Suits of Armor

The Hand Prop Room LP.   (323) 931-1534
great pcs; cust design & mfg

History For Hire, Inc.   (818) 765-7767

Sword & Stone   (818) 562-6548
poleaxes, knives, spears, swords, shields, crossbows

Weapons

See Also: Armor, Chainmail, Suits of Armor* Guns & Firearms* Knives* Military Props & Equipment* Non-Guns & Non-Pyro Flashes* Police Equipment* Swords & Swordplay

Dapper Cadaver   (818) 771-0818
Foam, rubber and plastic fake weapons. Knives, axes, hammers, crowbars, baseball bats, etc.

Eastern Costume   (818) 982-3611
Rifles, knives, retractable weapons, trick weapons, props, spears, 1920's to Present day

Emerson Knives   (310) 539-5633
1234 254th St, Harbor City, CA, 90710
Emerson Knives are the only choice of Elite Military and U.S. Covert Units. They are truly, "Famous In the Worst Places"
eknives@aol.com * www.emersonknives.com

The Hand Prop Room LP.   (323) 931-1534
great pcs; cust design & mfg

History For Hire, Inc.   (818) 765-7767
machetes, spears

J & M Special Effects, Inc.   (718) 875-0140
524 Sackett St, Brooklyn, NY, 11217
Formerly Jauchem & Meeh. rifles & shotguns, handguns, trick weapons, accessories
info@jmfx.net * www.jmfx.net

LCW Props   (818) 243-0707
Futuristic Weapons, Guns, Knives, Swords, Martial Arts Weapons, Training Equipment, Prepper Supplies

Old N Country Prop Shop, LLC   (818) 423-2599
Variety of weapons available, guns, knives, whip, etc.

Sony Pictures Studios-Prop House (Off Lot)   (310) 244-5999
Guns, gun accessories, blow guns, bow and arrows, clubs, crossbows, blades, maces, and more

Sword & Stone   (818) 562-6548
poleaxes, knives, spears, swords, retractable weapons. Experienced blacksmith. Man at Arms videos.

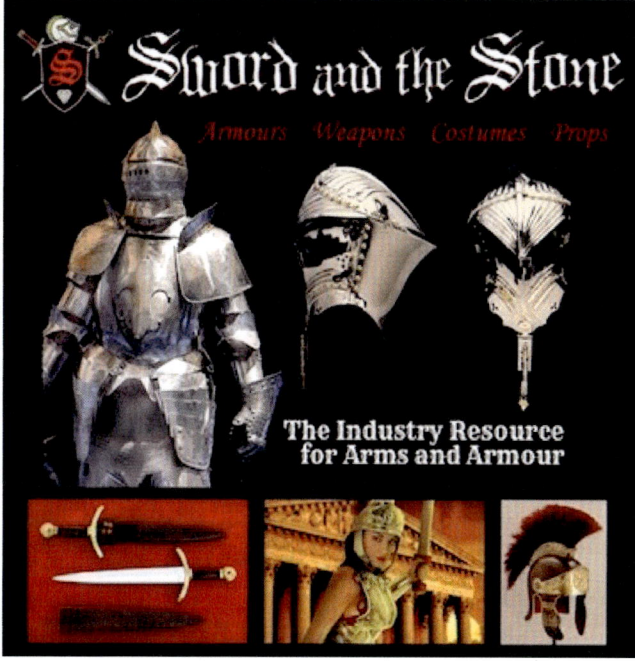

Weather Instruments

See: Lab Equipment* Nautical Dressing & Props* Science Equipment* Weather Vanes

Weather Vanes

See: Farm Equipment & Dressing* Rooftop Dressing

Wedding Attire

See Also: Formal Wear

CBS Costume Rental   (323) 575-2666
gowns, veils, bridesmaids

The Costume House   (818) 508-9933
gowns, tails & tuxes, 1890s through 1980s, veils, shoes

Dark Garden Unique Corsetry   (415) 431-7684
321 Linden St, San Francisco, CA, 94102
divine historical to fantasy custom made
www.darkgarden.com

David's Bridal   (818) 238-9001
2050 W. Empire Ave (Burbank Empire), Burbank, CA, 91504
Special occasion dresses, wedding consultant, alterations, also loc. in Northridge
www.davidsbridal.com

Sony Pictures Studios-Wardrobe   (310) 244-5995
alterations, call (310) 244-7260

Universal Studios Costume Dept   (818) 777-2722
Rental, mfg., & alterations

Warner Bros. Studios Costume Dept   (818) 954-1297
Bride, Bridesmaids, Flower Girl, Tuxedos, Ring Bearer, Bridal Party, Dresses, Veils

Western Costume Co.   (818) 760-0900

Wedding Cakes, Prop

See: Food, Artificial Food

Wedding Props

See Also: Balloons & Balloon Sculptures* Dance Floors* Events, Decorations, Supplies & Services* Florists/Floral Design* Wrapped Prop Gift Packages

Aah-Inspiring Balloons   **(562) 494-7605**
Call for an Appointment.
After 14 years in the TV and Film Industry, Aah-Inspiring Balloon Decor has been seen in over 200 TV shows and Films.
aahinspiring1@aol.com * www.aahinspiringballoons.com

Flower Art   **(323) 935-6800**
5859 West 3rd Street, Los Angeles, CA, 90036
Full-service Wedding florals: From lavish soap opera weddings, to an Indian-inspired theme we helped create for New Girl
info@flowerartla.com * www.flowerartla.com

FormDecor, Inc.   **(310) 558-2582**
America's largest event rental supplier of 20th Century furniture and accessories for Modern and Mid-Century styles.

Lux Lounge EFR   **(888) 247-4411**
106 1/2 Judge John Aiso St #318, Los Angeles, CA, 90012
Wedding Props for Rental
info@luxloungeefr.com * www.luxloungeefr.com

Sandy Rose Floral, Inc   **(818) 980-4371**
6850 Vineland Ave Unit C, N Hollywood, CA, 91605
Bouquets, boutonnieres, corsages, pedestals, urns, centerpieces. 24 hr service
www.sandyrose.com

ShopWildThings   **(928) 855-6075**
2880 Sweetwater Ave, Lake Havasu City, AZ, 86406
Event Decor, Beaded Curtains, Chain Curtains, String Curtains & Columns, Crystal Columns. Reliable service & delivery.
help@shopwildthings.com * www.shopwildthings.com

ZG04 DECOR   **(818) 853-8040**
Wedding props including wedding arches, wedding chairs, wedding flowers and more

Weightlifting Equipment

See Also: Physical Therapy* Exercise & Fitness Equipment

C. P. Two   **(323) 466-8201**
Weightlifting equipment for rent

Curtis Gym Equipment   **(818) 897-2804**
10275 Glenoaks Blvd Ste #7, Pacoima, CA, 91331
Prop Rentals and Servicing. Fitness Machines, Gymnastics & Weightlifting. Fake & Real Weights
curtisgymequipment@hotmail.com

The Hand Prop Room LP.   **(323) 931-1534**

History For Hire, Inc.   **(818) 765-7767**
strongman type barbells, dumbbells

Hollywood Gym Rentals   **(310) 663-6161**
200 West Chevy Chase Drive Unit B, Glendale, CA, 91204
Hollywood Gym Rentals specializes in short and long term rentals of fitness equipment in the Los Angeles area.
chris@hollywoodgymrentals.com * www.hollywoodgymrentals.com

I-Rep Therapy Products, Inc.   **(800) 828-0852**
508 Chaney St Ste B, Lake Elsinore, CA, 92530
Medical equipment, physical therapy equipment, fitness equipment and supplies.
btwilhelm@gmail.com * www.i-reptherapyproducts.com

Welding Equipment/Stations

See Also: Blacksmith Shop/Foundry* CNC Router & Laser Etching Services* Metalworking, Welding & Structural

AIR Designs   **(818) 768-6639**
Acetylene Torches, MIG Carts, Masks, Gloves, Screens

Alley Cats Studio Rentals   **(818) 982-9178**
tanks with gauges, hoses, push carts

E.C. Prop Rentals   **(818) 764-2008**
fully dressed carts & elec units, masks/goggles/gloves/aprons

History For Hire, Inc.   **(818) 765-7767**
period welding tanks, welding rigs

LCW Props   **(818) 243-0707**
Welding Carts, Electrical, Gas, Masks, Screens, Welding Salvage

Western Americana

History For Hire, Inc.   **(818) 765-7767**
Lots!

Western Ways Studio Prop Rentals   **(661) 269-2296**
Call for appt, Acton, CA, 93510
Western Props & Set Dressing, wagons, hand carts, luggage, directors chairs, mannequins
www.wwprops.com

Western Dressing

See Also: Cactus, Live & Artificial* Horse Saddles & Tack* Horses, Horse Equipment, Livestock* Native American* Wagons* Wheels, Wooden

C. P. Two　　　　　　　　　　　　　　　　**(323) 466-8201**
western barrels, troughs, water pumps, cast iron stoves, western tools, western lanterns

Caravan West Productions　　　　　　　　**(661) 268-8300**
35660 Jayhawker Rd, Aqua Dulce, CA, 91390
Western signage, Old West, cowboy, historically accurate, everything you need
caravanwest@earthlink.net * www.caravanwest.com

Dapper Cadaver　　　　　　　　　　　　　**(818) 771-0818**
Animal props & steer skulls. Apothecary props. Rattlesnake props. Gallows, toe pincher coffins & standing stocks.

FILM ART LA　　　　　　　　　　　　　　**(323) 461-4900**
Culver City Warehouse at Jefferson & Hauser. Call for address.
Large Inventory of cleared rentals 19th Century to Present. Western Art Rentals and High rez Images
filmartla@gmail.com * www.filmartla.com

Green Set, Inc.　　　　　　　　　　　　　**(818) 764-1231**
wagons, wagon wheels, F.G. horses, buffalos, straw bales, cows, carts, western & rustic decorations

The Hand Prop Room LP.　　　　　　　　　**(323) 931-1534**
saddles, gambling, saloon, cavalry equip, badges, etc.

History For Hire, Inc.　　　　　　　　　　**(818) 765-7767**
Lots, including: western advertising, period posters, American Indian, archery, wooden barrels, western drums, blacksmiths tools

Hollywood Studio Gallery　　　　　　　　**(323) 462-1116**
prints & paintings of rodeos

Jackson Shrub Supply, Inc.　　　　　　　**(818) 982-0100**
split rail fence, wagon wheels, cactus, hitching post, tumble weeds, carts, wagons, tumbleweeds

Old N Country Prop Shop, LLC　　　　　　**(818) 423-2599**
Variety of items for that Western set.

Sony Pictures Studios-Prop House (Off Lot)　　**(310) 244-5999**
Basin & pitchers, branding irons, western buckets, western barrels, horse gear, indian items, lassos, animal pelt, more

Universal Studios Property & Hardware Dept　　**(818) 777-2784**
Western dressing and western props for rent.

Warner Bros. Studios Property Department　　**(818) 954-2181**
Horse Bits, leather saddles, stirrups, saw horses, western smalls, stagecoaches, wagon wheels

Western Theme Events

See Also: Events, Decorations, Supplies & Services* Events, Design/Planning/Production

L. A. Party Works　　　　　　　　　　　　**(888) 527-2789**
9712 Alpaca St, S El Monte, CA, 91733
in Vancouver tel. 604-589-4101. Western theme parties, mech. bull, card sharks
partyworks@aol.com * www.partyworksinteractive.com

COMPLETE WESTERN THEME EVENTS AVAILABLE / MECHANICAL BULLS
PROPS / PHOTO OPS / GREEN SCREEN SYSTEMS / & MORE

LM Treasures　　　　　　　　　　　　　　**(626) 252-7354**
The place to find cowboys, indians, bulls, and all types of different western theme statues perfect for any occasions.

Western Wear

See Also: Horse Saddles & Tack* Native American* Wardrobe, Accessories* Wardrobe, Antique/Historical* Western Dressing* Western Theme Events

Alfonso of Hollywood Leather Co.　　　　**(818) 769-0362**
1512 W. Magnolia Blvd, Burbank, CA, 91506
Primarily fancy gunbelts/holsters, custom fitting/orders, we also do saddles!
www.alfonsosgunleather.com

Broken Horn Saddlery　　　　　　　　　　**(626) 337-4088**
1022 Leorita St, Baldwin Park, CA, 91706
10-6 Wed.- Sat. 10-5 Sun. Closed Mon & Tues
www.brokenhornsaddlery.com

LISTINGS FOR THIS CATEGORY CONTINUE ON THE FOLLOWING PAGE

Caravan West Productions   **(661) 268-8300**
35660 Jayhawker Rd, Aqua Dulce, CA, 91390
1800s-19002 cowboy western wear, cowboy chaps, pocket watches, belt
buckles, and more. Historically accurate, everything
caravanwest@earthlink.net * www.caravanwest.com

CBS Costume Rental   **(323) 575-2666**
Dr. Quinn western, Indian, buckskin, U.S. Cavalry
Country General Store   **(800) 269-9836**
6279 Van Nuys Blvd, Van Nuys, CA, 91401
complete contemp. western & work outfitters
www.countrygeneralstore.com
Falconhead   **(310) 471-7075**
Call for Custom Orders - El Paso TX & Cody WY
very special western wear/goods; custom belts, buckles, boots... If we don't
have it, we'll make it.
www.falconhead.com
Warner Bros. Studios Costume Dept   **(818) 954-1297**
Frontier, Pioneer, Cowboy, Chaps, Boots, Bolo Ties, Flannel, Jeans, Hats,
Bandanas
Western Costume Co.   **(818) 760-0900**

Wetsuits, Diving/Surfing

Action/Watersports   **(310) 827-2233**
4144 Lincoln Blvd, Marina del Rey, CA, 90292
kayaks, kiteboards, scuba, water skis, surf boards, wake boards, paddle board
www.actionwatersports.com
Body Glove   **(310) 374-3441**
504 N Broadway, Redondo Beach, CA, 90277
Ask for Scott, X200. regular/skin color
www.bodyglove.com
CBS Costume Rental   **(323) 575-2666**
flesh colored wetsuits
Dive and Surf   **(310) 372-8423**
504 N Broadway, Redondo Beach, CA, 90277
scuba diving & surfing equipment
customerservice@divensurf.com * www.divensurf.com
Scuba.com   **(949) 221-9300**
1752 Langley Ave, Irvine, CA, 92614
scuba diving equipment
www.diversdiscount.com
Scubahaus   **(310) 828-2916**
2501 Wilshire Blvd, Santa Monica, CA, 90403
swimming equipment, scuba diving equipment, underwater cameras
www.scubahaus.com
Universal Studios Costume Dept   **(818) 777-2722**
Rental, mfg., & alterations

Wharf Dock Lights

See: Lamp Posts & Street Lights

Wheel of Fortune

See: Gambling Equipment

Wheelchairs

The Hand Prop Room LP.   **(323) 931-1534**
period-present
History For Hire, Inc.   **(818) 765-7767**
all eras, big selection, FDR
LCW Props   **(818) 243-0707**
Electric, Manual
Sony Pictures Studios-Prop House (Off Lot)   **(310) 244-5999**

Wheels, Wooden

C. P. Two   **(323) 466-8201**
Wooden wheels/wagons wheels
Caravan West Productions   **(661) 268-8300**
35660 Jayhawker Rd, Aqua Dulce, CA, 91390
Old West, historically accurate & museum quality wagon wheels/wooden
wagon wheels and more
caravanwest@earthlink.net * www.caravanwest.com
History For Hire, Inc.   **(818) 765-7767**
wagon wheels

Whiteboards (Dry Erase)

See: Office Equipment & Dressing School Supplies, Desks &
Dressing*

Wi-Fi Boxes

Airwaves Wireless   **(818) 501-8200**
13400 Riverside Dr # 103 Sherman Oaks, CA, 91423
AT&T, Verizon, T-Mobile & Sprint USB Air card, MiFi or Wi-Fi wireless hotspot
devices with 4G LTE high speed connection
sales@airwaveswireless.com * www.airwaveswireless.com
Castex Rentals   **(323) 462-1468**
1044 N Cole Ave, Hollywood, CA, 90038
Wi Fi Boxes, WiFi boxes
service@castexrentals.com * www.castexrentals.com
LCW Props   **(818) 243-0707**
Wifi Disconnects, Bridges, Routers, Switches, Antennas, Rackmount Wifi
Equipment
Wireless for All   **(818) 551-9191**
919 S Glendale Ave Ste A1, Glendale, CA, 91205
Wifi boxes to rent, wifi boxes for purchase.
wirelessforallsocal@gmail.com * www.instagram.com/wirelessforall

Wicker

See: Furniture, Rattan & Wicker

Wigs

See Also: Clowns Make-up & Hair, Supplies & Services*
Charlie Wright, Ltd.   **(818) 347-4566**
18645 Hatteras St #121, Tarzana, CA 91356
custom only
www.wrighthair.com
The Costume House   **(818) 508-9933**
mens wigs, womens wigs, 18th century wigs, white wigs, brown wigs,fantasy
wigs, colored wigs
Favian Wigs   **(818) 388-0853**
5819 Capistrano Ave, Woodland Hills, CA, 91367
By appt. only: custom made lace front wigs, huge sel. of lace front rentals, all
human hair
favianwigs@gmail.com
Hollywood Wigs   **(323) 466-6479**
6530 Hollywood Blvd, Hollywood, CA, 90028
real/synthetic, period-contemp, men/women
www.hwigs.com
National Fiber Technology, LLC   **(978) 686-2964**
15 Union St, Lawrence, MA, 01840
catalog sales; hair & fur fabrics for wigs, headdresses, 'make-up' hair, & animal
costumes, wigs custom made.
www.nftech.com
Wilshire Wigs & Accessories, Inc.   **(800) 927-0874**
5241 Craner Ave, N Hollywood, CA, 91601
real/synthetic, period-contemp, men/women
www.wilshirewigs.com

Wind Machines

See: Special Effects, Equipment & Supplies

Windmill

See Also: Farm Equipment & Dressing

American Windmills   **(530) 644-3008**
PO Box 1187, Diamond Springs, CA, 95619
Vintage windmills & towers set up at your location. Last minute notice is our specialty.
www.windmills.net

Halsted & Hoggan, Inc.   **(800) 286-3303**
935 S Santa Fe Ave, Los Angeles, CA, 90021
small ones, for irrigation
www.pumpspecialists.com

Window Treatments

See Also: Awnings Drapery & Curtains* Flameproofing*

Collins Visual Media   **(818) 686-6581**
10518 Johanna Ave, Shadow Hills, CA, 91040
Complete range of window treatments, including removable, static cling, view-through, vinyl die-cut and hand-painted.
www.collinsvisualmedia.com

Linoleum City, Inc.   **(323) 469-0063**
4849 Santa Monica Blvd, Hollywood, CA, 90029
Custom window treatments. Blinds, shades, woven shades, natural shades, pleated shades, wood blinds, aluminum blinds.
sales@linocity.com * www.linoleumcity.com

Largest Selection of Floorcoverings in L.A.

Serving the Entertainment Industry for over 65 years.
We understand your needs and deliver promptly!

Carpet • Vinyl • Cork • Carpet Runners • Hardwood Floors
Linoleum • Tiles • Laminate Floors • Ceramic Tiles
Window Treatments • Wall Coverings

Lushes Curtains   **(626) 453-0337**
1855 Tyler Ave Unit C, S El Monte, CA, 91733
Your Direct Velvet Curtain Manufacture! Delivering Elegant and Quality Curtains to Every Industry World Wide!
Joe@LushesCurtains.com * www.LushesCurtains.com

Omega/Cinema Props   **(323) 466-8201**
drapery dept

Strickland's Window Coverings   **(910) 762-0944**
5422 Oleander Dr, Wilmington, NC, 28403
Strickland's Window Coverings Set Services has been providing window coverings to the film industry for over 26 years.
beckah@stricklandsblinds.com * www.stricklandsblinds.com

Universal Studios Drapery Dept   **(818) 777-2761**

Warner Bros. Drapery, Upholstery & Flooring **(818) 954-1831**
4000 Warner Blvd Bldg 30, Burbank, CA, 91522
Puffs; Balloon Shades; Beaded Curtains; Drapes; Sheers; Swags; Sunbursts; Tiebacks; Shades & Blinds
wbsfdrapery@warnerbros.com * www.wbdrapery.com

Warner Bros. Studios Property Department   **(818) 954-2181**
Custom fabrication, See WBSF Drapery department

Windsocks

Aradyne Industries, Inc.   **(281) 934-1776**
4631 11th St, Brookshire, TX, 77423
3' to 12', classic styles, & frames, masts, accessories
www.windsocks.com

E.C. Prop Rentals   **(818) 764-2008**
Many sizes with pole/bases optional

Windtek, Inc.   **(800) 468-7697**
Call to Order, Girard, PA, 16417
airport & industrial windsocks, also airport lights
www.bestwindsocks.com

The **10th anniversary of the iPhone** is here as Apple looks into creating original content for it's subscribers similar to HBO & Netflix; 40th Anniversary of Star Wars; a **full solar eclipse** came on August 21st; China's lunar expedition **Chang'e 5** will return the first lunar sample back to Earth since 1976; the 2017 World Expo will be held in Kazakhstan; and Debbies Book expands their Locations and Wardrobe categories while also launching it's new photo feature allowing companies to showcase a sample of their inventory in every category!

2017
40 YEARS OF DEBBIES BOOK

Wine Kegs

See Also: Barrels & Drums, Wood/Metal/Plastic
AIR Designs (818) 768-6639
Multiple Kegs, Winery Racks, Barrels, Racks
Alley Cats Studio Rentals (818) 982-9178
Wine kegs/wine barrels for rent
E.C. Prop Rentals (818) 764-2008
59 Gallon Oak Casks, With Wood Storage Racks

E.C. PROP RENTALS
11846 SHERMAN WAY NORTH HOLLYWOOD CA 91605
818-764-2008

Evans Family Barrels (818) 523-8174
7918 Fairchild Ave, Canoga Park, CA, 91306
59 gal oak wine barrels (casks or kegs) and 55 gal oak whiskey barrels and metal winery barrel racks, vintage barrels
evansbarrels@gmail.com * www.EvansFamilyBarrels.com
The Hand Prop Room LP. (323) 931-1534
Lennie Marvin Enterprises, Inc. (Prop Heaven) (818) 841-5882
Wine kegs, wine keg racks, whiskey barrels, whiskey barrel racks. Many multiples
Old N Country Prop Shop, LLC (818) 423-2599
Several different sizes of wine kegs available.

Wire
See: Electrical/Electronic Supplies & Services

Witchcraft
See: Crystal Balls* Occult/Spiritual/Metaphysical* Tarot Cards

Wood
See: Building Supply, Lumber, Hardware, Etc.* Greens

Wood Shop
See Also: Factory/Industrial* Tools
E.C. Prop Rentals (818) 764-2008
Carpentry dressing including power & hand tools, tables, signage & more.
LCW Props (818) 243-0707
Tools, Saws, Sanders, Presses, Planers, Dust Collector, Work Benches, Tech Benches & other Carpentry Dressing

Wood Turnings
See: Moulding, Wood

Woodworking
See: Doors* Moulding, Wood* Staff Shops

Workbenches
See: Benches* Tools* Wood Shop

Workrooms
See: Sewing Equipment & Workrooms

World Globe Maps
See: Globes, World Map

Worms
See: Fishing Equipment & Tackle

Wrap Parties
See: Events, Decorations, Supplies & Services* Events, Design/Planning/Production* Events, Entertainment

Wrap Party Gifts
See: Embroidery, Screen Printing, Etc.* Leather (Clothing, Accessories, Materials)

Wrapped Prop Gift Packages
See Also: Christmas* Gift Wrapping* Wedding Props
FROST (310) 704-8812
Call for Appointment - 21405 Madrona Ave, Torrance, CA, 90503
Individual wrapped gifts, stacked wrapped gifts, prop gifts of all kinds.
mdisplay@yahoo.com * www.frostchristmasprops.com
Jackson Shrub Supply, Inc. (818) 982-0100
Gift presents, boxed gifts, assorted wrapped gifts

Wrought Iron Furniture & Decorations
See Also: Bedroom Furniture & Decorations* Furniture, Rustic* Metalworking, Decorative* Metalworking, Welding & Structural
Badia Design, Inc. (818) 762-0130
5420 Vineland Ave, N Hollywood, CA, 91601
Our Moroccan Wrought Iron Furniture includes tables, chairs and stools for your indoor or outdoor decorating needs.
info@badiadesign.com * www.badiadesign.com
C. P. Two (323) 466-8201
Martin Iron Design (818) 760-3636
10750 Cumpston St, N Hollywood, CA, 91601
Wrought iron furniture and wrought iron decorations made to specifications.
martinirondesign@yahoo.com * www.martinirondesign.com
Prop Services West (818) 503-2790

Sword & Stone   (818) 562-6548
Wrought iron decorations including sword racks and more
Universal Studios Property & Hardware Dept   (818) 777-2784
Many wrought iron pieces; furniture, dressing, and decorations for rent.
Used Church Items, Religious Rentals   (412) 220-2272
115 East Barr Street, Mcdonald, PA, 15057
Wrought Iron Religious Furniture and Decorations. Kneelers, Baptismals,
Censers, Candlesticks, Lights, Lamps, Stands.
www.religiousrentals.com
Warner Bros. Studios Metal Shop   (818) 954-1265
4000 Warner Blvd Bldg 44, Burbank, CA, 91522
Custom metal fabrication creating anything from structural steel elements to
intricate custom furniture
WBDS@warnerbros.com * www.wbmetalshop.com
Warner Bros. Studios Property Department   (818) 954-2181
Wrought iron benches, barstools, andirons, tables, chairs, fireplace tools, patio
chairs, beds, plant stands

X-ray Machine

See Also: Hospital Equipment X-ray Viewer* X-rays & X-ray Viewers*
LCW Props   (818) 243-0707
Light Boxes, Baggage Checker, Industrial, pallet X-Ray Machines
Modern Props   (323) 934-3000
airport hangar, baggage & conveyor x-ray machines

X-rays & X-ray Viewers

See Also: Hospital Equipment X-ray Machine* MRI (Magnetic
Resonance Imaging)*
A-1 Medical Integration   (818) 753-0319
Medical devices for Set Decoration & Property, from minor procedures to
detailed hospital units.
Alpha Companies - Spellman Desk Co.   (818) 504-9090
The #1 source for medical equipment in the industry.
History For Hire, Inc.   (818) 765-7767
LCW Props   (818) 243-0707
Different Sizes Of X-Ray Light Boxes, Medical, Dental. X-rays for Medical,
Dental, Assortment, Head, Foot, Bones
Universal Studios Property & Hardware Dept   (818) 777-2784
X-ray lightboxes and x-ray viewers for rent.

Xerox Machines

See: Copy Machines Office Equipment & Dressing*

Xylophone

See: Musical Instruments

Yurts

See: Canopies, Tents, Gazebos, Cabanas

Guilds, Unions, Societies, Associations

Academy of Motion Picture Arts & Sciences   (310) 247-3000
8949 Wilshire Blvd, Beverly Hills, CA, 90211
www.oscars.org
Actors Equity Association (A.E.A)   (323) 978-8080
5636 Tujunga Ave, North Hollywood, CA, 91601
www.actorsequity.org
Alliance of Spec. Effects & Pyro. Oper.   (818) 506-8173
12522 Moorpark St Ste 100, Studio City, CA, 91604
www.asepo.org
American Assn. of Community Theatre   (817) 732-3177
1300 Gendy St, Fort Worth, TX, 76107
www.aact.org
American Pyrotechnics Association   (301) 907-8181
7910 Woodmont Ave Ste 1220, Bethesda, MD, 20814
Trade association for fireworks industry
www.americanpyro.com
American Rental Assn. (ARA)   (800) 334-2177
1900 19th St, Moline, IL, 61265
www.ararental.org
AMPTP - Alliance of M.P. & TV Producers   (818) 995-3600
15301 Ventura Blvd Bldg E, Sherman Oaks, CA, 91403
www.amptp.org
APA American Photographic Artists - LA   (323) 933-1631
9190 West Olympic Blvd #212, Beverly Hills, CA, 90212
Volunteer organization, run by photographers for photographers, many member
discounts throughout the industry
director@apa-la.com * http://apa-la.org/

Art Directors Guild   (818) 762-9995
11969 Ventura Blvd 2nd Floor, Studio City, CA, 91604
Art Directors Guild & Scenic, Title & Graphic Artists, Set Designers, Model
Makers, Illustrators, Matte/Digital Artists
www.adg.org
ASA Entertainment Group, LLC   (321) 722-9300
201 N Riverside Dr Ste C, Indialantic, FL, 32903
ASA demo skating team can spice up an event
www.asaentertainment.com
ASID - American Society Of Interior Designers   (202) 546-3480
1152 15th St NW Suite 910 Washington DC, 20005
Has chapters throughout the entire U.S.
www.asid.org
ASID CA Los Angeles Chapter   (310) 659-4716
8687 Melrose Ave Ste B245, W Hollywood, CA, 90069
cala.asid.org
ASID NY New York Metro Chapter   (212) 641-0018
555 Eighth Ave Ste 1902, New York, NY, 10018
nymetro.asid.org
Assn. of Independent Commercial Producers   (323) 960-4763
650 N Bronson Ave Ste 223b, Los Angeles, CA, 90004
7 offices in U.S., see web site for more info.
www.aicp.com
Contract Services Admin. Trust Fund   (818) 565-0550
2710 Winona, Burbank, CA, 91504
www.csatf.org
Dance/USA   (202) 833-1717
1029 Vermont Ave NW Ste 400, Washington, DC, 20005
Provide professional development & networking opportunities that advance &
support the art form of dance.
www.danceusa.org
Directors Guild of America (DGA)   (310) 289-2000
7920 Sunset Blvd, Los Angeles, CA, 90046
www.dga.org
Dramatists Guild   (212) 398-9366
1501 Broadway Ste 701, New York, NY, 10036
www.dramatistsguild.com
Exhibit Designers and Producers Assn.   (203) 557-6321
19 Compo Road South, Westport, CT, 06880
Provides leadership, education & networking for advancement of its members
& the exhibition industry.
info@edpa.com * www.edpa.com
Greater S.F. Bay Area Costumer's Guild   Not Listed
PO Box 6392, Alameda, CA, 94501
good links to resources for patterns, research, historical & vintage wardrobe, &
fashion shopping in garment districts
www.gbacg.org
IATSE General Office   (212) 730-1770
207 W 25th St 4th Fl, New York, NY, 10001
www.iatse-intl.org
IATSE West Coast Office   (818) 980-3499
10045 Riverside Dr, Toluca Lake, CA, 91602
www.iatse-intl.org
International Interior Design Association   (888) 799-4432
111 E Wacker Dr. Ste 222, Chicago IL 60601
Regional chapters throughout U.S. & the world
www.iida.org
International Stunt Association   (818) 501-5225
4454 Van Nuys Blvd Ste 214, Sherman Oaks, CA, 91403
www.isastunts.com
The League of Resident Theatres   (212) 944-1501
1501 Broadway Ste 1801, New York, NY, 10036   x19
www.lort.org
Local # 1 Theatrical Stage Employees   (212) 333-2500
320 West 46th Street, New York, NY, 10036
IATSE #1, New York, Westchester/Putnam counties
www.iatselocalone.org
Local # 4 Theatrical Stage Employees   (718) 252-8777
2917 Glenwood Rd, Brooklyn, NY, 11210
IATSE #4, Brooklyn & Queens
www.iatselocal4.org
Local # 33 Stage Technicians   (818) 841-9233
1720 W Magnolia Blvd, Burbank, CA, 91506
Local 33, IATSE, AFL
www.ia33.org
Local # 44 Affil. Property Craftspersons   (818) 769-2500
12021 Riverside Dr, N Hollywood, CA, 91607
Local 44, IATSE, AFL, Property Masters, Set Decorators, Greens, Special
Effects, Upholsterer-Draper, Sewing Persons, Pro
www.local44.com

**LISTINGS FOR THIS CATEGORY CONTINUE ON THE
FOLLOWING PAGE**

Guilds, Unions, Societies, Associations

Local # 52 Studio Mechanics (718) 906-9440
19-02 Steinway St, Astoria, NY, 11105
Allied Crafts, Electricians, Grips, Properties, Shop Crafts, Sound, Video; NY, NJ, CT, PA, DE
www.iatselocal52.org

Local # 53 NABET-CWA (818) 846-0490
1918 W Burbank Blvd, Burbank, CA, 91506
www.nabet53.org

Local # 80 M.P. Studio Grips & Craft Svc. (818) 526-0700
2520 W Olive Ave, Burbank, CA, 91505
Local 80, IATSE, AFL
www.iatselocal80.org

Local # 122 Theatrical & Stage, San Diego (619) 640-0042
3737 Camino Del Rio South Ste 307, San Diego, CA, 92108
www.iatse122.org

Local # 161 Script Sup. & Continuity Coor. (212) 977-9655
630 9th Ave Ste 1103, New York, NY, 10036
Script Sup., Continuity Coor., Prod. Office Coor., Accountants
www.local161.org

Local # B192 Amusement Area Employees (818) 509-9192
5250 Lankershim Blvd Ste 600, N Hollywood, CA, 91601
www.b192iatse.org

Local # 399 Studio Transportation Drivers (818) 985-7374
4747 Vineland Ave, N Hollywood, CA, 91602
Teamsters Local 399
www.ht399.org

Local # 442 Theatrical & Stage Employees (805) 898-0442
PO Box 413, Santa Barbara, CA, 93102
Serving Santa Barbara, Ventura, San Luis Obispo Counties
www.iatse442.org

Local # 480 Studio Mechanics (505) 986-9512
1418 Cerrillos Rd, Santa Fe, NM, 87505
Film & TV technicians of New Mexico
www.iatselocal480.com

Local # 504 Theatrical & Stage Employees (714) 774-5004
671 S Manchester Ave, Anaheim, CA, 92802
Orange County & parts of Corona
www.iatse504.com

Local # 600 Int'l Cinematographers Guild (323) 876-0160
7755 Sunset Blvd, Los Angeles, CA, 90046
Local 600, IATSE; also Publicist Guild
www.cameraguild.com

Local # 695 Int'l Sound/TV Eng./Video (818) 985-9204
5439 Cahuenga Blvd, N Hollywood, CA, 91601
IATSE Prod. Sound/TV Engineering/Video Assistants, Tech. & Studio Projectionists
www.local695.com

Local # 700 Motion Picture Editors Guild (323) 876-4770
7715 Sunset Blvd Suite #200, Hollywood, CA, 90046
www.editorsguild.com

Local # 705 Motion Picture Costumers (818) 487-5655
4731 Laurel Canyon Blvd Ste 201, Valley Village, CA, 91607
Local 705, IATSE, MPTAA, AFL-CIO
www.motionpicturecostumers.org

Local # 706 Make-up Artists & Hair Stylists (818) 295-3933
828 N Hollywood Way, Burbank, CA, 91505
Local 706, IATSE/MPMO of U.S. & Canada
www.local706.org

Local # 728 Studio Electrical Lighting Tech (818) 954-0728
1001 W Magnolia Blvd, Burbank, CA, 91506
Local 728
www.iatse728.org

Local # 729 Motion Picture Set Painters (818) 842-7729
1811 W Burbank Blvd, Burbank, CA, 91506
Local 729, IATSE, AFL-CIO
www.ialocal729.com

Local # 755 Sculpturers & Plasterers (818) 379-9711
13245 Riverside Dr Ste 350, Sherman Oaks, CA, 91423
Local 755, OP & CMIA
www.local755.com

Local # 764 Theatrical Wardrobe Union (212) 957-3500
545 W 45th Street 2nd Floor, New York, NY, 10036
www.ia764.org

Local # 768 Theatrical Wardrobe Union (818) 843-8768
1023 N Hollywood Way #203, Burbank, CA, 91505
(Live theatre only!) L.A., Long Beach, Pasadena, Santa Monica, Cerritos
www.wardrobe768.com

Local # 784 Theatrical Wardrobe (415) 861-8379
1182 Market St Ste 312, San Francisco, CA, 94102
All costume crewing needs for Northern California
www.iatwu784.org

Local # 798 Make-up Artist, Hair Stylists (212) 627-0660
70 West 36th St Suite 4A, New York, NY, 10018
www.local798.net

Local # 800 Art Directors Guild (818) 762-9995
11969 Ventura Blvd 2nd Floor, Studio City, CA, 91604
Art Directors Guild & Scenic, Title & Graphic Artists, Set Design Model Makers, Illustrators & Matte Artists, Digital Arti
www.adg.org

Local # 829 United Scenic Artists, LA (323) 965-0957
1200 Wilshire Blvd Ste 620, Los Angeles, CA 90017
IATSE Local 829 West Coast office
www.usa829.org

Local # 829 United Scenic Artists, NY (212) 581-0300
29 W 38th Street 15th floor, New York, NY, 10018
IATSE Local USA 829
www.usa829.org

Local # 839 The Animation Guild (818) 845-7500
1105 N Hollywood Way, Burbank, CA, 91505
www.animationguild.org

Local # 871 Script Supervisors (818) 509-7871
4011 W Magnolia Blvd, Burbank, CA, 91505
Script Supervisors/Continuity, Coordinators, Accountants, & Allied Production Specialists Guild
www.ialocal871.org

Local # 884 Studio Teachers (818) 559-9600
PO Box 461467, Los Angeles, CA, 90046
dispatch phone: (818) 559-9600. Studio Teachers/Welfare Workers
www.thestudioteachers.com

Local # 892 Costume Designers Guild (818) 848-2800
3919 West Magnolia Blvd, Burbank, CA, 91505
www.costumedesignersguild.com

Location Managers Guild International (310) 967-2007
8033 Sunset Blvd #1017, Los Angeles, CA, 90046
Founded in 2003, LMGI is dedicated to the promotion & interests of our members and our relations with the general public
contact@locationmanagers.org * locationmanagers.org

Motion Picture Assn. of America (818) 995-6600
15301 Ventura Blvd Bldg E, Sherman Oaks, CA, 91403
Advocate for American motion picture, home video & TV industries
www.mpaa.org

OPERA America (212) 796-8620
330 7th Ave 7th Floor, New York, NY, 10001
service & support opera companies
www.operaamerica.org

PLASA North America (212) 244-1505
630 9th Ave Ste 609, New York, NY, 10036
Non-profit trade association concerned with entertainment technology
www.esta.org

Producers Guild of America (310) 358-9020
8530 Wilshire Blvd Ste 400, Beverly Hills, CA, 90211
www.producersguild.org

SAG-AFTRA (323) 954-1600
5757 Wilshire Blvd 7th Floor, Los Angeles, CA, 90036
www.sagaftra.org

Set Decorators' Society of America (818) 255-2425
7100 Tujunga Ave Ste A, N Hollywood, CA, 91605
www.setdecorators.org

Society of American Fight Directors (818) 255-2425
1350 E Flamingo Rd #25, Las Vegas, NV, 89119
contact regional rep. via their web site
www.safd.org

Stage Directors & Choreographers Society (212) 391-1070
321 W 44th St Ste 804, New York, NY, 10036
www.sdcweb.org

Stuntmen's Assn. of Motion Pictures (818) 766-4334
5200 Lankershim Blvd Suite 190, N Hollywood, CA, 91601
www.stuntmen.com

Television Academy (818) 754-2800
5220 Lankershim Blvd, N Hollywood, CA, 91601
www.emmysfoundation.org

Themed Entertainment Association (818) 843-8497
150 E Olive Ave Ste 306, Burbank, CA, 91502
Alliance of themed entertainment companies
www.teaconnect.org

U. S. Institute for Theater Technology (800) 938-7488
290 Elwood Davis Rd Ste 100, Liverpool, NY, 13088
www.usitt.org

University Resident Theatre Assn (212) 221-1130
1560 Broadway Ste 1103, New York, NY, 10036
www.urta.com

Women In Film (323) 935-2211
4221 Wilshire Blvd Ste 130, Los Angeles, CA, 90010
www.wif.org

Writer's Guild of America (323) 951-4000
7000 W Third St, Los Angeles, CA, 90048
www.wga.org

Locations, Stages/Studios, Film/TV/Events

See Also: Locations, Insert Stages & Theatres

ABC 7 Broadcast Center (818) 560-7450
500 Circle Seven Dr, Glendale, CA, 91201

Ahmanson Theater (213) 628-2772
135 N Grand, Los Angeles, CA, 90012
for admin office, see Dorothy Chandler Pavillion, Filming (213) 972-7334,
Rentals (213) 972-7478
www.centertheatregroup.org

Albuquerque Studios (505) 227-2000
5650 University Blvd SE, Albuquerque, NM, 87106
www.abqstudios.com

Anaheim Convention Center (714) 765-8950
800 W Katella Ave, Anaheim, CA, 92802
www.anaheimconventioncenter.com

Anaheim Grove (714) 712-2700
2200 E Katella Ave, Anaheim, CA, 92806
event inquiries: (714) 712-2703
www.citynationalgroveofanaheim.com

Angel Stadium of Anaheim (714) 940-2000
2000 Gene Autry Way, Anaheim, CA, 92806
http://losangeles.angels.mlb.com/ana/ballpark/index.jsp

The Barker Hangar Santa Monica Air Center (310) 390-9071
3021 Airport Ave Ste 203, Santa Monica, CA, 90405
Large clearspan interior, high ceilings
www.barkerhangar.com

Ben Kitay Studios (323) 466-9015
1015 N Cahuenga Blvd, Hollywood, CA, 90038
www.benkitay.com

The Burbank Studios (818) 840-3000
3000 W Alameda Ave, Burbank, CA, 91523
www.theburbankstudios.com

California Theatre of Performing Arts (909) 885-5152
562 W 4th St, San Bernardino, CA, 92402
www.californiatheatre.net

CBS Studio Center (818) 655-5000
4024 Radford Ave, Studio City, CA, 91604
Residential streets, central park, new york street, and subway car mock up and
subway station mock up.
www.cbssc.com

CBS Television City (323) 575-2676
7800 Beverly Blvd, Los Angeles, CA, 90036
www.cbstelevisioncity.com

Cerritos P.A.C. (562) 916-8510
12700 Center Court Dr, Cerritos, CA, 90703
www.cerritoscenter.com

Chandler Valley Center Studios (818) 424-4551
13927 Saticoy St, Van Nuys, CA, 91402
Commercials & music videos, TV/Movies
www.cvcstudios.com

The Culver Studios (310) 202-1234
9336 W Washington Blvd, Culver City, CA, 90232
www.theculverstudios.com

Delfino Studios (818) 361-2421
12501 Gladstone Ave, Sylmar, CA, 91342
www.delfinostudios.com

depict (323) 222-1001
1460 Naud St, Los Angeles, CA, 90012
info@depict33.com * www.depict33.com

Dodger Stadium (866) 363-4377
1000 Elysian Park Ave, Los Angeles, CA, 90012
http://losangeles.dodgers.mlb.com

Dolby Theater (323) 308-6300
6801 Hollywood Blvd Ste 180 Admin, Hollywood, CA, 90028
www.dolbytheatre.com

Dorothy Chandler Pavilion (213) 972-7211
135 N Grand Ave, Los Angeles, CA, 90012
venue for Music Center, Opera, Master Chorale admin office for Ahmanson &
Mark Taper
www.musiccenter.org

El Capitan Theater (323) 467-7674
6838 Hollywood Blvd, Hollywood, CA, 90028
www.elcapitantheatre.com

Empire Studio (818) 840-1400
1845 Empire Ave, Burbank, CA, 91504
www.lbimedia.com

ENOX Filming & Concert Location (323) 770-4822
4550-4560 Worth St, Los Angeles, CA, 90063
Warehouse location complete with large parking lot, loading dock and high
ceiling.
catx4046@gmail.com * www.enoxevents.com

The Fonda Theater (323) 464-0808
6126 Hollywood Blvd, Hollywood, CA, 90028
www.fondatheatre.com

The Forum (310) 330-7300
3900 W Manchester Blvd, Inglewood, CA, 90305
www.fabulousforum.com

Glendale Production Center (818) 550-6000
1239 S Glendale Ave, Glendale, CA, 91205
www.glendalestudios.com

GMT Studios (310) 649-3733
5751 Buckingham Pkwy, Culver City, CA, 90230
www.gmtstudios.com

Greek Theatre (844) 524-7335
2700 N Vermont Ave, Los Angeles, CA, 90027
www.lagreektheatre.com

Historic Hudson Studios (323) 461-1044
1106 N Hudson Ave, Hollywood, CA, 90038
Boutique photo studio: wifi, meeting area, prep kitchen, set kitchen,
diffused/black out curtains & addl. equipment.
info@historichudsonstudios.com * www.historichudsonstudios.com

Historic Hudson Studios
www.historichudsonstudios.com
323.461.1044

Hollywood Bowl (323) 850-2000
2301 N Highland Ave, Los Angeles, CA, 90078
www.hollywoodbowl.com

Hollywood Center Studios (323) 860-0000
1040 N Las Palmas Ave, Los Angeles, CA, 90038
see floor plans, lighting/grip & tech dept on our website
www.hollywoodcenter.com

Hollywood Palladium (323) 962-7600
6215 Sunset Blvd, Hollywood, CA, 90028
www.thehollywoodpalladium.com

The Honda Center, AKA Arrowhead Pond (714) 704-2400
2695 E. Katella Ave, Anaheim, CA, 92806
www.hondacenter.com

John Anson Ford Theaters (323) 856-5793
2580 Cahuenga Blvd E, Los Angeles, CA, 90068
box office (323) 461-3673
www.fordtheatres.org

KCAL TV Studios (818) 655-2000
4200 Radford Ave, Studio City, CA, 91604
http://losangeles.cbslocal.com/station/cbs-kcal/

KCBS TV Studios (818) 655-2000
4200 Radford Ave, Studio City, CA, 91604
http://losangeles.cbslocal.com/station/cbs-kcal/

KCET TV Studios (747) 201-5258
2900 W Alameda Ave, Burbank, CA, 91505
contact@kcet.org * www.kcet.org

**LISTINGS FOR THIS CATEGORY CONTINUE ON THE
FOLLOWING PAGE**

KLCS TV Studios (213) 241-4000
1061 W Temple St, Los Angeles, CA, 90012
http://klcs.org/

KMEX TV Studios (Univision) (310) 216-3434
5999 Center Drive, Los Angeles, CA, 90045
losangeles.univision.com

Koch's Movie Ranch (661) 268-1341
7650 Soledad Canyon Road, Acton, CA, 93510
Locations: House, Cabin, Mineshaft, Cave, Barn, Outhouse, Restaurant,
70,000 gallon pond w/ waterfall & gazebo, Church
customerservice@kochs.com * www.kochsmovieranch.com

Koch's Movie Ranch
www.kochsmovieranch.com
(661) 268-1341 (661) 433-2854
7650 Soledad Canyon Road, Acton, CA

KTLA TV Studios (323) 460-5500
5800 Sunset Blvd, Los Angeles, CA, 90028
www.ktla.com

KTTV TV Fox 11 Studios (310) 584-2000
1999 S Bundy Dr, Los Angeles, CA, 90025
www.myfoxLA.com

The L. A. Lofts (323) 462-5880
6442 Santa Monica Blvd Ste 203, Los Angeles, CA, 90038
www.thelalofts.com

Lacy Street Production Center (323) 222-8872
2630 Lacy St, Los Angeles, CA, 90031
standing sets, music videos, commercials
www.lacystreet.com

Long Beach Convention Center (562) 436-3636
300 E Ocean Blvd, Long Beach, CA, 90802
www.longbeachcc.com

Los Angeles Center Studios (213) 534-3000
1201 W 5th Street Ste T-110, Los Angeles, CA, 90017
www.lacenterstudios.com

Los Angeles Convention Center (213) 741-1151
1201 S Figueroa St, Los Angeles, CA, 90015
Event Services X5360
www.lacclink.com

Los Angeles Memorial Coliseum (213) 747-7111
3911 S Figueroa St, Los Angeles, CA, 90037
www.lacoliseum.com

Los Angeles Sports Arena (213) 747-7111
3939 S Figueroa St, Los Angeles, CA, 90037
www.lacoliseumlive.com

The Lot (323) 850-3180
1041 N Formosa Ave, W Hollywood, CA, 90046
www.thelotstudios.com

Mack Sennett Studios (323) 660-8466
1215 Bates Ave, Los Angeles, CA, 90029
www.macksennettstudios.net

Mark Taper Forum (213) 628-2772
135 N Grand Ave, Los Angeles, CA, 90012
for admin office, see Dorothy Chandler Pavilion
www.centertheatregroup.org

Microsoft Theater (213) 763-6030
777 Chick Hearn Court, Los Angeles, CA, 90015
www.microsofttheater.com

Occidental Studios (213) 384-3331
201 N Occidental Blvd, Los Angeles, CA, 90026
12 locations, stages from 1,000 to 43,000 sq. ft., lighting, grip, offices, props,
etc.
www.occidentalentertainment.com

Panavision (Woodland Hills) (818) 316-1000
6101 Variel Ave, Woodland Hills, CA, 91367
Cameras & film. Commercials, music videos, hair & make-up test, trailers
www.panavision.com

Pantages Theatre (323) 468-1700
6233 Hollywood Blvd, Hollywood, CA, 90028
www.hollywoodpantages.com

Pasadena Civic Auditorium (626) 793-2122
300 E Green St, Pasadena, CA, 91101
Also, Pasadena Convention Center.
www.thepasadenacivic.com

The Pasadena Playhouse (626) 356-7529
39 S El Molino Ave, Pasadena, CA, 91101
www.pasadenaplayhouse.org

The Production Group (323) 469-8111
1626 N Wilcox Ave Ste 281, Hollywood, CA, 90028
www.productiongroup.tv

Prospect Studios (323) 671-4022
4151 Prospect Ave, Los Angeles, CA, 90027
http://studioservices.go.com/prospectstudios/index.html

Quixote Studios (323) 851-5030
1011 N Fuller Ave, W Hollywood, CA, 90046
trucks and stages, greenrooms, production stages
www.quixotestudios.com

Raleigh Studios (323) 960-3456
5300 Melrose Ave, Hollywood, CA, 90038
www.raleighstudios.com

Red Studios Hollywood (323) 463-0808
846 Cahuenga Blvd, Los Angeles, CA, 90038
http://www.redstudio.com/

Rose Bowl (626) 577-3100
1001 Rose Bowl Dr, Pasadena, CA, 91103
www.rosebowlstadium.com

Saban Theatre (888) 645-5006
8440 Wilshire Blvd, Beverly Hills, CA, 90211
www.sabantheatre.org

San Gabriel Mission Playhouse (626) 308-2865
320 S Mission Drive, San Gabriel, CA, 91776
Location, Sound Stage, Venue, Rehearsal Space, Theater, Spanish style,
wurlitzer organ
swilkinson@missionplayhouse.org * www.missionplayhouse.org

San Manuel Amphitheater (909) 880-6500
2575 Glen Helen Pkwy, San Bernardino, CA, 92407
www.sanmanuelamphitheater.net

Santa Barbara Bowl (805) 962-7411
1122 N Milpas St, Santa Barbara, CA, 93103
www.sbbowl.com

Santa Clarita Studios (661) 294-2000
25135 Anza Dr, Santa Clarita, CA, 91355
www.santaclaritastudios.com

Santa Monica Civic Auditorium (310) 458-8551
1855 Main St, Santa Monica, CA, 90401
www.santamonicacivic.org

Schmidli Backdrops LA (323) 938-2098
5830 W Adams Blvd, Culver City, CA, 90232
Providing hand painted Textured and Scenic backdrops to the commercial, film,
and fashion industry for over 20 years.
backdrops@schmidli.com * www.schmidli.com

Segerstrom Center (714) 556-2121
600 Town Center Dr, Costa Mesa, CA, 92626
Five performing arts & event venues
www.scfta.org

Shrine Auditorium (213) 748-5116
665 W Jefferson Blvd, Los Angeles, CA, 90007
www.shrineauditorium.com

Sony Pictures Studios (310) 244-6926
10202 W Washington Blvd, Culver City, CA, 90232
www.sonypicturesstudios.com

Stage 1001 (323) 876-1001
1001 N Poinsettia Pl, Los Angeles, CA, 90046
www.stage1001.com

Staples Center (213) 742-7100
1111 S Figueroa St, Los Angeles, CA, 90015
www.staplescenter.com

The Studios At Paramount (323) 956-5000
5555 Melrose, Hollywood, CA, 90038
Call (323) 956-8811 for booking stages.
www.thestudiosatparamount.com

Sunset Gower Studios (323) 467-1001
1438 North Gower Box 21, Hollywood, CA, 90028
Call (323) 315-9460 for new inquiries
www.sgsandsbs.com

Thunder Studios (310) 762-1360
20434 S Santa Fe Ave, Long Beach, CA, 90810
15 stages, hard cycs, fisher boxes/flats
www.thunderstudios.com

Twentieth Century Fox (310) 369-1000
10201 W Pico Blvd, Los Angeles, CA, 90035
www.foxstudios.com

Universal Studios Stages & Backlot (818) 777-3000
100 Universal City Plaza, Universal City, CA, 91608
universal.locations@nbcuni.com *
http://universalstudioslot.com/stages-and-backlot

The Walt Disney Concert Hall (213) 972-7211
135 N Grand Ave, Los Angeles, CA, 90012
http://www.wdch.com/

The Walt Disney Studios (818) 560-7450
500 S Buena Vista St, Burbank, CA, 91505
www.stu-ops.disney.com

Warner Bros. Studios (818) 954-6000
4000 Warner Blvd, Burbank, CA, 91522
For facilities, call (818) 954-3000
www.warnerbros.com

The Wiltern (213) 388-1400
3790 Wilshire Blvd, Los Angeles, CA, 90010
call (213) 380-5005 for box office
www.thewiltern.com

Prop Houses

See Also: Prop & Set Design Supplies, Parts, Tools Prop Design &
Manufacturing* Prop Reproduction & Fabrication* Scenery/Set
Construction*

A-1 Medical Integration (818) 753-0319
7344 Laurel Canyon Blvd, N Hollywood, CA, 91605
Medical devices for Set Decoration & Property, from minor procedures to
detailed hospital units.
a1medwarehouse@aol.com * www.a1props.com

Advanced Liquidators Office Furniture (818) 763-3470
11151 Vanowen St, N Hollywood, CA, 91605
Specializes in new and used office furniture as well as studio rentals.
rentals@advancedliquidators.com * www.advancedliquidators.com

Aero Mock-Ups (888) 662-5877
13126 Saticoy St, N Hollywood, CA, 91605
Aviation prop house. Complete airplane interiors & airport dressing, model
airplanes, jet engines, and airline costumes.
info@aeromockups.com * www.aeromockups.com

AIR Designs (818) 768-6639
11900 Wicks St, Sun Valley, CA, 91352
Auto, Gas, Racing, Fast Food, Coffee, Diner, Cafeteria, Store, Street, Vendor
Carts
info@airdesigns.net * www.airdesigns.net

Alley Cats Studio Rentals (818) 982-9178
7101 Case Ave, N Hollywood, CA, 91605
alleycatsprops@gmail.com * www.alleycatsprops.com

Alpha Companies - Spellman Desk Co. (818) 504-9090
7990 San Fernando Rd, Sun Valley, CA, 91352
The #1 source for medical equipment in the industry.
rentals@alphaprops.com * www.alphaprops.com
    Atlanta (470) 237-4490
    Los Angeles **(818) 504-9090**
    New York (718) 349-9090

Arenson Prop Center (917) 210-2562
1115 Broadway, 6th Floor, New York, NY 10010
info@aof.com * www.aof.com/p/props

Artkraft Taxidermy Rentals (818) 505-8425
10847 Vanowen St, N Hollywood, CA, 91605
Taxidermied animals of all kinds: birds, fish, mammals, and much more from
Africa, North America, and exotic locales.
info@artkrafttaxidermy.com * www.artkrafttaxidermy.net

Bridge Furniture & Props Los Angeles (818) 433-7100
3210 Vanowen St, Burbank, CA, 91505
We carry modern & traditional furniture, lighting, accessories, cleared art, &
rugs. Items are online for easy shopping.
la@bridgeprops.com * http://la.bridgeprops.com
    Atlanta (404) 549-7494
    Los Angeles **(818) 433-7100**
    New York (718) 916-9706

C. P. Two (323) 466-8201
5755 Santa Monica Blvd, Los Angeles, CA, 90038
www.omegacinemaprops.com

Central Atlanta Props & Sets (470)-225-6709
675 Metropolitan Parkway SW Ste 5121, Atlanta, GA, 30310
Atlanta prop house with industrial, office, rustic, exterior or classic furnishing
needs.
capsga@outlook.com * http://capsga.com

Dapper Cadaver (818) 771-0818
7648 San Fernando Rd, Sun Valley, CA, 91352
Specializes in horror, science, medical, crime, oddity & Halloween props.
Custom fabrication & FX. Rent & buy online.
info@dappercadaver.com * www.dappercadaver.com

E.C. Prop Rentals (818) 764-2008
11846 Sherman Way, N Hollywood, CA, 91605
Factory, Industrial, Loading Dock, Warehouse, Locker Room, Garage,
Street/Alley, Shipping Yard
ecprops@aol.com * www.ecprops.com

Eccentric Trading Company Ltd. 011 44 20
Unit 2 Frogmore Estate, Acton Lane, London NW10 7NQ 8453-1125
www.eccentrictrading.com

Eclectic/Encore Props (212) 645-8880
47-51 33rd St, Long Island City, NY 11101
sbieler@eclecticprops.com * www.eclecticprops.com

The Farley Group 011 44 20
1-17 Brunel Rd, London, W3 7XR UK 8749-9925
props@farley.co.uk * www.farley.co.uk

Faux Library Studio Props, Inc. (818) 765-0096
7100 Case Avenue, N Hollywood, CA, 91605
large selection of hollow books, office furniture, desk dressing, decorative
accessories and of course books
fauxlibrary@sbcglobal.net * fb.me/fauxlibrary

FormDecor, Inc. (310) 558-2582
5600 Argosy Circle Ste 200, Huntington Beach, CA, 92649
America's largest event rental supplier of 20th Century furniture and
accessories for Modern and Mid-Century styles.
info@formdecor.com * www.formdecor.com

Gorygirl Halloween Event Staging and Prop (818) 912-6902
Rental
5330 Derry Ave Unit G, Agoura Hills, CA, 91301
Halloween themed prop house renting the creepy, crawly and spooky
gorygirlevents@gmail.com * gorygirl.com

Green Set, Inc. (818) 764-1231
11617 Dehougne St, N Hollywood, CA, 91605
www.greenset.com

The Hand Prop Room LP. (323) 931-1534
5700 Venice Blvd, Los Angeles, CA, 90019
Large Prop House for prop rentals, prop weapons, custom graphic design &
custom graphic printing, expendables and more.
info@hpr.com * www.hpr.com
    The Hand Prop Room Prop House **(323) 931-1534**
    HPR Custom (323) 931-1534
    HPR Graphics (323) 556-2694

History For Hire, Inc. (818) 765-7767
7149 Fair Ave, N Hollywood, CA, 91605
info@historyforhire.com * www.historyforhire.com

Hollywood Cinema Arts (818) 504-7333
8110 Webb Ave, N Hollywood, CA, 91605
Hollywood Cinema Arts, "The Pro's Prop House."
hollywoodcinemaarts@gmail.com * www.hcarts.com

Hollywood Cinema Production Resources (310) 258-0123
9700 S. Sepulveda Blvd, Los Angeles, CA, 90045
props@hollywoodcpr.org * www.hollywoodcpr.org

Hollywood Studio Gallery (323) 462-1116
1035 Cahuenga Blvd, Hollywood, CA, 90038
hsginfo@hollywoodstudiogallery.com * www.hollywoodstudiogallery.com

Independent Studio Services, Inc (818) 951-5600
9545 Wentworth St, Sunland, CA, 91040
www.issprops.com

Jackson Shrub Supply, Inc. (818) 982-0100
11505 Vanowen St, N Hollywood, CA, 91605
Plant rentals, shrub rentals, tree rentals. Christmas decorations and Halloween
decorations and more.
gary@jacksonshrub.com * www.jacksonshrub.com

LCW Props (818) 243-0707
6439 San Fernando Rd, Glendale, CA, 91201
LCW Is Your 1-Stop Shop For Almost Anything. We Work With Any Budget.
props@lcwprops.com * www.lcwprops.com

LISTINGS FOR THIS CATEGORY CONTINUE ON THE
FOLLOWING PAGE

Lennie Marvin Enterprises, Inc. (Prop Heaven) (818) 841-5882
3110 Winona Ave, Burbank, CA, 91504
catering to the entertainment industry
info@propheaven.com * www.propheaven.com

LM Treasures (626) 252-7354
10557 Juniper Ave Unit A, Fontana, CA, 92337
Statue rentals of many types: movie props, lamps, prop rentals, figurines
rentals, prop store, prop showroom
lmtreasures.ll@gmail.com * www.lifesizestatues.net

Modern Props (323) 934-3000
972 Griswold Ave, San Fernando, CA, 91340
Modern Props, Contemporary Props, Futuristic Props, & Electronic Props
ken@modernprops.com * www.modernprops.com

Modernica Props (323) 664-2322
2805 Gilroy Street, Los Angeles, CA, 90039
huge inventory 50s-70s furniture & decor. From couches to record players,
multiples up to 500 for many
www.modernicaprops.net

NEST Studio Rentals, Inc. (818) 942-0339
7007 Lankershim Blvd, N Hollywood, CA, 91605
contemporary furniture, rugs, lighting, art, drapery, smalls
sales@neststudiorentals.net * www.neststudiorentals.net

Ob-jects (818) 351-4200
10623 Keswick St, Sun Valley, CA, 91352
Upscale props and furniture, wide variety in clean, large warehouse.
fred@ob-jects.com * www.ob-jects.com

Oceanic Arts (562) 698-6960
12414 Whittier Blvd, Whittier, CA, 90602-1017
We Rent and We Sell Hawaiian, Polynesian, Tropical, and Nautical Decor.
oceanicarts56@gmail.com * www.oceanicarts.net

Old N Country Prop Shop, LLC (818) 423-2599
12007 Vose St, Los Angeles, CA, 91605
We are a family owned prop house specializing in Americana and hard to find
antiques from the East Coast, and MUCH more!
propshop@oldncountry.com * www.oldncountry.com

Omega/Cinema Props (323) 466-8201
5857 Santa Monica Blvd, Los Angeles, CA, 90038
www.omegacinemaprops.com

  C. P. Two
  5755 Santa Monica Blvd, Los Angeles, CA, 90038

Picture Start Props (818) 255-5472
7040 Laurel Canyon Blvd UNIT B, N Hollywood, CA, 91605
jennifer@picturestartprops.com * www.picturestartprops.com

Pinacoteca Picture Props (818) 764-2722
7120 Case Ave, N Hollywood, CA, 91605
art rentals, linens, furniture & custom framing
sales@pinaprops.com * www.pinaprops.com

Premiere Props. (818) 768-3800
11500 Sheldon St, Sun Valley, CA, 91352
www.premiereprops.net

Prop Mart, Inc. (773) 772-7775
2343 W St Paul Ave, Chicago, IL, 60647
table top, mainly commercials; dishes, linens, flatware, more

Prop Services West (818) 503-2790
7040 Laurel Canyon Blvd, North Hollywood, CA, 91605
www.propserviceswest.com

Propabilities (773) 278-2384
1517 N Elston, Chicago, IL, 60642
hand props, set dressing, furniture, smalls, park benches, photo surfaces
www.propabilitiesonline.com

propNspoon / Props for Today (212) 244-9600
32-00 Skillman Ave, 3rd Floor, Long Island City, NY, 11101
www.propsfortoday.com

RC Vintage, Inc. (818) 765-7107
7100 Tujunga Ave, N Hollywood, CA, 91605
specializing in 40s, 50s, 60s & 70s
rcvintage@aol.com * www.rcvintage.com

RJR Props (404) 349-7600
5300 Westpark Drive SW Ste B, Atlanta, CA, 30336
RJR Props can provide working realistic Props for your feature film, show,
commercial, music video, or event.
rjrelectronics@aol.com * www.rjrprops.com

Seasons Textiles Ltd 011 44 20 8965-6161
9 Gorst Road, London NW10 6LA
enquiries@seasonstextiles.net * www.seasonstextiles.co.uk

Sony Pictures Studios
10202 W Washington Blvd, Los Angeles, CA, 90232
www.sonypicturesstudios.com
  Events (310) 244-4456

Sony Pictures Studios (Off Lot)
5933 W Slauson Ave, Culver City, CA, 90230
www.sonypicturesstudios.com
  Fixtures (310) 244-5996
  Linens, Drapes, Rugs (310) 244-5999
  Prop House (310) 244-5999
  Wardrobe (310) 244-5995

Studio Plumbing Rentals (323) 829-9339
7373 Atoll Ave, N Hollywood, CA, 91605
studioplumbingrentals@gmail.com * www.studioair.com

Studio Props, Inc. (661) 775-1655
21170 Centre Pointe Parkway #200, Santa Clarita, CA, 91350
Police Equip, SWAT, Replica Weapons, Press and Media, Cameras, EMT
Equip.
actionprops@yahoo.com * http://www.studioprops.net

The Surface Library (323) 546-9314
1106 N Hudson Ave 2nd Floor, Los Angeles, CA, 90038
A curated prop house specializing in surfaces and table top props for food,
product, and lifestyle shoots.
info@thesurfacelibrary.com * www.thesurfacelibrary.com

Sword & Stone (818) 562-6548
1100 W Isabel St, Burbank, CA, 91506
medieval & fantasy props
tony@swordandstone.com * www.swordandstone.com

Technical Props, Inc (818) 761-4993
6811 Farmdale Ave, N Hollywood, CA, 91605
techpropsinc@rr.com * www.techpropsinc.com

Trading Post Ltd. 011 44 20 8903-3727
1-3 Beresford Avenue, Wembley, Middlesex, HA0 1NU
info@tradingposthire.co.uk * www.tradingposthire.co.uk

Trevor Howsam Ltd 011 44 20 8838-6166
182 Acton Lane, Park Royal, London NW10 7NH
props@trevorhowsam.co.uk * www.retrowallpaper.co.uk

Universal Studios Departments
100 Universal City Plaza, Universal City, CA, 91608
www.filmmakersdestination.com

Costume Dept.	(818) 777-2722
Drapery Dept.	(818) 777-2761
Graphic Design & Sign Shop	(818) 777-2350
Grip Dept.	(818) 777-2291
Property & Hardware Dept.	**(818) 777-2784**
Set Lighting Dept.	(818) 777-2291
Special Effects Equip.	(818) 777-3333
Special Events	(818) 777-9466
Staff Shop	(818) 777-2337
Stages & Backlot	(818) 777-3000
NBCUniversal StudioPost Editorial Facilities	(818) 777-5163
Transportation	(818) 777-2966
Filmmaker Production Svcs - Atlanta	(404) 815-5202
Filmmaker Production Svcs - Chicago	(678) 628-1997
NBCUniversal LightBlade LED Lighting	(818) 777-1671
New Mexico Lighting & Grip	(505) 227-2500

Warner Bros. Studios Departments
4000 Warner Blvd, Burbank, CA, 91522
www.wbpropertydept.com

Cabinet & Furniture Shop	(818) 954-1339
Costume Dept.	(818) 954-1297
Design Studio	(818) 954-4430
Drapery, Upholstery & Flooring	(818) 954-1831
Grip Dept.	(818) 954-1590
Hardware Rentals	(818) 954-1335
Metal Shop	(818) 954-1265
Paint Dept.	(818) 954-1817
Photo Lab	(818) 954-7118
Production Sound & Video	(818) 954-2511
Property Dept.	**(818) 954-2181**
Scenic Art & Sign Shop	(818) 954-1815
Special Efects & Prop Shop	(818) 954-1365
Staff Shop	(818) 954-2269
The Collection	(818) 954-2181

Woody's Electrical Props (818) 503-1940
5323 Craner Ave, N Hollywood, CA, 91601-3313
Period to futuristic. Electronic equipment. Custom built to specifications.
Electrical paneling
woody@woodysprops.com * www.woodysprops.com

Zap Props (773) 376-2278
3611 S Loomis Pl, Chicago, IL, 60609
hand props, set dressing, street dressing, big & small
www.zapprops.com

ZG04 DECOR (818) 853-8040
12224 Montague St, Sun Valley, CA, 91331
Rental & Sale
saul@zg04decor.com * www.zg04decor.com

Made in the USA
Lexington, KY
14 March 2018